Langenscheid

Notebook Dictionary
Spanish

Revised and updated edition by Teresa Catarella, Ph.D. (C) 1992 Langenscheidt KG, Berlin and Munich.

Abbreviations — *Abreviaturas*

La tilde (~, si la inicial cambia: ℒ) sustituye la voz-guía entera, o bien la parte que precede a la raya vertical (|).

The tilde (~, when the initial letter changes: ℒ) stands for the catchword at the beginning of the entry or the part of it preceding the vertical bar (|).

Ejemplos:
abani|car; **~co** = abanico
chin|a; **ℒa** = China; **ℒese** = Chinese
Easter; **ℒn** = eastern

Examples:
abus|e; **~ive** = abusive
noche; **ℒbuena** = Noche buena
Españ|a; **ℒol(a)** = español(a)

a	adjective, *adjetivo*	fig	figurative, *figurado*	pl	plural, *plural*
adv	adverb, *adverbio*	for	forensic, law, *voz forense*	pol	politics, *política*
aer	aeronautics, *aeronáutica*	foto	photography, *fotografía*	pos, poss	possessive, *posesivo*
agr	agriculture, *agricultura*	f/pl	feminine plural, *femenino al plural*	prep	preposition, *preposición*
Am	America, *América*	geog	geography, *geografía*	pron	pronoun, *pronombre*
anat	anatomy, *anatomía*	geol	geology, *geología*	pron pers	personal pronoun, *pronombre personal*
arq	architecture, *arquitectura*	gram	grammar, *gramática*		
art	article, *artículo*	impr	printing, *imprenta*	quím	chemistry, *química*
aut	automobile, motoring, *automóvil*	Ingl	England, *Inglaterra*	rel	relative, *relativo*
biol	biology, *biología*	interj	interjection, *interjección*	relig	religion, *religión*
bot	botany, *botánica*	interrog	interrogative, *interrogativo*	s	substantive, *substantivo*
cine	films, *cinema*	LA	Latin American, *latino americano*	sp	sports, *deportes*
coc	cookery, *cocina*	lit	literature, *literatura*	superl	superlative, *superlativo*
com	commerce, *comercio*	m	masculine, *masculino*	t	also, *también*
compar	comparative, *comparativo*	mar	marine, *marina*	teat	theatre, *teatro*
conj	conjunction, *conjunción*	mat	mathematics, *matemática*	tecn	technology, *tecnología*
elec	electricity, *electricidad*	med	medical, *medicina*	tel	telephone, *teléfono*
esp	especially, *especialmente*	mil	military, *militar*	TV	television, *televisión*
etc	etcetera, *etcétera*	min	mining, *minería*	v/aux	auxiliary verb, *verbo auxiliar*
f	feminine, *femenino*	m/pl	masculine plural, *masculino al plural*	v/i	intransitive verb, *verbo intransitivo*
fam	familiar, *familiar*	mús	music, *música*		
farm	pharmacy, *farmacia*	ópt	optics, *óptica*	v/r	reflexive verb, *verbo reflexivo*
f c	railway, *ferrocarril*	pint	painting, *pintura*	v/t	transitive verb, *verbo transitivo*
				zool	zoology, *zoología*

Pronunciation Key to English Words
Llave de pronunciación para las palabras inglesas
Vocales y Diptongos

[ɑ:]	como en *bajo*: *father* ['fɑ:ðə], *palm* [pɑ:m]	[əu]	diptongo compuesto de un sonido como el de la *o* en *como* y una *u* débil: *soap* [səup], *go* [gəu]
[ʌ]	sonido parecido al de la *a* en *para*: *butter* ['bʌtə], *mother* ['mʌðə]	[ɔ:]	sonido largo algo parecido al de la *o* en *forma*: *ball* [bɔ:l], *or* [ɔ:]
[æ]	sonido parecido al de la *a* en *parra*: *fat* [fæt], *man* [mæn]	[ɔ]	sonido breve parecido al de la *o* en *porra* pero más cerrado: *dog* [dɔg], *wash* [wɔʃ]
[ɛə]	diptongo compuesto de una *e* muy abierta y una *e* átona: *there* [ðɛə], *care* [kɛə]	[ɔi]	diptongo parecido al sonido de *oy* en *soy*: *point* [pɔint], *boy* [bɔi]
[ai]	diptongo parecido al *ai* en *baile*: *time* [taim], *eye* [ai]	[ə]	sonido átono parecido al de la *e* en el artículo francés *le*: *silent* ['sailənt], *about* [ə'baut]
[au]	diptongo parecido al *au* en *causa*: *count* [kaunt], *how* [hau]	[ə:]	forma más larga del sonido anterior que se encuentra en sílabas acentuadas; su sonido es parecido al de *eu* en la palabra francesa *leur*: *bird* [bə:d], *learn* [lə:n]
[ei]	diptongo compuesto de un sonido como el de la *e* en *pelo* y una *i* débil: *day* [dei], *eight* [eit]		
[e]	como la *e* en *perro*: *men* [men], *said* [sed]	[u:]	sonido largo parecido al de la *u* en *una*: *do* [du:], *fruit* [fru:t]
[i:]	sonido como la *i* en *brisa*: *tea* [ti:], *meet* [mi:t]	[uə]	diptongo compuesto de [u] y [ə]: *poor* [puə], *lure* [ljuə]
[i]	sonido breve parecido al de la *i* en *esbirro* pero más abierto: *bit* [bit], *city* ['siti]	[u]	sonido corto como el de la *u* en *culpa*: *put* [put], *took* [tuk]
[iə]	diptongo compuesto de [i] y [ə]: *fear* [fiə], *here* [hiə]		

Consonantes

[b]	como la *b* en *ambos*: *hobby* ['hɔbi], *boat* [bəut]
[d]	como la *d* en *andar*: *ladder* ['lædə], *day* [dei]
[f]	como la *f* en *fácil*: *fall* [fɔːl], *fake* [feik]
[g]	como la *g* en *goma*: *go* [gəu], *again* [ə'gen]
[h]	como la *j* en *jerga*, pero mucho más suave: *hard* [hɑːd], *who* [huː]
[j]	como la *y* de *yo*: *yet* [jet], *few* [fjuː]
[k]	como la *c* en *casa*: *cat* [kæt], *back* [bæk]
[l]	como la *l* en *lágrima*: *leaf* [liːf], *along* [ə'lɔŋ]
[m]	como la *m* en *madre*: *make* [meik], *team* [tiːm]
[n]	como la *n* en *nata*: *no* [nəu], *tin* [tin]
[p]	como la *p* en *tapa*: *pay* [pei], *top* [tɔp]
[r]	se pronuncia sólo cuando precede a una vocal, sin la vibración de la *r* española: *rate* [reit], *worry* ['wʌri]
[s]	como la *s* en *cosa*: *sun* [sʌn], *fast* [fɑːst]

[t]	como la *t* en *tos*: *tip* [tip], *letter* ['letə]
[v]	no existe el sonido en español; es parecido al de la *v* en la palabra francesa *avec*: *vain* [vein], *above* [ə'bʌv]
[w]	como la *u* en *huevo*: *wine* [wain], *quaint* [kweint]
[z]	como la *s* en *mismo*: *zeal* [ziːl], *hers* [həːz]
[ʒ]	no existe en *español*; su sonido es parecido al de la *j* en la palabra francesa *jolie*: *vision* ['viʒən], *measure* ['meʒə]
[ʃ]	no existe en español; su sonido corresponde al de la *ch* en la palabra francesa *charmant*: *sheet* [ʃiːt], *dish* [diʃ]
[θ]	como la *c* en *dice* y la *z* en *zapato*: *thin* [θin], *path* [pɑːθ]
[ð]	sonido parecido a la *d* en *hada*: *there* [ðeə], *bother* ['bɔðə]
[ŋ]	como la *n* en *tengo*: *long* [lɔŋ], *singer* ['siŋə]
[dʒ]	combina la [d] y la [ʒ]: *jaw* [dʒɔː], *edge* [edʒ]
[tʃ]	combina la [t] y la [ʃ]; como la *ch* en *mucho*: *chest* [tʃest], *watch* [wɔtʃ]

Sufijos sin pronunciación figurada

Para ahorrar espacio, no se ha indicado pronunciación figurada para los sufijos siguientes:

-ability	[-əbiliti]	-ar	[-ə]	-ee	[-iː]	-ian	[-(jə)n]	-ist	[-ist]	-ly	[-li]	-(s)sion	[-ʃ(ə)n]
-able	[-əbl]	-ary	[-(ə)ri]	-en	[-n]	-ible	[-əbl]	-istic	[-istik]	-ment(s)	[-mənt(s)]	-sive	[-siv]
-age	[-idʒ]	-ation	[-eiʃ(ə)n]	-ence	[-(ə)ns]	-ic(s)	[-ik(s)]	-ite	[-ait]	-ness	[-nis]	-ties	[-tiz]
-al	[-(ə)l]	-cious	[-ʃəs]	-ent	[-(ə)nt]	-ical	[-ik(ə)l]	-ity	[-iti]	-oid	[-ɔid]	-tion	[-ʃ(ə)n]
-ally	[-(ə)li]	-cy	[-si]	-er	[-ə]	-ily	[-ili]	-ive	[-iv]	-oidic	[-ɔidik]	-tious	[-ʃəs]
-an	[-(ə)n]	-dom	[-dəm]	-ery	[-əri]	-iness	[-inis]	-ization	[-aizeiʃ(ə)n]	-or	[-ə]	-trous	[-trəs]
-ance	[-(ə)ns]	-ed	[-d; -t; -id]	-ess	[-is]	-ing	[-iŋ]	-ize	[-aiz]	-ous	[-əs]	-try	[-tri]
-ancy	[-ənsi]	-edness	[-dnis; -tnis; -idnis]	-fication	[-fikeiʃ(ə)n]	-ish	[-iʃ]	-izing	[-aiziŋ]	-ry	[-ri]	-y	[-i]
-ant	[-ənt]			-ial	[-(ə)l]	-ism	[-iz(ə)m]	-less	[-lis]	-ship	[-ʃip]		

A

a [ei; ə] un *m*, una *f*; not ~ ni un(a)
aback [ə'bæk]: taken ~ quedar desconcertado
abandon [ə'bændən] *v/t* abandonar; dejar
abate [ə'beit] *v/t* mitigar, reducir; *v/i* disminuir; ceder
abbess ['æbis] abadesa *f*
abbey ['æbi] abadía *f*
abbot ['æbət] abad *m*
abbreviat|e [ə'bri:vieit] *v/t* abreviar; ~ion [~'eiʃən] abreviatura *f*
abdicate ['æbdikeit] *v/t*, *v/i* abdicar, renunciar
abdomen ['æbdəmen] abdomen *m*, vientre *m*
abduct [æb'dʌkt] *v/t* secuestrar, raptar
abet [ə'bet] *v/t* instigar; aid and ~ encubrir, ser cómplice
abeyance [ə'beiəns] suspensión *f*; in ~ en suspenso
abhor [əb'hɔ:] *v/t* aborrecer, detestar; ~rent detestable
abide [ə'baid]: ~ by cumplir con; atenerse a; *v/t* aguantar; soportar
ability [ə'biliti] habilidad *f*, aptitud *f*, talento *m*, ingenio *m*
abject ['æbdʒekt] vil
abjure [əb'dʒuə] *v/t* abjurar; renunciar (a)
ablaze [ə'bleiz] ardiendo
able ['eibl] capaz, hábil, apto, competente; to be ~ poder; ~-bodied ['~'bɔdid] sano
abnormal [æb'nɔ:məl] anormal
aboard [ə'bɔ:d] a bordo
abode [ə'bəud] residencia *f*, domicilio *m*, morada *f*
aboli|sh [ə'bɔliʃ] *v/t* abolir; suprimir; ~tion [æbəu'liʃən] abolición *f*
abominable [ə'bɔminəbl] abominable
abortion [ə'bɔ:ʃən] aborto *m*
abound [ə'baund] *v/i* abundar; ~ in *o* with abundar en
about [ə'baut] *prep* alrededor, acerca (de); what is it ~? ¿de qué se trata?; *adv* casi; más o menos; a eso de; all ~ por todas partes; to be ~ to (do) estar a punto de (hacer); ~-face media vuelta *f*
above [ə'bʌv] *adv, prep* sobre, (por) encima (de); ~board legítimo; ~mentioned arriba citado
abreast [ə'brest] de frente; to keep ~ correr parejas; estar al corriente
abridge [ə'bridʒ] *v/t* abreviar, condensar
abroad [ə'brɔ:d] en el extranjero
abrupt [ə'brʌpt] rudo, brusco; precipitado
abscess ['æbsis] absceso *m*
absen|ce ['æbsəns] ausencia *f*; falta *f*; ~t ['æbsent] *a* ausente; *v/r* [æb'sent] ausentarse, retirarse; ~t-minded distraído
absolute ['æbsəlu:t] absoluto; ~ly absolutamente
absolution [æbsə'lu:ʃən] absolución *f*, perdón *m*
absolve [əb'zɔlv] *v/t* absolver, dispensar
absorb [əb'sɔ:b] *v/t* absorber
abstain [əb'stein] *v/t* abstenerse
abstinence ['æbstinəns] abstinencia *f*
abstract ['æbstrækt] *a* abstracto; *s* resumen *m*, extracto *m*; *v/t* [æb'strækt] abstraer, resumir
absurd [əb'sə:d] absurdo
abundan|ce [ə'bʌndəns] abundancia *f*, plenitud *f*; ~t abundante, copioso
abus|e [ə'bju:s] *s* abuso *m*; injuria *f*; *v/t* [ə'bju:z] abusar; insultar; ~ive abusivo; injurioso
abyss [ə'bis] abismo *m*, sima *f*
academ|ic [ækə'demik] *a, s* académico *m*; ~y [ə'kædəmi] academia *f*
accede [æk'si:d] *v/i* acceder, consentir
accelerat|e [æk'seləreit] *v/t* acelerar; *v/i* apresurarse; ~or acelerador *m*
accent ['æksənt] *s* acento *m*; *v/t* [æk'sent] acentuar; ~uate [~'sentjueit] *v/t* acentuar
accept [ək'sept] *v/t* aceptar, admitir; ~able aceptable; ~ance aceptación *f*; acogida *f*; *com* aceptación (*de un giro, de una letra*); ~ation [æksep'teiʃən] *gram* acepción *f*, significado *m*
access ['ækses] acceso *m*; paso *m*, entrada *f*; ~ible [ək'sesəbl] asequible, accesible
accessory [æk'sesəri] *a* accesorio, secundario; *s for* cómplice *m*
accident ['æksidənt] accidente *m*; by ~ por casualidad; ~al [~'dentl] accidental, casual
acclaim [ə'kleim] *v/t* aclamar, aplaudir
acclimate [ə'klaimit] *v/t* aclimatar; acostumbrarse (a)
accommodat|e [ə'kɔmədeit] *v/t* acomodar; alojar; complacer; ~e with proveer de; *v/i* acomodarse, conformarse; ~ion [əkɔmə'deiʃən] adaptación *f*; alojamiento *m*
accompan|iment [ə'kʌmpənimənt] acompañamiento *m*; ~y *v/t* acompañar
accomplice [ə'kɔmplis] cómplice *m*
accomplish [ə'kɔmpliʃ] *v/t* realizar, efectuar; ~ed consumado, perfecto; ~ment realización *f*; logro *m*; talento *m*, habilidad *f*
accord [ə'kɔ:d] *s* acuerdo *m*; armonía *f*; *v/t* conceder, otorgar; *v/i* convenir, concordar
accordance [ə'kɔ:dəns]: in ~ with conforme a
according [ə'kɔ:diŋ]: ~ to según; ~ly por consiguiente; en conformidad
accordion [ə'kɔ:diən] acordeón *m*
accost [ə'kɔst] *v/t* dirigirse a
account [ə'kaunt] *s* cuenta *f*; relación *f*; informe *m*; of no ~ sin importancia; on ~ a cuenta; on ~ of por; a causa de; on no ~ de ningún modo; to take into ~ tomar en cuenta; to turn to ~ sacar provecho de; *v/t* tener por, considerar; *v/i*: to ~ for explicar; responder de; ~ant contable *m*; ~ing contabilidad *f*
accrue [ə'kru:] *v/i* crecer, aumentar; *com* acumularse (*interés, capital*)
accumulate [ə'kju:mjuleit] *v/t*, *v/i* acumular(se)
accura|cy ['ækjurəsi] exactitud *f*, precisión *f*; ~te exacto, preciso; correcto
accus|ation [ækju:'zeiʃən] acusación *f*; *for* denuncia *f*; ~ative [ə'kju:zətiv] *gram* acusativo *m*; ~e [ə'kju:z] *v/t* acusar, culpar; ~er acusador *m*
accustom [ə'kʌstəm] *v/t* acostumbrar; ~ed acostumbrado
ace [eis] as *m* (*t fig*)
ache [eik] *v/i* doler; *s* dolencia *f*; dolor *m*
achieve [ə'tʃi:v] *v/t* conseguir, lograr; ~ment logro *m*, proeza *f*
acid ['æsid] *s, a* ácido *m*
acknowledg|e [ək'nɔlidʒ] *v/t* reconocer; confirmar; ~e receipt acusar recibo; ~ment reconocimiento *m*
acorn ['eikɔ:n] bellota *f*
acoustics [ə'ku:stiks] acústica *f*
acquaint [ə'kweint] *v/t* familiarizar (con); enterar, informar; to be ~ed with conocer; ~ance conocimiento *m*; conocido *m*
acquiesce [ækwi'es] *v/i* asentir, acceder
acqui|re [ə'kwaiə] *v/t* adquirir, obtener; ~sition [ækwi'ziʃən] adquisición *f*
acquit [ə'kwit] *v/t* absolver; ~ oneself desempeñarse; ~tal *for* absolución *f*, descargo *m*
acre ['eikə] acre *m* (= 40,47 áreas)
acrid ['ækrid] acre (*t fig*)
acrobat ['ækrəbæt] acróbata *m, f*
across [ə'krɔs] a través de; al otro lado de; to come ~ encontrarse con
act [ækt] *s* acto *m*; hecho *m*; *for* ley *f*; *v/i* actuar, obrar; *teat* actuar; to ~ a part desempeñar un papel; ~ion ['ækʃən] acción *f*, operación *f*; *mil* batalla *f*; *for* demanda *f*; proceso *m*; take ~ion tomar medidas; ~ive *a* activo, enérgico; *s gram* (voz) activa *f*; ~ivity [~'tiviti] actividad *f*; ~or actor *m*; ~ress actriz *f*
actual ['æktʃuel] real, verdadero; actual; ~ly en efecto
acute [ə'kju:t] agudo
adamant ['ædəmənt] firme, intransigente
adapt [ə'dæpt] *v/t* adaptar, ajustar; ~er *tecn* adaptador *m*
add [æd] *v/t* añadir, agregar; to ~ up sumar
addict ['ædikt] *med* adicto *m*, toxicómano *m*; ~ed [ə'diktid]: ~ed (to) adicto (*a drogas*)
addition [ə'diʃən] adición *f*; añadidura *f*; in ~ por añadidura; in ~ to además de; ~al adicional
address [ə'dres] *v/t* dirigir (*carta, sobre, protesta*); dirigir la palabra a; dirigirse a; *s* señas *f/pl*, dirección *f*; discurso *m*; ~ee [ædrə'si:] destinatario *m*
adequate ['ædikwit] suficiente; adecuado
adhere [əd'hiə] *v/i* adherirse (to a); ~nt [~rənt] adherente *m*
adhesive [əd'hi:siv] adhesivo; ~ plaster esparadrapo *m*
adjacent [ə'dʒeisənt] adyacente, contiguo
adjective ['ædʒiktiv] adjetivo *m*
adjoin [ə'dʒɔin] *v/t* juntar; *v/i* lindar; ~ing contiguo, colindante
adjourn [ə'dʒə:n] *v/t* diferir, aplazar; suspender
adjust [ə'dʒʌst] *v/t* ajustar, arreglar; ~ment ajuste *m*, arreglo *m*
ad-lib [æd'lib] *v/t*, *v/i*, *fam* improvisar
administ|er [əd'ministə] *v/t* administrar; suministrar; ~ration [~'streiʃən] administración *f*; gobierno *m*; ~rative [~trətiv] administrativo, gubernamental; ~rator [~treitə] administrador *m*
admir|able ['ædmərəbl] admirable; ~ation [ædmə'reiʃən] admiración *f*; ~e [əd'maiə] *v/t* admirar
admiss|ible [əd'misəbl] admisible; ~ion admisión *f*; entrada *f*
admit [əd'mit] *v/t* admitir; permitir; reconocer, confesar; ~tance admisión *f*, entrada *f*; no ~tance prohibida la entrada
admonish [əd'mɔniʃ] *v/t* amonestar, reprender
ado [ə'du:] bullicio *m*; dificultad *f*; fatiga *f*; much ~ about nothing mucho ruido y pocas nueces
adolescent [ædəu'lesnt] *s, a* adolescente *m, f*
adopt [ə'dɔpt] *v/t* adoptar; ~ion adopción *f*
ador|able [ə'dɔ:rəbl] adorable; ~ation [ædɔ:'reiʃən] adoración *f*; ~e *v/t* adorar
adorn [ə'dɔ:n] *v/t* adornar
adrift [ə'drift] a la deriva
adroit [ə'drɔit] diestro, hábil
adult ['ædʌlt] *a, s* adulto *m*; ~erate [ə'dʌltəreit] *v/t* adulterar; falsificar; ~ery adulterio *m*
advance [əd'vɑ:ns] *v/t* avanzar; adelantar (*hora, reloj, dinero*); *v/i* progresar; avanzar (*tropas*); *s* avance *m*, progreso *m*; anticipo *m*, adelanto *m*; aumento *m*; ~d avanzado; ~d in years entrado en años
advantage [əd'vɑ:ntidʒ] ventaja *f*; to take ~ of aprovecharse de; ~ous [ædvən'teidʒəs] ventajoso
advent ['ædvənt] advenimiento *m*; 2 Adviento *m*
adventur|e [əd'ventʃə] aventura *f*; ~er aventurero *m*; ~ous aventurado
adverb ['ædvə:b] adverbio *m*
advers|ary ['ædvəsəri] adversario *m*; enemigo *m*; ~e adverso; contrario
advertis|e ['ædvətaiz] *v/t* anunciar, publicar; ~ement [əd'və:tismənt] anuncio *m*; ~er anunciante *m*; ~ing publicidad *f*
advice [əd'vais] consejo *m*; *com* aviso *m*; comunicación *f*; to take ~ seguir un consejo
advis|able [əd'vaizəbl] aconsejable; ~e *v/t* aconsejar; *com* avisar, informar; ~er consejero *m*, asesor *m*
advocate ['ædvəkeit] *v/t* abogar por; defender; ['ædvəkit] *s* abogado *m*
aerial ['ɛəriəl] *a* aéreo; *s* antena *f*
aero... ['ɛərəu] aero; ~dynamic aerodinámico; ~nautics [ɛərə'nɔ:tiks] aeronáutica *f*; ~plane ['ɛərəplein] aeroplano *m*, avión *m*
affable ['æfəbl] afable
affair [ə'fɛə] asunto *m*; negocio *m*; aventura *f* amorosa
affect [ə'fekt] *v/t* afectar; impresionar; influir en; ~ed afectado, artificioso; emocionado, conmovido; ~ion afecto *m*, cariño *m*; ~ionate [~ʃnit] afectuoso, cariñoso
affinity [ə'finiti] afinidad *f*
affirm [ə'fə:m] *v/t* afirmar; ratificar; ~ation [æfə:'meiʃən] afirmación *f*; ~ative [ə'fə:mətiv] *a* afirmativo
afflict [ə'flikt] *v/t* afligir, acuitar, angustiar
affluen|ce ['æfluens] opulencia *f*; abundancia *f*; ~t *a* opulento, rico; *s* afluente *m*
afford [ə'fɔ:d] *v/t* permitirse el lujo de; proporcionar
affront [ə'frʌnt] *v/t* afrentar; insultar; ultrajar; *s* afrenta *f*, insulto *m*; injuria *f*
afire [ə'faiə] ardiendo
aflame [ə'fleim] en llamas
afloat [ə'fləut] a flote
afore|mentioned [əfɔ:'menʃənd] sobredicho; ~said antedicho; ~thought premeditado
afraid [ə'freid] temeroso, miedoso; to be ~ tener miedo
African ['æfrikən] *a, s* africano(a) *m* (*f*)
after ['ɑ:ftə] *prep* después de, detrás de; ~ all después de todo; ~ hours fuera de horas; ~math [~mæθ] consecuencias *f/pl*; ~noon tarde *f*; ~taste dejo *m*, resabio *m*; ~wards [~wədz] luego, después
again [ə'gein] otra vez, de nuevo; now and ~ de vez en cuando; once and ~ repetidas veces; ~st contra; to be ~st oponerse a
age [eidʒ] *s* edad *f*; época *f*; of ~, under ~ mayor, menor de edad; ~-old secular; *v/t*, *v/i* envejecer(se)
aged ['eidʒid] viejo
agen|cy ['eidʒənsi] agencia *f*, representación *f*; medio *m*; ~t agente *m*, representante *m*
aggravat|e ['ægrəveit] *v/t* agravar; ~ing agravante; irritante
aggress|ion [ə'greʃən] agresión *f*, asalto *m*; ~ive agresivo
aghast [ə'gɑ:st] espantado, horrorizado
agitat|e ['ædʒiteit] *v/t* agitar; ~ion agitación *f*; ~or agitador *m*
ago [ə'gəu] hace, ha; how long ~? ¿hace cuánto tiempo?; long ~ hace mucho tiempo
agon|ize ['ægənaiz] *v/i* agonizar; ~izing angustioso, agonizante; ~y agonía *f*; angustia *f*
agree [ə'gri:] *v/i* estar de acuerdo, concordar; ~ to convenir en; ~able agradable; ~d convenido; ~ment acuerdo *m*; convenio *m*
agricultur|al [ægri'kʌltʃərəl] agrícola; ~e agricultura *f*
ague ['eigju:] fiebre *f* intermitente; escalofríos *m/pl*
ahead [ə'hed] delante, al frente, adelante; go ~ with llevar adelante
aid [eid] *v/t* ayudar; *s* ayuda *f*; 2s *med* SIDA *m*
ail [eil] *v/t* afligir, molestar; *v/i* sufrir; ~ing enfermizo; ~ment enfermedad *f*
aim [eim] *v/t* apuntar (*arma*); dirigir; *v/i* aspirar; proponerse; *s* puntería *f*; designio *m*; finalidad *f*, fin *m*; to miss one's ~ errar el tiro; ~less sin objeto
air [ɛə] aire *m*; in the open ~ al aire libre; to be on the ~ transmitir (*por la radio*); ~ base base *f* aérea; ~ conditioned con aire *m* acondicionado; ~craft avión *m*; ~craft carrier portaaviones *m*; ~ cushion almohada *f* neumática; ~ force *mil* fuerza *f* aérea; ~ hostess azafata *f*, *LA* aeromoza *f*; ~line línea *f* aérea; ~liner avión *m* de pasajeros; ~mail correo *m* aéreo; ~plane aeroplano *m*, avión *m*; ~port aeropuerto *m*; ~ raid ataque *m* aéreo; ~sick mareado; ~tight hermético; *v/t* airear, ventilar
aisle [ail] pasillo *m*
ajar [ə'dʒɑ:] entreabierto

English

akin 4

akin [ə'kin] relacionado (**to** con)
alarm [ə'lɑːm] *v/t* alarmar, preturbar; *s* alarma *f*; tumulto *m*; **~ clock** despertador *m*; **~ing** alarmante, perturbador
alas! [ə'lɑːs] ¡ay!
alcohol ['ælkəhɔl] alcohol *m*; **~ic** [~'hɔlik] alcohólico
ale [eil] cerveza *f* inglesa
alert [ə'ləːt] *a* vivo, activo; vigilante; *s* alerta *f*; **on the ~** sobre aviso
algebra ['ældʒibrə] álgebra *f*
alibi ['ælibai] coartada *f*
alien ['eiliən] *a* ajeno, extraño; *s* extranjero *m*; forastero *m*; **~ate** *v/t* enajenar; quitar; ofender
alight [ə'lait] *v/i* apearse; *aer* aterrizar
alike [ə'laik] *adv* igualmente; del mismo modo; *a* parecido; **to look ~** parecerse
alimony ['æliməni] *for* alimentos *m/pl* (*de divorcio*)
alive [ə'laiv] vivo, viviente; activo
all [ɔːl] todo; todos; **above ~** sobre todo; **after ~** al fin y al cabo; **~ in ~** en definitiva; **~ but** casi; **not at ~** de ningún modo; **~ over** por todas partes; **it is ~ over** se acabó; **~ right** muy bien; satisfactorio; **~ the better** tanto mejor; **~ the worse** tanto peor
all-(a)round ['ɔːl(ə)'raund] completo; versátil; de uso variado
allay [ə'lei] *v/t* aliviar, mitigar
alleged [ə'ledʒd] supuesto
alleviate [ə'liːvieit] *v/t* aliviar
alley ['æli] callejón *m*
all|iance [ə'laiəns] alianza *f*; **~ied** aliado; **~y** aliado *m*
allot [ə'lɔt] *v/t* adjudicar, asignar; **~ment** asignación *f*; cuota *f*, lote *m*
all-out ['ɔːl'aut] *a* máximo (*esfuerzo*); *adv* con toda fuerza
allow [ə'lau] *v/t*, *v/i* permitir; conceder; **~ for** tener en cuenta; **~ance** concesión *f*; pensión *f*; subsidio *m*; *com* descuento *m*
alloy [ə'lɔi] aleación *f*
allu|de [ə'luːd] *v/i* aludir; **~sion** alusión *f*; **~sive** alusivo
allure [ə'ljuə] *v/t* atraer, fascinar, seducir
almanac ['ɔːlmənæk] almanaque *m*
almighty [ɔːl'maiti] *a*, *s* todopoderoso *m*
almond ['ɑːmənd] almendra *f*; **~ tree** almendro *m*
almost ['ɔlːməust] casi
alms [ɑːmz] limosna *f*
aloft [ə'lɔft] hacia arriba, en alto
alone [ə'ləun] *a* solo; *adv* sólo; **all ~** a solas; **to leave ~** dejar en paz; **let ~** mucho menos
along [ə'lɔŋ] *prep* a lo largo (de); por; al lado de; *adv.* **all ~** desde el principio
aloof [ə'luːf] reservado; apartado
aloud [ə'laud] en voz alta
alphabet ['ælfəbit] alfabeto *m*
Alps [ælps] Alpes *m/pl*
already [ɔːl'redi] ya
also ['ɔːlsəu] también
altar ['ɔːltə] altar *m*
alter ['ɔːltə] *v/t* alterar, modificar
alternat|e ['ɔːltəːneit] *v/t*, *v/i* alternar; [~'təːnit] *a* alterno; *s* suplente *m*; **~ing current** corriente *f* alterna; **~ive** *a* alternativo; *s* alternativa *f*
although [ɔːl'ðəu] aunque, a pesar de que
altitude ['æltitjuːd] altitud *f*; altura *f*
alto [æltəu] *mús* contralto *m*, *f*
altogether [ɔːltə'geðə] en conjunto; por completo
aluminium [ælju'minjəm] aluminio *m*
always ['ɔːlwəz] siempre
am [æm]: **I ~** soy; estoy
amass [ə'mæs] *v/t* acumular
amateur ['æmətəː] aficionado *m*
amaze [ə'meiz] *v/t* asombrar; **~ment** asombro *m*
Amazon ['æməzən] Amazonas *m*
ambassador [æm'bæsədə] embajador *m*
amber ['æmbə] ámbar *m*
ambiguous [æm'bigjuəs] ambiguo; equívoco
ambiti|on [æm'biʃən] ambición *f*; **~ous** ambicioso
ambulance ['æmbjuləns] ambulancia *f*
ambush ['æmbuʃ] *v/t* acechar; *s* emboscada *f*, celada *f*
amen ['ɑː'men] amén *m*
amend [ə'mend] *v/t* enmendar; rectificar; **~ment** enmienda *f*; **~s** reparación *f*; indemnización *f*
America [ə'merikə] América *f*; **~n** *a*, *s* americano(a) *m* (*f*)
amiable ['eimiəbl] afable, amable
amicable ['æmikəbl] amistoso, amigable
amid(st) [ə'mid(st)] en medio de, entre
amiss [ə'mis] fuera de lugar, inoportuno; **to take ~** tomar a mal
ammunition [æmju'niʃən] municiones *f/pl*
amnesty ['æmnisti] amnistía *f*; indulto *m*
among(st) [ə'mʌŋ(st)] entre (*varios*)
amorous ['æmərəs] enamoradizo, amoroso
amount [ə'maunt] *v/i* ascender (a), elevarse (a); *s* cantidad *f*, importe *m*
ampl|e ['æmpl] amplio; **~ifier** [~lifaiə] amplificador *m*; **~ify** *v/t* ampliar, amplificar
amputate ['æmpjuteit] *v/t* amputar
amuse [ə'mjuːz] *v/t* divertir, entretener; **to ~ oneself** divertirse; **~ment** diversión *f*; entretenimiento *m*
an [æn, ən] un, uno, una
an(a)emia [ə'niːmiə] anemia *f*
analog|ous [ə'næləgəs] análogo; **~y** [~dʒi] analogía *f*
analy|se ['ænəlaiz] *v/t* analizar; **~sis** [ə'næləsis] análisis *m*, *f*
anarch|ic [æ'nɑːkik] anárquico; **~ist** ['ænəkist] anarquista *m*, *f*; **~y** anarquía *f*
anatomy [ə'nætəmi] anatomía *f*
ancest|or ['ænsistə] antepasado *m*; **~ry** linaje *m*, abolengo *m*
anchor ['æŋkə] *v/i* anclar; *s* ancla *f*, áncora *f*; **drop ~** echar anclas; **weigh ~** levar anclas
anchovy ['æntʃəvi] anchoa *f*
ancient ['einʃənt] antiguo
and [ænd, ənd] y, e
anew [ə'njuː] de nuevo, otra vez
angel ['eindʒəl] ángel *m*
ang|er ['æŋgə] *s* ira *f*; enfado *m*; *v/t* enojar, provocar; **~ry** furioso, enfadado; **get ~ry** montar en cólera
angle ['æŋgl] *s* ángulo *m*, esquina *f*; *v/t* pescar con caña
Anglican ['æŋglikən] *s*, *a* anglicano(a) *m* (*f*)
Anglo-Saxon ['æŋgləu-'sæksən] *s*, *a* anglosajón
anguish ['æŋgwiʃ] angustia *f*, ansia *f*
animal ['æniməl] animal *m*
animate ['ænimeit] *v/t* animar, alentar; **~d cartoon** película *f* de dibujos animados
animosity [æni'mɔsiti] animosidad *f*; rencor *m*
anise ['ænis] anís *m*
ankle ['æŋkl] tobillo *m*
annex [ə'neks] *v/t* anexar (*territorio*); adjuntar, unir; ['æneks] *s arq* pabellón *m*
annihilate [ə'naiəleit] *v/t* aniquilar
anniversary [æni'vəːsəri] aniversario *m*
annotat|e ['ænəuteit] *v/t* anotar, glosar; **~ion** anotación *f*; apunte *m*
announce [ə'nauns] *v/t* anunciar; **~ment** anuncio *m*, aviso *m*; **~r** locutor *m*
annoy [ə'nɔi] *v/t* molestar; fastidiar; **~ance** molestia *f*; **~ed: to be ~ed** estar fastidiado, enfadado; **~ing** molesto, enojoso
annual ['ænjuəl] anual
annul [ə'nʌl] *v/t* anular; **~ment** anulación *f*
anomalous [ə'nɔmələs] anómalo
anonymous [ə'nɔniməs] anónimo
another [ə'nʌðə] otro
answer ['ɑːnsə] *v/t*, *v/i* contestar a; responder a; **~ for** responder de; *s* contestación *f*, respuesta *f*; solución *f*
ant [ænt] hormiga *f*; **~hill** hormiguero *m*
antagonis|m [æn'tægənizəm] antagonismo *m*; **~t** antagonista *m*, *f*
Antarctic [ænt'ɑːktik] antártico
antelope ['æntiləup] antílope *m*
antenna [æn'tenə] antena *f*
anthem ['ænθəm] motete *m*; **national ~** himno *m* nacional
anti|-aircraft ['ænti'ɛəkrɑːft] antiaéreo; **~biotic** [~bai'ɔtik] *s*, *a* antibiótico *m*; **~climax** [~'klaimæks] fin *m* (*de un libro*, *etc*) decepcionante
antics ['æntiks] payasadas *f/pl*
anticipat|e [æn'tisipeit] *v/t* anticipar; prever; adelantar(se); **~ion** anticipación *f*; previsión *f*
anti|dote ['ænti'dəut] antídoto *m*; contraveneno *m*; **~freeze** [~friːz] anticongelante *m*
antipathy [æn'tipəθi] antipatía *f*
antiqu|ated ['æntikweitid] anticuado; **~e** [æn'tiːk] antiguo; **~es** antigüedades *f/pl*; **~ity** [~'tikwiti] antigüedad *f*
antler ['æntlə] cuerno *m*
anvil ['ænvil] yunque *m*
anxi|ety [æŋ'zaiəti] ansia *f*; ansiedad *f*; **~ous** ['æŋkʃəs] ansioso, inquieto; anheloso
any ['eni] cualquier(a); **not ~** ningún(o), a, os, as; **~body, ~one** alguno; cualquiera, quienquiera; **not ~body, ~one** nadie; **~how** de cualquier modo; **~thing** cualquier cosa; **~way** de cualquier modo; **~where** en cualquier parte; **not ~where** en ninguna parte
apart [ə'pɑːt] aparte; **~ment** piso *m*; *LA* apartamento *m*
apath|etic [æpə'θetik] apático; **~y** ['æpəθi] apatía *f*
ape [eip] mono *m*
aperitif [ə'peritiv] aperitivo *m*
apiece [ə'piːs] (a, por, para) cada uno
apolog|ize [ə'pɔlədʒaiz] *v/i* disculparse; **~y** disculpa *f*; excusa *f*
apoplexy ['æpəupleksi] apoplejía *f*
apostle [ə'pɔsl] apóstol *m*
apostrophe [ə'pɔstrəfi] *gram* apóstrofo *m*
appal(l) [ə'pɔːl] *v/t* asombrar, pasmar; espantar
apparatus [æpə'reitəs] aparato *m*; aparejo *m*
apparel [ə'pærəl] *com* ropa *f*
apparent [ə'pærənt] aparente; **~ly** por lo visto
appeal [ə'piːl] *v/i* **for** apelar; **~ to** apelar a; interesar a, atraer; *s* **for** apelación *f*; petición *f*; atractivo *m*
appear [ə'piə] *v/i* aparecer; parecer; **for** comparecer; **~ance** apariencia *f*; aspecto *m*; aparición *f*; *for* comparecencia *f*
appease [ə'piːz] *v/t* apaciguar; **~ment** apaciguamiento *m*
append|icitis [əpendi'saitis] apendicitis *f*; **~ix** [ə'pendiks] apéndice *m*
appeti|te ['æpitait] apetito *m*; **~zing** apetitoso
applau|d [ə'plɔːd] *v/t* aplaudir; **~se** [~z] aplauso *m*
apple ['æpl] manzana *f*; **Adam's ~** nuez *f* de la garganta; **~ of one's eye** *fam fig* el ojo derecho de uno; **~ pie** pastel *m* de manzana; **~ tree** manzano *m*
appliance [ə'plaiəns] aparato *m*; dispositivo *m*; **household ~s** electrodomésticos *m/pl*
application [æpli'keiʃən] aplicación *f*; solicitud *f*
apply [ə'plai] *v/t* aplicar, utilizar; *v/i* ser pertinente, corresponder; **~ for** pedir
appoint [ə'pɔint] *v/t* nombrar; señalar; **~ment** cita *f*, compromiso *m*; nombramiento *m*
apportion [ə'pɔːʃən] *v/t* prorratear
apprecia|te [ə'priːʃieit] *v/t* apreciar, estimar; *v/i* *com* subir de valor; **~tion** aprecio *m*; estimación *f*
apprehen|d [æpri'hend] *v/t*, *v/i* comprender, percibir; recelar; aprehender, prender, capturar; **~sive** aprensivo, receloso; perspicaz
apprentice [ə'prentis] aprendiz *m*; **~ship** aprendizaje *m*
approach [ə'prəutʃ] *v/t*, *v/i* aproximar(se); acercar(se); *s* acceso *m*; aproximación *f*
appropriate [ə'prəuprieit] *v/t* apropiarse de; [ə'prəupriit] *a* apropiado, apto
approv|al [ə'pruːvəl] aprobación *f*; asentimiento *m*; **~e** *v/t* sancionar, aprobar
approximate [ə'prɔksimeit] *v/t*, *v/i* aproximar(se); [ə'prɔksimit] *a* aproximado
apricot ['eiprikɔt] albaricoque *m*; *LA* damasco *m*
April ['eipril] abril *m*
apron ['eiprən] delantal *m*
apse [æps] ábside *m*
apt [æpt] apto; propenso; **~itude** ['æptitjuːd] aptitud *f*
aqu|arium [ə'kwɛəriəm] acuario *m*; **~atic** [ə'kwætik] acuático; **~atics** deportes *m/pl* acuáticos
aquiline ['ækwilain] aguileño
Arab ['ærəb] *s*, *a* árabe; **~ic** árabe *m*; lengua *f* árabe
arable ['ærəbl] cultivable
arbitrary ['ɑːbitrəri] arbitrario
arbo(u)r ['ɑːbə] cenador *m*
arc [ɑːk] arco *m*; **~ade** [ɑː'keid] *arq* arcada *f*; galería *f*
arch [ɑːtʃ] *arq* arco *m*; bóveda *f*; *anat* empeine *m*; *a* socarrón; zumbón
archaeolog|ist [ɑːki'ɔledʒist] arqueólogo *m*; **~y** arqueología *f*
archaic [ɑː'keiik] arcaico
arch|angel ['ɑːkeindʒəl] arcángel *m*; **~bishop** ['ɑːtʃ-'biʃəp] arzobispo *m*; **~er** ['ɑːtʃə] arquero *m*; **~ery** [~əri] tiro *m* de arco
architect ['ɑːkitekt] arquitecto *m*; **~ure** arquitectura *f*
arctic ['ɑːktik] ártico
ard|ent ['ɑːdənt] ardiente, vehemente; **~o(u)r** ardor *m*, pasión *f*; **~uous** arduo, duro, muy difícil
are [ɑː]: **you ~** eres, sois; estás, estáis; **we ~** somos; estamos; **they ~** son; están
area ['ɛəriə] área *f*, zona *f*
arena [ə'riːnə] arena *f*
Argentine ['ɑːdʒəntain] *s* Argentina *f*; *a* argentino
argu|e ['ɑːgjuː] *v/t*, *v/i* argüir, discutir; razonar; **~ment** argumento *m*; discusión *f*, disputa *f*
arid ['ærid] árido
arise [ə'raiz] *v/i* alzarse; surgir; resultar (de)
arithmetic [ə'riθmətik] aritmética *f*
ark [ɑːk] arca *f*
arm [ɑːm] *s* brazo *m*; **~ in ~** cogidos del brazo; *v/t*, *v/i* armar; **~ament** [~əmənt] armamento *m*; **~ chair** butaca *f*; **~ful** brazada *f*; **~istice** armisticio *m*; **~o(u)r** armadura *f*; blindaje *m*; **~o(u)red** blindado; **~pit** sobaco *m*; **~rest** apoyabrazos *m*; **~s** armas *f/pl*; **~y** ejército *m*; tropas *f/pl*
around [ə'raund] *adv* alrededor; *prep* alrededor de
arouse [ə'rauz] *v/t* despertar, excitar
arrange [ə'reindʒ] *v/t* arreglar; disponer; **~ment** arreglo *m*; disposición *f*
arrears [ə'riəz]: **in ~** atrasado en pagos
arrest [ə'rest] *v/t* detener, arrestar; *s* detención *f*, arresto *m*; paro *m*
arriv|al [ə'raivəl] llegada *f*; (el que ha) llegado *m*; **~e** *v/i* llegar; alcanzar éxito
arrogan|ce ['ærəgəns] arrogancia *f*; **~t** arrogante
arrow ['ærəu] flecha *f*
arsenic ['ɑːsnik] arsénico *m*
arson ['ɑːsn] *for* incendio *m* premeditado
art [ɑːt] arte *m*; destreza *f*; maña *f*; **~s and crafts** artes *f/pl* y oficios; **fine ~s** bellas artes *f/pl*; **~ful** mañoso; artificioso; **~fulness** astucia *f*
artichoke ['ɑːtitʃouk] alcachofa *f*
article ['ɑːtikl] artículo *m*
articulate [ɑː'tikjuleit] *v/t* articular, pronunciar; [~'tikjulit] *a* articulado; inteligible
artific|e ['ɑːtifis] artificio *m*; **~ial** [~'fiʃəl] artificial
artillery [ɑː'tiləri] artillería *f*
artisan [ɑːti'zæn] artesano *m*
artist ['ɑːtist] artista *m/f*; **~ic** artístico
artless ['ɑːtlis] natural, sencillo
as [æz, əz] *adv* como; **~ ... ~** tan(to) ... como; **~ far ~** en cuanto; **~ for** en cuanto a; **~ if** como si; **~ many ~** tantos como; **~ soon ~** tan pronto como; **~ well** también; **~ yet** hasta ahora; *conj* como;

aunque; ~ to en cuanto a

ascen|d [ə'send] v/t, v/i ascender, subir; ~sion ascensión f; ~t subida f; ascenso m

ascertain [æsə'tein] v/t averiguar; cerciorarse de

ascetic [ə'setik] ascético

ascribe [əs'kraib] v/t atribuir, achacar; imputar

aseptic [æ'septik] aséptico

ash [æʃ] fresno m; ceniza f

ashamed [ə'ʃeimd] avergonzado; to be ~ tener vergüenza

ash|es ['æʃiz] cenizas f/pl; ~tray cenicero m

ashore [ə'ʃɔ:] en tierra, a tierra; to go ~ desembarcar

Asia ['eiʃə] Asia f; ~tic a, s [eiʃi'ætik] asiático(a) m (f)

aside [ə'said] de lado, al lado; aparte (t s teat)

ask [ɑ:sk] v/t preguntar; pedir; invitar; ~ a question hacer una pregunta; ~ about, ~ for preguntar por

askew [əs'kju:] torcido, ladeado

asleep [ə'sli:p] dormido; to fall ~ quedarse dormido

asparagus [əs'pærəgəs] espárrago m

aspect ['æspekt] aspecto m

aspir|ant [əs'paiərənt] aspirante m; candidato m; ~e v/i aspirar; ambicionar

aspirin ['æspərin] aspirina f

ass [æs] asno m, burro m

assail [ə'seil] v/t asaltar, acometer

assassin [ə'sæsin] asesino m; ~ate v/t asesinar; ~ation asesinato m

assault [ə'sɔ:lt] v/t asaltar; s asalto m

assembl|age [ə'semblidʒ] tecn montaje m; ~e [ə'sembl] v/t juntar; tecn montar; v/i reunirse; ~y asamblea f; montaje m; ~y line tecn línea f de montaje

assent [ə'sent] s asentimiento m; v/i ~ to asentir a; consentir en

assert [ə'sə:t] v/t afirmar; ~ion afirmación f

assess [ə'ses] v/t valorar; gravar; fijar (impuestos)

asset ['æset] posesión f; ventaja f; ~s activo m, haber m

assiduous [ə'sidjuəs] asiduo; perseverante

assign [ə'sain] v/t asignar; señalar, destinar; ~ment asignación f; cesión f

assimilate [ə'simileit] v/t asimilar

assist [ə'sist] v/t asistir, ayudar; ~ance ayuda f, auxilio m; ~ant ayudante m

associat|e [ə'səuʃieit] v/t asociar; v/i asociarse; adherirse; s socio m; ~ion asociación f, sociedad f

assort|ed [ə'sɔ:tid] surtido, mixto; ~ment surtido m

assum|e [ə'sju:m] v/t tomar; asumir; presumir; suponer; ~ed fingido; ~ption [ə'sʌmpʃən] asunción f; postulado m, presunción f

assur|ance [ə'ʃuərəns] seguridad f; promesa f; aplomo m; com seguro m; ~e v/t asegurar, afirmar; ~ed seguro; com asegurado

asterisk ['æstərisk] asterisco m

asthma ['æsmə] asma f

astonish [əs'tɔniʃ] v/t sorprender, asombrar; ~ed sorprendido; asombrado; ~ment asombro m; sorpresa f

astound [əs'taund] v/t, v/i pasmar, consternar

astray [ə'strei]: to go ~ extraviarse; lead ~ llevar por mal camino

astride [əs'traid] a horcajadas

astrology [əs'trɔlədʒi] astrología f

astronaut ['æstrənɔ:t] astronauta m

astronom|er [əs'trɔnəmə] astrónomo m; ~y astronomía f

astute [əs'tju:t] astuto, sagaz; perspicaz

asunder [ə'sʌndə]: tear ~ hacer pedazos

asylum [ə'sailəm] asilo m

at [æt, ət] a, en; por; ~ best en el mejor de los casos; ~ home en casa; ~ night por la noche; ~ school en la escuela; ~ the door a la puerta

atheist ['eiθiist] ateo m

athlet|e ['æθli:t] atleta m; ~ic [~'letik] atlético; ~ics atletismo m

Atlantic [ət'læntik] atlántico

atmosphere ['ætməsfiə] atmósfera f

atom ['ætəm] átomo m; ~ bomb bomba f atómica; ~ic atómico; ~ic age era f atómica; ~ic pile pila f atómica; ~izer pulverizador m

atone [ə'təun]: v/i to ~ for expiar

atroci|ous [ə'trəuʃəs] atroz; ~ty [~siti] atrocidad f

attach [ə'tætʃ] v/t atar, ligar; vincular; apegar; ~ment apego m; afecto m

attack [ə'tæk] v/t atacar; s ataque m

attain [ə'tein] v/t conseguir

attempt [ə'tempt] v/t intentar; s tentativa f, prueba f

attend [ə'tend] v/t asistir a, concurrir a; atender, cuidar; ~ance asistencia f; presencia f; be in ~ance asistir

attent|ion [ə'tenʃən] atención f; ~ion! ¡ojo!; pay ~ion prestar atención, hacer caso; ~ive atento

attest [ə'test] v/t atestiguar

attic ['ætik] desván m

attire [ə'taiə] atavío m; vestido m

attitude ['ætitju:d] actitud f

attorney [ə'tə:ni] abogado m

attract [ə'trækt] v/t, v/i atraer; ~ion atracción f; atractivo m; ~ive atractivo

attribute [ə'tribju(:)t] v/t atribuir; ['ætribju:t] s atributo m

auburn ['ɔ:bən] castaño rojizo

auction ['ɔ:kʃən] subasta f

audac|ious [ɔ:'deiʃəs] audaz; ~ity [ɔ:'dæsiti] audacia f

audi|ble ['ɔ:dəbl] audible; ~ence público m; audiencia f; ~tor interventor m, revisor m de cuentas; ~torium [~'tɔ:riəm] sala f

augment [ɔ:g'ment] v/t, v/i aumentar(se)

August ['ɔ:gəst] agosto m

aunt [ɑ:nt] tía f

auspicious [ɔ:s'piʃəs] propicio, favorable

auster|e [əs'tiə] austero; ~ity [~'teriti] austeridad f

Australia [ɔs'treiljə] Australia f; ~n a, s australiano(a) m (f)

Austria ['ɔstriə] Austria f; ~n a, s austríaco(a) m (f)

authentic [ɔ:'θentik] auténtico

author ['ɔ:θə] autor m; escritor m; ~itarian [ɔ:θɔri'tɛəriən] autoritario; ~itative [ɔ:'θɔritətiv] autorizado; perentorio; ~ity autoridad f; on good ~ity de buena tinta; ~ize [~raiz] autorizar; ~ship paternidad f literaria

auto|matic [ɔ:tə'mætik] automático; ~matic focus foto autoenfoque m; ~mation automatización f

automobile ['ɔ:təməubi:l] automóvil m

autonomy [ɔ:'tɔnəmi] autonomía f

autopsy ['ɔ:tɔpsi] autopsia f

autumn ['ɔ:təm] otoño m

avail [ə'veil]: of no ~ inútil; v/i valer; to ~ oneself of servirse de; ~able disponible; aprovechable

avalanche ['ævəlɑ:ntʃ] alud m

avaric|e ['ævəris] avaricia f; ~ious [~'riʃəs] avaro

avenge [ə'vendʒ] v/t, v/i vengar(se) (de)

avenue ['ævinju:] avenida f

average ['ævəridʒ] s promedio m; on the ~ por término medio, en promedio; a medio; corriente; mediano, ordinario

aversion [ə'və:ʃən] aversión f, repugnancia f

avert [ə'və:t] v/t desviar; prevenir

aviat|ion [eivi'eiʃən] aviación f; ~or ['~eitə] aviador m

avocado [ɑ:vəkɑ:'dəu] aguacate m

avoid [ə'vɔid] v/t evitar

await [ə'weit] v/t aguardar

awake [ə'weik] v/t, v/i despertar(se); a despierto

award [ə'wɔ:d] v/t, v/i otorgar; conceder, conferir; s for fallo m; premio m

aware [ə'wɛə] enterado

away [ə'wei] fuera, ausente; far ~ lejos; to go ~ marcharse

aw|e [ɔ:] temor m reverente; ~e-struck espantado, pasmado; ~ful terrible, espantoso; fam pésimo; fatal; tremendo

awhile [ə'wail] (por) un rato

awkward ['ɔ:kwəd] torpe; embarazoso, desagradable; delicado (situación, etc)

awning ['ɔ:niŋ] toldo m

awry [ə'rai]: to go ~ salir mal, fracasar

ax(e) [æks] hacha f

axis ['æksis] eje m; anat axis

axle ['æksl] tecn eje m

azure ['æʒə] azul m celeste

B

babble ['bæbl] v/t, v/i balbucear; parlotear; barbotar; s barboteo m; parloteo m

babe [beib] criatura f

baboon [bə'bu:n] mandril m

baby ['beibi] criatura f; bebé m; ~hood primera infancia f; ~ish infantil

bachelor ['bætʃələ] soltero m; confirmed ~ solterón m

back [bæk] s espalda(s) f (pl); dorso m; reverso m, revés m; sp zaguero m; to be ~ estar de vuelta; to turn one's ~ dar la espalda; v/t apoyar; apostar a; v/i retroceder, dar marcha atrás; ~ down volverse atrás; ~ out retirarse; adv de vuelta; atrás; ~bone espina f dorsal; ~fire petardeo m; ~gammon chaquete m; ~ground fondo m; fundamento m; fig antecedentes m/pl; ~ing apoyo m; ~lash (t pol) reacción f en contra; ~log atrasos m/pl; ~pack mochila f; ~stroke brazada f de espaldas (en natación); ~ward(s) a atrasado; adv (hacia) atrás; ~yard patio m trasero

bacon ['beikən] tocino m

bacterium [bæk'tiəriəm] bacteria f

bad [bæd] malo; podrido; dañoso; not ~ nada malo; from ~ to worse de mal en peor; too ~! ¡qué lástima!; ~ly mal

badge [bædʒ] insignia f

badger ['bædʒə] tejón m

badminton ['bædmintən] juego m del volante

baffle ['bæfl] v/t desconcertar; frustrar

bag [bæg] saco m; bolsa f; ~gage Am equipaje m; mil bagaje m

bagpipes ['bægpaips] gaita f

bail [beil] fianza f

bailiff ['beilif] alguacil m

bait [beit] cebo m

bake [beik] v/t cocer (al horno); ~r panadero m; ~ry panadería f

balance ['bæləns] s equilibrio m; balanza f; volante m (de reloj); com balance m; v/t balancear; equilibrar; com saldar

balcony ['bælkəni] balcón m; teat galería f

bald [bɔ:ld] calvo

bale [beil] s bala f; fardo m; v/t embalar; to ~ out lanzarse en paracaídas

Balearic [bæli'ærik] balear; ~ Islands Islas f/pl Baleares

balk [bɔ:k] v/t impedir, frustrar; v/i plantarse (caballo)

ball [bɔ:l] pelota f; bola f; baile m; globo m; yema f (del dedo); ~ad ['bæləd] romance m; balada f; ~ast ['bæləst] lastre m; ~ bearing(s) tecn cojinete m de bolas

ballet ['bælei] ballet m, baile m artístico

ballistics [bə'listiks] balística f

balloon [bə'lu:n] globo m

ballot ['bælət] balota f; votación f; ~ box urna f electoral

ballpoint pen ['bɔ:lpɔint pen] bolígrafo m

balm [bɑ:m] bálsamo m; ~y suave (brisa, etc)

Baltic ['bɔ:ltik] (Sea) (Mar) Báltico m

bamboo [bæm'bu:] bambú m

ban [bæn] s prohibición f (oficial); v/t prohibir; excluir

banana [bə'nɑ:nə] plátano m; LA banana f

band [bænd] cinta f; mús banda f; to ~ together asociarse; ~age venda f, vendaje m

bandit ['bændit] bandido m

bang [bæŋ] interj ¡pum!; s estallido m; golpe m resonante; v/t golpear; cerrar de golpe

banish ['bæniʃ] v/t desterrar; ~ment destierro m

banisters ['bænistəz] pasamano m; barandilla f

bank [bæŋk] s orilla f; banco m; banca f; v/t depositar en el banco; ~ account cuenta f bancaria; ~er banquero m; ~ing operaciones f/pl bancarias; ~note billete m de banco; ~rupt ['~rʌpt] quebrado; ~ruptcy quiebra f, bancarrota f

banner ['bænə] bandera f

banns [bænz] amonestaciones f/pl

banquet ['bæŋkwit] s banquete m

banter ['bæntə] v/i chancear

bapti|sm ['bæptizm] bautismo m; ~ze [~'taiz] v/t bautizar

bar [bɑ:] s barra f; mostrador m; bar m; fig obstáculo m; ~s rejas f/pl; behind ~s en la cárcel; v/t atrancar; enrejar; impedir

barbar|ian [bɑ:'bɛəriən] bárbaro m; ~ous ['~bərəs] bárbaro

barbecue ['bɑ:bikju:] barbacoa f

barbed [bɑ:bd]: ~ wire alambre m de púas

barber ['bɑ:bə] barbero m, peluquero m

bare [bɛə] desnudo; escaso; mero; ~faced descarado; ~foot(ed) descalzo; ~headed descubierto; ~ly apenas

bargain ['bɑ:gin] s pacto m; ganga f; ~ price precio m rebajado; v/t, v/i negociar; regatear

barge [bɑ:dʒ] barcaza f; ~ in fig irrumpir

baritone ['bæritəun] barítono m

bark [bɑ:k] s ladrido m; corteza f (de un árbol); v/i ladrar

barley ['bɑ:li] cebada f

barmaid ['bɑ:meid] tabernera f

barn [bɑ:n] granero m; establo m; cuadra f

barometer [bə'rɔmitə] barómetro m

barrack ['bærək] cuartel m

barrel ['bærəl] barril m; cañón m; ~ organ organillo m

barren ['bærən] estéril, árido

barricade [bæri'keid] s barricada f; v/t obstruir

barrier ['bæriə] barrera f

barrister ['bæristə] abogado m

bartender ['bɑ:tendə] barman m

barter ['bɑ:tə] s trueque m; v/t trocar; v/i traficar

base [beis] a bajo, vil, villano; s base f; mil, quím base f; v/t basar; apoyar; fundar; ~ball béisbol m; ~less infundado; ~ment sótano m

bashful ['bæʃful] tímido

basic ['beisik] básico

basil ['bæzl] albahaca f

basin ['beisn] palangana f; geog cuenca f

bask [bɑ:sk] v/i tomar el sol

basket ['bɑ:skit] cesta f; canasta f; ~ball baloncesto m

Basque [bæsk] a, s vasco(a) m (f)

bass [beis] mús bajo m

bastard ['bæstəd] bastardo m

bat [bæt] zool murciélago m; sp bate m

bath [bɑ:θ] s baño m; v/t bañar (niño, enfermo, etc); ~e [beið] v/t bañar; v/i bañarse (al aire libre); ~ing-suit traje m de baño; bañador m; ~robe albornoz m; ~ room cuarto m de baño; ~tub [bɑ:θ-] bañera f

baton ['bætən] mús batuta f

batter ['bætə] v/t golpear; demoler; ~ed magullado; ~y batería f; pila f

battle ['bætl] s batalla f; lucha f; v/i luchar; ~ship acorazado m

bawl [bɔ:l] v/i vocear; llorar a gritos

bay [bei] a bayo; s bahía f; rada f; bot laurel m; arq entrepaño m; at ~ acorralado; v/t ladrar, aullar; ~onet bayoneta f

be [bi:, bi] v/i ser; estar; to ~ in estar (en casa, etc); to ~ out haber salido; so ~ it así sea

beach [bi:tʃ] playa f

beacon ['bi:kən] almenara f, aer baliza f; faro m

bead [bi:d] cuenta f; abalorio m; ~s rosario m

beak [bi:k] pico m

beam [bi:m] s arq viga f; rayo m (de luz; sol); mar manga f; v/t emitir; v/i brillar

bean [bi:n] haba f; judía f; LA frijol m; habichuela f

bear [bɛə] s zool oso m; com bajista m/f; v/t aguantar; dar a luz; llevar; ~ out confirmar

beard [biəd] barba *f*; **~ed** barbudo
bear|er ['bɛərə] portador(a) *m(f)*; **~ing** porte *m*; **~ings** rumbo *m*, orientación *f*
beast [biːst] bestia *f*
beat [biːt] *v/t* batir; pegar; golpear; tocar; derrotar; *v/i* latir, palpitar; **~ about the bush** ir por rodeos; **~ it** largarse; **~ time** *mús* llevar el compás; **~ up** dar una paliza; *s* golpe *m*; latido *m*; ronda *f* (*del policía*); *mús* compás *m*
beaut|iful ['bjuːtəful] hermoso, bello; **~ify** ['~fai] *v/t* embellecer; **~y** hermosura *f*; belleza *f*; **~y parlo(u)r** salón *m* de belleza
beaver ['biːvə] castor *m*
because [bi'kɔz] *adv* porque; **~ of** *prep* por; a causa de
beckon ['bekən] *v/t* llamar por señas
becom|e [bi'kʌm] *v/i* llegar a ser; hacerse; volverse, ponerse; *v/t* convenir a; **~ing** que sienta bien (*vestido*)
bed [bed] cama *f*; lecho *m*; *bot* arriate *m*; **to go to ~** acostarse; **~ding** ropa *f* de cama; **~lam** ['bedləm] confusión *f*, caos *m*; **~ridden** postrado en cama; **~room** dormitorio *m*; alcoba *f*; **~spread** colcha *f*; **~time** hora *f* de acostarse
bee [biː] abeja *f*; **~hive** colmena *f*; **~line** línea *f* recta
beech [biːtʃ] haya *f*
beef [biːf] carne *f* de res *o* de vaca; **~steak** bistec *m*
beer [biə] cerveza *f*
beet [biːt] remolacha *f*
beetle ['biːtl] escarabajo *m*
befit [bi'fit] *v/t* convenir a
before [bi'fɔː] *adv* delante (*lugar*); antes (*tiempo*); *prep* delante de (*lugar*); ante; antes de (*tiempo*); **~hand** de antemano
beg [beg] *v/t* rogar; pedir; *v/i* mendigar
beggar ['begə] mendigo *m*
begin [bi'gin] *v/t, v/i* empezar, comenzar; iniciar; **~ner** principiante *m*; **~ning** comienzo *m*
beguile [bi'gail] *v/t* engañar; seducir
behalf [bi'hɑːf]: **on ~ of** en nombre de
behav|e [bi'heiv] *v/t, v/i* (com)portarse; obrar; conducirse; **~io(u)r** conducta *f*
behead [bi'hed] *v/t* decapitar
behind [bi'haind] *adv* atrás; detrás; *prep* detrás de; tras; **to be ~** estar atrasado; *s* trasero *m*
being ['biːiŋ] ser *m*; persona *f*; **for the time ~** por ahora
belated [bi'leitid] tardío; atrasado
belch [beltʃ] *v/i* eructar
belfry ['belfri] campanario *m*
Belgi|an ['beldʒən] *a, s* belga *m, f*; **~um** ['~əm] Bélgica *f*
belie [bi'lai] *v/t* desmentir
belie|f [bi'liːf] creencia *f*; **~vable** creíble; **~ve** *v/t, v/i* creer; **to make ~ve** fingir; **~ver** creyente *m*, fiel *m*
belittle [bi'litl] *v/t* menospreciar
bell [bel] (*iglesia*) campana *f*; (*eléctrico*) timbre *m*; (*ganado*) cencerro *m*; **~boy** botones *m*
belligerent [bi'lidʒərənt] *a, s* beligerante
bellow ['beləu] *v/i* bramar; gritar; **~s** fuelle *m*
belly ['beli] vientre *m*; panza *f*; **~ button** *fam* ombligo *m*
belong [bi'lɔŋ] *v/i* pertenecer; **~ings** posesiones *f/pl*
beloved [bi'lʌvid] *a, s* querido(a) *m (f)*
below [bi'ləu] *adv* abajo; *prep* bajo; debajo de
belt [belt] cinturón *m*; faja *f*; *tecn* correa *f*
bench [ben(t)ʃ] banco *m*; tribunal *m*
bend [bend] *s* vuelta *f*; curva *f*; *v/t* doblar; inclinar; *v/i* encorvarse; torcerse
beneath [bi'niːθ] *adv* abajo; debajo; *prep* bajo, debajo de
bene|diction [beni'dikʃən] bendición *f*; **~factor** ['~fæktə] bienhechor *m*; **~ficial** [~'fiʃəl] beneficioso; **~fit** ['~fit] beneficio *m*, provecho *m*; **~volent** [bi'nevələnt] benévolo
benign [bi'nain] benigno (*t med*)
bent [bent] encorvado; doblado; **to be ~ on** empeñarse en
benzine ['benziːn] bencina *f*
bequeath [bi'kwiːð] *v/t* legar
bequest [biː'kwest] legado *m*
bereaved [bi'riːvd]: **the ~** los afligidos
beret ['berei] boina *f*
berry ['beri] baya *f*
berth [bəːθ] *s* amarradero *m*; camarote *m*; litera *f*; *v/t* atracar
beseech [bi'siːtʃ] *v/t* implorar; suplicar
beside [bi'said] *prep* al lado de, junto a; **to be ~ oneself** estar fuera de sí; **~s** *adv* además
besiege [bi'siːdʒ] *v/t* sitiar; asediar
best [best] el (lo) mejor; óptimo; superior; **~ man** padrino *m* de boda; **~ seller** éxito *m* de librería; **to do one's ~** hacer todo lo posible; **to make the ~ of it** salir lo mejor posible
bestow [bi'stəu] *v/t* conferir; otorgar
bet [bet] *s* apuesta *f*; *v/t, v/i* apostar
betray [bi'trei] *v/t* traicionar; revelar; **~al** traición *f*; **~er** traidor *m*
betrothed [bi'trəuðd] prometido(a) *m (f)*
better ['betə] *a, adv* mejor; **to be ~** valer más; **to be ~ off** estar mejor; **so much the ~** tanto mejor; **to get ~** mejorarse; *v/t* mejorar
between [bi'twiːn] entre
beverage ['bevəridʒ] bebida *f*
beware [bi'wɛə] *v/t, v/i* precaverse; **~ of ...!** ¡cuidado con (*el perro, etc*)!
bewilder [bi'wildə] *v/t* dejar perplejo; aturdir; **~ment** aturdimiento *m*
bewitch [bi'witʃ] *v/t* hechizar, embrujar
beyond [bi'jɔnd] *adv* más allá; *prep* más allá de; además de; **it's ~ me** no lo entiendo; **~ the seas** allende los mares
bias ['baiəs] *s* prejuicio *m*, parcialidad *f*; sesgo *m*; *v/t* predisponer
bib [bib] babero *m*
Bible ['baibl] Biblia *f*
bicycle ['baisikl] bicicleta *f*
bid [bid] *v/t* mandar; licitar; pujar; **~ding** mandato *m*; oferta *f*, licitación *f*
bier [biə] féretro *m*
big [big] grande; **~ brother** hermano *m* mayor; **~ game** caza *f* mayor; **to talk ~** fanfarronear; echar bravatas; **~ot** ['bigət] fanático(a) *m(f)*
bike [baik] *fam* bicicleta *f*
bile [bail] bilis *f*; ira *f*
bill [bil] cuenta *f*; nota *f*; factura *f*; billete *m*; proyecto *m* de ley; cartel *m*, letrero *m*; pico *m* (*de ave*); **~ of exchange** letra *f* de cambio; **~ of fare** menú *m*; **~ of lading** conocimiento *m* de embarque; **~board** [~'bɔːd] *Am* cartelera *f*; **~fold** [~fəuld] *Am* billetero *m*
billet ['bilit] *s mil* acantonamiento *m*; *v/t* acantonar
billiards ['biljədz] billar *m*
billion ['biljən] billón *m*, *Am* mil millones *m/pl*
billow ['biləu] *v/i* ondular; *s* ola *f*, onda *f*
bind [baind] *v/t* sujetar; atar, ligar; encuadernar; obligar; **~ing** *a* obligatorio; *s* encuadernación *f*
binoculars [bi'nɔkjuləz] prismáticos *m/pl*
biography [bai'ɔgrəfi] biografía *f*
biology [bai'ɔlədʒi] biología *f*
birch [bəːtʃ] abedul *m*
bird [bəːd] ave *f*; pájaro *m*; **~ of passage** ave *f* de paso; **~ of prey** ave *f* de rapiña; **~'s-eye view** (a) vista *f* de pájaro
birth [bəːθ] nacimiento *m*; *med* parto *m*; **to give ~ (to)** dar a luz; **~ control** control *m* de la natalidad; **~day** cumpleaños *m*; **~mark** rosa *f* de nacimiento; **~-rate** natalidad *f*
biscuit ['biskit] galleta *f*
bishop ['biʃəp] obispo *m*; alfil *m* (*de ajedrez*)
bison ['baisn] bisonte *m*
bit [bit] poquito *m*; bocado *m*; **a little ~** un poquito; **~ by ~** poco a poco
bitch [bitʃ] perra *f*
bite [bait] *s* mordedura *f*; picadura *f*; bocado *m*; *v/t, v/i* morder; picar
bitter ['bitə] *a* amargo; encarnizado; cortante; **~ness** amargura *f*; **~sweet** agridulce
bizarre [bi'zɑː] grotesco; extraño
black [blæk] *a, s* negro(a) *m (f)*; *v/t* ennegrecer; *v/i*: **~ out** *med* desmayarse; **~ and blue** amoratado; **in ~ and white** por escrito; **~berry** zarzamora *f*; **~bird** mirlo *m*; **~board** pizarra *f*; **~ eye** ojo *m* amoratado; **~mail** chantaje *m*; **~ market** mercado *m* negro; **~out** apagón *m*; **~smith** herrero *m*
bladder ['blædə] vejiga *f*
blade [bleid] hoja *f* (*de espada, de cuchillo*); pala *f* (*de remo*); hoja *f* (*de hélice*)
blame [bleim] *s* culpa *f*; *v/t* culpar; **to be to ~ for** tener la culpa de; **~less** inocente
bland [blænd] blando
blank [blæŋk] *a* en blanco; vacío; sin expresión (*mirada, etc*); **~ verse** verso *m* libre; *s* formulario *m*; **draw a ~** intentar sin éxito
blanket ['blæŋkit] manta *f*; *LA* frazada *f*
blare [blɛə] *v/i* resonar
blast [blɑːst] *s* ráfaga *f*; soplo *m*; carga *f* explosiva; explosión *f*; *v/t* volar (*con dinamita*); **~ furnace** alto horno *m*; **~ (it)!** ¡maldito sea!; **~-off** despegue *m* (*de un cohete*)
blaze [bleiz] *s* llamarada *f*; *v/i* arder; llamear; **~ a trail** (*t fig*) abrir un camino
bleach [bliːtʃ] *v/t* blanquear
bleak [bliːk] desierto, frío; desolado, sombrío
bleat [bliːt] *v/i* balar; *s* balido *m*
bleed [bliːd] *v/t* sangrar; *v/i* sangrar, perder sangre
blemish ['blemiʃ] *s* mancha *f*; tacha *f*; defecto *m*
blend [blend] *s* mezcla *f*; combinación *f*; *v/t* mezclar, combinar
bless [bles] *v/t* bendecir; **~ my soul!** ¡válgame Dios!; **~ed** bendito; **~ing** bendición *f*; gracia *f*
blind [blaind] *a* ciego; *s* celosía *f*; persiana *f*; *fig* pretexto *m*; *v/t* cegar; deslumbrar; **~ alley** callejón *m* sin salida; **~folded** con los ojos vendados; **~ness** ceguera *f*, ceguedad *f*
blink [bliŋk] *s* parpadeo *m*; **on the ~** incapacitado; roto; *v/t* guiñar; *v/i* parpadear; **~er** *aut* intermitente *m*
bliss [blis] felicidad *f*
blister ['blistə] ampolla *f*
blizzard ['blizəd] ventisca *f*
bloat [bləut] *v/t* hinchar
block [blɔk] *s* bloque *m*; zoquete *m*; obstrucción *f*; manzana *f* (*casas*), *LA* cuadra *f*; *v/t* obstruir, bloquear; **~ade** [blɔ'keid] bloqueo *m*; **~head** zopenco *m*; **~ letter** letra *f* de imprenta
blond(e) [blɔnd] *a, s* rubio(a) *m (f)*
blood [blʌd] sangre *f*; **in cold ~** a sangre fría; **~ poisoning** envenenamiento *m* de la sangre; **~ pressure** tensión *f* arterial; **~shed** matanza *f*; **~shot** ensangrentado; **~-thirsty** sanguíneo; **~ vessel** vaso *m* sanguíneo; **~y** sangriento; *fam* maldito
bloom [bluːm] *s* florecimiento *m*; *v/i* florecer
blossom ['blɔsəm] *s* flor *f*; *v/i* florecer
blot [blɔt] *s* borrón *m*; mancha *f*; *v/t* **~ out** borrar, tachar; **~ting paper** papel *m* secante
blouse [blauz] blusa *f*
blow [bləu] *s* golpe *m*; *v/t* soplar; *mús* tocar; **~ one's nose** sonarse; **~ up** *foto* ampliar; *v/i* soplar; **~ out** apagarse; **~ over** pasar; **~ up** estallar; **~ out** *aut* pinchazo *m*
bludgeon ['blʌdʒən] cachiporra *f*
blue [bluː] azul; *fam* desanimado, triste; **~bell** campánula *f*; **~-blooded** de sangre noble; **~print** calco *m* azul; *fig* plan *m* de acción
bluff [blʌf] *s* fanfarronada *f*; *v/i* aparentar, baladronear
blunder ['blʌndə] *s* patochada *f*; desacierto *m*; *v/t, v/i* disparatar, equivocarse
blunt [blʌnt] desafilado; despuntado; obtuso; rudo; brusco
blur [bləː] aspecto *m* borroso
blush [blʌʃ] *s* sonrojo *m*; *v/i* sonrojarse, ruborizarse
bluster ['blʌstə] *v/i* bravear
boar [bɔː] verraco *m*; **wild ~** jabalí *m*
board [bɔːd] *s* tabla *f*; tablero *m*; **full ~** pensión *f* completa; **on ~** a bordo; *v/t* subir a bordo de; enmaderar; **~er** huésped *m*; alumno *m* interno; **~ing card** tarjeta *f* de embarque; **~ing house** casa *f* de huéspedes; **~ing school** internado *m*
boast [bəust] *s* jactancia *f*; *v/t* ostentar; *v/i* alardear; jactarse, vanagloriarse
boat [bəut] barca *f*; bote *m*; barco *m*; **~race** regata *f*; **~swain** ['bəusən] contramaestre *m*
bob [bɔb] *v/t, v/i* menear(se); **~sled** ['bɔbsled] bob *m*
bodice ['bɔdis] corpiño *m*
body ['bɔdi] cuerpo *m*; casco *m* (*de barco*); carrocería *f* (*de coche*); gremio *m*, corporación *f*; **in a ~** en comitiva; **~guard** guardaespaldas *m*
bog [bɔg] pantano *m*
boil [bɔil] *v/t, v/i* hervir, cocer; *s* furúnculo *m*; **~ over** rebosar(se); **~ed egg** huevo *m* pasado por agua; **~er** caldero *m*; caldera *f*
boisterous ['bɔistərəs] ruidoso, alborotado
bold [bəuld] atrevido, audaz; valiente
Bolivia [bə'liviə] Bolivia *f*; **~n** *a, s* boliviano(a) *m (f)*
bolster ['bəulstə] travesero *m*
bolt [bəult] *s* cerrojo *m*; perno *m*; rayo *m*; pasador *m*; *v/t* acerrojar; **~ upright** erguido
bomb [bɔm] *s* bomba *f*; *v/t* bombardear; **~er** bombardero *m*
bond [bɔnd] *s* lazo *m*; ligazón *f*; *com* bono *m*; **~age** esclavitud *f*; **~ed** depositado bajo fianza
bone [bəun] hueso *m*; espina *f*; **~ of contention** manzana *f* de la discordia
bonfire ['bɔnfaiə] hoguera *f*
bonnet ['bɔnit] gorra *f*; toca *f*
bonus ['bəunəs] prima *f*; sobrepaga *f*
bony ['bəuni] huesudo
boo [buː] *v/t* abuchear
booby ['buːbi]: **~ prize** premio *m* de consolación; **~ trap** trampa *f* explosiva
book [buk] *s* libro *m*; *teat* libreto *m*; *v/t* reservar (*cuarto, etc*); asentar; **~case** armario *m* para libros; **~ed up** (*hotel*) completo; **~ing clerk** taquillero *m*; **~ing office** despacho *m* de billetes; *teat* taquilla *f*; *LA* boletería *f*; **~keeper** tenedor *m* de libros; **~let** ['~lit] folleto *m*; **~maker** corredor *m* de apuestas; **~shop** librería *f*
boom [buːm] prosperidad *f*; auge *m* repentino; retumbo *m*
boor [buə] patán *m*
boost [buːst] *s tecn* incremento *m*; *v/t* levantar; fomentar
boot [buːt] bota *f*; portamaletas *m* (*de automóvil*); **to ~** para colmos, además; **~black** limpiabotas *m*
booth [buːð] puesto *m*; cabina *f*; tenderete *m*
booty ['buːti] botín *m*
border ['bɔːdə] borde *m*; frontera *f*
bor|e [bɔː] *v/t* taladrar; aburrir, dar la lata a; *s* latoso *m*, pelmazo *m*; **~edom** aburrimiento *m*; **~ing** aburrido, latoso
borough ['bʌrə] municipio *m*
borrow ['bɔrəu] *v/t, v/i* pedir prestado
bosom ['buzəm] seno *m*; pecho *m*
boss [bɔs] *s* jefe *m*, patrón *m*, amo *m*, cacique *m*; *v/t* dominar; mandar
botany ['bɔtəni] botánica *f*
botch [bɔtʃ] *v/t* frangollar, embarullar
both [bəuθ] *a* ambos; *pron* los (las) dos, ambos(as); **~ ... and** tanto ... como
bother ['bɔðə] *s* molestia *f*; fastidio *m*; *v/t* fastidiar, molestar; *v/i* preocuparse; molestarse
bottle ['bɔtl] *s* botella *f*; **baby ~** biberón *m*; **hit the ~** *fam* emborracharse; *v/t* **~ up** embotellar; *fig* reprimir; **~ opener** abrebotellas *m*
bottom ['bɔtəm] *s* fondo *m*; trasero *m*

bough [bau] rama *f*
boulder ['bəuldə] pedrón *m* rodado, pedrejón *m*
bounce [bauns] *v/i* rebotar
bound [baund] *v/t* confinar, limitar; *v/i* saltar; *s* límite *m*, término *m*; *a* atado, ligado; ~ ***for*** con rumbo a; **~ary** límite *m*, linde *m*; **~less** ilimitado
bounty ['baunti] generosidad *f*; merced *f*
bouquet [bu'kei] ramo *m* de flores; nariz *f* (*del vino*)
bout [baut] tanda *f*, turno *m*; *med* ataque *m*; *sp* asalto *m*
bow [bəu] *s* arco *m*; [bau] saludo *m*; *mar* proa *f*; *v/t* doblar; saludar; *v/i* inclinarse, hacer reverencia
bowels ['bauəlz] intestinos *m/pl*
bowl [bəul] *s* tazón *m*; escudilla *f*; bola *f*; *v/i* jugar a las bochas
bowlegged ['bəu'legid] estevado
bowler ['bəulə] (sombrero *m* de) hongo *m*
box [bɔks] *v/i* boxear; *v/t* abofetear; *s* caja *f*; *teat* palco *m*; casilla *f*; **~ing** boxeo *m*; ~ **office** taquilla *f*
boy [bɔi] muchacho *m*; niño *m*
boycott ['bɔikət] *v/t* boicotear
bra [brɑː] *fam* sostén *m*
brace [breis] *v/t* reforzar; asegurar; *s* abrazadera *f*, riostra *f*; **~let** brazalete *m*; pulsera *f*; **~s** tirantes *m/pl*
bracket ['brækit] *v/t* poner entre corchetes; agrupar; *s* ménsula *f*; soporte *m*; grupo *m*; **~s** corchetes *m/pl*
brag [bræg] *v/t*, *v/i* jactarse, fanfarronear; **~gart** ['~ət] bravucón *m*, fanfarrón *m*
braid [breid] *s* trenza *f*; *v/t* trenzar
brain [brein] cerebro *m*; **~s** *fig* sesos *m/pl*; ***rack one's ~s*** devanarse los sesos; **~washing** *fig* lavado *m* del cerebro
brake [breik] *s* freno *m*; *bot* helecho *m*; *v/t* frenar
bramble ['bræmbl] zarza *f*
branch [brɑːntʃ] *s* rama *f*; ramo *m*; ~ **office** sucursal *f*
brand [brænd] *s* tizón *m* (*fuego*); hierro *m* (*ganado*); marca *f*, estigma *m*; **~-new** flamante, novísimo
brandy ['brændi] coñac *m*
brass [brɑːs] latón *m*
brassière ['bræsiə] sostén *m*
brat [bræt] mocoso *m*
brave [breiv] *v/t* desafiar; *a* valiente; **~ry** valentía *f*; proeza *f*
bravo! ['brɑː'vəu] ¡olé!; ¡bravo!
brawl [brɔːl] *s* alboroto *m*; camorra *f*; *v/i* armar camorra
bray [brei] rebuzno *m*
brazen ['breizn] descarado
Brazil [brə'zil] (el) Brasil; **~ian** *a*, *s* brasileño(a) *m* (*f*)
breach [briːtʃ] *v/t*, *v/i* abrir una brecha (en); *s* rotura *f*; rompimiento *m*; *fig* infracción *f*, violación *f*; brecha *f*
bread [bred] pan *m*
breadth [bredθ] anchura *f*
break [breik] *s* pausa *f*; ruptura *f*; quiebra *f*; grieta *f*; ***without a ~*** sin parar; ~ ***of day*** alba *f*; *v/t* romper, quebrar; fracturar; infringir (*ley*); abatir; comunicar (*noticia*); hacer saltar (*la banca*); ~ ***down*** derribar; ~ ***in*** forzar; ~ ***in pieces*** hacer pedazos; *v/i* romperse; quebrar(se); ~ ***away*** escaparse; ~ ***down*** perder el ánimo; *aut* averiarse; ~ ***out*** estallar; **~down** colapso *m*; *tecn* avería *f*; **~fast** ['brekfəst] desayuno *m*; **~through** *fig* avance *m* importante; **~up** disolución *f*; desintegración *f*
breast [brest] pecho *m*; seno *m*; ***to make a clean ~ of*** confesar
breath [breθ] aliento *m*; ***out of ~*** sin aliento; ***to hold one's ~*** contener el aliento; **~e** [briːð] *v/i* respirar; **~less** ['breθlis] falto de aliento, sofocado
breeches ['briːtʃiz] calzones *m/pl*
breed [briːd] *s* casta *f*; raza *f*; *v/t* engendrar; criar; *v/i* multiplicarse; **~ing** crianza *f*; educación *f*
breeze [briːz] brisa *f*
brethren ['breðrin] *relig* hermanos *m/pl*
brew [bruː] *s* infusión *f*; mezcla *f*; *v/t* fabricar (*cerveza*); tramar; *v/i* amenazar (*tormenta*); **~ery** fábrica *f* de cerveza
bribe [braib] *s* soborno *m*; *v/t* sobornar; **~ry** soborno *m*; cohecho *m*
brick [brik] *s* ladrillo *m*; *v/t* enladrillar; **~layer** albañil *m*; **~work** albañilería *f*
brid|al ['braidl] nupcial; **~e** novia *f*, desposada *f*; **~egroom** novio *m*, desposado *m*; **~esmaid** madrina *f* de boda
bridge [bridʒ] *v/t* tender un puente sobre; ~ ***a gap*** *fig* llenar un vacío; *s* puente *m*, *f*; *anat* caballete *m*; bridge *m* (*juego de naipes*)
bridle ['braidl] *v/t* embridar; *v/i* erguirse; *s* brida *f*; ~ **path** camino *m* de herradura
brief [briːf] *a* corto, sumario; *s for* escrito *m*; *relig* breve *m* apostólico; *v/t* informar; **~case** cartera *f*; **~ing** informe *m*; **~s** calzoncillos *m/pl*
bright [brait] claro, brillante; despierto, inteligente; **~en** *v/t* iluminar; avivar; *v/i* aclararse; avivarse; **~ness** resplandor *m*; claridad *f*; agudeza *f*
brillian|ce, ~cy ['briljəns, '~si] brillantez *f*; **~t** brillante
brim [brim] borde *m*; labio *m* (*de vasija*); ala *f* (*de sombrero*); **~ful** repleto
brine [brain] salmuera *f*
bring [briŋ] *v/t* traer; conducir; rendir; ~ ***about*** originar, causar; ~ ***back*** devolver; ~ ***forth*** producir; parir; ~ ***forward*** *com* llevar (*saldo*); ~ ***off*** lograr; ~ ***round*** convencer; ~ ***up*** criar, educar
brink [briŋk] borde *m*
brisk [brisk] enérgico; rápido; activo
bristle ['brisl] *v/t*, *v/i* erizar(se); *s* cerda *f*
Britain ['britən] Gran Bretaña *f*
British ['britiʃ] inglés, británico
brittle ['britl] quebradizo; frágil
broach [brəutʃ] *v/t* introducir (*tópico*)
broad [brɔːd] ancho; amplio; **~cast** *v/t*, *v/i* emitir; radiar; *s* emisión *f*; **~en** *v/t*, *v/i* ensanchar(se); **~minded** tolerante
broccoli ['brɔkəli] brécol *m*
broil [brɔil] *v/t* asar a la parrilla
broke [brəuk]: ***to be ~*** estar sin blanca; **~n:** ***~n English*** inglés imperfecto; ***to be ~nhearted*** tener el corazón partido
broker ['brəukə] corredor *m*; agente *m*
bronze [brɔnz] bronce *m*
brooch [brəutʃ] broche *m*
brood [bruːd] *v/t* empollar; *v/i* ~ ***over*** rumiar; *s* cría *f*; camada *f*
brook [bruk] arroyo *m*
broom [bruːm] escoba *f*; retama *f*
broth [brɔθ] caldo *m*
brothel ['brɔθl] burdel *m*
brother ['brʌðə] hermano *m*; **~hood** hermandad *f*; **~-in-law** cuñado *m*; **~ly** fraternal
brow [brau] ceja *f*; frente *f*; ***knit one's ~*** fruncir las cejas
brown [braun] *a* marrón; moreno; castaño; pardo; ~ ***paper*** papel *m* de estraza; *v/t* dorar; broncear
bruise [bruːz] *s* contusión *f*; magulladura *f*; *v/t* magullar
brush [brʌʃ] *s* cepillo *m*; brocha *f*; *v/t* cepillar; ~ ***up*** pulir; *fig* repasar; *v/i* rozar
Brussels ['brʌslz] Bruselas; ~ **sprouts** col *f* de Bruselas
brut|al ['bruːtl] brutal; **~ality** ['~tæliti] brutalidad *f*; **~e** [bruːt] bruto *m*; bestia *f*
bubble ['bʌbl] *s* burbuja *f*; ~ ***bath*** baño *m* espumoso; *v/i* burbujear; bullir
buck [bʌk] macho *m* cabrío; gamo *m*; ***pass the ~*** echar la carga a otro
bucket ['bʌkit] cubo *m*
buckle ['bʌkl] *s* hebilla *f*
buckskin ['bʌkskin] piel *f* de ante
bud [bʌd] *v/t* echar hojas; *v/i* brotar; *s* brote *m*, capullo *m*; yema *f*; ***nip in the ~*** cortar de raíz
budget ['bʌdʒit] presupuesto *m*
buff|alo ['bʌfələu] búfalo *m*; **~er** ['bʌfə] amortiguador *m*; tope *m*; **~et** ['bʌfit] *v/t* abofetear; *s* bofetada *f*; ['bufei] aparador *m*
bug [bʌg] sabandija *f*; chinche *f*
bugle ['bjuːgl] corneta *f*; clarín *m*; **~r** corneta *m*
build [bild] *v/t* construir; edificar; establecer; **~er** constructor *m*; **~ing** construcción *f*; edificio *m*
built|-in ['bilt'in] empotrado; incorporado; **~-up** urbanizado
bulb [bʌlb] *bot* bulbo *m*; *elec* bombilla *f*
bulge [bʌldʒ] *v/t*, *v/i* combar(se); *s* comba *f*; protuberancia *f*
bulk [bʌlk] masa *f*; volumen *m*; (la) mayor parte *f*; ***in ~*** (*mercancías*) a granel; **~y** voluminoso
bull [bul] *zool* toro *m*; *relig* bula *f*; *com* alcista *m*; ~ **dozer** ['~dəuzə] aplanadora *f*
bullet ['bulit] bala *f*
bulletin ['bulitin] boletín *m*
bull|fight ['bulfait] corrida *f* de toros; **~fighter** torero *m*; **~headed** terco; **~ring** plaza *f* de toros
bullion ['buljən] lingote *m* (*de oro, etc*)
bully ['buli] *v/t* intimidar; *s* matón *m*
bum [bʌm] holgazán *m*, vagabundo *m*; **~blebee** ['~blbiː] abejorro *m*
bump [bʌmp] *v/t* golpear; *v/i* chocar contra; *s* choque *m*; chichón *m*; **~er** parachoques *m*
bun [bʌn] bollo *m*; (*de pelo*) moño *m*
bunch [bʌntʃ] manojo *m*; racimo *m*
bundle ['bʌndl] *s* lío *m*; haz *m* (*de leña*); *v/t* liar, atar
bungalow ['bʌŋgələu] casita *f* campestre
bungle ['bʌŋgl] *v/t* estropear, chapucear, frangollar
bunk [bʌŋk] litera *f*; tarima *f*; **~er** carbonera *f*
bunny ['bʌni] conejillo *m*
buoy [bɔi] *s* boya *f*; **~ant** boyante; animado
burden ['bəːdn] *s* carga *f*; *v/t* cargar; **~some** pesado; oneroso
bureau [bjuə'rəu] oficina *f*; **~cracy** [~'rɔkrəsi] burocracia *f*
burgl|ar ['bəːglə] ladrón *m*; **~ary** robo *m* con allanamiento (*de morada*)
burial ['beriəl] entierro *m*; ~ **ground** cementerio *m*
burly ['bəːli] corpulento
burn [bəːn] *v/t* quemar; *v/i* arder; *s* quemadura *f*; **~er** mechero *m*; **~ing** ardiente
burp [bəːp] *s* eructo *m*; *v/i* eructar
burst [bəːst] *v/t* reventar, romper; *v/i* estallar, reventar; ~ ***into tears*** desatarse en lágrimas; *s* estallido *m*; explosión *f*; ~ ***of laughter*** carcajada *f*
bury ['beri] *v/t* enterrar
bus [bʌs] autobús *m*; ~ ***stop*** parada *f* de autobús
bush [buʃ] arbusto *m*
business ['biznis] negocio *m*; empresa *f*; ocupación *f*; asunto *m*; ***to mind one's own ~*** no meterse en lo que no le toca; ~ **hours** horas *f/pl* de oficina; ~ **letter** carta *f* comercial; **~like** sistemático, formal; **~man** hombre *m* de negocios; ~ **trip** viaje *m* de negocios
bust [bʌst] busto *m*; pecho *m*
bustle ['bʌsl] *v/i* apresurarse; *s* animación *f*; ajetreo *m*
busy ['bizi] ocupado
but [bʌt] *conj* pero; sino; *prep* excepto; *adv* solamente; ~ ***for*** a no ser por; ~ ***then*** pero por otra parte
butcher ['butʃə] *v/t* matar; *s* carnicero *m*
butler ['bʌtlə] mayordomo *m*
butt [bʌt] tocón *m* (*de un árbol*); cabo *m*
butter ['bʌtə] *s* mantequilla *f*; *v/t* untar con mantequilla; **~cup** *bot* ranúnculo *m*; **~fly** mariposa *f*; **~milk** leche *f* de manteca
buttock ['bʌtək] nalga *f*
button ['bʌtn] *v/t* abotonar; *s* botón *m*; **~hole** ojal *m*
buttress ['bʌtris] *arq* contrafuerte *m*; ***flying ~*** arbotante *m*
buxom ['bʌksəm] persona *f* rolliza
buy [bai] *v/t* comprar; **~er** comprador *m*
buzz [bʌz] *v/i* zumbar; *s* zumbido *m*
by [bai] *prep* por; al lado de; junto a; *adv* al lado; aparte; cerca; ~ ***day*** de día; ~ ***and ~*** luego; ~ ***and large*** en general; **~gone** pasado; **~pass** desvío *m*; **~-product** producto *m* derivado; **~stander** espectador *m*; **~street** calcjuela *f*; **~way** camino *m* apartado; **~word** refrán *m*
bye-bye! ['bai'bai] *fam* ¡adiós!

C

cab [kæb] taxi *m*
cabbage ['kæbidʒ] col *f*; repollo *m*
cabin ['kæbin] cabaña *f*; *mar* camarote *m*; cabina *f*; **~et** ['~it] gabinete *m*; **~etmaker** ebanista *m*
cable ['keibl] *s* cable *m*; *v/t*, *v/i* cablegrafiar
caboose [kə'buːs] *f c* vagón *m* de cola
cabstand ['kæbstænd] parada *f* de taxis
cackle ['kækl] *s* cacareo *m*; *v/i* cacarear
cactus ['kæktəs] cacto *m*
cadger ['kædʒə] gorrón *m*
cafeteria [kæfi'tiəria] cafetería *f*; restaurante *m*
cage [keidʒ] *s* jaula *f*; *v/t* enjaular
cake [keik] pastel *m*; tarta *f*; pastilla *f* (*de jabón*)
calamity [kə'læmiti] calamidad *f*, desastre *m*
calcium ['kælsiəm] calcio *m*
calcula|te ['kælkjuleit] *v/t* calcular; **~tion** cálculo *m*; **~tor** calculadora *f*
calendar ['kælində] calendario *m*
calf [kɑːf] *zool* ternero(a) *m* (*f*); *anat* pantorrilla *f*
calibre ['kælibə] calibre *m* (*t fig*)
call [kɔːl] *s* llamada *f*; grito *m*; visita *f*; ***on ~*** disponible; ***port of ~*** puerto *m* de escala; *v/t* llamar; proclamar; calificar de; ~ ***back*** volver a llamar; ~ ***off*** cancelar; *v/i* llamar; dar voces; ~ ***at*** pasar por, visitar; ~ ***for*** ir por; pedir; ~ ***on*** visitar; **~-box** cabina *f* telefónica; **~er** visitante *m*; llamador *m*; **~ing** vocación *f*
calm [kɑːm] *a* sereno, tranquilo; *s* calma *f*; tranquilidad *f*; *v/t* calmar; *v/i* ~ ***down*** tranquilizarse
calorie ['kæləri] caloría *f*
camel ['kæməl] camello *m*
camera ['kæmərə] máquina *f* fotográfica; *TV*, *cine* cámara *f*
camomile ['kæməumail] manzanilla *f*
camouflage ['kæmuflɑːʒ] *s* camuflaje *m*; disfraz *m*
camp [kæmp] *s* campamento *m*; campo *m*; *v/i* acampar; ~ **bed** catre *m* (*de tijera*); ~ **ground** [~graund], ~ **site** [~sait] camping *m*; ~ **stool** silla *f* plegadiza
campaign [kæm'pein] campaña *f*
camphor ['kæmfə] alcanfor *m*
can [kæn] *s* lata *f*; bote *m*; *v/t* enlatar; **~opener** abrelatas *m*
can *defectivo usado como verbo auxiliar*: poder; saber hacer algo
Canada ['kænədə] el Canadá
Canadian [kə'neidjən] *a*, *s* canadiense *m*, *f*
canal [kə'næl] canal *m*
canary [kə'nɛəri] canario *m*
cancel ['kænsəl] *v/t* cancelar; revocar; **~lation** cancelación *f*; anulación *f*
cancer ['kænsə] cáncer *m*
candid ['kændid] franco; abierto, sincero
candidate ['kændidit] candidato *m*
candied ['kændid] azucarado
candle ['kændl] candela *f*; vela *f*; bujía *f*; **~stick** candelero *m*; palmatoria *f*
candy ['kændi] bombón *m*; dulce *m*
cane [kein] caña *f*; bastón *m*
canister ['kænistə] bote *m*; lata *f*
cannon ['kænən] cañón *m*
canoe [kə'nuː] canoa *f*; piragua *f*
canteen [kæn'tiːn] cantina *f*
canter ['kæntə] *s* medio galope *m*

canvas ['kænvəs] lona *f*; lienzo *m*; **~s** *v/t* solicitar (*votos, etc*)
canyon ['kænjən] cañón *m*
cap [kæp] gorra *f*; tapa *f*
capa|bility [keipə'biliti] capacidad *f*; **~ble** capaz; **~city** [kə'pæsiti] capacidad *f*; cabida *f*
cape [keip] *geog* cabo *m*; capa *f*
caper ['keipə] alcaparra *f*
capital ['kæpitl] *s com* capital *m*; (*ciudad*) capital *f*; *arq* capitel *m*; *a* capital; magnífico; **~ letter** mayúscula *f*; **~ism** capitalismo *m*
capitulate [kə'pitjuleit] *v/i* capitular
capricious [kə'priʃəs] caprichoso
capsize [kæp'saiz] *v/t, v/i* zozobrar; volcar(se)
capsule ['kæpsju:l] cápsula *f*
captain ['kæptin] capitán *m*
caption ['kæpʃən] encabezamiento *m*; leyenda *f*; *cine* subtítulo *m*
captiv|ate ['kæptiveit] *v/t* cautivar; **~e** *s, a* cautivo; **~ity** [~'tiviti] cautiverio *m*
capture ['kæptʃə] *v/t* capturar, apresar; *fig* cautivar; *s* captura *f*
car [kɑ:] coche *m*; auto *m*; *LA* carro *m*; *f c* vagón *m*
carafe [kə'rɑ:f] garrafa *f*
carat ['kærət] quilate *m*
caravan [kærə'væn] caravana *f*; remolque *m*
carbon ['kɑ:bən] carbono *m*; **~ dioxide** *quím* dióxido *m* de carbono
carbuncle ['kɑ:bʌŋkl] (*piedra*) carbúnculo *m*; *med* carbunclo *m*
carburet(t)or ['kɑ:bjuretə] carburador *m*
card [kɑ:d] *s* tarjeta *f*; carta *f*; (*baraja*) naipe *m*; *v/t* cardar; **~board** cartón *m*; **~igan** ['~igən] chaqueta *f* de punto
cardinal ['kɑ:dinl] cardenal *m*
care [kɛə] *s* cuidado *m*; atención *f*; preocupación *f*; **in ~ of** al cuidado de; **take ~** tener cuidado; **take ~ of** cuidar a; ocuparse de; *v/i* **~ for** cuidar; querer; **I don't ~** me da igual; **~free** despreocupado; **~ful** cuidadoso; **~less** descuidado; **~taker** guardián *m*; **~worn** agobiado
career [kə'riə] carrera *f*
caress [kə'res] *v/t* acariciar; *s* caricia *f*
cargo ['kɑ:gəu] carga *f*; cargamento *m*
caricature [kærikə'tjuə] caricatura *f*
carnation [kɑ:'neiʃən] clavel *m*
carnival ['kɑ:nivəl] carnaval *m*
carol ['kærəl] villancico *m*
carp [kɑ:p] *s* carpa *f*; *v/i* criticar
carpenter ['kɑ:pintə] carpintero *m*
carpet ['kɑ:pit] alfombra *f*
carriage ['kæridʒ] carruaje *m*; vagón *m*; coche *m*; porte *m* (*t com*)
Carribean [kæri'bi:ən] caribe; **~ Sea** [~si:] mar *m* caribe
carrier ['kæriə] compañía *f* de transportes; *med* portador *m*; *aer* portaaviones *m*
carrot ['kærət] zanahoria *f*
carry ['kæri] *v/t* llevar; transportar; tener (encima); traer consigo; **~ away** llevarse; **~ on** continuar, seguir; **~ out** realizar; *v/i* alcanzar
cart [kɑ:t] *s* carro *m*; carreta *f*; *v/t* acarrear
cartoon [kɑ:'tu:n] caricatura *f*; *cine* dibujo *m* animado; **~ist** caricaturista *m, f*
cartridge ['kɑ:tridʒ] cartucho *m*
carv|e [kɑ:v] *v/t, v/i* tallar; esculpir; (*carne*) trinchar; **~ing** escultura *f*
cascade [kæs'keid] cascada *f*
cas|e [keis] *s* caso *m*; caja *f*; estuche *m*; cubierta *f*; *for* causa *f*, pleito *m*; **in any ~e** de todas formas; **just in ~e** por si acaso; **~ement** ventana *f* a bisagra
cash [kæʃ] *s* dinero *m* efectivo; **~ down** al contado; **~ on delivery** pago *m* contra entrega; **~ register** caja *f* registradora; *v/t* cobrar; hacer efectivo; **~ier** [kæ'ʃiə] cajero *m*
cashmere [kæʃ'miə] cachemira *f*
cask [kɑ:sk] cuba *f*; barril *m*; **~et** cofrecito *m*; ataúd *m*
cassette [kæ'set] cassette *m, f*
cassock ['kæsək] sotana *f*
cast [kɑ:st] *s* echada *f*; tirada *f*; molde *m*; *teat* reparto *m*; *v/t* tirar, lanzar; fundir (*metales*); *teat* repartir (*papeles*); echar; **~ iron** hierro *m* fundido; **~ out** arrojar, expulsar; **~anet** [kæstə'net] castañuela *f*
caste [kɑ:st] casta *f*
castle ['kɑ:sl] castillo *m*; (*ajedrez*) torre *f*
castor ['kɑ:stə]: **~ oil** aceite *m* de ricino
casual ['kæʒjuəl] casual; indiferente; **~ty** víctima *m/f*; *mil* baja *f*
cat [kæt] gato(a) *m* (*f*)
catalogue ['kætələg] *s* catálogo *m*; *v/t* catalogar
cataract ['kætərækt] catarata *f*
catarrh [kə'tɑ:] catarro *m*
catastrophe [kə'tæstrəfi] catástrofe *f*
catcall ['kætkɔ:l] rechifla *f*, *LA* silbatina *f*
catch [kætʃ] *v/t, v/i* coger; agarrar, atrapar; captar, entender; **~ cold** resfriarse; **~ fire** prender fuego; encenderse; **~ on** caer en la cuenta; **~ up with** alcanzar; **~ as ~ can** lucha *f* libre; *s* cogida *f*; pesca *f*; cerradura *f*; trampa *f*; **~ing** pegadizo; contagioso; **~word** lema *m*, mote *m*
category ['kætigəri] categoría *f*
cater ['keitə]: **~ for** proveer, abastecer
caterpillar ['kætəpilə] oruga *f*
cathedral [kə'θi:drəl] catedral *f*
Catholic ['kæθəlik] *a, s* católico(a) *m* (*f*)
cattle [kætl] ganado *m*
cauldron ['kɔ:ldrən] caldera *f*
cauliflower ['kɔliflauə] coliflor *f*
cause ['kɔ:z] *s* causa *f*, motivo *m*; *v/t* causar, motivar; **~way** arrecife *m*; calzada *f* elevada
cauti|on ['kɔ:ʃən] *s* cautela *f*; advertencia *f*; *v/t* advertir; **~ous** cauteloso, cauto
cavalry ['kævəlri] caballería *f*
cav|e [keiv] *s* cueva *f*; *v/i*: **to ~ in** derrumbarse; **~ern** ['kævən] caverna *f*; **~ity** cavidad *f*
cease [si:s] *v/t* suspender, parar; *v/i* cesar; **~ fire** alto *m* el fuego; **~less** incesante
cedar ['si:də] cedro *m*
cede [si:d] *v/t, v/i* ceder
ceiling ['si:liŋ] techo *m*; **to hit the ~** poner el grito en el cielo; **~ price** precio *m* máximo
celebr|ate ['selibreit] *v/t* celebrar; **~ated** célebre; **~ation** fiesta *f*; **~ity** [si'lebriti] celebridad *f*
celery ['seləri] apio *m*
celestial [si'lestjəl] celestial
celibacy ['selibəsi] celibato *m*
cell [sel] celda *f*; célula *f* (*t elec*)
cellar ['selə] sótano *m*; bodega *f*
Celt [kelt] celta *m*; **~ic** céltico
cement [si'ment] *s* cemento *m*; *v/t* cimentar (*t fig*)
cemetery ['semitri] cementerio *m*
cens|or ['sensə] *s* censor *m*; *v/t* censurar; **~orship** censura *f*; **~ure** ['~ʃə] *s* censura *f*; *v/t* reprobar, reprender; **~us** censo *m*
cent [sent] céntimo *m*; centavo *m*; **per ~** por ciento; **~ennial** *a, s* centenario *m*; **~er** = **centre**
centi|grade ['sentigreid] centígrado; **~meter, ~metre** [~mi:tə] centímetro *m*
cent|ral ['sentrəl] central, céntrico; **~ral heating** calefacción *f* central; **~ralize** *v/t* centralizar; **~re** centro *m*; **~re-forward** delantero *m* centro; **~re-half** medio *m* centro.
century ['sentʃuri] siglo *m*
ceramic [si'ræmik] cerámico; **~s** cerámica *f*
cereal ['siəriəl] *a, s* cereal *m*
ceremon|ial [seri'məunjəl] *a, s* ceremonial; **~y** ['~məni] ceremonia *f*
certain ['sə:tn] cierto; **~ly** ciertamente, por cierto; **~ty** certeza *f*; certidumbre *f*
certif|icate [sə'tifikit] certificado *m*; diploma *m*; partida *f* (*de nacimiento, etc*); **~y** ['sə:rtifai] *v/t* certificar
chafe [tʃeif] *v/t, v/i* rozar(se); irritar(se)
chagrin ['ʃægrin] desazón *f*, mortificación *f*
chain [tʃein] *s* cadena *f*; serie *f*; *v/t* encadenar; **~ reaction** reacción *f* en cadena
chair [tʃɛə] silla *f*; cátedra *f* (*de universidad*); presidencia *f*; **~lift** telesilla *f*; **~man, ~woman** presidente(a) *m*(*f*)
chalk [tʃɔ:k] creta *f*; tiza *f*
challenge ['tʃælindʒ] *s* desafío *m*; *v/t* desafiar
chamber ['tʃeimbə] cámara *f*; recámara *f*
chamois ['ʃæmwɑ:] gamuza *f*
champagne [ʃæm'pein] champaña *m*
champion ['tʃæmpjən] campeón *m*; **~ship** campeonato *m*
chance [tʃɑ:ns] *a* accidental, casual; *s* casualidad *f*; ocasión *f*; suerte *f*; **by ~** por casualidad; **stand a ~** tener la posibilidad; **to take a ~** aventurarse
chancell|ery ['tʃɑ:nsələri] cancillería *f*
chandelier [ʃændi'liə] araña *f* de luces
change [tʃeindʒ] *s* cambio *m*; vuelta *f*; **for a ~** para variar; *v/t* cambiar; cambiar de (*ropa, tren, opinión*); **~able** variable; **~less** inmutable
channel ['tʃænl] *s* canal *m* (*t fig*); *v/t* encauzar
chaos ['keiɔs] caos *m*
chap [tʃæp] *s* grieta *f*; *fam* mozo *m*; tipo *m*
chapel ['tʃæpəl] capilla *f*
chaperon ['ʃæpərəun] *v/t* acompañar
chap|lain ['tʃæplin] capellán *m*; **~ter** ['~tə] *relig* cabildo *m*; capítulo *m*
character ['kæriktə] carácter *m*; *teat* personaje *m*; **~istic** [~'ristik] característico
charcoal ['tʃɑ:kəul] carbón *m* vegetal
charge [tʃɑ:dʒ] *s* carga *f*; cargo *m*; gasto *m*; acusación *f*; **free of ~** gratis; **in ~ of** encargado de; *v/t* cargar; encargar; acusar; *mil* atacar
charit|able ['tʃæritəbl] caritativo; **~y** caridad *f*
charm [tʃɑ:m] *s* gracia *f*; encanto *m*; hechizo *m*; amuleto *m*; *v/t* encantar; **~ing** encantador
chart [tʃɑ:t] *s* carta *f* de navegar; gráfica *f*; esquema *m*; **~er** ['~ə] *s* carta *f*; *v/t mar* fletar; **~er flight** vuelo *m* chárter
chase [tʃeis] *v/t* cazar; perseguir
chassis ['ʃæsi] armazón *f*; chasis *m*
chast|e [tʃeist] *a* casto, puro; **~ity** ['tʃæstiti] castidad *f*
chat [tʃæt] *s* charla *f*; *v/i* charlar; **~ter** *s* cháchara *f*; *v/i* parlotear; chacharear; **~terbox** parlanchín(ina) *m* (*f*)
chauffeur ['ʃəufə] chófer *m*
cheap [tʃi:p] barato
cheat [tʃi:t] *s* tramposo *m*; trampa *f*; *v/t* defraudar
check [tʃek] *s* freno *m*; impedimento *m*; nota *f*, cuenta *f*; control *m*; talón *m*, contraseña *f*; cuadro *m*; tela *f* de cuadros; (*ajedrez*) jaque *m*; *v/t* controlar; refrenar; comprobar; *v/i* **~ in** registrarse en (*un hotel*); facturar (*el equipaje*); **~ out** pagar la cuenta y salir (*de un hotel*); **~book** talonario *m* de cheques; **~ers** juego *m* de damas; **~mate** (*ajedrez*) jaque *m* mate; **~room** guardarropa *m*; *f c* consigna *f*
cheek [tʃi:k] mejilla *f*; descaro *m*; **~y** descarado
cheer [tʃiə] *v/t* aplaudir; alentar; *v/i* **~ up** animarse; **~ful** alegre; **~less** triste; **~s** (*brindis*) ¡salud!
cheese [tʃi:z] queso *m*
chemi|cal ['kemikəl] *a* químico; *s* producto *m* químico; **~st** químico *m*; farmacéutico *m*; **~stry** química *f*; **~st's shop** farmacia *f*
cheque [tʃek] cheque *m*; talón *m*; **~-book** talonario *m* de cheques
chequered ['tʃekəd] a cuadros (*tela, etc*); *fig* variado
cherish ['tʃeriʃ] *v/t* apreciar; acariciar (*esperanza*)
cherry ['tʃeri] cereza *f*
chess [tʃes] ajedrez *m*; **~-board** tablero *m* de ajedrez
chest [tʃest] cofre *m*, cajón *m*; pecho *m*; **~ of drawers** cómoda *f*
chestnut ['tʃesnʌt] *a* castaño; *s* castaña *f*
chew [tʃu:] *v/t, v/i* masticar; **~ing gum** chicle *m*
chicken ['tʃikin] pollo *m*; **~hearted** cobarde; **~ pox** ['~pɔks] varicela *f*
chickpea ['tʃikpi:] garbanzo *m*
chief [tʃi:f] *a* principal; *s* jefe *m*; **~tain** ['~tən] cacique *m*
chilblain ['tʃilblein] sabañón *m*
child [tʃaild] hijo(a), niño(a) *m* (*f*); **~birth** parto *m*; **~hood** niñez *f*; **~ish** pueril; **~like** como un niño; **~ren** ['tʃildrən] ninõs(as), hijos(as) *m/pl* (*f/pl*)
Chile ['tʃili] Chile *m*; **~an** *a, s* chileno (a) *m* (*f*)
chill [tʃil] *s* frío *m*; escalofrío *m*; *v/t* enfriar; **~y** frío
chime [tʃaim] *s* repique *m*; campaneo *m*; *v/i* repicar; *v/t* tocar
chimney ['tʃimni] chimenea *f*
chin [tʃin] barbilla *f*
chin|a ['tʃainə] porcelana *f*; **⁓a** China *f*; **⁓ese** *a, s* chino(a) *m* (*f*)
chip [tʃip] *s* astilla *f*; lasca *f*; *v/t* astillar; *v/i* desportillarse; **~munk** [~mʌŋk] ardilla *f* listada; **~s** patatas *f/pl* fritas
chirp [tʃə:p] *s* gorjeo *m*; *v/i* piar; chirriar
chisel ['tʃizl] *s* escoplo *m*; cincel *m*; *v/t, v/i* cincelar
chivalr|ous ['ʃivəlrəs] caballeroso; **~y** caballerosidad *f*
chive [tʃaiv] cebollino *m*
chlor|ide ['klɔ:raid] cloruro *m*; **~ine** ['~in] cloro *m*; **~oform** cloroformo *m*
chocolate ['tʃɔkəlit] chocolate *m*
choice [tʃɔis] *a* selecto; *s* elección *f*; preferencia *f*
choir ['kwaiə] coro *m*
choke [tʃəuk] *v/t, v/i* estrangular, sofocar(se); *s tecn* estrangulador *m*
cholera ['kɔlərə] cólera *m*
choose [tʃu:z] *v/t* escoger, elegir
chop [tʃɔp] *s* corte *m*; tajada *f*, *coc* chuleta *f*; *v/t* cortar; tajar; *coc* picar; **~sticks** palillos *m/pl*
chord [kɔ:d] cuerda *f*; *mús* acorde *m*
chore [tʃɔ:] faena *f* doméstica; quehacer *m*
chorus ['kɔ:rəs] coro *m*; estribillo *m*; **~ girl** *teat* corista *f*
Christ [kraist] Jesucristo *m*; **⁓en** ['krisn] *v/t* bautizar; **~ian** ['kristjən] *a, s* cristiano(a) *m* (*f*); **~mas** ['krisməs] Navidad *f*; **~mas Eve** Nochebuena *f*
chromium ['krəumjəm] cromo *m*
chronic ['krɔnik] crónico
chron|icle ['krɔnikəl] *s* crónica *f*; **~ological** [krɔnə'lɔdʒikəl] cronológico
chubby ['tʃʌbi] rechoncho
chuck [tʃʌk] *v/t fam* tirar
chuckle [tʃʌkl] *s* risa *f* ahogada; *v/i* reírse entre dientes
chum [tʃʌm] *fam* camarada *m, f*
chunk [tʃʌŋk] pedazo *m*; trozo *m*
church [tʃə:tʃ] iglesia *f*; **⁓ of England** iglesia anglicana; **~yard** cementerio *m*
churn [tʃə:n] *s* mantequera *f*; *v/t* (*leche*) batir; agitar
cider ['saidə] sidra *f*
cigar [si'gɑ:] cigarro *m*; puro *m*; **~ette** [sigə'ret] cigarrillo *m*; pitillo *m*; **~ette case** pitillera *f*; **~ette holder** boquilla *f*
cinder ['sində] carbonilla *f*; **~s** cenizas *f/pl*
cinema ['sinimə] cine *m*
cinnamon ['sinəmən] canela *f*
cipher ['saifə] *s* cifra *f*; clave *f*; cero *m* (*t fig*); *v/t* cifrar
circle ['sə:kl] *s* círculo *m*; *v/t* rodear, circundar
circuit ['sə:kit] circuito *m*
circula|r ['sə:kjulə] circular; **~te** *v/i* circular; **~tion** circulación *f*
circum|ference [sə'kʌmfərəns] circunferencia *f*; **~scribe** ['~skraib] *v/t* circunscribir
circumstance ['sə:kʌmstəns] circunstancia *f*; condición *f*
circus ['sə:kəs] circo *m*
cistern ['sistən] cisterna *f*; depósito *m*

cit|ation [sai'teiʃən] cita *f*, citación *f*; **~e** *v/t* citar

cit|izen ['sitizn] ciudadano(a) *m* (*f*); **~izenship** ciudadanía *f*

city ['siti] ciudad *f*

civ|ic ['sivik] cívico; municipal; **~ics** educación *f* cívica; **~il** civil; cortés; **~il service** administración *f* pública; **~ilian** [si'viljən] paisano *m*; **~ility** cortesía *f*; **~ilization** civilización *f*; **~ilize** ['sivilaiz] *v/t* civilizar

claim [kleim] *s* reclamación *f*; demanda *f*; *v/t* reclamar, demandar

clam [klæm] almeja *f*

clam|orous ['klæmərəs] ruidoso; **~o(u)r** *s* clamor *m*; ruido *m*; *v/i* gritar, vociferar

clamp [klæmp] *s* grapa *f*; *v/t* sujetar

clan [klæn] clan *m*

clandestine [klæn'destin] clandestino

clap [klæp] *s* palmoteo *m*; palmada *f*; **~ of thunder** trueno *m*; *v/t* **~ one's hands** dar palmadas; *v/i* aplaudir

clarity ['klæriti] claridad *f*

clash [klæʃ] *s* choque *m*; conflicto *m*; *v/i* chocar

clasp [klɑ:sp] *s* broche *m*; apretón *m* (de manos); **~ knife** navaja *f* (de muelle); *v/t* abrochar; apretar

class [klɑ:s] *s* clase *f*; **first ~** primera clase *f*; **economy ~** clase *f* turista; **lower ~** clase *f* baja; *v/t* clasificar

classic ['klæsik] *a, s* clásico *m*; **~al** clásico

class|ification [klæsifi'keiʃən] clasificación *f*; **~ify** ['klæsifai] *v/t* clasificar

class|mate ['klɑ:smeit] compañero(a) *m*(*f*) de clase; **~room** aula *f*

clatter ['klætə] *s* chacoloteo *m*; *v/i* chacolotear

clause [klɔ:z] cláusula *f*; artículo *m*

claw [klɔ:] *s* garra *f*; *v/t* arañar

clay [klei] arcilla *f*; barro *m*

clean [kli:n] *a* limpio; *v/t* limpiar; **~ up** poner en orden; **~ers** tintorería *f*, *LA* lavandería *f*; **~ing** limpieza *f*; aseo *m*; **~ness** limpieza *f*; **~se** [klenz] *v/t* limpiar, purificar

clear [kliə] *a* claro; libre; *v/t* aclarar; despejar (*camino, etc*); *v/i* despejarse; **~ out** marcharse; **~-cut** bien definido; **~ing** claro *m*

cleave [kli:v] *v/t* partir

clef [klef] *mús* clave *f*

clemency ['klemənsi] clemencia *f*

clench [klentʃ] *v/t* cerrar; apretar

cler|gy ['klə:dʒi] clero *m*; **~gyman** clérigo *m*; **~ical** ['klerikəl] de oficina (*error, etc*)

clerk [klɑ:k] oficinista *m*

clever ['klevə] hábil; listo; mañoso; inteligente

cliché ['kli:ʃei] cliché *m*; frase *f* hecha

click [klik] golpecito *m* seco; chasquido *m* (*de la lengua*); *v/t* chasquear

client ['klaiənt] cliente *m, f*

cliff [klif] risco *m*, acantilado *m*

climate ['klaimit] clima *m*

climax ['klaimæks] culminación *f*; punto *m* culminante; colmo *m*

climb [klaim] *s* subida *f*; *v/t, v/i* subir, escalar; trepar

clinch [klintʃ] *s* forcejeo *m* (*de boxeadores*); *v/t* agarrar; remachar

cling [kliŋ] *v/i* adherirse, pegarse, quedar fiel

clinic ['klinik] clínica *f*

clink [kliŋk] *v/i* tintinear

clip [klip] *s* prendedor *m*; recorte *m*; sujetapapeles *m*; grapa *f*; *v/t* cortar; (*ovejas*) esquilar; acortar; recortar; **~pings** recortes *m/pl*

clique [kli:k] pandilla *f*

cloak [kləuk] manto *m*; capa *f* (*t fig*); **~room** guardarropa *f*

clock [klɔk] reloj *m*

clog [klɔg] *s* zueco *m*; chanclo *m*; *v/t* atascar

cloister ['klɔistə] claustro *m*; monasterio *m*

clos|e [kləus] *a* estrecho; callado; cercano; exacto; tacaño; *adv* cerca; [kləuz] *s* fin *m*; **draw to a ~e** tocar a su fin; *v/t, v/i* cerrar; terminar; **~ed** cerrado; **~e down** cerrar definitivamente; **~e-knit** ['kləusnit] muy unido; **~et** ['klɔzit] ropero *m*; **~e-up** ['kləusʌp] primer plano *m*

clot [klɔt] *v/t* coagular

cloth [klɔθ] paño *m*; tela *f*; **~e** [kləuð] *v/t* vestir; **~es** [kləuðz] ropa *f*; **~es hanger** percha *f*; **~ing** ['kləuðiŋ] ropa *f*

cloud [klaud] *s* nube *f*; **~less** despejado; **~y** nublado

clove [kləuv] *bot* clavo *m*; **~r** trébol *m*

clown [klaun] payaso *m*

club [klʌb] porra *f*; palo *m*; club *m*; **~s** (*naipes*) tréboles *m/pl*

cluck [klʌk] *v/i* cloquear

clue [klu:] indicio *m*; pista *f*

clump [klʌmp] *s* masa *f*; grupo *m*

clumsy ['klʌmzi] desmañado; torpe

cluster ['klʌstə] *s bot* racimo *m*; (*gente*) grupo *m*; *v/i* arracimarse; apiñarse

clutch [klʌtʃ] *s* agarro *m*; garra *f*; *tecn* embrague *m*; *v/t* agarrar

c/o = **in care of** a cargo de

coach [kəutʃ] coche *m*; *sp* entrenador *m*; *v/t* entrenar; preparar

coal [kəul] carbón *m*

coalition [kəuə'liʃən] *pol* coalición *f*

coarse [kɔ:s] basto; vulgar; tosco

coast [kəust] *s* costa *f*; litoral *m*; **the ~ is clear** no hay moros en la costa; **~guard** guardacostas *m*

coat [kəut] *s* chaqueta *f*; americana *f*; abrigo *m*; capa *f*, mano *f* (*de pintura*); **~ of arms** escudo *m* de armas; *v/t* cubrir; **~ing** capa *f*; revestimiento *m*

coax [kəuks] *v/t* engatusar

cobalt [kəu'bɔ:lt] cobalto *m*

cobweb ['kɔbweb] telaraña *f*

cocaine [kə'kein] cocaína *f*

cock [kɔk] *s* gallo *m*; macho *m*; grifo *m*; llave *f*; *v/t* amartillar (*fusil*); **~-a-doodle-do** ['kɔkədu:dl'du:] *interj* ¡quiquiriquí!; **~-and-bull story** cuento *m* chino; **~atoo** [~ə'tu:] cacatúa *f*; **~le** ['kɔkl] berberecho *m*; **~pit** *aer* cabina *f* de piloto

cockroach ['kɔkrəutʃ] cucaracha *f*

cocktail ['kɔkteil] cóctel *m*

cocoa ['kəukəu] cacao *m*

coconut ['kəukənʌt] coco *m*; **~ palm** cocotero *m*

cocoon [kə'ku:n] capullo *m*

cod [kɔd] bacalao *m*

code [kəud] *s* código *m*; clave *f*; *v/t* cifrar

coerce [kəu'ə:s] *v/t* forzar, obligar

coexist ['kəuig'zist] *v/i* coexistir; **~ence** coexistencia *f*

coffee ['kɔfi] café *m*; **~ bean** grano *m* de café; **~house** café *m*; **~ mill** molinillo *m* de café; **~pot** cafetera *f*

coffin ['kɔfin] ataúd *m*

cog [kɔg] *tecn* diente *m*; **~nac** ['kɔnjæk] coñac *m*; **~wheel** rueda *f* dentada

coherence [kəu'hiərəns] coherencia *f*

coiffeur [kwa:'fjuə] peluquero *m*

coil [kɔil] *s* rollo *m*; bobina *f*; espiral *f*; *v/t, v/i* enrollar(se)

coin [kɔin] *s* moneda *f*; *v/t* acuñar (*t fig*)

coincide [kəuin'said] *v/i* coincidir; **~nce** [kəu'insidəns] coincidencia *f*

coke [kəuk] coque *m*; **2** *fam* Coca Cola *f*

cold [kəuld] *a* frío (*t fig*); *s* frío *m*; resfriado *m*; catarro *m*; **catch a ~** resfriarse; **have a ~** estar resfriado; **~blooded** *zool* de sangre fría; *fig* desalmado; **~ cuts** [~'kʌts] fiambres *m/pl*; **~ness** frialdad *f*, indiferencia *f*

coleslaw ['kəulslɔ:] ensalada *f* de col

colic ['kɔlik] cólico *m*

collaborat|e [kə'læbəreit] *v/t* colaborar; **~ion** colaboración *f*; **~or** colaborador *m*

collaps|e [kə'læps] *s* fracaso *m*; *med* colapso *m*; *v/i* desplomarse; **~ible** plegadizo

collar ['kɔlə] cuello *m*; collar *m* (*de perro*); **~bone** clavícula *f*

colleague ['kɔli:g] colega *m, f*

collect [kə'lekt] *v/t* reunir; coleccionar (*sellos, etc*); cobrar; **~ion** colección *f*; **~ive** colectivo; **~or** coleccionista *m*; recaudador *m*; *elec* colector *m*

college ['kɔlidʒ] colegio *m*

collide [kə'laid] *v/i* chocar

collision [kə'liʒən] choque *m*

colloquial [kə'ləukwiəl] popular; familiar

colon ['kəulən] *gram* dos puntos *m/pl*; *anat* colon *m*

colonel ['kə:nl] coronel *m*

colon|ial [kə'ləunjəl] colonial; **~ialism** colonialismo *m*; **~ist** ['kɔlənist] colono *m*; **~ize** *v/t* colonizar; **~y** colonia *f*

colo(u)r ['kʌlə] *s* color *m*; *v/t* colorar; colorear, teñir; **~ bar** discriminación *f* racial; **~-blind** daltoniano; **~ed** colorado; de color (*personas*); **~ful** lleno de color; **~ing** colorido *m*; **~less** incoloro; pálido; **~s** colores *m/pl* de la bandera

colt [kəult] potro *m*

column ['kɔləm] columna *f*

comb [kəum] *s* peine *m*; *v/t* peinar

combat ['kɔmbət] *s* combate *m*; *v/t, v/i* combatir; **~ant** combatiente *m*

combin|ation [kɔmbi'neiʃən] combinación *f*; **~e** [kəm'bain] *v/t, v/i* combinar(se); ['kɔmbain] *s agr* segadora *f* trilladora

combustion [kəm'bʌstʃen] combustión *f*

come [kʌm] *v/i* venir; **how ~?** ¿y eso?; **~ about** suceder; **~ across** encontrarse con; **~ along!** ¡vamos!; **~ back** volver; **~ by** conseguir; **~ down** bajar; **~ from** venir de; **~ in (to)** entrar (en); **~ in!** ¡pase!; **~ in handy** ser útil; **~ out** salir; **~ to** volver en sí; **~ true** realizarse; **~ up** subir; surgir; salir; **~back** rehabilitación *f*

comed|ian [kə'mi:diən] cómico *m*; **~y** ['kɔmidi] comedia *f*

comet ['kɔmit] cometa *m*

comfort ['kʌmfət] *s* comodidad *f*; consuelo *m*; *v/t* consolar; **~able** cómodo

comic ['kɔmik] gracioso; cómico; **~s, ~ strips** tiras *f/pl* cómicas; tebeos *m/pl*

command [kə'mɑ:nd] *s* mando *m*; orden *f*; dominio *m*; **to be in ~** estar al mando; *v/t* mandar; ordenar; *mil.* comandar; **~er** comandante *m*; **~ment** mandamiento *m*

commemorate [kə'meməreit] *v/t* conmemorar

commence [kə'mens] *v/t, v/i* comenzar, empezar; **~ment** comienzo *m*

commend [kə'mend] *v/t* encomendar; alabar; **~able** loable

comment ['kɔment] *s* comentario *m*; *v/i* comentar; **~ator** ['~enteitə] comentarista *m*; (*radio*) locutor *m*

commerc|e ['kɔmə:rs] comercio *m*; **~ial** [kə'mə:ʃəl] *a* comercial; *s* anuncio *m* publicitario

commission [kə'miʃən] *s* comisión *f*; *mil* nombramiento *m*; *v/t* encargar; nombrar; **~er** comisario *m*

commit [kə'mit] *v/t* cometer; entregar; **~ oneself** comprometerse; **~ment** compromiso *m*

committee [kə'miti] comité *m*; comisión *f*

commodity [kə'mɔditi] mercancía *f*

common ['kɔmən] *a* común; ordinario, corriente; **in ~** en común; **~er** plebeyo *m*; **~ market** mercado *m* común; **~place** *s* cosa *f* común; *a* trivial; **2s** Cámara *f* Baja; **~ sense** sentido *m* común

commotion [kə'məuʃən] tumulto *m*; alboroto *m*

commun|icate [kə'mju:nikeit] *v/t* comunicar; transmitir; **~ication** comunicación *f*; **~icative** [~kətiv] comunicativo; **~ion** [~jən] comunión *f*; **~ism** ['kɔmjunizəm] comunismo *m*; **~ist** *a, s* comunista; **~ity** [kə'mju:niti] comunidad *f*, sociedad *f*

commute [kə'mju:t] *v/t* conmutar; *v/i* viajar (al trabajo) a diario

compact [kəm'pækt] *a* compacto; ['kɔmpækt] *s* pacto *m*

companion [kəm'pænjen] compañero(a) *m* (*f*); **~able** sociable

company ['kʌmpəni] compañía *f*; **(limited) ~** *com* sociedad *f* anónima

compar|able ['kɔmpərəbl] comparable; **~ative** [kəm'pærətiv] comparativo; (*ciencia*) comparado; **~e** [~'pɛə] *s* comparación *f*; **beyond ~e** sin igual; *v/t* comparar; *v/i*: **to ~e (with)** compararse (con); **~ison** [~'pærisn] comparación *f*

compartment [kəm'pɑ:tmənt] compartimiento *m*; *f c* departamento *m*

compass ['kʌmpəs] *s* brújula *f*; alcance *m*; *v/t* circundar; lograr

compassion [kəm'pæʃən] compasión *f*; **~ate** [~it] compasivo

compatible [kəm'pætəbl] compatible

compel [kəm'pel] *v/t* obligar, forzar

compensat|e ['kɔmpenseit] *v/t* compensar, indemnizar; **~ion** compensación *f*; indemnización *f*

compet|e [kəm'pi:t] *v/i* competir; **~ence** ['kɔmpitəns] competencia *f*; **~ent** ['kɔmpitənt] competente; capaz; **~ition** [kɔmpi'tiʃən] competición *f*; **~itor** [kəm'petitə] competidor *m*, rival *m*

compile [kəm'pail] *v/t* recopilar

complacent [kəm'pleisənt] satisfecho de sí mismo

complain [kəm'plein] *v/i* quejarse; **~t** queja *f*; dolencia *f*; reclamación *f*

complaisant [kəm'pleizənt] afable, agradable

complet|e [kəm'pli:t] *a* completo; acabado; *v/t* completar; acabar; **~ion** terminación *f*; cumplimiento *m*

complex ['kɔmpleks] *a, s* complejo *m*; **~ion** [kəm'plekʃn] tez *f*; cutis *m*

complicat|e ['kɔmplikeit] *v/t* complicar; **~ion** complicación *f*

compliment ['kɔmplimənt] cumplido *m*; piropo *m*, galantería *f*; **~s** saludos *m/pl*

comply [kəm'plai]: **~ (with)** *v/i* cumplir (con); acatar

component [kəm'pəunənt] *a, s* componente *m*

compos|e [kəm'pəuz] *v/t* componer; **~e oneself** calmarse; **~ed** sereno; **~ed of** compuesto de; **~er** compositor *m*; **~ition** composición *f*; **~ure** [kəm'pəuʒə] compostura *f*, serenidad *f*

compound ['kɔmpaund] *a* compuesto; *s* mezcla *f*; [kəm'paund] *v/t* componer; **~ fracture** fractura *f* complicada; **~ interest** *com* interés *m* compuesto

comprehen|d [kɔmpri'hend] *v/t* comprender; contener; **~sible** inteligible; **~sion** comprensión *f*; **~sive** extenso

compress [kəm'pres] *v/t* comprimir; ['kɔmpres] *s med* compresa *f*

comprise [kəm'praiz] *v/t* comprender, incluir

compromise ['kɔmprəmaiz] arreglo *m*, componenda *f*

compuls|ion [kəm'pʌlʃən] compulsión *f*, coacción *f*; **~ory** obligatorio

computer [kəm'pju:tə] ordenador *m*; computador(a) *m* (*f*); **~ science** informática *f*

comrade ['kɔmreid] camarada *m, f*

concave ['kɔn'keiv] cóncavo

conceal [kən'si:l] *v/t* ocultar; **~ment** ocultación *f*

concede [kən'si:d] *v/t* conceder

conceit [kən'si:t] presunción *f*; **~ed** engreído, presumido

conceiv|able [kən'si:vəbl] concebible; **~e** *v/t, v/i* concebir

concentrat|e ['kɔnsentreit] *v/t, v/i* concentrar(se); **~ion** concentración *f*

conception [kən'sepʃən] concepción *f*

concern [kən'sə:n] *s* interés *m*; inquietud *f*; asunto *m*; empresa *f*; *v/t* concernir, interesar; tratar de; preocupar; **~ed** preocupado; **~ing** sobre, acerca de; **as ~s** respecto de

concert ['kɔnsət] *s* concierto *m*; **in ~ with** de concierto con; [kən'sə:t] *v/t* concertar; **~ed** unido, combinado

concession [kən'seʃən] concesión *f*

conciliate [kən'silieit] *v/t* conciliar

concise [kən'sais] conciso

conclu|de [kən'klu:d] *v/t* concluir, terminar; inferir; deducir; decidir; **~sion** [~ʒən] conclusión *f*; **~sive** decisivo

concord ['kɔŋkɔ:d] concordia *f*; *mús*, *gram* concordancia *f*

concrete ['kɔnkri:t] *s* hormigón *m*, *LA* concreto *m*; *a* concreto

concur [kən'kə:r] *v/i* concurrir, coincidir

concussion [kən'kʌʃən] *med* conmoción *f* cerebral

condemn [kən'dem] *v/t* condenar; censurar; **~ation** [kɔndem'neiʃən] condenación *f*

condens|e [kən'dens] *v/t*, *v/i* condensar(se)

condescend [kɔndi'send] *v/i* condescender, dignarse

condition [kən'diʃən] *s* condición *f*; *v/t* condicionar, estipular; ***on ~ that*** a condición (de) que

condolences [kən'dəulənsiz] pésame *m*

condominium ['kɔndə'miniəm] condominio *m*

conduct ['kɔndəkt] *s* conducta *f*; comportamiento *m*, dirección *f*; [kən'dʌkt] *v/t* conducir, dirigir; manejar; **~or** *mús* director *m* de orquesta; (*autobús*) cobrador *m*

cone [kəun] cono *m*

confectioner [kən'fekʃənə] repostero *m*; **~'s shop** repostería *f*; **~y** confites *m/pl*, confitura *f*

confedera|cy [kən'fedərəsi], **~tion** confederación *f*; alianza *f*; **~te** *a*, *s* aliado(a) *m* (*f*); *v/i* aliarse, confederar(se)

confer [kən'fə:] *v/t* conferir, otorgar; *v/i* conferenciar; consultar; **~ence** ['kɔnfərəns] conferencia *f*; congreso *m*

confess [kən'fes] *v/t*, *v/i* confesar(se); **~ion** confesión *f*; credo *m*

confid|e [kən'faid] *v/t*, *v/i*: ***to ~e in*** confiar en; fiarse de; **~ence** ['kɔnfidəns] confianza *f*; confidencia *f*; **~ent** seguro; **~ential** [~'denʃəl] confidencial

confine [kən'fain] *v/t* limitar; encerrar; ***to be ~d*** *med* estar de parto; **~ment** encierro *m*; prisión *f*; *med* sobreparto *m*; **~s** ['kɔnfainz] confines *m/pl*

confirm [kən'fə:m] *v/t* confirmar; ratificar; **~ation** [kɔnfə'meiʃən] confirmación *f*

confiscate ['kɔnfiskeit] *v/t* confiscar

conflict ['kɔnflikt] *s* conflicto *m*; [kən'flikt] *v/i* pugnar; contradecirse; **~ing** antagónico, opuesto

conform [kən'fɔ:m] *v/t*, *v/i* conformar(se); **~ity** conformidad *f*

confound [kən'faund] *v/t* confundir

confront [kən'frʌnt] *v/t* confrontar; afrontar; **~ation** [kɔnfrʌn'teiʃən] enfrentamiento *m*

confus|e [kən'fju:z] *v/t* confundir; **~ed** confuso; **~ion** [~ʒən] confusión *f*

congeal [kən'dʒi:l] *v/t*, *v/i* cuajar(se); coagular(se)

congenial [kən'dʒi:niəl] simpático, agradable

congestion [kən'dʒestʃən] *med* congestión *f*; *fig* aglomeración *f*

congratulat|e [kən'grætjuleit] *v/t* felicitar; **~ions!** ¡enhorabuena! *f*

congregat|e ['kɔŋgrigeit] *v/t*, *v/i* congregar(se); **~ion** *relig* fieles *m/pl*

congress ['kɔŋgres] congreso *m*

conifer ['kɔnifə] conífera *f*

conjecture [kən'dʒektʃə] conjetura *f*

conjugal ['kɔndʒugəl] conyugal

conjugat|e ['kɔndʒugeit] *v/t* conjugar; **~ion** conjugación *f*

conjunct|ion [kən'dʒʌŋkʃən] conjunción *f*; **~ive** conjuntivo *m*

conjur|e [kən'dʒuə] *v/t* suplicar; ['kʌndʒə] *v/t*, *v/i* hacer juegos de manos; ***~e up*** hacer aparecer; **~er** mago *m*

connect [kə'nekt] *v/t* juntar; unir; conectar; asociar; relacionar; *v/i* unirse; conectarse; empalmar (*tren*); **~ed** unido; conexo; **~ion** conexión *f*; *f c* correspondencia *f*; enlace *m*; relación *f*

connive [kə'naiv] *v/i* intrigar; hacer la vista gorda

connoisseur [kɔni'sə:] conocedor(a) *m* (*f*)

conque|r ['kɔŋkə] *v/t* conquistar; *fig* vencer; **~ror** conquistador *m*; vencedor *m*; **~st** ['kɔŋkwest] conquista *f*

consci|ence ['kɔnʃəns] conciencia *f*; **~entious** [~i'enʃəs] concienzudo; **~ous** ['kɔnʃəs] consciente; **~ousness** conciencia *f*; *med* conocimiento *m*

conscript ['kɔnskript] recluta *m*

consecrate ['kɔnsikreit] *v/t* consagrar

consecutive [kən'sekjutiv] consecutivo

consent [kən'sent] *s* consentimiento *m*; *v/i* ***to ~ to*** consentir en

consequen|ce ['kɔnsikwəns] consecuencia *f*; **~t** consiguiente; **~tly** por consiguiente

conserv|ation [kɔnsə'veiʃən] conservación *f*; **~ative** [kən'sə:vətiv] *a*, *s* conservativo(a) *m* (*f*); conservador(a) *m* (*f*); **~atory** *mús* conservatorio *m*; **~e** *v/t* conservar; *s* conserva *f*

consider [kən'sidə] *v/t* considerar; tomar en cuenta; **~able** considerable; **~ate** [~it] considerado, respetuoso; **~ation** consideración *f*; aspecto *m*; recompensa *f*

consign [kən'sain] *v/t* consignar; **~ment** *com* consignación *f*; envío *m*

consist [kən'sist] *v/i*: ~ (***of***) consistir (en); **~ence**, **~ency** consistencia *f*; **~ently** continuamente

consol|ation [kɔnsə'leiʃən] consolación *f*; consuelo *m*; **~e** [kən'səul] *v/t* consolar

consolidate [kən'sɔlideit] *v/t*, *v/i* consolidar(se)

consonant ['kɔnsənənt] consonante *f*

conspicuous [kən'spikjuəs] llamativo

conspir|acy [kən'spirəsi] conspiración *f*; **~ator** conspirador *m*; **~e** [~'spaiə] *v/i* conspirar; *v/t* urdir

constable ['kʌnstəbl] policía *m*

constant ['kɔnstənt] constante; firme

consternation [kɔnstə'neiʃən] consternación *f*

constipation [kɔnsti'peiʃən] *med* estreñimiento *m*

constituen|cy [kən'stitjuənsi] distrito *m* electoral; **~t** *s pol* elector *m*

constitut|e ['kɔnstitju:t] *v/t* constituir; **~ion** *pol*, *med* constitución *f*; **~ional** constitucional

constrain [kən'strein] *v/t* constreñir, compeler; obligar; **~t** constreñimiento *m*; encierro *m*

construct [kən'strʌkt] *v/t* construir; **~ion** construcción *f*; obra *f*; interpretación *f*; **~ive** constructivo

consul ['kɔnsəl] cónsul *m*; **~ar** ['~julə] consular; **~ate** ['~julit] consulado *m*

consult [kən'sʌlt] *v/t* consultar; **~ation** [kɔnsəl'teiʃən] consulta *f*; consultación *f*; **~ing hours** horas *f/pl* de consulta

consum|e [kən'sju:m] *v/t* consumir; comerse; beberse; *v/i* consumirse; **~er** consumidor *m*; **~er goods** artículos *m/pl* de consumo; **~mate** ['kɔnsəmeit] *v/t* consumar; [kən'sʌmit] *a* consumado

consumption [kən'sʌmpʃən] consunción *f*, consumo *m*; *med* tisis *f*

cont. = ***continued***

contact ['kɔntækt] *s* contacto *m*; [kən'tækt] *v/t* poner(se) en contacto con; **~ lenses** microlentillas *f/pl*

contagious [kən'teidʒəs] contagioso

contain [kən'tein] *v/t* contener; abarcar; **~er** envase *m*, recipiente *m*

contaminat|e [kən'tæmineit] *v/t* contaminar; **~ion** contaminación *f*

contemplat|e ['kɔntempleit] *v/t* contemplar; **~ion** contemplación *f*; **~ive** contemplativo

contemporary [kən'tempərəri] *a*, *s* contemporáneo(a) *m* (*f*)

contempt [kən'tempt] desprecio *m*, desdén *m*; *for* contumacia *f*; **~ible** despreciable; **~uous** [~juəs] desdeñoso, despreciativo

contend [kən'tend] *v/t* sostener, disputar; *v/i* contender

content [kən'tent] *a* contento, satisfecho; *s* satisfacción *f*; agrado *m*; **~ed** satisfecho, tranquilo; **~ion** contienda *f*; argumento *m*

contents ['kɔntents] contenido *m*; tabla *f* de materias

contest ['kɔntest] *s* concurso *m*; contienda *f*; disputa *f*; [kən'test] *v/t* debatir, disputar; *pol* ser candidato en; **~ant** concursante *m*, *f*

context ['kɔntekst] contexto *m*

continent ['kɔntinənt] continente *m*; **~al** [~'nentl] continental

contingent [kən'tindʒənt] contingente; ***~ upon*** dependiente de

continu|al [kən'tinjuəl] continuo; **~ally** constantemente; **~ation** continuación *f*; **~e** [~u(:)] *v/t* continuar, seguir; *v/i* continuar, durar, proseguir; ***to be ~ed*** continuará; **~ity** [kɔnti'njuiti] continuidad *f*; **~ous** continuo

contour ['kɔntuə] contorno *m*

contraceptive [kɔntrə'septiv] anticonceptivo *m*

contract [kən'trækt] *v/t* contraer; *v/i* contraerse; encogerse; ['kɔntrækt] *s* contrato *m*; **~or** [kən'træktə] contratista *m*, *f*

contradict [kɔntrə'dikt] *v/t* contradecir; desmentir; **~ion** contradicción *f*; **~ory** contradictorio

contrary ['kɔntrəri] *s*, *a* contrario; ***on the ~*** al contrario

contrast ['kɔntra:st] *s* contraste *m*; [kən'tra:st] *v/t*, *v/i* contrastar

contribut|e [kən'tribju(:)t] *v/t*, *v/i* contribuir; **~ion** [kɔntri'bju:ʃən] contribución *f*; colaboración *f*; **~or** contribuyente *m*, *f*

contrite ['kɔntrait] contrito

contrive [kən'traiv] *v/t* idear, inventar; lograr

control [kən'trəul] *s* control *m*; mando *m*; comprobación *f*, inspección *f*; puesto *m* de control; *v/t* controlar; gobernar; dominar; manejar; ***~ tower*** *aer* torre *f* de control; **~ler** inspector *m*

controver|sial [kɔntrə'və:ʃəl] contencioso; discutible; **~sy** ['~və:si] controversia *f*

convalesce [kɔnvə'les] *v/i* convalecer; **~nce** convalecencia *f*; **~t** convaleciente

convenien|ce [kən'vi:njəns] conveniencia *f*; comodidad *f*; **~ient** conveniente

convent ['kɔnvənt] convento *m*

convention [kən'venʃən] convención *f*; asamblea *f*; convenio *m*; **~al** convencional

convers|ation [kɔnvə'seiʃən] conversación *f*; **~e** [kən'və:s] *v/i* conversar; **~e** ['kɔnvə:s] *a* inverso

conver|sion [kən'və:ʃən] conversión *f*; **~t** *v/t* convertir; transformar; ['kɔnvə:t] *s* converso(a) *m* (*f*); **~tible** *a*, *s* convertible *m*; *aut* descapotable

convey [kən'vei] *v/t* transportar; transmitir; **~ance** transporte *m*; transmisión *f*; vehículo *m*; **~or belt** cinta *f* transportadora

convict ['kɔnvikt] *s* presidiario *m*; [kən'vikt] *v/t* condenar, declarar culpable; **~ion** convicción *f*; *for* condena *f*

convince [kən'vins] *v/t* convencer

convulsion [kən'vʌlʃən] convulsión *f*; **~s of laughter** paroxismo *m* de risa

coo [ku:] *v/i* arrullar

cook [kuk] *s* cocinero(a) *m* (*f*); *v/t* cocinar; guisar; cocer; *v/i* cocinar; **~ie** galleta *f*, pasta *f*; **~ing** arte *m* de cocinar

cool [ku:l] *a* fresco; *fig* indiferente; sereno; *v/t* enfriar; *v/i* ***~ down*** enfriarse; calmarse; **~ness** frescura *f*; frialdad *f*

coop [ku:p] gallinero *m*; ***~ up*** *v/t* encerrar

co-op ['kəuɔp] *fam* = ***cooperative*** cooperativa *f*

cooperat|e [kəu'ɔpəreit] *v/i* cooperar; **~ion** cooperación *f*; **~ive** [~ətiv] *a* cooperativo; *s* cooperativa *f*

co-opt [kəu'ɔpt] *v/t* apropiar

coordinate [kəu'ɔ:dineit] *v/t* coordinar; *s mat* coordenada *f*

copartner ['kəu'pa:tnə] consocio *m*, copartícipe *m*, *f*

cope [kəup] *v/i*: ***~ with*** hacer frente a; arreglárselas con; dar abasto para

copious ['kəupjəs] copioso

copper ['kɔpə] cobre *m*; caldera *f*; *fam* perra *f* (*moneda*)

copulat|e ['kɔpjuleit] *v/i* copularse; **~ion** cópula *f*

copy ['kɔpi] *s* copia *f*; ejemplar *m*; *v/i* copiar, imitar; **~book** cuaderno *m*; **~cat** *fam* imitador(a) *m* (*f*); **~right** derechos *m/pl* de autor

coral ['kɔrəl] coral *m*

cord [kɔ:d] *s* cuerda *f*; cordón *m*; *v/t* encordonar

cordial ['kɔ:djəl] cordial; **~ity** [~i'æliti] cordialidad *f*

corduroy ['kɔ:dərɔi] pana *f*

core [kɔ:] *bot* corazón *m*; núcleo *m*, centro *m*; *fig* esencia *f*

cork [kɔ:k] corcho *m*; **~screw** sacacorchos *m*

corn [kɔ:n] grano *m*; trigo *m*; maíz *m*; callo *m* (*de pie*); **~cob** mazorca *f* de maíz

corner ['kɔ:nə] *s* rincón *m*; esquina *f*; *v/t* arrinconar; ***cut ~s*** atajar; **~stone** *arq*, *fig* piedra *f* angular

cornet ['kɔ:nit] corneta *f*

corn starch ['kɔ:nsta:tʃ] almidón *m* de maíz

corny ['kɔ:ni] gastado; pesado (*broma*, *etc*)

coronation [kɔrə'neiʃən] coronación *f*

coroner ['kɔrənə] *for* pesquisidor *m*

corpora|l ['kɔpərəl] *a* corporal; físico; *s mil* cabo *m*; **~tion** corporación *f*; sociedad *f* anónima

corpse [kɔ:ps] cadáver *m*

corpuscle ['kɔ:pʌsl] glóbulo *m* (*de sangre*)

correct [kə'rekt] *a* correcto, exacto; *v/t* corregir; calificar; **~ion** corrección *f*; rectificación *f*

correspond [kɔris'pɔnd] *v/i* corresponder; **~ence** correspondencia *f*; **~ent** *a* correspondiente; *s* corresponsal *m*; **~ing** correspondiente

corridor ['kɔridɔ:] pasillo *m*

corroborate [kə'rɔbəreit] *v/t* corroborar

corro|de [kə:rəud] *v/t* corroer; **~sion** [~ʒən] corrosión *f*

corrugate ['kɔrugeit] *v/t* arrugar; acanalar; **~d iron** hierro *m* ondulado

corrupt [kə'rʌpt] *a* corrompido, corrupto; *v/t* corromper; viciar; **~ion** corrupción *f*

corsage [kɔ:'sa:ʒ] corpiño *m*; ramillete *m* (*de flores*)

cosmetic [kɔz'metik] *a*, *s* cosmético *m*; **~s** cosmética *f*

cosmic ['kɔsmik] cósmico

cosmonaut ['kɔzmənɔ:t] cosmonauta *m*, *f*

cosmopolitan [kɔsmə'pɔlitən] *a*, *s* cosmopolita *m*, *f*

cost [kɔst] *s* coste *m*; costo *m*; precio *m*; *v/i* costar; valer; **~ly** costoso

Costa Rica ['kɔstə'ri:kə] Costa *f* Rica; **~ ~n** *a*, *s* costarriqueño(a) *m* (*f*)

costume ['kɔstju:m] traje *m*; disfraz *m*; **~ jewel(l)ery** bisutería *f*

cosy ['kəuzi] cómodo; acogedor

cot [kɔt] cuna *f*; catre *m*

cottage ['kɔtidʒ] casita *f* de campo; **~ cheese** requesón *m*

cotton ['kɔtn] algodón *m*

couch [kautʃ] *s* canapé *m*; sofá *m*; *v/t* expresar

cough [kɔf] *s* tos *f*; *v/i* toser; ***~ up*** escupir; **~ drop** pastilla *f* para la tos

council ['kaunsl] *s* consejo *m*; *relig* concilio *m*; **~(l)or** concejal *m*

counsel ['kaunsəl] consejo *m*; abogado *m*; ***to take ~*** consultar; **~(l)or** ['~silə] consejero(a) *m* (*f*)

count [kaunt] *s* cuenta *f*; cómputo *m*; suma *f*; (*noble*) conde *m*; *v/t* contar; *v/i* valer; ***it doesn't ~*** no vale; ***~ on*** contar con; **~down** cuenta *f* regresiva (*al lanzar un cohete*); **~enance** ['~inəns] *s* semblante *m*; *v/t* aprobar; **~er** *s* mostrador *m*; ficha *f*; contador *m*; *v/t* combatir; contradecir; *v/i* oponerse;

run ~er to oponerse a; ~eract [kauntə'rækt] v/t contrarrestar; ~er-espionage contraespionaje m; ~erfeit ['~fit] falsificado, falso; ~erpart persona f correspondiente (a uno); ~ess condesa f; ~less innumerable
country ['kʌntri] país m; patria f; campo m; in the ~ en el campo; ~man paisano m; ~side campo m
county ['kaunti] condado m; ~ seat cabeza f de partido
coup [ku:] golpe m; ~ d'état golpe m de estado
couple ['kʌpl] s pareja f; par m; v/t acoplar; juntar; a married ~ matrimonio m; a ~ of un par de
courage ['kʌridʒ] valor m; ánimo m; ~ous [kə'reidʒəs] valiente
cour|ier ['kuriə] estafeta f; ~se [kɔ:s] curso m; rumbo m; vía f; ruta f; plato m; to change ~se cambiar de rumbo; in due ~se a su tiempo; of ~se por supuesto
court [kɔ:t] s patio m; corte f; tribunal m; v/t cortejar; ~eous ['kɔ:tjes] cortés; ~esy ['kɔ:tisi] cortesía f; ~ house palacio m de justicia; ~ier ['kɔ:tje] cortesano m; ~-martial consejo m de guerra; ~ship cortejo m; ~yard patio m
cousin ['kʌzn] primo(a) m (f); first ~ primo(a) m (f) carnal
cove [kəuv] cala f, ensenada f
cover ['kʌvə] s cubierta f; tapa f; envoltura f; amparo m; pretexto m; v/t cubrir; proteger; tapar; revestir; under ~ bajo techo; to ~ up ocultar; ~ charge precio m del cubierto
covert ['kʌvət] secreto, disimulado
covet ['kʌvit] v/t codiciar
cow [kau] s vaca f; hembra f (de elefante, etc); v/t acobardar; ~ard ['kauəd] cobarde m; ~ardice ['~is] cobardía f; ~boy vaquero m
co-worker ['kəu'wɔ:kə] colaborador m; compañero m de trabajo
coxswain ['kɔkswein] timonel m
coy [kɔi] tímido; coqueta
cozy ['kəuzi] = cosy
crab [kræb] cangrejo m; ~ apple manzana f silvestre
crack [kræk] s grieta f; chasquido m; fam chiste m; hendedura f; v/t agrietar; chasquear (un látigo); resquebrajar; hender; v/i restallar; henderse; agrietarse; ~ up med sufrir un colapso nervioso; ~er cracker m; petardo m
cradle ['kreidl] s cuna f
craft [krɑ:ft] habilidad f; oficio m; astucia f; embarcación f; ~sman artesano m; ~y astuto
crag [kræg] despeñadero m, peñasco m
cram [kræm] v/t rellenar; embutir; v/i empollar
cramp [kræmp] calambre m; grapa f
cranberry ['krænbəri] arándano m agrio
crane [krein] s tecn grúa f; orn grulla f; v/t, v/i estirar(se) (el cuello)
crank [kræŋk] s manubrio m; manivela f; chiflado(a) m (f); v/t hacer arrancar (motor); ~shaft eje m del cigüeñal
crash [kræʃ] s estrépito m; choque m; aer caída f; fig derrumbe m; com quiebra f; v/i estrellarse; ~ into chocar con
crate [kreit] cajón m de embalaje
crater ['kreitə] cráter m
crav|e [kreiv] v/t implorar; v/i ~e for anhelar; ~ing antojo m, anhelo m
crawl [krɔ:l] v/i arrastrarse; andar a gatas; s (natación) crol m
crayfish ['kreifiʃ] cangrejo m de río
crayon ['kreiən] creyón m
crazy ['kreizi] loco; extravagante
creak [kri:k] v/i crujir; chirriar
cream [kri:m] nata f (de leche), crema f (t fig); ~ cheese queso m crema; ~y cremoso
crease [kri:s] s arruga f; pliegue m; v/t arrugar; plegar
creat|e [kri(:)'eit] v/t crear; causar; ~ion creación f; ~ive creativo, creador; ~or creador(a) m (f); ~ure ['kri:tʃə] criatura f
credentials [kri'denʃəlz] credenciales f/pl
credible ['kredəbl] creíble
credit ['kredit] s crédito m; v/t acreditar, abonar en; ~ card tarjeta f de crédito; ~or acreedor m
creed [kri:d] credo m
creek [kri:k] cala f; riachuelo m
creep [kri:p] v/i arrastrarse; gatear; ~er bot trepadora f
cremate [kri'meit] v/t incinerar (cadáver)
crescent ['kresnt] a creciente; s (luna) cuarto m creciente
cress [kres] mastuerzo m
crest [krest] cresta f; cima f; ~fallen abatido
crevice ['krevis] grieta f; hendedura f
crew [kru:] tripulación f; equipo m
crib [krib] pesebre m; cuna f (de bebé); fam chuleta f
cricket ['krikit] grillo m; criquet m
crim|e [kraim] crimen m; ~inal ['kriminl] a, s criminal m
crimson ['krimzn] carmesí
cringe [krindʒ] v/i agacharse; encogerse (de miedo)
crinkle ['kriŋkl] v/t arrugar
cripple ['kripl] s lisiado(a) m (f); mutilado(a) m (f); v/t lisiar; fig incapacitar
crisis ['kraisis] crisis f
crisp [krisp] a crujiente; crespo; tostado; v/t encrespar; ~s rajas f/pl de patatas fritas
crisscrossed ['kriskrɔst] entrelazado
critic ['kritik] s crítico m; ~al crítico; ~ism ['~sizəm] crítica f; ~ize ['~saiz] v/t, v/i criticar
croak [krəuk] v/i graznar; croar
crochet ['krəuʃei] s labor f de ganchillo; v/t hacer ganchillo
crockery ['krɔkəri] loza f
crocodile ['krɔkədail] cocodrilo m
crony ['krəuni] compinche m
crook [kruk] gancho m; fam fullero m, estafador m; ~ed torcido
crop [krɔp] s cosecha f; v/t cortar; cosechar; v/i ~ up surgir
cross [krɔs] s cruz f; v/t cruzar; atravesar; ~ oneself santiguarse; ~ out borrar; tachar; a malhumorado; enfadado; ~ country a campo traviesa; ~eyed bizco; ~ing cruce m, intersección f; ~road camino m transversal; pl encrucijada f; ~ section sección f transversal; ~wise transverso; ~word puzzle crucigrama m
crouch [krautʃ] v/i agacharse
crow [krəu] s cuervo m; corneja f; v/i cantar (gallo); ~bar alzaprima m
crowd [kraud] s gentío m; muchedumbre f; v/t atestar; apiñar; v/i apiñarse; ~ed atestado; concurrido
crown [kraun] s corona f; v/t coronar
crucial ['kru:ʃəl] crucial; decisivo
cruci|fixion [kru:si'fikʃən] crucifixión f; ~fy ['kru:sifai] v/t crucificar
crude [kru:d] crudo; grosero
cruel ['kruəl] cruel; ~ty crueldad f
cruet ['kru:it] vinagrera f
cruise [kru:z] s crucero m; v/i cruzar; ~r crucero m
crumb [krʌm] miga f; ~le ['~bl] v/t desmigajar; v/i desmoronarse
crumple ['krʌmpl] v/t arrugar; v/i contraerse
crunch [krʌntʃ] v/t ronzar; v/i crujir
crusade [kru:'seid] cruzada f; ~r cruzado m
crush [krʌʃ] s apretón m, apretadura f; gentío m; v/t aplastar; estrujar; abrumar
crust [krʌst] s corteza f; costra f; v/t, v/i encostrar(se)
crutch [krʌtʃ] muleta f
cry [krai] s grito m; llanto m; v/t, v/i gritar; llorar
crypt [kript] cripta f
crystal ['kristl] cristal m
cub [kʌb] cachorro m
Cuba ['kju:bə] Cuba f; ~n a, s cubano(a) m (f)
cub|e [kju:b] s cubo m; v/t cubicar; ~ic cúbico
cuckoo ['kuku:] cuclillo m
cucumber ['kju:kʌmbə] pepino m
cuddle ['kʌdl] v/t acariciar
cudgel ['kʌdʒəl] s porra f
cue [kju:] apunte m; señal f; taco m (de billar)
cuff [kʌf] puño m de camisa; bofetada f; ~ links gemelos m/pl
culminate ['kʌlmineit] v/i culminar
culprit ['kʌlprit] culpable m, f
cult|ivate ['kʌltiveit] v/t cultivar; ~ure ['~tʃə] cultura f; ~ured culto
cunning ['kʌniŋ] a astuto; s ardid m; astucia f
cup [kʌp] taza f; copa f; ~board ['kʌbəd] armario m; aparador m
curb [kə:b] s = kerb; v/t refrenar
curd [kə:d] cuajada f
curdle ['kə:dl] v/t, v/i cuajar(se)
cure [kjuə] s cura f; v/t, v/i curar(se)
curfew ['kə:fju:] toque m de queda
curio|sity [kjuəri'ɔsiti] curiosidad f; ~us ['~əs] curioso
curl [kə:l] s rizo m; bucle m; v/t, v/i rizar(se); arrollar(se); ~y rizado
currant ['kʌrənt] pasa f de Corinto; red ~ grosella f
curren|cy ['kʌrənsi] moneda f; ~t s corriente f; a corriente; actual; ~tly actualmente
curriculum [kə'rikjuləm] plan m de estudios
curse [kə:s] s maldición f; v/t maldecir; v/i blasfemar
curt [kə:t] brusco, rudo; breve, lacónico
curtail [kə:'teil] v/t acortar; reducir
curtain ['kə:tn] cortina f; teat telón m
curtsy ['kə:tsi] s reverencia f; v/i hacer una reverencia
curve [kə:v] s curva f; v/t, v/i encorvar(se); hacer una curva
cushion ['kuʃən] s cojín m; almohadón m; v/t amortiguar; mitigar
custard ['kʌstəd] natillas f/pl
custody ['kʌstədi] custodia f; in ~ for detenido
custom ['kʌstəm] costumbre f; ~ary acostumbrado; ~er cliente m; ~ize v/t fabricar según especificaciones; ~-made Am hecho a la medida; ~s aduana f
cut [kʌt] a cortado; ~ off aislado; s cortadura f; corte m; reducción f; short ~ atajo m; v/t cortar; tallar; partir; v/i cortar; ~ down talar (árboles); reducir (gastos, precios); ~ out recortar; ~e [kju:t] mono; ~lery cuchillería f; ~let chuleta f; ~-throat asesino m; ~ting cortante; fig mordaz
cyanide ['saiənaid] cianuro m
cycl|e ['saikl] s ciclo m; bicicleta f; v/i ir en bicicleta; ~ist ciclista m
cyclone ['saikləun] ciclón m
cylinder ['silində] cilindro m
cyni|c ['sinik] cínico m; ~cal cínico; ~cism cinismo m
cypress ['saipris] ciprés m
cyst [sist] med quiste m
Czechoslovak ['tʃekəu'sləuvæk] s, a checo(e)slovaco(a) m (f); ~ia Checoslovaquia f

D

dab [dæb] pequeña cantidad f
dabble ['dæbl]: v/i ~ in ocuparse superficialmente en
dad [dæd], ~dy [~i] papá m
daffodil ['dæfədil] narciso m
daft [dɑ:ft] tonto, chiflado
dagger ['dægə] puñal m; daga f
daily ['deili] diario, cotidiano
dainty ['deinti] delicado, exquisito, fino
dairy ['dεəri] lechería f; vaquería f; ~ products productos m/pl lácteos
daisy ['deizi] margarita f
dam [dæm] s embalse m; presa f; v/t represar; embalsar
damage ['dæmidʒ] s daño m; perjuicio m; avería f; v/t dañar; perjudicar; v/i dañarse
dame [deim] dama f; fam tía f
damn [dæm] v/t maldecir; ~ it! ¡maldito sea!; I don't give a ~ no me importa un bledo; ~ation [~'neiʃən] condenación f
damp [dæmp] a húmedo; v/t mojar; humedecer; amortiguar; fig desanimar; ~ness humedad f
danc|e [dɑ:ns] s baile m; danza f; v/i bailar; ~er bailarín m, bailarina f; ~ing baile m
dandelion ['dændilaiən] diente m de león
dandruff ['dændrif] caspa f
danger ['deindʒə] peligro m; riesgo m; ~ous ['~dʒrəs] peligroso; arriesgado
dangle ['dæŋgl] v/t colgar; v/i pender
Danish ['deiniʃ] a, s danés m
dar|e [dεə] v/i osar; atreverse; v/t desfiar; ~ing a atrevido, temerario; s osadía f, arrojo m
dark [dɑ:k] a oscuro; tenebroso; s oscuridad f; ~en v/t oscurecer; v/i oscurecerse; ~ness oscuridad f; ~ room foto cuarto m oscuro
darling ['dɑ:liŋ] a, s querido(a) m (f); amor m
darn [dɑ:n] v/t zurcir
dart [dɑ:t] s dardo m; v/i lanzarse, precipitarse; ~board blanco m; ~s juego m de dardos
dash [dæʃ] s brío m; arremetida f; pizca f; raya f; v/i lanzarse; ~board aut salpicadero m; ~ing brioso; garboso; vistoso
data ['deitə] datos m/pl; ~ base base f de datos
date [deit] s fecha f; plazo m; cita f; bot dátil m; up to ~ al día; moderno; out of ~ anticuado; v/t fechar; ~d pasado de moda
daughter ['dɔ:tə] hija f; ~-in-law nuera f
dawdle ['dɔ:dl] v/i holgazanear
dawn [dɔ:n] s alba f; v/i amanecer; from ~ to dusk de sol a sol
day [dei] día m; all ~ todo el día; by ~ de día; ~ by ~ día por día; ~ in, ~ out día tras día; every ~ todos los días; every other ~ un día sí y otro no; the ~ after tomorrow pasado mañana; the ~ before yesterday anteayer; to this ~ hasta hoy; ~break amanecer m; ~dream ensueño m; ~light luz f del día; in broad ~light en pleno día
daze [deiz] v/t aturdir
dazzle ['dæzl] v/t deslumbrar
dead [ded] muerto; difunto; elec sin corriente; the ~ los muertos m/pl; ~ beat hecho polvo; ~beat ['dedbi:t] vago m; ~en v/t amortiguar; ~ end callejón m sin salida (t fig); ~line fecha f, línea f tope; ~lock fig punto m muerto; ~ly mortal
deaf [def] sordo; to turn a ~ ear hacerse el sordo; ~en v/t ensordecer; ~-mute a, s sordomudo(a) m (f); ~ness sordera f
deal [di:l] s negocio m; trato m; pacto m; a good ~ bastante; a great ~ (of) mucho; v/t distribuir; v/i ~ in comerciar en; ~ with tratar con; ocuparse de; ~er comerciante m
dean [di:n] decano m
dear [diə] querido; caro; ~ me! ¡válgame Dios!; ~ly profundamente; caramente; ~th [də:θ] falta f; escasez f
death [deθ] muerte f; fallecimiento m; freeze to ~ partírsele de frío los huesos; frightened to ~ muerto de susto; ~ly sepulcral; mortal; ~ rate mortalidad f
debase [di'beis] v/t degradar; envilecer
debate [di'beit] s debate m; v/t, v/i discutir, debatir
debauchery [di'bɔ:tʃəri] libertinaje m
debit ['debit] s com debe m; v/t cargar en cuenta, adeudar; ~ balance saldo m deudor
debris ['deibri:] escombros m/pl
debt [det] deuda f; ~or deudor(a) m (f)
début ['deibu:] estreno m
decade ['dekeid] decenio m; década f
decaden|ce ['dekədəns] decadencia f; ~t decadente
decaffeinated [di'kæfi:nətid] descafeinado

decay [di'kei] *s* podredumbre *f*; decaimiento *m*; *v/i* pudrirse; decaer
decease [di'si:s] *s* fallecimiento *m*; *v/i* fallecer; **~d** *a, s* difunto(a) *m (f)*
decei|t [di'si:t] engaño *m*; fraude *m*; **~tful** engañoso, falso; **~ve** *v/t* engañar
December [di'sembə] diciembre *m*
decen|cy ['di:snsi] decencia *f*; **~t** decente
decentralize [di:'sentrəlaiz] *v/t* descentralizar
decept|ion [di'sepʃən] engaño *m*; **~ive** engañoso
decide [di'said] *v/t, v/i* resolver; determinar; decidir(se)
decipher [di'saifə] *v/t* descifrar
decision [di'siʒən] decisión *f*; *for* fallo *m*
deck [dek] *mar* cubierta *f*; **~ chair** hamaca *f*
declar|ation [deklə'reiʃən] declaración *f*; **~e** [di'klɛə] *v/t* declarar, manifestar
decl|ension [di'klenʃən] *gram* declinación *f*; **~ine** [di'klain] *s* declive *m*; decadencia *f*; *v/t gram* declinar; rehusar; *v/i* declinar, decaer
decontamination [di:kən'tæmineiʃn] descontaminación *f*
decor|ate ['dekəreit] *v/t* decorar, adornar, condecorar; **~ation** adorno *m*; condecoración *f*; **~ator** decorador *m*; **~um** [di'kɔ:rəm] decoro *m*
decrease ['di:kri:s] *s* disminución *f*; *v/t, v/i* disminuir(se), reducir(se)
decree [di'kri:] *s* decreto *m*; edicto *m*; *v/t, v/i* decretar
decrepit [di'krepit] decrépito
dedicat|e ['dedikeit] *v/t* dedicar; consagrar; **~ion** dedicación *f*; *(en un libro)* dedicatoria *f*
deduce [di'dju:s] *v/t* deducir, inferir
deduct [di'dʌkt] *v/t* restar; descontar; **~ion** deducción *f*; descuento *m*
deed [di:d] acto *m*; hecho *m*; *for* escritura *f*
deem [di:m] *v/t* juzgar
deep [di:p] profundo, hondo; astuto; subido, oscuro *(color)*; *fig* astuto; **~en** *v/t* profundizar, intensificar; *v/i* intensificarse; **~-freeze** congeladora *f*; **~ly** profundamente; **~-sea** de alta mar; **~-set** hundido *(ojos)*
deer [diə] ciervo *m*
deface [di'feis] *v/t* desfigurar; estropear
defame [di'feim] *v/t* difamar, calumniar
default [di'fɔ:lt] *v/i* no pagar; *s* **by** ~ *for* en rebeldía; **~er** moroso(a) *m (f)*
defeat [di'fi:t] *s* derrota *f*; *v/t* vencer, derrotar
defect [di'fekt] defecto *m*; **~ive** defectuoso
defen|ce [di'fens] defensa *f*; protección *f*; **~celess** indefenso, desamparado; **~d** [di'fend] *v/t* defender; **~dant** *for* demandado(a) *m (f)*; acusado(a) *m (f)*; **~der** defensor(a) *m (f)*; **~se** = **defence**; **~sive** *s*: **on the ~sive** a la defensiva
defer [di'fə:] *v/t* diferir, aplazar; **~ential** [defə'renʃəl] deferente, respetuoso
defiance [di'faiəns] desafío *m*; **in ~ of** en contra de
deficien|cy [di'fiʃənsi] deficiencia *f*; **~t** deficiente; insuficiente
deficit ['defisit] déficit *m*
defin|e [di'fain] *v/t* definir; **~ite** ['definit] exacto; determinado; **~ition** definición *f*; **~itive** [di'finitiv] definitivo
deflate [di'fleit] *v/t* desinflar
deflect [di'flekt] *v/t, v/i* apartar(se), desviar(se)
deform [di'fɔ:m] *v/t* deformar; **~ed** deforme, desfigurado; **~ity** deformidad *f*
defrost ['di:'frɔst] *v/t* deshelar, descongelar
deft [deft] diestro, hábil
defunct [di'fʌŋkt] difunto
defy [di'fai] *v/t* desafiar
degenerate [di'dʒenərit] *s, a* degenerado(a) *m (f)*
degrade [di'greid] *v/t* degradar
degree [di'gri:] grado *m*; rango *m*; **by ~s** paso a paso, gradualmente
dehydrated [di:'haidreitid] deshidratado; **~ milk** leche *f* en polvo
de-ice ['di:'ais] *v/t* deshelar
deign [dein] *v/i*: **~ to** dignarse
deity ['di:iti] deidad *f*
dejected [di'dʒektid] abatido, desalentado
delay [di'lei] *s* dilación *f*; retraso *m*; tardanza *f*; *v/t* demorar, aplazar; dilatar; *v/i* tardar
delegat|e ['deligit] *a, s* delegado(a); diputado; ['deligeit] *v/t* delegar; **~ion** delegación *f*
deliberate [di'libəreit] *v/t, v/i* deliberar; [di'libərit] premeditado; **~ly** a propósito; pausadamente
delica|cy ['delikəsi] delicadeza *f*; *(salud)* delicadez *f*; golosina *f*; **~te** ['~it] delicado, fino; frágil; **~tessen** [delikə'tesn] tienda *f* de ultramarinos
delicious [di'liʃəs] delicioso, rico
delight [di'lait] *s* encanto *m*; deleite *m*; delicia *f*; *v/t* encantar; *v/i* deleitarse; **~ed** encantado; **~ful** delicioso, encantador
delinquen|cy [di'liŋkwənsi] delincuencia *f*; **~t** delincuente
deliver [di'livə] *v/t* librar; entregar; **~ a speech** pronunciar un discurso; **~y** entrega *f*; alumbramiento *m*; **~y room** paritorio *m*; **home ~y** servicio *m* a domicilio
delude [di'lu:d] *v/t* engañar; **~ oneself** engañarse
deluge ['delju:dʒ] diluvio *m*, inundación *f*
delusion [di'lu:ʒən] ilusión *f*; decepción *f*
de luxe [di'lʌks] de lujo
demand [di'mɑ:nd] *s* petición *f*; exigencia *f*; *v/t* exigir; **in ~** solicitado; **~ing** exigente
demeano(u)r [di'mi:nə] porte *m*; conducta *f*
demilitarized [di:'militəraizd] desmilitarizado
demise [di'maiz] fallecimiento *m*
demobilize [di:'məubilaiz] *v/t* desmovilizar
democra|cy [di'mɔkrəsi] democracia *f*; **~t** ['deməkræt] demócrata *m, f*; **~tic** [~'krætik] democrático
demolish [di'mɔliʃ] *v/t* demoler; derribar
demon ['di:mən] demonio *m*
demonstra|te ['demənstreit] *v/t* demostrar, probar; **~tion** demostración *f*; *pol* manifestación *f*
demur [di'mə:] *v/i* poner reparo; **~e** [di'mjuə] modesto; púdico
den [den] guarida *f*; estudio *m*; gabinete *m*
denial [di'naiəl] negación *f*; desmentida *f*
Denmark ['denmɑ:k] Dinamarca *f*
denomination [di'nɔmineiʃən] *relig* secta *f*; valor *m (de una moneda)*
denote [di'nəut] *v/t* significar
denounce [di'nauns] *v/t* denunciar
dense [dens] denso; espeso
dent [dent] *v/t* abollar; *s* abolladura *f*; **~al** dental
dent|ist ['dentist] dentista *m*; **~ure** ['~tʃə] dentadura *f*
deny [di'nai] *v/t* negar, denegar; desmentir
deodorant [di:'əudərənt] desodorante *m*
depart [di'pɑ:t] *v/i* partir, irse; marcharse; **~ment** departamento *m*; sección *f*; **~ment store** grandes almacenes *m/pl*; **~ure** [~tʃə] partida *f*, salida *f*
depend [di'pend]: *v/i* **~ on** depender de; contar con; **that ~s** según y conforme; **~able** seguro; de confianza; **~ence** dependencia *f*; confianza *f*; **~ent** *a, s* dependiente; subordinado(a) *m (f)*
deplor|able [di'plɔ:rəbl] deplorable; **~e** *v/t* deplorar
deployment [di'plɔimənt] *mil* despliegue *m*
depopulate [di'pɔpjuleit] *v/t* despoblar
deport [di'pɔ:t] *v/t* deportar; **~ment** comportamiento *m*
depos|e [di'pəuz] *v/t* deponer; **~it** [~'pɔzit] *s* depósito *m*; fianza *f*; sedimento *m*; *v/t* depositar
depot ['depəu] depósito *m*, almacén *m*
depraved [di'preivd] depravado
depreciate [di'pri:ʃieit] *v/i* depreciarse, perder valor
depress [di'pres] *v/t* deprimir; **~ed** deprimido; **~ing** deprimente; **~ion** depresión *f (t com)*
deprive [di'praiv] *v/t* privar, despojar
depth [depθ] profundidad *f*
deputy ['depjuti] diputado *m*, delegado *m*
derail [di'reil] *v/t, v/i* (hacer) descarrilar
derange [di'reindʒ] *v/t* desarreglar; **~d** trastornado mentalmente; **~ment** desarreglo *m*; trastorno *m* (mental)
deri|de [di'raid] *v/t* ridiculizar, mofarse de; **~sion** [di'riʒən] mofa *f*; burla *f*; **~sive** [~'raisiv] burlón; mofador
derive [di'raiv] *v/t* derivar
derogatory [di'rɔgətəri] despectivo; desdeñoso
descen|d [di'send] *v/t, v/i* descender, bajar; **~dant** *a, s* descendiente; **~t** [di'sent] descenso *m*; pendiente *f*; descendencia *f*
descri|be [dis'kraib] *v/t* describir; **~ption** [dis'kripʃən] descripción *f*; **~ptive** descriptivo
desecrate ['desikreit] *v/t* profanar
desert ['dezət] *a* desierto, yermo; *s* desierto *m*; [di'zə:t] *v/t* abandonar; *v/i* desertar; **~er** desertor *m*; **~ion** deserción *f*
deserve [di'zə:v] *v/t* merecer
design [di'zain] *s* designio *m*; proyecto *m*; dibujo *m*, diseño *m*; *v/t* proyectar; diseñar, dibujar
designate ['dezigneit] *v/t* designar; señalar; nombrar
designer [di'zainə] dibujante *m, f*; diseñador *m*; **fashion ~** modista *m/f*
desir|able [di'zaiərəbl] deseable; **~e** [~aiə] *s* deseo *m*; *v/t* desear
desk [desk] escritorio *m*; *(escuela)* pupitre *m*
desolat|e ['desəlit] *a* solitario; desierto; **~ion** desolación *f*; aflicción *f*
despair [dis'pɛə] *s* desesperación *f*; *v/i* desesperarse
desperate ['despərit] desesperado
despise [dis'paiz] *v/t* despreciar
despite [dis'pait] *prep* a pesar de, a despecho de
despondent [dis'pɔndənt] abatido, alicaído
dessert [di'zə:t] postre(s) *m(pl)*
destin|ation [desti'neiʃən] destino *m*; **~e** ['~in] *v/t* destinar; **~y** destino *m*
destitute ['destitju:t] indigente; desamparado
destr|oy [dis'trɔi] *v/t* destrozar; destruir; **~oyer** destructor *m*; **~uction** [dis'trʌkʃən] destrucción *f*; **~uctive** destructivo
detach [di'tætʃ] *v/t* separar, desprender; *mil* destacar; **~able** separable; **~ed** separado; imparcial; **~ment** separación *f*; *mil* destacamento *m*
detail ['di:teil] *s* detalle *m*; pormenor *m*; **in ~** en detalle; **~ed** detallado
detain [di'tein] *v/t* retener; detener
detect [di'tekt] *v/t* descubrir; averiguar; **~ion** descubrimiento *m*; **~ive** detective *m*; **~ive story** novela *f* policíaca
detention [di'tenʃən] detención *f*
deter [di'tə:] *v/t* disuadir; impedir; **~gent** *a, s* detergente *m*
deteriorate [di'tiəriəreit] *v/t, v/i* empeorar(se)
determin|ation [ditə:mi'neiʃən] determinación *f*, empeño *m*; **~e** [di'tə:min] *v/t* determinar; **~ed** resuelto
deterrent [di'terənt] *a* disuasivo
detest [di'test] *v/t* detestar; **~able** detestable
detonat|e ['detəuneit] *v/t* hacer detonar; **~ion** detonación *f*
detour ['di:tuə] desvío *m*; **make a ~** dar un rodeo
detract [di'trækt] *v/t*: **~ from** quitar mérito a
detriment ['detrimənt]: **to the ~ of** en perjuicio de; **~al** perjudicial
devalu|ation [di:vælju'eiʃən] desvalorización *f*; **~e** [~'vælju:] *v/t* desvalorizar
devastat|e ['devəsteit] *v/t* devastar; **~ing** abrumador
develop [di'veləp] *v/t* desarrollar; revelar; explotar; *v/i* desarrollarse, desenvolverse; **~ment** desarrollo *m*; suceso *m*; urbanización *f*; *foto* revelado *m*
deviat|e ['di:vieit] *v/t, v/i* desviar(se); **~ion** desviación *f*
device [di'vais] aparato *m*, dispositivo *m*; plan *m*
devil ['devl] diablo *m*, demonio *m*; **raise the ~** *fam* armarla; **~ish** diabólico; **~-may-care** *fam* despreocupado
devious ['di:viəs] tortuoso; intricado
devise [di'vaiz] *v/t* proyectar; idear
devoid [di'vɔid]: **~ of** desprovisto de
devot|e [di'vəut] *v/t* dedicar; **~ed** devoto; dedicado; **~ion** devoción *f*
devour [di'vauə] *v/t* devorar; tragar
devout [di'vaut] devoto
dew [dju:] rocío *m*
dexter|ity [deks'teriti] destreza *f*; habilidad *f*
diabetic [daiə'bətik] *a, s* diabético(a) *m (f)*
diagnose ['daiəgnəuz] *v/t* diagnosticar
diagram ['daiəgræm] diagrama *m*
dial ['daiəl] *s* cuadrante *m*; esfera *f*; *tel* disco *m* (selector); *v/t tel* marcar
dialect ['daiəlekt] dialecto *m*; **~ics** dialéctica *f*
dialogue ['daiəlɔg] diálogo *m*
diameter [dai'æmitə] diámetro *m*
diamond ['daiəmənd] diamante *m*
diaper ['daiəpə] *Am* pañal *m (para bebés)*
diaphragm ['daiəfræm] diafragma *m*
diarrh(o)ea [daiə'riə] diarrea *f*
diary ['daiəri] diario *m*
dice [dais] dados *m/pl*
dictat|e [dik'teit] *v/t* dictar; **~ion** dictado *m*; **~or** dictador *m*; **~orship** dictadura *f*
dictionary ['dikʃənri] diccionario *m*
die [dai] *v/i* morir; **~ down** extinguirse gradualmente; **~hard** intransigente *m, f*
diet ['daiət] *s* régimen *m* alimenticio, dieta *f*; *v/i* estar a dieta
differ ['difə] *v/i* diferenciarse; distinguirse; **~ence** ['difrəns] diferencia *f*; **it makes no ~ence** lo mismo da; **~ent** diferente
difficult ['difikəlt] difícil; **~y** dificultad *f*; **with utmost ~y** a duras penas
diffident ['difidənt] tímido
diffuse [di'fjus] *a* difuso; [di'fju:z] *v/t* difundir
dig [dig] *v/t, v/i* cavar; excavar; **~ out, up** desenterrar
digest ['daidʒest] *s* compendio *m*; [di'dʒest] *v/t* digerir *(t fig)*; compendiar, resumir; **~ion** digestión *f*
digni|fied ['dignifaid] serio, mesurado; **~ty** dignidad *f*
digress [dai'gres] *v/i*: **~ from** apartarse de; **~ion** digresión *f*
dike [daik] dique *m*
dilapidated [di'læpideitid] ruinoso
dilate [dai'leit] *v/t, v/i* dilatar(se)
diligen|ce ['dilidʒəns] diligencia *f*; **~t** diligente
dill [dil] eneldo *m*
dilute [dai'lju:t] *v/t, v/i* diluir(se)
dim [dim] *a* débil; indistinto, oscuro; opaco *(t fig)*; *v/t* oscurecer, opacar
dimension [di'menʃən] dimensión *f*
diminish [di'miniʃ] *v/t, v/i* disminuir(se)
dimple ['dimpl] hoyuelo *m*
din [din] estruendo *m*
din|e [dain] *v/i* cenar; **~e out** comer fuera de casa; **~ing car** coche-comedor *m*; **~ing room** comedor *m*; **~ner** ['dinə] comida *f*, cena *f*; **~ner jacket** esmoquin *m*
dip [dip] *s* inclinación *f*, inmersión *f*; *v/t* sumergir; *v/i* sumergirse; inclinarse
diphtheria [dif'θiəriə] difteria *f*

diploma [di'pləumə] diploma *m*; **~cy** diplomacia *f*; **~t** ['~əmæt] diplomático *m*; **~tic** [~ə'mætik] diplomático
dire ['daiə] horrendo
direct [di'rekt] *a* directo; derecho; recto; franco; *v/t* dirigir; mandar; **~ion** dirección *f*; **~ions** instrucciones *f/pl*; **~ions for use** modo *m* de empleo; **~ly** directamente; en seguida; **~or** director *m*
directory *s*: (**telephone**) ~ guía *f* telefónica
dirt [də:t] suciedad *f*; porquería *f*; **~ cheap** baratísimo, regalado; **~y** *a* sucio; indecente; *v/t* ensuciar
disab|ility [disə'biliti] incapacidad *f*; inhabilidad *f*; **~led** [dis'eibld] incapacitado; inválido; mutilado
disadvantage [disəd'vɑ:ntidʒ] desventaja *f*; detrimento *m*; **~ous** [disædvɑ:n'teidʒəs] desventajoso
disagree [disə'gri:] *v/i* discrepar; **~ with** no estar de acuerdo con; **~able** desagradable; **~ment** desacuerdo *m*; altercado *m*
disappear [disə'piə] *v/t* desaparecer; **~ance** desaparición *f*
disappoint [disə'pɔint] *v/t* decepcionar; defraudar; **~ment** desilusión *f*; decepción *f*
disapprov|al [disə'pru:vəl] desaprobación *f*; **~e** *v/t*, *v/i* desaprobar
disarm [dis'ɑ:m] *v/t* desarmar; **~ament** desarme *m*
disarray ['disə'rei] *s* desarreglo *m*; desorden *m*
disast|er [di'zɑ:stə] desastre *m*; **~er area** zona *f* siniestrada; **~rous** desastroso
disbelief ['disbi'li:f] incredulidad *f*
disburse [dis'bə:s] *v/t* desembolsar; **~ment** desembolso *m*, gasto *m*
disc [disk] disco *m*
discard [dis'kɑ:d] *v/t* descartar; tirar
discern [di'sə:n] *v/t*, *v/i* discernir; percibir; **~ing** perspicaz; **~ment** discernimiento *m*; juicio *m*
discharge [dis'tʃɑ:dʒ] *s* descarga *f*; (*arma*) disparo *m*; *com* descargo *m*; *mil* licenciamiento *m*; pago *m*; despedida *f*; *v/t* descargar; disparar; licenciar; desempeñar; despedir; dar de alta; *v/i* descargar
disciple [di'saipl] discípulo *m*
discipline ['disiplin] disciplina *f*
disc jockey ['disk 'dʒɔki] montadiscos *m*
disclaim [dis'kleim] *v/t* negar; *for* renunciar
disclose [dis'kləuz] *v/t* revelar
discomfort [dis'kʌmfət] incomodidad *f*; molestia *f*
disconcert [diskən'sə:t] *v/t* desconcertar; confundir
disconnect ['diskə'nekt] *v/t* desconectar; desacoplar; **~ed** inconexo
disconsolate [dis'kɔnsəlit] desconsolado
discontent ['diskən'tent] descontento *m*; desagrado *m*; **~ed** descontento
discontinue ['diskən'tinju] *v/t*, *v/i* interrumpir, suspender (*pagos*)
discord ['diskɔ:d] discordia *f*; desacuerdo *m*; **~ance** [~'kɔ:dəns] discordia *f*; *mús* disonancia *f*; **~ant** discordante; *mús* disonante
discotheque ['diskəutek] discoteca *f*
discount ['diskaunt] descuento *m*; rebaja *f*
discourage [dis'kʌridʒ] *v/t* desanimar, desalentar; **~ment** desaliento *m*
discourse ['diskɔ:s] discurso *m*
discourteous [dis'kə:tiəs] descortés
discover [dis'kʌvə] descubrir; **~er** descubridor *m*; **~y** descubrimiento *m*
discredit [dis'kredit] *s* descrédito *m*; *v/t* desacreditar
discre|et [dis'kri:t] discreto; **~pancy** [dis'krepənsi] discrepancia *f*; **~tion** [~'kreʃən] discreción *f*
discriminat|e [dis'krimineit] *v/t*: **~e between** distinguir entre; **~e against** discriminar contra; **~ing** discerniente; **~ion** discriminación *f*
discuss [dis'kʌs] *v/t* discutir; hablar de, tratar de; **~ion** discusión *f*
disdain [dis'dein] *s* desdén *m*; *v/t* desdeñar
disease [di'zi:z] enfermedad *f*; **~d** enfermo
disembark ['disim'bɑ:k] *v/t*, *v/i* desembarcar(se)
disengage ['disin'geidʒ] *v/t* desenganchar; soltar; *aut* desembragar
disentangle ['disin'tæŋgl] *v/t* desenredar
disfavo(u)r ['dis'feivə] *s* desaprobación *f*; desgracia *f*
disfigure [dis'figə] *v/t* desfigurar; deformar
disgrace [dis'greis] *s* deshonra *f*; vergüenza *f*; *v/t* deshonrar; **~ful** ignominioso
disgruntled [dis'grʌntld] disgustado, malhumorado
disguise [dis'gaiz] *s* disfraz *m*; *v/t* disfrazar
disgust [dis'gʌst] *s* asco *m*; repugnancia *f*; *v/t* repugnar; **~ing** asqueroso, repugnante
dish [diʃ] plato *m*; fuente *f*; **~es** vajilla *f*; **wash the ~es** fregar los platos; **~cloth** paño *m* de cocina
dishearten [dis'hɑ:tn] *v/t* desalentar
dishevel(l)ed [di'ʃevəld] desgreñado, desmelenado
dishonest [dis'ɔnist] fraudulento; tramposo; falso; **~y** falta *f* de honradez
dishono(u)r [dis'ɔnə] *s* deshonra *f*, deshonor *m*; *v/t* deshonrar; *com* rechazar (*cheque, etc*)
dishwasher ['diʃwɔʃə] *tecn* lavavajillas *m*
disillusion [disi'lu:ʒən] *s* desilusión *f*; *v/t* desilusionar
disinclined ['disin'klaind] renuente, poco dispuesto
disinfect [disin'fekt] *v/t* desinfectar; fumigar; **~ant** *a*, *s* desinfectante *m*
disinherit ['disin'herit] *v/t* desheredar
disintegrate [dis'intigreit] *v/i* disgregarse; desintegrarse
disinterested [dis'intristid] desinteresado
disk [disk] = **disc**
dislike [dis'laik] *s* aversión *f*; antipatía *f*; *v/t* tener aversión a; no gustarle a uno
dislocate ['disləukeit] *v/t* dislocar
dislodge [dis'lɔdʒ] *v/t* echar fuera; *mil* desalojar
disloyal ['dis'lɔiəl] desleal
dismal ['dizməl] lúgubre; sombrío; deprimente
dismantle [dis'mæntl] *v/t* desmontar
dismay [dis'mei] *s* consternación *f*; *v/t* consternar
dismiss [dis'mis] *v/t* despedir; destituir; dejar ir; **~al** despedida *f*; destitución *f*
dismount ['dis'maunt] *v/t* desmontar; *v/i* apearse
disobedien|ce [disə'bi:djəns] desobediencia *f*; **~t** desobediente
disobey ['disə'bei] *v/t*, *v/i* desobedecer
disorder [dis'ɔ:də] *s* desorden *m*; disturbio *m*; *med* trastorno *m*; *v/t* desordenar; **~ly** desordenado; alborotado
disown [dis'əun] *v/t* desconocer; negar; repudiar
disparage [dis'pæridʒ] *v/t* menospreciar; **~ment** menosprecio *m*
dispassionate [dis'pæʃənit] desapasionado
dispatch [dis'pætʃ] *s* despacho *m*; prontitud *f*; *v/t* despachar; expedir
dispel [dis'pel] *v/t* disipar; *fig* desvanecer
dispens|able [dis'pensəbl] dispensable; **~e** *v/t* distribuir, repartir; *v/i* **~e with** pasar sin, prescindir de
disperse [dis'pə:s] *v/t*, *v/i* dispersar(se)
displace [dis'pleis] *v/t* sacar de su sitio; **~d person** desplazado(a) *m* (*f*); **~ment** desalojamiento *m*; *mar* desplazamiento *m*
display [dis'plei] *s* exhibición *f*, ostentación *f*; **~ window** escaparate *m*; *v/t* exponer; ostentar
displeas|e [dis'pli:z] *v/t*, *v/i* disgustar, molestar; desagradar; **~ing** desagradable; **~ure** [~eʒə] desagrado *m*, disgusto *m*
dispos|al [dis'pəuzəl] disposición *f*; ajuste *m*; venta *f*; eliminación *f*; **~e** *v/t* disponer; *v/i* **~e of** disponer de; deshacerse de; **~ition** disposición *f*; propensión *f*; carácter *m*
disproportionate [disprə'pɔ:ʃnit] desproporcionado
disprove [dis'pru:v] *v/t* refutar
dispute [dis'pju:t] *s* disputa *f*, controversia *f*; *v/t*, *v/i* disputar
disqualify [dis'kwɔlifai] *v/t* descalificar; inhabilitar
disquieting [dis'kwaiətiŋ] inquietante
disregard [disri'gɑ:d] *s* descuido *m*; *v/t* desatender
disrepair ['disri'pɛə]: **fall into ~** deteriorarse
disreputable [dis'repjutəbl] de mala fama
disrespectful [disris'pektful] irrespetuoso
disrupt [dis'rʌpt] *v/t* romper; interrumpir
dissatisf|action ['dissætis'fækʃən] descontento *m*; **~ied** [~faid] descontento
dissen|sion [di'senʃən] disensión *f*, discordia *f*; **~t** *v/i* disentir; **~ter** disidente *m*
disservice ['dis'sə:vis]: **do a ~ to** perjudicar a
dissipate ['disipeit] *v/t*, *v/i* disipar(se)
dissociat|e [di'səuʃieit] *v/t* disociar; **~ion** disociación *f*
dissol|ute ['disəlu:t] disoluto; **~ution** disolución *f*; **~ve** [di'zɔlv] *v/t*, *v/i* disolver(se)
dissuade [di'sweid] *v/t* disuadir
distan|ce ['distəns] distancia *f*; **from a ~ce** desde lejos; **in the ~ce** a lo lejos; **keep at a ~ce** no tratar con familiaridad; **~t** distante, apartado; *fig* reservado
distaste ['dis'teist] aversión *f*; repugnancia *f*; **~ful** desagradable
distend [dis'tend] *v/t*, *v/i* hinchar(se); dilatar(se)
distil(l) [dis'til] *v/t* destilar; **~ery** destilería *f*
distinct [dis'tiŋkt] distinto; claro; **~ion** distinción *f*; **~ive** distintivo
distinguish [dis'tiŋgwiʃ] *v/t* distinguir; **~ed** distinguido, ilustre; marcado
distort [dis'tɔ:t] *v/t* torcer (*t fig*); distorsionar (*sonido, etc*); **~ion** distorsión *f*; deformación *f*
distract [dis'trækt] *v/t* distraer; perturbar; **~ed** aturdido; **~ion** distracción *f*; diversión *f*; perturbación *f*
distress [dis'tres] *s* angustia *f*; congoja *f*; apuro *m*, peligro *m*; miseria *f*; *v/t* afligir, angustiar; **to be in ~** estar en un apuro; **~ing** penoso
distribut|e [dis'tribju(:)t] *v/t* distribuir, repartir; **~ion** distribución *f*, reparto *m*
district ['distrikt] distrito *m*; comarca *f*; **~ attorney** *Am* [~ə'tɔ:ni] fiscal *m*, *f*
distrust [dis'trʌst] *s* desconfianza *f*; *v/t* desconfiar de; **~ful** desconfiado
disturb [dis'tə:b] *v/t* molestar; inquietar; **~ance** disturbio *m*; tumulto *m*; **~ing** perturbador, inquietante
disuse [dis'ju:s]: **to fall into ~** caer en desuso
ditch [ditʃ] zanja *f*; cuneta *f*
ditto ['ditəu] ídem, lo mismo
dive [daiv] *v/i* bucear; zambullirse; *mar* sumergirse; *aer* picar; *fig* lanzarse; *s* salto *m*; buceo *m*; *aer* picada *f*; **~r** buzo *m*; saltador(a) *m* (*f*)
diverge [dai'və:dʒ] *v/i* divergir
diver|se [dai'və:s] diverso; **~sion** diversión *f*; **~sity** diversidad *f*; **~t** *v/t* desviar; divertir
divid|e [di'vaid] *v/t* dividir, separar; *v/i* dividirse; **~end** ['dividend] dividendo *m*; **~ing** divisorio
divin|e [di'vain] *a* divino; **~g** ['daiviŋ] **board** trampolín *m*; **~g suit** escafandra *f*; **~ity** [di'viniti] divinidad *f*
division [di'viʒən] división *f*; *com* departamento *m*
divorce [di'vɔ:s] *s* divorcio *m*; *v/t* divorciar; *fig* separar; **get ~d** divorciarse; **~d** divorciado
divulge [dai'vʌldʒ] *v/t* divulgar
dizzy ['dizi] mareado; confundido; vertiginoso
do [du:] *v/t* hacer; ejecutar; rendir; servir; arreglar; recorrer; *v/i* actuar; convenir; estar; **how ~ you ~?** mucho gusto; **that will ~** eso basta; **~ away with** eliminar; **what can I ~ for you?** ¿en qué puedo servirle?; **~ over** volver a hacer; **make ~ with** contentarse con; **nothing to ~ with** nada que ver con; **~ without** prescindir de
docile ['dəusail] dócil
dock [dɔk] *s* dique *m*; dársena *f*; muelle *m*; *for* banquillo *m*; *v/t* cercenar; acortar; *v/i* atracar; **~er** estibador *m*; **~yard** astillero *m*
doctor ['dɔktə] *s* médico *m*, doctor *m*; *v/t* medicinar; falsificar; **~ate** doctorado *m*
doctrine ['dɔktrin] doctrina *f*
document ['dɔkjumənt] documento *m*; **~ary** *cine* documental *m*
dodge [dɔdʒ] *s* regate *m*; truco *m*; *v/t* regatear; evadir
doe [dəu] gama *f*; coneja *f*; **~skin** ante *m*
dog [dɔg] *s* perro *m*; *v/t* seguir, acosar; **~ days** canícula *f*; **~ged** tenaz
dogma ['dɔgmə] dogma *m*
doings ['du(:)iŋz] *fam* actividades *f/pl*
do-it-yourself ['du:itjə'self] bricolaje *m*
dole [dəul]: *s* **on the ~** subsidio *m* de paro; *v/t* **~ out** repartir; **~ful** triste, lúgubre
doll [dɔl] muñeca *f*
dollar ['dɔlə] dólar *m*
dolphin ['dɔlfin] delfín *m*
dome [dəum] cúpula *f*
domestic [dəu'mestik] doméstico; casero; **~ate** [~eit] *v/t* domesticar
domicile ['dɔmisail] *for* domicilio *m*
domin|ate ['dɔmineit] *v/t* dominar; **~ation** dominación *f*; **~eer** *v/t*, *v/i* dominar; tiranizar; **~eering** mandón; **~oes** ['dɔminəuz] juego *m* de dominó
dona|te [dəu'neit] *v/t* donar; **~tion** donativo *m*
done [dʌn] ejecutado; acabado; **well ~!** ¡muy bien hecho!; **well ~** *coc* bien hecho; **~ for** rendido; perdido
donkey ['dɔŋki] burro *m*
donor ['dəunə] donante *m*, *f*
doom [du:m] *s* fatalidad *f*; destino *m*; *v/t* condenar; **~sday** día *m* del juicio final
door [dɔ:] puerta *f*; **next ~** en la casa de al lado; **behind closed ~s** a puertas cerradas; **out of ~s** al aire libre; **~bell** timbre *m*; **~knob** perilla *f*; **~man** portero *m*; **~mat** esterilla *f*; **~way** portal *m*
dope [dəup] *s fam* narcótico *m*; droga *f*; tonto *m*, bobo *m*; *v/t* narcotizar
dormitory ['dɔ:mitri] dormitorio *m*
dose [dəus] *s* dosis *f*
dot [dɔt] punto *m*; **on the ~** en punto; **~ted with** salpicado de
double ['dʌbl] *a* doble; *s teat* doble *m*; *adv* dos veces, doble; *v/t* doblar; *v/i* doblarse; **at (on) the ~** rápidamente; **~ up** doblarse; **~bass** contrabajo *m*; **~breasted** cruzado; **~cross** *v/t* engañar; traicionar; **~decker** *fam* ómnibus *m* de dos pisos; **~entry** *com* partida *f* doble
doubt [daut] *s* duda *f*; *v/t*, *v/i* dudar; **no ~** sin duda; **~ful** dudoso; **~less** indudablemente
dough [dəu] masa *f*; pasta *f*; **~nut** buñuelo *m*
dove [dʌv] paloma *f*; **~tail** *v/i* encajar
dowdy ['daudi] desaliñado; mal vestido
down [daun] *adv* abajo; hacia abajo; *s* plumón *m*; **~ and out** arruinado; **~ to earth** realista; **~ with...!** ¡abajo!; **~cast** cabizbajo, abatido; **~fall** caída *f*; **~hill** cuesta abajo; **~pour** chaparrón *m*; **~right** absoluto, completo; **~stairs** abajo; **~town** centro *m* de la ciudad; **~ward(s)** ['~wəd(z)] hacia abajo; **~y** velloso
dowry ['dauəri] dote *f*
doze [dəuz] *s* sueño *m* ligero; *v/i* dormitar
dozen ['dʌzn] docena *f*
drab [dræb] gris; monótono
draft [drɑ:ft] bosquejo *m*;

borrador *m*; corriente *f* de aire; *com* letra *f* de cambio, giro *m*; *mil* quinta *f*; ~ **beer** cerveza *f* de barril; *v/t* bosquejar; hacer un proyecto de; **~sman** dibujante *m*
drag [dræg] *s mar* rastra *f*; *fam* lata *f*; *v/t* arrastrar; *mar* rastrear; *v/i* arrastrarse (*por el suelo*); ~ **on** ser interminable
dragon ['drægən] dragón *m*; **~fly** caballito *m* del diablo
drain [drein] *s* desagüe *m*; desaguadero *m*; *v/t* desaguar; drenar; **~age** desagüe *m*; drenaje *m*
drama ['drɑːmə] drama *m*; **~tic** [drə'mætik] dramático; **~tist** ['dræmətist] dramaturgo *m*
drape [dreip] *v/t* vestir, cubrir con colgaduras; **~r's shop** pañería *f*; **~s** cortinas *f/pl*
drastic ['dræstik] drástico
draught [drɑːft] corriente *f* (*de aire*); tiro *m* de chimenea; trago *m* (*de bebida*); *mar* calado *m*; ~ **animal** animal *m* de tiro
draw ['drɔː] *s sp* empate *m*; atracción *f*; sorteo *m*; *v/t* tirar, arrastrar; dibujar; atraer; sacar; tomar (*aliento*); *com* girar; ~ **aside** apartar a; ~ **back** retirar; ~ **forth** hacer salir; ~ **lots** echar suertes *f/pl*; ~ **money** cobrar; ~ **out** sacar; ~ **up** redactar; *v/i* atraer, dibujar; *sp* empatar; ~ **near** acercarse; ~ **up** detenerse; **~back** inconveniente *m*; **~-bridge** puente *m* levadizo; **~er** ['drɔːə] girador *m*; [drɔː] cajón *m*; **~ing** dibujo *m*; diseño *m*; **~ing pin** chincheta *f*; **~ing room** salón *m*
dread [dred] *s* temor *m*; pavor *m*; espanto *m*; *v/t*, *v/i* temer; **~ful** espantoso
dream [driːm] *s* sueño *m*; **day** ~ ensueño *m*; *v/t*, *v/i* soñar; soñar con; **~y** soñador
dreary ['driəri] monótono
dregs [dregz] heces *f/pl*
drench [drentʃ] *v/t* empapar; calar
dress [dres] *s* vestido *m*; traje *m*; atuendo *m*; *v/t* vestir; ataviar; arreglar; *med* curar; *v/i* vestirse; ~ **circle** galería *f* principal; ~ **coat** frac *m*; **~ing gown** bata *f*; **~ing table** tocador *m*; **~maker** modista *f*; ~ **rehearsal** ensayo *m* general
dribble ['dribl] *v/i* gotear; babear
drift [drift] *s* corriente *f*; rumbo *m*, tendencia *f*; *mar*, *aer* deriva *f*; *v/t* llevar, arrastrar la corriente; *v/i* ir a la deriva; amontonarse (*arena*, *nieve*)
drill [dril] *s* taladro *m*; barrena *f*; *mil* ejercicio *m*; surco *m* (*para siembra*); *v/t* taladrar; ejercitar; *mil* adiestrar
drink [driŋk] *s* bebida *f*; trago *m*; *v/t*, *v/i* beber
drip [drip] *s* goteo *m*; *v/i* gotear; chorrear; **~-dry** de lava y pon
driv|e [draiv] *s* paseo *m*, viaje *m* (*en coche*); calzada *f* particular; avenida *f*; energía *f*, empuje *m*; *tecn* propulsión *f*; *v/t* conducir; impulsar; empujar, llevar; *v/i* conducir; **~e at** querer decir; **~e-in** servicio *m* al coche (*banco*, *etc*); **~er** conductor *m*; **~ing** conducción *f*; **~ing licence** carnet *m* de conducir; **~ing school** autoescuela *f*
drizzle ['drizl] *s* llovizna *f*; *v/i* lloviznar
drone [drəun] *s* zángano *m*; zumbido *m*; *v/i* zumbar
drool [druːl] *v/i* babear
droop [druːp] *v/i* colgar; pender
drop [drɔp] *s* gota *f*; caída *f*; pastilla *f*; *v/t* dejar caer; *v/i* bajar, caer; ~ **in** visitar de paso; ~ **off** quedarse dormido
drought [draut] sequía *f*
drown [draun] *v/t* ahogar; anegar; *v/i* ahogarse
drowsy ['drauzi] soñoliento
drudge [drʌdʒ] *s* esclavo *m* del trabajo; *v/i* afanarse
drug [drʌg] *s* droga *f*; medicamento *m*; *v/t* narcotizar; ~ **addict** toxicómano *m*; **~gist** ['~gist] farmacéutico *m*; **~store** farmacia *f*
drum [drʌm] *s* tambor *m*; cilindro *m*; *anat* tímpano *m*; *v/i* tocar el tambor; tamborear (*con los dedos*); **~stick** *mús* palillo *m*; *coc* muslo *m*
drunk [drʌŋk] borracho; **get** ~ emborracharse; **~ard** borracho *m*
dry [drai] *a* seco, árido; desecado; *fig* aburrido; *v/t* secar, desecar; *v/i* secarse; **~-clean** *v/t* limpiar en seco; ~ **dock** dique *m* de carena; **~er** secador(a) *m* (*f*); ~ **goods** *Am* mercería *f*
dual ['djuːəl] doble
dubious ['djubjəs] dudoso
duchess ['dʌtʃis] duquesa *f*
duck [dʌk] *s* pato(a) *m* (*f*); *v/i* agacharse
due [djuː] *a* debido; merecido; *com* pagadero; **in ~ course** a su debido tiempo; ~ **to** debido a; *s* derecho *m*
duel ['dju(ː)əl] duelo *m*
duke [djuːk] duque *m*
dull [dʌl] *a* apagado; aburrido; opaco; estúpido; *v/t* entorpecer; embotar
duly ['djuːli] debidamente
dumb [dʌm] mudo; estúpido; **~founded** atónito
dummy ['dʌmi] *a* postizo; *s* maniquí *m*; chupete *m* (*de bebé*)
dump [dʌmp] *s* basurero *m*; *mil* depósito *m*; *v/t* descargar; verter; vaciar
dunce [dʌns] zopenco *m*
dune [djuːn] duna *f*
dung [dʌŋ] estiércol *m*; **~hill** estercolero *m*
dungeon ['dʌndʒən] calabozo *m*; mazmorra *f*
dupe [djuːp] *s* incauto *m*; primo *m*; *v/t* engañar
duplicat|e ['djuːplikit] *a*, *s* duplicado *m*; **~or** multicopista *f*
durable ['djuərəbl] duradero
duration [djuə'reiʃən] duración *f*
duress [djuə'res] compulsión *f*
during ['djuəriŋ] durante
dusk [dʌsk] anochecer *m*; crepúsculo *m*; **~y** obscuro; moreno
dust [dʌst] *s* polvo *m*; *v/t* desempolvar; quitar el polvo; empolvorear; **~bin** cubo *m* para basura; **~er** plumero *m*; trapo *m* de polvo; **~pan** cogedor *m*; **~y** polvoriento
Dutch [dʌtʃ] *s*, *a* holandés; **~man** holandés *m*; **~woman** holandesa *f*
duty ['djuːti] deber *m*; obligación *f*; **off** ~ libre (de servicio); **on** ~ de servicio; **~-free** libre de derechos de aduana
dwarf [dwɔːf] enano *m*
dwell [dwel] *v/i* habitar, morar; **~ing** vivienda *f*
dwindle ['dwindl] *v/i* disminuir(se); menguar
dye [dai] *s* tinte *m*; *v/t* teñir; **~r** tintorero *m*
dying ['daiiŋ] moribundo
dynamic [dai'næmik] dinámico; **~s** dinámica *f*
dynamite ['dainəmait] dinamita *f*
dynamo ['dainəməu] dínamo *f*
dysentery ['disntri] disentería *f*

E

each [iːtʃ] *a* cada; *pron* cada uno(a); ~ **other** mutuamente; el uno al otro
eager ['iːgə] ansioso; anhelante; **~ness** ansia *f*, anhelo *m*; afán *m*
eagle ['iːgl] águila *f*
ear [iə] oído *m*; oreja *f*; *bot* espiga *f*; **~drum** tímpano *m*
earl [əːl] conde *m*
early ['əːli] temprano; primitivo; ~ **in the morning** muy de mañana; **5 minutes** ~ (con) 5 minutos de anticipación
earmark ['iəmɑːk] *v/t* destinar; poner aparte
earn [əːn] *v/t* ganar(se); merecer; **~ings** ['~iŋz] sueldo *m*; ingresos *m/pl*
earnest ['əːnist] serio, formal; **in** ~ de veras, en serio
ear|phones ['iəfəunz] auriculares *m/pl*; **~rings** pendientes *m/pl*, aretes *m/pl*
earth [əːθ] *s* tierra *f*; *v/t elec* conectar a tierra; **~en** de barro; **~enware** loza *f* de barro; **~quake** terremoto *m*
ease [iːz] *s* tranquilidad *f*; alivio *m*; comodidad *f*; facilidad *f*; *v/t* facilitar; aliviar; **ill at** ~ incómodo
easel ['iːzl] caballete *m*
east [iːst] este *m*, oriente *m*; **the** ℒ el Oriente
Easter ['iːstə] Pascua *f* de Resurrección; **ℒly** del este; **ℒn** oriental
easy ['iːzi] fácil; cómodo; **take it** ~ tomarlo con calma; descansar; ~ **chair** sillón *m*; **~going** despreocupado
eat [iːt] *v/t* comer; ~ **up** comerse; acabar
eaves [iːvz] alero *m*; **~drop** *v/i* escuchar a escondidas (*a la conversación privada de otros*)
ebb [eb] menguante *m*; reflujo *m*; **at a low** ~ decaído; ~ **tide** marea *f* menguante
ebony ['ebəni] ébano *m*
eccentric [ik'sentrik] *a*, *s* excéntrico(a) *m* (*f*)
ecclesiastical [ikliːzi'æstikəl] eclesiástico
echo ['ekəu] *s* eco *m*; *v/i* reverberar, resonar
eclipse [i'klips] eclipse *m*
ecolo|gy [i'kɔlədʒi] ecología *f*; **~gist** ecologista *m*, *f*
economi|c [iːkə'nɔmik] económico; **~cal** económico, frugal; **~cs** economía *f* política; **~st** [i(ː)'kɔnəmist] economista *m*, *f*; **~ze** *v/t*, *v/i* economizar, ahorrar
economy [i(ː)'kɔnəmi] economía *f*
ecstasy ['ekstəsi] éxtasis *m*
Ecuador [ekwə'dɔː] El Ecuador; **~ian** *s*, *a* ecuatoriano(a) *m* (*f*)
edg|e [edʒ] *s* canto *m*; filo *m*; borde *m*; **on ~e** de canto; *fig* ansioso; nervioso; **~ing** borde *m*; ribete *m*
edible ['edibl] comestible
edifice ['edifis] edificio *m*
edit ['edit] *v/t* editar; dirigir; redactar; **~ion** [i'diʃən] edición *f*; tirada *f*; **~or** redactor *m*; **~orial** [~'tɔːriəl] *s* artículo *m* de fondo; **~orial staff** redacción *f*
educat|e ['edju(ː)keit] *v/t* educar; instruir; **~ion** educación *f*, instrucción *f*; **~ional** educacional; docente
eel [iːl] anguila *f*
effect [i'fekt] *s* efecto *m*; impresión *f*; *v/t* efectuar, ejecutar; **go into** ~ entrar en vigor; **~ive** efectivo, eficaz; vigente; **~s** efectos *m/pl*
effeminate [i'feminit] afeminado
effervescent [efə'vesnt] efervescente
efficien|cy [i'fiʃənsi] eficiencia *f*; eficacia *f*; **~t** eficiente
effort ['efət] esfuerzo *m*; **to make an** ~ esforzarse por
effusive [i'fjuːsiv] efusivo
egg [eg] huevo *m*; **to ~ on** *v/t* incitar; **~cup** huevera *f*; **~head** *fam* intelectual *m*; **~nog** ponche *m* de huevo; **~plant** berenjena *f*; **~shell** cáscara *f* de huevo
ego ['egou] (el) yo; **~tist** egoísta *m*, *f*
Egypt ['iːdʒipt] Egipto *m*; **~ian** [i'dʒipʃən] *a*, *s* egipcio(a) *m* (*f*)
eiderdown ['aidədaun] edredón *m*
eight [eit] ocho
either ['aiðə] *a*, *pron* uno u otro; ambos; *adv* (*en negación*) tampoco
eject [i(ː)'dʒekt] *v/t* expulsar; echar; **~ion** expulsión *f*
elaborate [i'læbərit] *a* elaborado; detallado; [~eit] *v/t* elaborar
elapse [i'læps] *v/i* transcurrir, pasar
elastic [i'læstik] *a*, *s* elástico *m*
elated [i'leitid]: **to be** ~ regocijarse
elbow ['elbəu] *s* codo *m*; *v/i* codear
elde|r ['eldə] *a*, *s* mayor *m*; *bot* saúco *m*; **~rly** *a* entrado en años; *s* la gente mayor; **~st** *a*, *s* (*el*, *la*) mayor (*de todos*)
elect [i'lekt] *a* elegido; *v/t* elegir; ~ **to** optar por; **~ion** elección *f*; **~or** elector *m*; **~orate** electorado *m*
electr|ic [i'lektrik] eléctrico; **~ical** eléctrico; **~ician** [~'triʃən] electricista *m*; **~icity** [~'trisiti] electricidad *f*; **~ify** *v/t* electrificar; *fig* electrizar
electron [i'lektrɔn] electrón *m*; **~ic** electrónico; **~ics** electrónica *f*
elegan|ce ['eligəns] elegancia *f*; **~t** elegante
element ['elimənt] elemento *m*; **~ary** [~'mentəri] elemental; **~ary school** escuela *f* primaria
elephant ['elifənt] elefante *m*
elevat|e ['eliveit] *v/t* elevar, ascender; **~ion** elevación *f*; altura *f*; **~or** *Am* ascensor *m*
eligible ['elidʒəbl] elegible
eliminat|e [i'limineit] *v/t* eliminar; descartar; **~ion** eliminación *f*
elitist [ei'liːtist] *a*, *s* elitista *m*, *f*
elk [elk] alce *m*
ellipse [i'lips] elipse *f*
elm [elm] olmo *m*
elongate ['iːlɔŋgeit] *v/t* alargar
elope [i'ləup] *v/i* fugarse (*con un amante*)
eloquen|ce ['eləukwəns] elocuencia *f*; **~t** elocuente
else [els] *a* otro; más; **everyone** ~ todos los demás; **nobody** ~ ningún otro; **nothing** ~ nada más; **somebody** ~ otra persona; **what ~?** ¿qué más?; **~where** en otra parte; a otra parte
elu|de [i'luːd] *v/t* eludir, esquivar; **~sion** evasión *f*; **~sive** evasivo
emaciated [i'meiʃieitid] demacrado
emanate ['eməneit] *v/i* emanar
emancipate [i'mænsipeit] *v/t* emancipar
embalm [im'bɑːm] *v/t* embalsamar; *fig* preservar
embankment [im'bæŋkmənt] terraplén *m*; dique *m*
embark [im'bɑːk] *v/t*, *v/i* embarcar(se); ~ **upon** emprender; lanzarse a
embarrass [im'bærəs] *v/t* desconcertar, avergonzar; estorbar; **~ing** embarazoso; molesto; **~ment** desconcierto *m*; perplejidad *f*; embarazo *m*; **financial ~ment** apuros *m/pl*
embassy ['embəsi] embajada *f*
embed [im'bed] *v/t* empotrar
embellish [im'beliʃ] *v/t* embellecer
embers ['embəz] rescoldo *m*
embezzle [im'bezl] *v/t* desfalcar; **~ment** desfalco *m*
embitter [im'bitə] *v/t* amargar
emblem ['embləm] emblema *m*
embody [im'bɔdi] *v/t* encarnar; incorporar
embrace [im'breis] *s* abrazo *m*; *v/t* abrazar; abarcar
embroider [im'brɔidə] *v/t* bordar; **~y** bordado *m*
embryo ['embriəu] embrión *m*
emerald ['emərəld] esmeralda *f*
emerge [i'məːdʒ] *v/i* salir, surgir; **~ncy** [~əns] emergencia *f*; **in an ~ncy** en caso de urgencia; **~ncy exit** salida *f* de emergencia; **~ncy landing** *aer* aterrizaje *m* forzoso
emigra|nt ['emigrənt] emigrante *m*; **~te** ['~eit] *v/i* emigrar; **~tion** emigración *f*
eminent ['eminənt] eminente
emit [i'mit] *v/t* emitir, despedir
emotion [i'məuʃən] emoción *f*; **~al** emocional; impresionable
emperor ['empərə] emperador *m*
empha|sis ['emfəsis] énfasis *m*; **~size** destacar, recalcar; **~tic** [im'fætik] enfático; categórico
empire ['empaiə] imperio *m*
employ [im'plɔi] *s* puesto *m*, empleo *m*; *v/t* emplear; **~ee** [emplɔi'iː] empleado *m*; **~er** patrón *m*; **~ment** empleo *m*; oficio *m*; **~ment agency** agencia *f* de colocaciones
empress ['empris] emperatriz *f*
empt|iness ['emptinis] vacío *m*; vacuidad *f*; **~y** *a* vacío; *v/t* vaciar
enable [i'neibl] *v/t* capacitar; permitir
enact [i'nækt] *v/t* decretar, promulgar; **~ment** promulgación *f* (*de una ley*)
enamel [i'næməl] *s* esmalte *m*; *v/t* esmaltar
enchant [in'tʃɑːnt] *v/t* encantar; **~ing** encantador
encircle [in'səːkl] *v/t* cercar; circundar; ceñir
encl. = **enclosed**
enclos|e [in'kləuz] *v/t* encerrar; incluir, adjuntar; **~ed** adjunto; **~ure** [~ʒə] cercado *m*; recinto *m*; carta *f* adjunta
encore [ɔŋ'kɔː] *teat* ¡bis!

encounter [in'kauntə] *s* encuentro *m*; choque *m*; *v/t, v/i* encontrar; dar con

encourag|e [in'kʌridʒ] *v/t* animar; alentar; **~ement** estímulo *m*; **~ing** animador, alentador

encumber [in'kʌmbə] *v/t* recargar; estorbar; **~ed with** tener que cargar con

end [end] *s* fin *m*; extremo *m*; cabo *m*; final *m*; conclusión *f*; ***in the ~*** al fin y al cabo; ***for hours on ~*** horas seguidas; ***put to an ~*** poner fin a; ***on ~*** de punta; ***stand on ~*** erizarse (*pelo*); ***to be at an ~*** tocar a su fin; ***to what ~?*** ¿a qué propósito?; *v/t, v/i* terminar, acabar; cesar; ***~ up at*** ir a parar en

endanger [in'deindʒə] *v/t* arriesgar; poner en peligro

endear [in'diə] *v/t* hacer querer; **~ment** cariño *m*

endeavo(u)r [in'devə] *s* esfuerzo *m*; empeño *m*; *v/i* esforzarse

end|ing ['endiŋ] conclusión *f*; desenlace *m* (*de un libro*); terminación *f*; final *m*; **~ive** ['endiv] endibia *f*; **~less** interminable

endorse [in'dɔ:s] *v/t* endosar; aprobar; **~ment** aprobación *f*

endow [in'dau] *v/t* dotar, fundar; **~ment** fundación *f*

endur|ance [in'djuərəns] aguante *m*, resistencia *f*; **~e** *v/t* soportar, aguantar; tolerar

enemy ['enimi] *a, s* enemigo(a) *m (f)*

energ|etic [enə'dʒetik] enérgico; **~y** ['enədʒi] energía *f*

enfold [in'fəuld] *v/t* envolver; abrazar

enforce [in'fɔ:s] *v/t* imponer; hacer cumplir (*ley*); poner en vigor; **~ment** ejecución *f* de una ley

engage [in'geidʒ] *v/t* contratar; emplear; ocupar; comprometer; *v/i tecn* engranar con; comprometerse; **~d** comprometido (*en matrimonio*); ocupado; *tel* comunicando; **~ment** compromiso *m*; contrato *m*; *mil* combate *m*; noviazgo *m*; **~ment ring** anillo *m* de prometida

engine ['endʒin] motor *m*; locomotora *f*; **~ driver** maquinista *m*; **~er** [endʒi'niə] *s* ingeniero *m*; *v/t fam* agenciar, gestionar; **~ering** ingeniería *f*

England ['iŋglənd] Inglaterra *f*

English ['iŋgliʃ] *a* inglés; *s* (*idioma*) inglés *m*; **the ~** los ingleses; **~ Channel** Canal *m* de la Mancha; **~man** inglés *m*; **~woman** inglesa *f*

engrav|e [in'greiv] *v/t* grabar; **~er** grabador *m*; **~ing** grabado *m*

engross [in'grəus] *v/t* absorber (*atención, etc*); **~ing** fascinante

engulf [in'gʌlf] *v/t* sumergir, hundir

enigma [i'nigmə] enigma *m*

enjoin [in'dʒɔin] *v/t* mandar; prescribir

enjoy [in'dʒɔi] *v/t* gozar de; disfrutar de; gustarle a uno; ***~ oneself*** divertirse; **~able** agradable; **~ment** goce *m*; uso *m*

enlarge [in'la:dʒ] *v/t foto* ampliar; extender; **~ment** aumento *m*; *foto* ampliación *f*

enlighten [in'laitn] *v/t* instruir; ilustrar; **~ment** ilustración *f*

enlist [in'list] *v/t* alistar

enliven [in'laivn] *v/t* avivar, vivificar; animar

enmity ['enmiti] enemistad *f*

enormous [i'nɔ:məs] enorme

enough [i'nʌf] bastante

enrage [in'reidʒ] *v/t* enfurecer

enrapture [in'ræptʃə] *v/t* embelesar

enrich [in'ritʃ] *v/t* enriquecer

enrol(l) [in'rəul] *v/t, v/i* inscribir(se), matricular(se); **~ment** inscripción *f*

en route [ɔn 'ru:t] en camino

ensign ['ensain, *mar* 'ensn] bandera *f*; alférez *m*

enslave [in'sleiv] *v/t* esclavizar

ensure [in'ʃuə] *v/t* asegurar

entail [in'teil] *v/t* suponer; ocasionar

entangle [in'tæŋgl] *v/t* enredar; **~ment** enredo *m*

enter ['entə] *v/t* entrar en; afiliarse a; anotar; *v/i* entrar; ***~ into*** establecer; tomar parte en; ***~ upon*** emprender

enterpris|e ['entəpraiz] empresa *f*; **~ing** emprendedor

entertain [entə'tein] *v/t* entretener; divertir; agasajar; **~er** artista *m, f*; **~ing** divertido, entretenido; **~ment** entretenimiento *m*; espectáculo *m*

enthusias|m [in'θju:ziæzəm] entusiasmo *m*; **~tic** [~'æstik] entusiástico

entice [in'tais] *v/t* atraer, seducir; tentar

entire [in'taiə] entero, íntegro; **~ly** enteramente

entitled [in'taitld]: ***to be ~ to*** tener derecho a

entourage [ɔntu'ra:ʒ] séquito *m*

entrails ['entreilz] entrañas *f/pl*

entrance ['entrəns] entrada *f*; admisión *f*; [in'tra:ns] *v/t* encantar, hechizar

entreat [in'tri:t] *v/t* rogar, suplicar

entrepreneur [ɔntrəprə'nə:] impresario *m*

entrust [in'trʌst]: *v/t* ***to ~ something to someone*** confiar algo a uno

entry ['entri] entrada *f*; acceso *m*; ***no ~*** prohibido el paso

enumerate [i'nju:məreit] *v/t* enumerar

envelop [in'veləp] *v/t* envolver; **~e** ['envələup] sobre *m*

env|ious ['enviəs] envidioso; **~y** ['envi] *s* envidia *f*; *v/t* envidiar

environment [in'vaiərənmənt] medio ambiente *m*

envisage [in'vizidʒ] *v/t* contemplar; prever

envoy ['envɔi] enviado *m*

epidemic [epi'demik] *a* epidémico; *s* epidemia *f*

epilepsy ['epilepsi] epilepsia *f*

episode ['episəud] episodio *m*

epoch ['i:pɔk] época *f*

equal ['i:kwəl] *a, s* igual *m*; ***to be ~ to*** estar a la altura de; **~ity** [i(:)'kwɔliti] igualdad *f*; **~ize** *v/t* igualar

equa|nimity [ekwə'nimiti] ecuanimidad *f*; **~te** [i'kweit] considerar equivalente (a)

equation [i'kweiʒən] ecuación *f*

equator [i'kweitə] ecuador *m*

equestrianism [i'kwestriənizəm] *sp* hípica *f*

equilibrium [i:kwi'libriəm] equilibrio *m*

equinox ['i:kwinɔks] equinoccio *m*

equip [i'kwip] *v/t* equipar; **~ped with** *tecn* dotado de; **~ment** equipo *m*; material *m*

equivalent [i'kwivələnt] *a, s* equivalente *m*

era ['iərə] época *f*; era *f*

eras|e [i'reiz] *v/t* borrar; **~er** goma *f* de borrar; **~ure** [~ʒə] borradura *f*

erect [i'rekt] *a* derecho; erguido; *v/t* erigir; levantar; **~ion** construcción *f*; erección *f*

ermine ['ə:min] armiño *m*

erotic [i'rɔtik] erótico

err [ə:] *v/i* errar; equivocarse

errand ['erənd] mandado *m*, recado *m*; ***run ~s*** hacer los mandados

erratic [i'rætik] irregular, inconstante

erroneous [i'rəunjəs] erróneo

error ['erə] error *m*, equivocación *f*

eruption [i'rʌpʃən] erupción *f*

escalat|ion [eskə'leiʃən] intensificación *f*; **~or** escalera *f* móvil

escape [is'keip] *v/t* escapar de, evitar; *v/i* escaparse, huir; *s* fuga *f*; escape *m* (*de gas*)

escort ['eskɔ:t] *s* escolta *f*; [is'kɔ:t] *v/t* escoltar

Eskimo ['eskiməu] esquimal *m, f*

esophagus [i'sɔfəgəs] esófago *m*

esoteric [esəu'terik] esotérico, recóndito

espadrille ['espədril] alpargata *f*

especially [is'peʃəli] especialmente

espionage [espiə'na:ʒ] espionaje *m*

essay ['esei] ensayo *m*; **~ist** ensayista *m*

essen|ce ['esns] esencia *f*; **~tial** [i'senʃəl] esencial

establish [is'tæbliʃ] *v/t* establecer; instituir; probar; **~ment** establecimiento *m*

estate [is'teit] finca *f*; hacienda *f*; propiedad *f*, bienes *m/pl*; caudal *m* hereditario

esteem [is'ti:m] *v/t* estimar; apreciar

estimat|e ['estimit] *s* estimación *f*, tasa *f*; ['~eit] *v/t* estimar, valorar, tasar; **~ion** estimación *f*; ***in my ~ion*** según mis cálculos

estrange [is'treindʒ] *v/t* enajenar

estuary ['estjuəri] estuario *m*, ría *f*

etching ['etʃiŋ] grabado *m*; aguafuerte *f*

etern|al [i(:)'tə:nl] eterno; **~ity** eternidad *f*

ether ['i:θə] éter *m*

ethic|al ['eθikl] ético; honrado; **~s** ['eθiks] ética *f*

etiquette [eti'ket] etiqueta *f*

eulogize ['julədʒaiz] *v/t* elogiar; preconizar

euphemism ['ju:fimizm] eufemismo *m*

Europe ['juərəp] Europa *f*; **~an** [~'pi(:)ən] *a, s* europeo(a) *m (f)*

evacuat|e [i'vækjueit] *v/t* evacuar; **~ion** evacuación *f*

evade [i'veid] *v/t* evadir, eludir

evaluate [i'væljueit] *v/t* evaluar

evangelist [i'vændʒilist] evangelizador *m*

evaporate [i'væpəreit] *v/t, v/i* evaporar(se)

evasion [i'veiʒən] evasión *f*

eve [i:v] víspera *f*; ***on the ~ of*** en vísperas de

even ['i:vən] *a* llano, liso; igual; constante; *mat* par; *adv* aun, hasta; siquiera; ***~ so*** aun así; ***~ though*** aunque; ***not ~*** ni siquiera; *v/t* igualar, nivelar; ***break ~*** ni ganar ni perder; ***get ~*** ajustar cuentas

evening ['i:vniŋ] *s* tarde *f*; anochecer *m*; noche *f*; ***good ~!*** ¡buenas tardes!; ¡buenas noches!; **~ dress** traje *m* de etiqueta

event [i'vent] suceso *m*, acontecimiento *m*; *sp* contienda *f*; ***at all ~s*** en todo caso; **~ful** memorable, notable; **~ual** subsiguiente; **~ually** finalmente

ever ['evə] siempre, jamás; alguna vez; nunca (*con verbo negativo*); ***for ~ and ~*** para siempre jamás; ***if ~*** si alguna vez; ***better than ~*** mejor que nunca; ***~ since*** desde entonces; **~green** de hoja perenne; **~lasting** eterno

every ['evri] *a* cada; todo, todos los; ***~ other day*** un día sí y otro no; **~body, ~one** todo el mundo; **~day** cada día; **~thing** todo; **~where** en todas partes

eviden|ce ['evidəns] evidencia *f*; *for* prueba *f*; testimonio *m*; **~t** evidente, patente

evil ['i:vl] *a* malo; maligno; *s* maldad *f*; mal *m*

evoke [i'vəuk] *v/t* evocar

evolution [i:və'lu:ʃən] evolución *f*; desarrollo *m*

evolve [i'vɔlv] *v/t* desenvolver; *v/i* desarrollarse

ewe [ju:] oveja *f* hembra

exact [ig'zækt] *a* exacto; *v/t* exigir; **~ing** exigente; **~ly** en punto (*hora*)

exaggerate [ig'zædʒəreit] *v/t* exagerar

exalt [ig'zɔ:lt] *v/t* exaltar

examin|ation [igzæmi'neiʃən] examen *m*; *med* reconocimiento *m*; **~e** [ig'zæmin] *v/t* examinar; *for* interrogar

example [ig'za:mpl] ejemplo *m*; ejemplar *m*; ***for ~*** por ejemplo

exasperate [ig'za:spəreit] *v/t* exasperar

excavate ['ekskəveit] *v/t* excavar

exceed [ik'si:d] *v/t* exceder; **~ingly** sumamente

excel [ik'sel] *v/t, v/i* superar; sobresalir; **~lence** ['eksələns] excelencia *f*; **~lent** excelente

except [ik'sept] *prep* excepto, salvo; ***~ for*** dejando aparte; sin contar; *v/t* exceptuar; **~ing** *prep* excepto, menos; **~ion** excepción *f*; ***with the ~ion of*** a excepción de; **~ional** excepcional

excess [ik'ses] exceso *m*; **~ luggage** exceso *m* de equipaje; **~ive** excesivo

exchange [iks'tʃeindʒ] *s* cambio *m*; intercambio *m*; *tel* central *f* (telefónica); *v/t* cambiar; **~-rate** tipo *m* de cambio

excite [ik'sait] *v/t* excitar; emocionar; **~ment** emoción *f*

excla|im [iks'kleim] *v/t, v/i* exclamar; **~mation** [eksklə'meiʃən] exclamación *f*; **~mation point** signo *m* de admiración

exclu|de [iks'klu:d] *v/t* excluir; **~sion** [~ʒən] exclusión *f*; **~sive** [~siv] exclusivo; selecto

excrement ['ekskrimənt] excremento *m*

excruciating [iks'kru:ʃieitiŋ] agudísimo, atroz

excursion [iks'kə:ʃən] excursión *f*

excuse [iks'kju:z] *s* excusa *f*, disculpa *f*; pretexto *m*; *v/t* excusar, disculpar, perdonar; ***~ me!*** ¡perdóneme!

execut|e ['eksikju:t] *v/t* ejecutar; llevar a cabo; cumplir; **~ion** ejecución *f*; cumplimiento *m*; **~ioner** verdugo *m*; **~ive** [ig'zekjutiv] *a, s* ejecutivo *m*; **~or** *for* albacea *m*; ejecutor *m* testamentario

exempt [ig'zempt] *a* exento; *v/t* eximir; **~ion** exención *f*

exercise ['eksəsaiz] *s* ejercicio *m*; *v/t* ejercer; *v/i* hacer ejercicios

exert [ig'zə:t] *v/t* ejercer; ***~ oneself*** *v/r* esforzarse, afanarse; **~ion** esfuerzo *m*

exhale [eks'heil] *v/t* exhalar; *v/i* disiparse

exhaust [ig'zɔ:st] *s* (tubo de) escape *m*; ***~ fumes*** gases *m/pl* de escape; *v/t* agotar; cansar; **~ed** agotado; **~ing** agotador; **~ion** agotamiento *m*; **~ive** exhaustivo, detallado

exhibit [ig'zibit] *s* objeto *m* expuesto; *for* prueba *f* instrumental; *v/t* manifestar; exponer; presentar; **~ion** [eksi'biʃən] exposición *f*

exhilarate [ig'ziləreit] *v/t* regocijar; vivificar

exile ['eksail] *s* destierro *m*; exilio *m*; *v/t* desterrar, exiliar

exist [ig'zist] *v/i* existir; vivir; **~ence** existencia *f*, vida *f*; **~ent, ~ing** existente

exit ['eksit] salida *f*

exonerate [ig'zɔnəreit] *v/t* exculpar

exotic [ig'zɔtik] exótico

expan|d [iks'pænd] *v/t, v/i* extender(se); **~se** [~s] extensión *f*; **~sion** expansión *f*; **~sive** expansivo

expect [iks'pekt] *v/t* esperar; suponer; contar con; **~ation** [ekspek'teiʃən] expectativa *f*; **~ing: *to be ~ing*** estar encinta

expedient [iks'pi:djənt] *a* conveniente; *s* expediente *m*, recurso *m*

expedition [ekspi'diʃən] expedición *f*

expel [iks'pel] *v/t* expulsar; expeler

expen|d [iks'pend] *v/t* gastar, derrochar; **~dable** prescindible; **~diture** [~ditʃə] gastos *m/pl*; desembolso *m*; **~se** [~s] gasto *m*; **~se account** cuenta *f* de gastos; **~sive** caro

experience [iks'piəriəns] *s* experiencia *f*; *v/t* experimentar; sufrir

experiment [iks'perimənt] *s* experimento *m*; *v/i* experimentar

expert ['ekspə:t] *a* experto; *s* perito *m*, experto *m*

expir|ation [ekspaiə'reiʃən] expiración *f*; *com* vencimiento *m*; **~e** [iks'paiə] *v/i* expirar; *com* vencer

expla|in [iks'plein] *v/t* explicar; **~nation** [eksplə'neiʃən] explicación *f*; **~natory** [iks'plænətəri] explicativo

explicit [iks'plisit] explícito

explode [iks'pləud] *v/t* detonar, volar; hacer saltar; *v/i* estallar; *fig* reventar

exploit ['eksplɔit] *s* hazaña *f*, proeza *f*; [iks'plɔit] *v/t* explotar; **~ation** explotación *f*

explor|ation [eksplɔ:'reiʃən] exploración *f*; **~e** [iks'plɔ:] *v/t* explorar; **~er** explorador *m*

explo|sion [iks'pləuʒən] explosión *f*; **~sive** [~siv] explosivo

export ['ekspɔ:t] *s* exportación *f*; [eks'pɔ:t] *v/t* exportar; **~er** exportador *m*

expos|e [iks'pəuz] *v/t* exponer; descubrir; poner al descubierto; **~ition** [ekspəu-

'ziʃən] exposición *f*; **~ure** [~ʒə] exposicón *f*; revelación *f*; **~ure meter** *foto* fotómetro *m*
express [iks'pres] *a*, *s* expreso *m*; (*tren*) rápido *m*; *v/t* exprimir; expresar; **~ion** expresión *f*; **~ive** expresivo; **~ly** expresamente
expulsion [iks'pʌlʃən] expulsión *f*
exquisite ['ekskwizit] exquisito
exten|d [iks'tend] *v/t* extender, alargar; prolongar; diluir; *v/i* extenderse; proyectarse: **~sion** extensión *f*; anexo *m*; *com* prórroga *f*; **~sive** extenso; amplio; **~t** extensión *f*; alcance *m*; ***to some ~t*** hasta cierto punto
exterior [eks'tiəriə] *a*, *s* exterior *m*
exterminat|e [iks'tə:mineit] *v/t* exterminar; **~ion** exterminación *f*
external [eks'tə:nl] externo, exterior
extin|ct [iks'tiŋkt] extinto; **~ction** extinción *f*; **~guish** [~'tiŋgwiʃ] *v/t* extinguir, apagar
extra ['ekstrə] *a* de más; de sobra; extraordinario; adicional; *s* recargo *m*; extra *m*; gasto *m* extraordinario
extract ['ekstrækt] *s* extracto *m*; [iks'trækt] *v/t* extraer; **~ion** extracción *f*
extraordinary [iks'trɔ:dnri] extraordinario
extravagan|ce [iks'trævigəns] extravagancia *f*; despilfarro *m*; **~t** extravagante
extrem|e [iks'tri:m] *a* extremo; extremado; *s* extremo *m*, extremidad *f*; **~e unction** [~ 'ʌŋkʃən] extremaunción *f*; **~ely** extremadamente; sumamente; **~ity** [~'tremiti] extremidad *f*
extricate ['ekstrikeit] *v/t* desenredar; sacar (de una dificultad)
exuberant [ig'zju:bərənt] exuberante
exult [ig'zʌlt] *v/i* exultar, alborozarse
eye [ai] *s* ojo *m*; *bot* yema *f*; ***to turn a blind ~*** hacer la vista gorda; ***to see ~ to ~*** estar de acuerdo; ***to keep an ~ on*** vigilar; ***with an ~ to*** con miras a; *v/t* ojear, mirar; **~ball** globo *m* del ojo; **~brow** ceja *f*; **~glasses** gafas *f/pl*, lentes *m/pl*; **~lash** pestaña *f*; **~let** ojete *m*; **~lid** párpado *m*; **~ shadow** sombreador *m* (de ojos); **~sight** vista *f*; **~ tooth** colmillo *m*; **~witness** testigo *m* ocular

F

fable ['feibl] *s* fábula *f*
fabric ['fæbrik] tejido *m*; tela *f*; **~ation** invención *f*
fabulous ['fæbjuləs] fabuloso
façade [fə'sɑ:d] fachada *f*
fac|e [feis] *s* cara *f*; rostro *m*, semblante *m*; esfera *f* (*del reloj*); ***lose ~e*** desprestigiarse; ***save ~e*** salvar las apariencias; ***~e down*** boca abajo; ***~e to ~e*** cara a cara; ***to make o pull ~es*** hacer muecas; *v/t* hacer frente a; mirar hacia; encararse con; **~e lift** cirugía *f* estética; **~e value** valor *m* nominal
facil|itate [fə'siliteit] *v/t* facilitar; **~ity** facilidad *f*
facing ['feisiŋ] frente (a)
fact [fækt] hecho *m*; realidad *f*; ***in ~*** en realidad; **~-finding** de investigación
factor ['fæktə] factor *m*
factory ['fæktəri] fábrica *f*
faculty ['fækəlti] facultad *f*; aptitud *f*
fad [fæd] novedad *f* pasajera
fade [feid] *v/t* marchitarse; descolorarse; ***~ away*** desvanecerse
fail [feil] *v/t* suspender; no aprobar; *v/i* acabarse; fallar; fracasar; *com* quebrar; ser suspendido; ***without ~*** sin falta; ***~ to*** dejar de; **~ure** [~jə] fracaso *m*; *com* quiebra *f*
faint [feint] *a* débil; casi imperceptible; ***to feel ~*** sentirse mareado; *s* desmayo *m*; *v/i* desmayarse; **~hearted** tímido, medroso
fair [fɛə] *a* claro; rubio; equitativo, justo; regular; favo-rable; ***it's not ~!*** ¡no hay derecho!; ***~ play*** juego *m* limpio; *s* feria *f*; **~ly** bastante; **~ness** rectitud *f*
fairy ['fɛəri] hada *f*; **~ tale** cuento *m* de hadas
faith [feiθ] fe *f*; confianza *f*; **~ful** fiel, leal; **~fully yours** atentamente le saluda; **~fulness** fidelidad *f*, lealtad *f*; **~less** desleal, pérfido
fake [feik] *s* falsificación *f*; impostor *m*; *v/t* falsificar; fingir
falcon ['fɔ:lkən] halcón *m*
fall [fɔ:l] *s* caída *f*; *com* baja *f*; otoño *m*; *v/i* caer(se); bajar; disminuir; ***~ apart*** deshacerse; ***~ back on*** recurrir a; ***~ behind*** quedarse atrás; ***~ due*** *com* vencerse; ***~ for*** dejarse engañar por; ***~ in love with*** enamorarse de; ***~ out*** reñir; ***~ short of*** no llegar a; ***~ through*** fracasar; **~out** ['fɔ:laut] lluvia *f* (radiactiva)
fals|e [fɔ:ls] falso, incorrecto; falsificado; ***~e teeth*** dentadura *f* postiza; **~ehood** falsedad *f*
falter ['fɔ:ltə] *v/i* vacilar
fame [feim] fama *f*; **~d** famoso, afamado
famil|iar [fə'miljə] familiar; conocido; ***to be ~iar with*** estar enterado de; **~iarity** [~i'æriti] familiaridad *f*; confianza *f*; **~y** ['fæmili] familia *f*; **~y name** apellido *m*; **~y tree** árbol *m* genealógico
fami|ne ['fæmin] hambre *f*; **~shed** hambriento
famous ['feiməs] famoso, célebre
fan [fæn] *s* abanico *m*; ventilador *m*; aficionado *m*; *v/t* abanicar; avivar
fanatic(al) [fə'nætik(əl)] *a* fanático; *s* fanático(a) *m* (*f*)
fancy ['fænsi] *s* fantasía *f*; capricho *m*; gusto *m*; *a* de adorno; ***~ ball*** baile *m* de disfraces; ***~ dress*** disfraz *m*; ***to take a ~ to*** aficionarse a
fang [fæŋ] colmillo *m*
fantastic [fæn'tæstik] fantástico
far [fɑ:] *a* lejano, remoto; *adv* lejos; ***as ~ as*** hasta; ***by ~*** con mucho; ***~ and wide*** por todas partes; ***~ better*** mucho mejor; ***~ off*** a lo lejos; ***to go too ~*** extralimitarse; **~away** lejano
farce [fɑ:s] farsa *f*
fare [fɛə] precio *m* (del billete); tarifa *f*; pasaje *m*; **~well** adiós *m*; despedida *f*
far-fetched ['fɑ:'fetʃid] improbable; **~-flung** ['~'flʌŋ] extenso
farm [fɑ:m] *s* granja *f*; *v/t* cultivar; **~er** granjero *m*; **~hand** labriego *m*, *LA* peón *m*; **~house** alquería *f*; **~ing** cultivo *m*; labranza *f*
far-sighted ['fɑ:'saitid] présbita; *fig* previsor
fart [fɑ:t] (*tabu*) *s* pedo *m*; *v/i* soltar pedos
farther ['fɑ:ðə] más lejos
fascinat|e ['fæsineit] *v/t* fascinar; **~ing** fascinador; **~ion** fascinación *f*
fascis|m ['fæʃizəm] fascismo *m*; **~t** *a*, *s* fascista *m*, *f*
fashion ['fæʃən] *s* moda *f*; uso *m*; ***out of ~*** pasado de moda; ***to be in ~*** estar de moda; **~able** de moda
fast [fɑ:st] *a* rápido, veloz; firme; (*reloj*) adelantado; disoluta (*mujer*); *adv* rápidamente; de prisa; ***hold ~*** mantenerse firme; *s* ayuno *m*; *v/i* ayunar; **~en** ['fɑ:sn] *v/t* fijar; atar; **~ener** cierre *m*
fastidious [fəs'tidiəs] delicado; quisquilloso
fat [fæt] *a* gordo, grueso; *fig* pingüe; ***to get ~*** engordar; *s* grasa *f*
fat|al ['feitl] fatal; funesto; **~ality** [fə'tæliti] fatalidad *f*; **~ally injured** herido a muerte; **~e** hado *m*, destino *m*; suerte *f*
father ['fɑ:ðə] *s* padre *m*; *v/t* engendrar; **~hood** paternidad *f*; **~-in-law** suegro *m*; **~land** patria *f*; **~ly** paternal
fathom ['fæðəm] *s mar* braza *f*; *v/t* sondear; *fig* comprender; **~less** insondable
fatigue [fə'ti:g] *s* fatiga *f*; *v/t* cansar, fatigar
fat|ten ['fætn] *v/t* cebar; *v/t*, *v/i* engordar; **~ty** grasiento
faucet ['fɔ:sit] grifo *m*
fault [fɔ:lt] *s* falta *f*; defecto *m*; culpa *f*; ***to be at ~*** tener la culpa; ***to find ~ with*** criticar, desaprobar; **~less** sin defecto, impecable; **~y** defectuoso
favo(u)r ['feivə] *s* favor *m*; apoyo *m*; aprobación *f*; ***do a ~*** hacer un favor; ***in ~ of*** a favor de; *v/t* favorecer; **~able** favorable; **~ite** [~rit] *a* favorito, predilecto; *s* favorito *m*; **~itism** favoritismo *m*
fawn [fɔ:n] *s* cervato *m*; *v/i* ***~ on*** lisonjear
fear [fiə] *s* miedo *m*; temor *m*; aprensión *f*; *v/t*, *v/i* temer; tener miedo; **~ful** miedoso; tímido; **~less** audaz
feast [fi:st] *s* fiesta *f*; banquete *m*; *v/t* festejar
feat [fi:t] hazaña *f*, proeza *f*
feather ['feðə] pluma *f*; *tecn* cuña *f*; lengüeta *f*; ***birds of a ~*** *fig* lobos *m/pl* de una camada; *v/t* emplumar; **~-bed** plumón *m*
feature ['fi:tʃə] *s* rasgo *m*, característica *f*; película *f o* artículo *m* principal; *v/t* hacer resaltar; **~s** facciones *f/pl*
February ['februəri] febrero *m*
federal ['fedərəl] federal
federation [fedə'reiʃən] federación *f*
fed up [fed 'ʌp]: ***to be ~*** estar harto
fee [fi:] honorarios *m/pl*; cuota *f* de ingreso; derechos *m/pl*
feeble ['fi:bl] débil; **~minded** imbécil
feed [fi:d] *v/t* nutrir, alimentar; dar de comer a; *v/i* pastar; alimentarse; **~er** *tecn* alimentador *m*
feel [fi:l] *v/t* tocar, palpar; sentir; experimentar; *v/i* sentirse, encontrarse; resultar (*al tacto*); ***~ cold*** tener frío; ***~ for*** compadecerse de; ***~ like*** tener ganas de; ***~ up to*** creerse capaz de; **~er** tentáculo *m*; sondeo *m*; **~ing** tacto *m*; sentimiento *m*; sensación *f*; ***hard ~ings*** rencor; ***hurt one's ~ings*** ofenderle
feign [fein] *v/t*, *v/i* fingir
fell [fel] *v/t* talar (*árbol*)
fellow ['feləu] compañero *m*; socio *m*; *fam* tipo *m*, tío *m*; mozo *m*; **~ being** prójimo *m*; **~ citizen** conciudadano *m*; **~ship** compañerismo *m*; beca *f*; **~ travel(l)er** compañero *m* de viaje; **~ worker** colega *m*, *f*
felon ['felən] criminal *m*; **~y** delito *m* mayor
felt [felt] fieltro *m*; **~-tip pen** rotulador *m*
female ['fi:meil] *a*, *s* hembra *f*
femini|ne ['feminin] femenino; **~st** feminista *m*, *f*
fenc|e [fens] *s* valla *f*, cerca *f*; *v/t* cercar; guardar; *v/i* esgrimir; **~ing** esgrima *f*
fend [fend] (***off***) *v/t* parar; repeler; **~er** *aut* guardabarro *m*
ferment ['fə:ment] *s* fermento *m*; [fə(:)'ment] *v/i* fermentar; **~ation** fermentación *f*
fern [fə:n] helecho *m*
ferocity [fə'rɔsiti] ferocidad *f*
ferry ['feri] transbordador *m*; **~man** barquero *m*
fertil|e ['fə:tail] fértil, fecundo; **~ity** [~'tiliti] fertilidad *f*; **~ize** ['~ilaiz] *v/t* fertilizar, *agr* abonar; **~izer** abono *m*
fervent ['fə:vənt] fervoroso, ardiente
fester ['festə] *v/i* ulcerarse
festiv|al ['festəvəl] fiesta *f*; *mús* festival *m*; **~e** festivo; **~ity** [~'tiviti] festividad *f*
fetch [fetʃ] *v/t* ir a buscar; ir por; *v/i* venderse a (*cierto precio*); **~ing** atractivo
fetter ['fetə] *v/t* encadenar, trabar; **~s** grillos *m/pl*
feud [fju:d] enemistad *f* (*entre familias*); odio *m* de sangre; **~alism** feudalismo *m*
fever ['fi:və] fiebre *f*, calentura *f*; **~ish** febril
few [fju:] *a*, *s* pocos(as); unos(as), algunos(as); ***a ~*** unos(as) cuantos(as); **~er** menos
fiancé [fi'ɑ:nsei] novio *m*; **~e** novia *f*
fib [fib] mentirilla *f*
fiber = **fibre**
fibr|e ['faibə] fibra *f*; **~eglass** fibra *f* de vidrio
fickle ['fikl] inconstante
ficti|on ['fikʃən] ficción *f*; novelas *f/pl*; **~tious** [~'tiʃəs] ficticio
fiddle ['fidl] *s* violín *m*; ***to be fit as a ~*** estar de buena salud; ***to play second ~*** hacer el papel de segundón; *v/i* tocar el violín; ***~ with*** jugar con; **~r** violinista *m*, *f*; **~sticks!** ¡ tonterías!
fidelity [fi'deliti] fidelidad *f*
fidget ['fidʒit] *v/i* moverse nerviosamente
field [fi:ld] campo *m*; prado *m*; esfera *f* (*de actividades*); **~ glasses** gemelos *m/pl*; **~gun** cañón *m* de campaña; **~ marshal** mariscal *m* de campo
fiend [fi:nd] demonio *m*, diablo *m*; **~ish** diabólico
fierce [fiəs] feroz; violento, intenso
fiery ['faiəri] ardiente; *fig* apasionado
fifth [fifθ] quinto
fifty ['fifti] cincuenta; ***to go ~-~*** ir a medias
fig [fig] higo *m*; **~ tree** higuera *f*
fight [fait] *s* lucha *f*; pelea *f*; *v/t* combatir; *v/i* luchar, pelear; **~er** combatiente *m*; avión *m* de caza; **~ing** lucha *f*, combate *m*
figur|ative ['figjurətiv] figurado; **~e** ['figə] *s* figura *f*; ilustración *f*; cifra *f*, número *m*; personaje *m*; *v/t* representar; imaginar; ***~e out*** entender; *v/i* figurar; **~e skating** patinaje *m* artístico
file [fail] *s* lima *f*; carpeta *f*; archivo *m*; fila *f*, hilera *f*; ***in single ~*** en fila india; ***on ~*** archivado; *v/t* limar; clasificar; archivar
fill [fil] *v/t* llenar; rellenar; empastar (*diente*); ***~ in*** llenar, completar; *v/i* llenarse
fil(l)et ['filit] filete *m*
filling ['filiŋ] relleno *m*; **~station** estación *f* de servicio
film [film] *s* película *f*; *v/t* filmar; rodar (*una escena, etc*); **~ star** estrella *f* de cine
filter ['filtə] *s* filtro *m*; *v/t* filtrar
filth [filθ] suciedad *f*; obscenidad *f*; **~y** sucio; obsceno
fin [fin] aleta *f*
final ['fainl] final, último; **~ exam** reválida *f*; **~ly** finalmente, por último
financ|e [fai'næns] *s* finanzas *f/pl*; *v/t* financiar; **~ing** financiación *f*, financiamiento *m*; **~ial** [~ʃəl] financiero; **~ier** [~siə] financiero *m*
find [faind] *v/t* encontrar, hallar; descubrir; ***~ out*** averiguar; *s* hallazgo *m*; **~er** hallador *m*; **~ing** descubrimiento *m*; *for* fallo *m*
fine [fain] *a* fino; bello; ***~ weather*** buen tiempo; ***that is ~!*** ¡de acuerdo!; *adv fam* muy bien; *s* multa *f*; *v/t* multar; **~ arts** bellas artes *f/pl*; **~ry** ['~əri] aderezo *m*, galas *f/pl*; **~sse** [fi'nes] sutileza *f*
finger ['fiŋgə] *s* dedo *m* (*de la mano*); manecilla *f* (*del reloj*); ***not lift a ~*** no hacer nada; ***little ~*** dedo *m* meñique; ***middle ~*** dedo *m* del corazón; ***ring ~*** dedo *m* anular; *v/t* manosear, tocar; teclear; **~nail** uña *f*; **~prints** huellas *f/pl* dactilares; **~tip** punta *f* del dedo
finish ['finiʃ] *s* fin *m*; final *m*, remate *m*; acabado *m*; *v/t* acabar, terminar; ***~ off*** acabar con; *v/i* acabar; **~ing touch** última mano *f*
Finland ['finlənd] Finlandia *f*
Finnish ['finiʃ] *a*, *s* finlandés(esa) *m* (*f*)
fir [fə:] abeto *m*
fire ['faiə] *s* fuego *m*; incendio *m*; ***to be on ~*** estar en llamas; ***to set on ~*** incendiar; *v/t* encender; incendiar; *fig* excitar; *fam* despedir; disparar; **~arm** arma *f* de fuego; **~ brigade**, *Am* **department** cuerpo *m* de bomberos; **~ engine** bomba *f* de incendios; **~ escape** escalera *f* de escape de incendios; **~man** bombero *m*; **~place** chimenea *f*; **~proof** a prueba de fuego; **~works** fuegos *m/pl* artificiales
firm [fə:m] *a* firme; *s* casa *f* comercial; empresa *f*; **~ness** firmeza *f*
first [fə:st] *a* primero; primitivo; original; *adv* primero; ***~ of all*** ante todo; (***the***) **~** *s* (el) primero; ***at ~*** al principio; **~ aid** primeros auxilios *m/pl*; **~-aid kit** botiquín *m*; **~ born** primogénito; **~-class** excelente, de primera clase; **~ cousin** primo hermano *m*; **~ hand** de primera mano; **~ly** en primer lugar; **~ name**

nombre m de pila; ~ night teat estreno m; ~-rate de primera (clase)
firth [fə:θ] brazo m de mar
fish [fiʃ] s pez m; peces m/pl; pescado m; v/t, v/i pescar; ~bone espina f de pescado; ~bowl pecera f; ~erman ['fiʃəmən] pescador m; ~ing rod caña f de pescar; ~ing tackle aparejo m de pesca; ~monger's pescadería f; ~y a pescado (sabor, olor); fig dudoso, sospechoso
fiss|ion ['fiʃən] fisión f; ~ure ['fiʃə] s grieta f, hendedura f; v/i agrietarse
fist [fist] puño m; ~ful puñado m
fit [fit] a en buen estado físico; sp en forma; a propósito; apropiado; adecuado, digno; to see ~ juzgar conveniente; s ataque m; ajuste m; v/t acomodar; cuadrar con; sentar bien a (ropa); ~ out equipar; v/i ajustarse; ~ in caber; ~ in with llevarse bien con; ~ness aptitud f; buena salud f; ~ter ajustador m; ~ting a conveniente; s ajuste m; prueba f; ~tings guarniciones f/pl
five [faiv] cinco
fix [fiks] s apuro m; in a ~ en un aprieto; v/t fijar; asegurar; arreglar; ~ up arreglar; reparar; ~ed fijo; ~tures instalaciones f/pl
flabbergasted ['flæbəgɑ:stid] pasmado
flabby ['flæbi] flojo; gordo
flag [flæg] s bandera f; pabellón m; v/i flaquear; fig aflojar (interés, etc); ~pole asta f de bandera; ~ship capitana f; ~stone losa f
flagrant ['fleigrənt] notorio
flair [flɛə] aptitud f especial
flake [fleik] s escama f; copo m (de nieve); v/i desprenderse en escamillas
flamboyant [flæm'bɔiənt] extravagante; flamante
flame [fleim] s llama f; fig novio(a) m (f); v/i to ~ up inflamarse
flank [flæŋk] s lado m, costado m; flanco m; v/t mil flanquear
flannel ['flænl] franela f
flap [flæp] s faldilla f; solapa f (del sobre); aletazo m; palmada f; v/i aletear; sacudirse; v/t batir
flare [flɛə] s llamarada f; señal f luminosa; v/i fulgurar; brillar; ~ up encenderse
flash [flæʃ] s destello m; fogonazo m de cañón; instante m; foto flash m; v/i relampaguear; v/t blandir; fam ostentar; ~light linterna f eléctrica; ~y chillón, llamativo
flask [flɑ:sk] frasco m
flat [flæt] a llano, liso; insípido; apagado; mús bemol; desafinado; adv to fall ~ caer mal; s piso m, LA departamento m; aut pinchazo m; ~footed de pies planos; ~ iron plancha f; ~ten v/t allanar, aplastar; v/i aplanarse
flatter ['flætə] v/t adular, lisonjear; ~ing halagüeño; ~y adulación f, lisonja f
flaunt [flɔ:nt] v/t ostentar, lucir
flavo(u)r ['fleivə] s sabor m, gusto m; aroma m; v/t sazonar; condimentar
flaw [flɔ:] falta f; defecto m; grieta f; ~less intachable
flax [flæks] lino m
flay [flei] v/t desollar
flea [fli:] pulga f
flee [fli:] v/i huir
fleec|e [fli:s] s vellón m; lana f; v/t esquilar; fig desplumar, pelar
fleet [fli:t] s flota f; a veloz; ~ing fugaz; pasajero
flesh [fleʃ] carne f; pulpa f (de una fruta); in the ~ en persona; of ~ and blood de carne y hueso
flexible ['fleksəbl] flexible
flexitime ['fleksitaim] horario m flexible
flick [flik] s golpecito m; v/t dar un capirotazo a
flicker ['flikə] s parpadeo m; luz f oscilante; v/i flamear; vacilar
flight [flait] huida f, fuga f; vuelo m; ~ of stairs tramo m de escalera; ~y frívolo; casquivano
flimsy ['flimzi] débil, frágil
flinch [flintʃ] v/i acobardarse, echarse atrás
fling [fliŋ] v/t arrojar, tirar; ~ open abrir de golpe (puerta, etc)
flint [flint] pedernal m; piedra f
flip [flip] v/t dar la vuelta a; (moneda) echar a cara o cruz
flippant ['flipənt] impertinente; poco serio
flipper ['flipə] aleta f
flirt [flə:t] s coqueta f; galanteador m; v/i coquetear, flirtear, galantear; ~ation coqueteo m, flirteo m
flit [flit] v/i volar, revolotear
float [fləut] s boya f; balsa f; v/i flotar
flock [flɔk] s congregación f; rebaño m (de ovejas); v/i congregarse, afluir
flog [flɔg] v/t azotar
flood [flʌd] s inundación f; diluvio m; pleamar f; fig flujo m; torrente m; v/t inundar; v/i desbordar; ~ gate compuerta f de esclusa; ~ light faro m
floor [flɔ:] s suelo m; piso m; ground ~, Am first ~ planta f baja; v/t solar; fig derribar, vencer
flop [flɔp] s fracaso m; v/i aletear; moverse bruscamente; fig fracasar; ~ down dejarse caer pesadamente
florist ['flɔrist] florista m, f
flour ['flauə] harina f
flourish ['flʌriʃ] v/t blandir; v/i florecer; prosperar; ~ing floreciente
flow [fləu] s corriente f; flujo m; v/i correr, fluir
flower ['flauə] s flor f; ~bed macizo m; ~ bowl, ~ vase florero m; ~pot tiesto m, maceta f
flu [flu:] fam gripe f
fluctuate ['flʌktjueit] v/i fluctuar
fluent ['flu(:)ənt] fluido, fácil; corriente
fluff [flʌf] pelusa f; ~y velloso
fluid ['flu(:)id] fluido m; líquido m
flurry ['flʌri] ráfaga f, remolino m (de viento); agitación f
flush [flʌʃ] a parejo, igual; ~ with a ras de; ~ with money adinerado; s rubor m, sonrojo m; flujo m rápido; v/i fluir, brotar (agua); ruborizarse
fluster ['flʌstə] s agitación f, confusión f; v/t confundir
flut|e [flu:t] s flauta f; arq estría f; v/t acanalar; ~ist flautista m, f
flutter ['flʌtə] s revolteo m; aleteo m; palpitación f; v/i palpitar; aletear; agitarse
flux [flʌks] flujo m
fly [flai] s mosca f; bragueta f; v/i volar; huir; ir en avión; ~ into a rage montar en cólera; ~ off desprenderse; ~catcher papamoscas m; ~ing: ~ing boat hidroavión m; with ~ing colors con gran éxito; ~ing saucer platillo m volante; ~ swatter atrapamoscas m; ~wheel volante m
foal [fəul] s potro m; v/t, v/i parir (una yegua)
foam [fəum] s espuma f; v/i espumar; ~y espumoso
focus ['fəukəs] s foco m; in ~ enfocado; v/t enfocar
foe [fəu] enemigo m
f(o)etus ['fi:təs] feto m
fog [fɔg] s niebla f; fig nebulosidad f; v/t obscurecer; ~gy brumoso; fig nebuloso
foible ['fɔibl] punto m débil, flaqueza f
foil [fɔil] s hojuela f; fig contraste m; v/t frustrar
fold [fəuld] s pliegue m, arruga f; corral m, aprisco m; relig rebaño m; v/t doblar; plegar; cruzar (brazos); v/i doblarse, plegarse; ~er carpeta f; folleto m; ~ing bed cama f plegadiza; ~ing chair silla f de tijera; ~ing door puerta f plegadiza; ~ing screen biombo m
foliage ['fəuliidʒ] follaje m
folk [fəuk] gente f; nación f; pueblo m; ~lore ['~lɔ:] folklore m; ~s fam parentela f; ~song canción f folklórica
follow ['fɔləu] v/t, v/i seguir; resultar; ~ through llevar hasta el fin; ~er seguidor(a) m (f), partidario m; ~ing a siguiente; s partidarios m/pl; séquito m
folly ['fɔli] locura f
fond [fɔnd] cariñoso, afectuoso; to be ~ of tener cariño a; ser aficionado a
fondle ['fɔndl] v/t acariciar
food [fu:d] comida f; alimento m; provisiones f/pl; ~stuffs comestibles m/pl
fool [fu:l] s tonto(a) m (f); to make a ~ of oneself ponerse en ridículo; v/t engañar; v/i bromear, chancear; ~ around malgastar el tiempo; ~hardy temerario; ~ish tonto; imprudente; ~ishness tontería f, disparate m; ~proof a prueba de impericia; infalible
foot [fut] pie m; pata f (de animal); on ~ de pie; to put one's ~ in it meter la pata; ~ball fútbol m; ~baller futbolista m; ~ brake freno m de pie; ~hold pie m firme; ~ing fig posición f; ~lights candilejas f/pl; ~note nota f (al pie de la página); ~print huella f; ~step paso m; ~wear calzado m
for [fɔ:, fə] prep para, con destino a; por, a causa de; as ~ en cuanto a; what ~? ¿para qué?; ~ good para siempre; conj pues, porque; as ~ me por mi parte
forbear [fɔ:'bɛə] v/t, v/i abstenerse (de)
forbid [fə'bid] v/t prohibir; ~ding lúgubre
force [fɔ:s] s fuerza f; by ~ a la fuerza; in ~ en vigor; v/t forzar; violar; ~d landing aer aterrizaje m forzoso; ~ful vigoroso, enérgico
forceps ['fɔ:seps] tenazas f/pl
forcible ['fɔ:səbl] forzado
ford [fɔ:d] s vado m; v/t vadear
fore [fɔ:] delantero; ~arm antebrazo m; ~boding presagio m; ~cast s pronóstico m; v/t predecir; ~fathers antepasados m/pl; ~finger índice m; ~front vanguardia f; ~going anterior; ~ground primer plano m; ~head ['fɔrid] frente f
foreign ['fɔrin] extranjero, exterior; extraño; ~er extranjero(a) m (f); ~ exchange divisas f/pl, moneda f extranjera; ~ policy política f exterior
fore|man ['fɔ:mən] capataz m; ~most primero; ~runner precursor m; ~see v/t prever; ~sight previsión f
fore|st ['fɔrist] s bosque m; ~-stall [fɔ:'stɔ:l] v/t prevenir
fore|taste ['fɔ:teist] anticipo m; ~thought prevención f
forever [fə'revə] para siempre
foreword ['fɔ:wə:d] prefacio m
forfeit ['fɔ:fit] s prenda f; multa f; v/t perder (derecho a)
forge [fɔ:dʒ] s fragua f; v/t fraguar; forjar; falsificar; ~ ahead seguir avanzando; ~ry falsificación f
forget [fə'get] v/t olvidar; ~ful olvidadizo; descuidado; ~-me-not bot nomeolvides f
forgiv|e [fə'giv] v/t perdonar; ~eness perdón m
fork [fɔ:k] s tenedor m; agr horca f; bifurcación f (de caminos, etc); v/i bifurcarse
forlorn [fə'lɔ:n] abandonado; desamparado
form [fɔ:m] s forma f; figura f; formulario m; banco m; clase f; v/t formar; constituir; in top ~ en plena forma
formal ['fɔ:məl] formal; ceremonioso; ~ity [~'mæliti] formalidad f; etiqueta f
formation [fɔ:'meiʃən] formación f
former ['fɔ:mə] a anterior; precedente; the ~ pron aquél m, aquélla f; ~ly antiguamente, antes
formidable ['fɔ:midəbl] formidable
formulate ['fɔ:mjuleit] v/t formular
forsake [fə'seik] v/t dejar, abandonar
fort [fɔ:t] fuerte m, fortaleza f
forth [fɔ:θ]: back and ~ de acá para allá; and so ~ etcétera; ~coming próximo, venidero; ~right franco; directo
fortify ['fɔ:tifai] v/t fortificar
fortitude ['fɔ:titjud] fortaleza f
fortnight ['fɔ:tnait] quincena f; ~ly quincenal
fortress ['fɔ:tris] fortaleza f
fortunate ['fɔ:tʃnit] afortunado, feliz; ~ly afortunadamente
fortune ['fɔ:tʃən] fortuna f
forward ['fɔ:wəd] a adelantado, delantero; s sp delantero m; v/t promover, fomentar; reexpedir; ~s adelante, hacia adelante
foster| brother ['fɔstə-] hermano m de leche; ~ mother madre f adoptiva; ~ sister hermana f de leche
foul [faul] a sucio, asqueroso; vil; malo, desagradable; obsceno, grosero; s sp falta f; v/t ensuciar
found [faund] v/t fundar; tecn fundir; ~ation fundación f; ~er fundador m; ~ling niño m expósito
fountain ['fauntin] fuente f; ~ pen pluma f estilográfica
four [fɔ:] cuatro; ~fold ['fɔ:fəuld] cuádruple; ~-square firme; sincero
fowl [faul] ave f (de corral)
fox [fɔks] zorro m (t fig); ~-glove bot dedalera f; ~y fig astuto
foyer ['fɔiei] vestíbulo m
fraction ['frækʃən] fracción f
fracture ['fræktʃə] s fractura f; v/t, v/i fracturar(se)
fragile ['frædʒail] frágil
fragment ['frægmənt] fragmento m
fragran|ce ['freigrəns] fragancia f; ~t fragante
frail [freil] delicado, frágil; quebradizo
frame [freim] s marco m; tecn armazón f, m; estructura f; cuerpo m; v/t formar; formular; enmarcar; ~s (para gafas) montura f
France [frɑ:ns] Francia f
franchise ['fræntʃaiz] sufragio m; derecho m político
frank [fræŋk] franco, abierto
frankfurter ['fræŋkfətə] perrito m caliente
frantic ['fræntik] frenético, furioso
fratern|al [frə'tə:nl] fraternal; ~ity fraternidad f
fraud [frɔ:d] fraude m, timo m; ~ulent fraudulento
fray [frei] s refriega f, riña f; v/i desgastarse
freak [fri:k] rareza f; monstruosidad f; tipo m excéntrico
freckle ['frekl] peca f
free [fri:] a libre; liberal; suelto; gratuito; get off scot ~ salir impune; set ~ poner en libertad; ~ and easy despreocupado; ~ of charge gratis; ~ on board (f o b) franco a bordo; v/t liberar, libertar; eximir; desembarazar; ~dom libertad f; inmunidad f; ~hand hecho a pulso; ~ly sin reserva; libremente; ~mason francmasón m; ~ port puerto m franco; ~ trade librecambio m; ~way Am autopista f; ~ will libre albedrío m
freez|e [fri:z] v/t helar, congelar; v/i congelarse; fig helarse; ~er congelador m; ~ing point punto m de congelación
freight [freit] s flete m; carga f; v/t cargar; fletar; ~er buque m de carga
French [frentʃ] a, s francés; the ~ los franceses m/pl; ~man francés m; ~ window puerta f ventana; ~woman francesa f
frenzy ['frenzi] frenesí m
frequen|cy ['fri:kwənsi] frecuencia f; ~t frecuente
fresh [freʃ] fresco; nuevo; dulce (agua); ~en v/t, v/i refrescar(se); ~ness frescura f
fret [fret] v/t rozar, raer; v/i inquietarse; ~ful irritable, enojadizo; ~fully de mala gana
friar ['fraiə] fraile m
friction ['frikʃən] fricción f; fig rozamiento m
Friday ['fraidi] viernes m
fridge [fridʒ] fam refrigeradora f
fried [fraid] frito
friend [frend] amigo(a) m (f); to make ~s hacerse amigos; ~ly amistoso; ~ship amistad f
fright [frait] susto m; ~en v/t asustar, espantar; ~en away ahuyentar; ~ened of tener miedo a; ~ful espantoso, terrible
frigid ['fridʒid] frío; hostil: med frígido
frill [fril] volante m
fringe [frindʒ] fleco m; borde m; periferia f; grupo m marginal

frisk [frisk] *v/i* brincar; cabriolar; **~y** juguetón, retozón
fritter ['fritə]: **~ away** desperdiciar
frivolous ['frivələs] frívolo
fro [frəu]: **to and ~** de una parte a otra
frog [frɔg] rana *f*
frolic ['frɔlik] *v/i* juguetear
from [frɔm, frəm] de, desde; **~ day to day** de día en día
front [frʌnt] *s* frente *f*; fachada *f*; **in ~ of** delante de; *a* delantero; frontero; **~ door** puerta *f* principal; **~ier** ['~iə] frontera *f*; **~ page** primera plana *f*
frost [frɔst] *s* helada *f*; escarcha *f*; *v/t* cubrir con escarcha; escarchar (*pasteles, etc*); **~bite** congelación *f*
froth [frɔθ] espuma *f*
frown [fraun] *s* ceño *m*; *v/i* fruncir el entrecejo
frozen ['frəuzn] congelado, helado
frugal ['fru:gəl] frugal
fruit [fru:t] fruta *f*; fruto *m*; producto *m*, resultado *m*; **~ful** provechoso; **~ion** [fru'iʃn]: **to come to ~ion** verse logrado; **~ juice** zumo *m* (*LA* jugo *m*) de frutas; **~less** infructuoso
frustrate [frʌs'treit] *v/t* frustrar; **~d** frustrado
fry [frai] *v/t*, *v/i* freír(se); **~ing pan** sartén *f*
fuel [fjuəl] combustible *m*
fugitive ['fju:dʒitiv] fugitivo *m*
fulfil(l) [ful'fil] *v/t* cumplir; realizar; **~ment** cumplimiento *m*; satisfacción *f*
full [ful] lleno, repleto; completo; máximo; pleno; **in ~** (*citar*) íntegramente; **~-length** de cuerpo entero; **~ moon** luna *f* llena; **~ness** plenitud *f*; **~ stop** punto *m* final; **~ time** de jornada completa; **~y** completamente
fumble ['fʌmbl] *v/t*, *v/i* manosear *o* tentar torpemente
fume [fju:m] *v/i* humear; *fig* echar rayos; **~s** humo *m*
fun [fʌn] diversión *f*; alegría *f*; **for ~, in ~** en broma; **to have ~** divertirse; **to make ~ of** burlarse de
function ['fʌŋkʃən] *s* función *f*; *v/i* funcionar; **~al** funcional; **~ary** funcionario *m*
fund [fʌnd] *s* fondo *m*; *v/t* proveer de fondos
fundamental [fʌndə'mentl] fundamental
funeral ['fju:nərəl] entierro *m*; **~ service** funerales *m/pl*
funnel ['fʌnl] embudo *m*; *mar* chimenea *f*
funny ['fʌni] gracioso; raro
fur [fə:] piel *f*; pelo *m*; **~ coat** abrigo *m* de pieles
furious ['fjuəriəs] furioso
furl [fə:l] *v/t* aferrar
furnace ['fə:nis] horno *m*
furni|sh ['fə:niʃ] *v/t* amueblar; suministrar; **~ture** ['fə:nitʃə] muebles *m/pl*
furrier ['fʌriə] peletero *m*
furrow ['fʌrəu] surco *m*
furth|er ['fə:ðə] *a* más distante; adicional; *adv* más allá; además; *v/t* fomentar; **~ermore** además; **~est** *a* más lejano; *adv* más lejos
furtive ['fə:tiv] furtivo
fury ['fjuəri] furia *f*, rabia *f*
fuse [fju:z] *s* espoleta *f*; *elec* fusible *m*; *v/t*, *v/i* fundir(se)
fuselage ['fju:zila:ʒ] *aer* fuselaje *m*
fusion ['fju:ʒən] fusión *f*
fuss [fʌs] *s* agitación *f*; conmoción *f*; lío *m*; **make a ~** armar un lío; *v/i* agitarse por pequeñeces; **~y** exigente
futile ['fju:tail] inútil
future ['fju:tʃə] *a* futuro, venidero; *s* futuro *m*
fuzz [fʌz] borra *f*; vello *m*

G

gab [gæb] *fam* parloteo *m*; **to have the gift of the ~** tener mucha labia
gable ['geibl] *arq* aguilón *m*
gadfly ['gædflai] tábano *m*
gadget ['gædʒit] aparato *m*; artilugio *m*
gag [gæg] *s* mordaza *f*; *teat* morcilla *f*; *fam* chiste *m*; *v/t* amordazar
gaiety ['geiəti] alegría *f*
gaily ['geili] alegremente
gain [gein] *s* ganancia *f*; beneficio *m*; *v/t* ganar, conseguir, lograr; *v/i* crecer; engordar; ganar terreno
gait [geit] marcha *f*, paso *m*
gale [geil] vendaval *m*; ventarrón *m*
gall [gɔ:l] hiel *f*; bilis *f*; *fig* rencor *m*; descaro *m*; **~ bladder** vejiga *f* de la bilis
gallant ['gælənt] valiente; garboso; **~ry** valentía *f*; galantería *f*
gallery ['gæləri] galería *f*
galley ['gæli] galera *f*
gallon ['gælən] galón *m* (*ingl*: 4,5 litros; *EU*: 3,8 *litros*)
gallop ['gæləp] *s* galope *m*; *v/i* galopar
gallows ['gæləuz] horca *f*
gallstone ['gɔ:lstəun] cálculo *m* biliar
galore [gə'lɔ:] en abundancia
gambl|e ['gæmbl] *s* jugada *f* arriesgada; *v/t* apostar; *v/i* jugar al azar; **~er** jugador *m*; tahúr *m*
game [geim] *s* juego *m*; partida *f* (*de naipes*); partido *m* (*de fútbol, etc*); caza *f*; **big ~** caza *f* mayor; **~keeper** guardabosque *m*
gang [gæŋ] *s* banda *f*; pandilla *f*; cuadrilla *f*; **~ up on** *v/i* atacar en conjunto contra
gangster ['gæŋstə] pistolero *m*, gánster *m*
gangway ['gæŋwei] pasillo *m*; *mar* portalón *m*
gaol [dʒeil] = **jail**
gap [gæp] abertura *f*; brecha *f*; vacío *m*; intervalo *m*
gape [geip] *v/i* estar boquiabierto
garage ['gæra:dʒ] *s* garaje *m*; *v/t* guardar en un garaje
garbage ['ga:bidʒ] basura *f*
garden ['ga:dn] jardín *m*; huerto *m*; huerta *f*; **~er** jardinero *m*; **~ing** jardinería *f*
gargle ['ga:gl] *v/i* hacer gárgaras
garland ['ga:lənd] guirnalda *f*
garlic ['ga:lik] ajo *m*
garment ['ga:mənt] prenda *f* de vestir
garnish ['ga:niʃ] *v/t* adornar, guarnecer
garrison ['gærisn] *s* guarnición *f*
garter ['ga:tə] liga *f*
gas [gæs] *s* gas *m*; *Am* gasolina *f*; **~eous** ['~jəs] gaseoso; **~ket** *tecn* junta *f*; **~mask** careta *f* antigás
gasp [ga:sp] *v/i* boquear; jadear
gas|-station ['gæsteiʃən] gasolinera *f*; **~stove** ['gæstəuv] cocina *f* de gas
gate [geit] puerta *f*, portal *m*; taquilla *f*; **~keeper** portero *m*; **~way** puerta *f*, entrada *f*
gather ['gæðə] *v/t* recoger; reunir; deducir; cobrar (*velocidad, fuerzas, etc*); entender; *v/i* reunirse, congregarse; **~ing** reunión *f*; agrupación *f*
gaudy ['gɔ:di] llamativo, chillón
ga(u)ge [geidʒ] *s* medida *f*; calibre *m*; *f c* entrevía *f*; *tecn* calibrador *m*; *v/t* medir; calibrar; estimar
gaunt [gɔ:nt] flaco; sombrío; **~let** ['gɔ:ntlit]: **run the ~let** correr baquetas; **throw down the ~let** arrojar el guante
gauze [gɔ:z] gasa *f*
gay [gei] alegre; jovial, festivo; *fam* homosexual
gaze [geiz] *s* mirada *f* fija; *v/i* mirar fijamente
gear [giə] *s* prendas *f/pl*; equipo *m*; pertrechos *m/pl*; *mar* aparejo *m*; *tecn* engranaje *m*; transmisión *f*; *aut* marcha *f*; **in ~** engranado; **~box** caja *f* de engranajes; **~shift** cambio *m* de velocidades
gelatine ['dʒelətin] gelatina *f*
gem [dʒem] gema *f*; *fig* joya *f*
gender ['dʒendə] género *m*
gene [dʒi:n] gen *m*
general ['dʒenərəl] *a* general; *s* general *m*; **in ~** en general, por lo general; **~ize** *v/i* generalizar; **~ly** generalmente
generat|e ['dʒenəreit] *v/t* engendrar; procrear; producir; *elec* generar; **~ion** generación *f*; **~or** generador *m*
genero|sity [dʒenə'rɔsiti] generosidad *f*; **~us** ['dʒenərəs] generoso
genetics [dʒi'netiks] genética *f*
genial ['dʒi:njəl] afable; suave
genitals ['dʒenitlz] órganos *m/pl* genitales
genitive ['dʒenitiv] genitivo *m*
genius ['dʒi:njəs] genio *m*
gentle ['dʒentl] suave, dulce; manso; cortés, fino; bien nacido, noble; **~man** caballero *m*; señor *m*; **~ness** bondad *f*; mansedumbre *f*; dulzura *f*
gently ['dʒentli] suavemente
gentry ['dʒentri] alta burguesía *f*
genuine ['dʒenjuin] genuino, auténtico
geography [dʒi'ɔgrəfi] geografía *f*
geolog|ist [dʒi'ɔlədʒist] geólogo *m*; **~y** geología *f*
geometry [dʒi'ɔmitri] geometría *f*
geophysics [dʒiəu'fiziks] geofísica *f*
geranium [dʒi'reinjəm] geranio *m*
geriatrics [dʒeri'ætriks] geriatría *f*
germ [dʒə:m] germen *m*; **~ warfare** guerra *f* bacteorológica
German ['dʒə:mən] *a*, *s* alemán(ana) *m* (*f*); **~ measles** rubéola *f*; **~y** Alemania *f*
germinate ['dʒə:mineit] *v/i* germinar
gest|iculate [dʒes'tikjuleit] *v/i* gesticular; **~ure** ['dʒestʃə] gesto *m*
get [get] *v/t* conseguir, lograr; obtener; recibir; traer; aprender, comprender; *v/i* volverse, ponerse; **~ about** andar; viajar; **~ across** hacer entender; **~ ahead** prosperar; **~ along** marcharse; progresar; **~ along with** llevarse bien; **~ along without** pasarse sin; **~ away** escaparse; **~ back** recobrar; **~ back at** pagar en la misma moneda; **~ by** ir tirando; **~ down** bajar; **~ going** ponerse en marcha; **~ in** entrar; subir; **to ~ it** *fam* caer en la cuenta; **~ lost** perderse; **~ off** bajar, apearse de; **~ on** progresar; subir; **~ on with** congeniar con; **~ out** salir; *interj* ¡fuera!; **~ over** reestablecerse de; **~ ready** prepararse; **~ up** levantarse; **have got** tener; **have got to ...** tener que, deber ...
geyser ['gaizə] géiser *m*; ['gi:zə] calentador *m*
ghastly ['ga:stli] horrible, espantoso; pálido
gherkin ['gə:kin] pepinillo *m*
ghost [gəust] fantasma *m*; espectro *m*; **to give up the ~** rendir el alma
giant ['dʒaiənt] gigante *m*
gibe [dʒaib] *v/i* mofarse (de)
giblets ['dʒiblits] menudillos *m/pl*
giddy ['gidi] mareado; vertiginoso; atolondrado
gift [gift] regalo *m*; dádiva *f*; don *m*, dote *f*, talento *m*; **~ed** talentoso, dotado
gigantic [dʒai'gæntik] gigantesco
giggle ['gigl] *s* risita *f* tonta; *v/i* reírse tontamente
gild [gild] *v/t* dorar
gilt [gilt] dorado
gin [dʒin] *s* ginebra *f*
ginger ['dʒindʒə] *s* jengibre *m*; *fam* brío *m*, vivacidad *f*; **~bread** pan *m* de jengibre; **~ly** cautelosamente
gipsy ['dʒipsi] *a*, *s* gitano(a) *m* (*f*)
giraffe [dʒi'ra:f] jirafa *f*
gird [gə:d] *v/t* ceñir; **~er** viga *f* maestra; **~le** ['gə:dl] *s* cinturón *m*; faja *f*; *v/t* ceñir
girl [gə:l] muchacha *f*; chica *f*; moza *f*; **~ish** de niña
girth [gə:θ] cincha *f*; circunferencia *f*
gist [dʒist] lo esencial
give [giv] *v/t* dar; entregar; causar (*enfermedad*); indicar (*temperatura, etc*); **~ away** regalar; revelar; **~ back** devolver; **~ birth to** dar a luz; **~ off** emitir; **~ up** renunciar a; **~ oneself up** rendirse, entregarse; **~n to** propenso a; *v/i* dar, hacer regalos; ceder; **~ in** ceder; **~ up** darse por vencido; **~-and-take** ['givən'teik] toma y daca *m*
glacier ['glæsjə] glaciar *m*
glad [glæd] contento, alegre; **to be ~** alegrarse; estar contento; **~ly** con mucho gusto; **~den** *v/t* alegrar
glamo(u)r ['glæmə] encanto *m*; **~ous** encantador
glance [gla:ns] *s* mirada *f*; vistazo *m*; **at first ~** a primera vista; *v/i* echar un vistazo; **~ at** dar un vistazo a
gland [glænd] glándula *f*
glare [glɛə] *s* relumbrón *m*; mirada *f* feroz; *v/i* relumbrar; **~ at** mirar con ira
glass [gla:s] *s* cristal *m*; vidrio *m*; vaso *m*; espejo *m*; barómetro *m*; catalejo *m*; **~es** gafas *f/pl*, *LA* anteojos *m/pl*; *a* de cristal, de vidrio; **~house** invernadero *m*; **~y** vítreo; vidrioso (*ojos, etc*)
glaz|e [gleiz] *s* barniz *m*; *v/t* barnizar; lustrar; poner vidrios a (*una ventana*); **~ier** ['~jə] vidriero *m*
gleam [gli:m] *s* destello *m*; brillo *m*; *v/i* brillar, centellear
glee [gli:] júbilo *m*
glen [glen] hoya *f*
glib [glib] suelto de lengua
glide [glaid] *s* deslizamiento *m*; *v/i* deslizarse; *aer* planear; **~r** *aer* planeador *m*
glimmer ['glimə] *s* vislumbre *f*; *fig* rastro *m*; *v/i* rielar, brillar
glimpse [glimps] *s* ojeada *f*, vista *f* fugaz; *v/t* vislumbrar
glint [glint] *s* destello *m*; *v/i* destellar
glisten ['glisn] *v/i* relucir, brillar
glitter ['glitə] *s* brillo *m*; *v/i* brillar; relucir
gloat [gləut]: **~ over** *v/i* saborear maliciosamente
glob|al ['gləubl] mundial; global; **~e** globo *m*; **~e trotter** trotamundos *m*, *f*
gloom [glu:m] lobreguez *f*; tristeza *f*; **~y** obscuro, tenebroso; triste, abatido
glor|ify ['glɔ:rifai] *v/t* glorificar; **~ious** glorioso; **~y** gloria *f*
gloss [glɔs] *s* lustre *m*, brillo *m*; glosa *f*; **~ary** ['~əri] glosario *m*; **~y** lustroso; satinado
glove [glʌv] guante *m*
glow [gləu] *s* brillo *m*; luminosidad *f*; *v/i* brillar, fulgurar; **~er** ['glauə]: **~er at** *v/i* mirar con ceño; **~worm** luciérnaga *f*
glue [glu:] *s* cola *f*; goma *f*; *v/t* pegar, encolar
glut [glʌt] *s* superabundancia *f*; *v/t* inundar (*el mercado*)
glutt|on ['glʌtn] glotón *m*; **~ony** gula *f*
glycerine ['glisərin] glicerina *f*
gnarled [na:ld] nudoso
gnash [næʃ] *v/t* rechinar (*dientes*)
gnat [næt] mosquito *m*
gnaw [nɔ:] *v/t* roer
go [gəu] *v/i* ir; irse; andar; viajar; funcionar; pasar, correr (*el tiempo*); alcanzar; **~ ahead** seguir adelante; **~ away** irse, marcharse; **~ back** regresar; **~ between** mediar; **~ by** pasar (por); **~ down** ponerse (*sol*); bajar; **~ for** ir a buscar, ir por; **~ home** volver a casa; **~ in for** dedicarse a; **~ into** entrar en; investigar; **~ off** irse, dispararse; **~ on** seguir, continuar; **~ out** salir; extinguirse; apagarse; **~ over** recorrer; repasar; **~ through** pasar por; sufrir; **~ through with** llevar a cabo; **~ to bed** acostarse; **~ to school** ir al colegio; **to be ~ing to** ir a (*hacer*); **~ under** hundirse; perderse; **~ with** hacer juego con; **~ without** pasarse sin; *s* energía *f*, fuerza *f*; empuje *m*; **no ~** es inútil; **on the ~** en actividad; activo; **have a ~ at** probar suerte con
goad [gəud] *v/t* aguijonear; incitar
go-ahead ['gəuəhed] *fig* luz *f* verde
goal [gəul] meta *f*, gol *m*; **~keeper** guardameta *m*, portero *m*
goat [gəut] cabra *f*; macho *m* cabrío
go-between ['gəu-bitwi:n] mediador(a) *m* (*f*)
gobble ['gɔbl]: *v/t* **~ up** engullirse
goblet ['gɔblit] copa *f*
goblin ['gɔblin] duende *m*
God [gɔd] Dios *m*; **ᘓ** deidad *f*, dios *m*; **~ forbid!** ¡por Dios!; **~ willing** si Dios quiere
god|child ahijado(a) *m* (*f*); **~dess** diosa *f*; **~father** padrino *m*; **~less** descreído; **~like** (de aspecto) divino; **~liness** santidad *f*; **~mother** madrina *f*; **~parents** padrinos *m/pl*; **~send** don *m* del cielo

goggles ['gɔglz] gafas *f/pl* submarinas

going ['gəuiŋ] *s* ida *f*, partida *f*; *a* en marcha; existente; ***the ~ rate*** la tarifa en vigor; **~s-on** actividades *f/pl* dudosas

gold [gəuld] oro *m*; **~ digger** buscador *m* de oro; *fig Am* aventurera *f*; **~en** de oro; **~fish** pez *m* de colores; **~smith** orfebre *m*

golf [gɔlf] golf *m*; **~ course** campo *m* de golf; **~er** jugador *m* de golf

gone [gɔn] ido; perdido, arruinado; pasado; muerto

good [gud] *a* bueno; ***for ~*** para siempre; ***to make ~*** cumplir (*promesa*); reparar; prosperar; ***as ~ as*** tan bueno como; casi; ***a ~ deal*** mucho; ***~ afternoon*** buenas tardes; ***~ at*** hábil en; ***~ breeding*** buena educación *f*; ***~ for*** servir para; ***2 Friday*** Viernes *m* Santo; ***in ~ time*** a tiempo; ***~ luck!*** ¡buena suerte!; ***~ morning*** buenos días; *s* bien *m*; ***it's no ~*** no vale para nada, es inútil; ***for the ~ of*** para el bien de; **~bye** adiós *m*; **~-for-nothing** haragán *m*; **~looking** guapo; **~-natured** bondadoso; **~ness** bondad *f*; benevolencia *f*; **~s** [gudz] bienes *m/pl*; **~ turn** favor *m*; **~ will** buena voluntad *f*

goose [gu:s] ganso *m*; **~berry** ['guzbəri] grosella *f* espina; **~flesh**, *Am* **~bumps** *fig* carne *f* de gallina

gore [gɔ:] *v/t* cornear

gorge [gɔ:dʒ] *s anat, geog* garganta *f*; barranco *m*; *v/t* engullir; *v/i* hartarse; **~ous** ['~əs] magnífico, hermosísimo

gorilla [gə'rilə] gorila *m*

gory ['gɔ:ri] sangriento

gospel ['gɔspəl] evangelio *m*

gossip ['gɔsip] *s* chismorreo *m*; chisme *m*; chismoso(a) *m* (*f*); *v/i* chismear

gourd [guəd] calabaza *f*

gout [gaut] gota *f*; **~y** gotoso

govern ['gʌvən] *v/t* gobernar; dirigir; regir, guiar; *v/i* gobernar; **~ess** institutriz *f*; **~ing board** junta *f* directiva; **~ment** gobierno *m*; **~or** gobernador *m*; director *m*

gown [gaun] vestido *m* de mujer; toga *f*

grab [græb] *v/t* agarrar; arrebatar; coger

grace [greis] *s* gracia *f*; finura *f*; *relig* bendición *f*; ***to say ~*** bendecir la mesa; *v/t* adornar; favorecer; **~ful** agraciado; elegante; **~ note** *mús* nota *f* de adorno

gracious ['greiʃəs] benigno; grato, ameno; ***good ~!*** ¡válgame Dios!

grad|e [greid] *s* grado *m*; pendiente *f*; clase *f*; nota *f*; **~e crossing** *f c* paso *m* a nivel; *v/t* graduar; nivelar; **~ient** ['~jənt] pendiente *f*; **~ual** ['grædʒuəl] gradual; **~uate** ['grædjueit] *v/t, v/i* graduar(se); ['~dʒuət] *s* graduado *m*; **~uation** [~dju'eiʃən] graduación *f*

graft [grɑ:ft] *s med* injerto *m*; soborno *m*; *v/i* injertar; transferir

grain [grein] *s* grano *m*; (*de tejido*) fibra *f*; cereales *m/pl*; ***against the ~*** a contrapelo

gramm|ar ['græmə] gramática *f*; **~atical** [grə'mætikəl] gramático

gram(me) [græm] gramo *m*

gramophone ['græməfəun] gramófono *m*

grand [grænd] grandioso, ilustre; magnífico; **~daughter** ['~ndɔ:tə] nieta *f*; **~eur** ['~ndʒə] magnificencia *f*; **~father** ['~df~] abuelo *m*; **~father clock** reloj *m* de péndulo; **~ma** ['~nmɑ:] abuelita *f*; **~mother** ['~nm~] abuela *f*; **~pa** ['~npɑ:] abuelito *m*; **~parents** ['~np~] abuelos *m/pl*; **~son** nieto *m*; **~stand** tribuna *f* principal

granny ['græni] *fam* abuelita *f*

grant [grɑ:nt] *s* concesión *f*; otorgamiento *m*; donación *f*; beca *f*; *v/t* conceder, otorgar; permitir; ***to take for ~ed*** dar por sentado; ***~ed that*** dado que

granulated ['grænjuleitid] **sugar** azúcar *m* granulado

grape [greip] uva *f*; ***sour ~s*** *fam* envidia *f*; **~fruit** pomelo *m*; toronja *f*; **~shot** metralla *f*; **~vine** vid *f*

graph [græf] gráfica *f*; **~ic** gráfico

grapple ['græpl]: *v/i* ***~ with*** esforzarse por resolver

grasp [grɑ:sp] *v/t* empuñar, asir; agarrar; *s* asimiento *m*; alcance *m*; **~ing** codicioso

grass [grɑ:s] hierba *f*; yerba *f*; césped *m*; **~hopper** saltamontes *m*; **~land** pradera *f*; **~ roots** *pol* básico; popular

grate [greit] *s* parrilla *f* de hogar; *v/t* rallar; enrejar; *v/i* ***~ on*** *fig* irritar

grateful ['greitful] agradecido, reconocido

grati|fication [grætifi'keiʃən] satisfacción *f*; **~fy** ['~fai] *v/t* satisfacer, complacer

grating ['greitiŋ] *s* verja *f*, reja *f*; *a* áspero; irritante

gratitude ['grætitju:d] agradecimiento *m*

gratuit|ous [grə'tju(:)itəs] gratuito; **~y** gratificación *f*

grave [greiv] *a* grave, serio; importante; *s* tumba *f*, sepultura *f*; **~digger** sepulturero *m*

gravel ['grævəl] grava *f*

graveyard ['greivjɑ:d] cementerio *m*

gravitation [grævi'teiʃən] gravitación *f*

gravity ['græviti] gravedad *f*; seriedad *f*

gravy ['greivi] jugo *m* de carne; salsa *f*

gray [grei] = **grey**

graze [greiz] *v/t* apacentar; rozar; *v/i* pacer

greas|e [gri:s] *f* grasa *f*; lubricante *m*; [~z] *v/t* engrasar; **~y** ['~zi] grasiento, pringoso

great [greit] grande; importante; estupendo; largo; principal; ***a ~ deal*** mucho; ***a ~ many*** muchos(as); **~aunt** tía *f* abuela; **2 Britain** ['~ 'britn] Gran Bretaña *f*; **~est** mayor, máximo; **~grandchild** bisnieto(a) *m* (*f*); **~-grandfather** bisabuelo *m*; **~-grandmother** bisabuela *f*; **~ly** mucho; muy; **~ness** grandeza *f*

Greece [gri:s] Grecia *f*

greed [gri:d] codicia *f*, avidez *f*; gula *f*; voracidad *f*; **~y** codicioso, avaro; goloso; voraz

Greek [gri:k] *a, s* griego(a) *m* (*f*)

green [gri:n] *a* verde; fresco; *s* pradera *f*; césped *m*; **~ bean** judía *f* verde; **~grocer** verdulero *m*; **~horn** bisoño *m*; novato *m*; **~house** invernadero *m*; **~s** verduras *f/pl*

greet [gri:t] *v/t* saludar; **~ing** saludo *m*

gregarious [gre'gɛəriəs] gregario

grenade [gri'neid] granada *f*

grey [grei] gris; **~ hair** canas *f/pl*; **~-haired** canoso; **~hound** galgo *m*; **~ish** pardusco

grid [grid] *s* rejilla *f*; **~iron** parrilla *f*

grie|f [gri:f] *s* pesar *m*; pena *f*; dolor *m*; ***to come to ~f*** fracasar; **~vance** agravio *m*; motivo *m* para quejarse; **~ve** *v/t* afligir; *v/i* apenarse; **~vous** penoso; doloroso

grill [gril] *s* parrilla *f*; *v/t* asar a la parrilla

grim [grim] ceñudo, torvo; sombrío; severo; siniestro

grimace [gri'meis] *s* mueca *f*; *v/i* hacer muecas

grim|e [graim] mugre *f*; **~y** sucio; mugriento

grin [grin] *v/i* sonreír bonachonamente *o* abiertamente

grind [graind] *s* trabajo *m* pesado y aburrido; *v/t* moler; afilar; hacer rechinar (*los dientes*)

grip [grip] *s* apretón *m*; agarro *m*; *v/t* apretar, agarrar; ***come to ~s with*** luchar a brazo partido

grisly ['grizli] espantoso, horrible

grit [grit] arena *f*, cascajo *m*; valor *m*

groan [grəun] *s* gemido *m*; quejido *m*; *v/i* gemir

grocer ['grəusə] tendero *m* (de ultramarinos); abacero *m*; **~y** tienda *f* de comestibles; *LA* tienda *f* de abarrotes

groin [grɔin] ingle *f*

groom [grum] *s* mozo *m* de cuadra; novio *m*; *v/t* cuidar

groove [gru:v] *s* ranura *f*, surco *m*; *v/t* acanalar

grope [grəup] *v/t, v/i* ir a tientas; ***~ for*** buscar a tientas

gross [grəus] *a* grueso; denso; grosero; *com* bruto; *s* gruesa *f* (*doce docenas*); **~ly** excesivamente

grotesque [grəu'tesk] grotesco

grotto ['grɔtəu] gruta *f*

grouch [grautʃ] *fam, Am* quejoso(a) *m* (*f*)

ground [graund] *s* suelo *m*, tierra *f*; causa *f*; *mar* fondo *m*; *v/t* fundar; *v/i mar* encallar; **~ control** *aer* control *m* desde tierra; **~floor** planta *f* baja; **~less** sin fundamento; **~nut** cacahuete *m*; **~s** terreno *m*; poso *m*; **~work** cimientos *m/pl*

group [gru:p] *s* grupo *m*; *v/t, v/i* agrupar(se)

grove [grəuv] arboleda *f*

grow [grəu] *v/t* cultivar; *v/i* crecer; volverse; ***~ dark*** obscurecer; ***~ fat*** engordar; ***~ into*** llegar a ser; ***~ old*** envejecer; ***~ up*** crecer; salir de la niñez; **~er** cultivador *m*; **~ing** *a* creciente

growl [graul] *s* gruñido *m*; *v/i* gruñir

grown-up ['grəunʌp] adulto

growth [grəuθ] crecimiento *m*; desarrollo *m*; vegetación *f*; *med* tumor *m*

grub [grʌb] *s* larva *f*; gusano *m*; *v/t, v/i* desarraigar, desyerbar; **~by** sucio; desaliñado

grudg|e [grʌdʒ] *s* rencor *m*; inquina *f*; ***bear a ~e*** guardar rencor; **~ingly** de mala gana

gruel [gruəl] gachas *f/pl*; **~(l)ing** duro, riguroso

gruff [grʌf] áspero; ceñudo; bronco

grumble ['grʌmbl] *v/i* refunfuñar, regañar; **~r** gruñón *m*

grunt [grʌnt] *s* gruñido *m*; *v/i* gruñir

guarant|ee [gærən'ti:] *s* garantía *f*; *v/t* garantizar, responder por; **~or** [~'tɔ] garante *m*; fiador *m*; **~y** ['gærənti] garantía *f*; fianza *f*

guard [gɑ:d] *s* guarda *m, f*; *mil* guardia *m*; centinela *m, f*; protección *f*; ***off ~*** desprevenido; ***on ~*** en guardia; *v/t, v/i* guardar, proteger; custodiar; **~ian** guardián *m*; *for* tutor *m*

Guatemala [gwɑ:ti'mɑ:lə] Guatemala *f*; **~n** *a, s* guatemalteco(a) *m* (*f*)

guess [ges] *s* suposición *f*, conjetura *f*; *v/t, v/i* suponer, conjeturar

guest [gest] huésped(a) *m* (*f*); invitado(a) *m* (*f*); **~house** casa *f* de huéspedes

guffaw [gʌ'fɔ:] carcajada *f*

guid|ance ['gaidəns] *s* gobierno *m*, dirección *f*; **~e** guía *m, f*; *v/t* guiar, conducir; **~e book** guía *f* del viajero; **~elines** normas *f/pl* generales

guild [gild] gremio *m*

guile [gail] astucia *f*; maña *f*; **~less** inocente, cándido

guilt [gilt] culpa *f*, culpabilidad *f*; **~less** inocente; **~y** culpable

guinea pig ['ginipig] conejillo *m* de Indias

guise [gaiz] apariencia *f*; ***under the ~ of*** so capa de

guitar [gi'tɑ:] guitarra *f*

gulf [gʌlf] golfo *m*, bahía *f*

gull [gʌl] gaviota *f*

gull|et ['gʌlit] esófago *m*; **~ible** ['gʌləbl] crédulo; **~y** barranco *m*

gulp [gʌlp] *s* trago *m*; *v/t* tragar; ***~ down*** engullir

gum [gʌm] *s* goma *f*; *v/t* engomar; **~s** encías *f/pl*

gun [gʌn] *s* fusil *m*; cañón *m*; *Am fam* revólver *m*, pistola *f*; ***jump the ~*** precipitarse; **~man** pistolero *m*; **~metal** bronce *m* de cañón; **~ner** artillero *m*; **~powder** pólvora *f*; **~shot** cañonazo *m*, escopetazo *m*

gurgle ['gɔ:gl] *v/i* gorgotear

gush [gʌʃ] *s* chorro *m*; *fam* efusión *f*; *v/i* salir en chorros

gust [gʌst] ráfaga *f*

guts [gʌts] intestinos *m/pl*, tripas *f/pl*; ***to have ~*** *fig* tener agallas *f/pl*

gutter ['gʌtə] arroyo *m*, zanja *f*; gotera *f*

guy [gai] *fam* tipo *m*; tío *m*; ***wise ~*** *fam* sabelotodo *m*

guzzle ['gʌzl] *v/t* engullir

gymnas|ium [dʒim'neizjəm] gimnasio *m*; **~tics** [~'næstiks] gimnasia *f*

gyn(a)ecologist [gaini'kɔlədʒist] ginecólogo *m*

gypsum ['dʒipsəm] yeso *m*

gyr|ate [dʒaiə'reit] *v/i* girar; **~ation** giro *m*, vuelta *f*

H

haberdashery ['hæbədæʃəri] mercería *f*

habit ['hæbit] hábito *m*; costumbre *f*; **~able** habitable

habitual [hə'bitjuəl] habitual, acostumbrado

hack [hæk] *s* caballo *m* de alquiler; corte *m*; *v/t* picar; machetear; **~ney coach** coche *m* de alquiler; **~neyed** trillado; **~saw** sierra *f* para metales

h(a)emorrhage ['heməridʒ] hemorragia *f*

h(a)emorrhoids ['hemərɔidz] hemorroides *f/pl*

hag [hæg] bruja *f*

haggard ['hægəd] emaciado; trasnochado, ojeroso

haggle ['hægl] *v/i* discutir; regatear (*el precio*)

hail [heil] *s* granizo *m*; pedrisco *m*; saludo *m*; *v/i* granizar; *v/t* llamar a; aclamar; **~storm** granizada *f*

hair [hɛə] pelo *m*; cabello *m*; vello *m* (*de brazo o pierna*); ***let one's ~ down*** comportarse con desenvoltura; ***make one's ~ stand on end*** ponerle los pelos de punta; ***split ~s*** andar en quisquillas; **~curlers** rulos *m/pl*; **~cut** corte *m* de pelo; **~do** peinado *m*; **~dresser** peluquero(a) *m* (*f*); **~drier** secador *m*; **~net** redecilla *f*; **~pin** horquilla *f*; **~-raising** horripilante; **~-splitting** quisquilloso; **~y** peludo

half [hɑ:f] *s* mitad *f*; ***in ~*** en dos mitades; ***cut in ~*** cortar por la mitad; *a, adv* medio (a); semi; casi; a medias; ***~an hour*** media hora; ***an hour and a ~*** hora y media; **~blood** mestizo *m*; **~ brother** medio hermano *m*; **~-caste** mestizo(a) *m* (*f*); **~hearted** con poco entusiasmo; **~ price** a mitad del precio; **~ sister** media hermana *f*; **~ time** *sp* intermedio *m*; **~way** a medio camino; en el medio; **~-witted** bobo; imbécil

hall [hɔ:l] vestíbulo *m*; sala *f*

hallo [hə'ləu] ¡hola!

hallow ['hæləu] *v/t* santificar; **~ed** sagrado

hallucinate [hə'lu:sineit] *v/t* alucinar

halo ['heiləu] halo *m*; aureola *f*

halt [hɔ:lt] *s* alto *m*; parada *f*; *v/t* parar; detener; *v/i* detenerse, hacer alto

halter ['hɔ:ltə] cabestro *m*; dogal *m*

halve [hɑ:v] *v/t* dividir en dos partes iguales

ham [hæm] jamón *m*

hamburger ['hæmbə:gə] hamburguesa *f*

hamlet ['hæmlit] caserío *m*; aldea *f*

hammer ['hæmə] *s* martillo *m*; *v/t* martillar

hammock ['hæmək] hamaca *f*

hamper ['hæmpə] *s* canasta *f*, cesta *f* grande; *v/t* estorbar

hand [hænd] *s* mano *f*; obrero *m*; *mar* tripulante *m*; manecilla *f* (*de reloj*); aplausos *m/pl*; escritura *f*; ***at ~*** a la mano; inminente; ***at first ~*** de primera mano; ***by ~*** a mano; ***~ in ~*** cogidos de la mano; ***on ~*** disponible; ***on the one ~*** por una parte; ***on the other ~*** por otra parte; ***to change ~s*** mudar de manos; ***to get out of ~*** desmandarse; ***to have the upper ~*** dominar la situación; ***to lend a ~*** echar una mano a; *v/t* dar; entregar, pasar; ***~ in*** presentar; ***~ over*** entregar; **~bag** bolsa *f* de mano; **~ball** balonmano *m*; **~bill** volante *m*; **~book** manual *m*; **~cuffs** esposas *f/pl*; **~ful** manojo *m*

handi|cap ['hændikæp] *s* handicap *m*; *fig* desventaja *f*; *v/t* estorbar; ***the ~capped*** los minusválidos *m/pl*; **~craft** artesanía *f*; **~craftsman** artesano *m*

handkerchief ['hæŋkətʃif] pañuelo *m*

handl|e ['hændl] *s* mango *m*, puño *m*; tirador *m*; picaporte *m*; **~ebar** manillar *m* (*de bicicleta*); **~ing** manejo *m*

hand|made ['hændmeid] hecho a mano; **~rail** pasamano *m*; **~shake** apretón *m* de manos; **~some** ['hænsəm] guapo; **~writing** escritura *f*; **~y** a mano; diestro; práctico; **come in ~y** venir bien

hang [hæŋ] *v/t* colgar; suspender; ahorcar (*el criminal*); *v/i* pender, colgar

hangar ['hæŋə] hangar *m*

hanger ['hæŋə] percha *f*

hangman ['hæŋmən] verdugo *m*

hangover ['hæŋəuvə] *fam* resaca *f*

haphazard ['hæp'hæzəd] *a* casual; fortuito

happen ['hæpən] *v/i* suceder, acontecer, ocurrir, pasar; **~ to (do) ...** (hacer) por casualidad; **~ing** acontecimiento *m*; espectáculo *m* improvisado

happ|ily ['hæpili] *adv* felizmente; **~iness** felicidad *f*; **~y** feliz; dichoso; **~y-go-lucky** despreocupado

harass ['hærəs] *v/t* acosar; hostigar

harbo(u)r ['ha:bə] *s* puerto *m*; *v/t* abrigar; albergar

hard [ha:d] *a* duro; sólido; firme; inflexible; riguroso, severo; difícil; **~ luck** mala suerte *f*; **~ of hearing** duro de oído; *adv* fuertemente; duramente, muy; **~ by** muy cerca; **~ up** apurado; **~en** *v/t* endurecer; empedernir; **~headed** testarudo; poco sentimental; **~hearted** duro de corazón; insensible; **~ly** apenas; **~ness** dureza *f*; **~ship** penuria *f*; penas *f/pl*; **~ware** quincalla *f*, ferretería *f*; **~y** robusto; audaz

hare [hεə] liebre *f*; **~brained** casquivano

harm [ha:m] *s* daño *m*; perjuicio *m*; *v/t* dañar, perjudicar; herir; **~ful** dañino, perjudicial; **~less** inofensivo

harmon|ious [ha:'məunjəs] armonioso; **~ize** ['~'naiz] *v/i* armonizar; **~y** armonía *f*

harness ['ha:nis] *s* arreos *m/pl*, guarniciones *f/pl*; *v/t* enjaezar; *fig* utilizar

harp [ha:p] *s* arpa *f*; *v/i* **to ~ on** repetir constantemente

harpoon [ha:'pu:n] *s* arpón *m*; *v/t* arponear

harrow ['hærəu] *s* grada *f*; *v/t* gradar; **~ing** horroroso

harsh [ha:ʃ] áspero, duro; chillón (*color*)

hart [ha:t] ciervo *m*

harvest ['ha:vist] *s* cosecha *f*, recolección *f*; *v/t* cosechar, recoger; **~er** segador(a) *m (f)*; cosechadora *f*

hash [hæʃ] *s* picadillo *m*

hashish ['hæʃi:ʃ] hachís *m*

hassle ['hæsl] *Am s* riña *f*; *v/t* molestar a

hast|e [heist] prisa *f*; **to make ~e** darse prisa; **~en** ['~sn] *v/i* darse prisa; *v/t* apresurar; apremiar; **~y** apresurado; precipitado

hat [hæt] sombrero *m*

hatch [hætʃ] *s* pollada *f*, nidada *f*; compuerta *f*; *mar* escotilla *f*; *v/t* empollar, incubar; tramar; *v/i* empollarse; (*ideas*) madurarse

hatchet ['hætʃit] machado *m*, hacha *f*; **bury the ~** hacer las paces

hat|e [heit] *s* odio *m*; *v/t* odiar, detestar; **~eful** odioso; **~red** ['~rid] odio *m*

haughty ['hɔ:ti] altanero; altivo

haul [hɔ:l] *s* redada *f* (*de peces*); botín *m*; tirón *m*; trayecto *m*; transporte *m*; *v/t* arrastrar, tirar de; transportar

haunt [hɔ:nt] *s* guarida *f*; lugar *m* favorito; *v/t* frecuentar; **~ed** visitado por fantasmas; **~ed house** casa *f* de fantasmas

have [hæv, həv] *v/t* tener; poseer; *v/aux* haber; **to ~ a mind to** tener ganas de; **to ~ had it** no poder más; **to ~ it out** poner las cosas en claro; **to ~ on** llevar puesto; **to ~ to** tener que

haven ['heivn] puerto *m*; *fig* refugio *m*

havoc ['hævək] estrago *m*; destrucción *f*; **to play ~ with** causar estragos en

hawk [hɔ:k] *s* halcón *m*; *v/t* pregonar

hawthorn ['hɔ:θɔ:n] espino *m*

hay [hei] heno *m*; **~ fever** fiebre *f* del heno; **~loft** henil *m*; **~stack** almiar *m*, **~wire** en desorden

hazard ['hæzəd] *s* azar *m*; *v/t* arriesgar; **~ous** arriesgado

haze [heiz] calina *f*

hazel ['heizl] avellano *m*; **~nut** avellana *f*; neblina *f*

hazy ['heizi] calinoso; nebuloso; confuso

he [hi:] *pron* él; **~ who** el que, quien

head [hed] *s* cabeza *f*; cara *f* (*de moneda*); jefe *m*; *geog* cabo *m*; *tecn* cabezal *m*; **not to make ~ nor tail of it** no verle ni pies ni cabeza; **~ or tails** cara o cruz; **~ over heels** precipitadamente; locamente; **off one's ~** loco; *v/t* dirigir; encabezar; encaudillar; *v/i* adelantarse, dirigirse; **~ache** ['~eik] dolor *m* de cabeza; **~ing** título *m*; **~land** promontorio *m*; **~lights** faros *m/pl*; **~line** titular *m*; **~master** director *m* (*de colegio*); **~ office** central *f*, oficina *f* principal; **~phones** auriculares *m/pl*; **~quarters** cuartel *m* general; **~rest** reposacabezas *m*; **~strong** voluntarioso; **~way: make ~way** avanzar

heal [hi:l] *v/t* curar; *v/i* cicatrizarse

health [helθ] salud *f*; sanidad *f*; **~ful** sano; **~y** sano, saludable

heap [hi:p] *s* montón *m*; *v/t* amontonar, acumular; colmar de

hear [hiə] *v/t* oír; sentir; escuchar; *v/i* oír; oír decir; **~er** oyente *m, f*, **~ing** oído *m*; audiencia *f*; **within ~ing** al alcance del oído; **~say** rumores *m/pl*

hearse [hə:s] coche *m* fúnebre

heart [ha:t] corazón *m*; *fig* fondo *m*; copa *f* (*de naipes*); **at ~** en el fondo; **by ~** de memoria; **to lose ~** descorazonarse; **to take ~** cobrar ánimo; **~ attack** ataque *m* cardíaco; **~beat** latido *m* del corazón; **~breaking** desgarrador; **~burn** acedía *f*; **~en** *v/t* alentar, animar

hearth [ha:θ] fogón *m*

heart|ily ['ha:tili] sinceramente; cordialmente; **~less** ['ha:tlis] despiadado; **~y** cordial; sincero; sano

heat [hi:t] *s* calor *m*; ardor *m*, vehemencia *f*; celo *m* (*animales*); *v/t* calentar; *fig* acalorar; *v/i* calentarse; **~er** calentador *m*

heath [hi:θ] brezal *m*; brezo *m*

heathen ['hi:ðən] *a, s* paga-

no(a) *m (f)*

heather ['heðə] brezo *m*

heating ['hi:tiŋ] calefacción *f*

heave [hi:v] *v/t* levantar; elevar; alzar

heaven ['hevn] cielo *m*; **good ~s!** ¡cielos!; **~ly** divino, celeste

heavy pesado; denso; fuerte; *fig* importante; fuerte, potente (*producto*); **~handed** opresivo

Hebrew ['hi:bru:] *a, s* hebreo(a) *m (f)*

hectic ['hektik] agitado

hedge [hedʒ] *s* seto *m* vivo; *v/t* cercar; rodear; dar respuestas evasivas; **~hog** erizo *m*

heed [hi:d] *s* caso *m*; hacer caso; *v/t* hacer caso de, atender a; escuchar; *v/i* prestar atención; **~less** descuidado

heel [hi:l] talón *m*; tacón *m* (*de zapato*); **to take to one's ~s** *fam* largarse, poner pies en polvorosa

hefty ['hefti] fornido; fuerte

heifer ['hefə] novilla *f*

height [hait] altura *f*; altitud *f*; talle *f*; *geog* cerro *m*; cima *f*, cumbre *f*; *fig* colmo *m*; **~en** *v/t* realzar; aumentar

heinous ['heinəs] horrendo

heir [εə] heredero *m*; **~ess** heredera *f*

helicopter ['helikɔptə] helicóptero *m*

hell [hel] infierno *m*

hello ['he'ləu] ¡hola!; *tel* ¡diga!

helm [helm] timón *m*

helmet ['helmit] casco *m*

help [help] *s* ayuda *f*; socorro *m*; remedio *m*; ayudante *m*; **~!** ¡socorro!; *v/t* ayudar, socorrer; **to ~ oneself** servirse; **it can't be ~ed** no hay más remedio; **~er** ayudante *m*; **~ful** útil; servicial; **~ing** porción *f*; **~less** desvalido; impotente; indefenso

helter-skelter ['heltəskeltə] *a* troche y moche

hem [hem] *s* dobladillo *m*; *v/t* dobladillar; **~ in** cercar, encerrar

hemisphere ['hemisfiə] hemisferio *m*

hemlock ['hemlɔk] cicuta *f*

hemp [hemp] cáñamo *m*

hen [hen] gallina *f*

hence [hens] *adv* de aquí; por esto; por lo tanto; **~forth** de aquí en adelante

hen|coop ['henku:p] gallinero *m*; **~peck** *v/t* tiranizar (*al marido*)

her [hə:] *pron pos* su (*de ella*); *pron pers* la, le, a ella; ella (*después de preposición*)

herald ['herəld] *s* heraldo *m*; precursor *m*; *v/t* anunciar; **~ry** heráldica *f*

herb [hə:b] hierba *f*

herd [hə:d] *s* hato *m*; rebaño *m*; manada *f*; *fig* tropel *m*; **~sman** vaquero *m*

here [hiə] *adv* aquí, acá; **~!** ¡presente!; **~ and there** aquí y allá; **~ goes!** ¡ahí va!; **~ you are!** ¡tenga!; **~'s to you!** ¡a su salud!; **in ~** aquí dentro; **over ~** por aquí; **right ~** aquí mismo; **~abouts** por aquí; **~after** en lo futuro; **~by** por la presente

heredity [hi'rediti] herencia *f*

here|sy ['herəsi] herejía *f*; **~tic** ['herətik] hereje *m, f*

here|upon ['hiərə'pɔn] en seguida; **~with** con ésta

heritage ['heritidʒ] herencia *f*

hermit ['hə:mit] ermitaño *m*; **~age** ermita *f*

hernia ['hə:njə] hernia *f*

hero ['hiərəu] héroe *m*; protagonista *m*; **~ic** [hi'rəuik]

heróico, **~in** ['herəuin] heroína *f farm*; **~ine** ['herəuin] heroína *f*; **~ism** heroísmo *m*

heron ['herən] garza *f*

herring ['heriŋ] arenque *m*; **red ~** pista *f* falsa

hers [hə:z] *pron pos* suyo, suya; el suyo, la suya; los suyos, las suyas (*de ella*); **~elf** [hə:'self] ella misma; sí misma; se

hesita|te ['heziteit] *v/i* vacilar, titubear; **~tion** vacilación *f*; hesitación *f*

heterosexual [hetərəu'seksjuəl] *a, s* heterosexual *m, f*

hew [hju:] *v/t* cortar; talar (*árboles*); labrar (*piedra*)

hey [hei] ¡oiga!; ¡eh!

heyday ['heidei] auge *m*; apogeo *m*

hi [hai] ¡hola!

hiccup ['hikʌp] hipo *m*

hid|den ['hidn] escondido, oculto; **~e** [haid] *v/t, v/i* esconder(se), ocultar(se); *s* cuero *m*; piel *f*; **~e-and-seek** escondite *m*

hideous ['hidiəs] horrible; feo; deforme

hid|e-out ['haidaut] escondrijo *m*; **~ing** *fam* paliza *f*; **go into ~ing** ocultarse; **~ing place** escondrijo *m*

hierarchy ['haiəra:ki] jerarquía *f*

hi-fi ['hai'fai] (de) alta fidelidad *f*

high [hai] alto; elevado; fuerte; extremo; **it is ~ time** ya es hora; **~ and dry** en seco; **~ and mighty** encopetado; **~ altar** altar *m* mayor; **~brow** intelectual *m, f*; **~chair** silla *f* alta; **~class** de clase superior; **~command** alto mando *m*; **~diving** saltos *m/pl* de palanca; **~fidelity** (de) alta fidelidad *f*; **~handed** despótico; **~heeled** de tacón alto; **~jump** salto *m* de altura; **~lights** puntos *m/pl* salientes; **~ly** altamente; muy bien; suma altura *f*; **2ness** Alteza *f*; **~pitched** agudo; **~powered** de gran potencia; *fig* deforme de presión; **~ rise** edificio *m* de muchos pisos; **~ school** *Am* colegio *m* de segunda enseñanza; **~ season** temporada *f* alta; **~spirited** animado; **~ tide** marea *f* alta; **~way** carretera *f*

hijack ['haidʒæk] *v/t* secuestrar (*avión*)

hike [haik] *v/i* hacer excursiones; *s* caminata *f*; excursión *f*; **~r** excursionista *m*

hilarious [hi'lεəriəs] hilarante; muy chistoso

hill [hil] colina *f*; cerro *m*; cuesta *f*; **~side** ladera *f*; **~y** ondulado, montuoso

hilt [hilt] puño *m*; empuñadura *f*

him [him] *pron pers* le; lo; él (*después de preposición*); **~self** ['~self] él mismo; sí mismo; se

hind [haind] *s* cierva *f*; *a* trasero, posterior

hind|er ['hində] *v/t* impedir, estorbar; **~rance** impedimento *m*, estorbo *m*, obstáculo *m*

hinge [hindʒ] *s* bisagra *f*; *v/t* engoznar

hint [hint] *s* indirecta *f*, sugestión *f*; **take the ~** darse por aludido; *v/t* insinuar, sugerir; *v/i* echar una indirecta

hinterland ['hintəlænd] traspaís *m*

hip [hip] cadera *f*

hippopotamus [hipə'potə-

məs] hipopótamo *m*

hire ['haiə] *s* alquiler *m*; arriendo *m*; sueldo *m*; *v/t* alquilar, arrendar

his [hiz] *pron pos* su, de él; (el) suyo, (la) suya; (los) suyos, (las) suyas (*de él*)

Hispanic [his'pænik] hispánico

hiss [his] *s* siseo *m*; silbido *m*; *v/t, v/i* silbar; sisear (*hablando*)

histor|ian [his'tɔ:riən] historiador(a) *m (f)*; **~ic(al)** [~'tɔrik(əl)] histórico; **~y** ['~əri] historia *f*

hit [hit] *s* golpe *m*; choque *m*; acierto *m*; *mús, teat* éxito *m*; *v/t* pegar, golpear; dar con; **~ or miss** a la buena ventura; **~ the nail on the head** dar en el clavo; **it ~s you in the eye** le salta a la vista

hitch [hitʃ] *s* tropiezo *m*, dificultad *f*; *v/t* atar; amarrar; **~hike** *v/i* hacer autostop

hither ['hiðə] *lit* acá, hacia acá; **~to** hasta ahora

hive [haiv] *s* colmena *f*

hoard [hɔ:d] *s* provisión *f*; *v/t, v/i* acumular y guardar; acaparar; **~ing** acaparamiento *m*; atesoramiento *m*

hoarfrost ['hɔ:'frost] escarcha *f*

hoarse [hɔ:s] ronco; **~ness** ronquera *f*

hoax [həuks] *s* engaño *m*; trampa *f*; *v/t* chasquear, engañar

hobble ['hɔbl] *v/t* manear; poner trabas a; *v/i* cojear

hobby ['hɔbi] pasatiempo *m*; afición *f*; **~horse** caballito *m* de madera

hobgoblin ['hɔbgɔblin] duende *m*

hobo ['həubəu] *Am* vagabundo *m*

hock [hɔk] *v/t* empeñar

hockey ['hɔki] hockey *m*

hoe [həu] *s* azada *f*, azadón *m*; *v/t* azadonar

hog [hɔg] *s* cerdo *m*, puerco *m*; *v/t* *fig* acaparar

hoist [hɔist] *s* montacargas *m*; *v/t* alzar, elevar; levantar; izar (*bandera*)

hold [həuld] *s* presa *f*; *fig* posesión *f*; dominio *m*; autoridad *f*; *mar* bodega *f* (*de un barco*); **to catch (get) ~ of** coger, agarrar; *v/t* tener; poseer; ocupar; sostener; **~ one's own** mantenerse firme; **~ up** detener; mostrar; **~ back** detener; asaltar; *v/i* no ceder; ser válido; **~ on** agarrarse bien; **~ out for** insistir en; **~ the line!** *tel* ¡no cuelgue!; **~er** titular *m/f*; arrendatario *m*; **~ing** posesión *f*; propiedad *f*; **~up** atraco *m*

hole [həul] agujero *m*; hoyo *m*; boquete *m*; *fig* aprieto *m*; **~ puncher** ['~pʌntʃə] perforadora *f*

holiday ['hɔlədi] día *m* de fiesta; **~s** vacaciones *f/pl*

Holland ['hɔlənd] Holanda *f*

hollow ['hɔləu] *a* hueco; vacío; hundido; *s* cavidad *f*; hondonada *f*; *v/t* excavar; ahuecar

holly ['hɔli] acebo *m*

holster ['həulstə] pistolera *f*

holy ['həuli] santo; 2 **Ghost, Spirit** Espíritu *m* Santo; 2 **Land** Tierra *f* Santa; **~ water** agua *f* bendita; **the 2 Writ** la Sagrada Escritura

homage ['hɔmidʒ] homenaje *m*; **to pay ~** rendir homenaje

home [həum] casa *f*, hogar *m*; domicilio *m*; residencia *f*; asilo *m*; **at ~** en casa; **to make**

oneself at ~ ponerse cómodo; ***to strike*** ~ dar en lo vivo; **~less** sin hogar; **~ly** acogedor; sencillo; feo; **~-made** casero, de fabricación casera; **~maker** ama *f* de casa; **~ rule** autonomía *f*; **~sick** nostálgico; ***to be ~sick*** tener morriña; **~ team** *sp* equipo *m* de casa; **~town** ciudad *f* natal; **~ward(s)** a casa, hacia casa; **~work** deberes *m/pl*

homicide ['hɔmisaid] homicidio *m*; homicida *m, f*

homosexual ['həuməu'seksjuəl] *a, s* homosexual *m, f*

Hondura|n [hɔn'djuərən] *a, s* hondureño(a) *m (f)*; **~s** Honduras *f*

honest ['ɔnist] honrado; recto; probo; honesto; **~ly** honradamente; **~y** honradez *f*; rectitud *f*

honey ['hʌni] miel *f*; **~comb** panal *m*; **~moon** luna *f* de miel; **~suckle** madreselva *f*

honk [hɔŋk] *aut* bocinazo *m*; *zool* graznido *m*

honorary ['ɔnərəri] honorario

hono(u)r ['ɔnə] *s* honor *m*; honra *f*; *v/t* honrar; respetar; condecorar; *com* aceptar; **~able** honorable

hood [hud] capucha *f*; *tecn* capota *f*; *Am* capó *m*

hoodlum ['hu:dləm] maleante *m*, matón *m*

hoodwink ['hu:dwiŋk] *v/t* engañar

hoof [hu:f] casco *m*; pezuña *f*

hook [huk] *s* gancho *m*; anzuelo *m* (*de pescar*); ***by ~ or by crook*** por fas o por nefas; *v/t* enganchar, encorvar; **~ed** ganchudo; **~y**: ***play ~y*** hacer novillos

hoop [hu:p] aro *m*

hoot [hu:t] *s* ululación *f*; grito *m*; bocinazo *m* (*de coche*); *v/i* ulular; gritar; tocar la bocina

hop [hɔp] *s* brinco *m*, salto *m*; *bot* lúpulo *m*; *v/i* brincar, saltar

hope [həup] *s* esperanza *f*; confianza *f*; *v/t*, *v/i* esperar, confiar; **~ful** lleno de esperanzas; prometedor; **~less** sin esperanza, desesperado

horizon [hə'raizn] horizonte *m*; **~tal** [hɔri'zɔntl] horizontal

hormone ['hɔ:məun] hormona *f*

horn [hɔ:n] cuerno *m*; asta *f*; *mús* cuerno *m*; trompa *f*; *aut* bocina *f*

hornet ['hɔ:nit] avispón *m*

horny ['hɔ:ni] córneo; calloso

horoscope ['hɔrəskəup] horóscopo *m*

horr|ible ['hɔrəbl] horrible; espantoso; **~id** ['~id] espantoso; **~ify** ['~ifai] *v/t* horrorizar; **~or** horror *m*, espanto *m*; **~or film** película *f* de terror

horse [hɔ:s] caballo *m*; *mil* caballería *f*; ***on ~back*** a caballo; **~ chestnut** castaño *m* de Indias; **~hair** crin *f*; **~man** jinete *m*; **~play** payasadas *f/pl*; **~power** caballo *m* de fuerza; **~ race** carrera *f* de caballos; **~radish** rábano *m* picante; **~shoe** herradura *f*; **~whip** látigo *m*; **~woman** amazona *f*

horticulture ['hɔ:tikʌltʃə] horticultura *f*

hose [həuz] manguera *f*

hosiery ['həuziəri] calcetería *f*

hospi|table ['hɔspitəbl] hospitalario; **~tal** hospital *m*; **~tality** [~'tæliti] hospitalidad *f*

host [həust] anfitrión *m*; multitud *f*; *relig* hostia *f*

hostage ['hɔstidʒ] rehén *m*

hostel ['hɔstəl] posada *f*; ***youth*** ~ albergue *m* juvenil

hostess ['həustis] anfitriona *f*; ***air*** ~ azafata *f*

hostil|e ['hɔstail] hostil; **~ity** [~'tiliti] hostilidad *f*

hot [hɔt] muy caliente; caluroso; *fig* acalorado, ardiente; (*comida*) picante; ***it is*** ~ hace mucho calor; ***to be*** ~ tener calor; **~-blooded** apasionado

hotel [həu'tel] hotel *m*

hot|head ['hɔthed] exaltado *m*; **~house** invernadero *m*

hound [haund] *s* perro *m* de caza; sabueso *m*; *v/t* acosar, perseguir

hour ['auə] hora *f*; ***by the*** ~ por horas; ***rush*** ~ hora(s) *f*/(*pl*) punta; ***keep late ~s*** trasnochar; ***wee ~s*** (*of the morning*) altas horas *f/pl* (*de la madrugada*); **~ly** cada hora

house [haus] *s* casa *f*; residencia *f*; *teat* sala *f*; ***it's on the*** ~ va por cuenta de la casa; ***to keep*** ~ llevar la casa; *v/t* [hauz] alojar; almacenar; **~coat** bata *f*; **~hold** casa *f*; familia *f*; **~keeper** ama *f* de llaves; **~maid** sirvienta *f*, criada *f*; **~warming party** fiesta *f* de estreno de casa; **~wife** ama *f* de casa; **~work** quehaceres *m/pl* domésticos

housing ['hauziŋ] alojamiento *m*; **~ estate** urbanización *f*

hover ['hɔvə] *v/i* revolotear, cernerse; **~craft** aerodeslizador *m*; **~ing** revoloteo *m*

how [hau] *adv* cómo; (*exclamación ante adjetivo o adverbio*) qué, cuán(to, -ta, -tos, -tas); ~ ***about that?*** ¿qué le parece?; ~ ***are you?*** ¿qué tal?; ~ ***do you do?*** mucho gusto; ~ ***far?*** ¿a qué distancia?; ~ ***long?*** ¿cuánto tiempo?; ~ ***many?*** ¿cuántos(as)?; ~ ***much?*** ¿cuánto?; ~ ***much is it?*** ¿cuánto cuesta?

however [hau'evə] *conj* no obstante; sin embargo; *adv* por muy ... que sea; aunque sea

howl [haul] *s* aullido *m*, alarido *m*; *v/i* aullar, dar alaridos (*animales*); bramar (*viento*); berrear (*niños*)

hub [hʌb] cubo *m* (*de rueda*); eje *m*, centro *m*

hubbub ['hʌbʌb] alboroto *m*, tumulto *m*

hubcap ['hʌbkæp] tapacubos *m*

huddle ['hʌdl] *v/t* amontonar; *v/i* ~ (***up***) acurrucarse

hue [hju:] color *m*; matiz *m*; ~ ***and cry*** alarma *f*

huff [hʌf]: ***get into a*** ~ ofenderse

hug [hʌg] *s* abrazo *m* fuerte; *v/t* abrazar

huge [hju:dʒ] enorme, vasto, inmenso

hull [hʌl] *s* vaina *f*; casco *m* (*de un buque*); *v/t* mondar, descascarar

hullaballoo [hʌləbə'lu:] alboroto *m*, jaleo *m*

hullo ['hʌ'ləu] ¡hola!

hum [hʌm] *s* zumbido *m*; *v/t* tararear; *v/i* zumbar

human ['hju:mən] humano; **~e** [~'mein] humano, humanitario; **~itarian** [~mæni'teəriən] humanitario; **~ity** [~'mæniti] humanidad *f*

humble ['hʌmbl] *a* humilde; *v/t* humillar

humbug ['hʌmbʌg] *s* farsa *f*; patraña *f*; (*persona*) farsante *m*, embustero *m*

humdrum ['hʌmdrʌm] monótono; rutinario

humidity [hju(:)'miditi] humedad *f*

humili|ate [hju(:)'milieit] *v/t* humillar; **~ation** humillación *f*; **~ty** [~'militi] humildad *f*

hummingbird ['hʌmiŋ'bə:d] colibrí *m*

humo(u)r ['hju:mə] *s* humor *m*; genio *m*; humorismo *m*; ***in a good*** (***bad***) ~ de buen (mal) humor; *v/t* complacer; **~ist** humorista *m*; **~ous** gracioso, chistoso

hump [hʌmp] joroba *f*

hunch [hʌntʃ] presentimiento *m*; **~back** jorobado *m*

hundred ['hʌndrəd] *a* ciento, cien; *s* ciento *m*

Hungar|ian [hʌŋ'geəriən] *a, s* húngaro(a) *m (f)*; **~y** Hungría *f*

hung|er ['hʌŋgə] *s* hambre *m*; *v/i* tener hambre; ansiar; **~ry** ['hʌŋgri] hambriento; ***to be ~ry*** tener hambre

hunt [hʌnt] *s* caza *f*; cacería *f*; *v/t* cazar; ~ ***for*** buscar; **~er** cazador *m*; **~ing** caza *f*, cacería *f*, montería *f*

hurdle ['hə:dl] *sp* valla *f*

hurl [hə:l] *v/t* tirar, lanzar

hurrah! [hu'rɑ:] ¡viva!

hurricane ['hʌrikən] huracán *m*

hurried ['hʌrid] apresurado; precipitado

hurry ['hʌri] *s* prisa *f*; ***to be in a*** ~ tener prisa; *v/i* apresurarse; *v/t* acelerar

hurt [hə:t] *s* daño *m*; herida *f*; *v/t* lastimar; dañar; hacer mal a; ***get*** ~ lastimarse; *v/i* doler

husband ['hʌzbənd] *s* marido *m*, esposo *m*; *v/t* economizar; **~ry** labranza *f*, agricultura *f*

hush [hʌʃ] *s* silencio *m*; *v/t* apaciguar; aquietar; *interj* **~!** ¡chito!; ¡silencio!; ~ ***up*** callar; encubrir

husk [hʌsk] *s* cáscara *f*; vaina *f*; pellejo *m*; *v/t* descascarar; desvainar

husky [hʌski] *s* ronco; robusto, fornido

hustle ['hʌsl] *s* ajetreo *m*; *v/t* empujar; apresurar; *v/i fam* menearse

hut [hʌt] cabaña *f*, choza *f*

hutch [hʌtʃ] conejera *f*

hyacinth ['haiəsinθ] jacinto *m*

hybrid ['haibrid] *a, s* híbrido *m*

hydrant ['haidrənt] boca *f* de riego

hydraulic [hai'drɔ:lik] hidráulico

hydro|carbon ['haidrəu'kɑ:bən] hidrocarburo *m*; **~chloric** [~'klɔrik] clorhídrico; **~gen** ['~ədʒən] hidrógeno *m*; **~gen bomb** bomba *f* de hidrógeno; **~plane** hidroavión *m*

hyena [hai'i:nə] hiena *f*

hygiene ['haidʒi:n] higiene *f*

hymn [him] himno *m*

hyphen ['haifən] guión *m*

hypnotize ['hipnətaiz] *v/t* hipnotizar

hypocri|sy [hi'pɔkrisi] hipocresía *f*; **~te** ['hipəkrit] hipócrita *m, f*; **~tical** [hipəu'kritikəl] hipócrita

hypothesis [hai'pɔθisis] hipótesis *f*

hysteri|a [his'tiəriə] histeria *f*, histerismo *m*; **~cal** [~'terikəl] histérico; **~cs** paroxismo *m* histérico

I

I [ai] yo

Iberian [ai'biəriən] *a* ibérico; *s* ibero(a) *m (f)*

ice [ais] *s* hielo *m*; *v/t* helar; alcorzar; *v/i* ~ ***over***, ~ ***up*** helarse; **~berg** ['~bə:g] iceberg *m*; **~box** nevera *f*; *LA* refrigerador *m*; **~cream** helado *m*; **~cube** cubito *m* de hielo; **~ hockey** hockey *m* sobre hielo

Iceland ['aislənd] Islandia *f*

ice|rink ['aisriŋk] pista *f* de hielo; **~ skating** patinaje *m* sobre hielo

ic|icle ['aisikl] carámbano *m*; **~ing** alcorza *f*; **~y** helado

idea [ai'diə] idea *f*; concepto *m*; **~l** *a, s* ideal *m*; **~list** idealista *m, f*

identi|cal [ai'dentikəl] idéntico; **~fication** [aidentifi'keiʃən] identificación *f*; **~fy** [~'dentifai] *v/t* identificar; **~ty** [~'dentiti] identidad *f*

ideology [aidi'ɔlədʒi] ideología *f*

idiom ['idiəm] lenguaje *m*; modismo *m*

idiot ['idiət] idiota *m, f*, necio *m*; **~ic** [~'ɔtik] idiota, tonto

idle ['aidl] *a* ocioso; perezoso; inútil; frívolo; ~ ***hours*** horas *f/pl* desocupadas; *v/t* ~ ***away the time*** malgastar el tiempo; *v/i* holgazanear; *tecn* marchar en vacío; **~ness** ociosidad *f*

idol ['aidl] ídolo *m*; **~atry** idolatría *f*; **~ize** ['~əulaiz] *v/t* idolatrar

idyll ['idil] idilio *m*

if [if] *conj* si; aunque; ***as*** ~ como si; ~ ***so*** de ser así

igloo ['iglu] iglú *m*

ign|ite [ig'nait] *v/t* encender; *v/i* inflamarse; **~ition** [ig'niʃən] ignición *f*; *aut* encendido *m*

ignoble [ig'nəubl] innoble

ignoran|ce ['ignərəns] ignorancia *f*; **~nt** ignorante; **~nt of** ignorar, desconocer

ignore [ig'nɔ:] *v/t* pasar por alto; desatender

ill [il] *a* enfermo; malo; ***fall*** ~ ponerse enfermo; ***feel*** ~ sentirse mal; *adv* mal; difícilmente; **~-advised** malaconsejado; **~-at-ease** incómodo; **~-bred** malcriado

il|legal [i'li:gəl] ilegal; **~legible** [i'ledʒəbl] ilegible; **~legitimate** ilegítimo; **~l-fated** malogrado; **~licit** [i'lisit] ilícito; **~literate** [i'litərit] *a, s* analfabeto *m*

ill|-mannered ['il'mænəd] maleducado; **~ness** enfermedad *f*; **~ogical** ilógico; **~-tempered** de mal genio; **~-timed** inoportuno

illuminat|e [i'lju:mineit] *v/t* iluminar; **~ion** iluminación *f*; alumbrado *m*

illus|ion [i'lu:ʒən] ilusión *f*; **~ory** [~səri] ilusorio

illustrat|e ['iləstreit] *v/t* ilustrar; explicar; **~ion** ilustración *f*; grabado *m*; lámina *f*; **~ive** ilustrativo

illustrious [i'lʌstriəs] ilustre

imag|e ['imidʒ] imagen *f*; **~inary** [i'mædʒinəri] imaginario; **~ination** imaginación *f*; fantasía *f*; **~ine** [~in] *v/t* imaginar; imaginarse

imbecile ['imbisi:l] *a, s* imbécil *m, f*

imitat|e ['imiteit] *v/t* imitar; **~ion** imitación *f*

immature [imə'tjuə] inmaduro

immediate [i'mi:djət] inmediato; **~ly** inmediatamente, en seguida

im|mense [i'mens] inmenso, vasto; **~merse** [i'mə:s] *v/t* sumergir, hundir

immigra|nt ['imigrənt] inmigrante *m, f*; **~te** ['~eit] *v/i* inmigrar

im|mobile ['iməubail] inmóvil; **~modest** [i'mɔdist] impúdico; **~moral** inmoral; **~mortal** inmortal; **~mortality** [imɔ:'tæliti] inmortalidad *f*; **~movable** inmóvil; **~mune** [i'mju:n] inmune

imp [imp] diablillo *m*

impact ['impækt] impacto *m*

impair [im'pɛə] *v/t* perjudicar; deteriorar; debilitar

impart [im'pɑ:t] *v/t* comunicar, impartir; **~ial** [~'pɑ:ʃəl] imparcial

im|passable [im'pasəbl] intransitable; **~passive** impasible; **~patience** impaciencia *f*; **~patient** impaciente; **~peccable** impecable

imped|e [im'pi:d] *v/t* estorbar, dificultar; **~iment** impedimento *m*

impending [im'pendiŋ] inminente

imperative [im'perətiv] *a* imperioso; *s gram* imperativo *m*

imperfect [im'pə:fikt] *a* imperfecto, defectuoso; *s gram* imperfecto *m*

imperial [im'piəriəl] imperial; **~ism** imperialismo *m*

imperil [im'peril] *v/t* arriesgar; poner en peligro

im|personate [im'pə:səneit] *v/t teat* hacer el papel de; **~pertinent** [~'pə:tinənt] impertinente; **~pervious** [~'pə:vjəs] **to** insensible a

impetuous [im'petjuəs] impetuoso

impetus ['impitəs] ímpetu *m*

impinge [im'pindʒ]: *v/t* ~ ***on*** abusar de

implausible [im'plɔ:zəbl] inverosímil

implement ['implimənt] instrumento *m*; herramienta *f*; utensilio *m*

implicat|e ['implikeit] *v/t* implicar; **~ion** implicación *f*; inferencia *f*

implicit [im'plisit] implícito

implore [im'plɔ:] *v/t* suplicar, implorar

imply [im'plai] *v/t* implicar; significar

impolite [impə'lait] descortés

import [im'pɔ:t] *v/t com* importar; *v/i* importar; ['impɔ:t] *s com* importación *f*; significado *m*

importan|ce [im'pɔ:təns] importancia *f*; **~t** importante

importer [im'pɔ:tə] importador *m*

impos|e [im'pəuz] *v/t* imponer; **~e upon** molestar; **~ing** imponente; **~ition** molestia *f*; carga *f*

impossib|ility [impɔsə'biliti] imposibilidad *f*; **~le** [~'pɔsibl] imposible

impostor [im'pɔstə] impostor *m*

impotence ['impətens] impotencia *f*

impoverish [im'pɔvəriʃ] *v/t* empobrecer; **~ed** necesitado

impractical [im'præktikəl] poco práctico

impregnate ['impregneit] *v/t* impregnar

impress [im'pres] *v/t* impresionar; imprimir; estampar; **~ion** impresión *f*; marca *f*; **~ive** impresionante

imprint ['imprint] *s* impresión *f*; huella *f*; [im'print] *v/t* imprimir; grabar

imprison [im'prizn] *v/t* encarcelar; **~ment** encarcelamiento *m*

improbable [im'prɔbəbl] improbable

impromptu [im'prɔmtju:] improvisado

improper [im'prɔpə] impropio; incorrecto

improve [im'pru:v] *v/t* mejorar; *v/i* progresar; mejorarse; **~ment** mejora *f*; progreso *m*

im|provise ['imprəvaiz] *v/t*, *v/i* improvisar; **~prudent** [im'pru:dənt] imprudente

impuden|ce ['impjudəns] descaro *m*; **~t** descarado

impuls|e ['impʌls] impulso *m*; impulsión *f*; **~ive** [im'pʌlsiv] impulsivo

impur|e [im'pjuə] impuro; adulterado; **~ity** impureza *f*

in [in] *prep* dentro de; en; *adv* dentro; de moda; **~ the distance** a lo lejos; **~ the house** en la casa; **~ the morning** por la mañana; **~ this way** de este modo; **to go ~ for** dedicarse a; *s* **the ~s and outs** recovecos *m/pl*

in|accessible [inæk'sesəbl] inasequible, inaccesible; **~accurate** inexacto; **~adequate** insuficiente; **~advertent** [~əd'və:tənt] inadvertido; accidental; **~advisable** no aconsejable; **~ane** [i'nein] necio, fatuo; **~animate** [~'ænimit] inanimado; **~appropriate** inoportuno; **~articulate** incapaz de expresarse

inasmuch [inəz'mʌtʃ]: **~ as** puesto que, ya que

inattentive [inə'tentiv] distraído; desatento

inaugurat|e [i'nɔ:gjureit] *v/t* inaugurar; **~ion** inauguración *f*

in|born ['in'bɔ:n] innato; **~capable** [in'keipəbl] incapaz

Inc. = **incorporated** *Am* sociedad *f* anónima

incapacitate [inkə'pæsiteit] *v/t* incapacitar

incendiary [in'sendjəri] *a*, *s* incendiario *m*

incense ['insens] *s* incienso *m*; [in'sens] *v/t* encolerizar

incentive [in'sentiv] estímulo *m*

incessant [in'sesnt] incesante

incest ['insest] incesto *m*

inch [intʃ] pulgada *f* (2,54 cm); **within an ~ of** a dos dedos de; **~ by ~** palmo a palmo

inciden|t ['insidənt] incidente *m*; **~tal** [~'dentl] no esencial, accesorio; **~tally** a propósito, de paso

incis|ion [in'siʒn] incisión *f*; corte *m*; **~ive** penetrante; tajante; **~or** incisivo *m* (*diente*)

incite [in'sait] *v/t* incitar, provocar

inclin|ation [inkli'neiʃən] inclinación *f*; declive *m*; tendencia *f*; **~e** [in'klain] *v/t* inclinar; *v/i* inclinarse; tender a

inclu|de [in'klu:d] *v/t* incluir; comprender; **~sive** inclusivo

incoherent [inkəu'hiərənt] incoherente

incom|e ['inkʌm] ingresos *m/pl*; entrada *f*; **~e tax** impuesto *m* sobre la renta; **~ing** entrante

incompa|rable [in'kɔmpərəbl] incomparable; sin igual; **~tible** incompatible

in|competent [in'kɔmpitənt] incompetente; **~complete** incompleto; **~comprehensible** [~'kɔmpri'hensəbl] incomprensible; **~conceivable** inconcebible; **~conclusive** inconcluyente; **~congruous** [in'kɔŋgruəs] absurdo; disonante; **~considerate** desconsiderado

inconsistent [inkən'sistənt] inconsistente; contradictorio

inconspicuous [inkən'spikjuəs] poco llamativo; modesto

inconstant [in'kɔnstənt] inconstante, variable

inconvenien|ce [inkən'vi:njəns] *s* inconvenientes *m/pl*; *v/t* incomodar; **~t** incómodo, inoportuno

incorporat|e [in'kɔ:pəreit] *v/t* incorporar; agregar; **~ed** *com* sociedad *f* anónima; **~ion** incorporación *f*

in|correct [inkə'rekt] incorrecto; **~corrigible** [in'kɔridʒəbl] incorregible

increas|e [in'kri:s] *s* aumento *m*; *v/t* aumentar; incrementar; *v/i* crecer; multiplicarse; **~ingly** cada vez más

incredible [in'kredəbl] increíble; **it seems ~** parece mentira

incredulous [in'kredjuləs] incrédulo

incriminate [in'krimineit] *v/t* incriminar

incumbent [in'kʌmbent] *s* ocupante *m/f*; *a* **to be ~ upon** incumbir a uno

incur [in'kə:] *v/t* incurrir en; contraer (*deuda*)

indebted [in'detid] adeudado; **to be ~ to** estar en deuda con; **~ness** deuda *f*; obligación *f*

indecent [in'di:sənt] indecente

indecisive [indi'saisiv] indeciso; incierto

indeed [in'di:d] en efecto; **~?** ¿de veras?; **yes, ~!** ¡sí, por cierto!

indefatigable [indi'fætigəbl] incansable

in|definite [in'definit] indefinido; incierto; **~delible** [~'delibl] indeleble; imborrable

indelicate [in'delikit] indelicado; indecoroso

indemni|fy [in'demnifai] *v/t* indemnizar; **~ty** indemnización *f*

indent [in'dent] *v/t* (en)dentar; *impr* sangrar; **~ation** mella *f*; *impr* sangría *f*

independent [indi'pendənt] independiente

in-depth [in'depθ] detallado; completo; trabajado

indescribable [indis'kraibəbl] indescriptible

indeterminate [indi'tə:minit] indeterminado

index ['indeks] índice *m*; **~ card** ficha *f*; **~ finger** índice *m*

India ['indjə] India *f*; **~n** *a*, *s* indio(a) *m* (*f*); **~n corn** maíz *m*; **~n summer** veranillo *m* de San Martín

indicat|e ['indikeit] *v/t* indicar; **~ion** indicio *m*; señal *f*; **~ive** indicativo; **~or** indicador *m*

indict [in'dait] *v/t* acusar; procesar; **~ment** acusación *f*; *for* sumaria *f*

indifferen|ce [in'difrəns] indiferencia *f*; **~t** indiferente; imparcial

indigenous [in'didʒinəs] indígena

indigent ['indidʒənt] indigente, pobre

indigesti|ble [indi'dʒestəbl] indigestible; **~on** indigestión *f*; empacho *m*

indign|ant [in'dignənt] indignado; **~ation** indignación *f*; **~ity** indignidad *f*; ultraje *m*

indirect [indi'rekt] indirecto

indiscre|et [indis'kri:t] indiscreto; **~tion** indiscreción *f*

indiscriminate [indis'kriminit] promiscuo; sin criterio; indistinto

indispensable [indis'pensəbl] imprescindible

indisposed [indis'pəuzd] indispuesto

indisputable [indis'pju:təbl] incontestable

indistinct [indis'tiŋkt] indistinto, confuso

individual [indi'vidjuəl] *a* individual; *s* individuo(a) *m* (*f*); **~ist** individualista *m/f*

indolent ['indələnt] indolente, haragán

indomitable [in'dɔmitəbl] indomable; invincible

indoor ['indɔ:] interior; de casa; *sp* en sala; **~s** en casa; (a)dentro; bajo techado

induce [in'dju:s] *v/t* inducir; **~ment** aliciente *m*

induct [in'dʌkt] *v/t* instalar; admitir; **~ion** *elec* inducción *f*

indulge [in'dʌldʒ] *v/t* consentir a; *v/i* **~ in** darse a, permitirse; **~nce** indulgencia *f*; **~nt** indulgente

industr|ial [in'dʌstriəl] industrial; **~ialist** industrial *m*; **~ialize** *v/t* industrializar; **~ious** aplicado; **~y** ['indʌstri] industria *f*

inedible [in'edibl] incomestible

ineffective [ini'fektiv] ineficaz

inefficient [ini'fiʃənt] ineficaz

inept [i'nept] inepto

inequality [ini'kwɔliti] desigualdad *f*; disparidad *f*

inert [i'nə:t] inerte

in|evitable [in'evitəbl] inevitable; **~excusable** imperdonable; **~exhaustible** inagotable; **~expensive** económico; **~experienced** inexperto; **~explicable** [~'eksplikəbl] inexplicable

inexpressible [iniks'presəbl] indecible

infallible [in'fæləbl] infalible

infam|ous ['infəməs] infame; **~y** infamia *f*

infan|cy ['infənsi] infancia *f*; **~t** criatura *f*; **~tile** ['~tail] infantil, pueril

infantry ['infəntri] infantería *f*

infatuat|e [in'fætjueit] *v/t* amartelar; atontar; **~ed with** encaprichado por; enamorado de

infect [in'fekt] *v/t* infectar; contagiar; **~ion** infección *f*; **~ious** infeccioso; contagioso

infer [in'fə:] *v/t* inferir, deducir; **~ence** ['infərəns] deducción *f*

inferior [in'fiəriə] *a*, *s* inferior *m*; **~ity** [~'ɔriti] inferioridad *f*

infernal [in'fə:nl] infernal

infertile [in'fə:tail] estéril

infest [in'fest] *v/t* infestar; **~ed with** plagado de

infidelity [infi'deliti] infidelidad *f*

infiltrate ['infiltreit] *v/t*, *v/i* infiltrar(se), penetrar

infinit|e ['infinit] infinito; **~ive** [~'finitiv] *gram* infinitivo *m*; **~y** infinidad *f*

infirm [in'fə:m] enfermizo; **~ity** debilidad *f*; enfermedad *f*

inflame [in'fleim] inflamar (*t fig*)

inflamma|ble [in'flæməbl] inflamable; **~tion** [~ə'meiʃən] inflamación *f*; **~tory** [~'flæmətəri] *med* inflamatorio; *fig* incitante

inflat|e [in'fleit] *v/t* inflar; **~ion** inflación *f*

inflect [in'flekt] *v/t* torcer; doblar; **~ion** inflexión *f*

inflexible [in'fleksəbl] inflexible

inflict [in'flikt] *v/t* infligir; imponer

influen|ce ['influəns] *s* influencia *f*; influjo *m*; *v/t* influir sobre, en; **~tial** [~'enʃəl] influente

influenza [influ'enzə] gripe *f*

inform [in'fɔ:m] *v/t* informar; avisar; **to be ~ed about** estar al corriente de; *v/i* **~ against** denunciar; **~al** informal; familiar; **~ation** información *f*; informes *m/pl*; conocimientos *m/pl*; **~er** denunciante *m*

infraction [in'frækʃn] infracción *f*

infrequent [in'fri:kwənt] poco frecuente

infringe [in'frindʒ]: *v/i* **~ on** abusar de

infuriate [in'fjuərieit] *v/t* enfurecer

infuse [in'fju:z] *v/t* infundir; inculcar

ingenious [in'dʒi:njəs] ingenioso; inventivo

ingenu|ity [indʒi'nju(:)iti] ingeniosidad *f*; **~ous** ingenuo

ingot ['iŋgət] lingote *m*; barra *f*

ingrained ['in'greind] arraigado; innato

ingrati|ate [in'greiʃieit]: *v/r* **~ate oneself** congraciarse; **~tude** [~'grætitju:d] ingratitud *f*

ingredient [in'gri:djənt] ingrediente *m*

inhabit [in'hæbit] *v/t* habitar; **~ant** habitante *m*

inhale [in'heil] *v/t* inhalar

inherit [in'herit] *v/t* heredar; **~ance** herencia *f*

inhibit [in'hibit] *v/t* inhibir; **~ion** inhibición *f*

in|hospitable [in'hɔspitəbl] inhospitalario; **~human** inhumano; **~imitable** inimitable

initia|l [i'niʃəl] *a*, *s* inicial *f*; **~te** [~ʃieit] *v/t* iniciar; **~tive** [~ʃiətiv] iniciativa *f*

inject [in'dʒekt] *v/t* inyectar; **~ion** inyección *f*

injunction [in'dʒʌŋkʃn] *for* entredicho *m*

injur|e ['indʒə] *v/t* lastimar; herir; dañar; lesionar; **~ious** [in'dʒuəriəs] dañoso; **~y** herida *f*; lesión *f*; daño *m*

injustice [in'dʒʌstis] injusticia *f*

ink [iŋk] tinta *f*

inkling ['iŋkliŋ] atisbo *m*; noción *f* vaga

ink|pot ['iŋkpɔt], **~well** ['~wel] tintero *m*

inland ['inlənd] *a* interior; *adv* tierra adentro

in-laws ['inlɔ:z] parientes *m/pl* políticos

inlay ['in'lei] *v/t* embutir; taracear

inlet ['inlet] cala *f*

inmate ['inmeit] inquilino *m*; paciente *m*; preso *m*

inmost ['inməust] más íntimo; más profundo

inn [in] posada *f*; fonda *f*

inner ['inə] interior; interno; **~ tube** *aut* cámara *f*

innocen|ce ['inəsns] inocencia *f*; **~t** inocente

innovation ['inəuveiʃən] novedad *f*

innuendo [inju'endəu] insinuación *f*

inoffensive [inə'fensiv] inofensivo

inordinate [i'nɔ:dinit] desmesurado

in-patient ['inpeiʃənt] paciente *m* (*f*) interno(a)

inquest ['inkwest] pesquisa *f* judicial

inquir|e [in'kwaiə] *v/t*, *v/i* pedir informes; **~e about** preguntar por; **~e into** indagar; **~y** consulta *f*; investigación *f*

inquisit|ion [inkwi'ziʃən] inquisición *f*; **~ive** [~'kwizitiv] inquisitivo; preguntón

insan|e [in'sein] loco; demente; **~ity** [~'sæniti] locura *f*; demencia *f*

inscri|be [in'skraib] *v/t* inscribir; **~ption** [~ipʃən] inscripción *f*; dedicatoria *f*

insect ['insekt] insecto *m*

insecure [insi'kjuə] inseguro

insensitive [in'sensətiv] insensible

insert [in'sə:t] *v/t* insertar; intercalar; introducir

inside [in'said] *a* interior; interno; *s* interior *m*; parte *f* de dentro; *adv* por dentro; **~ out** al revés; **~ and out** por dentro y por fuera; **~s** entrañas *f/pl*

insight ['insait] perspicacia *f*

in|significant [insig'nifikənt] insignificante; **~sincere** [insin'siə] poco sincero, falso; **~sinuate** [~'sinjueit] *v/t* insinuar; **~sipid** [~'sipid] insípido

insist [in'sist] *v/i* insistir; persistir; **~ence** insistencia *f*; empeño *m*

insolent ['insələnt] descarado, insolente

in|soluble [in'sɔljubl] insoluble; **~solvent** insolvente

insomnia [in'sɔmniə] insomnio *m*

inspect [in'spekt] *v/t* inspeccionar; **~ion** inspección *f*; **~or** inspector *m*

inspir|ation [inspə'reiʃən] inspiración *f*; **~e** [in'spaiə] *v/t* inspirar

install [in'stɔ:l] *v/t* instalar; **~ation** [~ə'leiʃən] instalación *f*

instal(l)ment [in'stɔ:lmənt] entrega *f*; *com* plazo *m*; **~ plan** pago *m* a plazos

instan|ce ['instəns] ejemplo *m*; caso *m*; **for ~ce** por ejemplo; **~t** *a* inmediato; instantáneo; *s* instante *m*; momento *m*; **~t coffee** café *m* en polvo; **~tly** en seguida

instead [in'sted] *adv* en cambio; **~ of** *prep* en vez de; en lugar de

instep ['instep] empeine *m*

instigate ['instigeit] *v/t* instigar

instil(l) [in'stil]: *v/t* **~ into** inculcar en

instinct ['instiŋkt] instinto *m*; **~ive** [in'stiŋktiv] instintivo

institut|e ['institju:t] *s* instituto *m*; *v/t* instituir; establecer; **~ion** institución *f*; establecimiento *m*

instruct [in'strʌkt] *v/t* instruir; mandar; **~ion** instrucción *f*; **~ions for use** modo *m* de empleo; **~ive** instructivo; aleccionador; **~or** instructor *m*

instrument ['instrumənt] instrumento *m*

in|subordinate [insə'bɔ:dnit] insubordinado; **~sufferable** [~'sʌfərəbl] insufrible; **~sufficient** insuficiente

insular ['insjulə] insular; *fig* de miras estrechas

insulat|e ['insjuleit] *v/t* *tecn* aislar; **~ion** aislamiento *m*

insulin ['insjulin] insulina *f*

insult ['insʌlt] *s* insulto *m*; [in'sʌlt] *v/t* insultar; injuriar
insur|ance [in'ʃuərəns] seguro *m*; **~ance policy** póliza *f* de seguro; **~e** *v/t* asegurar
insurrection [insə'rekʃən] insurrección *f*
intact [in'tækt] intacto
intake ['inteik] *tecn* toma *f*; cantidad *f* admitida
intangible [in'tænʒəbl] intangible
integ|rate ['intigreit] *v/t*, *v/i* intergrar(se); **~rity** [in'tegriti] entereza *f*; integridad *f*
intellect ['intilekt] intelecto *m*; **~ual** [~'lektjuəl] *a*, *s* intelectual *m, f*
intelligen|ce [in'telidʒəns] inteligencia *f*; información *f*; **~t** inteligente
intend [in'tend] *v/t* proponerse; querer hacer; pensar en; **~ for** destinar a
intens|e [in'tens] intenso; **~ity** intensidad *f*; **~ive** intensivo
intent [in'tent] *a* atento; empeñado; *s* propósito *m*; intento *m*; **~ion** intención *f*; **~ionally** adrede
inter [in'tə:] *v/t* enterrar
interact [intər'ækt] *v/i* influirse mutuamente
inter|cede [intə(:)'si:d] *v/t* interceder; **~cept** [~'sept] *v/t* interceptar
interchange ['intə(:)'tʃeindʒ] *s* intercambio *m*; [intə(:)'tʃeindʒ] *v/t*, *v/i* alternar(se); trocar(se)
intercourse ['intə(:)kɔ:s] trato *m*; comercio *m*; coito *m*
interest ['intrist] *s* interés *m*; beneficio *m*; **to earn ~** devengar intereses; **take an ~ in** interesarse por; *v/t* interesar; **~ing** interesante
interfer|e [intə'fiə] *v/i* entremeterse; **~e with** estorbar; **~ence** intromisión *f*; *elec* interferencia *f*
interim ['intərim]: **in the ~** entretanto
interior [in'tiəriə] *a* interior; interno; *s* interior *m*
interlude [intə(:)'lu:d] intervalo *m*; *teat.* intermedio *m*
intermediary [intə(:)'mi:djəri] intermediario *m*
intermission [intə'miʃn] *teat* descanso *m*
intermittent [intə'mitənt] intermitente
internal [in'tə:nl] interno
inter|national [intə(:)'næʃənl] internacional; **~play** interacción *f*
interpret [in'tə:prit] *v/t* interpretar; **~ation** interpretación *f*; **~er** intérprete *m, f*
interrogate [in'terəugeit] *v/t* interrogar
interrupt [intə'rʌpt] *v/t* interrumpir; **~ion** interrupción *f*
intersect [intə'sekt] *v/t*, *v/i* cruzar(se); **~ion** cruce *m*
intertwine [intə'twain] *v/t*, *v/i* entrelazar(se)
interval ['intəvəl] intervalo *m*
interven|e [intə(:)'vi:n] *v/i* intervenir; sobrevenir; **~tion** intervención *f*
interview ['intəvju:] *s* entrevista *f*; interviú *f*; *v/t* entrevistar(se con)
intestine [in'testin] intestino *m*
intima|cy ['intiməsi] intimidad *f*; **~te** ['~it] *a* íntimo; [~'eit] *v/t* insinuar
intimidate [in'timideit] *v/t* intimidar
into ['intu, 'intə] en; a; hacia dentro; adentro
intolerant [in'tɔlərənt] intolerante
intoxicate [in'tɔksikeit] *v/t* embriagar; *med* intoxicar; **~d** embriagado
intransigent [in'trænsidʒənt] intransigente
intravenous ['intrə'vi:nəs] intravenoso
intrepid [in'trepid] intrépido
intricate ['intrikit] intrincado
intrigu|e [in'tri:g] *s* intriga *f*; trama *f*; *v/i* intrigar; *v/t* fascinar; **~ing** intrigante
introduc|e [intrə'dju:s] *v/t* introducir; presentar; **~tion** [~'dʌkʃən] introducción *f*; **~tory** [~'dʌktəri] preliminar
intru|de [in'tru:d] *v/i* entremeterse; **~sion** [~ʒən] intrusión *f*
intuition [intju(:)'iʃən] intuición *f*
invade [in'veid] *v/t* invadir; **~r** invasor *m*
invalid ['invəli:d] *s* inválido *m*; [in'vælid] *a* inválido, nulo; **~ate** [~eit] *v/t* invalidar
invaluable [in'væljuəbl] inestimable
invariable [in'vɛəriəbl] invariable
invasion [in'veiʒən] invasión *f*
invent [in'vent] *v/t* inventar; idear; **~ion** invento *m*; invención *f*; **~ory** ['invəntri] inventario *m*
inver|se ['in'və:s] inverso; **~sion** inversión *f*; **~t** *v/t* invertir; **~ted commas** comillas *f/pl*
invest [in'vest] *com* invertir
investigat|e [in'vestigeit] *v/t* investigar; examinar; **~ion** investigación *f*; **~or** investigador *m*
invest|ment [in'vestmənt] *com* inversión *f*; **~or** *com* inversionista *m, f*
invigorat|e [in'vigəreit] *v/t* vigorizar; *fig* estimular; **~ing** vigorizador
invincible [in'vinsəbl] invencible
inviolable [in'vaiələbl] inviolable
invisible [in'vizibl] invisible
invit|ation [invi'teiʃən] invitación *f*; convite *m*; **~e** [in'vait] *v/t* invitar; convidar; instar; **~ing** atractivo; tentador
invoice ['invɔis] *com* factura *f*
in|voke [in'vəuk] *v/t* invocar; apelar a; **~voluntary** involuntario; **~volve** [~'vɔlv] *v/t* envolver; implicar; **~volved** complicado; **get ~volved in** embrollarse en
inward ['inwəd] interno; interior; **~ly** para sí
iodine ['aiəudi:n] yodo *m*
I. O. U. ['aiəu'ju:] *com* pagaré *m*
irascible [i'ræsibl] irascible
irate [ai'reit] airado; enojado
Ireland ['aiələnd] Irlanda *f*
iris ['aiəris] *anat* iris *m*; *bot* lirio *m*
Irish ['airiʃ] *a*, *s* irlandés *m*; **the ~** los irlandeses; **~man, ~woman** irlandés *m*, irlandesa *f*
iron ['aiən] *s* hierro *m*; plancha *f*; *a* férreo; de hierro; *v/t* planchar; **~clad** acorazado; **~ curtain** telón *m* de acero
iron|ic(al) [ai'rɔnik(əl)] irónico; **~ing board** tabla *f* de planchar; **~monger** ['aiənmʌŋgə] ferretero *m*; **~y** ['airəni] ironía *f*
ir|rational [i'ræʃənl] irracional; **~reconcilable** irreconciliable
irregular [i'regjulə] irregular; desigual
ir|relevant [i'relivənt] ajeno al caso; inaplicable; **~replaceable** [iri'pleisəbl] irreemplazable
irreproachable [iri'prəutʃəbl] intachable
irresistible [iri'sistəbl] irresistible
irresolute [i'rezəlu:t] indeciso
irrespective [iris'pektiv]: **~ of** sin consideración a
irresponsible [iri'spɔnsəbl] irresponsable; poco serio
irrevocable [i'revəkəbl] irrevocable; inalterable
irrigat|e ['irigeit] *v/t* regar; *med* irrigar; **~ion** riego *m*; *med* irrigación *f*
irritate ['iriteit] *v/t* irritar
Islam ['izlɑ:m] islam *m*
island ['ailənd] *s* isla *f*; *a* isleño
isolat|e ['aisəleit] *v/t* aislar, separar; **~ion** aislamiento *m*
Israel ['izreil] Israel *m*; **~i** *a*, *s* israelí *m, f*
issue ['iʃju:] *s* cuestión *f*; resultado *m*; sucesión *f*, prole *f*; emisión *f* (*de bonos, moneda, etc*); edición *f*; número *m* (*de revista, etc*); **at ~** en discusión; **evade the ~** esquivar la pregunta; *v/t* emitir; extender (*cheque, etc*); impartir (*orden, etc*); publicar (*libro, etc*); *v/i* salir; surtir; provenir
isthmus ['isməs] istmo *m*
it [it] *pron* él; ella; ello; *acc* la, lo; *dat* le; *impers* (*no se traduce cuando es sujeto gramatical*); **~ is hot** hace calor; **~ is late** es tarde; **~ is impossible** es imposible; **who is ~?** ¿quién es?
Italian [i'tæljən] *a*, *s* italiano(a) *m(f)*
italics [i'tæliks] *impr* letra *f* bastardilla
Italy ['itəli] Italia *f*
itch [itʃ] *s* picazón *m*; *v/i* picar
item ['aitəm] artículo *m*; detalle *m*; asunto *m* a tratar
itinerary [ai'tinərəri] itinerario *m*
its [its] *pron pos* su, sus (de él, de ello, de ella); **~elf** [it'self] *pron* él mismo, ella misma; ello mismo; **by ~elf** sólo; separado
ivory ['aivəri] marfil *m*
ivy ['aivi] hiedra *f*

J

jab [dʒæb] *s* pinchazo *m*; codazo *m*; *v/t* dar un codazo a; golpear
jack [dʒæk] *aut* gato *m*; sota *f* (*de cartas*)
jackal ['dʒækɔ:l] chacal *m*
jackdaw ['dʒækdɔ:] grajo *m*
jacket ['dʒækit] americana *f*; chaqueta *f*
jackknife ['dʒæknaif] navaja *f*
jade [dʒeid] jade *m*; **~d** hastiado
jagged ['dʒægid] dentado
jail [dʒeil] cárcel *f*, prisión *f*; **~er** carcelero *m*
jam [dʒæm] *s* confitura *f*; *fam* enredo *m*, lío *m*; *v/t* apretar; apiñar; obstruir; (*radio*) perturbar; *v/i* atascarse
janitor ['dʒænitə] portero *m*, conserje *m*
January ['dʒænjuəri] enero *m*
Japan [dʒə'pæn] Japón *m*; **~ese** [dʒæpə'ni:z] *a*, *s* japonés(esa) *m (f)*
jar [dʒɑ:] *s* tarro *m*; jarra *f*; cántaro *m*; sacudida *f*; choque *m*; *v/t* sacudir
jargon ['dʒɑ:gən] jerga *f*
jaundice ['dʒɔ:ndis] ictericia *f*
jaunt [dʒɔ:nt] excursión *f*; **~y** alegre
javelin ['dʒævlin] jabalina *f*
jaw [dʒɔ:] *s* mandíbula *f*; quijada *f*
jealous ['dʒeləs] celoso, envidioso; **~y** celos *m/pl*; envidia *f*
jeans [dʒi:nz] pantalones *m/pl* vaqueros
jeer [dʒiə] *v/i* burlarse, mofar; *s* burla *f*, mofa *f*
jelly ['dʒeli] jalea *f*; gelatina *f*; **~fish** medusa *f*
jeopardize ['dʒepədaiz] *v/t* arriesgar; comprometer
jerk [dʒə:k] *s* sacudida *f*; tirón *m*; *v/t* sacudir; tirar; *v/i* mover a empujones
jersey ['dʒə:zi] jersey *m*
jest [dʒest] *s* broma *f*, burla *f*; *v/i* bromear, burlar; **~er** bufón *m*
jet [dʒet] azabache *m*; chorro *m*; surtidor *m*; mechero *m* (*de gas*); avión *m* a reacción; **~ fighter** caza *m* a (de) reacción; **~ lag** síndrome *m* de los vuelos intercontinentales; **~-propelled** a reacción; a chorro
jetty ['dʒeti] muelle *m*
Jew [dʒu:] judío(a) *m (f)*
jewel ['dʒu:əl] joya *f*; alhaja *f*; rubí *m* (*de reloj*); **~(l)er** joyero *m*; **~(l)er's** joyería *f*; **~(l)ery** joyas *f/pl*
Jewish judío
jiffy ['dʒifi]: **in a ~** en un santiamén
jigsaw ['dʒigsɔ:]: **~ puzzle** rompecabezas *m*
jingle ['dʒiŋgl] *s* tintineo *m*, retintín *m*; *v/i* retiñir
job [dʒɔb] tarea *f*; empleo *m*, puesto *m*; asunto *m*
jocular ['dʒɔkjulə] jocoso
jog [dʒɔg] *v/t* empujar; *v/i* hacer footing; *s* empujón *m*, trote *m* corto; **~ging suit** chandal *m*; *LA* sudadera *f*
join [dʒɔin] *v/t* juntar, unir, acoplar; anexar; *com* asociarse a; *v/i* unirse; juntarse; confluir; **~ in** participar en; **~er** ebanista *m*; **~t** *s* junta *f*, juntura *f*; *anat* articulación *f*; asado *m* (*de carne*); *a* unido, junto; colectivo; común; **by ~t agreement** por común acuerdo; **~tly** en común
joke [dʒəuk] *s* chiste *m*, broma *f*; **play a ~ on** gastar una broma a; *v/i* bromear, hacer chistes; **~r** bromista *m*; comodín *m* (*de naipes*)
jolly ['dʒɔli] *a* alegre; divertido; jovial; *adv* muy
jolt [dʒəult] *v/t*, *v/i* sacudir, traquetear; *s* traqueteo *m*
jostle ['dʒɔsl] *v/t*, *v/i* empujar; codear
jot [dʒɔt] *s* pizca *f*; jota *f*; *v/t* **~ down** apuntar
journal ['dʒə:nl] *s* diario *m*; periódico *m* (*diario*); revista *f*; **~ism** ['~əlizəm] periodismo *m*; **~ist** periodista *m, f*
journey ['dʒə:ni] *s* viaje *m*; pasaje *m*; *v/i* viajar
joy [dʒɔi] alegría *f*, júbilo *m*; **~ful** alegre, jubiloso
jubil|ant ['dʒu:bilənt] jubiloso; **~ation** júbilo *m*; **~ee** aniversario *m*; *relig* jubileo *m*
judg|e [dʒʌdʒ] *s* juez *m*; árbitro *m*; conocedor *m*; *v/i* juzgar, opinar; *v/t* juzgar, sentenciar; **~ment** juicio *m*; fallo *m*; sentencia *f*; **2ment Day** día *m* del juicio final
judic|ial [dʒu(:)'diʃəl] judicial; **~ious** juicioso
jug [dʒʌg] jarro *m*
juggle ['dʒʌgl] *v/i* hacer juegos malabares; **~ with** engañar; falsificar; **~r** malabarista *m, f*
Jugoslav ['ju:gəu'slɑ:v] *a*, *s* yugoeslavo(a) *m (f)*
juic|e [dʒu:s] jugo *m*; zumo *m*; **~er** exprimidor *m*; **~y** jugoso, suculento; *fig* picante, sabroso
juke-box ['dʒu:k-] tocadiscos *m* automático
July [dʒu(:)'lai] julio *m*
jumble ['dʒʌmbl] *s* confusión *f*, mezcla *f*; *v/t* mezclar, confundir
jump [dʒʌmp] *s* salto *m*, brinco *m*; *v/i* saltar, brincar; sobresaltarse; **~y** nervioso
junction ['dʒʌŋkʃən] unión *f*; *elec, f c* empalme *m*
juncture ['dʒʌŋktʃə] coyuntura *f*
June [dʒu:n] junio *m*
jungle ['dʒʌŋgl] jungla *f*; selva *f*
junior ['dʒu:njə] *s* joven *m*; *a* menor, más joven
juniper ['dʒu:nipə] enebro *m*
junk [dʒʌŋk] junco *m* (*barca*); *fam* trastos *m/pl* viejos
juri|sdiction [dʒuəris'dikʃən] jurisdicción *f*; **~sprudence** ['~pru:dəns] jurisprudencia *f*; **~st** jurista *m*
jury ['dʒuəri] jurado *m*
just [dʒʌst] *a* justo, recto; merecido; genuino, legítimo; *adv* precisamente; exactamente; apenas; solamente; **~ about** poco más o menos; **~ as** en el momento en que; **~ as well** menos mal; **~ like that** así como así; **~ now** ahora mismo; **he has ~ come** acaba de venir
justice ['dʒʌstis] justicia *f*; juez *m*
justif|ication [dʒʌstifi'keiʃən] justificación *f*; **~y** ['~fai] *v/t* justificar
justly ['dʒʌstli] justamente; debidamente
jut [dʒʌt] *v/i* sobresalir; **~ out** proyectarse
juvenile ['dʒu:vinail] juvenil
juxtapose [dʒʌkstə'pəuz] *v/t* yuxtaponer

K

kaleidoscope [kə'laidəskəup] cal(e)idoscopio *m*
kangaroo [kæŋgə'ru:] canguro *m*
keel [ki:l] *s* quilla *f*; *v/i* **~ over** dar de quilla
keen [ki:n] agudo; afilado; sutil, vivo; entusiasta, interesado; **~ on** aficionado a; **~ness** agudeza *f*; entusiasmo *m*
keep [ki:p] *s* mantenimiento *n*; **earn one's ~** ganarse la vida; *v/t* guardar, conservar; mantener; llevar; proteger; seguir por; cumplir con, observar; **~ back** retener; **~ from doing** no dejar hacer; **~ in mind** tener presente, recordar; **~ up** mantener; **~ waiting** hacer esperar; *v/i* quedar(se); conservarse; continuar, seguir; **~ aloof, ~ away** mantenerse apartado; **~ on** continuar; **~ out!** ¡prohibida la entrada!; **~ to** adherirse a; **~ up** mantenerse firme; **~ up with** ir al paso de; **~er** guardián *m*; **~ing** preservación *f*; custodia *f*; **in ~ing with** en conformidad con; **~sake** ['ki:pseik] recuerdo *m*
kennel ['kenl] perrera *f*
kerb [kə:b] bordillo *m*
kerchief ['kə:tʃif] pañuelo *m*
kernel ['kə:nl] grano *m*; meollo *m*, núcleo *m*
ketchup ['ketʃəp] salsa *f* dulce de tomate
kettle ['ketl] caldera *f*; **a pret-**

ty ~ ***of fish*** bonito lío *m*; **~drum** atabal *m*; timbal *m*
key [ki:] *s* llave *f*; clave *f*; *mús* tono *m*; tecla *f* (*de piano o máquina de escribir*); *v/t tecn* enchavetar; **~board** teclado *m*; **~hole** ojo *m* de la cerradura; ~ **ring** llavero *m*; **~stone** *arq* piedra *f* clave
khaki ['kɑ:ki] caqui
kick [kik] *s* coz *f*, patada *f*, puntapié *m*; *fig* fuerza *f*, vigor *m*; ***for ~s*** para divertirse; *v/t* dar coces a; dar una patada a; ~ ***the bucket*** *fam* morirse; *v/i* dar coces
kid [kid] *s* cabrito *m*; *fam* niño(a) *m* (*f*); chico(a) *m* (*f*); *v/i fam* bromearse; ***no ~ding!*** ¡en serio!; ~ **gloves** guantes *m/pl* de cabritilla; **~nap** ['kidnæp] *v/t* secuestrar, raptar; **~napper** secuestrador *m*; **~napping** secuestro *m*
kidney ['kidni] riñón *m*; ~ **bean** judía *f*, frijol *m*
kill [kil] *v/t* matar; destruir; **~er** asesino *m*; **~ing** matanza *f*; asesinato *m*
kiln [kiln] horno *m*
kilogram ['kiləugræm] kilo *m*, kilogramo *m*
kilometre ['kiləumi:tə] kilómetro *m*
kilt [kilt] tonelete *m* escocés
kin [kin] parentela *f*; linaje *m*; **~ship** parentesco *m*
kind [kaind] *a* amable; cordial; bondadoso; cariñoso; ~ ***regards*** muchos recuerdos *m/pl*; *s* clase *f*, especie *f*; ***in*** ~ en especie
kindergarten ['kindəgɑ:tn] jardín *m* de infancia
kind-hearted ['kaind'hɑ:tid] bondadoso
kindle ['kindl] *v/t* encender; *v/i* arder
kind|ly ['kaindli] *a* bondadoso; *adv* amablemente; **~ness** bondad *f*
kindred ['kindrid] semejante; afín
king [kiŋ] rey *m*; **~dom** ['~dəm] reino *m*; **~ly** real; regio; **~-size** de tamaño extra
kinky [kiŋki] enroscado; *fam* excéntrico; pervertido
kipper ['kipə] arenque *m* ahumado
kiss [kis] *s* beso *m*; *v/t* besar
kit [kit] equipo *m*; caja *f* de herramientas
kitchen ['kitʃin] cocina *f*; **~ette** [~'net] cocina *f* pequeña
kite [kait] cometa *f*
kitten ['kitn] gatito *m*
knack [næk] destreza *f*; treta *f*, truco *m*
knapsack ['næpsæk] mochila *f*
knave [neiv] bribón *m*, pícaro *m*; sota *f* (*de naipes*)
knead [ni:d] *v/t* amasar
knee [ni:] rodilla *f*; **~cap** ['ni:kæp] rótula *f*; **~l** [ni:l] *v/i*: **~l *down*** arrodillarse
knickerbockers ['nikəbɔkəz], **knickers** ['nikəz] pantalones *m/pl* bombachos; bragas *f/pl*
knick-knack ['niknæk] baratija *f*
knife [naif] *s* cuchillo *m*; navaja *f*; *tecn* cuchilla *f*; *v/t* acuchillar
knight [nait] *s* caballero *m*; caballo *m* (*de ajedrez*); *v/t* armar caballero
knit [nit] *v/i* hacer punto, tejer, hacer calceta; fruncir (*el entrecejo*); *fig* unir; **~ting** labor *f* de punto; **~ting needle** aguja *f* de hacer punto; **~wear** géneros *m/pl* de punto
knob [nɔb] botón *m*; perilla *f*; bulto *m*
knock [nɔk] *s* golpe *m*; llamada *f* (*a la puerta*); *v/t*, *v/i* golpear, pegar; llamar (*a la puerta*); ~ ***down*** tumbar, derribar; atropellar; ~ ***out*** dejar sin sentido; **~er** aldaba *f*; llamador *m*; **~ing** golpeto *m*
knot [nɔt] *s* nudo *m*; lazo *m*; grupo *m*; *mar* nudo *m*; *v/t* atar, anudar; **~ty** nudoso; *fig* difícil
know [nəu] *v/t* saber; conocer; comprender; *v/i* saber; estar informado; ~ ***about*** estar enterado de; **~-how** pericia *f*; **~ing** hábil; sagaz; despierto; **~ingly** a sabiendas; **~ledge** ['nɔlidʒ] conocimiento *m*; saber *m*; ***to my ~ledge*** que yo sepa; **~n** conocido, sabido; ***to make ~n*** dar a conocer, hacer saber
knuckle ['nʌkl] *s* nudillo *m*, artejo *m*; *v/i* ~ ***under*** someterse
Koran [kɔ'rɑ:n] Alcorán *m*, Corán *m*

L

label ['leibl] *s* etiqueta *f*, rótulo *m*; *v/t* poner etiqueta a, rotular
laboratory [lə'bɔrətəri] laboratorio *m*
laborious [lə'bɔ:riəs] laborioso
labo(u)r ['leibə] *s* labor *f*; trabajo *m*; fatiga *f*; tarea *f*; faena *f*; mano *f* de obra; dolores *m/pl* de parto; ***hard*** ~ trabajos *m/pl* forzados; ***to be in*** ~ estar de parto; *v/i* trabajar; fatigarse; **~er** trabajador *m*; obrero *m*; **~-saving** que ahorra trabajo
lace [leis] *s* encaje *m*; cordón *m* de zapato; *v/t* atar
lack [læk] *s* falta *f*, carencia *f*; *v/t* carecer de; faltarle a uno; **~ing** carente de
laconic [lə'kɔnik] lacónico
lacquer ['lækə] laca *f*
lad [læd] muchacho *m*, joven *m*
ladder ['lædə] *s* escalera *f*; carrera *f* (*de media*); *v/i* correrse, desmallarse (*la media*)
laden ['leidn] cargado
ladle ['leidl] *s* cucharón *m*, cazo *m*; *v/t* sacar con cucharón
lady ['leidi] señora *f*; señorita *f*; **~bird** mariquita *f*; **~-in-waiting** dama *f* de honor; **~like** elegante, bien educada
lag [læg] *s* retraso *m*; *v/i* ~ ***behind*** quedarse atrás
lager ['lɑ:gə] cerveza *f* (añeja)
lagoon [lə'gu:n] laguna *f*
lair [lɛə] guarida *f*
lake [leik] lago *m*
lamb [læm] *s* cordero *m*; *v/i* parir (*la oveja*); ~ **chop** chuleta *f* de cordero
lame [leim] cojo; lisiado; *fig* débil, insatisfactorio
lament [lə'ment] *s* lamento *m*, queja *f*; *v/t*, *v/i* lamentar(se) (de); **~able** ['læməntəbl] lamentable, deplorable; **~ation** lamentación *f*
lamp [læmp] lámpara *f*; **~oon** [læm'pu:n] *v/t* satirizar; **~post** poste *m* de farol; **~shade** pantalla *f* de lámpara
lance [lɑ:ns] *s* lanza *f*; *v/t* lancear; **~r** lancero *m*; **~t** lanceta *f*
land [lænd] *s* tierra *f*; terreno *m*; finca *f*; campo *m*; país *m*; ***by*** ~ por tierra; *v/t* desembarcar; *v/i* desembarcar; aterrizar; **~ed** hacendado; **~ing** desembarque *m*; aterrizaje *m*; **~ing field** *aer* campo *m* de aterrizaje; **~ing gear** tren *m* de aterrizaje; **~lady** patrona *f*; **~locked** cercado de tierra; **~lord** patrón *m*; **~mark** mojón *m*; hito *m*; **~scape** paisaje *m*; **~slide** desprendimiento *m* de tierra
lane [lein] senda *f*; callejuela *f*; carril *m* (*de carretera*)
language ['læŋgwidʒ] idioma *m*; lengua *f*; lenguaje *m*
langu|id ['læŋgwid] lánguido; **~ish** *v/i* languidecer, consumirse; **~or** ['læŋgə] languidez *f*; **~orous** lánguido
lank [læŋk] flaco; lacio (*pelo*); **~y** delgaducho, larguirucho
lantern ['læntən] linterna *f*
lap [læp] *s* regazo *m*; falda *f*; *v/t*, *v/i* traslapar(se); **~el** [lə'pel] solapa *f*
lapse [læps] *s* lapso *m*; desliz *m*; transcurso *m* de tiempo; *v/i* transcurrir, pasar (*tiempo*); recaer; *for* caducar
larceny ['lɑ:səni] hurto *m*, robo *m*
lard [lɑ:d] manteca *f* de cerdo; **~er** despensa *f*
large [lɑ:dʒ] grande; amplio, vasto; grueso; ***at*** ~ en libertad; **~ly** en buena parte, mayormente; **~-scale** en gran escala
lark [lɑ:k] alondra *f*; *fam* travesura *f*
larynx ['læriŋks] laringe *f*
lascivious [lə'siviəs] lascivo
lash [læʃ] *s* tralla *f* (*del látigo*); latigazo *m*; azote *m*; **(eye)~** pestaña *f*; *v/t* azotar; *mar* amarrar; *v/i* ~ ***out*** atacar violentamente
lass, ~ie [læs, '~i] muchacha *f*, mozuela *f*
lasso [læ'su:] *s* lazo *m*; *v/t* lazar
last [lɑ:st] *a* último; pasado; final; extremo; ~ ***but one*** penúltimo; ~ ***night*** anoche; ~ ***week*** la semana pasada; ***the ~ time*** la última vez; ***this is the ~ straw!*** ¡no faltaba más que esto!; *adv* por último; finalmente; *s* último *m*; ***at*** ~ por fin; ~ ***but not least*** no hay que olvidar; *v/i* durar; continuar; subsistir; sobrevivir; **~ing** duradero, permanente; **~ly** por último; ~ **name** apellido *m*
latch [lætʃ] *s* aldaba *f*; picaporte *m*; *v/i* cerrar con aldaba; **~key** llavín *m*
late [leit] *a* tarde; tardío; difunto; último; antiguo; ***to get*** ~ hacerse tarde; *adv* tarde; ***to come*** ~ llegar tarde; ~ ***at night*** muy entrada la noche; ~ ***in life*** a una edad avanzada; **~r *on*** más tarde; ***at the ~st*** a más tardar; **~ly** últimamente
lathe [leið] torno *m*
lather ['lɑ:ðə] *s* espuma *f* (*de jabón*); *v/t* enjabonar
Latin ['lætin] *a* latino; *s* latín *m*; ~ **American** *a*, *s* latinoamericano(a) *m* (*f*)
latitude ['lætitju:d] latitud *f*
latter ['lætə] *a* posterior; último; segundo (*de dos*); *pron* ***the*** ~ éste, ésta, esto
lattice ['lætis] celosía *f*
laudable ['lɔ:dəbl] laudable
laugh [lɑ:f] *s* risa *f*; *v/i* reír; reírse; ~ ***at*** reírse de; ~ ***off*** tomar a risa; **~able** risible; **~ing stock** hazmerreír *m*; **~ter** risa *f*
launch [lɔ:ntʃ] *s* lancha *f*; *v/t* botar; lanzar; **~ing** lanzamiento *m* (*de cohetes*); *mar* botadura *f*; **~ing pad** plataforma *f* de lanzamiento
laund|erette [lɔ:ndə'ret] lavandería *f* automática; **~ry** lavadero *m*; lavandería *f*; ropa *f* de lavar; ropa *f* lavado o por lavar
laurel ['lɔrəl] laurel *m*
lavatory ['lævətəri] lavabo *m*; retrete *m*
lavender ['lævində] lavanda *f*
lavish ['læviʃ] *a* profuso; pródigo; *v/t* ~ ***on*** colmar a
law [lɔ:] ley *f*; derecho *m*, jurisprudencia *f*; *sp* regla *f*; ~ ***and order*** orden *m* público; ~ **court** tribunal *m* de justicia; **~ful** legal, lícito, legítimo; **~less** ilegal; anárquico
lawn [lɔ:n] césped *m*; **~mower** ['~məuə] cortacésped *m*
law|suit ['lɔ:sju:t] pleito *m*; **~yer** ['~jə] abogado *m*
lax [læks] laxo, flojo; **~ative** ['~ətiv] *a*, *s* laxante *m*
lay [lei] *s* laico *m*; *v/t* poner; colocar; tumbar; ~ ***aside*** dejar a un lado; ~ ***bare*** poner al descubierto; ~ ***before*** exponer a; ~ ***out*** tender; gastar; planificar; ~ ***up*** acumular; guardar; ***to be laid up*** guardar cama; *v/i* poner (*huevos*); ~ ***off*** *fam* quitarse de encima
layer ['leiə] capa *f*
layette [lei'et] ajuar *m* (*de niño*)
layman ['leimən] lego *m*
lay|off ['leiɔf] despido *m* provisional; **~out** trazado *m*; *impr* composición *f*
lazy ['leizi] perezoso, holgazán
lead [li:d] *s* delantera *f*; dirección *f*; *teat* papel *m* principal; *elec* conductor *m*; traílla *f*; *v/t* guiar, conducir; acaudillar; *v/i* ir primero; ~ ***to*** llevar a; ~ ***to nothing*** no dar resultado; ~ ***up to*** conducir a
lead [led] plomo *m*; mina *f* (*de lápiz*); *mar* sonda *f*; **~en** plomoso
lead|er ['li:də] guía *m*, *f*; líder *m*, caudillo *m*; editorial *m*; **~ing** principal
leaf [li:f] *s* hoja *f*; ***turn over a new*** ~ reformarse; *v/i* ~ ***through*** hojear; **~let** folleto *m*; **~y** frondoso
league [li:g] *s* liga *f*
leak [li:k] *s* gotera *f*; escape *m*; *v/i* gotear; salirse; escaparse; **~age** goteo *m*; escape *m*, fuga *f*; **~y** agujerado; llovedizo (*techo, etc*)
lean [li:n] *a* flaco; magro; *v/i* apoyarse; inclinarse; ~ ***out*** asomarse; **~ing** propensión *f*, inclinación *f*
leap [li:p] *s* salto *m*, brinco *m*; *v/i* saltar, brincar; ~ **year** año *m* bisiesto
learn [lə:n] *v/t*, *v/i* aprender; enterarse de; **~ed** ['~id] docto, erudito; **~er** principiante *m*, *f*; estudiante *m*, *f*; **~ing** saber *m*
lease [li:s] *s* arriendo *m*; *v/t* arrendar
leash [li:ʃ] *s* traílla *f*; correa *f*
least [li:st] *a* mínimo; menor; más pequeño; ***that's the ~ of it*** eso es lo de menos; *s* lo menos; ***at*** ~ por lo menos; ***not in the*** ~ de ninguna manera; *adv* menos
leather ['leðə] cuero *m*
leave [li:v] *s* permiso *m*, vacaciones *f/pl*; *mil* licencia *f*; ***to take (one's)*** ~ despedirse; *v/i* salir, marcharse; *v/t* dejar; abandonar, salir de; ~ ***out*** omitir
leaven ['levn] levadura *f*
lecherous ['letʃərəs] lascivo
lecture ['lektʃə] *s* conferencia *f*; reprimenda *f*; *v/i* dictar conferencias, disertar; *v/t* sermonear; **~r** conferenciante *m*
ledge [ledʒ] repisa *f*; reborde *m*
ledger ['ledʒə] *com* libro *m* mayor
lee [li:] sotavento *m*
leech [li:tʃ] *s* sanguijuela *f*
leek [li:k] puerro *m*
leer [liə] *v/i* mirar de reojo (*maliciosa o socarronamente*); *s* mirada *f* de soslayo
left [left] *a* izquierdo; *s* izquierda *f*; ***to be ~ over*** sobrar; ***on the*** ~ a la izquierda; ***to the*** ~ a la izquierda; **~handed** zurdo; **~ist** *a*, *s* izquierdista *m*, *f*
left-luggage office ['left-'lʌgidʒ'ɔfis] consigna *f*
leg [leg] pierna *f*; pata *f* (*de animales*); ***to pull one's*** ~ tomarle el pelo a alguien
legacy ['legəsi] herencia *f*, legado *m*
legal ['li:gəl] legal, jurídico; legítimo, lícito; ***to take ~ action*** entablar juicio; **~ize** *v/t* legitimar, legalizar
legation [li'geiʃən] legación *f*
legend ['ledʒənd] leyenda *f*; **~ary** legendario, fabuloso
legible ['ledʒəbl] legible
legion ['li:dʒən] legión *f*
legislat|ion [ledʒis'leiʃən] legislación *f*; **~ive** ['~lətiv] legislativo; **~or** ['~leitə] legislador *m*
legitimate [li'dʒitimit] *a* legítimo; [~eit] *v/t* legitimar
leisure ['leʒə] ocio *m*; tiempo *m* libre; ***at*** ~ con sosiego; ***a life of*** ~ una vida regalada; ~ ***time*** ratos *m/pl* libres; **~ly** pausadamente; despacio
lemon ['lemən] limón *m*; **~ade** [~'neid] limonada *f*
lend [lend] *v/t* prestar; **~ing library** biblioteca *f* circulante
length [leŋθ] *s* longitud *f*, largo *m*; trozo *m*; duración *f*; ***at*** ~ por fin; **~en** *v/t*, *v/i* alargar(se), estirar(se); prolongar(se); **~wise** ['~waiz] de largo; **~y** largo; extenso
lenient ['li:njənt] indulgente, clemente
lens [lenz] lente *f*
Lent [lent] cuaresma *f*
lentil ['lentil] lenteja *f*
leopard ['lepəd] leopardo *m*
leprosy ['leprəsi] lepra *f*
less [les] *a* menor; menos; *adv* menos; ***to grow*** ~ disminuir, menguar; ~ ***and*** ~ cada vez menos; ***more or*** ~ más o menos
less|en ['lesn] *v/t* disminuir, reducir; **~er** menor, más pequeño
lesson ['lesn] lección *f*
lest [lest] *conj* para que no; no sea que; por miedo de
let [let] *v/t* dejar, permitir; alquilar; ~ ***alone*** menos aún; ~ ***down*** bajar; *fam* decepcionar; ~ ***go*** soltar; ~ ***in*** admitir; ~ ***off*** disparar, descargar; ~ ***out*** dejar salir; *v/i* alquilarse; ~ ***up*** moderarse; ***to*** ~ se alquila; **~down** decepción *f*
lethal ['li:θəl] mortal
letter ['letə] *s* carta *f*; letra *f*; ~ ***of credit*** carta de crédito; ***to the*** ~ al pie de la letra; *v/t* estampar con letras; ~ **box** buzón *m*; **~head** membrete *m*
lettuce ['letis] lechuga *f*
level ['levl] *s* nivel *m*, altura *f*; llanura *f*; ***on the*** ~ *fam* honesto; *a* llano; igual, plano; ~ ***crossing*** paso *m* a nivel; *v/t* nivelar; igualar; derribar; allanar; **~-headed** sensato
lever ['li:və] palanca *f*
levity ['leviti] ligereza *f*
levy ['levi] *s* leva *f*; recauda-

ción *f* (*de impuestos*); *v/t* imponer tributo; *mil* reclutar
lewd [lu:d] lascivo; obsceno
liab|ility [laiə'biliti] responsabilidad *f*; obligación *f*; *pl com* pasivo *m*; **~le** ['laiəbl] responsable; expuesto (a)
liaison [li'eizɔ:n] enlace *m*
liar ['laiə] mentiroso(a) *m* (*f*)
libel ['laibəl] *s* difamación *f*; *v/t* difamar; calumniar
liberal ['libərəl] *a* liberal, generoso; *s* liberal *m, f*; **~ism** liberalismo *m*
liberat|e ['libəreit] *v/t* liberar; **~ion** liberación *f*
liberty ['libəti] libertad *f*; **at ~** libre, en libertad; **take the ~ of** tomarse la libertad de
librar|ian [lai'brɛəriən] bibliotecario(a) *m* (*f*); **~y** ['~əri] biblioteca *f*
lice [lais] *pl* de **louse** piojos *m/pl*
licen|ce ['laisəns] licencia *f*; permiso *m*; autorización *f*; título *m*; **~ce plate** placa *f* de matrícula; **~se** ['~səns] *v/t* licenciar, autorizar; **~see** [~'si:] concesionario *m*
lick [lik] *s* lamedura *f*; *v/t* lamer; *fam* cascar; derrotar; **~ing** *fam* paliza *f*
licorice ['likəris] regaliz *m*
lid [lid] tapa *f*; *anat* párpado *m*
lie [lai] *s* mentira *f*; embuste *m*; **white ~** mentirilla *f*; *v/i* mentir
lie [lai] *s* posición *f*; *v/i* estar acostado; yacer; estar colocado, situado; **~ down** acostarse, echarse
lieu [lju:]: **in ~ of** en lugar de
lieutenant [lef'tenənt, *Am* lu:'tenənt] teniente *m*
life [laif] vida *f*; existencia *f*; **for ~** de por vida; **never in my ~** en mi vida; **~ annuity** renta *f* vitalicia; **~belt** cinturón *m* salvavidas; **~boat** bote *m* salvavidas; **~guard** vigilante *m* de playa; **~ jacket** chaleco *m* salvavidas; **~less** exánime; muerto; **~like** natural; **~long** de toda la vida; **~time** (el curso de la) vida *f*
lift [lift] *s* ascensor *m*; montacargas *m*; alza *f*; **to give someone a ~** llevar a uno en auto; *v/t* elevar, subir, levantar; *v/i* disiparse; **~-off** *aer* despegue *m*
light [lait] *s* luz *f*; claridad *f*; lumbre *f*; día *m*; **have you got a ~?** ¿tiene fuego?; *a* ligero; claro; *v/t* encender; alumbrar, iluminar; **~ bulb** bombilla *f*; **~en** *v/t* alumbrar; aligerar (*peso*); aliviar; **~er** mechero *m*, encendedor *m*; **~headed** ligero de cascos; **~house** faro *m*; **~ing** alumbrado *m*; **~ly** ligeramente; **~ning** ['~niŋ] relámpago *m*; **~ning conductor** pararrayos *m*; **~weight** peso *m* ligero
like [laik] *a* semejante, parecido; **what is he ~?** ¿cómo es?; *prep* como, a manera de; tal como; *s* semejante *m*; **and the ~** y cosas por el estilo; *v/t* querer, tener afecto a; gustar; **I ~ tea** me gusta el té; **~ better** preferir; **~able** simpático; **~lihood** ['laiklihud] probabilidad *f*; **~ly** probable; verosímil; **~ness** parecido *m*, semejanza *f*; retrato *m*; **~wise** ['~waiz] igualmente
liking ['laikiŋ] simpatía *f*; agrado *m*
lilac ['lailək] lila *f*
lily ['lili] lirio *m*
limb [lim] *anat* miembro *m*; *bot* rama *f*
lime [laim] *s* cal *f*; *bot* lima *f*; *v/t* encalar, abonar con cal; **~light** luz *f* de calcio; **to be in the ~light** *fig* ser el centro de atención; **~ tree** limero *m*; tilo *m*
limit ['limit] *s* límite *m*; **that's the ~!** *fam* ¡esto es el colmo!; **to the ~** hasta no más; *v/t* limitar, restringir; **~ation** limitación *f*
limousine ['limuzi:n] limusina *f*
limp [limp] *a* flojo; *v/i* cojear
line [lain] *s* línea *f*; raya *f*, hilera *f*; cuerda *f*; *f c* vía *f*, *impr* renglón *m*; *com* especialidad *f*, ramo *m*; **draw the ~** fijar límites; detenerse; **to stand in ~** hacer cola; *v/t* alinear; rayar; revestir, forrar; *v/i* **~ up** ponerse en fila; **~age** ['liniidʒ] linaje *m*; **~ar** linear, lineal
linen ['linin] hilo *m*, lino *m*; lienzo *m*; lencería *f*; ropa *f* blanca
liner ['lainə] transatlántico *m*; vapor *m* de línea
line-up ['lainʌp] alineación *f*
linger ['liŋgə] *v/i* tardar, demorarse
lingerie ['lænʒəri] ropa *f* interior de mujer
lining ['lainiŋ] forro *m*
link [liŋk] *s* eslabón *m*; enlace *m*; *v/t* enlazar, unir; **~ up** enlazarse; *aer* acoplarse
lion ['laiən] león *m*; **~ess** leona *f*
lip [lip] labio *m*; **to lick one's ~s** chuparse los dedos; **~stick** barra *f* de labios
liquid ['likwid] *a, s* líquido *m*; **~ate** *v/t* liquidar
liquor ['likə] licor *m*; bebidas *f/pl* alcohólicas
liquorice ['likəris] regaliz *m*
lisp [lisp] *s* ceceo *m*; *v/i* cecear
list [list] *s* lista *f*; *v/t* catalogar; registrar; inscribir
listen ['lisn] *v/i* escuchar; oír; **~er** oyente *m, f* (*de radio*)
listless ['listlis] indiferente
litany ['litəni] letanía *f*
liter = **litre**
literal ['litərəl] literal
litera|ry ['litərəri] literario; **~ture** ['~ritʃə] literatura *f*
lithe [laið] ágil; flexible
litre ['li:tə] litro *m*
litter ['litə] *s* litera *f*; camilla *f*; camada *f*; desechos *m/pl*; *v/t* esparcir
little ['litl] *a* pequeño; poco; **a ~** un poquito *m*; **~ finger** meñique *m*; *s* poco *m*; **~ by ~** poco a poco; *adv* poco
liv|e [laiv] *a* vivo; *elec* cargado; *TV* vivo; [liv] *v/i* vivir; **long ~e!** ¡viva!; **~e and learn** vivir para ver; *v/t* llevar; tener; pasar; **~e it up** darse la buena vida; **~elihood** ['laivlihud] sustento *m*; **~ely** animado
liver ['livə] hígado *m*
livestock ['laivstɔk] ganado *m*
livid ['livid] lívido; furioso
living ['liviŋ] *a* vivo; *s* **make a ~** ganarse la vida; **~ room** sala *f* de estar
lizard ['lizəd] lagarto *m*
load [ləud] *s* carga *f*; *v/t* cargar; colmar
loaf [ləuf] *s* barra *f* de pan; *v/i* holgazanear
loam [ləum] marga *f*
loan [ləun] *s* préstamo *m*, empréstito *m*; **on ~** prestado; *v/t* prestar
loath [ləuθ] renuente; **~e** *v/t* detestar; **~some** ['~ðsəm] repugnante
lobby ['lɔbi] vestíbulo *m*, antesala *f*; **~ing** cabildeo *m*
lobe [ləub] lóbulo *m*
lobster ['lɔbstə] langosta *f*
loca|l ['ləukəl] *a* local; *s fam* taberna *f* del barrio; **~lity** [~'kæliti] localidad *f*; **~lize** *v/t* localizar; **~te** [~'keit] *v/t* situar, localizar; **~tion** colocación *f*; localidad *f*; *cine* **on ~tion** (*rodaje*) exterior
loch [lɔk] lago *m*, laguna *f*
lock [lɔk] *s* cerradura *f*; cerrojo *m* (*del fusil*); *sp* llave *f*; esclusa *f*; *v/t* cerrar con llave; entrelazar; **~er** armario *m*; **~jaw** trismo *m*; **~out** cierre *m* forzoso (*de fábrica, etc*) por los patronos; **~smith** cerrajero *m*
locomotive ['ləukəməutiv] locomotora *f*
locust ['ləukəst] cigarra *f*
lodg|e [lɔdʒ] *s* casita *f* (del portero); casa *f* de campo; *v/t* alojar; **~er** huésped *m*; **~ings** hospedaje *m*; habitación *f*
loft [lɔft] desván *m*; **~y** elevado; altivo; eminente
log [lɔg] tronco *m*; **~book** *aer* libro *m* de vuelo
logic ['lɔdʒik] *s* lógica *f*; *a* lógico; **~al** lógico
loin [lɔin] ijada *f*; *coc* lomo *m*
loiter ['lɔitə] *v/i* holgazanear, vagar
London ['lʌndən] Londres; **~er** londinense *m, f*
lonel|iness ['ləunlinis] soledad *f*; **~y** solitario
long [lɔŋ] *a* largo; prolongado; **in the ~ run** a la larga; *adv* mucho tiempo; **all day ~** todo el santo día; **as ~ as** mientras; **before ~** en breve; **~ ago** hace mucho; **~ before** mucho antes; **how ~?** ¿cuánto tiempo?; **~ since** hace mucho; **so ~!** ¡hasta luego!; **to take ~** tardar mucho; *v/i* **~ for** anhelar, ansiar; **~-distance** de larga distancia; *tel* interurbano; **~ing** anhelo *m*; **~itude** ['lɔndʒitu:d] longitud *f*; **~-playing** de larga duración; **~-range** de gran alcance; **~standing** de mucho tiempo; **~-suffering** sufrido; **~-term** *com* a largo plazo; **~-winded** verboso
look [luk] *s* mirada *f*; *pl* aspecto *m*; **to take a ~ at** echar una mirada a; *v/t* mirar, contemplar; **~ over** examinar; *v/i* mirar; tener aspecto de; **~ after** cuidar (de); **~ at** mirar, observar; **~ back** mirar hacia atrás; **~ down on** despreciar; **~ for** buscar; **~ forward to** esperar con ilusión; **~ in** entrar al pasar; **~ into** investigar; **~ like** parecerse a; **~ out!** ¡ojo!; ¡cuidado!; **~ up to** respetar, admirar; **~ well** tener buen aspecto; **~ing glass** espejo *m*; **~out** vigía *f*; atalaya *f*; *fig* perspectiva *f*; asunto *m*
loom [lu:m] *s* telar *m*; *v/i* asomarse en forma vaga
loop [lu:p] *s* lazo *m*; presilla *f*; *aer* rizo *m*; **~hole** escapatoria *f*
loose [lu:s] suelto; flojo; disoluto; **~n** ['~sn] *v/t* soltar, desatar, aflojar
loot [lu:t] *s* botín *m*; *v/t* pillar, saquear
lop [lɔp] *v/t* desmochar; **~ off** cortar; **~sided** desequilibrado
loquacious [ləu'kweiʃəs] locuaz
lord [lɔ:d] señor *m*; lord (*título*); **ℒ's Prayer** padrenuestro *m*; **~ly** señorial; **~ship** señoría *f*
lorry ['lɔri] camión *m*
los|e [lu:z] *v/t* perder; *v/i* sufrir una pérdida; perder; **~s** [lɔs] pérdida *f*; **to be at a ~s** no saber qué hacer; **~t** [lɔst] perdido; **to get ~t** perderse
lot [lɔt] lote *m*; suerte *f*; parcela *f*; **a ~** mucho
lotion ['ləuʃən] loción *f*
lottery ['lɔtəri] lotería *f*
loud [laud] alto; fuerte; ruidoso; chillón; **~ly** en alta voz, fuertemente; **~speaker** altavoz *m*, *LA* altoparlante *m*
lounge [laundʒ] *s* salón *m*; *v/i* haraganear; reposar
lous|e [laus] piojo *m*; **~y** piojoso; ['lauzi] *fam* pésimo, miserable
lout [laut] patán *m*, gamberro *m*
lov|e [lʌv] *s* amor *m*; cariño *m*; **to fall in ~e** enamorarse; *v/t* amar, querer; **~e affair** aventura *f* amorosa; amorío *m*; **~e letter** carta *f* de amor; **~ely** encantador, bello, hermoso; **~er** amante *m, f*; **~ing** cariñoso, afectuoso
low [ləu] *a* bajo; abatido; débil; estrecho; escotado; *adv* bajo; en voz baja; *v/i* mugir; *s meteor* área *f* de baja presión; *fam* punto *m* bajo; **~-cost** ecónomico; **~er** *a* más bajo, inferior; *v/t* bajar; reducir; disminuir; *v/i* bajar; menguar; **~land** tierra *f* baja; **~liness** humildad *f*; **~ly** humilde; **~ tide** marea *f* baja
loyal ['lɔiəl] leal, fiel; **~ty** lealtad *f*; fidelidad *f*
lozenge ['lɔzindʒ] pastilla *f*
Ltd. = ***limited company*** S.A.
lubrica|nt ['lu:brikənt] *a, s* lubri(fi)cante *m*; **~te** ['~eit] *v/t* lubri(fi)car, engrasar
lucid ['lu:sid] lúcido
luck [lʌk] suerte *f*, ventura *f*; **good ~** buena suerte *f*; **~y** afortunado, dichoso
ludicrous ['lu:dikrəs] ridículo, absurdo
lug [lʌg] *s* tirón *m*; *v/t* tirar; arrastrar
luggage ['lʌgidʒ] equipaje *m*; **~ rack** portaequipajes *m*, rejilla *f*
lukewarm ['lu:kwɔ:m] tibio (*t fig*)
lull [lʌl] *s* momento *m* de calma; *v/t* arrullar, adormecer; calmar; **~aby** ['~əbai] canción *f* de cuna; nana *f*
lumber ['lʌmbə] *s* maderos *m/pl*; madera *f* aserrada; *fam* trastos *m/pl*; *v/i* andar pesadamente; **~jack** leñador *m*
luminous ['lu:minəs] luminoso
lump [lʌmp] *s* bulto *m*; pedazo *m*; terrón *m* (*de azúcar*); nudo *m* (*en la garganta*); *v/t* **~ together** amontonar; **~ sum** cantidad *f* global
lunacy ['lu:nəsi] locura *f*
lunar ['lu:nə] lunar
lunatic ['lu:nətik] *a, s* loco *m*, demente *m*; **~ asylum** manicomio *m*
lunch [lʌntʃ] *s* almuerzo *m*; comida *f*; *v/i* almorzar; comer; **~ hour** pausa *f* para almorzar
lung [lʌŋ] pulmón *m*
lunge [lʌndʒ] *v/i* arremeter; **~ at** abalanzarse sobre
lurch [lə:tʃ] *s* sacudida *f*; **to leave in the ~** dejar a uno plantado; *v/i* dar tumbos
lure [ljuə] *s* atractivo *m*; señuelo *m*; *v/t* atraer, seducir
lurk [lə:k] *v/i* estar al acecho; *fig* estar latente
luscious ['lʌʃəs] suculento, sabroso; delicioso
lust [lʌst] *s* lujuria *f*; codicia *f*; *v/i* **~ after** codiciar; **~y** robusto; vigoroso
luster = **lustre**
lustr|e ['lʌstə] lustre *m*, brillo *m*; **~ous** lustroso
lute [lu:t] laúd *m*
luxur|ious [lʌg'zjuəriəs] lujoso, suntuoso; **~y** ['lʌkʃəri] lujo *m*
lye [lai] lejía *f*
lying ['laiiŋ] falso, mentiroso; yacente, situado; **~-in** parto *m*
lymph [limf] linfa *f*
lynch [lintʃ] *v/t* linchar
lynx [liŋks] lince *m*
lyric ['lirik] *a* lírico; *s* poema *m* lírico; **~s** letra *f* (*de una canción*)

M

macaroni [mækə'rəuni] macarrones *m/pl*
machine [mə'ʃi:n] *s* máquina *f*; mecanismo *m*; *v/t* trabajar, acabar a máquina; **~ gun** ametralladora *f*; **~ry** maquinaria *f*; **~ tool** máquina *f* herramienta
mackintosh ['mækintɔʃ] impermeable *m*
mad [mæd] loco; demente; furioso; **to be ~ about** estar loco por; **to get ~** enfadarse; **to go ~** volverse loco; enloquecerse
madam ['mædəm] señora *f*
madden ['mædn] *v/t*, *v/i* enloquecer
made [meid] hecho; fabricado; **~-to-order** hecho a la medida; **~-up** ficticio
mad|man ['mædmən] loco *m*; **~ness** locura *f*
magazine [mægə'zi:n] *impr* revista *f*; *mil* recámara *f* (*del cañón*); almacén *m* de explosivos
maggot ['mægət] gusano *m*
magic ['mædʒik] *s* magia *f*; *a*: **~ wand** varita *f* mágica; **~al** mágico; **~ian** [me'dʒiʃən] mago *m*
magistrate ['mædʒistreit] magistrado *m*
magnanimous [mæg'næniməs] magnánimo
magnet ['mægnit] imán *m*; **~ic** [~'netik] magnético
magni|ficence [mæg'nifisns] magnificencia *f*; **~ficent** magnífico; **~fy** ['~fai] *v/t* amplificar; exagerar; **~fying glass** lupa *f*; **~tude** ['~tju:d] magnitud *f*
magpie ['mægpai] urraca *f*
mahogany [mə'hɔgəni] caoba *f*
maid [meid] criada *f*; **~en** *a* virgen; soltera; *s* doncella *f*; joven *f* soltera; **~en name** nombre *m* de soltera
mail [meil] *s* correo *m*; correspondencia *f*; *v/t* despachar; echar al correo; **~bag** valija *f* (postal); **~box** buzón *m*; **~man** cartero *m*; **~-order house** almacén *m* de ventas por correo
maim [meim] *v/t* mutilar; *fig* estropear
main [mein] principal; mayor; **~land** tierra *f* firme; **~s** tubería *f* maestra (*de gas, agua*); red *f* eléctrica; **~stay** *fig* pilar *m*; **~stream** corriente *f* principal
maint|ain [mein'tein] *v/t* mantener; sostener; **~enance** ['meintənəns] mantenimiento *m*
maize [meiz] maíz *m*
majest|ic [mə'dʒestik] majes-

tuoso; **~y** ['mædʒisti] majestad *f*
major ['meidʒə] *a* mayor; más importante; *s* comandante *m*
Majorca [mə'dʒɔ:kə] Mallorca *f*
majority [mə'dʒɔriti] mayoría *f*; mayor parte *f*
make [meik] *s* marca *f*; fabricación *f*; *v/t* hacer; crear; producir; ganar (*dinero*); obligar; causar; *fam* recorrer (*distancia*); **~ do with** contentarse con; **~ fun of** burlarse de; **~ known** dar a conocer; **~ the most of** aprovechar; **~ out** descifrar; comprender; divisar; extender (*documento*); **~ over** traspasar; **~ up** formar; inventar; arreglar; **~ up one's mind** resolverse; **~ it up** hacer las paces; **~ use of** servirse de; *v/i* **~ for** ir hacia; **~ off** largarse; **~ ready** prepararse; **~-believe** *a* fingido; *s* ficción *f*; invención *f*; **~r** fabricante *m*; **~shift** improvisado; provisional; **~-up** maquillaje *m*
malady ['mælədi] enfermedad *f*
male [meil] *s* varón *m*; *a* masculino
malevolent [mə'levələnt] malévolo
malfunction [mæl'fʌŋkʃn] funcionamiento *m* defectuoso
malic|e ['mælis] malicia *f*; **~ious** [mə'liʃəs] malicioso
malignant [mə'lignənt] maligno
mallet ['mælit] mazo *m*
malnutrition ['mælnju(:)'triʃən] desnutrición *f*
malpractice ['mæl'præktis] procedimientos *m/pl* impropios *o* injuriosos (*esp. de médicos*)
malt [mɔ:lt] malta *f*
mam(m)a [mə'mɑ:] mamá *f*
mammal ['mæməl] mamífero *m*
man [mæn] *s* hombre *m*; el hombre *m*, la humanidad *f*; sirviente *m*; **the ~ in the street** hombre *m* corriente; *v/t* tripular; guarnecer
manage ['mænidʒ] *v/t* manejar; manipular; dirigir; arreglar; administrar; *v/i* arreglárselas; **~able** manejable; dócil; **~ment** dirección *f*; manejo *m*; *com* gerencia *f*; **~r** *com* gerente *m*; director *m*; empresario *m*
mandatory ['mændətəri] obligatorio
mane [mein] crin *f*; melena *f*
manger ['meindʒə] pesebre *m*
mangle ['mæŋgl] *v/t* mutilar; magullar
mangy ['meindʒi] sarnoso, roñoso
manh|andle ['mænhændl] *v/t* maltratar; **~ood** [~hud] virilidad *f*; edad *f* adulta
mania ['meinjə] manía *f*; **~c** ['~iæk] *a*, *s* maníaco *m*
manicure ['mænikjuə] manicura *f*
manifest ['mænifest] *a* manifiesto; evidente; *v/t* manifestar; revelar
manifold ['mænifəuld] múltiple; vario; variado
man|kind [mæn'kaind] la humanidad; **~ly** varonil
manner ['mænə] manera *f*; modo *m*; conducta *f*; **~s** modales *m/pl*; **bad ~s** mala educación *f*
manœuvre [mə'nu:və] *s* maniobra *f*; *v/t*, *v/i* maniobrar
manor ['mænə] casa *f* solariega
manpower ['mænpauə] mano *f* de obra
mansion ['mænʃən] casa *f* señorial
manslaughter ['mænslɔ:tə] *for* homicidio *m* no premeditado
mantelpiece ['mæntlpi:s] repisa *f* de chimenea
manual ['mænjuəl] *a*, *s* manual *m*
manufactur|e [mænju'fæktʃə] *s* fabricación *f*; *v/t* fabricar
manure [mə'njuə] *s* estiércol *m*; *v/t* abonar
many ['meni] muchos; **a great ~** muchísimos; **as ~ as** tantos como; **how ~?** ¿cuántos?; **too ~** demasiados
map [mæp] *s* mapa *m*; plano *m* (*de una ciudad*); *v/t* **~ out** planear
maple ['meipl] arce *m*
marble ['mɑ:bl] mármol *m*; canica *f*
March [mɑ:tʃ] marzo *m*; **⁲** *v/i* marchar; *s* marcha *f*
mare [mεə] yegua *f*
margarine [mɑ:dʒə'ri:n] margarina *f*
margin ['mɑ:dʒin] margen *m*; **in the ~** al margen
marine [mə'ri:n] *a* marino; *s* marina *f*; **merchant ~** marina *f* mercante; **~r** ['mærinə] marinero *m*; **~s** infantería *f* de marina
marital ['mæritl]: **~ status** estado *m* civil
maritime ['mæritaim] marítimo
mark [mɑ:k] *s* marca *f*; señal *f*; impresión *f*; huella *f*; calificación *f*; blanco *m*; *v/t* marcar; notar; señalar; **~down** rebaja *f*; **~ed** [mɑ:kt] marcado, pronunciado
market ['mɑ:kit] *s* mercado *m*; *v/t* llevar al mercado; vender; **~able** vendible; **~ing** marketing *m*, compra *f* y venta *f*; **~ place** plaza *f* del mercado
marksman ['mɑ:ksmən] tirador *m* (certero)
marmalade ['mɑ:məleid] mermelada *f* de frutas cítricas
marmot ['mɑ:mət] marmota *f*
marquee [mɑ:'ki:] entoldado *m*; marquesina *f*
marri|age ['mæridʒ] matrimonio *m*; boda *f*; **~age certificate** partida *f* de matrimonio; **~ed** casado; **to get ~ed** casarse
marrow ['mærəu] médula *f*; calabacín *m*
marry ['mæri] *v/t* casar; casarse con; *v/i* casarse
marsh [mɑ:ʃ] pantano *m*; marisma *f*
marshal ['mɑ:ʃəl] *s* mariscal *m*; *v/t* dirigir; ordenar, formar (*las tropas*)
marshmallow ['mɑ:ʃ'mæləu] malvavisco *m*
martial ['mɑ:ʃəl] marcial; **~ law** ley *f* marcial
martyr ['mɑ:tə] mártir *m*, *f*
marvel ['mɑ:vəl] *s* maravilla *f*; *v/i* admirarse; **~lous** maravilloso
mascara [mæs'kɑ:rə] rímel *m*
masculine ['mæskjulin] masculino
mash [mæʃ] *s* masa *f*; *v/t* majar; **~ed potatoes** puré *m* de patatas, *LA* de papas
mask [mɑ:sk] máscara *f*
mason ['meisn] albañil *m*; **~ry** mampostería *f*
mass [mæs] *s* masa *f*; montón *m*; muchedumbre *f*; *relig* misa *f*; **~ media** los media *m/pl*; **~ production** fabricación *f* en serie; *v/t*, *v/i* juntar(se)
massacre ['mæsəkə] matanza *f*
massage ['mæsɑ:ʒ] *s* masaje *m*; *v/t* dar masaje a
massive ['mæsiv] macizo; grande, grueso
mast [mɑ:st] palo *m*; mástil *m*
master ['mɑ:stə] *s* amo *m*; dueño *m*; maestro *m*; **~ of ceremonies** presentador *m*; *v/t* superar; domar; dominar; **~ly** magistral; **~piece** obra *f* maestra; **~y** maestría *f*
mat [mæt] *s* estera *f*; felpudo *m*; *v/i* enredarse; *a* mate
match [mætʃ] *s* cerilla *f*, fósforo *m*; partido *m*; matrimonio *m*; *v/t* aparear; emparejar; igualar; *v/i* hacer juego, corresponderse; **~box** cajita *f* de fósforos; **~less** sin igual
mate [meit] *s* cónyuge *m*, *f*; compañero(a) *m* (*f*); *mar* maestre *m*; (*ajedrez*) mate *m*; *v/t*, *v/i* casar; parear(se)
material [mə'tiəriəl] *s* material *m*; materia *f*; tejido *m*; tela *f*; *a* material; esencial; **~ize** *v/i* concretarse; realizarse
matern|al [mə'tə:nl] maternal; materno; **~ity** maternidad *f*
mathematic|ian [mæθimə'tiʃən] matemático(a) *m* (*f*); **~s** [~'mætiks] matemáticas *f/pl*
matinée ['mætinei] función *f* de tarde
matriculate [mə'trikjuleit] *v/t*, *v/i* matricular(se)
matrimony ['mætriməni] matrimonio *m*
matron ['meitrən] matrona *f*
matter ['mætə] *s* materia *f*; sustancia *f*; asunto *m*; **as a ~ of course** por rutina; **as a ~ of fact** en realidad; **for that ~** en cuanto a eso; **no ~** no importa; **what's the ~?** ¿qué pasa?; *v/i* importar; **it doesn't ~** no importa; **~-of-fact** prosaico; práctico
mattress ['mætris] colchón *m*
matur|e [mə'tjuə] *a* maduro; *v/i* madurar; *com* vencer; **~ity** madurez *f*; *com* vencimiento *m*
mauve [məuv] color *m* de malva
maxim ['mæksim] máxima *f*; **~um** ['~əm] máximo *m*
May [mei] mayo *m*
may [mei] *v/i* poder; ser posible; **~ I come in?** ¿puedo entrar?; **~be** quizá
mayonnaise [meiə'neiz] mayonesa *f*
mayor [mεə] alcalde *m*
maze [meiz] laberinto *m*
me [mi:, mi] *pron pers* me, mí; **with ~** conmigo
meadow ['medəu] pradera *f*
meager = **meagre**
meagre ['mi:gə] magro; pobre
meal [mi:l] comida *f* (*preparada*); **~time** hora *f* de comer
mean [mi:n] *a* medio; humilde; tacaño; *v/t* querer decir; significar; *v/i* tener (buenas, malas) intenciones; *s* medio *m*; término *m* medio; **~s** medios *m/pl*; recursos *m/pl*; **by all ~s** de todos modos; **by no ~s** de ninguna manera; **by ~s of** mediante
meaning ['mi:niŋ] significado *m*; **~ful** significativo; **~less** sin sentido
mean|time ['mi:n'taim], **~while** ['~'wail]: **in the ~** mientras tanto
measles ['mi:zlz] *med* sarampión *m*; **German ~** rubéola *f*
measur|e ['meʒə] *s* medida *f*; cantidad *f*; **beyond ~e** excesivamente; *v/t*, *v/i* medir; **~ement** dimensión *f*
meat [mi:t] carne *f*; **~ball** albóndiga *f*; **~y** carnudo; *fig* substancioso
mechani|c [mi'kænik] mecánico *m*; **~cs** mecánica *f*; **~sm** ['mekənizəm] mecanismo *m*; **~ze** ['~naiz] *v/t* mecanizar
medal ['medl] medalla *f*
meddle ['medl] *v/i* entrometerse
mediat|e ['mi:dieit] *v/t*, *v/i* mediar; **~ion** mediación *f*
medic|al ['medikəl] *a* médico; **~ament** [mə'dikəmənt] medicamento *m*; **~ine** ['medsin] medicina *f*
mediocre [mi:di'əukə] mediocre; mediano
meditat|e ['mediteit] *v/i* meditar; **~ion** meditación *f*; **~ive** ['~ətiv] meditativo
Mediterranean [meditə'reinjən] (**Sea**) (Mar *m*) mediterráneo *m*
medium ['mi:djəm] *a* mediano; regular; *s* medio *m*
medley ['medli] mezcolanza *f*; *mús* potpurrí *m*
meek [mi:k] manso, dócil
meet [mi:t] *v/t* encontrar(se) (con); tropezar con; esperar; conocer; hacer frente a; cumplir; satisfacer; *v/i* encontrarse; reunirse; **~ with** toparse con; sufrir; **~ing** reunión *f*; junta *f*
melancholy ['melənkəli] melancolía *f*
meld [meld] *v/t*, *v/i* unir(se), fusionar(se)
melee ['melei] pelotera *f*; confusión *f*
mellow ['meləu] maduro; suave
melod|ious [mi'ləudjəs] melodioso; **~y** ['melədi] melodía *f*
melon ['melən] melón *m*
melt [melt] *v/t* derretir; *v/i* fundirse; **~ away** esfumarse
member ['membə] miembro *m*; socio *m*; **~ship** calidad *f* de socio
membrane ['membrein] membrana *f*
memo|irs ['memvɑ:z] *pl* memorias *f/pl*; **~rial** [mi'mɔ:riəl] conmemorativo; **~rize** ['meməraiz] *v/t* aprender de memoria
memory ['meməri] memoria *f*; recuerdo *m*
menace ['menəs] *s* amenaza *f*; *v/t*, *v/i* amenazar
mend [mend] *v/t* componer; remendar; reparar; *v/i* curarse
menial ['mi:njəl] *a* servil
mental ['mentl] mental; **~ity** [~'tæliti] mentalidad *f*
mention ['menʃən] *s* mención *f*; *v/t* mencionar; **don't ~ it!** ¡no hay de qué!
menu ['menju:] menú *m*, minuta *f*
meow [mi:'au] *s* maullido *m*; *v/i* maullar
mercantile ['mə:kəntail] mercantil
mercenary ['məsinəri] *a*, *s* mercenario *m*
merchan|dise ['mə:tʃəndaiz] mercancías *f/pl*; *LA* mercadería *f*; **~t** comerciante *m*
merc|iful ['mə:siful] clemente; compasivo; **~iless** despiadado
mercury ['mə:kjuri] mercurio *m*
mercy ['mə:si] misericordia *f*; piedad *f*; **at the ~ of** a la merced de
mere [miə] mero; puro
merge [mə:dʒ] *v/t* unir; *v/i* fundirse; **~r** *for*, *com* fusión *f*
meridian [mə'ridiən] meridiano *m*
meringue [mə'ræŋ] merengue *m*
merit ['merit] *s* mérito *m*; *v/t* merecer
mermaid ['mə:meid] sirena *f*
merr|iment ['merimənt] alegría *f*; **~y** alegre; feliz; **to make ~y** divertirse; **~y-go-round** tiovivo *m*
mesh [meʃ] *s* malla *f*; *tecn* engranaje *m*; *v/i* engranar
mess [mes] *s* lío *m*; confusión *f*; *mil* comedor *m*; *v/t* **~ up** desordenar
mess|age ['mesidʒ] mensaje *m*; recado *m*; **~enger** mensajero *m*
messy ['mesi] desordenado
metal ['metl] *s* metal *m*; *a* de metal; **~lic** [mi'tælik] metálico
mete [mi:t] *v/t* **~ out** repartir; imponer (*castigo*)
meteor ['mi:tjə] meteoro *m*; **~ology** [~'rɔlədʒi] meteorología *f*
meter ['mi:tə] = **metre**; contador *m* (*gas, etc*); medidor *m*
method ['meθəd] método *m*; **~ical** [mi'θɔdikəl] metódico
meticulous [mi'tikjuləs] meticuloso
metr|e ['mitə] metro *m*; **~ical** ['metrikəl] métrico
metropolitan [metrə'pɔlitən] metropolitano
mew [mju:] *s* maullido *m*; lugar *m* de reclusión; *v/i* maullar
Mexic|an ['meksikən] *a*, *s* mexicano(a) *m* (*f*); **~o** ['~əu] México *m*
mezzanine ['mezəni:n] entresuelo *m*
miaow [mi(:)'au] = **meow**
micro|phone ['maikrəfəun] micrófono *m*; **~processor** microprocesador *m*; **~scope** microscopio *m*; **~wave oven** horno *m* microondas
mid [mid] medio; pleno; **in ~ winter** en pleno invierno; **~day** mediodía *m*
middl|e ['midl] *a* medio; intermedio; mediano; *s* centro *m*; mitad *f*; **~e-aged** de mediana edad; **⁲e Ages** *pl* Edad *f* Media; **~eman** intermediario *m*; **~e name** segundo nombre *m*; **~ing** mediano
midget ['midʒit] enano *m*
midnight ['midnait] medianoche *f*
mid|st [midst]: **in the ~st of** entre; en medio de; **~way** a mitad del camino
midwife ['midwaif] comadrona *f*
might [mait] poder *m*; poderío *m*; **~y** *a* poderoso; potente; *adv* sumamente
migrane ['mi:grein] jaqueca *f*
migra|te [mai'greit] *v/i* emigrar; **~tion** migración *f*; **~tory** ['~ətəri] migratorio
mild [maild] suave, benigno, templado; manso
mildew ['mildju:] moho *m*
mile [mail] milla *f*
mil(e)age ['mailidʒ] millaje *m*; recorrido *m* en millas
milestone ['mailstəun] piedra *f* miliaria; hito *m* (*t fig*)
militant ['militənt] militante
military ['militəri] militar
milk [milk] *s* leche *f*; *v/t* ordeñar; **~man** lechero *m*; **~shake** batido *m* de leche; **~y** lechoso; **⁲y Way** Vía *f* Láctea

mill [mil] *s* molino *m*; fábrica *f* de tejidos; *v/t* moler; **~er** molinero *m*
millet ['milit] mijo *m*
milliner ['milinə] modista *f* de sombreros
million ['miljən] millón *m*; **~aire** [~'nɛə] millonario *m*
mime [maim] mimo *m*; mímica *f*
mimeograph ['mimiəgrɑːf] mimeógrafo *m*
mimic ['mimik] *a* mímico; *s* remedador *m*; *v/t* imitar
mince [mins] *v/t* desmenuzar; picar (*carne*); **~ no words** no tener pelos en la lengua; *v/i* andar con pasos menuditos; **~meat** carne *f* picada
mind [maind] *s* mente *f*; inteligencia *f*; opinión *f*; intención *f*; **out of one's ~** loco, fuera de su juicio; **to bear in ~** tener en cuenta; **to change one's ~** cambiar de opinión; **to cross one's ~** ocurrírsele; **to have a ~ to** tener ganas de; **to make up one's ~** decidirse; *v/t* fijarse en; cuidar; oponerse a; tener inconveniente en; **~ your own business!** ¡no se meta en cosas ajenas!; **I don't ~** me es igual; **never ~!** ¡no importa!; **~blowing** *fam* alucinante; **~boggling** abrumador; **~ful of** consciente de; **~less** estúpido
mine [main] *pron pos* mío, mía, míos, mías, el mío, la mía, los míos, las mías, lo mío
min|e [main] *s* mina *f*; *v/t* minar; extraer (*mineral, etc*); **~er** minero *m*
mineral ['minərəl] mineral *m*; **~ water** agua *f* mineral
mingle ['miŋgl] *v/t, v/i* mezclar(se)
miniature ['minjətʃə] miniatura *f*
minimum ['minimәm] mínimo *m*
mining ['mainiŋ] minería *f*
miniskirt ['miniskəːt] minifalda *f*
minist|er ['ministə] *s pol, relig* ministro *m*; *v/t relig* administrar (*sacramento*); *v/i* ayudar; **~ry** ministerio *m*; *relig* sacerdocio *m*
mink [miŋk] visón *m*
minor ['mainə] *a* menor (*t mús*); inferior; secundario; *s* menor *m, f* de edad; **~ity** [~'nɔriti] minoría *f*
minster ['minstə] catedral *f*
minstrel ['minstrəl] juglar *m*; trovador *m*
mint [mint] *bot* menta *f*; casa *f* de la moneda
minus ['mainəs] *prep* menos; *a* negativo; *fam* sin, desprovisto de
minute [mai'njuːt] *a* menudo; diminuto; ['minit] *s* minuto *m*; momento *m*; **at the last ~** a última hora; **~ hand** minutero *m*; **~s** *pl* actas *f/pl*
mirac|le ['mirəkl] milagro *m*; **~ulous** [mi'rækjuləs] milagroso
mirage ['mirɑːʒ] espejismo *m*
mire ['maiə] cenagal *m*
mirror ['mirə] *s* espejo *m*; *v/t* reflejar
mirth [məːθ] regojico *m*; alegría *f*
misadventure ['misəd'ventʃə] desgracia *f*
misapprehen|d ['misæpri'hend] *v/t* malentender; **~sion** equivocación *f*
misbehav|e ['misbi'heiv] *v/i* portarse mal; **~io(u)r** mala conducta *f*
miscarr|iage [mis'kæridʒ] aborto *m*; error *m*; fracaso *m*; **~y** *v/i* abortar; malparir; malograrse
miscellaneous [misi'leinjəs] misceláneo
mischie|f ['mistʃif] travesura *f*; daño *m*; **~vous** ['~vəs] travieso; malicioso
misconception ['miskən'sepʃən] concepto *m* erróneo
misdeed ['mis'diːd] delito *m*
misdemeanour [misdi'miːnə] *for* delito *m* menor
miser ['maizə] avaro *m*; **~able** ['mizərəbl] triste; abatido; despreciable; **~y** miseria *f*
misfit ['misfit] malajuste *m*; inadaptado(a) *m* (*f*)
mis|fortune [mis'fɔːtʃən] desgracia *f*; infortunio *m*; percance *m*; **~giving** recelo *m*; desconfianza *f*; **~guided** equivocado, mal aconsejado
mishandle ['mis'hændl] *v/t* manejar mal; maltratar
mishap ['mishæp] contratiempo *m*; accidente *m*
mislay [mis'lei] *v/t* extraviar; traspapelar
mislead [mis'liːd] *v/t* engañar; despistar
mismanage ['mis'mænidʒ] *v/t* administrar mal; **~ment** desgobierno *m*; mala administración *f*
misplace ['mis'pleis] *v/t* colocar mal; extraviar
misprint [mis'print] *s impr* errata *f*; *v/t* imprimir mal
misrepresent ['misrepri'zent] *v/t* tergiversar; desfigurar, falsificar
miss [mis] señorita *f*
miss [mis] *v/t* perder; no acertar; fallar; echar de menos; *v/i* errar el blanco
missal ['misəl] misal *m*
misshapen ['mis'ʃeipən] deforme
missile ['missail] proyectil *m*; cohete *m*
missing ['misiŋ] *mil* desaparecido; perdido; **to be ~** faltar
mission ['miʃən] *relig, pol* misión *f*; *mil* tarea *f*; **~ary** ['~ʃnəri] misionero(a) *m* (*f*)
mist [mist] *s* neblina *f*; niebla *f*; vaho *m*; *v/t* empañar
mistake [mis'teik] *s* equivocación *f*; error *m*; **by ~** por equivocación; *v/t* confundir; entender mal; **~n** erróneo; **to be ~n** estar equivocado
mister ['mistə] señor *m*
mistletoe ['misltəu] muérdago *m*
mistress ['mistris] maestra *f*; dueña *f*; querida *f*
mistrust ['mis'trʌst] *s* desconfianza *f*; *v/t* desconfiar de; dudar de
misty ['misti] nebuloso
misunderstand ['misʌndə'stænd] *v/t* entender mal; **~ing** malentendido *m*
misuse ['mis'juːs] *s* abuso *m*; ['~'juːz] *v/t* abusar de; maltratar; *com* malversar (*fondos*)
mite [mait] pizca *f*
mitigate ['mitigeit] *v/t* mitigar
mitten ['mitn] manopla *f*
mix [miks] *v/t* mezclar; **~ up** *fig* confundir; *v/i* mezclarse; asociarse; **~ed** mixto; mezclado; **~er** batidora *f*; **~ture** ['~tʃə] mezcla *f*; mescolanza *f*; **~-up** confusión *f*
moan [məun] *s* gemido *m*; *v/i* quejarse; gemir
moat [məut] *mil* foso *m*
mob [mɔb] chusma *f*; gentío *m*; muchedumbre *f*
mobil|e ['məubail] móvil; movible; **~ize** ['məubilaiz] *v/t* movilizar
mock [mɔk] *a* imitado; fingido; *v/t, v/i* mofarse (de), burlarse (de); **~ery** mofa *f*; burla *f*
mode [məud] moda *f*; manera *f*; modo *m*
model ['mɔdl] *a* modelo; *s* modelo *m, f*; patrón *m*; maqueta *f*; *v/t* modelar
moderat|e ['mɔdərit] *a* moderado; ['mɔdəreit] *v/t* moderar; **~ion** [~'reiʃən] moderación *f*
modern ['mɔdən] moderno; **~ize** *v/t* modernizar
modest ['mɔdist] modesto; **~y** modestia *f*; pudor *m*
modif|ication [mɔdifi'keiʃən] modificación *f*; **~y** ['~fai] *v/t* modificar
modul|ate ['mɔdjuleit] *v/t* modular; **~e** ['~uːl] módulo *m* (*lunar, etc*)
mohair ['məuhɛə] mohair *m*
Mohammedan [məu'hæmidən] *a, s* mahometano(a) *m* (*f*)
moist [mɔist] húmedo; **~en** ['~sn] *v/t* humedecer; **~ure** ['~stʃə] humedad *f*
molar ['məulə] muela *f*
mole [məul] *zool* topo *m*; lunar *m*; muelle *m*
molecule ['mɔlikjuːl] molécula *f*
molest [məu'lest] *v/t* molestar; importunar; **~ation** [~'teiʃən] molestia *f*
mollify ['mɔlifai] *v/t* apaciguar
moment ['məumənt] momento *m*; instante *m*; importancia *f*; **at the ~** de momento, por ahora; **~ary** momentáneo; **~ous** [məu'mentəs] importante
monarch ['mɔnək] monarca *m*; **~y** monarquía *f*
monastery ['mɔnəstəri] monasterio *m*
Monday ['mʌndi] lunes *m*
monetary ['mʌnitəri] monetario
money ['mʌni] dinero *m*; moneda *f*; **make ~** ganar dinero; **ready ~** fondos *m/pl* disponibles; **~ed** adinerado; **~lender** prestamista *m*; **~ order** giro *m* postal
monitor ['mɔnitə] *s* monitor *m*; *TV* receptor *m*; *v/t* controlar; vigilar
monk [mʌŋk] monje *m*, fraile *m*
monkey ['mʌŋki] *s* mono *m*
monologue ['mɔnələg] monólogo *m*
monopol|ize [mə'nɔpəlaiz] monopolizar (*t fig*); **~y** monopolio *m*
monotone ['mɔnətəun] monotonía *f*; **speak in a ~** hablar en un solo tono
monotonous [mə'nɔtnəs] monótono
monsoon [mɔn'suːn] monzón *m, f*
monst|er ['mɔnstə] monstruo *m*; **~rous** enorme; monstruoso
month [mʌnθ] mes *m*; **~ly** mensual
monument ['mɔnjumənt] monumento *m*
moo [muː] *v/i* mugir
mood [muːd] humor *m*; disposición *f*; **to be in a good (bad) ~** estar de buen (mal) humor; **~y** malhumorado; caprichoso
moon [muːn] luna *f*; **~light** luz *f* de la luna
Moor [muə] moro(a) *m* (*f*)
moor [muə] *s* páramo *m*; brezal *m*; *v/t mar* amarrar; *v/i* atracar; **~ings** *pl* amarras *f/pl*; amarradero *m*
moose [muːs] alce *m*
mop [mɔp] *s* fregona *f*; greña *f*; *v/t* fregar; enjugar, *LA* trapear
mope [məup] *v/i* estar abatido; **~ around** andar alicaído
moral ['mɔrəl] *a* virtuoso; moral; recto; *s* moraleja *f*; **~e** [mɔ'rɑːl] estado *m* de ánimo; **~ity** [mə'ræliti] moralidad *f*; **~ize** ['mɔrəlaiz] *v/t, v/i* moralizar
morass [mə'ræs] ciénaga *f*
morbid ['mɔːbid] morboso
more [mɔː] *a* (*compar de* **much, many**) más; *adv* más; además; **~ and ~** cada vez más; **~ or less** más o menos; **once ~** una vez más; **the ~ the merrier** cuanto más, ... tanto mejor; **~over** además
morgue [mɔːg] depósito *m* de cadáveres
morning ['mɔːniŋ] *s* mañana *f*; **early ~** madrugada *f*; **good ~!** ¡buenos días!; **this ~** esta mañana; **tomorrow ~** mañana por la mañana; *a* matutino; matinal
Morocc|an [mə'rɔkən] *a, s* marroquí *m, f*; **~o** Marruecos *m*
morose [mə'rəus] malhumorado; hosco
morphine ['mɔːfiːn] morfina *f*
morsel ['mɔːsəl] pedacito *m*, bocado *m*
mortal ['mɔːtl] *a, s* mortal *m*; **~ity** [~'tæliti] mortalidad *f*
mortar ['mɔːtə] *mil, arq* mortero *m*
mortgage ['mɔːgidʒ] *s* hipoteca *f*; *v/t* hipotecar
mortify ['mɔːtifai] *v/t* mortificar, humillar
mortuary ['mɔːtjuəri] depósito *m* de cadáveres
mosaic [məu'zeiik] mosaico *m*
Moslem ['mɔzlem] *a, s* musulmán(ana) *m* (*f*)
mosque [mɔsk] mezquita *f*
mosquito [məs'kiːtəu] mosquito *m*
moss [mɔs] musgo *m*
most [məust] *a* (*superl de* **much, many**) el, la, los, las más; la mayor parte de; *adv* más; muy; sumamente; **at (the) ~** a lo más; **~ likely** muy probable; **make the ~ of** sacar el mejor partido de; **~ly** principalmente
moth [mɔθ] polilla *f*; **~-eaten** apolillado
mother ['mʌðə] *s* madre *f*; **~hood** maternidad *f*; **~-in-law** suegra *f*; **~less** huérfano de madre; **~ly** maternal; **~-of-pearl** nácar *m*; **~ tongue** lengua *f* materna
motif [məu'tiːf] motivo *m*
motion ['məuʃən] *s* movimiento *m*; gesto *m*; ademán *m*; moción *f*; *v/t* indicar con un gesto de la mano; **~less** inmóvil; **~ picture** película *f*
motiv|ate ['məutiveit] *v/t* motivar; **~e** motivo *m*
motor ['məutə] *s* motor *m*; automóvil *m*; *v/i* ir en coche; **~bike** moto *f*; **~car** automóvil *m*; coche *m*; **~cycle** motocicleta *f*; **~cyclist** motociclista *m, f*; **~ing** automovilismo *m*; **~ist** automovilista *m, f*; **~ize** motorizar; **~way** autopista *f*
motto ['mɔtəu] lema *m*; divisa *f*
mo(u)ld [məuld] *s* molde *m*; moho *m*; *v/t* moldear; formar; **~er** *v/i* desmoronarse; **~y** mohoso
mound [maund] montículo *m*
mount [maunt] *s* monte *m*; montura *f*; *v/t* montar; elevar; subir, escalar; *v/i* subir; crecer; montar a caballo
mountain ['mauntin] montaña *f*; **~ chain, ~ range** cordillera *f*; sierra *f*; **~eer** [~'niə] alpinista *m*; montañés *m*; **~ous** montañoso
mourn [mɔːn] *v/t* llorar; lamentar; *v/i* lamentarse; **~er** doliente *m, f*, plañidera *f*; **~ful** triste; doloroso; **~ing** luto *m*; **to be in ~ing** estar de luto
mouse [maus] ratón *m*; **~trap** ratonera *f*
moustache [məs'tɑːʃ] bigote *m*
mouth [mauθ] *s* boca *f*; desembocadura *f* (*de río*); [mauð] *v/t* pronunciar; **~ful** bocado *m*; **~piece** boquilla *f*; portavoz *m*; **~wash** enjuague *m*; **~watering** apetitoso
mov|e [muːv] *s* movimiento *m*; paso *m*; jugada *f*; *v/t* mover; trasladar; conmover; *v/i* moverse; mudarse; **~e into** (*casa*) instalarse en; **~e on** seguir caminando; **~ement** movimiento *m*; **~ies** *fam* cine *m*; **~ing** conmovedor
mow [mau] *v/t* segar; **~er** segador(a) *m* (*f*)
much [mʌtʃ] *a* mucho; *adv* mucho; muy; **as ~ as** tanto como; **how ~ is it?** ¿cuánto es?; **so ~ the better** tanto mejor; **so ~ the worse** tanto peor; **too ~** demasiado; **very ~** muchísimo
mucus ['mjuːkəs] moco *m*
mud [mʌd] barro *m*; fango *m*; lodo *m*
muddle ['mʌdl] *s* embrollo *m*; perplejidad *f*; *v/t* confundir; **~ up** embrollar
mud|dy ['mʌdi] lodoso; **~guard** guardabarros *m*
muezzin [mu(ː)'ezin] almuecín *m*
muff [mʌf] manguito *m*
muffin ['mʌfin] mollete *m*
muffle ['mʌfl] *v/t* tapar; embozar; amortiguar (*sonido, etc*); **~r** bufanda *f*; *aut* silenciador *m*
mug [mʌg] cubilete *m*; *v/t* asaltar para robar; **~ging** asalto *m*; **~gy** bochornoso
mulberry ['mʌlbəri] mora *f*; moral *m*
mule [mjuːl] mulo *m*; mula *f*; **~teer** [~i'tiə] arriero *m*
mull [mʌl] *v/t* **~ over** meditar sobre
multicolored ['mʌltikʌləd] multicolor
multifarious ['mʌlti'fɛəriəs] múltiple, vario
multipl|e ['mʌltipl] *a* múltiple; *s* múltiplo *m*; **~y** ['~plai] *v/t, v/i* multiplicar(se)
multitude ['mʌltitjuːd] multitud *f*
mumble ['mʌmbl] *v/t, v/i* hablar entre dientes
mummy ['mʌmi] momia *f*; mami *f*
mumps [mʌmps] paperas *f/pl*
munch [mʌntʃ] *v/t* mascar
mundane [mʌn'dein] mundano
municipal [mju(ː)'nisipəl] municipal; **~ity** [~'pæliti] municipio *m*
mural ['mjuərəl] *a, s* mural *m*
murder ['məːdə] *s* asesinato *m*; *v/t* asesinar; **~er** asesino *m*; **~ous** asesino; homicida; *fig* feroz
murmur ['məːmə] *s* murmullo *m*; *v/t, v/i* murmurar
musc|le ['mʌsl] músculo *m*; **~ular** ['~kjulə] musculoso; muscular

muse [mju:z] *v/i* reflexionar; meditar; *s* musa *f*
museum [mju(:)'ziəm] museo *m*
mush [mʌʃ] gachas *f/pl*
mushroom ['mʌʃrum] seta *f*; champiñón *m*
music ['mju:zik] música *f*; **~al** musical; músico; **~ hall** teatro *m* de variedades; **~ian** [~'ziʃən] músico(a) *m (f)*
musk [mʌsk] almizcle *m*
Muslim ['mʌslim] *a, s* musulmán(ana) *m (f)*
muslin ['mʌslin] muselina *f*
mussel ['mʌsəl] mejillón *m*
must [mʌst] *v/aux* deber, tener que, haber de, deber de; ***I ~ write*** debo escribir; ***it ~ be late*** debe de ser tarde; *s* ***it's a ~*** es imprescindible
must [mʌst] mosto *m*; moho *m*
mustard ['mʌstəd] mostaza *f*
muster ['mʌstə] *v/t* reunir; *v/i* juntarse; *s* asamblea *f*
musty ['mʌsti] mohoso; rancio
mute [mju:t] silencioso; mudo; **~d** sordo, apagado
mutilate ['mju:tileit] *v/t* mutilar
mutin|eer [mju:ti'niə] amotinado *m*; **~ous** ['~nəs] sedicioso; **~y** ['~ni] motín *m*
mutter ['mʌtə] *v/t, v/i* murmurar; rezongar
mutton ['mʌtn] carne *f* de carnero
mutual ['mju:tʃuəl] mutuo
muzzle ['mʌzl] *s* hocico *m*; bozal *m*; boca *f* (*de arma de fuego*); *v/t* amordazar
my [mai] *pron pos* mi, mis
myopic [mai'ɔpik] miope
myrrh [mə:] mirra *f*
myrtle ['mə:tl] mirto *m*
myself [mai'self] *pron* yo mismo; me; mí
myst|erious [mis'tiəriəs] misterioso; **~ery** ['~təri] misterio *m*; **~ic** ['mistik] *a, s* místico(a) *m (f)*; **~ify** ['~tifai] *v/t* mistificar; desconcertar
myth [miθ] mito *m*

N

nab [næb] *v/t* arrestar, atrapar
nag [næg] *v/t, v/i* regañar
nail [neil] *s* uña *f*; clavo *m*; ***to hit the ~ on the head*** dar en el clavo; *v/t* clavar; **~ file** lima *f* para las uñas; **~ polish** laca *f* de uñas
naïve [nai'i:v] ingenuo
naked ['neikid] desnudo
name [neim] *s* nombre *m*; apellido *m*; título *m*; *v/t* poner nombre a; apellidar; designar; mencionar; ***maiden ~*** nombre *m* de soltera; ***what's your ~?*** ¿cómo se llama?; **~less** sin nombre; anónimo
namely ['neimli] a saber
nanny ['næni] niñera *f*; **~ goat** cabra *f*
nap [næp] sueño *m* ligero; ***to take a ~*** echar una siesta
nape [neip] nuca *f*
nap|kin ['næpkin] servilleta *f*; **~py** *fam* pañal *m*
narcotic [nɑ:'kɔtik] *a, s* narcótico *m*; **~s** estupefacientes *m/pl*
narrat|e [næ'reit] *v/t* narrar; **~ion** narración *f*; **~ive** ['~ətiv] narrativa *f*
narrow ['nærəu] *a* estrecho; limitado; *v/t* estrechar; limitar; *v/i* estrecharse; **~ly** por poco; **~-minded** intolerante, de miras estrechas
nasty ['nɑ:sti] horrible; sucio; repulsivo; peligroso
nation ['neiʃən] nación *f*; **~al** ['næʃənl] nacional; **~ality** [~'næliti] nacionalidad *f*; **~alize** ['næʃnəlaiz] *v/t* nacionalizar; **~wide** ['~waid] a nivel nacional
nativ|e ['neitiv] *a* nativo; natural; indígena; *s* natural *m, f*, nacional *m, f*, nativo(a) *m (f)*; **~ity** [nə'tiviti] natividad *f*
natural ['nætʃrəl] natural; **~ize** *v/t* naturalizar; **~ly** naturalmente; desde luego
nature ['neitʃə] naturaleza *f*; carácter *m*; índole *f*
naught [nɔ:t] nada *f*; cero *m*
naughty ['nɔ:ti] travieso; desobediente
nause|a ['nɔ:sjə] náusea *f*; **~ate** ['~ieit] *v/t* dar asco; **~ating** nauseabundo
nautical ['nɔ:tikəl] náutico; **~ mile** milla *f* marina
naval ['neivəl] naval
nave [neiv] *relig* nave *f*
navel ['neivəl] ombligo *m*
naviga|te ['nævigeit] *v/t, v/i* navegar; **~tor** navegante *m*
navy ['neivi] marina *f*; armada *f*; **~ blue** azul marino
near [niə] *prep* cerca de; junto a; próximo a; *adv* cerca; *a* cercano; próximo; contiguo; íntimo; inmediato; *v/i* acercarse a; **~by** cerca; **~ly** casi; por poco; **~ness** proximidad *f*; inminencia *f*; **~sighted** miope
neat [ni:t] pulcro; ordenado; **~ness** pulcritud *f*
necessary ['nesisəri] necesario; preciso
necessit|ate [ni'sesiteit] *v/t* necesitar, requerir; **~y** necesidad *f*; requisito *m*
neck [nek] cuello *m*; pescuezo *m*; gollete *m* (*de una botella*); **~lace** ['~lis] collar *m*; **~tie** corbata *f*
née [nei] nacida
need [ni:d] *s* necesidad *f*; carencia *f*; urgencia *f*; pobreza *f*; ***in ~*** necesitado; *v/t* necesitar; precisar
needle ['ni:dl] aguja *f*
needless ['ni:dlis] innecesario, inútil; ***~ to say*** huelga decir
needy ['ni:di] necesitado
negati|on [ni'geiʃən] negación *f*; **~ve** ['negətiv] *s* negativa *f*; *foto* negativo *m*; *a* negativo
negl|ect [ni'glekt] *s* descuido *m*; abandono *m*; *v/t* descuidar; abandonar; **~igent** ['neglidʒənt] negligente, descuidado; **~igible** insignificante
negotia|te [ni'gəuʃieit] *v/i* negociar; tratar; *v/t* negociar; tramitar; **~tion** negociación *f*; **~tor** negociador(a) *m (f)*
neigh [nei] *v/i* relinchar
neighbo(u)r ['neibə] vecino(a) *m (f)*; **~hood** vecindad *f*; barrio *m*; **~ing** cercano, vecino; **~ly** sociable
neither ['naiðə] *a* ningún (*de dos*); *pron* ninguno(a) (*de dos*); ni uno ni otro; *conj* ni; tampoco; ***~ ... nor*** ni ... ni
neon ['ni:ən] neón *m*
nephew ['nevju(:)] sobrino *m*
nerv|e [nə:v] nervio *m*; valor *m*; descaro *m*; ***what ~e!*** ¡qué caradura!; ***it gets on my ~es*** me crispa los nervios; **~ous** nervioso
nest [nest] *s* nido *m*
net [net] *s* red *f*; redecilla *f* (*para el pelo*); *a* neto; *v/t* coger con la red
Netherlands ['neðələndz] Países *m/pl* Bajos
nettle ['netl] ortiga *f*
network ['netwə:k] *radio, TV* red *f* de emisoras
neut|er ['nju:tə] *a* neutro; **~ral** ['~trəl] *a, s* neutral *m, f*; **~rality** [~'træliti] neutralidad *f*
neutron ['nju:trɔn] neutrón *m*
never ['nevə] nunca; jamás; **~ending** interminable; **~more** nunca más; **~theless** no obstante; sin embargo
new [nju:] nuevo; fresco; novicio; reciente; **~born** recién nacido; **~comer** recién llegado *m*; novato *m*; **~ly** nuevamente; **~lyweds** recién casados *m/pl*; **~ness** novedad *f*
news [nju:z] noticia *f*; noticias *f/pl*; **~cast** (*radio, TV*) telediario *m*; **~paper** periódico *m*; **~reel** noticiario *m*; actualidades *f/pl*; **~stand** quiosco *m* de periódicos
New| Year ['nju:'jə:] año *m* nuevo; ***~ Year's Eve*** Nochevieja *f*
next [nekst] *a* siguiente, venidero; próximo; ***~ time*** la próxima vez; ***~ to*** junto a; ***~ year*** el año que viene; *adv* luego; después; en seguida; **~-door** al lado
nibble [nibl] *v/t* mordiscar
Nicaragua [nikə'rægjuə] Nicaragua *f*; **~n** *a, s* nicaragüense *m, f*
nice [nais] simpático; amable; agradable; bonito; **~ly** muy bien; agradablemente; **~ness** amabilidad *f*; **~ties** ['~itiz] sutilezas *f/pl*
niche [nitʃ] nicho *m*
nick [nik] *s* mella *f*; *v/t* mellar
nickel ['nikl] níquel *m*
nickname ['nikneim] apodo *m*; mote *m*
nicotine ['nikəti:n] nicotina *f*
niece [ni:s] sobrina *f*
niggardly ['nigədli] tacaño
night [nait] noche *f*; ***at ~*** por la noche; ***by ~*** de noche; ***good ~!*** ¡buenas noches!; ***last ~*** anoche; ***tomorrow ~*** mañana por la noche; **~cap** gorro *m* de dormir; *fam* último trago *m* (*de la noche*); **~fall** anochecer *m*; **~gown** camisón *m*; **~ingale** ['~iŋgeil] ruiseñor *m*; **~ly** de noche; todas las noches; **~mare** ['~mεə] pesadilla *f*; **~ school** escuela *f* nocturna; **~time** noche *f*
nil [nil] nada
nimble ['nimbl] ágil, ligero
nine [nain] nueve
nip [nip] *s* pellizco *m*; traguito *m*; *v/t* pellizcar
nipple ['nipl] pezón *m*
nit|rate ['naitreit] nitrato *m*; **~rogen** ['~trədʒən] nitrógeno *m*
no [nəu] *adv* no; *a* ninguno; ***~ one*** nadie
nobility [nəu'biliti] nobleza *f*
nobl|e ['nəubl] noble; **~eman** noble *m*
nobody ['nəubədi] nadie; ***~ else*** nadie más
nod [nɔd] *s* seña *f* con la cabeza; *v/i* afirmar con la cabeza; inclinar la cabeza; dormitar
nois|e [nɔiz] ruido *m*; **~eless** silencioso; **~y** ruidoso
nomad ['nɔməd] *a, s* nómada *m, f*
nomina|l ['nɔminl] nominal; **~te** ['~eit] *v/t* proponer; nombrar; **~tion** nombramiento *m*; **~tive** ['~ətiv] nominativo *m*
non ['nɔn] *prefijo* no; des...; in...; falta de; **~acceptance** rechazo *m*; **~aligned** (*país*) neutral; **~chalant** [nɔnʃə'lɑ:nt] indiferente; **~-committal** evasivo; **~descript** ['~diskript] indefinido; indeterminado
none [nʌn] nadie, ninguno
non|entity [nɔ'nentiti] nulidad *f*; **~etheless** [nʌnðəles] no obstante; **~fiction** no ficción; **~observance** incumplimiento *m*; **~plus** ['nɔn'plʌs] *v/t* dejar perplejo; **~profit** sin fin lucrativo
nonsense ['nɔnsəns] disparate *m*; tontería *f*
non|reflecting ['nɔnri'flektiŋ] antirreflejo; **~skid** ['nɔn'skid] antideslizante; **~smoker** no fumador; **~stop** directo (*tren*); sin escalas
noodle ['nu:dl] fideo *m*
nook [nuk] rincón *m*
noon [nu:n] mediodía *m*
nor [nɔ:] tampoco; ni
norm [nɔ:m] norma *f*; **~al** normal
north [nɔ:θ] *s* norte *m*; *a* del norte; septentrional; *adv* hacia el norte; **2 America** América *f* del Norte; **2 American** *a, s* norteamericano(a) *m (f)*; **~ern** del norte; **2 Pole** Polo *m* Norte; **2 Sea** Mar *m* del Norte; **~wards** ['~wədz] hacia el norte
Norw|ay ['nɔ:wei] Noruega *f*; **~egian** [~'wi:dʒən] *a, s* noruego(a) *m (f)*
nose [nəuz] *s* nariz *f*; olfato *m*; ***blow one's ~*** sonarse; *v/i* ***~ about*** curiosear; **~ dive** *v/i* *aer* lanzarse de morro; **~gay** ['~gei] ramillete *m* de flores
nostalgia [nɔs'tældʒiə] nostalgia *f*, añoranza *f*
nostril ['nɔstril] ventana *f* de la nariz
nosy ['nəuzi] *fam* curioso
not [nɔt] no; ***why ~?*** ¿por qué no?; ***~ at all*** de ninguna manera; en absoluto; ***~ yet*** todavía no
notable ['nəutəbl] notable
notary ['nəutəri] notario *m*
notch [nɔtʃ] *s* muesca *f*
note [nəut] *s* nota *f*; billete *m*; señal *f*; apunte *m*; distinción *f*; *com* vale *m*; *v/t* apuntar; observar; advertir; **~book** libreta *f*; cuaderno *m*; **~d** afamado, conocido; **~paper** papel *m* de carta; **~worthy** notable
nothing ['nʌθiŋ] nada *f*; cero *m*; ***for ~*** gratis; ***~ if not*** más que todo; ***~ to do with*** nada que ver con; ***to say ~ of*** sin mencionar
notice ['nəutis] *s* aviso *m*; atención *f*; ***take ~ of*** hacer caso de; ***to give ~*** despedir (*a uno*); informar; ***short ~*** corto plazo *m*; *v/t* notar; advertir; **~able** perceptible; evidente
notify ['nəutifai] *v/t* notificar
notion ['nəuʃən] noción *f*; idea *f*; opinión *f*
notorious [nəu'tɔ:riəs] notorio
notwithstanding [nɔtwiθ'stændiŋ] *prep* a pesar de; *adv* no obstante
nought [nɔ:t] nada *f*; cero *m*
noun [naun] nombre *m*, sustantivo *m*
nourish ['nʌriʃ] *v/t* nutrir, alimentar; **~ing** nutritivo; **~ment** alimento *m*, sustento *m*
novel ['nɔvəl] *a* nuevo; *s* novela *f*; **~ist** novelista *m, f*; **~ty** novedad *f*
November [nəu'vembə] noviembre *m*
now [nau] ahora; ***right ~*** ahora mismo; ***~ and then*** de vez en cuando; **~adays** ['~ədeiz] hoy en día
nowhere ['nəuwεə] en ninguna parte
noxious ['nɔkʃəs] nocivo
nozzle ['nɔzl] boquilla *f*; *tecn* tobera *f*
nucle|ar ['nju:kliə] nuclear; **~us** ['nju:kliəs] núcleo *m*
nude [nju:d] *a, s* desnudo *m*
nudge [nʌdʒ] *s* codazo *m*; *v/t* dar un codazo
nudism ['nju:dizm] naturismo *m*
nugget ['nʌgit] pepita *f* (de oro)
nuisance ['nju:sns] fastidio *m*; molestia *f*
null [nʌl] nulo; ***~ and void*** nulo, sin efecto ni valor
numb [nʌm] entumecido; *v/t* entumecer, entorpecer
number ['nʌmbə] *s* número *m*; *v/t* numerar; **~ plate** *aut* placa *f* de matrícula
numer|al ['nju:mərəl] *a* numeral; *s* número *m*, cifra *f*; **~ous** numeroso
nun [nʌn] monja *f*
nuptials ['nʌpʃəlz] nupcias *f/pl*
nurs|e [nə:s] *s* enfermera *f*; niñera *f*; *v/t* criar; cuidar; **~ery** cuarto *m* de los niños; **~ery rhyme** canción *f* infantil; **~ery school** parvulario *m*; **~ing** crianza *f*; cuidado *m*; **~ing home** clínica *f* de inválidos
nut [nʌt] nuez *f*; *tecn* tuerca *f*; *fam* loco *m*; **~cracker** cascanueces *m*; **~meg** nuez *f* moscada; **~shell** cáscara *f* de nuez; ***in a ~shell*** en resumidas cuentas
nutritious [nju'triʃəs] nutritivo
nylon ['nailən] nilón *m*

O

oak [əuk] roble *m*
oar [ɔ:] remo *m*
oasis [əu'eisis] oasis *m*
oat [əut] avena *f*
oath [əuθ] juramento *m*; ***to take an ~*** prestar juramento
oatmeal ['əutmi:l] harina *f* de avena
obedien|ce [ə'bi:djəns] obediencia *f*; sumisión *f*; **~t** obediente; sumiso
obes|e [əu'bi:s] obeso; **~ity** obesidad *f*
obey [ə'bei] *v/t* obedecer; cumplir
obituary [ə'bitjuəri] necrología *f*
object ['ɔbdʒikt] *s* objeto *m*; materia *f*; propósito *m*; *gram* complemento *m*; [əb'dʒekt] *v/t* objetar; *v/i* oponerse; **~ion** objeción *f*, reparo *m*; ***to have no ~ion*** no ver ningún inconveniente; **~ionable** ofensivo; **~ive** *a, s* objetivo *m*
obligat|ion [ɔbli'geiʃən] obligación *f*; **~ory** [ɔ'bligətəri] obligatorio
oblig|e [ə'blaidʒ] *v/t* obligar; complacer; ***much ~ed*** muy agradecido; **~ing** servicial, atento
oblique [ə'bli:k] oblicuo; indirecto
obliterate [ə'blitəreit] *v/t* obliterar, borrar; aniquilar
oblivi|on [ə'bliviən] olvido *m*; **~ous:** ***to be ~ous of*** inconsciente de
oblong ['ɔblɔŋ] *s* figura *f* oblonga; *a* oblongo
obnoxious [əb'nɔkʃəs] ofensivo, detestable
obscene [əb'si:n] obsceno
obscure [əb'skjuə] *a* oscuro; vago; confuso; *v/t* oscurecer; anublar

obsequious [əb'si:kwiəs] obsequioso; servil
observan|ce [əb'zə:vəns] prática f; ~t observador
observ|ation [ɔbzə(:)'veiʃən] observación f; under ~ation vigilado; ~atory [əb'zə:vətri] observatorio m; ~e v/t observar; ~er observador m
obsess [əb'ses] v/t obsesionar; ~ion obsesión f
obsolete ['ɔbsəli:t] anticuado, desusado
obstacle ['ɔbstəkl] obstáculo m; inconveniente m
obstina|cy ['ɔbstinəsi] terquedad f; ~te [~it] terco; obstinado
obstruct [əb'strʌkt] v/t obstruir; estorbar; bloquear; ~ion obstrucción f; obstáculo m; estorbo m
obtain [əb'tein] v/t obtener, conseguir; ~able asequible
obtrusive [əb'tru:siv] intruso; importuno
obvious ['ɔbviəs] obvio; evidente; patente
occasion [ə'keiʒən] s ocasión f, oportunidad f; acontecimiento m; motivo m; v/t ocasionar; on the ~ of con motivo de; ~al poco frecuente; ~ally de vez en cuando
occupant ['ɔkjupənt] ocupante m; inquilino m
occup|ation [ɔkju'peiʃən] ocupación f; tenencia f; empleo m; profesión f; ~y ['~pai] v/t ocupar; vivir en; emplear (tiempo)
occur [ə'kə:] v/i ocurrir; suceder; ~rence [ə'kʌrəns] ocurrencia f; acontecimiento m; caso m
ocean ['əuʃən] océano m; ~ liner transatlántico m
o'clock [ə'klɔk]: it is two ~ son las dos
octane ['ɔktein] octano m
octave ['ɔktiv] octava f
October [ɔk'təubə] octubre m
octopus ['ɔktəpəs] pulpo m
ocul|ar ['ɔkjulə] ocular; ~ist oculista m, f
odd [ɔd] impar; y tanto; suelto; sobrante; raro; estrambótico; ocasional; ~ numbers impares m/pl; thirty ~ treinta y tanto; ~ity rareza f; ~ly curiosamente; ~s ventaja f; probabilidad f; at ~s en desacuerdo; ~s and ends retazos m/pl
odious ['əudjəs] odioso
odorous ['əudərəs] oloroso
odo(u)r ['əudə] olor m; ~less inodoro
of [ɔv, əv] prep de; all ~ them todos ellos; most ~ all más que nada; a cup ~ coffee una taza de café; it smells ~ fish huele a pescado; I dream ~ you sueño contigo; a friend ~ mine un amigo mío; ~ late últimamente; ~ course por supuesto
off [ɔf] prep lejos de; fuera de; a day ~ un día libre; 10% ~ 10% de descuento; ~ the road fuera de la carretera; adv lejos; fuera de servicio; to take ~ quitarse; despegar (el avión); to go ~ marcharse; ~ and on a intervalos; ~ with you! ¡lárgate! a tecn desconectado; apagado (luz)
offen|ce, ~se [ə'fens] ofensa f; delito m; to take ~ce ofenderse; ~d v/t ofender; v/i ~d against pecar contra; ~der ofensor m; delincuente m; ~sive s ofensiva f; a ofensivo
offer ['ɔfə] s oferta f; propuesta f; proposición f; v/t ofrecer; proponer; v/i ofrecerse, presentarse; ~ing relig ofrenda f; sacrificio m
offhand [ɔf'hænd] adv de improviso; a espontáneo
office ['ɔfis] oficina f; despacho m; oficio m; empleo m; to take ~ asumir un cargo; ~r oficial m; funcionario m; policía m
official [ə'fiʃəl] a oficial; s funcionario m; ~dom burocracia f
offing ['ɔfiŋ]: to be in the ~ estar en perspectiva
off|shoot ['ɔfʃu:t] vástago m; fig ramal m; ~shore cerca de la costa; ~side sp fuera de juego
offspring ['ɔfspriŋ] descendiente m, f; descendencia f
often ['ɔfn] adv muchas veces; frecuentemente; a menudo; how ~? ¿cuántas veces?
oil [ɔil] s aceite m; petróleo m; v/t aceitar, lubri(fi)car; engrasar; ~cloth encerado m; ~ gauge aut mediador m del aceite; ~ painting pintura f al óleo; ~skin impermeable m, chubasquero m; ~ well pozo m de petróleo; ~y aceitoso; grasiento
ointment ['ɔintmənt] ungüento m
OK, okay ['əu'kei] interj fam muy bien; ¡vale!; s visto m bueno
old [əuld] viejo; antiguo; añejo; grow ~ envejecer; how ~ is he? ¿cuántos años tiene?; ~ age vejez f; ~est el (la) más viejo(a); ~-fashioned pasado de moda; ~ maid solterona f; ♀ Testament Antiguo Testamento m
olive ['ɔliv] aceituna f; ~ tree olivo m
Olympic [əu'limpik] games juegos m/pl olímpicos
omelet(te) ['ɔmlit] tortilla f
omen ['əumen] agüero m; augurio m
ominous ['ɔminəs] siniestro; de mal agüero
omi|ssion [ə'miʃən] omisión f; olvido m; ~t v/t omitir; pasar por alto
omni|potent [ɔm'nipətənt] omnipotente; ~scient [~sient] omnisciente
on [ɔn] prep encima de; sobre; en; ~ account of a causa de; ~ Monday el lunes; ~ foot a pie; ~ holiday de vacaciones; ~ horseback a caballo; ~ purpose a propósito; adv adelante; sucesivamente; encima; puesto; encendido (gas, luz, etc); go ~! ¡siga!; to go ~ seguir adelante; come ~! ¡vamos!; ¡venga!; and so ~ y así sucesivamente; from then ~ desde entonces
once [wʌns] una vez; antiguamente; all at ~ de repente; at ~ en seguida; ~ in a while de vez en cuando; ~ more otra vez; ~ upon a time érase una vez
one [wʌn] a un, uno(a); único; cierto; un tal; ~ hundred ciento, cien; s, pron uno m; una f; la una (hora) f; this ~ éste(a); that ~ ése(a), aquél(la); ~ another el uno al otro; ~ by ~ uno a uno; ~'s su, sus; ~self uno(a) mismo(a); sí mismo(a); ~-armed manco; ~-sided parcial; ~-way street calle f de dirección única; ~-way ticket billete m de ida
onion ['ʌnjən] cebolla f
onlooker ['ɔnlukə] espectador(a) m (f)
only ['əunli] a único; solo; an ~ child un hijo m único; adv solamente, sólo; únicamente; recién; ~ just apenas; conj sólo que; pero
onrush ['ɔnrʌʃ] arremetida f
onset ['ɔnset] ataque m; comienzo m
onward ['ɔnwəd] a progresivo; ~(s) adv adelante
ooze [u:z] s cieno m; v/t exudar
opaque [əu'peik] opaco
open ['əupən] a abierto; libre; franco; manifiesto; descubierto; susceptible de; com pendiente; v/t abrir; descubrir; dar comienzo a; in the ~ al aire libre; bring into the ~ hacer público; ~er abridor m; ~ing abertura f; comienzo m; oportunidad f; ~ly abiertamente; ~-minded imparcial; ~ness franqueza f
opera ['ɔpərə] ópera f; ~ glasses gemelos m/pl de teatro
operat|e ['ɔpəreit] v/t impulsar; hacer funcionar; v/i operar; obrar, actuar; med operar; ~ing room sala f de operaciones; ~ion operación f; funcionamiento m; ~ive ['~ətiv] a eficaz; activo; ~or operador m
opinion [ə'pinjən] opinión f; juicio m; parecer m; in my ~ a mi parecer; ~ated testarudo (en sus opiniones)
opium ['əupjəm] opio m
opponent [ə'pəunənt] antagonista m; adversario m
opportunity [ɔpə'tju:niti] oportunidad f
oppos|e [ə'pəuz] v/t oponerse a; ~ed opuesto; ~ing contrario; divergente; ~ite ['ɔpəzit] de enfrente; opuesto; ~ition [ɔpə'ziʃən] oposición f; resistencia f
oppress [ə'pres] v/t oprimir; ~ion opresión f; ~ive opresivo; agobiante
optic|(al) ['ɔptik(əl)] a óptico; ~ian [ɔp'tiʃən] óptico m; ~s óptica f
optimism ['ɔptimizəm] optimismo m
or [ɔ:] conj o; u; ~ else de otro modo; si no; either ... ~ o ... o
oral ['ɔ:rəl] oral
orange ['ɔrindʒ] naranja f; ~ade ['~eid] naranjada f
orator ['ɔrətə] orador m
orbit ['ɔ:bit] órbita f
orchard ['ɔ:tʃəd] huerto m
orchestra ['ɔ:kistrə] orquesta f
orchid ['ɔ:kid] orquídea f
ordeal [ɔ:'di:l] prueba f dura
order ['ɔ:də] s mandato m; orden m; arreglo m; com pedido m; orden f (militar o religiosa); condecoración f; in ~ that para que; in ~ to para; in short ~ en breve plazo; on ~ por encargo; out of ~ estropeado; "no funciona"; to put in ~ arreglar; v/t ordenar, mandar; dirigir; com pedir; ~ly a ordenado; metódico; s mil ordenanza m
ordinary ['ɔ:dnri] ordinario; común; corriente
ore [ɔ:] mineral m
organ ['ɔ:gən] órgano m
organic [ɔ:'gænik] orgánico
organiz|ation [ɔ:gənai'zeiʃən] organización f; ~e ['~aiz] v/t, v/i organizar(se)
Orient ['ɔ:riənt] Oriente m; ♀ation orientación f
origin ['ɔridʒin] origen m; principio m; procedencia f; ~al [ə'ridʒənl] a original, primitivo; legítimo; s original m; prototipo m; ~ality [əridʒi'næliti] originalidad f; ~ate [ə'ridʒineit] v/t crear; ocasionar; v/i originarse; provenir
orna|ment ['ɔ:nəmənt] s ornamento m; adorno m; [~'ment] v/t adornar; decorar; ~mental ornamental
orphan ['ɔ:fən] huérfano(a) m (f); ~age orfanato m
ortho|dox ['ɔ:θədɔks] ortodoxo; ~pedic [~'pidik] ortopédico
oscillat|e ['ɔsileit] v/i oscilar; ~ion oscilación f
ostentatious [ɔsten'teiʃəs] ostentativo; aparatoso
ostrich ['ɔstritʃ] avestruz m
other ['ʌðə] a otro(a, os, as); adv ~ than otra cosa que; pron el otro, la otra; one after the ~ uno tras otro; ~wise ['~waiz] de otra manera
ought [ɔ:t] v/aux deber; he ~ to write debería escribir
ounce [auns] onza f
our ['auə] a nuestro(a, os, as); ♀ Father padrenuestro m; ~s pron pos el nuestro, la nuestra, los nuestros, las nuestras; ~selves nosotros(as) mismos(as)
oust [aust] v/t desalojar, expulsar
out [aut] adv fuera; afuera; de fuera; ausente; terminado; apagado; de huelga; pasado de moda; al descubierto; get ~! ¡fuera!; prep ~ of fuera de; ~ of danger fuera de peligro; to go ~ salir
out|board fuera de borda; ~break erupción f; estallido m; ~burst explosión f; ~cast paria m, f; ~come resultado m; ~cry protesta f; ~do v/t superar, exceder; ~doors al aire libre; ~er externo; ~fit s equipo m; pertrechos m/pl; v/t equipar; ~flow efusión f; ~going saliente; extrovertido; ~grow v/t superar; salirse de; ~ing excursión f; ~law s proscrito m; v/t proscribir; ~lay gasto m; ~let salida f; desahogo m; ~line s contorno m; v/t trazar; ~live v/t sobrevivir a; ~look perspectiva f; ~lying remoto; ~moded anticuado; ~number v/t exceder en número; ~patient paciente m, f externo(a); ~post puesto m de avanzada; ~put producción f; ~rage s ultraje m; atrocidad f; v/t ultrajar; ~rageous [aut'reidʒəs] escandaloso; ~right ['aut'rait] a completo; definitivo; adv de una vez; ~run v/t correr más que; ~set principio m; ~side a externo, exterior; s exterior m; adv fuera; prep fuera de; ~sider extraño m; forastero m; ~skirts alrededores m/pl; ~spoken franco; ~standing destacado; com pendiente; ~strip v/t aventajar; ~ward [~'wəd] a exterior; externo; ~wards adv hacia fuera; ~weigh v/t exceder; valer más que; ~wit v/t ser más listo que
oval ['əuvəl] oval, ovalado
oven [ʌvn] horno m
over ['əuvə] prep sobre; encima de; por encima de; durante; por; adv encima; ~ here acá; ~ there allá; it's all ~! ¡se acabó!; ~ and out mil cambio y corte; ~ and ~ repetidamente; ~alls mono m; ~bearing despótico; ~board al agua; ~booking sobreocupación f; ~cast anublado; ~charge v/t cobrar en demasía; ~coat abrigo m; ~come v/t vencer; ~crowding sobrepoblación f; ~do v/t excederse en; exagerar; ~dose sobredosis f; ~draw v/t girar en descubierto; ~due retrasado; ~flow v/i desbordarse; derramarse; ~haul v/i revisar (coche etc); ~head a de arriba; s com gastos m/pl generales; ~hear v/t oír por casualidad; ~joyed contentísimo; ~lap v/i traslaparse; ~load v/t sobrecargar; ~look v/t dominar (con la vista); pasar por alto; no hacer caso de; ~night durante la noche; ~pass f c paso m superior; ~power v/t subyugar; vencer; ~rate v/t sobrestimar; ~rule v/t for denegar; ~run v/t invadir; ~seas ultramar; ~seer capataz m; superintendente m; ~shadow v/t obscurecer; fig eclipsar; ~sight inadvertencia f; descuido m; ~sleep quedarse dormido; ~state v/t exagerar; ~strung muy tenso; ~take v/t alcanzar; aut adelantar; ~throw v/t volcar; derribar; ~time horas f/pl extraordinarias
overture ['əuvətjuə] mús obertura f
over|turn [əuvə'tə:n] v/t volcar; derribar; v/i volcar; ~weight exceso m de peso; ~whelm [~'welm] v/t abrumar; aplastar; ~work v/i trabajar en exceso
owe [əu] v/t deber
owing ['əuiŋ] to debido a
owl [aul] búho m; lechuza f
own [əun] v/t poseer; reconocer; a propio; on one's ~ por su propia cuenta; ~er propietario m; ~ership posesión f; propiedad f
ox [ɔks] buey m
ox|ide ['ɔksaid] óxido m; ~ygen ['ɔksidʒən] oxígeno m
oyster ['ɔistə] ostra f
ozone ['əuzəun] ozono m

P

pace [peis] s paso m; marcha f; v/i to ~ up and down pasearse de un lado a otro; ~maker med marcapasos m
pacif|ic [pə'sifik] pacífico; ~ist ['pæsifist] a, s pacifista m, f; ~y ['~fai] v/t pacificar; apaciguar
pack [pæk] s paquete m; fardo m; cajetilla f (de cigarrillos); baraja f (de naipes); pandilla f (de ladrones); jauría f (de perros); manada f (de lobos); v/t empaquetar; embalar; ~ off despachar; v/i hacer las maletas
pack|age ['pækidʒ] paquete m; bulto m; ~er embalador m; ~et ['~it] paquete m pequeño; ~ing embalaje m
pact [pækt] pacto m
pad [pæd] s almohadilla f; ~ of paper bloc m; v/t forrar; rellenar
paddle ['pædl] s canalete m; paleta f; v/t remar (con paleta)
paddock ['pædək] corral m
padlock ['pædlɔk] candado m
pagan ['peigən] a, s pagano(a) m (f)
page [peidʒ] s página f (de libro); plana f (de periódico); paje m (chico); botones m; v/t paginar
pageant ['pædʒənt] desfile m espectacular; ~ry pompa f, boato m
pail [peil] cubo m, balde m

pain [pein] *s* dolor *m*; *v/t* doler; dar lástima; ***to feel ~*** sentir dolor; sufrir; ***to take ~s*** empeñarse; **~ful** doloroso; **~less** sin dolor; **~staking** esmerado; concienzudo
paint [peint] *s* pintura *f*; *v/t* pintar; *v/i* ser pintor; maquillarse; **~er** pintor(a) *m* (*f*); **~ing** pintura *f*; cuadro *m*
pair [pɛə] *s* par *m*; pareja *f*; yunta *f* (*de bueyes*); ***~ of scissors*** tijeras *f/pl*; ***~ of glasses*** gafas *f/pl*; ***~ of trousers*** pantalones *m/pl*; *v/t* ***~ off*** aparear; acoplar
pajamas [pə'dʒæməz] *Am* pijama *m*, *LA f*
pal [pæl] *fam* compañero *m*
palace ['pælis] palacio *m*
palate ['pælit] paladar *m*
pal|e [peil] *a* pálido; ***to grow ~e*** palidecer; *s* estaca *f*; **~ing** estacada *f*; **~isade** [pæli'seid] palizada *f*
pallor ['pælə] palidez *f*
palm [pɑ:m] palma *f*; palmera *f*; **♀ Sunday** Domingo *m* de Ramos
palpitation [pælpi'teiʃən] palpitación *f*
paltry ['pɔ:ltri] baladí
pamper ['pæmpə] *v/t* mimar
pamphlet ['pæmflit] folleto *m*
pan [pæn] cacerola *f*; ***frying ~*** sartén *f*
Panama ['pænəmɑ:] Panamá *m*; **~nian** *a*, *s* panameño(a) *m* (*f*)
pancake ['pænkeik] hojuela *f*, tortita *f*, *LA* panqueque *m*
pane [pein] cristal *m*; hoja *f* de vidrio
panel ['pænl] *s* entrepaño *m*; tablero *m*; panel *m*; *v/t* cubrir de paneles; **~(l)ing** paneles *m/pl*
pang [pæŋ] dolor *m* agudo; punzada *f*; ***~s of conscience*** remordimiento *m*
panic ['pænik] *s* pánico *m*; terror *m*; *v/t*, *v/i* aterrar(se); **~-stricken** despavorido
pansy ['pænzi] *bot* pensamiento *m*
pant [pænt] *v/i* jadear
panther ['pænθə] pantera *f*
panties ['pæntiz] *fam* bragas *f/pl*; *LA* pantaletas *f/pl*
pantry ['pæntri] despensa *f*
pants ['pænts] calzoncillos *m/pl*; *Am* pantalones *m/pl*; **~ suit** traje *m* pantalón
panty ['pænti] **hose** media *f* panty
papa [pə'pɑ:] papá *m*
papacy ['peipəsi] papado *m*
paper ['peipə] *s* papel *m*; documento *m*; artículo *m*; *v/t* empapelar; **~back** libro *m* de bolsillo; **~ clip** sujetapapeles *m*, clip *m*; **~-hanger** empapelador *m*; **~ money** papel *m* moneda; **~ towels** papel *m* de cocina; **~weight** pisapapeles *m*; **~ work** papeleo *m*
par [pɑ:] par *f*; *sp m*; ***on a ~ with*** estar a la par con
parachut|e ['pærəʃu:t] *s* paracaídas *m*; *v/i* saltar con paracaídas; **~ist** paracaidista *m*
parade [pə'reid] *s* desfile *m*; *v/t* ostentar; *v/i* desfilar
paradise ['pærədais] paraíso *m*
paragraph ['pærəgrɑ:f] párrafo *m*
Paraguay ['pærəgwai] el Paraguay; **~an** *a*, *s* paraguayo(a) *m* (*f*)
parallel ['pærəlel] *a* paralelo; *s* paralela *f*; paralelo *m*
paraly|se ['pærəlaiz] *v/t* paralizar; **~sis** [pə'rælisis] parálisis *f*; **~tic** [pærə'litik] *a*, *s* paralítico(a) *m* (*f*)
paramount ['pærəmaunt] sumo; supremo
parasite ['pærəsait] parásito *m*
parcel ['pɑ:sl] *s* paquete *m*; lío *m*; bulto *m*; parcela *f* (*de tierra*); *v/t* **~ out** parcelar; repartir
parch [pɑ:tʃ] *v/t* (re)secar; **~ment** pergamino *m*
pardon ['pɑ:dn] *s* perdón *m*; *for* indulto *m*; *v/t* perdonar; ***I beg your ~*** perdone
pare [pɛə] *v/t* cortar; mondar; ***~ down*** reducir
parent ['pɛərənt] padre *m*; madre *f*; **~s** padres *m/pl*
parenthesis [pə'renθisis] paréntesis *m*
parings ['pɛəriŋz] peladuras *f/pl*, mondaduras *f/pl*
parish ['pæriʃ] parroquia *f*; **~ioner** [pə'riʃənə] parroquiano *m*
parity ['pæriti] paridad *f*
park [pɑ:k] *s* parque *m*; *v/t*, *v/i* estacionar; **~ing: *~ing attendant*** guardacoches *m*; ***~ing lot*** estacionamiento *m*; aparcamiento *m*; ***no ~ing*** prohibido estacionarse; **~ing meter** parquímetro *m*
Parliament ['pɑ:ləmənt] parlamento *m*; **♀ary** [~'mentəri] parlamentario
parlo(u)r ['pɑ:lə] salón *m*
parody ['pærədi] parodia *f*
parole [pə'rəul]: ***on ~*** *for* libre bajo palabra
parquet ['pɑ:kei] parqué *m*
parrot ['pærət] loro *m*; papagayo *m*
parsley ['pɑ:sli] perejil *m*
parson ['pɑ:sn] clérigo *m*
part [pɑ:t] *s* parte *f*; porción *f*; trozo *m*; paraje *m*; *teat* papel *m*; ***for my ~*** en cuanto a mí; ***to take ~ in*** tomar parte en; *v/t* dividir; repartir; *v/i* separarse; partir; ***~ from*** despedirse de; ***~ with*** privarse de; deshacerse de
partial ['pɑ:ʃəl] parcial; **~ity** [~ʃi'æliti] parcialidad *f*
particip|ant [pɑ:'tisipənt] participante *m*, *f*; **~ate** [~eit] *v/t* participar; *v/i* tomar parte (en); **~ation** participación *f*
participle ['pɑ:tisipl] participio *m*
particle ['pɑ:tikl] partícula *f*
particular [pə'tikjulə] particular; especial; quisquilloso; **~ity** [~'læriti] particularidad *f*; peculiaridad *f*
parting ['pɑ:tiŋ] separación *f*
partition [pɑ:'tiʃən] *s* división *f*; *v/t* repartir; dividir; **~ wall** tabique *m*
partly ['pɑ:tli] en parte
partner ['pɑ:tnə] socio(a) *m* (*f*); pareja *f*; **~ship** asociación *f*; sociedad *f*; ***to enter into ~ship with*** asociarse con
partridge ['pɑ:tridʒ] perdiz *f*
part-time ['pɑ:t'taim] de media jornada; por horas (*trabajo etc*)
party ['pɑ:ti] partido *m*; grupo *m*; partida *f*; fiesta *f*
pass [pɑ:s] *s* puerto *m* (*de montaña*); *sp* pase *m*; permiso *m*, licencia *f*; *v/t* pasar; traspasar; llevar; superar; aprobar (*examen*); ***~ out*** distribuir; ***~ over*** pasar por alto; ***~ up*** no aprovechar; *v/i* pasar; ser aceptable; ***~ away*** fallecer; ***~ out*** *fam* desmayarse; ***~ through*** estar de paso por; **~able** transitable; tolerable; **~age** paso *m*; pasaje *m*; travesía *f*; corredor *m*; **~enger** ['pæsindʒə] pasajero *m*; **~er-by** ['pɑ:sə'bai] transeúnte *m*; **~ing** pasajero
passion ['pæʃən] pasión *f*; cólera *f*; **~ate** ['~it] apasionado; colérico
passiv|e ['pæsiv] *a*, *s* pasivo *m*; **~ity** [~'siviti] pasividad *f*
pass|port ['pɑ:spɔ:t] pasaporte *m*; **~word** contraseña *f*
past [pɑ:st] *s* pasado *m*; *a* pasado; último; concluido; *prep* más de, más allá de; ***half ~ six*** las seis y media
paste [peist] *s* pasta *f*; engrudo *m*; *v/t* empastar; pegar; **~board** cartón *m*
pastime ['pɑ:staim] pasatiempo *m*; recreo *m*
pastry ['peistri] pasteles *m/pl*; pastas *f/pl*
pasture ['pɑ:stʃə] *s* pasto *m*; dehesa *f*; *v/t* apacentar; *v/i* pacer
pat [pæt] *s* palmadita *f*, golpecillo *m* de mano; *v/t* acariciar; dar golpecitos con la mano
patch [pætʃ] *s* remiendo *m*; parche *m*; *agr* terreno *m*; *v/t* remendar; ***~ up*** reparar; chapucear; **~work** obra *f* de retazos; **~y** desigual
patent ['peitənt] *a* patente; manifiesto; *s* patente *f* (*de invención*); privilegio *m*; *v/t* patentar; **~ leather** charol *m*; **~ly** evidentemente
patern|al [pə'tə:nl] paterno; paternal; **~ity** paternidad *f*
path [pɑ:θ] senda *f*, sendero *m*; camino *m*
pathetic [pə'θetik] patético, conmovedor
patien|ce ['peiʃəns] paciencia *f*; **~t** *a* paciente; *s* paciente *m*, *f*
patio ['pɑ:tiəu] patio *m*
patriot ['peitriət] *a*, *s* patriota *m*, *f*; **~ic** [pætri'ɔtik] patriótico; **~ism** ['pætriətizəm] patriotismo *m*
patrol [pə'trəul] *s* patrulla *f*; ronda *f*; *v/t*, *v/i* patrullar; **~ car** coche *m* patrullero
patron ['peitrən] cliente *m*; patrocinador *m*; ***~ saint*** patrono(a) *m* (*f*); **~age** ['pætrənidʒ] patrocinio *m*; **~ize** *v/t* patrocinar; frecuentar
patter ['pætə] *s* pasos *m/pl* ligeros; *v/i* andar con pasos ligeros; tamborilear
pattern ['pætən] *s* modelo *m*; dibujo *m*; *costura* patrón *m*; *v/t* modelar
paunch [pɔ:ntʃ] panza *f*
pause [pɔ:z] *s* pausa *f*; *v/i* cesar; hacer una pausa
pave [peiv] *v/t* pavimentar; **~ment** pavimento *m*
pavilion [pə'viljən] pabellón *m*
paw [pɔ:] *s* pata *f*, zarpa *f*; garra *f*; *v/t* piafar; manosear
pawn [pɔ:n] *s* (*ajedrez*) peón *m*; *v/t* empeñar; **~broker** prestamista *m*; **~shop** prendería *f*; monte *m* de piedad
pay [pei] *s* paga *f*; sueldo *m*; *v/t* pagar; abonar; ***it doesn't ~*** no vale la pena; ***~ back*** reembolsar; ***~ cash*** pagar al contado; ***~ down*** pagar a cuenta; ***~ in advance*** adelantar; ***~ off*** amortizar; ***~ a visit*** hacer una visita; **~able** pagadero; **~ee** [~'i:] tenedor *m*; **~er** pagador *m*; **~load** carga *f* útil; **~ment** pago *m*; ***make a ~ment*** efectuar un pago; ***stop ~ment*** detener el cobro; **~roll** nómina *f*, *LA* planilla *f*
pea [pi:] guisante *m*
peace [pi:s] paz *f*; **~ful** apacible, pacífico; sosegado; **~maker** pacificador *m*
peach [pi:tʃ] melocotón *m*; *LA* durazno *m*
peacock ['pi:kɔk] pavo *m* real
peak [pi:k] *s* pico *m*; cumbre *f*; *a* máximo; **~ hours** horas *f/pl* punta
peal [pi:l] *v/i* repicar; *s* repique *m* (*de las campanas*)
peanut ['pi:nʌt] cacahuete *m*
pear [pɛə] pera *f*; ***~ tree*** peral *m*
pearl [pə:l] perla *f*
peasant ['pezənt] campesino *m*
peat [pi:t] turba *f*
pebble ['pebl] guijarro *m*
peck [pek] *s* picotazo *m*; *v/t*, *v/i* picotear
peculiar [pi'kju:ljə] raro; peculiar; especial; **~ity** [~i'æriti] peculiaridad *f*; singularidad *f*
pedal ['pedl] *s* pedal *m*; *v/i* pedalear
pedant ['pedənt] pedante *m*
pedestal ['pedistl] pedestal *m*
pedestrian [pi'destriən] *s* peatón *m*; **~ crossing** paso *m* de peatones
pedigree ['pedigri:] linaje *m*
peek [pi:k] *s* mirada *f* furtiva; *v/i* mirar furtivamente
peel [pi:l] *v/t* pelar; *s* cáscara *f*; corteza *f*
peep [pi:p] *s* pío *m* (*pájaros*); atisbo *m*; *v/i* piar; atisbar
peer [piə] *s* par *m*; igual *m*; *v/t* mirar de cerca; **~age** nobleza *f*; **~less** sin par
peevish ['pi:viʃ] malhumorado; irritable
peg [peg] *s* clavija *f*; gancho *m*; pretexto *m*; pinzas *f/pl*; *v/t* estaquillar; fijar
pejorative ['pi:dʒərətiv] peyorativo
pelican ['pelikən] pelícano *m*
pelt [pelt] *v/t* lanzar, arrojar
pen [pen] *s* pluma *f*; corral *m*; *v/t* **~ (up)** encerrar
penal ['pi:nl] penal; **~ty** ['penlti] pena *f*, castigo *m*
penance ['penəns] penitencia *f*
pencil ['pensl] lápiz *m*; **~ sharpener** sacapuntas *m*
pendant ['pendənt] medallón *m*; pendiente *m*
pending ['pendiŋ] *a* pendiente; *prep* antes de
penetrate ['penitreit] *v/t* penetrar
penguin ['peŋgwin] pingüino *m*
penicillin [peni'silin] penicilina *f*
peninsula [pi'ninsjulə] península *f*
penis ['pi:nis] pene *m*
peniten|t ['penitənt] *s* penitente *m*; *a* arrepentido; **~tiary** cárcel *f*
penknife ['pennaif] cortaplumas *m*, navaja *f*
penniless ['penilis] indigente; sin dinero
pennant ['penənt] banderola *f*
penny ['peni] penique *m*
pension ['penʃən] *s* pensión *f*; retiro *m*; jubilación *f*; *v/t* pensionar; **~er** pensionado(a) *m* (*f*); pensionista *m*, *f*
pensive ['pensiv] pensativo
penthouse ['penthaus] apartamento *m* de azotea
pent-up ['pent'ʌp] contenido; reprimido
people ['pi:pl] *s* gente *f*; pueblo *m*; *v/t* poblar
pep [pep] *s* ánimo *m*, vigor *m*; *v/t* **~ up** animar
pepper ['pepə] pimienta *f*; ***green ~*** pimiento *m*; **~mint** menta *f*; pastilla *f* de menta
per [pə:] por
perceive [pə'si:v] *v/t* percibir; comprender
per|cent [pə'sent] por ciento *m*; **~centage** porcentaje *m*
percept|ible [pə'septəbl] perceptible; **~ion** percepción *f*; perspicacia *f*
perch [pə:tʃ] *s* percha *f*; *v/i* posarse
percussion [pə'kʌʃən] percusión *f*
peremptory [pə'remptəri] perentorio, terminante
perfect ['pə:fikt] *a* perfecto; acabado; [pə'fekt] *v/t* perfeccionar; **~ion** perfección *f*; **~ly** perfectamente
perforat|e ['pə:fəreit] *v/t* perforar; **~ion** perforación *f*; agujero *m*
perform [pə'fɔ:m] *v/t* ejecutar; llevar a cabo; cumplir; *v/i* actuar, representar; **~ance** ejecución *f*; *teat*, *mús* función *f*; actuación *f*
perfume ['pə:fju:m] *s* perfume *m*; fragancia *f*; [pə'fju:m] *v/t* perfumar
perhaps [pə'hæps, præps] quizá, quizás; tal vez; ***~ not*** puede que no
peril ['peril] peligro *m*; riesgo *m*; **~ous** peligroso; arriesgado
period ['piəriəd] período *m*; época *f*; punto *m*; *med* regla *f*; **~ical** [~'ɔdikəl] *a*, *s* periódico *m*
perish ['periʃ] *v/i* perecer; **~able** perecedero
perjury ['pə:dʒəri] perjurio *m*
perk [pə:k] *v/i* erguirse; **~ up** animarse; sentirse mejor
perm [pə:m] *fam* permanente *f*; **~anence** ['~ənəns] permanencia *f*; **~anent** permanente, duradero
permeate ['pə:mieit] *v/t* penetrar; impregnar
permi|ssion [pə'miʃən] permiso *m*; **~ssive** tolerante, permisivo; **~t** [~'mit] *v/t* permitir; ['pə:mit] *s* permiso *m*; licencia *f*
perpendicular [pə:pən'dikjulə] perpendicular
perpetual [pə'petʃuəl] perpetuo, continuo
perplex [pə'pleks] *v/t* confundir; **~ed** perplejo
persecut|e ['pə:sikju:t] *v/t* perseguir; acosar; **~ion** persecución *f*
persevere [pə:si'viə] *v/i* perseverar, persistir
Persian ['pə:ʃn] *a*, *s* persa *m*, *f*
persist [pə'sist] *v/i* persistir; empeñarse; **~ence** persistencia *f*, empeño *m*; **~ent** persistente, tenaz
person ['pə:sn] persona *f*; ***in ~*** en persona; **~age** personaje *m*; **~al** personal; particular; **~ality** [~sə'næliti] personalidad *f*; **~ify** [~'sɔnifai] *v/t* personificar; **~nel** [~sə'nel] personal *m*
perspective [pə'spektiv] perspectiva *f*
perspir|ation [pə:spə'reiʃən] transpiración *f*; sudor *m*; **~e** [pəs'paiə] *v/t* transpirar, sudar
persua|de [pə'sweid] *v/t* persuadir; **~sion** [~ʒən] persuasión *f*; **~sive** [~siv] persuasivo
pert [pə:t] descarado, fresco, respondón
pertain [pə:'tein] *v/i*: ***~ to*** referirse a
Peru [pə'ru:] el Perú
perus|al [pə'ru:zəl] lectura *f* cuidadosa; **~e** *v/t* leer; examinar
Peruvian [pə'ru:viən] *a*, *s* peruano(a) *m* (*f*)
pervade [pə:'veid] *v/t* penetrar; saturar
perver|se [pə'və:s] perverso;

~**sion** perversión f; corrupción f; ~**t** ['pəːvəːt] s pervertido m; [pə'vəːt] v/t pervertir; falsear

pessimis|m ['pesimizəm] pesimismo m; ~**t** pesimista m, f

pest [pest] plaga f; insecto m; ~**er** v/t molestar, fastidiar; ~**icide** ['~isaid] insecticida m

pet [pet] s favorito m; animal m doméstico; v/t mimar; acariciar

petal ['petl] pétalo m

petition [pi'tiʃən] s petición f; instancia f; ruego m; v/t suplicar; ~**er** suplicante m

pet name ['pet'neim] apodo m cariñoso

petrify ['petrifai] v/t, v/i petrificar(se)

petrol ['petrəl] gasolina f; ~ ***station*** gasolinera f

petroleum [pi'trəuljəm] petróleo m

petticoat ['petikəut] enagua f

petty ['peti] mezquino; insignificante; ~ **cash** gastos m/pl menores

petulant ['petjulənt] malhumorado; irritable

pew [pjuː] banco m de iglesia

phantom ['fæntəm] fantasma m

pharmacy ['fɑːməsi] farmacia f, botica f

phase [feiz] s fase f; v/t ~ ***out*** reducir por etapas

pheasant ['feznt] faisán m

phenomen|al [fi'nɔminl] fenomenal; ~**on** fenómeno m

philantropist [fi'lænθrəpist] filántropo m

Philippine ['filipain] a, s filipino(a) m (f); ~**s** (Islas) Filipinas f/pl

philolog|ist [fi'lɔlədʒist] filólogo m; ~**y** filología f

philosoph|er [fi'lɔsəfə] filósofo m; ~**ize** v/i filosofar; ~**y** filosofía f

phone [fəun] fam s teléfono m; v/t, v/i telefonear

phonetic [fəu'netik] fonético; ~**s** fonética f

phon(e)y ['fəuni] s farsante m, f; a falso; insincero

photo ['fəutəu] foto f; ~**copy** fotocopia f; ~**genic** [~'dʒenik] fotogénico; ~**grapher** [fə'tɔgrəfə] fotógrafo m; ~**graphy** fotografía f; ~**synthesis** fotosíntesis f

phrase [freiz] frase f; locución f

physic|al ['fizikəl] físico; ~**ian** [fi'ziʃən] médico m; ~**ist** ['~sist] físico m; ~**s** física f

physique [fi'zik] físico m

piano [pi'ænəu] piano m

pick [pik] s pico m; piqueta f; v/t picar; coger; seleccionar; ~ ***on*** meterse con; ~ ***out*** escoger; discernir; ~ ***up*** recoger; aprender; ~**et** s estaca f; piquete m; ~**et line** línea f de huelguistas

pickle ['pikl] s escabeche m; v/t escabechar; salar

pick|pocket ['pikpɔkit] ratero m; ~**up** furgoneta f; camioneta f

picnic ['piknik] jira f; merienda f campestre

pictorial [pik'tɔːriəl] a pictórico; s revista f ilustrada

picture ['piktʃə] s cuadro m; ilustración f, grabado m; cine película f; v/t describir, pintar, retratar

picturesque [piktʃə'resk] pintoresco

pie [pai] pastel m (de frutas)

piece [piːs] s trozo m; pieza f; pedazo m; ***a ~ of advice*** un consejo m; ***a ~ of news*** una noticia f; ***in ~s*** hecho pedazos; v/t remendar; juntar; ~**work** trabajo m a destajo

pier [piə] muelle m; embarcadero m

pierc|e [piəs] v/t penetrar; taladrar; atravesar; conmover; ~**ing** agudo

piety ['paiəti] piedad f

pig [pig] cerdo m, puerco m, marrano m, LA chancho m

pigeon ['pidʒin] pichón m, paloma f

pig|headed ['pig'hedid] testarudo; ~**sty** ['~stai] pocilga f; ~**tail** trenza f (de pelo), coleta f

pike [paik] pica f; lucio m

pile [pail] s pila f; montón m; v/t ~ ***up*** amontonar; v/i amontonarse

pilfer ['pilfə] v/t ratear

pilgrim ['pilgrim] peregrino m; ~**age** peregrinación f; romería f

pill [pil] píldora f

pillar ['pilə] pilar m; columna f; fig soporte m

pillow ['piləu] almohada f; ~**case**, ~**slip** funda f de almohada

pilot ['pailət] s piloto m; mar práctico m; v/t pilotar; guiar

pimp [pimp] chulo m

pimple ['pimpl] grano m

pin [pin] s alfiler m; broche m; tecn perno m; v/t prender con alfileres; ~ ***up*** sujetar; clavar

pincers ['pinsəz] tenazas f/pl; pinzas f/pl

pinch [pintʃ] s pellizco m; pizca f; aprieto m; apuro m; v/t pellizcar; hurtar, birlar; v/i apretar

pine [pain] s pino m; v/i ~ ***away*** desfallecer; languidecer; ~ ***for*** ansiar; ~**apple** ananás m; piña f; ~**cone** piña f (del pino)

ping [piŋ] sonido m metálico

pink [piŋk] a rosado; s clavel m

pinnacle ['pinəkl] ápice m; cima f; cumbre f

pinpoint ['pinpɔint] v/t indicar con precisión

pint [paint] pinta f (1/8 de galón)

pioneer [paiə'niə] s explorador m; pionero m; v/t explorar; fig promover

pious ['paiəs] piadoso, devoto

pip [pip] semilla f, pepita f

pip|e [paip] s tubo m, caño m; cañería f; cañón m (del órgano); pipa f (de fumar); ~**eline** tubería f; oleoducto m; ~**ing** cañería f

piquant ['pikənt] picante (t fig)

pique [pik] pique m; ***in a ~*** resentido

pirate ['paiərit] pirata m

pistol ['pistl] pistola f

piston ['pistən] émbolo m, pistón m

pit [pit] s hoyo m; pozo m; teat patio m; Am hueso m (de frutas); abismo m; v/t ***to ~ against*** oponer a

pitch [pitʃ] s pez f; grado m de inclinación; puesto m; tono m; tiro m; v/t tirar; arrojar; mús entonar; v/i caerse; mar cabecear; ~ ***into*** embestir; ~**er** cántaro m; sp lanzador m; ~**fork** agr horca f

piteous ['pitiəs] lastimero, lastimoso

pitfall ['pitfɔːl] trampa f

pith [piθ] médula f

pithy ['piθi] sucinto

piti|able ['pitiəbl] lastimoso; ~**ful** lastimoso, triste; lamentable; ~**less** despiadado; inhumano

pity ['piti] s piedad f, lástima f, compasión f; ***it's a ~*** es una lástima; v/t compadecer

pivot ['pivət] s pivote m; v/i girar sobre un eje

placard ['plækɑːd] cartel m

place [pleis] s lugar m; sitio m; puesto m; situación f; localidad f; región f; ***in ~ of*** en lugar de; ***out of ~*** fuera de lugar; ***to take ~*** ocurrir; tener lugar; v/t colocar; emplear; recordar

placid ['plæsid] plácido, sosegado; apacible

plagiarism ['pleidʒjərizəm] plagio m

plague [pleig] s peste f; plaga f; v/t atormentar

plaid [plæd] manta f escocesa

plain [plein] a llano, liso; sencillo; corriente; manifiesto; s llanura f; ~**clothes man** policía m vestido de civil; ~**ness** sencillez f; franqueza f; ~**spoken** franco

plaint|iff ['pleintif] demandante m, f; ~**ive** plañidero; dolorido

plait [plæt] trenza f (de cabello)

plan [plæn] s plan m; esquema m; plano m; proyecto m; v/t proyectar, planear

plane [plein] a plano; s plano m; fam avión m; tecn cepillo m; v/t alisar

planet ['plænit] planeta m

plank [plæŋk] s tabla f, tablón m; v/t entarimar

planning ['plæniŋ] planificación f

plant [plɑːnt] s planta f, instalación f industrial; equipo m; v/t plantar; sembrar, sentar; ~**ation** plantación f; ~**er** ['plɑːntə] cultivador m; hacendado m

plaque [plɑːk] placa f

plaster ['plɑːstə] s yeso m; argamasa f, enlucido m; med emplasto m, parche m; ~ ***of Paris*** yeso m blanco; v/t enyesar, enlucir; emplastar

plastic ['plæstik] a, s plástico m; ~**s** plástica f

plate [pleit] s plato m; plancha f, chapa f; lámina f; foto placa f; ~**au** ['plætəu] meseta f

platform ['plætfɔːm] plataforma f (t fig); f c andén m; estrado m

platinum ['plætinəm] platino m

platitude ['plætitjuːd] lugar m común

platter ['plætə] plato m grande; bandeja f

plausible ['plɔːzəbl] verosímil, plausible

play [plei] s juego m; teat obra f; tecn funcionamiento m; ***foul ~*** juego m sucio; v/t jugar a (algún juego); teat representar; tocar (música o instrumento); ~ ***dead*** hacerse el muerto; ~ ***down*** quitar importancia a; ~**back** reproducción f (de lo grabado); ~**boy** señorito m amante de los placeres; ~**er** jugador m; actor m, actriz f; ~**ful** juguetón; ~**mate** compañero m de juegos; ~**pen** parque m de niño; ~**thing** juguete m; ~**wright** dramaturgo m

plea [pliː] argumento m; súplica f; pretexto m; disculpa f; for alegato m

plead [pliːd] v/t for defender una causa; alegar; excusarse con; v/i suplicar; for abogar; ~ ***guilty*** confesarse culpable

pleas|ant ['pleznt] agradable; ameno; grato; simpático; ~**e** [pliz] v/t gustar, complacer; contentar; agradar; v/i gustar de; dignarse; ~**e!** ¡por favor!; ~**ed** satisfecho; ~**ing** agradable; placentero; ~**ure** ['pleʒə] placer m; gusto m

pleat [pliːt] s pliegue m; v/t plegar, plisar

pledge [pledʒ] s prenda f; fianza f; promesa f; v/t empeñar; prometer

plent|iful ['plentiful] abundante; ~**y** s abundancia f; profusión f; ~**y of** muchos, bastante

pliable ['plaiəbl] flexible; plegable; dócil

pliers ['plaiəz] alicates m/pl

plight [plait] aprieto m, apuro m

plod [plɔd] v/i fatigarse; andar laboriosamente

plot [plɔt] s solar m, parcela f; conspiración f; teat argumento m; v/t tramar; v/i conspirar; ~**ter** conspirador m

plough [plau] s arado m; v/t, v/i arar; ~**share** reja f de arado

ploy [plɔi] truco m; artimaña f

pluck [plʌk] s ánimo m; valor m; v/t sacar, arrancar; desplumar (aves); ~ ***up courage*** recobrar ánimo; ~**y** animoso, valiente

plug [plʌg] s taco m; tapón m; elec enchufe m; v/t tapar; ~ ***in*** enchufar

plum [plʌm] ciruela f; ~ ***tree*** ciruelo m

plumage ['pluːmidʒ] plumaje m

plumb [plʌm] plomada f; ~**er** fontanero m; LA gasfitero m; ~**ing** fontanería f

plume [pluːm] pluma f; penacho m, plumero m

plump [plʌmp] a rollizo, regordete; v/t soltar, dejar caer; v/i caer a plomo; engordar

plunder ['plʌndə] s pillaje m; botín m; v/t saquear, pillar; ~**er** saqueador m

plunge [plʌndʒ] s zambullida f; v/t sumergir; v/i caer; hundirse; arrojarse; ~**r** tecn émbolo m

plunk [plʌŋk] v/t puntear (cuerdas)

pluperfect ['pluː'pəːfikt] pluscuamperfecto m

plural ['pluərəl] plural m

plus [plʌs] prep más; a mat positivo; adicional

plush [plʌʃ] felpa f

ply [plai] s ***three ~*** de tres cordones; v/t ejercer (un oficio); v/i hacer servicio regular (entre puertos, etc); ~**wood** madera f contrachapada

pneumatic [nju(ː)'mætik] neumático

pneumonia [nju(ː)'məuniə] pulmonía f

poach [pəutʃ] v/t escalfar (huevos); v/i cazar clandestinamente; ~**er** cazador m furtivo

pocket ['pɔkit] s bolsillo m; bolsa f; cavidad f; v/t embolsar; ~**book** monedero m; Am bolsa f; ~ **book** libro m de bolsillo; ~**knife** cortaplumas m

pod [pɔd] vaina f; cápsula f

poem ['pəuim] poema m

poet ['pəuit] poeta m; ~**ic** [~'etik] poético; ~**ry** poesía f

poignant ['pɔinənt] intenso; agudo, conmovedor

point [pɔint] s punto m; punta f; cabo m; finalidad f; ~ ***of view*** punto m de vista; ***that's beside the ~*** no viene al caso; ***to come to the ~*** ir al grano; ***to make a ~*** hacerse entender; ***to see the ~*** caer en la cuenta; v/t apuntar; aguzar; ~ ***out*** indicar; v/i ~ ***at*** señalar; ~**-blank** a quemarropa; ~**ed** puntiagudo; evidente; ~**er** indicador m, puntero m; aguja f; ~**less** inútil, sin sentido

poise [pɔiz] s equilibrio m; serenidad f; v/t equilibrar

poison ['pɔizn] s veneno m; v/t envenenar; ~**ous** venenoso

poke [pəuk] s empuje m; v/t atizar (fuego); meter; asomar; ~ ***one's nose into*** meter las narices en; ~**r** hurgón m, atizador m; póquer m

polar ['pəulə] polar; ~ **bear** oso m blanco; ~**ize** v/t polarizar

Pol|and ['pəulənd] Polonia f; ~**e** polaco(a) m (f)

pole [pəul] s polo m; palo m; vara f; sp pértiga f

police [pə'liːs] policía f; ~**man** policía m; guardia m; ~ **station** comisaría f; ~**woman** mujer f policía

policy ['pɔlisi] política f (práctica); póliza f (de seguros)

Polish ['pəuliʃ] polaco

polish ['pɔliʃ] v/t pulir, barnizar; lustrar (zapatos); s lustre m, brillo m; betún m (de zapatos); ~**ed** culto; refinado

polite [pə'lait] cortés; atento; ~**ness** cortesía f

politic|al [pə'litikəl] político; ~**ian** [pɔli'tiʃən] político m; ~**s** ['pɔlitiks] política f (abstracta)

polka ['pəulkə] polca f; ~ **dots** lunares m/pl

poll [pəul] s votación f; votos m/pl; ***public opinion ~*** sondeo m; ***to go to the ~s*** acudir a las urnas

pollut|e [pə'luːt] v/t contaminar, corromper; ~**ion** contaminación f, polución f

polyester ['pɔliestə] poliéster m

poly|gamy [pə'ligəmi] poligamia f; ~**glot** ['~glɔt] a, s polígloto(a) m (f)

pomegranate ['pɔməgrænit] granada f

pomp [pɔmp] pompa f; ~**ous** pomposo

pond [pɔnd] estanque m; charco m

ponder ['pɔndə] v/t ponderar, examinar; v/i reflexionar; ~**ous** pesado, laborioso

pontif|f ['pɔntif] pontífice m; ~**ical** [~'tifikəl] pontifical; ~**icate** [~'tifikit] pontificado m

pony ['pəuni] jaca f

poodle ['puːdl] perro m de lanas

pool [puːl] s charca f; estanque m; piscina f; LA alberca f; quinielas f/pl; v/t mancomunar, juntar

poor [puə] pobre; malo; ***the ~*** los pobres; ~**ly** enfermizo; indispuesto

pop [pɔp] s taponazo m; detonación f; bebida f gaseosa; música f popular; v/t disparar; v/i estallar; ~ ***in*** visitar de paso; ~**corn** palomitas f/pl de maíz

Pope [pəup] papa m

poplar ['pɔplə] álamo m

poppy ['pɔpi] amapola f

popula|r ['pɔpjulə] popular; ~**rity** [~'læriti] popularidad f; ~**te** ['~eit] v/t poblar; ~**tion** población f

porcelain ['pɔːsəlin] porcelana f

porch [pɔːtʃ] porche m

porcupine ['pɔːkjupain] puerco *m* espín
pore ['pɔː] *s* poro *m*; *v/i* ~ **over** estudiar detenidamente
pork [pɔːk] carne *f* de cerdo
pornography [pɔː'nɔgrəfi] pornografía *f*
porous ['pɔːrəs] poroso
porpoise ['pɔːpəs] marsopa *f*
porridge ['pɔridʒ] gachas *f/pl* de avena
port [pɔːt] puerto *m*; *mar* babor *m*
portable ['pɔːtəbl] portátil
porter ['pɔːtə] portero *m*; conserje *m*; mozo *m*
portfolio [pɔːt'fəuljəu] carpeta *f*; cartera *f*
porthole ['pɔːthəul] portilla *f*
portion ['pɔːʃən] *s* porción *f*; parte *f*; dote *m*; *v/t* ~ **out** repartir; distribuir
portly ['pɔːtli] corpulento
portra|it ['pɔːtrit] retrato *m*; **~y** *v/t* retratar; describir; **~yal** [pɔː'treiəl] representación *f*
Portugal ['pɔːtjugəl] Portugal *m*
Portuguese [pɔːtju'giːz] *a, s* portugués(esa) *m (f)*
pose [pəuz] *s* postura *f*; afectación *f*; *v/t* poner; plantear (*problema*); *v/i* posar
position [pə'ziʃən] posición *f*; puesto *m*; opinión *f*; **to be in a ~** estar en condiciones de
positive ['pɔzətiv] *a* positivo (*t foto, mat, elec*); cierto; absoluto; seguro
possess [pə'zes] *v/t* poseer; **~ed** poseído, poseso; **~ion** posesión *f*; **~ive** posesivo; **~or** poseedor(a) *m (f)*
possib|ility [pɔsə'biliti] posibilidad *f*; **~le** ['pɔsəbl] posible; **as soon as ~le** cuanto antes; **~ly** posiblemente; quizás, quizá
post [pəust] *s* poste *m*; *mil* plaza *f*; puesto *m*, empleo *m*; correo *m*; **by return of ~** a vuelta de correo; *v/t* echar al correo; situar; contabilizar; "**~ no bills**" "prohibido fijar carteles"; **~age** franqueo *m*; **~age stamp** sello *m*, *LA* estampilla *f*; **~box** buzón *m*; **~card** tarjeta *f* postal; **~ed: to keep ~ed** tener al corriente; **~er** cartel *m*; **~erior** [pɔs'tiəriə] *a* posterior; *s* trasero *m*; **~erity** [pɔs'teriti] posteridad *f*; **~humous** ['pɔstjuməs] póstumo; **~man** cartero *m*; **~mark** matasellos *m*; **~ office** estafeta *f* de correos; **~-office box** apartado *m* de correos; **~paid** con porte pagado
postpone [pəust'pəun] *v/t* posponer, aplazar; **~ment** aplazamiento *m*
postscript ['pəusskript] pos(t)data *f*
posture ['pɔstʃə] postura *f*
postwar ['pəust'wɔː] de pos(t)guerra
pot [pɔt] *s* marmita *f*; olla *f*; maceta *f*, tiesto *m*; *v/t* envasar; plantar en tiestos
potato [pə'teitəu] patata *f*, *LA* papa *f*
potent ['pəutənt] potente; poderoso; **~ial** [pə'tenʃl] *a, s* potencial *m*
pot|hole ['pɔthəul] bache *m*; **~luck** comer lo que haya; **~shot** tiro *m* al azar
potter ['pɔtə] alfarero *m*; **~y** alfarería *f*
pouch [pautʃ] saquito *m*
poultice ['pəultis] cataplasma *m*
poultry ['pəultri] aves *f/pl* del corral
pounce [pauns] *v/i* lanzarse, saltar; ~ **upon** precipitarse sobre
pound [paund] *s* libra *f* (*451 gramos*); ~ **sterling** libra esterlina; *v/t* golpear; moler; machacar
pour [pɔː] *v/t* verter; echar; *v/i* fluir, correr
pout [paut] *s* puchero *m*; mueca *f*; *v/i* hacer pucheros
poverty ['pɔvəti] pobreza *f*
powder ['paudə] *s* polvo *m*; pólvora *f*; *v/t* pulverizar; **~ room** tocador *m*; **~y** polvoriento; empolvado
power ['pauə] poder *m*; poderío *m*; potencia *f*; facultad *f*; ~ **of attorney** poder *m* notarial; ~ **failure** apagón *m*; **~ful** poderoso; potente; enérgico; **~less** impotente; ineficaz; ~ **plant** central *f* eléctrica
practi|cable ['præktikəbl] practicable; **~cal** práctico; **~ce** ['~tis] costumbre *f*; ejercicio *m*; práctica *f*; **~se**, *Am* **~ce** *v/t* practicar; ejercitar; ejercer (*profesión*); *v/i* practicar, ejercer; entrenarse; **~tioner** [~'tiʃnə] profesional *m, f*
pragmatic [præg'mætik] pragmático
prairie ['prɛəri] llanura *f*, pampa *f*, pradera *f*
praise [preiz] *s* alabanza *f*; *v/t* alabar, loar, elogiar; **~worthy** loable
pram [præm] cochecillo *m* de niño
prance [prɑːns] *v/i* cabriolar
prank [præŋk] travesura *f*
prattle ['prætl] *s* parloteo *m*; *v/i* parlotear
prawn [prɔːn] camarón *m*
pray [prei] *v/t* rogar; pedir; *v/i* rezar, orar; **~er** [prɛə] oración *f*, rezo *m*; súplica *f*; **~er book** devocionario *m*
preach [priːtʃ] *v/t, v/i* predicar; **~er** predicador *m*
precarious [pri'kɛəriəs] precario
precaution [pri'kɔːʃən] precaución *f*
preced|e [pri(ː)'siːd] *v/t* preceder; **~ent** ['presidənt] precedente *m*
precept ['priːsept] precepto *m*; mandato *m*
precinct ['priːsiŋkt] recinto *m*; **~s** inmediaciones *f/pl*
precious ['preʃəs] *a* precioso; *adv fam* muy
precipi|ce ['presipis] precipicio *m*; **~tate** [pri'sipitit] *a* precipitado; [~eit] *v/t, v/i* precipitar(se); **~tation** precipitación *f*; **~tous** escarpado
precis|e [pri'sais] preciso, exacto; meticuloso; **~ely** precisamente; **~ion** [~'siʒən] precisión *f*, exactitud *f*
preclude [pri'kluːd] *v/t* excluir
precocious [pri'kəuʃəs] precoz; **~ness** precocidad *f*
predatory ['predətəri] rapaz
predecessor ['priːdisesə] predecesor *m*
predica|ment [pri'dikəmənt] apuro *m*; **~te** ['predikit] *gram* predicado *m*
predict [pri'dikt] *v/t* pronosticar; **~ion** pronóstico *m*
predisposition ['priːdispə'ziʃən] predisposición *f*
predomina|nt [pri'dɔminənt] predominante; **~te** [~eit] *v/i* predominar
prefabricated ['priː'fæbrikeitid] prefabricado
preface ['prefis] prefacio *m*
prefer [pri'fəː] *v/t* preferir; **~able** ['prefərəbl] preferible; **~ence** ['prefərəns] preferencia *f*; **~ential** [prefə'renʃəl] preferente; privilegiado
prefix ['priːfiks] prefijo *m*
pregnan|cy ['pregnənsi] embarazo *m*; **~t** embarazada, encinta; *fig* fecundo, repleto
prehistoric ['priːhis'tɔrik] prehistórico
prejudice ['predʒudis] *s* prejuicio *m*; *v/t* predisponer, prevenir; perjudicar
preliminary [pri'liminəri] *a, s* preliminar *m*
prelude ['preljuːd] preludio *m*
premature [premə'tjuə] prematuro
premeditate [pri(ː)'mediteit] *v/t, v/i* premeditar
premier ['premjə] primer ministro *m*
première ['premiɛə] estreno *m*
premises ['premisiz] local *m*, establecimiento *m*
premium ['priːmjən] premio *m*; **at a ~** ser muy solicitado
premonition [priːmə'niʃn] presentimiento *m*
preoccupied [pri(ː)'ɔkjupaid] preocupado
prepar|ation [prepə'reiʃən] preparación *f*; **~ations** preparativos *m/pl*; **~e** [pri'pɛə] *v/t* preparar; disponer; confeccionar; *v/i* ~ **for** prepararse para
prepay ['priː'pei] *v/t* pagar por adelantado
preposition [prepə'ziʃən] preposición *f*
preposterous [pri'pɔstərəs] absurdo
prerequisite ['priː'rekwizit] requisito *m* previo
prerogative [pri'rɔgətiv] prerrogativa *f*
prescri|be [pris'kraib] *v/t* prescribir; *med* recetar; **~ption** [~'kripʃən] prescripción *f*; *med* receta *f*
presence ['prezns] presencia *f*; ~ **of mind** presencia *f* de ánimo
present ['preznt] *s* actualidad *f*; regalo *m*; *a* presente; actual; **at ~** actualmente; **to be ~ at** asistir a; [pri'zent] *v/t* presentar; explicar; dar; **~ation** presentación *f*
presently ['prezntli] dentro de poco; *Am* ahora, al presente
preserv|ation [prezə(ː)'veiʃən] preservación *f*; conservación *f*; **~e** [pri'zəːv] *v/t* preservar; conservar; **~es** conservas *f/pl*
preside [pri'zaid] *v/t* presidir; **~ncy** ['prezidənsi] presidencia *f*; **~nt** presidente *m*
press [pres] *s* prensa *f*; imprenta *f*; apretón *m*; *v/t* prensar; planchar (*ropa*); apretar; instar; **~ed for time** tener poco tiempo; ~ **conference** rueda *f* de prensa; **~ing** *a* urgente; **~ure** ['~ʃə] presión *f*; urgencia *f*; **~ure cooker** olla *f* de presión; **~ure gauge** manómetro *m*; **~ure group** grupo *m* de presión
prestige [pres'tiːʒ] prestigio *m*; fama *f*
presum|able [pri'zjuːməbl] presumible; **~e** *v/t* presumir, suponer; *v/i* presumir
presumpt|ion [pri'zʌmpʃən] presunción *f*, conjetura *f*; atrevimiento *m*; **~uous** presumido; arrogante
presuppose [priːsə'pəuz] *v/t* presuponer
preten|ce, *Am* **~se** [pri'tens] pretexto *m*; pretensión *f*; **~d** *v/t* aparentar, fingir; *v/i* fingir; **~der** pretendiente *m* (*al trono*); **~sion** pretensión *f*; demanda *f*; **~tious** presuntuoso; presumido; afectado
pretext ['priːtekst] pretexto *m*
pretty ['priti] *a* bonito, lindo; *adv* bastante; casi
prevail [pri'veil] *v/i* prevalecer; estar en boga; ~ **on** persuadir a; **~ing** reinante; predominante
prevalent ['prevələnt] predominante; corriente
prevent [pri'vent] *v/t* impedir; **~ion** prevención *f*; **~ive** preventivo; impeditivo
previous ['priːvjəs] previo; anterior; **~ly** previamente, con anterioridad
prewar ['priː'wɔː] de preguerra
prey [prei] *s* presa *f*; **bird of ~** ave *f* de rapiña; *v/i* ~ **on** pillar; agobiar
price [prais] *s* precio *m*; valor *m*; **fixed ~** precio fijo; **at any ~** cueste lo que cueste; *v/t* valuar, tasar; **~less** inapreciable; ~ **list** lista *f* de precios
prick [prik] *s* pinchazo *m*, picadura *f*; *v/t* picar, pinchar, punzar; ~ **one's ears** aguzar las orejas; **~le** púa *f*; espina *f*; **~ly** espinoso
pride [praid] *s* orgullo *m*; soberbia *f*; *v/r* ~ **oneself on** enorgullecerse de
priest [priːst] sacerdote *m*
prim [prim] decoroso; estirado
primar|ily ['praimərili] ante todo; **~y** primario; **~y school** escuela *f* primaria
prime [praim] principal, primero; primo, selecto; ~ **minister** primer ministro *m*; **~r** cartilla *f*
primitive ['primitiv] primitivo; rudimentario
primrose ['primrəuz] *bot* primavera *f*, prímula *f*
prince [prins] príncipe *m*; **~ss** [~'ses] princesa *f*
principal ['prinsəpəl] *a* principal; *s* principal *m*, director *m*; **~ity** [prinsi'pæliti] principado *m*
principle ['prinsəpl] principio *m*; **on ~** por principio
print [print] *s* marca *f*; estampado *m*; impresión *f*; grabado *m*; **out of ~** agotado; *v/t* imprimir; escribir con letra de imprenta; *foto* copiar; **~ed matter** impresos *m/pl*; **~er** impresor(a) *m (f)*; **~ing** impresión *f*; tipografía *f*; **~ing office** imprenta *f*
prior ['praiə] *a* anterior; previo; *s* prior *m*; **~ity** [~'ɔriti] prioridad *f*
prison ['prizn] prisión *f*; cárcel *f*; **~er** preso *m*; prisionero *m*; **to take ~er** apresar
priva|cy ['privəsi] retiro *m*; secreto *m*; intimidad *f*; **~te** ['praivit] privado; particular; secreto
privation [prai'veiʃən] privación *f*
privilege ['privilidʒ] privilegio *m*; **~d** privilegiado
prize [praiz] *s* premio *m*; *v/t* apreciar; estimar
probab|ility [prɔbə'biliti] probabilidad *f*; **~le** ['~əbl] probable, verosímil
prob|ation [prə'beiʃən]: **on ~ation** de prueba *f*; *for* libertad *f* condicional; **~e** [prəub] *v/t* sondar; indagar; *s* sonda *f*; tienta *f*
problem ['prɔbləm] problema *m*
proce|dure [prə'siːdʒə] *s* procedimiento *m*; trámites *m/pl*; **~ed** [~'siːd] *v/i* proceder; seguir su curso; **~edings** *for* proceso *m*; actas *f/pl*; **~eds** ['prəusiːdz] ganancias *f/pl*
process ['prəuses] *s* proceso *m*; método *m*; *v/t* elaborar; tratar; **~ion** [prə'seʃən] procesión *f*, desfile *m*; cortejo *m* (*fúnebre*)
procla|im [prə'kleim] *v/t* proclamar; **~mation** [prɔklə'meiʃən] proclamación *f*
procure [prə'kjuə] *v/t* conseguir
prod [prɔd] *s* empuje *m*; codazo *m*; *v/t* empujar; *fig* estimular
prodig|ious [prə'didʒəs] prodigioso; **~y** ['prɔdidʒi] prodigio *m*; **infant ~y** niño *m* prodigio
produce ['prɔdjuːs] *s* producto *m* (*de la tierra*); [prə'djuːs] *v/t* producir; rendir; fabricar; poner en escena (*obra de cine, teatro*); **~r** productor *m*; director *m* (*de obras de teatro o cine*)
product ['prɔdʌkt] producto *m*, resultado *m*; **~ive** [prə'dʌktiv] productivo
profane [prə'fein] profano; sacrílego
profess [prə'fes] *v/t* profesar; manifestar; simular; **~ed** declarado; supuesto; **~ion** carrera *f*, profesión *f*; **~ional** profesional; **~or** catedrático *m*; profesor *m*
proficien|cy [prə'fiʃənsi] pericia *f*; habilidad *f*; **~t** experimentado; perito
profile ['prəufail] perfil *m*, silueta *f*
profit ['prɔfit] *s* provecho *m*; ganancia *f*; beneficio *m*; ~ **and loss** pérdidas y ganancias; *v/i* ganar; *v/t* servir a; aprovechar a; **~able** provechoso
profound [prə'faund] profundo
profu|se [prə'fjuːs] profuso; pródigo; **~sion** profusión *f*
prognosis [prɔg'nəusis] pronóstico *m*
program|(me) ['prəugræm] programa *m*; **~(m)ing** programación *f*
progress ['prəugres] *s* progreso *m*; [~'gres] *v/i* progresar, adelantar; **~ive** *a* progresivo; *a, s pol* progresista *m, f*
prohibit [prə'hibit] *v/t* prohibir; **~ion** [prəui'biʃən] prohibición *f*; **~ive** [~'hibitiv] prohibitivo
project ['prɔdʒekt] *s* proyecto *m*; plan *m*; [prə'dʒekt] *v/t* proyectar; *v/i* sobresalir; **~ion** proyección *f*; **~or** proyector *m*
proletarian [prəule'tɛəriən] *a, s* proletario(a) *m(f)*
prolog(ue) ['prəulɔg] prólogo *m*
prolong [prəu'lɔŋ] *v/t* extender, prolongar; **~ation** extensión *f*, prórroga *f*
promenade [prɔmi'nɑːd] *s* paseo *m*; *v/i* pasearse
prominent ['prɔminənt] prominente; saliente
promiscuous [prə'miskjuəs] promiscuo
promis|e ['prɔmis] *s* promesa *f*; esperanza *f*; *v/t, v/i* prometer; **~ing** prometedor
promontory ['prɔməntri] promontorio *m*
promot|e [prə'məut] *v/t* promover; fomentar; ascender; **~er** promotor *m*; gestor *m*; **~ion** promoción *f*; *com* fomento *m*
prompt [prɔmpt] *a* pronto; *adv* puntualmente; *v/t* incitar; impulsar; **~er** *teat* apuntador *m*

prone [prəun] postrado; ~ ***to*** propenso a

prong [prɔŋ] púa *f*, diente *m* (*de tenedor*)

pronoun ['prəunaun] pronombre *m*

pronounc|e [prə'nauns] *v/t* pronunciar; articular; **~ed** marcado; fuerte

pronunciation [prənʌnsi'eiʃən] pronunciación *f*

proof [pru:f] *s* prueba *f*; comprobación *f*; *a* a prueba de; **~s** *impr* pruebas *f/pl*

prop [prɔp] *s* soporte *m*; puntal *m*; *v/t* apuntalar

propaga|nda [prɔpə'gændə] propaganda *f*; **~te** ['prɔpəgeit] *v/t* propagar

propel [prə'pel] *v/t* impulsar; **~ler** hélice *f*

proper ['prɔpə] propio; conveniente; atinado, correcto; decoroso; **~ly** debidamente; **~ty** propiedad *f*

prophe|cy ['prɔfisi] profecía *f*; **~sy** ['~ai] *v/t* profetizar; **~t** ['~fit] profeta *m*

proportion [prə'pɔ:ʃən] *s* proporción *f*; **~s** dimensiones *f/pl*

propos|al [prə'pəuzəl] propuesta *f*; **~e** *v/t* proponer; *v/i* declararse, pedir la mano; **~ition** [prɔpə'ziʃən] proposición *f*

propriet|ary [prə'praiətəri] patentado; **~or, ~ress** [~ris] propietario(a) *m* (*f*)

propulsion [prə'pʌlʃən] propulsión *f*

prosaic [prəu'zeiik] prosaico

prose [prəuz] prosa *f*

prosecut|e ['prɔsikju:t] *v/t for* procesar; proseguir; **~ion** prosecución *f*; *for* parte *f* acusadora; **~or** demandante *m*; fiscal *m*

prospect ['prɔspekt] *s* perspectiva *f*; expectativa *f*; vista *f*; [prəs'pekt] *v/i*, *v/t* explorar; **~or** prospector *m*

prospectus [prəs'pektəs] prospecto *m*

prosper ['prɔspə] *v/i* prosperar; **~ity** [~'periti] prosperidad *f*; **~ous** ['~pərəs] próspero

prostitute ['prɔstitju:t] *s* prostituta *f*

prostrate ['prɔstreit] *a* postrado; [prɔs'treit] *v/t* postrar; ~ ***oneself*** postrarse

protect [prə'tekt] *v/t* proteger; **~ion** protección *f*, amparo *m*; **~ive** protector

protein ['prəuti:n] proteína *f*

protest ['prəutest] *s* protesta *f*; [prə'test] *v/t* protestar; afirmar; **2ant** ['prɔtistənt] *a*, *s* protestante *m, f*

protocol ['prəutəkɔl] protocolo *m*

protract [prə'trækt] *v/t* alargar; prolongar

protrude [prə'tru:d] *v/i* salir fuera

proud [praud] orgulloso; soberbio; imponente

prove [pru:v] *v/t* probar; *v/i* resultar

proverb ['prɔvə:b] refrán *m*; proverbio *m*; **~ial** [prə'və:bjəl] proverbial

provide [prə'vaid] *v/t* proveer; abastecer; proporcionar; *v/i* ~ ***against*** precaverse de; **~d (that)** con tal que, siempre que

providence ['prɔvidəns] providencia *f*

provinc|e ['prɔvins] provincia *f*; **~ial** [prə'vinʃəl] provincial

provision [prə'viʒən] provisión *f*; disposición *f*, medida *f*; **~al** provisional; **~s** provisiones *f/pl*

proviso [prə'vaizəu] estipulación *f*

provo|cation [prɔvə'keiʃən] provocación *f*; **~cative** [prə'vɔkətiv] provocativo; **~ke** [~'vəuk] *v/t* provocar; irritar

prow [prau] *mar* proa *f*

prowess ['prauis] destreza *f*

prowl [praul] *v/i* rondar

proximity [prɔk'simiti] proximidad *f*

proxy ['prɔksi] poder *m*; apoderado *m*; ***by*** ~ por poder(es)

prud|e [pru:d] mojigato(a) *m* (*f*); **~ence** prudencia *f*; discreción *f*; **~ent** prudente, discreto; **~ish** gazmoño

prune [pru:n] *s* ciruela *f* pasa; *v/t*, *v/i* podar

psalm [sɑ:m] salmo *m*

pseudonym ['psju:dənim] seudónimo *m*

psychiatr|ist [sai'kaiətrist] psiquiatra *m/f*; **~y** psiquiatría *f*

psychic ['saikik] psíquico

psycho|analysis [saikəuə'næləsis] psicoanálisis *m*; **~logical** [saikə'lɔdʒikəl] psicológico; **~logist** [sai'kɔlədʒist] psicólogo *m*; **~logy** [~'kɔlədʒi] psicología *f*; **~therapy** psicoterapia *f*

pub [pʌb] *fam* taberna *f*, cantina *f*, bar *m*

puberty ['pju:bəti] pubertad *f*

publi|c ['pʌblik] *a* público; **~c *house*** taberna *f*, bar *m*; **~c *prosecutor*** fiscal *m*; **~c *spirited*** de buen ciudadano; **~c *welfare*** salud *f* pública; *s* público *m*; ***in*** **~c** públicamente; **~cation** publicación *f*; **~city** [~'lisiti] publicidad *f*; **~cize** *v/t* publicar; **~sh** ['pʌbliʃ] *v/t* publicar; editar; **~shing house** casa *f* editorial

pudding ['pudiŋ] budín *m*

puddle ['pʌdl] charco *m*

Puerto Ri|can ['pwə:təu'ri:kən] *a*, *s* puertorriqueño(a) *m* (*f*); **~co** Puerto *m* Rico

puff [pʌf] *s* soplo *m*; bocanada *f*; borla *f*; *v/t* soplar; chupar (*pipa*); ~ ***up*** hinchar; *v/i* resoplar, jadear; ~ **pastry** hojaldre *m*; **~y** hinchado

pull [pul] *v/t* tirar (de); sacar; arrastrar; ~ ***down*** demoler; ~ ***off*** concluir con éxito; ~ ***one's leg*** tomarle el pelo; ~ ***oneself together*** componerse; ~ ***out*** arrancar; ~ ***up*** detener, parar; *s* tirón *m*; tirador *m*; trago *m*; influencia *f*

pulley ['puli] polea *f*

pullover ['puləuvə] jersey *m*, *LA* pulóver *m*

pulp [pʌlp] pulpa *f*

pulpit ['pulpit] púlpito *m*

puls|ate [pʌl'seit] *v/i* latir; **~ation** latido *m*, pulsación *f*; **~e** pulso *m*

pulverize ['pʌlvəraiz] *v/t* pulverizar; triturar

pumice ['pʌmis] **stone** piedra *f* pómez

pump [pʌmp] *s* bomba *f*; *v/t* bombear; sonsacar

pumpkin ['pʌmpkin] calabaza *f*

pun [pʌn] juego *m* de palabras

punch [pʌntʃ] *s* puñetazo *m*; punzón *m*; ponche *m*; *v/t* dar puñetazos; punzar

punctual ['pʌŋktjuəl] puntual

punctua|te ['pʌŋktjueit] *v/t* puntuar; **~tion** puntuación *f*; **~tion mark** signo *m* de puntuación

puncture ['pʌŋktʃə] *s* pinchazo *m*; puntura *f*; *v/t* pinchar; punzar

pungent ['pʌndʒənt] picante; mordaz; acre

punish ['pʌniʃ] *v/t* castigar; **~ment** castigo *m*

punt [pʌnt] *s* batea *f*; *v/i* ir en batea

puny ['pju:ni] diminuto; débil

pup [pʌp] cachorro(a) *m* (*f*)

pupil ['pju:pl] alumno(a) *m* (*f*); *anat* pupila *f*

puppet ['pʌpit] títere *m*

puppy ['pʌpi] cachorro(a) *m* (*f*)

purchas|e ['pə:tʃəs] *s* compra *f*; *v/t* comprar; **~ing power** poder *m* adquisitivo

pure [pjuə] puro; **~ly** puramente

purg|ative ['pə:gətiv] purgante; **~atory** purgatorio *m*; **~e** [pə:dʒ] *s med* purgante *m*; *pol* purga *f*; depuración *f*; *v/t med* purgar; *pol* depurar

purify ['pjuərifai] *v/t* purificar, depurar

purity ['pjuəriti] pureza *f*

purple ['pə:pl] *a* purpúreo; morado; *s* púrpura *f*

purpose ['pə:pəs] *s* propósito *m*; intención *f*; resolución *f*; ***on*** ~ de propósito, adrede; ***to no*** ~ en vano; *v/t*, *v/i* proponer(se); **~ful** resuelto; **~ly** de propósito

purr [pə:] *v/i* ronronear

purse [pə:s] *s* portamonedas *m*; bolso *m*; *LA* bolsa *f*; *v/t* fruncir (*labios*); **~r** *mar* cortador *m*

pursu|e [pə'sju:] *v/t* perseguir; seguir; acosar; **~er** perseguidor *m*; **~it** [~u:t] persecución *f*; ocupación *f*, actividad *f*; ***in*** **~*it of*** en pos de

purveyor [pə:'veiə] proveedor *m*

pus [pʌs] pus *m*

push [puʃ] *s* empujón *m*; impulso *m*; empuje *m*, brío *m*; *v/t* empujar; apretar; presionar; ~ ***back*** echar atrás, rechazar; *v/i* empujar; ~ ***off*** *fam* largarse; ~ ***through*** abrirse camino a empujones; **~y** agresivo

puss [pus], **pussy(-cat)** minino *m*, michino *m*

put [put] *v/t* poner, colocar; echar; exponer; presentar; ~ ***across*** hacer entender; ~ ***back*** devolver a su lugar; ~ ***down*** apuntar; reprimir; atribuir; ~ ***in*** meter; ~ ***it to*** decirlo a; ~ ***off*** aplazar; ~ ***on*** ponerse (*ropa, etc*); encender; ~ ***out*** poner afuera; extender, apagar; irritar; desconcertar; ~ ***through*** *tel* comunicar; ~ ***up*** hospedar; montar (*una máquina*); elevar; *v/i* ~ ***about*** *mar* cambiar de rumbo; ~ ***up with*** aguantar

putrefy ['pju:trifai] *v/i* pudrirse

putrid ['pju:trid] podrido, putrefacto

putty ['pʌti] masilla *f*

puzzle ['pʌzl] *s* rompecabezas *m*; problema *m*; *v/t* embrollar, confundir; *v/i* devanarse los sesos

pyjamas [pə'dʒɑ:məs] pijama *m*

pyramid ['pirəmid] pirámide *f*

Q

quack [kwæk] *s* curandero *m*; graznido *m*; *v/i* graznar; **~ery** curandería *f*

quadrangle ['kwɔdræŋgl] cuadrángulo *m*

quadruple ['kwɔdrupl] cuádruplo; **~ts** ['~lits] cuatrillizos *m/pl*

quail [kweil] *s zool* codorniz *f*; *v/i* acobardarse

quaint [kweint] pintoresco; curioso; extraño; exótico

quake [kweik] *s* temblor *m*; *v/i* temblar; trepidar

Quaker ['kweikə] cuáquero(a) *m* (*f*)

qualif|ication [kwɔlifi'keiʃən] calificación *f*, idoneidad *f*; reserva *f*; **~ied** ['~faid] calificado; capacitado; apto; limitado, condicional; **~y** ['~fai] *v/t* calificar, habilitar; *v/i* ser apto; ser aprobado; *sp* clasificarse

quality ['kwɔliti] cualidad *f*; calidad *f*, clase *f*

qualm [kwɑ:m] náusea *f*; escrúpulo *m*

quandary ['kwɔndəri]: ***to be in a*** ~ estar en un dilema

quantity ['kwɔntiti] cantidad *f*

quarantine ['kwɔrənti:n] *s* cuarentena *f*

quarrel ['kwɔrəl] *s* disputa *f*, querella *f*; *v/i* disputarse; reñir; **~some** pendenciero

quarry ['kwɔri] cantera *f*; presa *f*

quarter ['kwɔ:tə] *s* cuarta *f*, cuarta parte *f*; cuarto *m*; *mil* cuartel *m*; barrio *m* (*de ciudad*); ***a*** ~ ***to, past*** un cuarto para (la hora), (la hora) y cuarto; *v/t* hospedar; *mil* acuartelar; **~ly** *a* trimestral; **~s** alojamiento *m*; *mil* cuartel *m*; ***at close*** **~*s*** de cerca

quartet(te) [kwɔ:'tet] *mús* cuarteto *m*

quartz [kwɔ:ts] cuarzo *m*

quaver ['kweivə] *v/i* temblar; hablar en tono trémulo

quay [ki:] muelle *m*, (des)embarcadero *m*

queasy ['kwi:zi] *med* bascoso

queen [kwi:n] reina *f*

queer [kwiə] *a* raro, extraño; indispuesto; *s fam* maricón *m*

quench [kwentʃ] *v/t* apagar

querulous ['kweruləs] quejumbroso; irritable

query ['kwiəri] *s* pregunta *f*; cuestión *f*

quest [kwest] búsqueda *f*; indigación *f*

question ['kwestʃən] *s* pregunta *f*; cuestión *f*; asunto *m*; ***ask a*** ~ hacer una pregunta; ***out of the*** ~ imposible; ~ ***mark*** signo *m* de interrogación; *v/t*, *v/i* interrogar, preguntar; dudar de; **~able** discutible; dudoso; **~naire** [~stiə'nɛə] cuestionario *m*

queue [kju:] *s* cola *f*; *v/i* ~ ***up*** hacer cola

quick [kwik] rápido; ágil; vivo; agudo; ***to be*** ~ darse prisa; **~en** *v/t* apresurar; acelerar; **~ly** de prisa; pronto; **~ness** rapidez *f*; **~sand** arena *f* movediza; **~silver** mercurio *m*; **~-witted** listo, despierto

quid [kwid] *fam* libra *f* esterlina

quiet ['kwaiət] *a* callado; tranquilo; quieto; *s* sosiego *m*; calma *f*; silencio *m*; *v/t* calmar, aquietar; **~ness** silencio *m*; tranquilidad *f*

quilt [kwilt] edredón *m*

quince [kwins] membrillo *m*

quinine [kwi'ni:n] quinina *f*

quintuple ['kwintjupl] quíntuplo; **~ts** ['~lits] quintillizos *m/pl*

quip [kwip] pulla *f*

quirk [kwə:k] peculiaridad *f*

quit [kwit] *v/t* dejar; abandonar; *v/i* desistir, cesar

quite [kwait] totalmente; bastante, muy; ~ ***a few*** bastantes; ~ ***so!*** ¡ así es!

quits [kwits]: ***call it*** ~ dar por terminado

quiver ['kwivə] *s* vibración *f*; temblor *m*; *v/i* temblar; estremecerse

quiz [kwiz] *s* interrogatorio *m*; serie *f* de preguntas; *TV* concurso *m*; *v/t* examinar; interrogar

quota ['kwəutə] cuota *f*

quot|ation [kwəu'teiʃən] cita *f*; *com* cotización *f*; **~ation marks** comillas *f/pl*; **~e** *v/t* citar; *com* cotizar

quotient ['kwəuʃənt] c(u)ociente *m*

R

rabbi ['ræbai] rabino *m*

rabbit ['ræbit] conejo *m*

rabble ['ræbl] chusma *f*

rabi|d ['ræbid] rabioso; **~es** ['reibi:z] rabia *f*

raccoon [rə'ku:n] mapache *m*

race [reis] *s* raza *f*, casta *f*; carrera *f* (*de caballos, coches*); *v/i* correr de prisa; competir; **~course** hipódromo *m*, *LA* cancha *f*

raci|al ['reiʃəl] racial; **~sm** ['reisizm] racismo *m*; **~st** *a*, *s* racista *m, f*

rack [ræk] *s* colgadero *m*; percha *f*; rejilla *f*; potro *m*; pesebre *m*; *v/t* atormentar

racket ['rækit] raqueta *f*; alboroto *m*; *fam* estafa *f*

racy ['reisi] vigoroso; picante; salado

radar ['reidə] radar *m*

radian|ce ['reidjəns] brillo *m*, resplandor *m*; **~t** brillante, resplandeciente

radi|ate ['reidieit] *v/t* radiar; emitir; **~ation** radiación *f*; **~ator** radiador *m*; **~o** ['reidiəu] radio *f* (*emisión*); radio *f*, *LA* *m* (*aparato*); **~oactive** radiactivo

radish ['rædiʃ] rábano *m*

radius ['reidjəs] radio *m*

raffle ['ræfl] *s* rifa *f*; lotería *f*; *v/i* rifar; sortear

raft [rɑ:ft] balsa *f*

rag [ræg] trapo *m*

rag|e [reidʒ] *s* rabia *f*; furia *f*; *v/i* rabiar; ***to be all the*** ~ hacer furor; **~ing** violento

raid [reid] *s* incursión *f*; ataque *m*; *v/t* atacar; invadir

rail [reil] baranda *f*; *f c* riel *m*, carril *m*; ***by*** ~ por ferrocarril; **~ings** barandilla *f*; balaustrada *f*; **~road** *Am t*, **~way** ferrocarril *m*

rain [rein] *s* lluvia *f*; *v/i* llover; ~ ***cats and dogs*** llover a cántaros; **~bow** ['~bəu] arco *m* iris; **~coat** impermeable *m*; **~y** lluvioso

raise [reiz] *v/t* levantar; elevar; criar, educar (*niños*); formular (*preguntas, etc*); subir (*precio*); juntar (*dinero*); ~ ***one's glass to*** brindar por; ~ ***one's voice*** alzar la voz

raisin ['reizn] pasa *f*

rake [reik] *s* rastrillo *m*; libertino *m*; *v/t* rastrillar; barrer

rally ['ræli] *s* reunión *f* popular; *aut* rallye *m*; *med* recuperación *f*; *v/t* reunir; *v/i* congregarse; reanimarse

ram [ræm] *s zool* morueco *m*; carnero *m*; *tecn* pisón *m*; *mil* ariete *m*; *v/t* apisonar; chocar con

ramble ['ræmbl] *s* paseo *m*; *v/i* vagar; divagar; perder el hilo

ramp [ræmp] rampa *f*; **~age**: ***to be on the*** **~*age*** desbocarse; **~ant** prevaleciente; desenfrenado; **~art** ['~ɑ:t] terraplén *m*; muralla *f*

ranch [rɑ:ntʃ] estancia *f*; hacienda *f*; *LA* rancho *m*; **~er** ganadero *m*, hacendado *m*; *LA* ranchero *m*

rancid ['rænsid] rancio

ranco(u)r ['ræŋkə] rencor *m*
random ['rændəm]: **at ~** a la ventura; al azar
range [reindʒ] *s* extensión *f*; alcance *m*; fila *f*; orden *m*; pradera *f*; **mountain ~** sierra *f*, cordillera *f*; **within ~ of** al alcance de; *v/t* recorrer; clasificar; *v/i* vagar por; extenderse; fluctuar; **~r** guardabosques *m*
rank [ræŋk] *s mil* fila *f*; grado *m*, rango *m*; calidad *f*; **the ~ and file** las masas; **break ~s** romper filas; *v/t* clasificar; ordenar; *v/i* tener un grado; *a* exuberante; espeso; de mal olor; acabado
ransack ['rænsæk] *v/t* saquear; registrar
ransom ['rænsəm] *s* rescate *m*; *v/t* rescatar
rant [rænt] *v/i* vociferar; hablar con violencia
rap [ræp] *v/t* golpear; *v/i* dar golpes; *s* golpe *m* seco
rapacious [rə'peiʃəs] rapaz
rape [reip] *s* estupro *m*; violación *f*; *v/t* violar, estuprar
rapid ['ræpid] rápido; **~ity** [rə'piditi] rapidez *f*; velocidad *f*
rapt [ræpt] transportado, extasiado; **~ure** rapto *m*, éxtasis *m*
rar|e [rɛə] raro; precioso; poco hecho (*carne*); **~ity** rareza *f*; singularidad *f*
rascal ['rɑ:skəl] pícaro *m*; bellaco *m*; granuja *m*
rash [ræʃ] *a* temerario; imprudente; *s* salpullido *m*
rasher ['ræʃə] lonja *f* de tocino
rasp [rɑ:sp] *s* escofina *f*; sonido *m* estridente; *v/t* raspar; rallar; **~berry** ['rɑ:zbəri] frambuesa *f*
rat [ræt] *zool* rata *f*; **~ race** lucha *f* diaria competitiva; **to smell a ~** haber gato encerrado; *v/t* cazar ratas
rate [reit] *s* tasa *f*; proporción *f*, razón *f*; tipo *m*; valor *m*; **at any ~** de todos modos; **~ of exchange** tipo *m* de cambio; *v/t* tasar; clasificar; estimar
rather ['rɑ:ðə] más bien; antes; mejor dicho; bastante, algo; **would ~** preferir
ratify ['rætifai] *v/t* ratificar
ration ['ræʃən] *s* ración *f*; *v/t* racionar
rational ['ræʃənl] racional; razonable; **~ize** ['~ʃnəlaiz] *v/t* racionalizar
rationing ['ræʃniŋ] racionamiento *m*
rattle ['rætl] *s* matraca *f*, cascabel *m*; cascabeleo *m*, traqueteo *m*; golpeteo *m*; *v/t* sacudir con ruido; *v/i* traquetear; sonar; **~d** desconcertado; **~snake** serpiente *f* de cascabel
raucous ['rɔ:kəs] estridente
ravage ['rævidʒ] *v/t* devastar, asolar; *s* devastación *f*, estrago *m*
rave [reiv] *v/i* delirar; **~ about** entusiasmarse por
raven ['reivn] *zool* cuervo *m*; **~ous** ['rævənəs] voraz, rapaz; famélico; hambriento
ravine [rə'vi:n] barranco *m*
ravish ['ræviʃ] *v/t* arrebatar, encantar
raw [rɔ:] crudo; novato; rudo; *com* en bruto; **~ material** materia *f* prima
ray [rei] rayo *m*; *zool* raya *f*
rayon ['reiɔn] rayón *m*
razor ['reizə] navaja *f* de afeitar; máquina *f* de afeitar; **~ blade** hoja *f* de afeitar
reach [ri:tʃ] *s* alcance *m*; extensión *f*; facultad *f*; **within ~ of** al alcance de; *v/t* alcanzar; llegar a; lograr; *v/i* extenderse; llegar; **~ out one's hand** tender la mano
react [ri(:)'ækt] *v/i* reaccionar; **~ion** reacción *f*; **~ionary** [~ʃnəri] *a*, *s* reaccionario(a) *m* (*f*); **~or** reactor *m* (*nuclear*)
read [ri:d] *v/t* leer; interpretar; registrar; *v/i* rezar; saber leer; **~ aloud** leer en voz alta; **~able** legible; **~er** lector *m*
readi|ly ['redili] pronto; fácilmente; **~ness** disposición *f* favorable; estado *m* de alerta
reading ['ri:diŋ] lectura *f*; interpretación *f*
readjust ['ri:ə'dʒʌst] *v/t* reajustar; **~ment** reajuste *m*
ready ['redi] listo, preparado, dispuesto; **get ~** prepararse(se); **~-made** hecho; confeccionado
real [riəl] real, verdadero; genuino; **~ estate, ~ property** bienes *m/pl* raíces; inmuebles *m/pl*; **~ism** realismo *m*; **~ist** realista *m*, *f*; **~istic** realista; **~ity** [ri:'æliti] realidad *f*; **~ize** *v/t com* realizar; darse cuenta de; hacerse cargo de; **~ly** realmente, efectivamente; **~ly?** ¿de veras?
realm [relm] reino *m*
realtor ['riəltə] *Am* corredor *m* de bienes raíces
reap [ri:p] *v/t* segar; cosechar; **~er** segador *m*; segadora *f* mecánica
reappear ['ri:ə'piə] *v/i* reaparecer; **~ance** reaparición *f*
rear [riə] *a* trasero; posterior; *s* fondo *m*; *v/t* levantar; construir; criar; **~ guard** retaguardia *f*
rearm ['ri:'ɑ:m] *v/t* rearmar; **~ament** rearme *m*
reason ['ri:zn] *s* razón *f*, motivo *m*; sensatez *f*; **by ~ of** a causa de; **it stands to ~** es lógico que; *v/t* razonar que; *v/i* discutir; **~able** razonable, justo; módico (*precio*); **~ing** razonamiento *m*
reassure [ri:ə'ʃuə] *v/t* tranquilizar; *com* reasegurar
rebate ['ri:beit] *s* descuento *m*; rebaja *f*; *v/t*, *v/i* rebajar, descontar
rebel ['rebl] *a*, *s* rebelde *m*, *f*; [ri'bel] *v/i* sublevarse; rebelarse; **~lion** [~'beljən] rebelión *f*; sublevación *f*; **~lious** [~'beljəs] rebelde; revoltoso
rebirth ['ri:bə:θ] renacimiento *m*
rebound [ri'baund] *v/i* rebotar; repercutir
rebuff [ri'bʌf] *s* repulsa *f*; desaire *m*; *v/t* rechazar; desairar
rebuild ['ri:'bild] *v/t* reconstruir
rebuke [ri'bju:k] *s* reproche *m*; reprimenda *f*; *v/t* reprender; censurar; reprochar
rebuttal [ri'bʌtl] refutación *f*
recalcitrant [ri'kælsitrənt] recalcitrante
recall [ri'kɔ:l] *s* revocación *f*; recordación *f*; retirada *f*; **beyond ~** irrevocable; *v/t* revocar; retirar; recordar
recap [ri:'kæp] *v/t*, *v/i* recapitular
recapture ['ri:'kæptʃə] *s* represa *f*; *v/t* recobrar
recede [ri(:)'si:d] *v/i* retroceder, retirarse
receipt [ri'si:t] *s* recepción *f*; recibo *m*; **~s** ingresos *m/pl*
receive [ri'si:v] *v/t* recibir, cobrar; aceptar, admitir; acoger; **~r** recibidor *m*; (*teléfono*) auricular *m*; *for* síndico *m*
recent ['ri:snt] reciente; **~ly** recientemente; **until ~ly** hasta hace poco
reception [ri'sepʃən] recepción *f*; acogida *f*; **~ist** recibidor(a) *m* (*f*), *LA* recepcionista *m*, *f*
receptive [ri'septiv] receptivo
recess [ri'ses] nicho *m*; retiro *m*; recreo *m*; **~ion** recesión *f* (*económica*)
recipe ['resipi] receta *f*
recipient [ri'sipiənt] recipiente *m*, *f*
reciprocal [ri'siprəkəl] recíproco; mutuo
recit|al [ri'saitl] narración *f*; *mús*, *teat* recital *m*; **~e** *v/t* recitar, declamar; narrar
reckless ['reklis] temerario, imprudente
reckon ['rekən] *v/t* contar; considerar; **~ with** tomar en cuenta; **~ing** ['~niŋ] cálculo *m*; cómputo *m*
reclaim [ri'kleim] *v/t* reclamar; recuperar
recline [ri'klain] *v/t* recostar; *v/i* recostarse; reclinarse
recogni|tion [rekəg'niʃən] reconocimiento *m*; **~ze** ['rekəgnaiz] *v/t* reconocer; admitir
recoil [ri'kɔil] *v/i* retroceder; recular
recollect [rekə'lekt] *v/t* recordar, acordarse de; **~ion** recuerdo *m*
recommend [rekə'mend] *v/t* recomendar; **~ation** recomendación *f*
recompense ['rekəmpens] *s* recompensa *f*; compensación *f*; *v/t* recompensar
reconcil|e ['rekənsail] *v/t* (re)conciliar; **~e oneself to** resignarse a; **~iation** [~sili'eiʃən] (re)conciliación *f*
reconsider ['ri:kən'sidə] *v/t* volver a considerar; repensar
reconstruct ['ri:kəns'trʌkt] *v/t* reconstruir; reedificar
record ['rekɔ:d] *s* registro *m*; acta *f*, documento *m*; relación *f*; *sp* récord *m*; disco *m*; **on ~** registrado; **off the ~** confidencialmente; inoficial; [ri'kɔ:d] *v/t* registrar; relatar; marcar; grabar (*discos o cintas*); **~er** registrador *m*; (*máquina*) grabadora *f*; *mús* flauta *f* dulce; **~ing** grabación *f*; **~ player** tocadiscos *m*
recourse [ri'kɔ:s] recurso *m*; **to have ~ to** recurrir a
recover [ri'kʌvə] *v/t* recuperar, recobrar; *v/i* reponerse; **~y** recuperación *f*; restablecimiento *m*
recreation [rekri'eiʃən] recreación *f*; recreo *m*
recruit [ri'kru:t] *s* recluta *m*; *v/t*, *v/i* reclutar
rectangle ['rektæŋgl] rectángulo *m*
rectify ['rektifai] *v/t* rectificar
rector ['rektə] rector(a) *m* (*f*); **~y** rectoría *f*
recumbent [ri'kʌmbənt] reclinado; recostado
recur [ri'kə:] *v/i* repetirse; volver (*enfermedad*, *etc*); **~rent** [ri'kʌrənt] periódico; recurrente; repetido
recycl|able [ri'saikələbl] reciclable; **~ing** reciclaje *m*
red [red] rojo; encarnado; colorado; (*vino*) tinto; **~den** *v/i* ruborizarse
rede|em [ri'di:m] *v/t* redimir, rescatar; compensar; **~emer** redentor *m*; **~mption** [ri'dempʃən] redención *f*
red|-handed ['red'hændid]: **caught ~** cogido con las manos en la masa; **~-headed** pelirrojo; **~-hot** candente
redo ['ri:'du:] *v/t* rehacer
redouble [ri'dʌbl] *v/t*, *v/i* redoblar(se); intensificar(se)
redress [ri'dres] *s* reparación *f*; compensación *f*; *v/t* reajustar
redtape ['red'teip] papeleo *m*
red|uce [ri'dju:s] *v/t* reducir; abreviar; degradar; **~uction** [~'dʌkʃən] reducción *f*; rebaja *f*
reed [ri:d] caña *f*; *mús* lengüeta *f*
reef [ri:f] *s* arrecife *m*
reek [ri:k] *v/i* heder; oler mal; **~ of** oler a
reel [ri:l] *s* carrete *m*, broca *f*; *v/t tecn* devanar; *v/i* tambalear, bambolear
re|elect ['ri:i'lekt] *v/t* reelegir; **~emerge** *v/i* volver a salir; **~enter** *v/i* reingresar; **~establish** *v/t* restablecer
refer [ri'fə:] *v/t* referir, remitir; *v/i*: **~ to** referirse a; **~ee** [refə'ri:] árbitro *m*; **~ence** ['refrəns] referencia *f*; alusión *f*; certificado *m*; **~ence book** libro *m* de consulta; **~endum** [refə'rendəm] plebiscito *m*
refill ['ri:fil] *s* recambio *m*; ['ri:'fil] *v/t* rellenar
refine [ri'fain] *v/t* refinar, purificar; *fig* pulir; *v/i* refinarse; **~d** refinado; culto; **~ment** refinamiento *m*; urbanidad *f*; **~ry** refinería *f*
reflect [ri'flekt] *v/t*, *v/i* reflejar, reflectar; reflexionar; **~ion** reflexión *f*; reflejo *m*; meditación *f*
reflex ['ri:fleks] *a*, *s* reflejo *m*; **~ive** [ri'fleksiv] reflexivo
reform [ri'fɔ:m] *s* reforma *f*; reformación *f*; *v/t* reformar; **~ation** [refə'meiʃən] *relig* Reforma *f*; **~er** reformador(a) *m* (*f*)
refract [ri'frækt] *v/t* refractar; **~ory** refractorio
refrain [ri'frein] *v/i* abstenerse; *s* estribillo *m*
refresh [ri'freʃ] *v/t* refrescar; **~ment** refresco *m*
refrigerator [ri'fridʒəreitə] refrigerador *m*, nevera *f*, frigorífico *m*
refuel ['ri:'fjuəl] *v/t*, *v/i* reabastecer(se) de combustible
refuge ['refju:dʒ] *s* refugio *m*; asilo *m*; **~e** [~u(:)'dʒi:] refugiado(a) *m* (*f*)
refund [ri:'fʌnd] *s* re(e)mbolso *m*; *v/t* re(e)mbolsar; devolver
refus|al [ri'fju:zəl] negativa *f*, denegación *f*; **~e** [ri'fju:z] *v/t* denegar; rehusar; ['refju:s] *s* desperdicios *m/pl*; basura *f*
refute [ri'fju:t] *v/t* refutar
regain [ri'gein] *v/t* recuperar, recobrar
regal ['ri:gəl] regio; real
regard [ri'gɑ:d] *s* consideración *f*; atención *f*; respeto *m*; mirada *f*; **with ~ to** en cuanto a; *v/t* mirar; considerar; **~ing** con respecto a; **~less** *adv* a pesar de todo; **~less of** sin tomar en consideración; **~s** recuerdos *m/pl*, saludos *m/pl*
regent ['ri:dʒənt] regente *m*, *f*
régime [rei'ʒi:m] régimen *m*
regiment ['redʒimənt] regimiento *m*
region ['ri:dʒən] región *f*; comarca *f*
regist|er ['redʒistə] *s* registro *m*; inscripción *f*; asiento *m*; *v/t* registrar; inscribir; **~ered letter** carta *f* certificada; **~rar** [~'rɑ:] registrador *m*; **~ration** registro *m*; inscripción *f*; *aut*, *mar etc* matrícula *f*
regret [ri'gret] *s* sentimiento *m*, pesar *m*; remordimiento *m*; *v/t* sentir, lamentar; **~s** excusas *f/pl*; **~table** lamentable
regula|r ['regjulə] regular; corriente; normal; **~rity** [~'læriti] regularidad *f*; **~rize** ['regjuləraiz] *v/t* regularizar; **~te** *v/t* regular; **~tion** regulación *f*; reglamento *m*
rehears|al [ri'hə:səl] *teat*, *mús* ensayo *m*; **~e** *v/t*, *v/i* ensayar
reign [rein] *v/i* reinar; prevalecer; *s* reinado *m*; **~ing** reinante; prevaleciente
reimburse [ri:im'bə:s] *v/t* reembolsar; **~ment** reembolso *m*
rein [rein] rienda *f*; **to give ~ to** dar rienda suelta a
reindeer ['reindiə] *zool* reno *m*
reinforce ['ri:in'fɔ:s] *v/t* reforzar; (*cemento*) armar
reinstate ['ri:in'steit] *v/t* reintegrar; volver a emplear
reject [ri'dʒekt] *v/t* rechazar, rehusar, desechar; **~ion** rechazo *m*
rejoic|e [ri'dʒɔis] *v/t*, *v/i* regocijar(se), alegrar(se); **~ing** regocijo *m*; alegría *f*
rejoin ['ri:'dʒɔin] *v/t* reunirse con; **~der** réplica *f*
relapse [ri'læps] *s med* recaída *f*; reincidencia *f*; *v/i* recaer; reincidir
relat|e [ri'leit] *v/t* relatar, narrar; relacionar; *v/i* **~e to** referirse a; relacionarse con; **~ion** relación *f*; **~ive** ['relətiv] *a* relativo; *s* pariente(a) *m* (*f*); **~ively** relativamente
relax [ri'læks] *v/t* relajar; aflojar; *v/i* relajarse; descansar; **~ation** [ri:læk'seiʃən] relajamiento *m*; descanso *m*; esparcimiento *m*; **~ed** relajado
relay ['ri:'lei] *s* tanda *f*; *elec* relé *m*; *v/t* retransmitir (*radio*); **~-race** carrera *f* de relevos
release [ri'li:s] *s* liberación *f*; exoneración *f*; publicación *f*; *for* descargo *m*; *tecn* disparador *m*; *v/t* soltar; libertar; emitir; disparar; divulgar
relent [ri'lent] *v/i* ablandarse; **~less** implacable
relevant ['relivənt] pertinente; oportuno
reliab|ility [rilaiə'biliti] confiabilidad *f*; seguridad *f* de funcionamiento; **~le** fidedigno, de confianza
reliance [ri'laiəns] confianza *f*, dependencia *f*
relic ['relik] reliquia *f*
relief [ri'li:f] alivio *m*; desahogo *m*; socorro *m*; *mil* relevo *m*; *for* desagravio *m*; *arte*, *geog* relieve *m*
relieve [ri'li:v] *v/t* aliviar; socorrer; relevar
religio|n [ri'lidʒən] religión *f*; **~us** religioso
relinquish [ri'liŋkwiʃ] *v/t* renunciar a; abandonar
relish ['reliʃ] *s* gusto *m*; sabor *m*; apetito *m*; condimento *m*; *v/t* saborear; gustar de
reluctan|ce [ri'lʌktəns] desgana *f*; renuencia *f*; **~t** renuente; **~tly** de mala gana, a regañadientes
rely [ri'lai]: **~ on** *v/i* confiar en; fiarse de; contar con
remain [ri'mein] *v/i* quedar; permanecer; quedarse; so-

brar; **~der** resto *m*; **~ing** demás, restante; **~s** restos *m/pl*; sobras *f/pl*
remark [ri'mɑ:k] *s* observación *f*; *v/t, v/i* observar; **~able** notable; **~ably** extraordinariamente
remarry ['ri:'mæri] *v/i* volver a casarse
remedy ['remidi] *s* remedio *m*; *v/t* remediar
rememb|er [ri'membə] *v/t* recordar; acordarse de; tener presente; **~rance** recuerdo *m*, memoria *f*
remind [ri'maind] *v/t* recordar; **~er** recordatorio *m*; advertencia *f*
reminiscent [remi'nisnt] recordativo
remiss [ri'mis] negligente; **~ion** [~'miʃən] perdón *m*
remit [ri'mit] *v/t* remitir; **~tance** *com* remesa *f*
remnant ['remnənt] resto *m*; residuo *m*; retazo *m*
remonstrate ['remənstreit] *v/i* protestar
remorse [ri'mɔ:s] remordimiento *m*; **~ful** arrepentido; **~less** despiadado
remote [ri'məut] lejano; distante; **~ *control*** mando *m* a distancia
remov|al [ri'mu:vəl] deposición *f*; eliminación *f*; traslado *m*; mudanza *f*; **~e** *v/t* quitar; eliminar; trasladar; deponer
Renaissance [rə'neisəns] Renacimiento *m*
rend [rend] *v/t* desgarrar
render ['rendə] *v/t* rendir; dar; prestar (*servicios*); hacer; volver; *mús, teat* representar, interpretar
renegade ['renigeid] *a, s* renegado(a) *m* (*f*)
renew [ri'nju:] *v/t* renovar; extender; prorrogar; **~al** renovación *f*; prórroga *f*
renounce [ri'nauns] *v/t* renunciar; abandonar
renovate ['renəuveit] *v/t* renovar
renown [ri'naun] fama *f*; **~ed** renombrado, famoso
rent [rent] *s* alquiler *m*; *com* renta *f*; *v/t* alquilar, arrendar
repair [ri'pɛə] *v/t* reparar; componer; remendar; *s* reparación *f*; compostura *f*; **~ shop** taller *m* de reparaciones
reparation [repə'reiʃən] reparación *f*; satisfacción *f*; **~s** *pol* indemnizaciones *f/pl*
repartee [repɑ:'ti:] réplica *f* aguda
repay [ri:'pei] *v/t* reembolsar; devolver; pagar; **~ment** reembolso *m*
repeat [ri'pi:t] *v/t* repetir; reiterar; **~edly** repetidamente
repel [ri'pel] *v/t* repeler; rechazar; repugnar
repent [ri'pent] *v/i, v/t* arrepentirse (de); sentir; **~ance** arrepentimiento *m*; **~ant** arrepentido
repertoire ['repətwɑ:] repertorio *m*
repetition [repi'tiʃən] repetición *f*
replace [ri'pleis] *v/t* reemplazar; sustituir; **~ment** sustitución *f*; repuesto *m*
replenish [ri'pleniʃ] *v/t* rellenar; reponer
replete [ri'pli:t] repleto
replica ['replikə] copia *f*
reply [ri'plai] *s* respuesta *f*, contestación *f*; *v/t, v/i* contestar; responder
report [ri'pɔ:t] *s* relato *m*; parte *f*; informe *m*; (*arma*) estampido *m*; *v/t* relatar; denunciar; *v/i* presentar informe; **~er** reportero *m*
repose [ri'pəuz] *s* reposo *m*; *v/i* descansar; reposar
represent [repri'zent] *v/t* representar; **~ation** [~'teiʃən] representación *f*; **~ative** *a* representativo; *s* representante *m, f*; *for* apoderado *m*
repress [ri'pres] *v/t* reprimir; **~ion** represión *f*
reprieve [ri'pri:v] *s* suspensión *f*; respiro *m*; *v/t* indultar; suspender la pena
reprimand ['reprimɑ:nd] *s* reprimenda *f*; *v/t* reprender
reprint ['ri:'print] reimpresión *f*
reprisal [ri'praizəl] represalia *f*
reproach [ri'prəutʃ] *s* reproche *m*; *v/t* reprochar
reproduc|e [ri:prə'dju:s] *v/t* reproducir; **~tion** [~'dʌkʃən] reproducción *f*
repro|of [ri'pru:f] reproche *m*; **~ve** [ri'pru:v] *v/t* reprochar; reprender
reptile ['reptail] reptil *m*
republic [ri'pʌblik] república *f*; **~an** *a, s* republicano(a) *m* (*f*)
repudiate [ri'pju:dieit] *v/t* rechazar; repudiar; descartar
repugnan|ce [ri'pʌgnəns] repugnancia *f*; **~t** repugnante, repulsivo
repuls|e [ri'pʌls] *s* repulsa *f*; rechazo *m*; *v/t* repulsar, rechazar; **~ion** [~'pʌlʃən] repulsión *f*; repugnancia *f*; **~ive** repulsivo, repugnante
reput|able ['repjutəbl] respetable; honrado; **~ation** reputación *f*; renombre *m*; **~e** [ri'pju:t] *s* reputación *f*; *v/t* reputar; ***to be ~ed*** pasar por; tener fama de; **~edly** según se cree
request [ri'kwest] *s* ruego *m*, petición *f*, instancia *f*; *v/t* solicitar; pedir; suplicar
requi|re [ri'kwaiə] *v/t* necesitar; requerir; exigir; **~red** necesario; **~rement** necesidad *f*; requisito *m*; exigencia *f*; **~site** ['rekwizit] necesario
rer|oute ['ri:'ru:t] *v/t* desviar; **~un** ['ri:rʌn] *TV* programa *m* repetido
rescue ['reskju:] *s* salvamento *m*; rescate *m*; liberación *f*; *v/t* salvar; liberar; rescatar
research [ri'sə:tʃ] *v/t, v/i* investigar; *s* investigación *f*; **~er** investigador(a) *m* (*f*)
resembl|ance [ri'zembləns] parecido *m*, semejanza *f*; **~e** *v/t* parecerse a
resent [ri'zent] *v/t* resentirse de; **~ful** resentido; **~ment** resentimiento *m*
reserv|ation [rezə'veiʃən] reservación *f*; reserva *f*; **~e** [ri'zə:v] *s* reserva *f*; *v/t* reservar; guardar; **~ed** reservado; callado
reservoir ['rezəvwɑ:] depósito *m*; embalse *m*
reside [ri'zaid] *v/i* residir, vivir; **~nce** ['rezidəns] residencia *f*; domicilio *m*; **~nt** *a, s* residente *m, f*
residue ['rezidju:] residuo *m*; resto *m*
resign [ri'zain] *v/t* dimitir, renunciar; *v/r* resignarse; someterse; **~ation** [rezig'neiʃən] dimisión *f*; resignación *f*; **~ed** resignado
resin ['rezin] resina *f*
resist [ri'zist] *v/t, v/i* resistir; oponerse a; **~ance** resistencia *f*; **~ant** resistente
resolut|e ['rezəlu:t] resuelto; **~ion** [~'lu:ʃən] resolución *f*; acuerdo *m*
resolve [ri'zɔlv] *s* determinación *f*; propósito *m*; *v/t* resolver; decidir; *v/i* decidirse; ***to be ~d to*** estar resuelto a
resonance ['reznəns] resonancia *f*
resort [ri'zɔ:t] *s* recurso *m*; punto *m* de reunión; lugar *m* de temporada; ***as a last ~*** en último caso; *v/i* **~ *to*** acudir a; echar mano de; recurrir a
resound [ri'zaund] *v/i* resonar; **~ing** sonoro
resource [ri'sɔ:s] recurso *m*; expediente *m*; **~ful** ingenioso; **~s** recursos *m/pl*
respect [ris'pekt] respeto *m*; consideración *f*; respecto *m*; aspecto *m*; ***with ~ to*** con respecto a; ***in every ~*** en todo concepto; ***in this ~*** en cuanto a esto; **~able** respetable; **~ful** respetuoso; **~ive** respectivo, relativo; **~s** recuerdos *m/pl*
respiration [respə'reiʃən] respiración *f*
respite ['respait] *s* respiro *m*, pausa *f*; ***without ~*** sin tregua *f*
resplendent [ris'plendənt] resplandeciente
respon|d [ris'pɔnd] *v/i* responder, reaccionar; **~dent** *for* demandado(a) *m* (*f*); **~se** [~ns] respuesta *f*; contestación *f*; *fig* reacción *f*; **~sibility** [rispɔnsə'biliti] responsabilidad *f*; **~sible** [~'pɔnsəbl] responsable
rest [rest] *s* descanso *m*; resto *m*; apoyo *m*; pausa *f*; ***come to ~*** pararse; ***the ~*** el resto, lo demás; **~ *assured*** tener la seguridad; *v/i* descansar, reposar; **~ (*up*)*on*** apoyarse en; posarse en; ***to ~ with*** depender de
restaurant ['restərɔnt] restaurante *m*
rest|ful ['restful] descansado; sosegado; **~ home** residencia *f* de jubilados; **~ive** inquieto; **~less** intranquilo; agitado
restor|ation [restə'reiʃən] restauración *f*; renovación *f*; **~e** [ris'tɔ:] *v/t* restaurar
restrain [ris'trein] *v/t* refrenar, reprimir; **~ *oneself*** contenerse, dominarse; **~t** moderación *f*; restricción *f*; reserva *f*
restrict [ris'trikt] *v/t* restringir; **~ion** restricción *f*
rest room ['restru:m] excusado *m*; servicios *m/pl*
result [ri'zʌlt] *s* resultado *m*; *v/i* resultar; **~ *in*** terminar en
resum|e [ri'zju:m] *v/t* reanudar; **~ption** [~'zʌmpʃən] reanudación *f*
resurrection [rezə'rekʃən] resurrección *f*
resuscitate [ri'sʌsiteit] *v/t* resucitar
retail ['ri:teil] *s* venta *f* al por menor; [ri:'teil] *v/t* vender al por menor; **~er** detallista *m*
retain [ri'tein] *v/t* retener; guardar; contratar; **~er** partidario(a) *m* (*f*); criado(a) *m* (*f*); *for* anticipo *m*
retaliat|e [ri'tælieit] *v/i* tomar represalias; **~ion** represalias *f/pl*; desquite *m*
retard [ri'tɑ:d] *v/t* retrasar; **~ed** retrasado
retenti|on [ri'tenʃən] retención *f*; conservación *f*; **~ve** retentivo
reticent ['retisənt] reservado
retinue ['retinju:] comitiva *f*
retir|e [ri'taiə] *v/t* retirar, jubilar; *v/i* retirarse; jubilarse; **~ed** retirado; jubilado; **~ement** retiro *m*; jubilación *f*; **~ing** retraído
retort [ri'tɔ:t] *s* réplica *f*; *quim* retorta *f*; *v/t* replicar
retrace [ri'treis] *v/t* seguir (*las huellas*); desandar; volver a trazar
retract [ri'trækt] *v/t* retractar; retraer; *v/i* retractarse, retraerse; **~able** retráctil
retreat [ri'tri:t] *s* retiro *m*, refugio *m*; retirada *f*; *v/i* retirarse, refugiarse
retribution [retri'bju:ʃən] justo castigo *m*
retrieve [ri'tri:v] *v/t* recuperar; recobrar
retro|active ['retrəu'æktiv] retroactivo; **~spect**: ***in ~spect*** mirando hacia atrás
return [ri'tə:n] *s* vuelta *f*; regreso *m*; devolución *f*, retorno *m*; recompensa *f*; respuesta *f*; *com* utilidad *f*, ganancia *f*; relación *f*; ***by ~ mail*** a vuelta de correo; ***in ~*** en cambio; ***income tax ~*** declaración *f* de renta; *v/t* devolver; restituir; corresponder; producir; elegir; *v/i* volver, regresar; **~s** informe *m* oficial; *com* devoluciones *f/pl*; ***many happy ~s!*** ¡muchas felicidades!; **~ ticket** billete *m* de ida y vuelta
reunion ['ri:'ju:njən] reunión *f*
reveal [ri'vi:l] *v/t* revelar; descubrir
revel ['revl] *s* jarana *f*; *v/i* **~ *in*** deleitarse en
revelation [revi'leiʃən] revelación *f*
revenge [ri'vendʒ] *s* venganza *f*; ***to take ~ on*** vengarse de; **~ful** vengativo
revenue ['revinju:] ingresos *m/pl*; renta *f*; rédito *m*
reverberate [ri'və:bəreit] *v/i* resonar, retumbar
revere [ri'viə] *v/t* reverenciar, venerar; **~nce** ['revərəns] reverencia *f*; **~nd** reverendo
reverse [ri'və:s] *s* lo contrario; revés *m*; desgracia *f*; reverso *m*; *tecn* marcha *f* atrás; *v/t* volver al revés; invertir, trastornar; cambiar (*opinión, etc*); *a* inverso; opuesto
review [ri'vju:] *s* repaso *m*; reexaminación *f*; reseña *f*; revista *f*; *for* revisión *f*; *v/t* reexaminar, repasar; reseñar; *mil* pasar revista a; **~er** crítico *m*
revile [ri'vail] *v/t* injuriar
revis|e [ri'vaiz] *v/t* revisar; corregir; refundir; **~er** revisor(a) *m* (*f*); **~ion** [~iʒən] revisión *f*; repaso *m*; corrección *f*
reviv|al [ri'vaivəl] renacimiento *m*, restauración *f*; *teat* reposición *f*; **~e** *v/t* reanimar; restablecer; *v/i* reanimarse; volver en sí
revoke [ri'vəuk] *v/t* revocar
revolt [ri'vəult] *s* rebelión *f*, sublevación *f*; *v/t* repugnar, dar asco a; *v/i* rebelarse, sublevarse; **~ing** repugnante
revolution [revə'lu:ʃən] revolución *f*; **~ary** [~ʃnəri] *a, s* revolucionario *m*; **~ize** [~ʃnaiz] *v/t* revolucionar
revolv|e [ri'vɔlv] *v/i* revolver, girar; rodar; dar vueltas; *v/t* hacer girar *o* rodar; revolver; **~er** revólver *m*; **~ing** giratorio
revue [ri'vju:] *teat* revista *f*
revulsion [ri'vʌlʃən] asco *m*; *med* revulsión *f*
reward [ri'wɔ:d] *s* recompensa *f*; premio *m*; *v/t* recompensar; gratificar; **~ing** provechoso, valioso
rewind [ri:'waind] *v/t* dar cuerda a (*reloj*); rebobinar
rhapsod|ize ['ræpsədaiz]: *v/i* ***to ~ize over*** extasiarse ante; **~y** rapsodia *f*
rheumatism ['ru:mətizəm] reumatismo *m*
rhinoceros [rai'nɔsərəs] rinoceronte *m*
rhubarb ['ru:bɑ:b] ruibarbo *m*
rhyme [raim] *s* rima *f*; *v/t, v/i* rimar; ***without ~ or reason*** sin ton ni son
rhythm ['riðəm] ritmo *m*; **~ic, ~ical** rítmico
rib [rib] *anat* costilla *f*; *arq* nervio *m*; arista *f*; *mar* cuaderna *f*; varilla *f* (*de paraguas*)
ribald ['ribəld] obsceno
ribbon ['ribən] cinta *f*
rice [rais] arroz *m*; **~ field** arrozal *m*
rich [ritʃ] rico; fértil (*tierra*); sustancioso (*comida*); **~es** riqueza *f*; **~ness** riqueza *f*, opulencia *f*
ricket|s ['rikits] raquitismo *m*; **~y** raquítico
rid [rid] *v/t* desembarazar, librar; ***to get ~ of*** librarse de
riddle ['ridl] *s* adivinanza *f*, enigma *m*; criba *f*; *v/t* cribar; acribillar
rid|e [raid] *s* paseo *m* a caballo *o* en vehículo; *v/i* cabalgar; ir en coche; **~e *at anchor*** estar fondeado; *v/t* montar; **~e *someone*** tiranizar a uno; **~er** jinete *m*
ridge [ridʒ] lomo *m*; loma *f*; cresta *f*; *arq* caballete *m*
ridicul|e ['ridikju:l] *s* irrisión *f*; mofa *f*; *v/t* ridiculizar; burlarse de; **~ous** [~'dikjuləs] ridículo
riding ['raidiŋ] montar *m* a caballo
rife [raif] corriente; endémico
rifle ['raifl] *s* rifle *m*, fusil *m*; *v/t* robar; pillar
rift [rift] hendedura *f*; grieta *f*
right [rait] *s* derecho *m*; razón *f*; justicia *f*; derecha *f*; *a* correcto; recto, derecho; justo; ***to be ~*** tener razón; ***to have a ~ to*** tener derecho a; ***to set ~*** arreglar; *adv* directamente; bien; *v/t* enderezar; rectificar; ***all ~!*** ¡muy bien!; ***that's ~*** eso es; **~ *and left*** a diestro y siniestro; **~ *away*** en seguida; **~ *now*** ahora mismo; **~ *angle*** ángulo *m* recto; **~eous** ['~ʃəs] honrado, virtuoso; **~ful** legítimo; **~ly** con razón; **~ist** *a, s* derechista *m, f*
rigid ['ridʒid] rígido
rigor ['rigə] rigor *m*; **~ous** riguroso; severo; duro
rim [rim] canto *m*; borde *m*
rind [raind] corteza *f* (*de queso*); pellejo *m*
ring [riŋ] *s* anillo *m*; círculo *m* (*de gente*); aro *m*; *sp* cuadrilátero *m*; cerco *m* (*de montañas*); sonido *m* (*de timbre*); repique *m* (*de campanas*); ojera *f* (*bajo los ojos*); telefonazo *m*; *v/t* cercar; tocar; **~ *the bell*** tocar el timbre; **~ *up*** telefonear, llamar; *v/i* sonar; resonar; repicar; zumbar (*oídos*); **~leader** cabecilla *m*; **~let** bucle *m*, rizo *m*
rink [riŋk] pista *f*
rinse [rins] *v/t* enjuagar; aclarar
riot ['raiət] *s* motín *m*; tumulto *m*; *v/i* amotinarse; alborotarse; **~er** amotinado(a) *m* (*f*); **~ous** sedicioso; licencioso
rip [rip] *s* rasgón *m*, rasgadura *f*; *v/t* rasgar; descoser
ripe [raip] maduro; **~n** *v/t, v/i* madurar; **~ness** madurez *f*, sazón *f*
rip-off ['ripɔf] *fam* estafa *f*; timo *m*

ripple ['ripl] *s* rizo *m*; ondita *f*; *v/t, v/i* rizar(se)
rise [raiz] *s* subida *f*; *com* alza *f*; cuesta *f*; elevación *f*; aumento *m*; ***to give ~ to*** dar origen a; *v/i* subir, ascender; elevarse; ponerse de pie; surgir; sublevarse; salir (*el sol*); ***~ early*** madrugar
rising ['raiziŋ] levantamiento *m*; salida *f* (*del sol*)
risk [risk] *s* riesgo *m*; peligro *m*; *v/t* arriesgar; **~y** arriesgado; aventurado
rite [rait] rito *m*; ***funeral ~s*** exequias *f/pl*
rival ['raivəl] *a, s* rival *m, f*; competidor(a) *m* (*f*); *v/t* rivalizar; competir con; **~ry** rivalidad *f*
river ['rivə] río *m*; ***down ~*** río abajo; ***up ~*** río arriba; **~basin** cuenca *f* de río; **~bed** lecho *m* fluvial; **~side** orilla *f*, ribera *f*
rivet ['rivit] *s* remache *m*; *v/t* remachar
road [rəud] camino *m*; carretera *f*; vía *f*; *fig* senda *f*; **~ block** barricada *f*; **~ map** mapa *m* de carreteras; **~ sign** señal *f* de tráfico
roam [rəum] *v/i* vagar; errar
roar [rɔː] *s* rugido *m*; grito *m*; *v/i* rugir; gritar
roast [rəust] *a, s* asado *m*; *v/t, v/i* asar; tostar; **~ beef** rosbif *m*
rob [rɔb] *v/t* robar, hurtar; **~ber** ladrón *m*; salteador *m*; **~bery** robo *m*
robe [rəub] *s* túnica *f*; *for* toga *f*; manto *m*; ***bath ~*** albornoz *m*; bata *f*
robin ['rɔbin] petirrojo *m*
robot ['rəubɔt] robot *m*, autómata *m*
robust [rəu'bʌst] robusto; vigoroso
rock [rɔk] *s* roca *f*; peñasco *m*, peña *f*; ***on the ~s*** con hielo (*bebida*); *v/t* mecer; balancear; *v/i* mecerse; **~ bottom** punto *m* más bajo; **~ crystal** cristal *m* de roca; **~er** rockero(a) *m* (*f*)
rocket ['rɔkit] cohete *m*; **~ry** cohetería *f*
rocking chair ['rɔkiŋ'tʃɛə] mecedora *f*
rocky ['rɔki] rocoso; ***~ Mountains*** Montañas *f/pl* Rocosas
rod [rɔd] vara *f*; varilla *f*
rodent ['rəudənt] *zool* roedor *m*
roe [rəu] hueva *f* (*de pescado*); *zool* corzo *m*
rogu|e [rəug] pícaro *m*, bribón *m*; **~ish** pícaro, bellaco
role [rəul] papel *m*; ***to play a ~*** desempeñar un papel
roll [rəul] *s* rollo *m*; bollo *m*, panecillo *m*; lista *f*; redoble *m*, retumbo *m*; *fam* fajo *m* (*de dinero*); *v/t* hacer rodar, girar; enrollar; liar (*cigarillo*); *metal* laminar; vibrar (*la lengua*); ***~ up*** envolver; *v/i* rodar, dar vueltas; revolverse; bambolearse; balancearse; **~er** rodillo *m*; aplanadora *f*; **~er coaster** montaña *f* rusa; **~er skate** patín *m* de ruedas; **~film** película *f* en carrete; **~icking** alegre, divertido; **~ing** rodante; **~ing stock** material *m* rodante
Roman ['rəumən] *a, s* romano(a) *m* (*f*)
roman|ce [rəu'mæns] amoríos *m/pl*; novela *f* romántica; **~tic** romántico
rompers ['rɔmpəz] mameluco *m* (*para niños*); pelele *m*
roof [ruːf] *s* techo *m*; tejado *m*; azotea *f*; *v/t* techar; tejar
rook [ruk] graja *f*; (*ajedrez*) torre *f*
room [rum] cuarto *m*, pieza *f*; habitación *f*; sala *f*; espacio *m*, sitio *m*, cabida *f*; ***to make ~*** hacer sitio; **~mate** compañero(a) *m* (*f*) de cuarto; **~y** espacioso
roost [ruːst] percha *f* de gallinero; **~er** gallo *m*
root [ruːt] *s* raíz *f*; origen *m*; base *f*; *v/t, v/i* arraigar; ***~ out*** extirpar; arrancar
rope [rəup] cuerda *f*; soga *f*; cable *m*
rosary ['rəuzəri] *relig* rosario *m*
ros|e [rəuz] *s* rosa *f*; roseta *f* (*de ducha, etc*); *a* color *m* de rosa; **~ebush** rosal *m*; **~emary** romero *m*; **~y** sonrosado; rosado
rot [rɔt] *s* putrefacción *f*; descomposición *f*; *v/i* pudrirse; echarse a perder; *v/t* pudrir
rota|ry ['rəutəri] rotatorio; **~te** [~'teit] *v/t, v/i* (hacer) girar; **~tion** rotación *f*
rotor ['rəutə] *aer* rotor *m*
rotten ['rɔtn] podrido; corrompido; *fam* pésimo
rotund [rəu'tʌnd] rotundo
rouge [ruːʒ] colorete *m*
rough [rʌf] áspero; tosco; quebrado; crudo; rudo; aproximado; **~ly** ásperamente; aproximadamente; **~ness** aspereza *f*
round [raund] *a* redondo; rotundo; lleno; *s* esfera *f*; curvatura *f*; redondez *f*; vuelta *f*; *mil* ronda *f*; circuito *m*; *adv* alrededor; ***to go ~*** dar vueltas; ***all the year ~*** todo el año; *prep* alrededor de; a la vuelta de; *v/t* ***~ off, ~ out*** redondear; ***~ up*** recoger; **~about** *a* indirecto; *s* tiovivo *m*; **~ly** rotundamente
rouse [rauz] *v/t* despertar; excitar; levantar; ***~ oneself*** animarse
rout|e [ruːt] ruta *f*; **~ine** [~'tiːn] rutina *f*
rov|e [rəuv] *v/i* vagar; **~er** vagabundo *m*; **~ing** ambulante
row [rau] *s* alboroto *m*; tumulto *m*; disputa *f*
row [rəu] *s* hilera *f*; fila *f*; *v/i* remar; **~boat** bote *m* de remos
royal ['rɔiəl] real; **~ty** realeza *f*; derechos *m/pl* de autor
rub [rʌb] *s* frotamiento *m*; roce *m*; *v/t* frotar; restregar
rubber ['rʌbə] caucho *m*, goma *f*; *LA* jebe *m*, hule *m*
rubbish ['rʌbiʃ] basura *f*; desperdicios *m/pl*; *fam* tontería *f*; disparates *m/pl*
rubble ['rʌbl] escombros *m/pl*
ruby ['ruːbi] rubí *m*
rucksack ['ruksæk] mochila *f*
rudder ['rʌdə] timón *m*
ruddy ['rʌdi] rojizo
rude [ruːd] grosero; rudo; **~ness** grosería *f*; rudeza *f*
rue [ruː] *v/t* arrepentirse de
ruffian ['rʌfjən] bellaco *m*, rufián *m*
ruffle ['rʌfl] *s* volante *m*; *v/t* fruncir; erizar; arrugar; irritar; descomponer
rug [rʌg] alfombra *f*; manta *f*; **~ged** áspero; abrupto; rudo; robusto
ruin [ruin] *s* ruina *f*; *v/t* arruinar; estropear; **~ous** ruinoso
rul|e [ruːl] *s* regla *f*; reglamento *m*; norma *f*; ***as a ~e*** por regla general; ***home ~e*** autonomía *f*; *v/t* gobernar, mandar; ***~e out*** descartar, excluir; *v/i* gobernar; prevalecer; **~er** gobernador *m*; regla *f* (*para trazar líneas*); **~ing** *a* predominante; *s for* fallo *m*
rum [rʌm] ron *m*
Rumania [ruː'meinjə] Rumania *f*; **~n** *a, s* rumano(a) *m* (*f*)
rumble ['rʌmbl] *v/i* retumbar; *s* retumbo *m*
rumina|nt ['ruːminənt] *a, s* rumiante *m*; **~te** ['~eit] *v/t, v/i* rumiar
rummage ['rʌmidʒ] *v/t, v/i* revolverlo todo
rumo(u)r ['ruːmə] *s* rumor *m*; *v/i* ***it is ~ed*** se dice
rump [rʌmp] cuarto *m* trasero; ancas *f/pl*
rumple ['rʌmpl] *v/t* arrugar (*ropa*); desgreñar (*cabellos*)
run [rʌn] *s* carrera *f*; curso *m*; serie *f*, racha *f*; demanda *f* general; ***in the long ~*** a la larga; *v/t* explotar; manejar; llevar; ***~ across*** dar con; ***~ out of*** quedar sin; ***~ over*** atropellar; ***to be ~ down*** *med* estar debilitado; *v/i* correr; funcionar; fluir; ***~ away*** huir; ***~ down*** quedarse sin cuerda (*reloj*); ***~ out*** agotarse; ***~ over*** desbordar; ***~ up against*** chocar con
rung [rʌŋ] pedaño *m*
runner ['rʌnə] corredor(a) *m* (*f*); cuchilla *f* (*del patín*); *bot* trepadora *f*; **~-up** *sp* subcampeón *m*
running ['rʌniŋ] dirección *f*, manejo *m*; *tecn* funcionamiento *m*; **~ board** estribo *m*
runway ['rʌnwei] *aer* pista *f* de despegue *o* de aterrizaje
rupture ['rʌptʃə] *s* ruptura *f*, rotura *f*; *v/t* quebrarse
rural ['ruərəl] rural, rústico
rush [rʌʃ] *s* acometida *f*; prisa *f*, precipitación *f*; ajetreo *m*; *bot* junco *m*; ***~ hours*** horas *f/pl* punta; *v/t* apresurar; *v/i* precipitarse; ir de prisa
Russi|a ['rʌʃə] Rusia *f*; **~an** *a, s* ruso(a) *m* (*f*)
rust [rʌst] *s* herrumbre *f*; *v/i* oxidarse
rustic ['rʌstik] rústico
rustle ['rʌsl] *s* crujido *m*; *v/i* crujir; susurrar
rust|proof ['rʌstpruːf] a prueba de herrumbre; **~y** ['rʌsti] mohoso, oxidado
rut [rʌt] rodada *f*; carril *m*; celo *m* (*de animales*); *fig* rutina *f*
ruthless ['ruːθlis] inexorable; despiadado
rye [rai] centeno *m*

S

sable ['seibl] *zool* marta *f* cebellina
sabotage ['sæbətɑːʒ] *s* sabotaje *m*; *v/t* sabotear
saccharin ['sækərin] sacarina *f*
sack [sæk] *s* saco *m*; talego *m*; ***to get the ~*** ser despedido; *v/t* saquear; *fam* despedir, echar
sacrament ['sækrəmənt] sacramento *m*
sacred ['seikrid] sagrado
sacrifice ['sækrifais] *s* sacrificio *m*; *v/t, v/i* sacrificar
sacrilege ['sækrilidʒ] sacrilegio *m*
sad [sæd] triste; melancólico; **~den** *v/t* entristecer
saddle ['sædl] *s* silla *f* (*de montar*); sillín *m* (*de bicicleta*); collado *m* (*de monte*); *v/t* ensillar; **~-bag** alforja *f*
sadis|m ['sædizm] sadismo *m*; **~t** sadista *m, f*
sadness ['sædnis] tristeza *f*
safe [seif] *a* seguro; salvo; ileso; fuera de peligro; *s* caja *f* fuerte; ***~ and sound*** sano y salvo; ***to be on the ~ side*** por mayor seguridad; **~ conduct** salvoconducto *m*; **~guard** salvaguardia *f*; garantía *f*; **~ly** con seguridad; sin peligro; **~ty** seguridad *f*; **~ty belt** cinturón *m* de seguridad; **~ty pin** imperdible *m*; **~ty razor** maquinilla *f* de afeitar; **~ty valve** válvula *f* de seguridad
saffron ['sæfrən] azafrán *m*
sag [sæg] *s* comba *f*; *v/i* combarse; hundirse; aflojarse
sage [seidʒ] *s* sabio *m*; *bot* salvia *f*; *a* sabio
said [sed] dicho; ***when all is ~ and done*** al fin y al cabo
sail [seil] *s mar* vela *f*; *v/i* navegar; darse a la vela; **~(ing)boat** velero *m*; **~or** marinero *m*, marino *m*
saint [seint] *a, s* santo(a) *m* (*f*); San (*delante de nombres masculinos no empezando con t o d*)
sake [seik]: ***for God's ~!*** ¡por amor de Dios!; ***for the ~ of*** por; por respeto a
salad ['sæləd] ensalada *f*; **~ bowl** ensaladera *f*
salary ['sæləri] sueldo *m*
sale [seil] venta *f*; ***for ~*** se vende; **~sman, ~swoman** vendedor(a) *m* (*f*), dependiente *m*, dependienta *f*
saliva [sə'laivə] saliva *f*
sallow ['sæləu] cetrino; amarillento
sally ['sæli] *s* salida *f*; *v/i* ***~ forth*** salir resueltamente
salmon ['sæmən] salmón *m*
saloon [sə'luːn] sala *f* grande; *Am* bar *m*, taberna *f*
salt [sɔːlt] sal *f*; *fig* agudeza *f*; **~cellar** salero *m*; **~petre,** *Am* **~peter** ['~piːtə] salitre *m*; **~works** salinas *f/pl*; **~y** salado
salu|brious [sə'luːbriəs], **~tary** ['sæljutəri] salubre, saludable
salut|ation [sælju(ː)'teiʃən] salutación *f*; **~e** [sə'luːt] *s* saludo *m*; *mil* salva *f*; *v/t, v/i* saludar
salvage ['sælvidʒ] salvamento *m*; objetos *m/pl* salvados
salvation [sæl'veiʃən] salvación *f*
salve [sɑːv] ungüento *m*; *fig* bálsamo *m*
same [seim] mismo, idéntico; ***all the ~*** aun así; sin embargo; ***it is all the ~ to me*** a mí me da lo mismo
sample ['sɑːmpl] *s* muestra *f*; *v/t* probar; catar
sanatorium [sænə'tɔːriəm] sanatorio *m*
sancti|fy ['sæŋktifai] *v/t* santificar; **~monious** [~'məunjəs] santurrón; **~on** ['sæŋkʃən] *s* sanción *f*; *v/t* sancionar
sanctuary ['sæŋktjuəri] santuario *m*; asilo *m*
sand [sænd] *s* arena *f*; *v/t* enarenar
sandal ['sændl] sandalia *f*
sand|paper papel *m* de lija; **~stone** piedra *f* arenisca
sandwich ['sænwidʒ] bocadillo *m*; sandwich *m*
sandy ['sændi] arenoso
sane [sein] cuerdo, sensato
sanguine ['sæŋgwin] sanguíneo
sanita|ry ['sænitəri] sanitario; **~ry napkin** compresa *f*; **~tion** medidas *f/pl* sanitarias
sanity ['sæniti] cordura *f*, sensatez *f*
Santa Claus [sæntə'klɔːz] San Nicolás
sap [sæp] *s* savia *f*; vitalidad *f*; *mil* zapa *f*; *v/i mil* zapar; minar; *v/t* socavar; **~phire** ['sæfaiə] zafiro *m*
sarcasm ['sɑːkæzəm] sarcasmo *m*
sardine [sɑː'diːn] sardina *f*
Sardini|a [sɑː'diniə] Cerdeña *f*; **~an** *a, s* sardo(a) *m* (*f*)
sardonic [sɑː'dɔnik] burlón
sash [sæʃ] faja *f*; banda *f*
Satan ['seitən] Satanás *m*; **~ic** [sə'tænik] satánico
satchel ['sætʃəl] cartapacio *m*; bolso *m*
satellite ['sætəlait] satélite *m*
satin ['sætin] raso *m*
satir|e ['sætaiə] sátira *f*; **~ize** ['~əraiz] *v/t* satirizar
satisf|action [sætis'fækʃən] satisfacción *f*; **~actory** satisfactorio; **~y** ['~fai] *v/t* satisfacer
Saturday ['sætədi] sábado *m*
sauc|e [sɔːs] salsa *f*; **~epan** cacerola *f*; **~er** platillo *m*; ***flying ~er*** platillo *m* volador; **~y** fresco, insolente
saunter ['sɔntə] *v/i* deambular
sausage ['sɔsidʒ] salchicha *f*; embutido *m*
savage ['sævidʒ] salvaje *m, f*
sav|e [seiv] *prep* salvo; excepto; *conj* a menos que; *v/t* salvar; ahorrar (*dinero*); evitar; **~ings** ahorros *m/pl*; **~ings bank** caja *f* de ahorros
savio(u)r ['seivjə] salvador *m*; **~** *relig* Redentor *m*, Salvador *m*
savo(u)r ['seivə] *s* gusto *m*; sabor *m*; *v/t* saborear; **~y** sabroso, apetitoso
saw [sɔː] *s* sierra *f*; *v/t* serrar; **~dust** serrín *m*; **~mill** aserradero *m*
Saxon ['sæksn] *a, s* sajón *m*, sajona *f*
saxophone ['sæksəfəun] saxofón *m*
say [sei] *v/t, v/i* decir; recitar; ***they ~*** dicen; ***that is to ~*** es decir; ***~ grace*** bendecir la mesa; ***~ mass*** decir misa; ***~ no (yes)*** decir que no (sí); **~ing** dicho *m*; refrán *m*
scab [skæb] *med* costra *f*; *zool* roña *f*; **~by** sarnoso
scaffold ['skæfəld] andamio *m*; patíbulo *m*
scald [skɔːld] *s* escaldadura *f*; *v/t* escaldar
scale [skeil] *s* escala *f*; gama *f*; escama *f* (*de pez*); *v/t* escamar (*pescado*); escalar; **~s** balanza *f*
scalp [skælp] *s* cuero *m* cabelludo; *v/t* escalpar; **~el** escalpelo *m*
scamp [skæmp] diablillo *m*; **~er away** *v/i* escaparse corriendo
scan [skæn] *v/t* escudriñar; **~ner** escaner *m*
scandal ['skændl] escándalo *m*; **~ize** *v/t* escandalizar; **~ous** escandaloso
Scandinavian [skændi'neivjən] *a, s* escandinavo(a) *m* (*f*)
scant [skænt], **~y** escaso; magro
scapegoat ['skeipgəut] chivo *m* expiatorio
scar [skɑː] *s* cicatriz *f*; *v/i* cicatrizar(se)
scarc|e [skɛəs] escaso; **~ely** apenas; **~ity** escasez *f*
scare [skɛə] *s* espanto *m*; *v/t* espantar; **~crow** espantapájaros *m*
scarf [skɑːf] bufanda *f*; *LA* chalina *f*
scarlet ['skɑːlit] *s* escarlata *f*; *a* de color escarlata; **~ fever** escarlatina *f*
scary ['skɛəri] asustadizo
scathing ['skeiðiŋ] *fig* devastador; mordaz
scatter ['skætə] *v/t* esparcir; desparramar; dispersar

scavenge ['skævindʒ] *v/t* barrer (*calles, etc*); recoger (*entre la basura*)
scene [si:n] escena *f*; paisaje *m*; **~ry** escenario *m*; *teat* decorado *m*; ***behind the ~s*** entre bastidores
scent [sent] *s* perfume *m*; olor *m*; olfato *m*; rastro *m*; *v/t* perfumar; *v/i* olfatear; husmear
sceptic ['skeptik] *s, a* escéptico(a) *m* (*f*); **~al** escéptico; **~ism** ['~sizəm] escepticismo *m*
schedule ['ʃedju:l] *s* lista *f*; programa *m*; horario *m*; *v/t* fijar la hora de; catalogar
scheme [ski:m] *s* esquema *m*; proyecto *m*; intriga *f*; *v/t* proyectar; idear; tramar
schola|r ['skɔlə] estudiante *m, f*; erudito(a) *m* (*f*); **~rly** erudito; **~rship** beca *f*; erudición *f*; **~stic** [skə'læstik] escolar
school [sku:l] *s* escuela *f*; *v/t* instruir; entrenar; ***at ~*** en la escuela; **~boy** colegial *m*; **~girl** colegiala *f*; **~ing** enseñanza *f*; **~mate** compañero(a) *m* (*f*) de clase; **~teacher** maestro(a) *m* (*f*); profesor(a) *m* (*f*)
schooner ['sku:nə] goleta *f*
scien|ce ['saiəns] ciencia *f*; **~ce fiction** ciencia-ficción *f*; **~ces** ciencias *f/pl* naturales; **~tific** [~'tifik] científico; **~tist** ['~tist] científico *m*
scissors ['sizəz] tijeras *f/pl*
scoff [skɔf] *s* mofa *f*; *v/i* burlarse
scold [skəuld] *v/t* regañar, reprender
scoop [sku:p] *v/t* sacar con cuchara; ***~ out*** ahuecar
scooter ['sku:tə] patinete *m*; moto *f*
scope [skəup] alcance *m*; campo *m* de acción
scorch [skɔ:tʃ] *v/t* chamuscar; tostar
score [skɔ:] *s* marca *f*; raya *f*; cuenta *f*; veintena *f*; *sp* tanteo *m*; *mús* partitura *f*; *v/t* marcar; rayar; apuntar; *v/i* tantear; marcar un gol
scorn [skɔ:n] *s* desprecio *m*; *v/t* despreciar; **~ful** desdeñoso
scorpion ['skɔ:pjən] escorpión *m*
Scot [skɔt] escocés(esa) *m* (*f*)
Scotch [skɔtʃ], **Scottish** escocés
scot-free ['skɔt'fri:] impune
scoundrel ['skaundrəl] canalla *m*
scour [skauə] *v/t* fregar; limpiar
scourge [skə:dʒ] azote *m*
scout [skaut] *s* (niño *m*) explorador *m*; *v/t, v/i* explorar; reconocer
scowl [skaul] *s* ceño *m*; *v/i* mirar con ceño
scramble ['skræmbl] *s* arrebatiña *f*; *v/i* trepar; **~d eggs** huevos *m/pl* revueltos
scrap [skræp] *s* pedazo *m*; fragmento *m*; **~s** desperdicios *m/pl*; *v/t* desmontar; *fig* desechar; **~book** álbum *m* de recortes
scrap|e [skreip] *s* raspadura *f*; apuro *m*; *v/t* raspar; ***~e together*** reunir a duras penas; **~er** raspador *m*
scrap iron ['skræp'aiən] chatarra *f*
scratch [skrætʃ] *s* rasguño *m*; arañazo *m*; *v/t* rascar; arañar; ***~ out*** borrar
scrawl [skrɔ:l] *s* garabato *m*; *v/t, v/i* garabatear
scream [skri:m] *s* chillido *m*, grito *m*; *v/i* gritar, chillar
screech [skri:tʃ] chillido *m*
screen [skri:n] *s* biombo *m*; pantalla *f* (*de cine*; *radiología*); tabique *m*; *v/t* abrigar, ocultar; proyectar (*película*); investigar (*personas*)
screw [skru:] *s* tornillo *m*; *v/t* atornillar; **~driver** destornillador *m*
scribble ['skribl] *s* garabato *m*; *v/t, v/i* escribir mal; garabatear
script [skript] escritura *f*; guión *m* (*de película*); **Ձure** Escritura *f*
scroll [skrəul] rollo *m* de papel *o* de pergamino
scrounge [skraundʒ] *v/i* gorronear; sablear
scrub [skrʌb] *s* maleza *f*; *v/t* fregar; restregar
scruffy ['skrʌfi] sucio; desaliñado
scrup|le ['skru:pl] escrúpulo *m*; **~ulous** ['~pjuləs] escrupuloso
scrutin|ize ['skru:tinaiz] *v/t* escudriñar; **~y** escrutinio *m*
scuba diving ['skubə 'daiviŋ] submarinismo *m*
scuffle ['skʌfl] *s* refriega *f*; *v/i* pelear
sculpt|or ['skʌlptə], **~ress** escultor(a) *m* (*f*); **~ure** escultura *f*; *v/t, v/i* esculpir; tallar
scum [skʌm] espuma *f*; *fig* heces *f/pl*
scurvy ['skə:vi] escorbuto *m*
scuttle ['skʌtl] *mar* escotilla *f*
scythe [saið] guadaña *f*
sea [si:] mar *m, f*; ***at ~*** en el mar; ***on the high ~s*** en alta mar; ***to be all at ~*** estar despistado; **~dog** lobo *m* de mar; **~farer** marinero *m*; **~ food** mariscos *m/pl*; **~gull** gaviota *f*
seal [si:l] *s zool* foca *f*; sello *m*; *v/t* sellar; ***~ up*** encerrar herméticamente
sea|level ['si:'levl] nivel *m* del mar; **~ling wax** lacre *m*; **~ lion** león *m* marino
seam [si:m] *s* costura *f*; *tecn* juntura *f*; *med* sutura *f*
sea|man ['si:mən] marinero *m*; **~mstress** ['semstris] costurera *f*; **~plane** hidroavión *m*; **~port** puerto *m* de mar; **~ power** poderío *m* naval
search [sə:tʃ] *s* busca *f*, búsqueda *f*; registro *m*; *v/t, v/i* investigar; buscar; ***~ light*** reflector *m*
sea|shore ['si:'ʃɔ:] playa *f*; **~sick** mareado
season ['si:zn] *s* estación *f* (*del año*); temporada *f*; tiempo *m*; sazón *f*; *v/t* condimentar; madurar, curar; **~able** oportuno; **~ing** condimento *m*; **~ ticket** abono *m*
seat [si:t] *s* asiento *m*; localidad *f*; silla *f*; sede *f*; fondillos *m/pl* (*de calzones*); ***to take a ~*** tomar asiento; *v/t* sentar; colocar; tener asientos para; ***be ~ed!*** ¡siéntese!; **~ belt** *aut, aer* cinturón *m* de seguridad
sea|weed ['si:wi:d] alga *f* marina; **~worthy** marinero
secession [si'seʃən] secesión *f*
secluded [si'klu:did] apartado; retirado
second ['sekənd] *a* segundo; otro; *s* segundo *m*; ayudante *m*; padrino *m*; *v/t* apoyar; secundar; **~ary** secundario; **~-class** de segunda clase, inferior; **~hand** de segunda mano; **~ly** en segundo lugar; **~ thoughts** reflexión *f*
secre|cy ['si:krisi] secreto *m*; discreción *f*; **~t** ['~it] *a* secreto; oculto; *s* secreto *m*
secretary ['sekrətri] secretario(a) *m* (*f*)
secret|e [si'kri:t] *v/t med* secretar; esconder; **~ive** reservado; callado
sect [sekt] secta *f*
sect|ion ['sekʃən] sección *f*; parte *f*; **~or** sector *m*
secular ['sekjulə] seglar, secular; **~ize** ['~raiz] *v/t* secularizar
secur|e [si'kjuə] *a* seguro; cierto; firme; *v/t* asegurar; afirmar; conseguir; **~ity** seguridad *f*; firmeza *f*; protección *f*; *com* fianza *f*; **~ities** valores *m/pl*
sedative ['sedətiv] *a, s* sedativo *m*
sedentary ['sedntəri] sedentario
sediment ['sedimənt] *s* sedimento *m*
seduc|e [si'dju:s] *v/t* seducir; **~er** seductor *m*; **~tion** [~'dʌkʃən] seducción *f*
see [si:] *v/t, v/i* ver; observar; comprender; acompañar; ***let's ~*** a ver; ***~ off*** despedirse de; ***~ to*** atender a; ***~ you later!*** ¡hasta luego!
seed [si:d] *s* semilla *f*; simiente *f*; *v/t* sembrar; **~y** *fam* destartalado
seek [si:k] *v/t* buscar; anhelar; procurar
seem [si:m] *v/i* parecer; **~ing** aparente; **~ly** decente; decoroso
seep [si:p] *v/i* filtrarse
seesaw ['si:sɔ:] balancín *m*, *LA* subibaja *f*
seethe [si:ð] *v/i* bullir; *fig* hervir
segment ['segmənt] segmento *m*
segregat|e ['segrigeit] *v/t, v/i* segregar(se); **~ion** segregación *f*
seiz|e [si:z] *v/t* asir, agarrar, prender; capturar; *fig* comprender; ***~e upon*** valerse de; **~ure** ['~ʒə] confiscación *f*; embargo *m*; *med* ataque *m* apoplético
seldom ['seldəm] rara vez
select [si'lekt] *a* selecto; *v/t* escoger; seleccionar; **~ion** selección *f*; surtido *m*
self [self] *a* propio; *s* (*pl* **selves**) una misma, uno mismo; *pron pers* se; sí mismo; **~-assurance** confianza *f* en sí mismo; **~-centred**, *Am* **~-centered** egocéntrico; **~-conscious** cohibido; **~-control** dominio *m* de sí mismo; **~-defence**, *Am* **~-defense** defensa *f* propia; **~-denial** abnegación *f*; **~-evident** patente; **~-government** autonomía *f*; **~ish** egoísta; **~-made man** hombre que debe su posición a sí mismo; **~-pity** compasión *f* de sí mismo; **~-portrait** autorretrato *m*; **~-possessed** sereno; **~-respect** amor *m* propio; **~-righteous** santurrón; **~-sacrifice** abnegación *f*; **~-service** autoservicio *m*; **~-taught** autodidacta
sell [sel] *v/t* vender; *v/i* venderse; ***~ off*** liquidar las existencias; ***~ out*** transigir; **~er** vendedor(a) *m* (*f*); **~out** traición *f*; éxito *m* de taquilla
semblance ['sembləns] parecido *m*; semejanza *f*
semi|colon ['semi'kəulən] punto *m* y coma; **~nar** seminario *m*; **~sweet** semiamargo
senat|e ['senit] senado *m*; **~or** ['~ətə] senador *m*
send [send] *v/t* enviar, mandar; despachar; (*radio*) transmitir; ***~ away for*** despachar por; ***~ back*** devolver; ***~ on*** reexpedir; ***~ word*** avisar; *v/i* ***~ for*** enviar por; **~er** remitente *m*
senile ['si:nail] senil
senior ['si:njə] *a* mayor (de edad); más antiguo; *s* persona *f* mayor; oficial *m* más antiguo
sensation [sen'seiʃən] sensación *f*; **~al** sensacional
sens|e [sens] *v/t* percibir; *s* sentido *m*; juicio *m*; significado *m*; ***~e of humo(u)r*** sentido *m* de humor; ***common ~e*** sentido *m* común; ***in a ~e*** en cierto sentido; ***make ~e*** tener sentido; ***to be out of one's ~es*** haber perdido el juicio; **~eless** sin sentido, disparatado; **~ibility** [sensi'biliti] sensibilidad *f*; discernimiento *m*; **~ible** sensato, prudente (*juicio*); sensible; **~itive** ['sensitiv] sensible; **~ual** ['~juəl] sensual
sentence ['sentəns] *s* oración *f*; frase *f*; *for* sentencia *f*; *v/t* ***~ to*** *for* condenar a
sentiment ['sentimənt] sentimiento *m*; **~al** [~'mentl] sentimental; **~ality** [~men'tæliti] sentimentalismo *m*
sentry ['sentri] *mil* centinela *m, f*
separat|e ['sepəreit] *v/t, v/i* separar(se); ['seprit] *a* separado; privado; **~ely** por separado; **~ion** [~'reiʃən] separación *f*
sephardic [sə'fɑ:dik] *a, s* sefardí *m, f*
September [sep'tembə] se(p)tiembre *m*
septic ['septik] séptico
sepulcher = ***sepulchre***
sepulchre ['sepəlkə] sepulcro *m*
seque|l ['si:kwəl] secuela *f*; continuación *f*; resultado *m*; **~nce** ['~wəns] serie *f*; sucesión *f*
sequin ['si:kwin] lentejuela *f*
seren|e [si'ri:n] sereno, sosegado; **~ity** serenidad *f*, calma *f*
sergeant ['sɑ:dʒənt] sargento *m*
seri|al ['siəriəl] *a* consecutivo; *s* novela *f* por entregas; *radio, TV* serial *m*; **~es** ['~iz] serie *f*; ciclo *m*
serious ['siəriəs] serio; grave; **~ly** seriamente; gravemente
sermon ['sə:mən] sermón *m*
serpent ['sə:pənt] serpiente *f*; sierpe *f*
serum ['siərəm] suero *m*
serv|ant ['sə:vənt] criado(a) *m* (*f*); sirviente *m, f*; **~e** *v/t* servir; trabajar para; *v/i* servir; ser criado; *sp* sacar; **~ice** ['~vis] servicio *m*; *relig* oficio *m*; **~iceable** servible; útil; **~ice station** estación *f* de servicio
session ['seʃən] sesión *f*
set [set] *s* juego *m*, serie *f*; batería *f* (*de cocina*); plató *m* (*cine*); tendencia *f*; aparato *m* (*de radio*); puesta *f* (*del sol*); ***shampoo and ~*** lavar y marcar; *a, prep* rígido; listo; fijo; ***to be all ~*** estar listo; *v/t* poner, colocar; montar; fijar; ***~ aside*** reservar; desechar; poner aparte; ***~ eyes on*** avistar; ***~ free*** poner en libertad; ***~ on fire*** pegar fuego a; ***~ up*** establecer; *v/i* ponerse (*el sol*); cuajarse; fraguar (*cemento*); ***~ about*** empezar; ***~ off*** partir; **~back** revés *m*
setting ['setiŋ] montadura *f*; puesta *f* (*del sol*); colocación *f*
settle ['setl] *v/t* arreglar; colocar; *com* saldar; ajustar (*cuentas*); resolver; *v/i* posarse, asentarse; ***~ down*** sentar la cabeza; ***~ for*** conformarse con; ***~ on*** ponerse de acuerdo; **~ment** arreglo *m*; establecimiento *m*; colonia *f*; pago *m*; **~r** colono(a) *m* (*f*)
seven ['sevn] siete
sever ['sevə] *v/t* separar; cortar; *v/i* separarse
several ['sevrəl] varios; diversos
sever|e [si'viə] severo; riguroso; grave; duro; **~ity** [~'veriti] severidad *f*
sew [səu] *v/t, v/i* coser
sew|age ['sju(:)idʒ] aguas *f/pl* residuales; **~er** alcantarilla *f*; **~erage** alcantarillado *m*
sewing ['səuiŋ] costura *f*; **~ machine** máquina *f* de coser
sex [seks] sexo *m*; **~ appeal** atracción *f* sexual
sexual ['seksjuəl] sexual
shabby ['ʃæbi] gastado
shack [ʃæk] choza *f*
shad|e [ʃeid] *s* sombra *f*; matiz *m*; celosía *f*; pantalla *f* (*de lámpara*); *v/t* sombrear; matizar; **~ow** ['ʃædəu] *s* sombra *f*; *v/t* sombrear; seguir de cerca; **~owy** umbroso; vago; **~y** ['ʃeidi] sombreado; *fig* sospechoso
shaft [ʃɑ:ft] flecha *f*; caña *f*, vara *f*; mango *m*; *tecn* eje *m*; *min* pozo *m*
shaggy ['ʃægi] peludo
shak|e [ʃeik] *s* sacudida *f*; meneo *m*; vibración *f*; *v/t* sacudir; debilitar (*fe, etc*); ***~e hands*** estrecharse las manos; ***~e up*** agitar; *v/i* temblar; **~y** trémulo, tembloroso
shall [ʃæl] *v/aux para el futuro*: ***we ~ read*** leeremos; ***he ~ go*** irá; ***you ~ have it*** lo tendrás
shallow ['ʃæləu] poco profundo; *fig* superficial; **~s** bajío *m*
sham [ʃæm] *a* fingido; falso; *s* impostura *f*; *v/i* simular, fingir; **~bles** lío *m*, desorden *m*
shame [ʃeim] *s* vergüenza *f*; ignominia *f*; *v/t* avergonzar; **~faced** avergonzado; **~ful** vergonzoso; escandaloso; **~less** desvergonzado; descarado
shampoo [ʃæm'pu:] *s* champú *m*; *v/t* lavar (*la cabeza*)
shamrock ['ʃæmrɔk] trébol *m*
shank [ʃæŋk] zanca *f*; *tecn* mango *m*
shape [ʃeip] *s* forma *f*; figura *f*; condición *f*; *v/t* formar; moldear; *fig* idear; **~less** informe; **~ly** bien formado
share [ʃɛə] *s* porción *f*; participación *f*; parte *f*; *com* acción *f*; *v/t* compartir; ***~ out*** repartir; **~holder** accionista *m*
shark [ʃɑ:k] tiburón *m*
sharp [ʃɑ:p] *a* agudo; afilado; distinto; penetrante; definido; *mús* sostenido; *adv* en punto; ***four o'clock ~*** las 4 en punto; **~en** *v/t* afilar; aguzar; sacar punta a (*lápiz*); **~ener** afilador *m*; sacapuntas *m*; **~ness** agudeza *f*; nitidez *f*
shatter ['ʃætə] *v/t* estrellar; destrozar; *v/i* destrozarse
shav|e [ʃeiv] *v/t* afeitar; *tecn* acepillar; *v/i* afeitarse; **~ing** viruta *f* (*de madera*)

English
shawl 38

shawl [ʃɔːl] mantón *m*; chal *m*
she [ʃiː] *pron f* ella; *s* hembra *f*; **~-cat** gata *f*
sheaf [ʃiːf] gavilla *f*; haz *f*
shear [ʃiə] *v/t* esquilar, trasquilar; **~s** tijeras *f/pl* de jardín
sheath [ʃiːθ] vaina *f*; estuche *m*; **~e** [ʃiːð] *v/t* envainar; aforrar
shed [ʃed] *s* cobertizo *m*; *v/t* verter; despojarse (de)
sheep [ʃiːp] oveja(s) *f(pl)*; carnero *m*; **~dog** perro *m* pastor; **~ish** tímido
sheer [ʃiə] puro; transparente
sheet [ʃiːt] sábana *f*; hoja *f* (*de metal, papel*); lámina *f*; *mar* escota *f*
shelf [ʃelf] anaquel *m*, estante *m*
shell [ʃel] cáscara *f* (*de nuez, huevo, etc*); vaina *f* (*de legumbres*); *zool* concha *f*; armazón *f*; *mil* granada *f*; cápsula *f* (*para cartuchos*)
shellfish [ˈʃelfiʃ] marisco *m*
shelter [ˈʃeltə] *s* refugio *m*; asilo *m*; *v/t* abrigar; amparar; *v/i* refugiarse
shelve [ʃelv] *v/t fig* aplazar
shepherd [ˈʃepəd] *s* pastor *m*
sherry [ˈʃeri] jerez *m*
shield [ʃiːld] *s* escudo *m* (*t fig*); *v/t* proteger
shift [ʃift] *s* cambio *m*; recurso *m*; maña *f*, evasión *f*; turno *m*, tanda *f* (*de obreros*); *v/t* cambiar; desplazar; *v/i* cambiar; moverse; **~y** furtivo, taimado
shilling [ˈʃiliŋ] chelín *m*
shimmer [ˈʃimə] *s* reflejo *m* trémulo; *v/i* relucir
shin [ʃin] espinilla *f*; *v/t*, *v/i* **~ up** trepar
shine [ʃain] *s* lustre *m*; brillo *m*; *v/i* resplandecer; brillar (*t fig*); *v/t* sacar lustre a (*zapatos*)
shingle [ˈʃiŋgl] guijos *m/pl* (*playa*); tabla *f* de ripia; **~s** *med* herpes *m/pl o f/pl*
shiny [ˈʃaini] brillante
ship [ʃip] *s* buque *m*, barco *m*; navío *m*; nave *f*; *v/t* embarcar; despachar; **~ment** embarque *m*; envío *m*; **~owner** naviero *m*, armador *m*; **~wreck** naufragio *m*; **~yard** astillero *m*
shirk [ʃəːk] *v/t* evadir, eludir
shirt [ʃəːt] camisa *f*; **~sleeve** manga *f* de camisa
shiver [ˈʃivə] *s* escalofrío *m*; temblor *m*; *v/i* tiritar; temblar; tener escalofríos
shock [ʃɔk] *s* choque *m*; sacudida *f*; golpe *m*; *v/t* chocar; sacudir; disgustar; escandalizar; **~ absorber** amortiguador *m*; **~ing** chocante; escandaloso
shoddy [ˈʃɔdi] de pacotilla
shoe [ʃuː] *s* zapato *m*, calzado *m*; *v/t* calzar; herrar (*caballo*); **~horn** calzador *m*; **~lace** cordón *m*; **~maker** zapatero *m*; **~shop** zapatería *f*
shoot [ʃuːt] *s bot* vástago *m*; retoño *m*; *v/t* disparar; tirar; matar *o* herir a tiros; filmar, rodar (*una película*); *mil* fusilar; *v/i* tirar; germinar, brotar (*planta*); **~ing** tiro *m*; caza *f* con escopeta; **~ing star** estrella *f* fugaz; **~-out** pelea *f* a toros
shop [ʃɔp] tienda *f*; almacén *m*; taller *m*; **~ assistant** dependiente *m*; **~keeper** tendero *m*; **~lifter** mechero *m*; **~ping** compras *f/pl*; **to go ~ping** ir de compras; **~ping centre,** *Am* **center** centro *m* comercial; **~ steward** dirigente *m* obrero; **~walker** vigilante *m* de tienda; **~ window** escaparate *m*
shore [ʃɔː] orilla *f*; playa *f*
short [ʃɔːt] corto; breve; bajo (*de estatura*); **to be ~ of** andar escaso de; **in ~** en suma; **to cut ~** interrumpir; abreviar; **to run ~** escasear; **~age** escasez *f*; falta *f*; **~circuit** cortocircuito *m*; **~coming** defecto *m*; **~cut** atajo *m*; **~en** *v/t* acortar; abreviar; **~hand** taquigrafía *f*; **~hand typist** taquimecanógrafa *f*; **~ly** dentro de poco; **~ness** brevedad *f*; deficiencia *f*; **~s** pantalones *m/pl* cortos; **~-sighted** miope; **~tempered** enojadizo; **~-term** a corto plazo
shot [ʃɔt] tiro *m*, disparo *m*; balazo *m*; tirador(a) *m* (*f*) (*persona*); *foto, cine* toma *f*
should [ʃud] *v/aux para formar el condicional de los verbos*: **I ~ go** iría; debería irme
shoulder [ˈʃəuldə] *s* hombro *m*; *v/t* llevar a hombros; *fig* cargar con; **~ blade** omóplato *m*
shout [ʃaut] *s* grito *m*; *v/t*, *v/i* gritar; **~ing** vocerío *m*
shove [ʃʌv] *s* empujón *m*; *v/t*, *v/i* empujar
shovel [ˈʃʌvl] pala *f*
show [ʃəu] *s* exposición *f*; espectáculo *m*; *teat* función *f*; ostentación *f*; *v/t* mostrar; enseñar; exhibir; proyectar (*una película*); *v/i* parecer; **~ off** alardear; presumir; **~ up** asistir; presentarse; **~ business** el mundo del espectáculo; **~case** vitrina *f*
shower [ˈʃauə] *s* chaparrón *m*; ducha *f*; *v/t* regar; mojar; **~ with** colmar de; *v/i* llover; ducharse
showy [ˈʃəui] vistoso; ostentoso
shrapnel [ˈʃræpnl] metralla *f*
shred [ʃred] *s* triza *f*; fragmento *m*; *v/t* desmenuzar; hacer trizas
shrew [ʃruː] arpía *f*; mujer *f* de mal genio
shrewd [ʃruːd] astuto
shriek [ʃriːk] *s* chillido *m*; *v/i* chillar
shrill [ʃril] estridente; penetrante
shrimp [ʃrimp] *zool* gamba *f*
shrine [ʃrain] santuario *m*
shrink [ʃriŋk] *v/i* encogerse; disminuir; **~ from** evadir; **~age** encogimiento *m*
shrivel [ˈʃrivl] *v/t*, *v/i* arrugar(se); avellanarse
Shrove [ʃrəuv] **Tuesday** martes *m* de carnaval
shrub [ʃrʌb] arbusto *m*
shrug [ʃrʌg] *s* encogimiento *m* de hombros; *v/i* encogerse de hombros
shudder [ˈʃʌdə] *s* estremecimiento *m*; *v/i* estremecerse
shuffle [ˈʃʌfl] *s* barajadura *f* (*de naipes*); *v/t*, *v/i* barajar (*naipes*); arrastrar los pies
shun [ʃʌn] *v/t*, *v/i* esquivar
shut [ʃʌt] *v/t* cerrar; encerrar; *v/i* **~ up** callarse la boca; **~down** cierre *m*, suspensión *f* del trabajo; **~ter** contraventana *f*; *foto* obturador *m*
shuttle [ˈʃʌtl] *aer* lanzadera *f*
shy [ʃai] tímido; **~ness** timidez *f*
Sicil|ian [siˈsiljən] *a*, *s* siciliano(a) *m* (*f*); **~y** Sicilia *f*
sick [sik] enfermo; **~ of** harto de; **to be ~** tener náuseas; vomitar; **~en** *v/t* enfermar; dar asco a; *v/i* enfermarse; hartarse
sickle [ˈsikl] hoz *f*
sick| leave [ˈsikliːv] licencia *f* por enfermedad; **~ly** enfermizo; **~ness** enfermedad *f*; náuseas *f/pl*
sid|e [said] *s* lado *m*; costado *m*; ladera *f*; **~e by ~e** lado a lado; **on all ~es** por todas partes; *v/t*, *v/i* **to take ~es** tomar partido; **~eboard** aparador *m*; **~eburns** patillas *f/pl*; **~elong** de soslayo; **~estep** *v/t fig* esquivar; **~etrack** *v/t fig* desviar (a su propósito); **~ewalk** *Am* acera *f*; **~eways** de lado
siege [siːdʒ] sitio *m*; **to lay ~ to** sitiar
sieve [siv] *s* criba *f*; tamiz *m*; *v/t* tamizar
sift [sift] *v/t* tamizar; cribar; *fig* escudriñar
sigh [sai] *s* suspiro *m*; *v/i* suspirar; **~ for** añorar
sight [sait] *s* vista *f*; visión *f*; espectáculo *m*; lugar *m* de interés; mira *f*; **at first ~** a primera vista; **by ~** de vista; **in ~** a la vista; **to catch ~ of** avistar; *v/t* ver; divisar; **~seeing** turismo *m*; **~seer** turista *m*, *f*
sign [sain] *s* signo *m*; seña *f*, señal *f*; indicio *m*; letrero *m*; **show ~s of** dar muestras de; *v/t* firmar; señalar
signal [ˈsignl] *s* señal *f*; *v/t*, *v/i* indicar; hacer señales
signature [ˈsignitʃə] firma *f*
signboard [ˈsainbɔːd] letrero *m*
signet [ˈsignit] sello *m*
signif|icance [sigˈnifikəns] significación *f*; **~icant** significante; significativo; **~y** [ˈsignifai] *v/t* significar
signpost [ˈsainpəust] poste *m* indicador
silen|ce [ˈsailəns] *s* silencio *m*; *v/t* hacer callar; **~cer** *tecn* silenciador *m*; **~t** silencioso; callado; mudo (*filme*); **~t partner** *com* socio *m* comanditario
silhouette [siluːˈet] silueta *f*
silicon [ˈsilikən] silicio *m*
silk [silk] seda *f*; **~y** sedoso
sill [sil] antepecho *m* (*de la ventana*); repisa *f*
silly [ˈsili] tonto; necio; simple
silt [silt] sedimento *m*
silver [ˈsilvə] *s* plata *f*; **~-plated** plateado; **~smith** platero *m*; **~ware** vajilla *f* de plata; **~y** plateado; argentino (*tono, etc*)
similar [ˈsimilə] parecido, semejante; **~ity** [~ˈlæriti] semejanza *f*; **~ly** igualmente; del mismo modo
simmer [ˈsimə] *v/i* hervir a fuego lento
simpl|e [ˈsimpl] simple; mero; sencillo; tonto; **~icity** [simˈplisiti] sencillez *f*; **~ification** simplificación *f*; **~ify** *v/t* simplificar
simulate [ˈsimjuleit] *v/t* simular, fingir
simultaneous [siməlˈteinjəs] simultáneo
sin [sin] *s* pecado *m*; *v/i* pecar
since [sins] *adv* desde entonces; después; **long ~** hace mucho; *conj* ya que; puesto que; *prep* desde; después de
sincer|e [sinˈsiə] sincero; **~ity** [~ˈseriti] sinceridad *f*
sinew [ˈsinjuː] tendón *m*; **~s** *fig* fibra *f*; **~y** fibroso; *fig* fuerte
sing [siŋ] *v/t*, *v/i* cantar; trinar (*pájaros*)
singe [sindʒ] *v/t* chamuscar; quemar (*las puntas del pelo*)
singer [ˈsiŋə] cantante *m*, *f*
single [ˈsiŋgl] *a* solo; único; soltero; *v/t* **~ out** escoger, separar; *s* billete *m* de ida; persona *f* soltera; **~-handed** solo, sin ayuda; **~-minded** sincero; con un solo propósito
singular [ˈsiŋgjulə] singular; extraño; **~ity** [~ˈlæriti] singularidad *f*; rareza *f*
sinister [ˈsinistə] siniestro
sink [siŋk] *s* fregadero *m*; *v/t* sumergir; hundir; bajar; *v/i* hundirse; ponerse (*sol*); declinar; **~ in** penetrar; **~ing** hundimiento *m*
sinner [ˈsinə] pecador(a) *m* (*f*)
sinus [ˈsainəs] seno *m*
sip [sip] *s* sorbo *m*; *v/t* sorber
sir [səː] señor *m*
siren [ˈsaiərən] sirena *f*
sirloin [ˈsəːlɔin] solomillo *m*
sister [ˈsistə] hermana *f*; *relig* sor *f*; **~-in-law** cuñada *f*
sit [sit] *v/i* estar sentado; reunirse; sentar (*ropa*); **~ down** sentarse; **~ for** posar para; **~ up** velar; incorporarse; prestar atención; *v/t* sentar; dar asiento
site [sait] sitio *m*
sitting [ˈsitiŋ] *a* sentado; *s* sesión *f*; **~room** sala *f* de estar
situat|ed [ˈsitjueitid] *a* situado; **~ion** situación *f*
six [siks] seis
size [saiz] *s* tamaño *m*; talla *f*; número *m* (*zapatos*); *v/t* clasificar por tamaño; **~able** considerable
sizzle [ˈsizl] *v/t*, *v/i* chisporrotear, chirriar
skat|e [skeit] *s* patín *m*; *v/i* patinar; **~eboard** patinete *m*; **~er** patinador(a) *m* (*f*); **~ing rink** pista *f* de patinaje
skeleton [ˈskelitn] esqueleto *m*; *fig* armadura *f*; **~ key** llave *f* maestra
skeptic = **sceptic**
sketch [sketʃ] *s* bosquejo *m*, boceto *m*; *teat* pieza *f* corta; *v/t* bosquejar, trazar; **~y** superficial, incompleto
ski [skiː] *s* esquí *m*; *v/i* esquiar
skid [skid] *s* patinazo *m*, resbalón *m*; *v/i* patinar, resbalar
ski|er [ˈskiːə] esquiador(a) *m* (*f*); **~ing** esquí *m*; **~ lift** telesquí *m*
skil(l)ful [ˈskilful] hábil, diestro; **~l** habilidad *f*, destreza *f*; **~led** experto; **~led worker** obrero *m* calificado
skim [skim] *v/t* desnatar (*leche*); espumar; **~ through** hojear
skin [skin] *s* piel *f*; cutis *m*, *f*; pellejo *m*; cuero *m*; corteza *f*; *v/t* desollar, pelar; **~-deep** superficial; **~ny** flaco, magro
skip [skip] *s* brinco *m*; *v/i* brincar
skipper [ˈskipə] capitán *m*
skirmish [ˈskəːmiʃ] escaramuza *f*
skirt [skəːt] *s* falda *f*; faldón *m*; borde *m*; *v/t* bordear; moverse por el borde de
skittles [ˈskitlz] juego *m* de bolos
skull [skʌl] cráneo *m*; calavera *f*
skunk [skʌŋk] mofeta *f*
sky [skai] cielo *m*; **~diving** paracaidismo *m*; **~jack** [ˈ~dʒæk] *v/t* secuestrar en vuelo; **~lark** alondra *f*; **~light** tragaluz *m*; claraboya *f*; **~line** perfil *m* arquitectónico; **~scraper** rascacielos *m*
slab [slæb] losa *f*; plancha *f*
slack [slæk] *a* flojo; negligente; *s* lo flojo; período *m* inactivo; cisco *m* (*de carbón*); **~en** *v/t* aflojar; disminuir; *v/i* aflojarse; **~s** pantalones *m/pl*
slam [slæm] *s* golpe *m*; portazo *m*; *v/t* cerrar de golpe
slander [ˈslɑːndə] *s* calumnia *f*; *v/t* calumniar
slang [slæŋ] jerga *f*; argot *m*
slant [slɑːnt] *s* inclinación *f*; *v/t*, *v/i* inclinar(se)
slap [slæp] *s* palmada *f*; bofetada *f*; *v/t* pegar; abofetear; **~stick comedy** *teat* comedia *f* de payasadas
slash [slæʃ] *s* cuchillada *f*; *v/t* acuchillar
slate [sleit] *s* pizarra *f*
slaughter [ˈslɔːtə] *s* matanza *f*; carnicería *f*; *v/t* matar; *LA* carnear; *Am* masacrar; **~ house** matadero *m*
slav|e [sleiv] *s* esclavo(a) *m* (*f*); siervo(a) *m* (*f*); *v/i* **~e away** sudar tinta; **~ery** [ˈ~əri] esclavitud *f*; **~ish** servil
slay [slei] *v/t* matar; **~er** asesino *m*
sled [sled], **sledge** [sledʒ] trineo *m*; **~hammer** acotillo *m*
sleek [sliːk] *a* alisado; lustroso; *v/t* alisar
sleep [sliːp] *s* sueño *m*; **to go to ~** dormirse; *v/t*, *v/i* dormir; **~ soundly** dormir a pierna suelta; **~er** *f c* coche *m* cama; **~ing bag** saco *m* de dormir; **~ing partner** socio *m* secreto; **~lessness** insomnio *m*; **~walker** somnámbulo(a) *m* (*f*); **~y** soñoliento
sleet [sliːt] aguanieve *f*
sleeve [sliːv] manga *f*; *tecn* manguito *m*; **to have something up one's ~** tener preparado en secreto
sleigh [slei] trineo *m*
slender [ˈslendə] delgado; *fig* escaso, débil
slice [slais] *s* rebanada *f* (*de pan*); tajada *f* (*de carne*); *v/t* cortar; tajar
slick [slik] hábil, diestro; tramposo
slide [slaid] *s* tapa *f* corrediza; deslizadero *m*; tobogán *m*; *foto* diapositiva *f*; *v/i* resbalar; deslizarse; **~ rule** regla *f* de cálculo
slight [slait] *a* leve, ligero; escaso; pequeño; *v/t* despreciar; **~ly** un poco
slim [slim] *a* delgado; esbelto; escaso; *v/i* adelgazar
slim|e [slaim] limo *m*; cieno *m*; babaza *f*; **~y** viscoso; baboso; limoso
sling [sliŋ] *s mil* honda *f*; *med* cabestrillo *m*; *v/t* arrojar, tirar
slip [slip] *s* papeleta *f*; tira *f*; funda *f*; combinación *f*; resbalón *m*; *fig* desliz *m*; *v/i* deslizarse, resbalarse; **~ away** escabullirse; **~ up** equivocarse; *v/t* hacer deslizar; **~per** zapatilla *f*; **~pery** resbaladizo; **~shod** descuidado
slit [slit] *s* hendedura *f*; *v/t* hender, rajar
slobber [ˈslɔbə] *s* baba *f*; *v/i* babear
slogan [ˈsləugən] lema *m*; eslogan *m*
slop [slɔp] *v/t*, *v/i* **~ over** derramar(se)
slope [sləup] *s* cuesta *f*; inclinación *f*; *v/i* **~ down** estar en declive
sloppy [ˈslɔpi] descuidado; desaliñado
slot [slɔt] muesca *f*; ranura *f*
sloth [sləuθ] pereza *f*; *zool* perezoso *m*
slot machine [ˈslɔtməˈʃiːn] máquina *f* tragaperras
slouch [slautʃ] *v/i* **~ about** andar con un aire gacho
slough [slau] *s* fangal *m*; [slʌf] **~ off** *v/t* echar de sí; *v/i* desprenderse

slovenly ['slʌvnli] desaseado, descuidado

slow [sləu] *a* lento; atrasado (*reloj*); *v/t, v/i* ~ **down** aflojar el paso; **~ly** despacio; **~ motion** cámara *f* lenta; **~ness** lentitud *f*; torpeza *f*

sluggish ['slʌgiʃ] perezoso

sluice [slu:s] esclusa *f*

slum [slʌm] barrio *m* bajo, *LA* barriada *f*

slumber ['slʌmbə] *s* sueño *m*; *v/i* dormitar

slump [slʌmp] *s* declive *m* económico; *v/i* hundirse (*precios*)

slush [slʌʃ] fango *m*; nieve *f* acuosa

slut [slʌt] marrana *f*

sly [slai] disimulado; astuto; **on the ~** a escondidas

smack [smæk] *s* dejo *m*; palmada *f*; *v/t* dar una palmada a; *v/i* ~ **of** saber a; tener resabios de

small [smɔ:l] pequeño; menudo; reducido; poco; insignificante; **~ hours** primeras horas *f/pl* de la madrugada; **~ness** pequeñez *f*; **~pox** viruela *f*; **~ talk** cháchara *f*

smart [smɑ:t] *a* listo, vivo; elegante; alerto; *v/i* escocer; picar

smash [smæʃ] *s* choque *m*; colisión *f* violenta; *v/t, v/i* romper; destrozar; **~ing** *a* extraordinario

smattering ['smætəriŋ] tintura *f*; nociones *f/pl*

smear [smiə] *s* mancha *f*; *v/t* ensuciar; untar; calumniar

smell [smel] *s* olor *m*; aroma *m*; hedor *m* (*malo*); olfato *m* (*sentido*); *v/t* oler; olfatear; *v/i* ~ **of** oler a; **~ing salts** sales *f/pl* aromáticas; **~y** que huele mal

smelt *v/t* fundir

smil|e [smail] *s* sonrisa *f*; *v/i* sonreír(se); **~ing** risueño

smirk [smə:k] sonrisa *f* afectada

smith [smiθ] herrero *m*; **~y** ['~ði] herrería *f*

smock [smɔk] bata *f* (*de artista*); delantal *m* (*de niño*)

smog [smɔg] mezcla *f* nociva de humo y niebla

smok|e [sməuk] *s* humo *m*; *v/t* ahumar; fumar; *v/i* echar humo; fumar; **~er** fumador *m*; *f c* coche *m* de fumadores; **~e screen** cortina *f* de humo

smok|ing ['sməukiŋ] el fumar *m*; **no ~ing** prohibido fumar; **~y** humeante; ahumado

smooth [smu:ð] *a* liso; suave; llano; *v/t* alisar; suavizar

smother ['smʌðə] *v/t* sofocar, apagar; ahogar

smoulder ['sməuldə] *v/i* arder en rescoldo; *fig* estar latente

smudge [smʌdʒ] *s* tiznón *m*; *v/t* tiznar

smug [smʌg] pagado de sí mismo; presumido

smuggl|e ['smʌgl] *v/t* pasar de contrabando; **~er** contrabandista *m*; **~ing** contrabando *m*

smut [smʌt] *s* tizne *m*; obscenidad *f*; *v/t* tiznar; **~ty** tiznado; sucio; *fig* obsceno

snack [snæk] piscolabis *m*; **~ bar** cafetería *f*, merendero *m*

snail [sneil] caracol *m*; **at a ~'s pace** a paso de tortuga

snake [sneik] serpiente *f*; culebra *f*; víbora *f*

snap [snæp] *s* castañetazo *m* (*de dedos*); chasquido *m* (*ruido*); cierre *m* de resorte; *a* repentino; *adv* **~!** ¡crac!; *v/t* castañetear; romper; hacer crujir; *v/i* ~ **at** replicar con irritación; romperse con un chasquido; **~ fastener** corchete *m* de presión; **~pish** regañón, arisco; **~shot** *foto* instantánea *f*

snare [snɛə] lazo *m*; trampa *f*

snarl [snɑ:l] *s* gruñido *m* agresivo; *v/i* gruñir

snatch [snætʃ] *s* arrebatamiento *m*; **~es of** trozos de *m/pl*; *v/t* arrebatar

sneak [sni:k] *v/i* ir a hurtadillas; **~ers** zapatillas *f/pl*; playeras *f/pl*

sneer [sniə] *s* risa *f* de desprecio; mofa *f*; *v/i* mofarse (de)

sneeze [sni:z] *s* estornudo *m*; *v/i* estornudar

sniff [snif] *s* husmeo *m*; *v/t* husmear; olfatear; *v/i* ~ **at** oliscar; *fig* despreciar

snip [snip] *s* recorte *m*; pedacito *m*; *v/i* tijeretear

snipe [snaip] *zool* agachadiza *f*; **~r** tirador *m* emboscado

snivel ['snivl] *v/i* lloriquear

snob [snɔb] (e)snob *m, f*

snoop [snu:p] *v/i* curiosear, fisgonear

snooze [snu:z] *v/i* dormitar

snore [snɔ:] *s* ronquido *m*; *v/i* roncar

snort [snɔ:t] *v/i* bufar; *s* bufido *m*

snout [snaut] hocico *m*

snow [snəu] *s* nieve *f*; *v/i* nevar; **~ball** bola *f* de nieve; **~drift** ventisquero *m*; **~drop** campanilla *f* de invierno; **~fall** nevada *f*; **~flake** copo *m* de nieve; **~man** figura *f* de nieve; **~plough, *Am* ~plow** quitanieves *m*; **~storm** ventisca *f*; **~y** de mucha nieve

snub [snʌb] *a* desaire; *v/t* repulsar; desairar; **~-nosed** chato

snuff [snʌf] *s* rapé *m*, tabaco *m* en polvo; *v/t* aspirar; ~ **out** apagar

snug [snʌg] cómodo; abrigado; **~gle** *v/i* arrimarse

so [səu] *adv, pron* así; de este modo; tan; por tanto; ~ **far** hasta ahora; ~ **long!** ¡hasta luego!; ~ **much** tanto; **I think ~** creo que sí; **Mr. ~-and-~** don Fulano de tal; **~-~** así así; *conj* con tal que

soak [səuk] *s* remojo *m*; *v/t* remojar; empagar; ~ **up** absorber

soap [səup] *s* jabón *m*; *v/t* enjabonar; **~ dish** jabonera *f*; **~ opera** telenovela *f*; **~y** jabonoso

soar [sɔ:] *v/i* encumbrarse

sob [sɔb] *s* sollozo *m*; *v/i* sollozar

sob|er ['səubə] *a* sobrio; grave, serio; apagado (*color*); *v/i* **~er up** desintoxicarse; **~erness, ~riety** [~'braiəti] sobriedad *f*

so-called ['səu'kɔ:ld] llamado, supuesto

soccer ['sɔkə] fútbol *m*

sociable ['səuʃəbl] sociable

socia|l ['səuʃəl] social; **~l climber** arribista *m, f*; **~lism** socialismo *m*; **~list** *a, s* socialista *m, f*; **~lize** *v/t* socializar

society [sə'saiəti] sociedad *f*; asociación *f*

sock [sɔk] calcetín *m*; tortazo *m*

socket ['sɔkit] cuenca *f* (*del ojo*); *tecn* casquillo *m*; *elec* enchufe *m*

sod [sɔd] terrón *m* herboso; tepe *m*; **~den** empapado

sofa ['səufə] sofá *m*

soft [sɔft] blando; muelle; suave; no alcohólico (*bebida*); **~en** ['sɔfn] *v/t, v/i* ablandar(se); **~ness** suavidad *f*

soil [sɔil] *s* tierra *f*; suelo *m*; *v/t* ensuciar

sojourn ['sɔdʒə:n] permanencia *f*; estancia *f*

solace ['sɔləs] consuelo *m*

sold [səuld]: ~ **out** agotado; "no hay billetes"

soldier ['səuldʒə] soldado *m*, militar *m*

sole [səul] *s* planta *f* (*del pie*); suela *f* (*del zapato*); *zool* lenguado *m*; *v/t* echar suela; *a* único, solo, exclusivo

solemn ['sɔləm] solemne; grave

solicit [sə'lisit] *v/t* demandar, reclamar; **~or** abogado *m*; **~ous** solícito

solid ['sɔlid] sólido; macizo; bien fundado; **~arity** [sɔli'dæriti] solidaridad *f*; **~ity** [sə'liditi] solidez *f*

soliloquy [sə'liləkwi] soliloquio *m*

solit|ary ['sɔlitəri] solitario; **~ude** ['~tju:d] soledad *f*

solo ['səuləu] solo *m*; **~ist** solista *m, f*

solu|ble ['sɔljubl] soluble; **~tion** solución *f*

solve [sɔlv] *v/t* resolver; **~nt** *a, s* solvente *m*

somber = ***sombre***

sombre ['sɔmbə] sombrío; triste

some [sʌm, səm] *a* un poco de; algo de; algún; unos pocos; algunos; *pron* alguno(as); unos; algo; **~body** ['sʌmbədi], **~one** alguien; **~body else** algún otro; **~day** algún día; **~how** de algún modo

somersault ['sʌməsɔ:lt] salto *m* mortal, voltereta *f*

some|thing ['sʌmθiŋ] algo; **~time** algún día; **~times** a veces; **~what** algo; un tanto; **~where** en alguna parte

son [sʌn] hijo *m*

song [sɔŋ] canción *f*, canto *m*, cantar *m*; **~bird** pájaro *m* cantor; **~book** cancionero *m*

sonic ['sɔnik] sónico

son-in-law ['sʌninlɔ:] yerno *m*

sonnet ['sɔnit] soneto *m*

soon [su:n] pronto; **as ~ as** tan pronto como; **as ~ as possible** cuanto antes; **~er** más temprano; **no ~er ... than** apenas ... cuando; **~er or later** tarde o temprano

soot [sut] hollín *m*

soothe [su:ð] *v/t* calmar

sophisticated [sə'fistikeitid] sofisticado

soporific [sɔpə'rifik] soporífico *m*; narcótico *m*

sopping ['sɔpiŋ]: ~ **wet** empapado

sorcer|er ['sɔ:sərə] brujo *m*; **~y** brujería *f*

sordid ['sɔ:did] sórdido; asqueroso; vil

sore [sɔ:] *a* dolorido; inflamado; disgustado; ~ **throat** dolor *m* de garganta; *s* llaga *f*

sorrow ['sɔrəu] *s* dolor *m*; pesar *m*; **~ful** pesaroso

sorry ['sɔri] arrepentido; lastimoso; **to be ~** sentir; **to be ~ for (someone)** compadecerse de (alguien)

sort [sɔ:t] *s* clase *f*; especie *f*; **something of the ~** algo por el estilo; ~ **of** en cierta medida; *v/t* clasificar

soul [səul] alma *f*, espíritu *m*

sound [saund] *a* sano; ileso; correcto; profundo (*sueño*); *com* solvente; *s* sonido *m*; *v/t* sonar; tocar; *med* auscultar; sondear; *v/i* sonar; resonar; **~ barrier** barrera *f* del sonido; **~ing** sondeo *m*; **~less** silencioso *m*; **~proof** insonorizado; **~ track** *cine* banda *f* sonora; **~ wave** onda *f* sonora

soup [su:p] sopa *f*

sour ['sauə] *a* agrio, ácido; cortado (*leche*); *fig* desabrido; *v/t, v/i* agriar(se)

source [sɔ:s] fuente *f*, origen *m*

south [sauθ] *s* sur *m*; *a* meridional; **~ America** América *f* del Sur; **~ American** *a, s* sudamericano(a) *m* (*f*); **~erly** ['sʌðəli], **~ern** meridional; **~ward(s)** ['sauθwəd(z)] hacia el sur

souvenir ['su:vəniə] recuerdo *m*

soviet ['səuviət] soviético; **the ~ Union** la Unión Soviética

sow [sau] puerca *f*, cerda *f*

sow [səu] *v/t, v/i* sembrar; esparcir; diseminar; **~ one's wild oats** correr sus mocedades

soy [sɔi] soja *f*; **~bean** semilla *f* de soja

spa [spɑ:] balneario *m*

space [speis] *s* espacio *m*; intervalo *m*; *v/t* espaciar; **~craft, ~ship** nave *f* espacial; **~ shuttle** transbordador *m* espacial

spacious ['speiʃəs] amplio

spade [speid] laya *f*; pala *f*; (*naipes*) espada *f*

Spain [spein] España *f*

span [spæn] palmo *m* (*de la mano*); luz *f* (*del puente*); *arq* tramo *m*; *aer* envergadura *f*; lapso *m*; *v/t* medir; extender sobre

spangle ['spæŋgl] lentejuela *f*

Spaniard ['spænjəd] español(a) *m* (*f*)

spaniel ['spænjəl] perro *m* de aguas

Spanish ['spæniʃ] *a, s* español(a) *m* (*f*); hispánico

spank [spæŋk] *v/t* zurrar; **~ing** zurra *f*

spar|e [spɛə] *a* de repuesto; disponible; libre; enjuto; frugal; **~e parts** piezas *f/pl* de recambio; **~e time** tiempo *m* libre; *v/t* ahorrar; evitar; privarse de; perdonar (*vida*); **to ~e** de sobra; **~ing** frugal; escaso

spark [spɑ:k] *s* chispa *f*; *v/i* chispear; **~le** *v/i* centellear; **~ling** brillante; **~ plug** bujía *f*

sparrow ['spærəu] *zool* gorrión *m*

sparse [spɑ:s] esparcido

spasm ['spæzəm] espasmo *m*; **~odic** [~'mɔdik] espasmódico

spatter ['spætə] *s* salpicadura *f*; *v/t, v/i* salpicar

spawn [spɔ:n] *s zool* huevas *f/pl*; *v/t, v/i zool* desovar

speak [spi:k] *v/t, v/i* hablar; decir; **~ one's mind** hablar en plata; ~ **up** hablar en alta voz; hablar claro; **~er** orador(a) *m* (*f*); hablante *m, f*

spear [spiə] lanza *f*; **~head** punta *f* de lanza

special ['speʃəl] especial; particular; **~ist** especialista *m, f*; **~ity** [~i'æliti] especialidad *f*; **~ize** *v/i* especializarse

species ['spi:ʃi:z] especie *f*

speci|fic [spi'sifik] específico; **~fy** ['spesifai] *v/t* especificar

specimen ['spesimin] muestra *f*; ejemplar *m*

speck [spek] manchita *f*; grano *m*; **~le** *v/t* motear; manchar

specta|cle ['spektəkl] espectáculo *m*; **~cles** gafas *f/pl*; **~cular** [~'tækjulə] espectacular, aparatoso; **~tor** [~'teitə] espectador(a) *m* (*f*)

speculat|e ['spekjuleit] *v/t, v/i* especular; **~ion** especulación *f*

speech [spi:tʃ] discurso *m*; habla *f*; **~less** mudo

speed [spi:d] *s* velocidad *f*; rapidez *f*; **at full ~** a toda velocidad; *v/t* ~ **up** acelerar; **~ limit** límite *m* de velocidad; **~ometer** [spi'dɔmitə] taquímetro *m*; **~y** rápido

spell [spel] *s* hechizo *m*, encanto *m*; turno *m*; rato *m*; *v/t, v/i* deletrear; **~ing** ortografía *f*

spen|d [spend] *v/t* gastar (*dinero*); emplear, pasar (*tiempo*); **~dthrift** derrochador; **~t** gastado; agotado

sperm [spə:m] esperma *m*

spher|e [sfiə] esfera *f*; **~ical** ['sferikəl] esférico

sphinx [sfiŋks] esfinge *f*

spic|e [spais] *s* especia *f*; *v/t* condimentar; **~y** picante

spider ['spaidə] araña *f*; **~'s web** telaraña *f*

spike [spaik] *s* púa *f*; escarpia *f*; *v/t* clavar, escarpiar

spill [spil] *s fam* vuelco *m*; *v/t, v/i* derramar(se)

spin [spin] *s* vuelta *f*; giro *m*; *v/t, v/i* hilar; girar

spinach ['spinidʒ] espinaca *f*

spinal ['spainl] espinal; **~ column** columna *f* vertebral

spindle ['spindl] huso *m*

spine [spain] espina *f* dorsal; **~less** sin energía; servil

spinster ['spinstə] solterona *f*

spiny ['spaini] espinoso

spiral ['spaiərəl] *a, s* espiral *f*

spire ['spaiə] aguja *f* (*de iglesia*)

spirit ['spirit] *s* espíritu *m*; ánimo *m*; humor *m*; alcohol *m*; **high ~s** animación *f*; **low ~s** abatimiento *m*; *v/t* **~ away** llevarse en secreto; **~ed** vivo; brioso; **~ual** ['~tjuəl] espiritual

spit [spit] *s coc* asador *m*; saliva *f*; *v/t, v/i* escupir

spite [spait] rencor *m*; **in ~ of** a pesar de; **~ful** rencoroso; malévolo

spitt|le ['spitl] saliva *f*; **~oon** [~'tu:n] escupidera *f*

splash [splæʃ] *s* salpicadura *f*; *v/t* rociar; salpicar; *v/i* ~ **about** chapotear; **~down** amerizaje *m*

spleen [spli:n] *anat* bazo *m*

splend|id ['splendid] espléndido; **~o(u)r** pompa *f*; esplendor *m*

splint [splint] *med s* tablilla *f*; *v/t* entablillar; **~er** *s* astilla *f*; *v/t* astillar

split [split] *s* hendedura *f*; raja *f*; *fig* cisma *m*; *v/t* hender; rajar; ~ **up** dividir; *v/i* partirse; ~ **off**, ~ **up** separarse

splurge [splə:dʒ] *v/t* gastar de modo extravagante

splutter ['splʌtə] *s* farfulla *f*; *v/t, v/i* farfullar; chisporrotear

spoil [spɔil] *v/t* estropear; mimar; *v/i* echarse a perder; **~s** *s/pl* despojo *m*, botín *m*; **~sport** aguafiestas *m, f*; **~t child** niño *m* consentido

spoke [spəuk] rayo *m* (*de rueda*)

spokesman portavoz *m*

spong|e [spʌndʒ] *s* esponja *f*; *v/i* gorrear; **~e cake** bizcocho *m*; **~er** gorrista *m, f*; **~y** esponjoso

sponsor ['spɔnsə] *s* patrocinador *m*; *v/t* patrocinar

spontaneous [spɔn'teinjəs] espontáneo

spook [spu:k] espectro *m*

spool [spu:l] carrete *m*

spoon [spu:n] cuchara *f*; **~ful** cucharada *f*

sporadic [spə'rædik] esporádico

sport [spɔːt] s deporte m; diversión f; v/t ostentar; v/i jugar; divertirse; **~ing** deportivo; **~sman, ~swoman** deportista m, f

spot [spɔt] s lugar m; sitio m; punto m; tacha f; mancha f; **on the ~** en el acto; en un aprieto; v/t descubrir, encontrar; manchar; **~less** inmaculado; nítido; **~light** proyector m; **~ test** prueba f selectiva

spouse [spauz] cónyuge m, f

spout [spaut] s pitón m; pico m (de cafetera); v/t, v/i arrojar

sprain [sprein] s torcedura f; v/t torcer

sprat [spræt] sardineta f

spray [sprei] s rociada f; espuma f (del mar); atomizador m; v/t, v/i pulverizar; rociar; **~ gun** pistola f pulverizadora

spread [spred] s extensión f; expansión f; propagación f; cobertor m; v/t extender; divulgar; desplegar; untar

spree [spriː]: **go on a ~** ir de juerga

sprig [sprig] ramita f

spring [spriŋ] s primavera f; fuente f (de agua); tecn resorte m; muelle m; salto m; v/i saltar; brincar; brotar; nacer; surgir; **~board** trampolín m; **~iness** elasticidad f; **~s** aut ballestas f/pl; **~y** elástico

sprinkle ['spriŋkl] v/t rociar; **~r** regadera f rotativa

sprint [sprint] s corrida f; v/i correr a toda carrera; **~er** velocista m, f

sprout [spraut] s vástago m; v/i brotar

spruce [spruːs] a pulcro, galano; s pícea f

spur [spəː] s espuela f (t fig); v/t ~ **on** fig estimular; **on the ~ of the moment** de improviso; **~n** [spəːn] v/t rechazar

spy [spai] s espía m, f; v/t, v/i espiar

squabble ['skwɔbl] v/i reñir; s riña f; disputa f

squad [skwɔd] pelotón m; cuadrilla f; **~ron** ['~rən] mar, aer escuadra f

squall [skwɔːl] ráfaga f

squalor ['skwɔlə] suciedad f; miseria f

squander ['skwɔndə] v/t, v/i derrochar; malgastar

square [skwɛə] a cuadrado; honesto; fam abundante (comida); s plaza f; cuadrado m; v/t cuadrar; arreglar, saldar (cuentas); **~ly** honradamente

squash [skwɔʃ] s aplastamiento m; calabaza f; v/t aplastar

squat [skwɔt] v/i agacharse

squeak [skwiːk] s chirrido m; v/i chirriar

squeal [skwiːl] v/i chillar

squeamish ['skwiːmiʃ] escrupuloso; remilgado

squeeze [skwiːz] s estrujón m; v/t estrujar; **~ out** exprimir

squid [skwid] calamar m

squint [skwint] s mirada f bizca; v/t, v/i bizquear

squire ['skwaiə] hacendado m, terrateniente m

squirm [skwəːm] v/i retorcerse

squirrel ['skwirəl] ardilla f

squirt [skwəːt] s chorretada f; v/t, v/i (hacer) salir a chorros

stab [stæb] s puñalada f; v/t apuñalar

---

stab|ility [stə'biliti] estabilidad f; solidez f; **~ilize** ['steibilaiz] v/t estabilizar

stable ['steibl] s cuadra f; establo m; a estable

stack [stæk] s montón m; pila f; v/t amontonar

stadium ['steidjəm] estadio m

staff [staːf] s palo m; vara f; bastón m; personal m; mil estado m mayor; v/t dotar de personal

stag [stæg] ciervo m

stage [steidʒ] s escena f; plataforma f; escenario m; etapa f; v/t representar en escena; **~ fright** miedo m al público

stagger ['stægə] s tambaleo m; v/i tambalear; vacilar; v/t asombrar; hacer tambalear

stagnant ['stægnənt] estancado; fig paralizado

staid [steid] formal, sobrio, serio

stain [stein] s mancha f; tintura f; v/t, v/i manchar; **~ed glass** vidrio m de color; **~less steel** acero m inoxidable

stair [stɛə] s escalón m; peldaño m; **~s** escalera f

stake [steik] s estaca f; posta f; com interés m; **at ~** en juego; v/t estacar; arriesgar

stale [steil] viejo; viciado; rancio; **~mate** ['~meit] (ajedrez) tablas f/pl (por ahogado); fig paralización f

stalk [stɔːk] s bot tallo m; paso m majestuoso; v/t cazar al acecho

stall [stɔːl] s pesebre m; casilla f; puesto m (en el mercado); teat butaca f; v/t meter en establo; atascar; v/i atascarse; ahogarse (motor); buscar evasivas

stallion ['stæljən] caballo m padre

stalwart ['stɔːlwət] forzudo; pol leal

stamina ['stæminə] resistencia f

stammer ['stæmə] s balbuceo m; v/t, v/i tartamudear, balbucear

stamp [stæmp] s sello m, LA estampilla f; estampado m, marca f; impresión f; v/t sellar; marcar; franquear; **~ out** extirpar; v/i patear; **~ collecting** filatelia f

stand [stænd] s puesto m; tenderete m; posición f; pedestal m; estrado m, tribuna f; parada f (de taxis); **take a ~** aferrarse a un principio; v/t resistir; aguantar, tolerar; colocar; v/i estar de pie; erguirse; **~ by** estar alerta; apoyar; **~ in for** suplir a; **~ off** apartarse; **~ out** destacarse; **~ up** ponerse en pie; **~ up for** defender; **~ up to** hacer frente a

standard ['stændəd] a normal; s norma f; patrón m; tipo m; estandarte m; **~ of living** nivel m de vida; **~ize** v/t normalizar

standing ['stændiŋ] s reputación f; duración f; a de pie, derecho, LA parado; **~ room** teat entrada f para estar de pie

stand|-offish ['stænd'ɔfiʃ] reservado, poco amistoso; **~point** punto m de vista; **~still** parada f

stapler ['steiplə] grapadora f

star [staː] s estrella f (t teat, cine figurar como estrella

starboard ['staːbəd] estribor m

starch [staːtʃ] s almidón m

stare [stɛə] s mirada f fija; v/i abrir grandes ojos; mirar fijamente

---

stark [staːk] a escueto; severo; **~ naked** en cueros

star|ling ['staːliŋ] estornino m; **~lit** iluminado por las estrellas; **~ry** estrellado; **~ry-eyed** ingenuo

start [staːt] s comienzo m, principio m; salida f; sobresalto m; v/i arrancar; empezar; v/t comenzar; iniciar; **~er** aut arranque m; **~ing point** punto m de partida

startl|e ['staːtl] v/t asustar; **~ing** alarmante

starv|ation [staː'veiʃən] inanición f; hambre f; **~e** v/i hambrear; morir de hambre; v/t hacer morir de hambre; **~ing** famélico

state [steit] s estado m; condición f; **in ~** de gran ceremonia; **to lie in ~** estar de cuerpo presente; v/t, v/i declarar; manifestar; afirmar; **~ly** majestuoso; **~ment** declaración f; relato m; com estado m de cuenta; **~room** camarote m; **~sman** hombre m de estado; estadista m

static ['stætik] estático

station ['steiʃən] s estación f; puesto m; v/t colocar; **~ary** fijo; **~er's** papelería f; **~ery** útiles m/pl de escritorio; **~ master** jefe m de estación; **~ wagon** rubia f

statistics [stə'tistiks] estadística f

statue ['stætʃuː] estatua f

statute ['stætjuːt] estatuto m

staunch [stɔːntʃ] a firme; leal; v/t restañar (la sangre)

stay [stei] s estancia f, permanencia f; soporte m; v/i quedarse; hospedarse; **~ away** ausentarse; **~ behind** quedar atrás; **~ put** seguir en el mismo sitio; **~ up** velar

stead [sted]: **in his ~** en su lugar; **~fast** ['~fəst] firme; constante; **~y** seguro; uniforme; firme

steak [steik] biftec m; tajada f

steal [stiːl] v/t, v/i hurtar; robar; **~thy** ['stelθi] furtivo

steam [stiːm] s vapor m; vaho m; v/i emitir vapor; navegar a vapor; **~ up** empañarse (vidrio); **~boat, ~ship** (buque m de) vapor m; **~roller** apisonadora f

steel [stiːl] s acero m; a de acero; v/t tecn acerar; **~ oneself** acorazarse; **~works** fábrica f siderúrgica

steep [stiːp] a empinado; s precipicio m; v/t remojar, empapar

steeple ['stiːpl] campanario m; **~chase** carrera f de obstáculos

steer [stiə] s novillo m; v/t dirigir; gobernar; v/i navegar; **~age** dirección f; **~ing wheel** volante m

stem [stem] s bot tallo m; caña f; mar roda f; **from ~ to stern** de proa a popa; v/t contener; v/i ~ **from** provenir de

stench [stentʃ] hedor m

stenograph|er [stə'nɔgrəfə] taquígrafo(a) m (f); **~y** taquigrafía f

step [step] s paso m; escalón m; grado m; **to take ~s** tomar medidas; v/i dar un paso; andar; **~ down** retirarse; **~ in** entrar; **~brother** hermanastro m; **~child** hijastro(a) m (f); **~father** padrastro m; **~mother** madrastra f; **~s** escaleras f/pl; **~sister** hermanastra f

stereo ['stiəriəu] estéreo m; **~type** estereotipo m

---

steril|e ['sterail] estéril; **~ity** [~'riliti] esterilidad f; **~ize** ['~ilaiz] v/t esterilizar

sterling ['stəːliŋ] s libra f esterlina; a genuino; de ley

stern [stəːn] a austero, severo; s popa f

stew [stjuː] s estofado m; v/t, v/i estofar

steward [stjuəd] mayordomo m; camarero m (del buque); **~ess** azafata f, aeromoza f

stick [stik] s palo m; barra f; v/t clavar, picar; pegar; fijar; v/i quedar atascado; adherirse; perseverar; **~ by** ser fiel; **~ it out** perseverar; **~ out** sobresalir; **~ up for** defender a; **~er** pegatina f; etiqueta f; **~iness** viscosidad f; **~ing plaster** esparadrapo m; **~y** pegajoso, viscoso

stiff [stif] tieso, rígido; espeso; fuerte (bebida); difícil; **~en** v/t atiesar; endurecer; v/i endurecerse

stifle ['staifl] v/t sofocar

stigma ['stigma] estigma m

still [stil] a inmóvil; quieto; silencioso; adv aún, todavía; conj no obstante; s quietud f; silencio m; v/t calmar; **~born** nacido muerto; **~ life** naturaleza f muerta; **~ness** sosiego m; calma f

stilt [stilt] zanco m; **~ed** pomposo

stimul|ant ['stimjulənt] a, s estimulante m; **~ate** ['~eit] v/t estimular; **~us** ['~əs] estímulo m

sting [stiŋ] s aguijón m; picadura f; v/t picar

stingy ['stindʒi] tacaño

stink [stiŋk] s hedor m; v/i apestar, heder; **~ing** hediondo

stipulat|e ['stipjuleit] v/t estipular; **~ion** estipulación f

stir [stəː] s conmoción f; v/t remover; revolver; **~ up** agitar; fomentar

stirrup ['stirəp] estribo m

stitch [stitʃ] s puntada f; med punto m; v/t coser; med suturar

stock [stɔk] s linaje m; raza f; ganado m; com existencias f/pl, capital m; acciones f/pl; **in ~** en existencia; out of ~ agotado; **to take ~ of** hacer inventario de; v/t proveer; almacenar; **~breeder** ganadero m; **~broker** corredor m de bolsa; **~ exchange** bolsa f (de valores o de comercio); **~holder** accionista m

stocking ['stɔkiŋ] media f

stockpile ['stɔkpail] reserva f; v/t formar una reserva de

stocky ['stɔki] rechoncho

stomach ['stʌmək] s estómago m; fig apetito m; v/t fig tragar; **~ ache** dolor m de estómago

ston|e [stəun] s piedra f; med cálculo m; hueso m (de fruta); v/t apedrear; deshuesar; **~eware** gres m; **~y** pedregoso; pétreo

stool [stuːl] taburete m

stoop [stuːp] s inclinación f de hombros; v/i encorvarse; inclinarse

stop [stɔp] s alto m, parada f; pausa f; fin m; paradero m; tecn retén m; v/t detener; parar; tapar; **~ up** atascar; obturar; v/i pararse; cesar; **~ doing** dejar de hacer; **~gap** ['~gæp] recurso m provisional; **~over** escala f; **~page** interrupción f; suspensión f; tecn obturación f; **~per** tapón m; **~watch** cronómetro m

---

stor|age ['stɔːridʒ] almacenaje m; **~e** [stɔː] s provisión f; tienda f; almacén m; v/t almacenar; surtir; **~ehouse** depósito m, almacén m

stor(e)y ['stɔːri] piso m; planta f

stork [stɔːk] cigüeña f

storm [stɔːm] s tormenta f; tempestad f; v/t asaltar; tomar por asalto; v/i rabiar; **~y** borrascoso, tempestuoso

story ['stɔːri] cuento m; arq piso m, planta f

stout [staut] a fuerte; sólido; s cerveza f negra

stove [stəuv] estufa f; hornillo m

stow [stəu] v/t guardar, almacenar; mar arrumar; **~away** polizón m

straddle ['strædl] v/i ponerse a horcajadas; v/t no tomar partido (en un asunto)

straggling ['strægliŋ] disperso

straight [streit] a derecho; recto; erguido (espalda); lacio (pelo); adv directamente; correctamente; **~ ahead** todo seguido; **~ away** sin vacilar, en seguida; **~en** v/t enderezar; arreglar; **~forward** franco; recto

strain [strein] s tensión f; esfuerzo m; med torcedura f; raza f; v/t forzar; estirar; filtrar; v/i esforzarse; **~er** colador m

strait [streit] a estrecho; **~s** geog estrecho m

strand [strænd] v/t varar; fig abandonar; s hebra f

strange [streindʒ] extraño; raro; ajeno; **~r** forastero(a) m (f); desconocido(a) m (f)

strangl|e ['stræŋgl] v/t estrangular; **~ulation** [~ju-'leiʃən] estrangulación f

strap [stræp] s tira f; correa f; **~ping** robusto

strat|egic [strə'tiːdʒik] estratégico; **~egy** ['strætidʒi] estrategia f

straw [strɔː] paja f; **~berry** fresa f

stray [strei] a extraviado; perdido; v/i perderse; extraviarse

streak [striːk] s raya f; vena f; **winning ~** racha f de victorias; **~ of lightning** relámpago m; v/t rayar; **~y** rayado; entreverado (tocino)

stream [striːm] s arroyo m, corriente f; chorro m; flujo m; v/t, v/i correr; manar; **~lined** aerodinámico

street [striːt] calle f; **~car** Am tranvía m

strength [streŋθ] fuerza f; resistencia f; **~en** v/t fortalecer; robustecer

strenuous ['strenjuəs] vigoroso; arduo; enérgico

stress [stres] s esfuerzo m; tensión f; acento m; med estrés m; v/t acentuar; someter a esfuerzo

stretch [stretʃ] s estiramiento m; alcance m; trecho m; v/t extender; estirar; v/i extenderse; tenderse; **~er** camilla f

stricken ['strikən] herido; afectado; afligido (por)

strict [strikt] estricto

stride [straid] s tranco m; zancada f; v/i andar a trancos

strife [straif] contienda f; lucha f

strik|e [straik] s golpe m; huelga f; hallazgo m; mil ataque m; **on ~e** en huelga; v/t pegar; golpear; dar contra;

encender (*cerilla*); dar (*la hora*); hallar; arriar (*bandera, etc*); parecer a; **~e up** *mús* empezar a tocar; trabar (*una amistad*); *v/i* golpear; sonar (*campana*); declararse en huelga (*obreros*); **~er** huelguista *m, f*; **~ing** llamativo; sorprendente

string [striŋ] *s* cuerda *f*; hilera *f*; sarta *f*; *v/t* ensartar; encordar; **~ bean** judía *f* verde; **~y** fibroso; correoso

strip [strip] *s* tira *f*; faja *f*; *v/t, v/i* despojar(se); desnudar(se)

stripe [straip] raya *f*; lista *f*; *mil* galón *m*; **~d** rayado

strive [straiv] *v/i* esforzarse; disputar

stroke [strəuk] golpe *m*; *med* ataque *m* (*de apoplejía*); *sp* brazada *f*, remada *f*; **~ of luck** golpe *m* de fortuna

stroll [strəul] *s* paseo *m*; *v/i* pasearse; **~er** paseante *m*; *Am* cochecito *m* (*de niño*)

strong [strɔŋ] fuerte; robusto; intenso; **~ box** caja *f* fuerte; **~hold** fortaleza *f*; **~-willed** resuelto, obstinado

structure ['strʌktʃə] estructura *f*

struggle ['strʌgl] *s* lucha *f*; *v/i* luchar

strum [strʌm] *v/t, v/i* rasguear

strut [strʌt] *s arq* riostra *f*; *v/i* pavonearse

stub [stʌb] tocón *m*; colilla *f* (*de cigarro*); talón *m* (*de billete*)

stubble ['stʌbl] rastrojo *m*

stubborn ['stʌbən] terco, testarudo

stud [stʌd] *s* tachón *m*; botón *m* de cuello; caballeriza *f*; *v/t* tachonar

stud|ent ['stju:dənt] estudiante *m, f*; **~io** ['~diəu] estudio *m*, taller *m*; **~ious** ['~djəs] estudioso; **~y** ['stʌdi] *s* estudio *m*; *v/i, v/t* estudiar

stuff [stʌf] *s* materia *f*; material *m*; paño *m*; *fig* cosa *f*; *v/t* henchir; atestar; llenar; **~ing** relleno *m*; **~y** mal ventilado

stumble ['stʌmbl] *v/i* tropezar

stump [stʌmp] tocón *m*; muñón *m*

stun [stʌn] *v/t* aturdir; dejar pasmado; **~ning** asombroso; *fam* magnífico

stunt [stʌnt] truco *m*; *aer* acrobacia *f*; **publicity ~** ardid *m* publicitario

stupefy ['stju:pifai] *v/t* dejar estupefacto

stupendous [stju:'pendəs] estupendo

stupid ['stju:pid] estúpido; tonto; **~ity** [~'piditi] estupidez *f*

stupor ['stju:pə] estupor *m*

sturdy ['stə:di] fuerte, robusto

stutter ['stʌtə] *v/i* tartamudear; *s* tartamudeo *m*

sty [stai] pocilga *f*

styl|e [stail] estilo *m*; **~ish** elegante, de moda

suave [swa:v] afable; cortés

subdue [səb'dju:] *v/t* sojuzgar; **~d** amortiguado; tenue (*luz*)

subject ['sʌbdʒikt] *a* sujeto; **~ to** sujeto a; propenso a; *s* asunto *m*; tema *m*; súbdito *m*; [səb'dʒekt] *v/t* someter; exponer; **~ion** sujeción *f*; **~ive** subjetivo

subjunctive [səb'dʒʌŋktiv] subjuntivo *m*

sublime [sə'blaim] sublime, exaltado

submachine gun ['sʌbmə'ʃi:ngʌn] metralleta *f*

submarine ['sʌbmə'ri:n] *a, s* submarino *m*

submerge [səb'mə:dʒ] *v/t, v/i* sumergir(se)

submi|ssion [səb'miʃən] sumisión *f*; **~ssive** sumiso; **~t** [~'mit] *v/t* someter; *v/i* someterse; conformarse

subordinate [sə'bɔ:dnit] *a, s* subordinado(a) *m* (*f*); [~neit] *v/t* **~ to** subordinar a

subscri|be [səb'skraib] *v/t, v/i* suscribir, abonarse; **~be for** suscribirse a (*libro, acciones*); **~be to** abonarse a (*periódico, etc*); **~ber** *a, s* abonado(a) *m* (*f*); **~ption** [~'skripʃən] suscripción *f*; abono *m*

subsequent ['sʌbsikwənt] subsiguiente; **~ly** posteriormente, seguido

subside [səb'said] *v/i* sumirse; amainarse

subsid|iary [səb'sidjəri] *a* subsidiario; *s* sucursal *f*; **~ize** ['sʌbsidaiz] *v/t* subvencionar; **~y** ['~sidi] subvención *f*

subsist [səb'sist] *v/t* subsistir, existir

substan|ce ['sʌbstəns] sustancia *f*; esencia *f*; **~tial** [səb'stænʃəl] sustancial; sustancioso

substantive ['sʌbstəntiv] sustantivo *m*

substitute ['sʌbstitju:t] *s* sustituto *m*; *v/t* sustituir

subtitle ['sʌbtaitl] subtítulo *m*

subtle ['sʌtl] sutil; **~ty** sutileza *f*; astucia *f*

subtract [səb'trækt] *v/t, v/i* restar; sustraer

suburb ['sʌbə:b] suburbio *m*; **~an** [sə'bə:bən] suburbano

subway ['sʌbwei] pasaje *m* subterráneo; *Am* metro *m*

succ|eed [sək'si:d] *v/i* tener éxito; **~eed in** lograr; **~eed to** suceder; **~eeding** sucesivo; **~ess** [~'ses] éxito *m*; **~essful** exitoso; próspero; **~essive** sucesivo; **~essor** sucesor(a) *m* (*f*)

succinct [sək'siŋkt] sucinto

succulent ['sʌkjulənt] suculento

succumb [sə'kʌm] *v/i* sucumbir

such [sʌtʃ] *a* tal; semejante; **~ as** tal como; *pron* los que, las que; *adv* tan

suck [sʌk] *v/t, v/i* chupar; **~le** *v/t* amamantar

sudden ['sʌdn] repentino; súbito; **~ly** de repente; repentinamente

suds [sʌdz] jabonaduras *f/pl*

sue [sju:] *v/t, v/i* demandar

suède [sweid] ante *m*

suet ['sjuit] sebo *m*

suffer ['sʌfə] *v/t, v/i* sufrir; padecer; soportar; **~er** víctima *f*; **~ing** sufrimiento *m*

suffic|e [sə'fais] *v/t, v/i* bastar; **~cient** bastante, suficiente

suffix ['sʌfiks] sufijo *m*

suffocate ['sʌfəkeit] *v/t, v/i* sofocar(se); asfixiar(se)

sugar ['ʃugə] *s* azúcar *m*; *v/t* azucarar; **~ beet** remolacha *f*; **~ cane** caña *f* de azúcar; **~y** azucarado

suggest [sə'dʒest] *v/t* sugerir; aconsejar; **~ion** sugerencia *f*; **~ive** sugestivo

suicide ['sjuisaid] suicidio *m*; suicida *m, f*

suit [sju:t] *s* traje *m*; (*naipes*) palo *m*; *for* pleito *m*; *v/t* adaptar; ajustar; convenir; **~ oneself** hacer como guste; *v/i* **~ with** convenir; ir bien con; **~able** conveniente; apropiado; **~case** maleta *f*

suite [swi:t] séquito *m*; serie *f* (*de muebles*; *habitaciones*); *mús* suite *f*

suitor ['sju:tə] galán *m*; pretendiente *m*

sulk [sʌlk] *v/i* tener mohino; **~y** malhumorado

sullen ['sʌlən] hosco; malhumorado

sulphur ['sʌlfə] azufre *m*

sultry ['sʌltri] bochornoso; sensual

sum [sʌm] *s* suma *f*; **to do ~s** hacer cálculos; *v/t, v/i* **~ up** resumir; compendiar

summar|ize ['sʌməraiz] *v/t* resumir; **~y** resumen *m*, sumario *m*

summer ['sʌmə] verano *m*; **to spend the ~** veranear; **~ resort** lugar *m* de veraneo

summit ['sʌmit] cima *f*; cumbre *f*; **~ meeting** reunión *f* en la cumbre

summon ['sʌmən] *v/t* citar; convocar; **~s** llamamiento *m*; *for* citación *f*

sun [sʌn] sol *m*; **~bathe** *v/i* tomar el sol; **~beam** rayo *m* de sol; **~burn** quemadura *f* del sol

Sunday ['sʌndi] domingo *m*

sundial ['sʌndaiəl] reloj *m* de sol

sundries ['sʌndriz] *com* géneros *m/pl* diversos

sun|flower ['sʌnflauə] girasol *m*; **~glasses** gafas *f/pl*, *Am* lentes *m/pl* de sol

sunken ['sʌŋkən] hundido

sun|ny ['sʌni] soleado; **~rise** salida *f* del sol; **~set** puesta *f* del sol; **~shade** parasol *m*; **~shine** sol *m*; **~stroke** insolación *f*; **~tan** bronceado

superb [sju(:)'pə:b] soberbio; magnífico

super|cilious [sju:pə'siliəs] desdeñoso, arrogante; **~ficial** superficial; **~fluous** superfluo; **~human** sobrehumano

superintend [sju:pərin'tend] *v/t* vigilar; **~ent** inspector *m*; capataz *m*

superior [sju(:)'piəriə] superior; altivo; **~ity** [~'ɔriti] superioridad *f*

superlative [sju(:)'pə:lətiv] *a, s* superlativo *m*

super|man ['sju:pə'mən] superhombre *m*; **~market** supermercado *m*; **~natural** sobrenatural; **~sede** *v/t* suplantar; **~sonic** supersónico; **~stition** [~'stiʃən] superstición *f*; **~stitious** supersticioso; **~vise** ['~vaiz] *v/t* supervisar; controlar; **~visor** supervisor *m*; inspector *m*

supper ['sʌpə] cena *f*

supple ['sʌpl] flexible

supplement ['sʌplimənt] *s* suplemento *m*; ['~ment] *v/t* suplir, complementar

suppl|ier [sə'plaiə] proveedor(a) *m* (*f*), suministrador(a) *m* (*f*); **~y** [~ai] *s* abasto *m*; provisiones *f/pl*; **~y and demand** oferta y demanda; *v/t* suministrar; abastecer

support [sə'pɔ:t] *s* apoyo *m*; *v/t* mantener; sostener; apoyar; **~er** partidario(a) *m* (*f*); *sp* hincha *m, f*

suppos|e [sə'pəuz] *v/t* suponer; presumir; **~ed to do** deber hacer; **~edly** [~idli] según cabe suponer; **~ition** [sʌpə'ziʃən] suposición *f*

suppress [sə'pres] *v/t* suprimir; **~ion** represión *f*

suprem|acy [sju'preməsi] supremacía *f*; **~e** [~'pri:m] supremo

surcharge ['sə:tʃɑ:dʒ] sobreprecio *m*; sobrecarga *f* (*en sellos*); resello *m* (*en billetes*)

sure [ʃuə] seguro; firme; **~ enough** efectivamente; **to make ~ of** verificar; **~ly** seguramente; **~ness** seguridad *f*; **~ty** garantía *f*

surf [sə:f] oleaje *m*; olas *f/pl*

surface ['sə:fis] *s* superficie *f*; *v/i* emerger

surge [sə:dʒ] *s* oleada *f*; *v/i* agitarse

surg|eon ['sə:dʒən] cirujano *m*; **~ery** gabinete *m* de cirujano; cirugía *f*; **~ical** quirúrgico

surly ['sə:li] áspero, hosco

surmise ['sə:maiz] *s* conjetura *f*; [~'maiz] *v/t* conjeturar

surmount [sə:'maunt] *v/t* superar

surname ['sə:neim] apellido *m*

surpass [sə:'pɑ:s] *v/t* aventajar; exceder

surplus ['sə:pləs] *a, s* sobrante *m*; *com* superávit *m*

surprise [sə'praiz] *s* sorpresa *f*; *v/t* sorprender

surrender [sə'rendə] *s* abandono *m*; entrega *f*; rendición *f*; *v/t, v/i* entregar(se); rendir(se)

surround [sə'raund] *v/t* circundar; cercar; **~ings** alrededores *m/pl*

surveillance [sə:'veiləns] vigilancia *f*

survey [sə:'vei] *s* examen *m*; escrutinio *m*; *v/t* inspeccionar; **~or** topógrafo *m*; agrimensor *m*

surviv|al [sə'vaivəl] supervivencia *f*; **~e** *v/t, v/i* sobrevivir; **~or** sobreviviente *m, f*

susceptible [sə'septəbl] susceptible; sensible

suspect [səs'pekt] *a* sospechoso; *v/t, v/i* sospechar

suspen|d [səs'pend] *v/t* suspender; **~ders** ligas *f/pl* (*de medias*), *Am* tirantes *m/pl*; **~sion** suspensión *f*; aplazamiento *m*; **~sion bridge** puente *m* colgante

suspicio|n [səs'piʃən] sospecha *f*; **~us** sospechoso

sustain [səs'tein] *v/t* sostener; sustentar; sufrir

sustenance ['sʌstinəns] sustento *m*, alimento *m*

swab [swɔb] estropajo *m*; *med* torunda *f*

swaddle ['swɔdl] empañar (*criatura*)

swagger ['swægə] *v/i* pavonearse

swallow ['swɔləu] *s* trago *m*; *zool* golondrina *f*; *v/t* tragar

swamp [swɔmp] pantano *m*; marisma *f*; **~y** pantanoso

swan [swɔn] cisne *m*

swarm [swɔ:m] *s* enjambre *m*; *v/t, v/i* enjambrar; pulular

swarthy ['swɔ:ði] moreno

swat [swɔt] *v/t* aplastar (*mosca etc*)

sway [swei] *s* balanceo *m*; dominio *m*; *v/i* tambalear; oscilar; *v/t* mover; influir en

swear [swεə] *v/t, v/i* jurar; blasfemar; **~ word** palabrota *f*, *fam* taco *m*

sweat [swet] *s* sudor *m*; *v/i* sudar; **~er** suéter *m*, *LA* chompa *f*; **~y** sudoroso; sudado

Swed|e [swi:d] sueco(a) *m* (*f*); **~en** Suecia *f*; **~ish** sueco

sweep [swi:p] *s* barredura *f*; extensión *f*; **chimney ~** deshollinador *m*; *v/t, v/i* barrer; pasar (por); pasar la vista (sobre); **~er** barredor *m*; **~ing** extenso; comprensivo

sweet [swi:t] *a* dulce; *s* dulce *m*; bombón *m*; **~en** *v/t* endulzar; **~heart** enamorado(a) *m* (*f*); **~ly** dulcemente; **~ness** dulzura *f*; suavidad *f*; **~ pea** guisante *m* de olor; **~ potato** batata *f*, camote *m*

swell [swel] *a* estupendo; *s* marejada *f*; *v/i* hincharse; **~ing** hinchazón *f*

sweltering ['sweltəriŋ] sofocante (*calor*)

swerve [swə:v] *v/t, v/i* desviar(se)

swift [swift] rápido; veloz; **~ness** rapidez *f*

swim [swim] *v/i* nadar; dar vueltas (*la cabeza*); *s* **to take a ~** ir a nadar; **~mer** nadador(a) *m* (*f*); **~ming** natación *f*; **~ming pool** piscina *f*; **~suit** traje *m* de baño

swindle ['swindl] *s* estafa *f*; *v/t* estafar; **~r** estafador *m*

swine [swain] cerdo *m*; puerco *m*; *fig* canalla *m*

swing [swiŋ] *s* balanceo *m*; columpio *m*; **in full ~** en plena marcha; *v/t* balancear; *v/i* oscilar; mecerse; **~ door** puerta *f* giratoria

swipe [swaip] *v/t* golpear fuerte; *fam* hurtar

swirl [swə:l] *s* remolino *m*; *v/t, v/i* arremolinar(se)

Swiss [swis] *a, s* suizo(a) *m* (*f*)

switch [switʃ] *s* agujas *f/pl* (*de ferrocarril*); *elec* interruptor *m*; *v/t, v/i* desviar(se); cambiar(se); **~ on** encender (*la luz*); **~ off** desconectar; apagar (*la luz*); **~board** cuadro *m* de distribución

Switzerland ['switsələnd] Suiza *f*

swollen ['swəulən] hinchado

swoon [swu:n] *s* desmayo *m*; *v/i* desmayarse

swoop [swu:p] *v/i*: **~ down on** precipitarse sobre

sword [sɔ:d] espada *f*

syllable ['siləbl] sílaba *f*

syllabus ['siləbəs] programa *m* de estudios

symbol ['simbəl] símbolo *m*; **~ic, ~ical** [~'bɔlik(əl)] simbólico

symmetry ['simitri] simetría *f*

sympath|etic [simpə'θetik] compasivo; **~ize** [~'θaiz] compadecerse; **~y** ['simpəθi] compasión *f*

symphony ['simfəni] sinfonía *f*

symptom ['simptəm] síntoma *m*

synagogue ['sinəgɔg] sinagoga *f*

synchronize ['siŋkrənaiz] *v/t* sincronizar

syndicate ['sindikit] sindicato *m*

syndrome ['sindrəum] síndrome *m*

synonym ['sinənim] sinónimo *m*; **~ous** [si'nɔniməs] sinónimo

syntax ['sintæks] sintaxis *f*

synthe|sis ['sinθisis] síntesis *f*; **~tic** [~'θetik] sintético

syringe ['sirindʒ] jeringa *f*

syrup ['sirəp] almíbar *m*

system ['sistim] sistema *m*; método *m*; **~atic** [~'mætik] sistemático

T

tab [tæb] lengüeta *f*; oreja *f* de zapato

table ['teibl] mesa *f*; tabla *f*; **set the ~** poner la mesa; **~cloth** mantel *m*; **~land** meseta *f*; **~spoon** cuchara *f* grande

tablet ['tæblit] tableta *f*; pastilla *f*; comprimido *m*

taboo [tə'bu:] *a, s* tabú *m*

tacit ['tæsit] tácito; **~urn** ['~ə:n] taciturno

tack [tæk] *s* tachuela *f*; *v/t* clavar con tachuelas; hilvanar; **~le** ['tækl] *s* avíos *m/pl*; *mar* aparejo *m*; *v/t* abordar (*problema, etc*); enfrentar

English

tact 42

tact [tækt] tacto *m*; discreción *f*; **~ful** discreto

tactics ['tæktiks] táctica *f*

tactless ['tæktlis] indiscreto; falto de tacto

tadpole ['tædpəul] renacuajo *m*

taffeta ['tæfitə] tafetán *m*

tag [tæg] *s* herrete *m*; rabito *m*; etiqueta *f*

tail [teil] cola *f*, rabo *m*; **~ coat** frac *m*; **~light** luz *f* trasera; **~s** cruz *f* (*de moneda*); *fam* frac *m*

tailor ['teilə] sastre *m*

taint [teint] *s* corrupción *f*; *v/t* corromper

take [teik] *v/t* tomar; coger; asir; llevar; recibir; **~ advantage of** aprovecharse de; **~ along** llevar consigo; **~ away** quitar; **~ back** devolver; retractar; **~ in** admitir; abarcar; comprender; *fam* engañar; **~ off** quitarse; **~ out** sacar; **~ over** encargarse de; **~ pains** esmerarse; **~ place** ocurrir; **~ to heart** tomar a pecho; **~ up** recoger; empezar algo; *v/i* tener efecto; arraigar; **~ after** salir a; **~ off** marcharse; *aer* despegar; **~ to** aficionarse a; *s* presa *f*; *cine* toma *f*; **~off** *aer* despegue *m*; **~over** toma *f* de posesión

tale [teil] cuento *m*; fábula *f*

talent ['tælənt] talento *m*; capacidad *f*; **~ed** talentoso

talk [tɔ:k] *s* conversación *f*; charla *f*; conferencia *f*, discurso *m*; *v/t* hablar; **~ into** persuadir a; **~ out of** disuadir de; *v/i* hablar; charlar; **~ to** hablar a; **~ative** ['~ətiv] hablador; **~er** conversador(a) *m* (*f*)

tall [tɔ:l] alto; grande

tallow ['tæləu] sebo *m*

talon ['tælən] garra *f*

tambourine [tæmbə'ri:n] pandereta *f*

tame [teim] *a* manso; domesticado; *v/t* domar; domesticar

tamper ['tæmpə]: **~ with** *v/i* manipular indebidamente

tan [tæn] *s* bronceado *m*; *v/t* curtir; tostar

tangent ['tændʒənt] tangente *f*

tangerine [tændʒə'ri:n] mandarina *f*

tangible ['tændʒəbl] tangible

tangle ['tæŋgl] *s* enredo *m*; embrollo *m*; *v/t* enredar; embrollar

tank [tæŋk] tanque *m*; depósito *m*; **~er** *mar* petrolero *m*

tanner ['tænə] curtidor *m*

tantalizing ['tæntəlaiziŋ] tentador

tantrum ['tæntrəm] rabieta *f*

tap [tæp] *s* palmadita *f*; golpecito *m*; llave *f* (*de agua*); espita *f* (*del barril*); *v/t* tocar; espitar (*barril*); utilizar

tape [teip] cinta *f*; **~ measure** cinta *f* métrica

taper ['teipə] *s* cirio *m*; *v/i* ahusarse

tape recorder ['teipri'kɔ:də] magnetofón *m*

tapestry ['tæpistri] tapiz *m*; tapicería *f*; tenia *f*

tapeworm ['teipwə:m] solitaria *f*

tar [tɑ:] *s* alquitrán *m*; brea *f* líquida; *v/t* alquitranar

target ['tɑ:git] blanco *m*; objetivo *m*

tariff ['tærif] tarifa *f*; arancel *m*

tarnish ['tɑ:niʃ] *v/t*, *v/i* empañar(se); deslustrar(se)

tarpaulin [tɑ:'pɔ:lin] alquitranado *m*

tart [tɑ:t] *a* ácido; seco; *s* torta *f*

tartan ['tɑ:tən] tartán *m*

task [tɑ:sk] tarea *f*; **take to ~** reprender

tassel ['tæsəl] borla *f*

tast|e [teist] *s* gusto *m*; sabor *m*; *v/t* gustar; saborear; *v/i* **~e of** *o* **like** saber a; **~eful** de buen gusto; **~eless** insípido; **~y** sabroso

tatters ['tætəz]: **in ~** hecho jirones

tattoo [tə'tu:] tatuaje *m*

taunt [tɔ:nt] mofa *f*

taut [tɔ:t] tenso; tirante

tavern ['tævən] taberna *f*; tasca *f*

tawdry ['tɔ:dri] cursi, de mal gusto

tax [tæks] *s* impuesto *m*; *v/t* gravar; tasar; **~ation** impuestos *m/pl*; **~ collector** recaudador *m* de impuestos

taxi ['tæksi] *s* taxi *m*; *v/i aer* carretear; **~ driver** taxista *m*

tax|payer ['tækspeiə] contribuyente *m, f*; **~ return** declaración *f* de renta

tea [ti:] té *m*

teach [ti:tʃ] *v/t*, *v/i* enseñar; **~er** maestro(a) *m* (*f*); profesor(a) *m* (*f*); **~ing** enseñanza *f*

tea|cup ['ti:kʌp] taza *f* de té; **~ kettle** tetera *f*

team [ti:m] *s* equipo *m*; tiro *m* (*de caballos*); yunta *f* (*de bueyes*); *v/i* **~ up** asociarse con; **~work** trabajo *m* de equipo

teapot ['ti:pɔt] tetera *f*

tear [tεə] *s* rasgón *m*; *v/t* rasgar; romper; **~ off** arrancar; **~ up** romper; desarraigar; *v/i* rasgarse

tear [tiə] lágrima *f*; **~ful** lacrimoso; lloroso

tease [ti:z] *v/t fam* tomar el pelo a; fastidiar

teaspoon ['ti:spu:n] cucharita *f* de té

teat [ti:t] teta *f*

techn|ical ['teknikəl] técnico; **~ician** [~'niʃən] técnico *m*; **~ique** [~'ni:k] técnica *f*; **~ocrat** tecnócrata *m*; **~ology** tecnología *f*

teddy bear ['tedibεə] osito *m* de felpa

tedious ['ti:djəs] aburrido

teen|ager ['ti:neidʒə] adolescente *m, f*; **~s** años desde 13 a 19

teethe [ti:θ] *v/i* endentecer

teetotaler [ti:'təutlə] abstemio(a) *m* (*f*)

telegra|m ['teligræm] telegrama *m*; **~ph** ['~grɑ:f] telégrafo *m*

telepathy [ti'lepəθi] telepatía *f*

telephone ['telifəun] *s* teléfono *m*; *v/t*, *v/i* telefonear; **~ booth** cabina *f* telefónica; **~ call** llamada *f* (telefónica); **~ directory** guía *f* telefónica; **~ exchange** central *f* telefónica

tele|printer ['teliprintə] teleimpresor *m*; **~scope** [~'skəup] telescopio *m*

televis|e ['telivaiz] *v/t* televisar; **~ion** ['~viʒən] televisión *f*; **to watch ~ion** ver (por) televisión; **~ion set** televisor *m*

telex ['teleks] télex *m*

tell [tel] *v/t*, *v/i* contar; informar; **~er** cajero(a) *m* (*f*) (*en bancos*); **~tale** revelador

temper ['tempə] *s* humor *m*; mal genio *m*; temple *m* (*metal*); **to lose one's ~** perder la paciencia; *v/t* templar (*metal*); moderar; **~ament** temperamento *m*; **~ance** templanza *f*; **~ate** ['~rit] templado; **~ature** ['~pritʃə] temperatura *f*; fiebre *f*

tempest ['tempist] tempestad *f*; tormenta *f*

temple ['templ] templo *m*; *anat* sien *f*

tempora|l ['tempərəl] temporal; **~ry** temporáneo; provisional

tempt [tempt] *v/t* tentar; seducir; **~ation** tentación *f*; **~ing** tentador

ten [ten] diez

tenacious [ti'neiʃəs] tenaz

tenant ['tenənt] arrendatario *m*; inquilino *m*

tend [tend] *v/t* cuidar; atender; *v/i* tender a; **~ency** tendencia *f*

tender ['tendə] *a* tierno; delicado; *med* dolorido; *s* oferta *f*; *v/t* ofrecer; presentar; **~loin** ['~lɔin] filete *m* de solomillo; **~ness** ternura *f*

tendon ['tendən] tendón *m*

tenement house ['tenimənthaus] casa *f* de vecindad, *Am esp* de los barrios pobres

tennis ['tenis] tenis *m*; **~ court** pista *f*, *LA* cancha *f* de tenis

tenor ['tenə] *mús* tenor *m*

tense [tens] *a* tieso; tenso; *s gram* tiempo *m*; **~ness** tirantez *f*

tension ['tenʃən] tensión *f*

tent [tent] tienda *f* de campaña, *LA* carpa *f*

tentacle ['tentəkl] tentáculo *m*

tenuous ['tenjuəs] tenue

tepid ['tepid] tibio

term [tə:m] *s* término *m*; plazo *m*; período *m* académico; *v/t* nombrar; llamar; **~s** condiciones *f/pl*; **to be on good ~s with** estar en buenas relaciones con; **to come to ~s** llegar a un acuerdo

termina|l ['tə:minl] *s* estación *f* terminal; *a* terminal; mortal (*enfermedad*); **~te** ['~eit] *v/t* terminar; **~tion** terminación *f*

terrace ['terəs] terraza *f*; terraplén *m*

terrain ['terein] terreno *m*

terrible ['terəbl] terrible

terrif|ic [tə'rifik] fantástico, estupendo; **~y** ['terifai] *v/t* aterrar

territor|ial [teri'tɔ:riəl] territorial; **~y** ['~təri] territorio *m*

terror ['terə] terror *m*; espanto *m*; **~ism** terrorismo *m*; **~ist** terrorista *m, f*; **~ize** *v/t* aterrorizar

terse [tə:s] breve, conciso

test [test] *s* prueba *f*, ensayo *m*, experimento *m*; *v/t* ensayar; probar; examinar

testament ['testəmənt] testamento *m*

testify ['testifai] *v/t*, *v/i* atestiguar

testimony ['testiməni] testimonio *m*; atestación *f*

test tube ['testtju:b] probeta *f*; **~ baby** niño probeta *m*

testy ['testi] irritable

tetanus ['tetənəs] tétano *m*

text [tekst] texto *m*; **~book** libro *m* de texto

textile ['tekstail] textil; **~s** tejidos *m/pl*

texture ['tekstʃə] textura *f*

Thames [temz] Támesis *m*

than [ðæn, ðən] *conj* que (*después del comparativo*); **more ~ you** más que tú; de (*después de números*); **there are more ~ ten** hay más de diez

thank [θæŋk] *v/t* agradecer; dar las gracias; **~ you!** ¡gracias!; **~ful** agradecido; **~less** ingrato; **~s** gracias *f/pl*

that [ðæt, ðət] *a* ese, esa; aquel, aquella; *pron dem* ése, ésa, eso; aquél, aquélla, aquello; *pron rel* que; quien; el cual, la cual, lo cual; **~ which** el que, la que, lo que

thatch [θætʃ] barda *f*; **~ed roof** techumbre *f* de paja

thaw [θɔ:] *s* deshielo *m*; *v/t*, *v/i* deshelar(se)

the [ðe, ð, ði:] *art* el, la, lo; los, las; *adv* (*con comparativo*) cuanto ... tanto, mientras más ... tanto más; **~ sooner ~ better** cuanto antes mejor

theater = **theatre**

theatr|e ['θiətə] teatro *m*; arte *m* dramático; **~ical** [θi'ætrikəl] teatral

theft [θeft] hurto *m*, robo *m*

their [ðεə] *pron pos* su, sus; suyo(a, os, as); **~s** el suyo, la suya, los suyos, las suyas

them [ðem, ðəm] *pron* los, las, les; *con prep* ellos, ellas

theme [θi:m] tema *m*

themselves [ðəm'selvz] *pron pl* ellos mismos; ellas mismas; *con prep* sí mismos, sí mismas

then [ðen] *adv* entonces; luego; después; en otro tiempo; **from ~ on** desde entonces; *conj* en tal caso; pues; por consiguiente

theolog|ian [θiə'ləudʒjən] teólogo *m*; **~y** [θi'ɔlədʒi] teología *f*

theor|etical [θiə'retikəl] teórico; **~y** ['~ri] teoría *f*

therapy ['θerəpi] terapia *f*

there [ðεə] *adv* ahí, allí, allá; **~ is, ~ are** hay; **~ was, ~ were** había; hubo; *interj* ¡mira!; **~about(s)** por ahí; aproximadamente; **~after** después de eso; **~by** por eso; **~fore** por lo tanto; **~upon** en seguida; **~with** con eso

thermal ['θə:məl] termal

thermo|meter [θə'mɔmitə] termómetro *m*; **~s (flask)** termos *m*

these [ði:z] *a* estos, estas; *pron* éstos, éstas

thesis ['θi:sis] tesis *f*

they [ðei] *pron* ellos, ellas

thick [θik] espeso; grueso; tupido; denso; **~en** *v/t*, *v/i* espesar(se); **~et** ['~it] matorral *m*; **~ness** espesor *m*; densidad *f*; espesura *f*

thief [θi:f] ladrón(ona) *m* (*f*)

thigh [θai] muslo *m*

thimble ['θimbl] dedal *m*

thin [θin] *a* delgado; fino; ralo; escaso; raro (*aire*); *v/t*, *v/i* adelgazar; aclarar; reducirse

thing [θiŋ] cosa *f*; asunto *m*; objeto *m*; **the only ~** lo único; **tell him a ~ or two** decirle cuántos son cinco

think [θiŋk] *v/t*, *v/i* pensar; reflexionar; creer; **~ of** pensar en; acordarse de; idear; **~ over** pensar bien; **~ up** inventar; **~er** pensador(a) *m* (*f*); **~ing** pensamiento *m*

third party insurance ['θə:d-'pɑ:ti] seguro *m* de responsabilidad civil; **~-rate** de calidad baja; **2 World** el Tercer Mundo

thirst [θə:st] sed *f*; **~y** sediento

this [ðis] *a* este, esta; *pron* éste, ésta, esto

thistle ['θisl] cardo *m*

thorn [θɔ:n] espina *f*

thorough ['θʌrə] completo; cabal; perfecto; minucioso; **~bred** ['~bred] caballo *m* de pura sangre; **~fare** camino *m* público; **~ly** a fondo; **~ness** minuciosidad *f*

those [ðəuz] *a* esos, esas; aquellos, aquellas; *pron* ésos, ésas; aquéllos, aquéllas

though [ðəu] *conj* aunque; *adv* sin embargo

thought [θɔ:t] pensamiento *m*; idea *f*; **~ful** pensativo; atento; **~less** descuidado; desatento

thousand ['θauzənd] mil

thrash [θræʃ] *v/t* trillar; apalear; **~ing** paliza *f*

thread [θred] *s* hilo *m*; *tecn* rosca *f*; *v/t* enhebrar; **~bare** raído

threat [θret] amenaza *f*; **~en** *v/t*, *v/i* amenazar; **~ening** amenazador

three [θri:] tres

thresh [θreʃ] *v/t* trillar; **~er** (máquina) trilladora *f*

threshold ['θreʃhəuld] umbral *m*

thrift [θrift] economía *f*, frugalidad *f*; **~y** económico, ahorrativo

thrill [θril] *s* emoción *f*; *v/t* emocionar; **~er** novela *f* o película *f* escalofriante; **~ing** emocionante, excitante

thriv|e [θraiv] *v/i* prosperar; **~ing** floreciente, próspero

throat [θrəut] garganta *f*

throb [θrɔb] *v/i* latir

throne [θrəun] trono *m*

throng [θrɔŋ] *s* muchedumbre *f*; *v/t* atestar; *v/i* apiñarse

throttle ['θrɔtl] *s aut* obturador *m*; **to give full ~** acelerar al máximo; *v/t* ahogar; estrangular

through [θru:] *a* de paso libre; directo (*tren*); *adv* a través; de un extremo a otro; **~ and ~** por los cuatro costados; *prep* por; a través de; **~out** [~'aut] *prep* por todo; *adv* por todas partes

throw [θrəu] *v/t*, *v/i* echar; tirar; lanzar; **~ away** arrojar, *LA* botar; **~ out** echar fuera; expeler; *LA* botar; **~ up** vomitar; *s* tiro *m*, tirada *f*; lanzamiento *m*

thrush [θrʌʃ] tordo *m*

thrust [θrʌst] *s* empuje *m*; empujón *m*; estocada *f*; arremetida *f*; *tecn* empuje *m* axial; *v/t* empujar; meter

thud [θʌd] *s* golpe *m* sordo

thumb [θʌm] pulgar *m*; **~tack** chincheta *f*

thump [θʌmp] *s* porrazo *m*; baque *m*; *v/t*, *v/i* aporrear

thunder ['θʌndə] *s* trueno *m*; *v/i* tronar; **~bolt** rayo *m*; **~storm** tronada *f*; **~struck** atónito, pasmado

Thursday ['θə:zdi] jueves *m*

thus [ðʌs] así, de este modo; por consiguiente

thwart [θwɔ:t] *v/t* frustrar

thyme [taim] tomillo *m*

tick [tik] *s* garrapata *f*; funda *f*; contramarca *f*; *v/i* hacer tictac; *v/t* contramarcar

ticket ['tikit] billete *m*, *LA* boleto *m*; entrada *f*; **~ office** taquilla *f*, *LA* boletería *f*

tickl|e ['tikl] *v/t* hacer cosquillas a; **~ish** cosquilloso (*t fig*)

tid|al ['taidl] **wave** ola *f* de marejada; **~e** [taid] *s* marea *f*; *fig* corriente *f*; **high ~e** pleamar *f*; **low ~e** bajamar *f*

tidy ['taidi] *a* arreglado; limpio; *v/t*, *v/i* poner en orden

tie [tai] *s* corbata *f*; lazo *m*; *sp* empate *m*; *v/t* atar

tier [tiə] grada *f*; *teat* fila *f*

tiger ['taigə] tigre *m*

tight [tait] apretado; ajustado, ceñido; estrecho; **~en** *v/t*, *v/i* apretar(se); estrechar(se); **~rope** cuerda *f* floja

tigress ['taigris] tigresa *f*

tile [tail] *s* teja *f* (*de tejado*); baldosa *f* (*de piso*); azulejo *m* (*de color*)

till [til] *v/t* labrar; cultivar; *s* caja *f* (*de tienda*); *prep* hasta; *conj* hasta que

tilt [tilt] *s* inclinación *f*; *v/t*, *v/i* inclinar(se)

timber ['timbə] madera *f* de construcción; viga *f*, madero *m*

time [taim] *s* tiempo *m*; hora *f*; vez *f*; época *f*; ocasión *f*; compás *m*; ***for the ~ being*** por lo pronto; ***from ~ to ~*** a veces; ***in ~*** a tiempo; ***on ~*** puntual; ***to have a good ~*** divertirse; ***what ~ is it?*** ¿qué hora es?; ***at ~s*** a veces; *v/t* fijar para el momento oportuno; regular; **~ limit** fecha *f* tope; **~ly** oportuno; **~table** horario *m*

tim|id ['timid] tímido; **~orous** ['~ərəs] miedoso

tin [tin] *s* estaño *m*; lata *f*; *v/t* estañar; **~foil** papel *m* de estaño

tinge [tindʒ] *v/t* teñir; *fig* matizar; *s* tinte *m*; matiz *m*

tingle ['tiŋgl] *v/i* sentir picazón

tinkle ['tiŋkl] *v/i* tintinear

tin|ned [tind] en lata; **~ opener** abrelatas *m*; **~plate** hojalata *f*; **~sel** ['tinsl] oropel *m*

tint [tint] *v/t* teñir; *s* matiz *m*, tinte *m*

tiny ['taini] diminuto

tip [tip] *s* punta *f*; boquilla *f*; propina *f*; aviso *m* confidencial; *v/t* dar un golpecito a; dar una propina a; **~ *off*** advertir; **~ *out*** verter; **~ *over*** volcar

tipsy ['tipsi] achispado

tiptoe ['tiptəu] *v/i* andar de puntillas

tire ['taiə] neumático *m*, *LA* llanta *f*

tir|e ['taiə] *v/t* cansar; **~ed** cansado; **~edness** cansancio *m*; **~esome** pesado; aburrido; latoso

tissue ['tiʃu:] gasa *f*; **~ paper** papel *m* de seda

tit [tit] *zool* herrerillo *m*

titbit ['titbit] golosina *f*, bocadito *m*

titillate ['titileit] *v/t* estimular

title ['taitl] título *m*; *for* título *m*, derecho *m*; **~ page** portada *f*

to [tu:, tu, tə] *prep* para; a; hasta; hacia; menos (*de la hora*); ***it is five minutes ~ ten*** son las diez menos cinco; ***~ and fro*** de un lado para otro; ***to have ~*** tener que

toad [təud] sapo *m*

toast [təust] *s* tostada *f*; brindis *m*; *v/t* tostar; brindar por; **~er** tostador *m*

tobacco [tə'bækəu] tabaco *m*; **~nist's (shop)** estanco *m*

toboggan [tə'bɔgən] tobogán *m*

today [tə'dei] hoy

toddle ['tɔdl] *v/i* hacer pinitos; andar tambaleando

toe [təu] *s* dedo *m* del pie; punta *f* (*de media, etc*)

toff|ee, ~y ['tɔfi] caramelo *m*

together [tə'geðə] *a* juntos; *adv* juntamente; junto; a la vez

toil [tɔil] *s* trabajo *m* duro; *v/i* afanarse; esforzarse

toilet ['tɔilit] *m* tocado *m*; excusado *m*; **~ paper** papel *m* higiénico; **~ries** artículos *m/pl* de aseo

token ['təukən] señal *f*; prenda *f*

tolera|ble ['tɔlərəbl] tolerable; **~nce** tolerancia *f*; **~nt** tolerante; **~te** ['~eit] tolerar; aguantar

toll [təul] *s* peaje *m*; *v/i* doblar (*campanas*)

tomato [tə'mɑ:təu] tomate *m*

tomb [tu:m] tumba *f*; **~oy** ['tɔmbɔi] marimacho *m*; **~stone** lápida *f* sepulcral

tomorrow [tə'mɔrəu] *s*, *adv* mañana *f*; **~ *night*** mañana por la noche; ***the day after ~*** pasado mañana

ton [tʌn] tonelada *f*

tone [təun] *s* tono *m*; *v/t mús* entonar; **~ *down*** suavizar

tongs [tɔŋz] tenacillas *f/pl*

tongue [tʌŋ] lengua *f*; ***to hold one's ~*** callarse; **~ twister** trabalenguas *m*

tonic ['tɔnik] tónico *m*; *mús* tónica *f*

tonight [tə'nait] esta noche

tonnage ['tʌnidʒ] tonelaje *m*

tonsil ['tɔnsl] amígdala *f*; **~litis** [~si'laitis] amigdalitis *f*

too [tu:] *adv* demasiado; también; **~ *many*** demasiados(as); **~ *much*** demasiado

tool [tu:l] herramienta *f*

toot [tu:t] bocinazo *m*; silbido *m*

tooth [tu:θ] diente *m*; **~ache** dolor *m* de muelas; **~brush** cepillo *m* de dientes; **~paste** pasta *f* dentífrica; **~pick** palillo *m*

top [tɔp] *s* cima *f*, cumbre *f*; cabeza *f* (*de una lista etc*); tapa *f*; *aut* capota *f*; superficie *f*; ***at the ~ of*** a la cabeza de; ***from ~ to bottom*** de arriba abajo; ***on ~ of*** encima de; *a* más alto; máximo; *v/t* coronar; superar; llenar al tope; **~coat** sobretodo *m*; **~ hat** *fam* sombrero *m* de copa

topic ['tɔpik] asunto *m*; tema *m*

topsy-turvy ['tɔpsi'tə:vi] trastornado; patas arriba

torch [tɔ:tʃ] linterna *f*; antorcha *f*

torment ['tɔ:ment] *s* tormento *m*; suplicio *m*; [tɔ:'ment] *v/t* atormentar

tornado [tɔ:'neidəu] tornado *m*

torpedo [tɔ:'pi:dəu] torpedo *m*

torp|id ['tɔ:pid] tórpido; inerte; **~or** entumecimiento *m*

torrent ['tɔrənt] torrente *m*

torrid ['tɔrid] tórrido, ardiente

tortoise ['tɔ:təs] tortuga *f*

torture ['tɔ:tʃə] *s* tortura *f*; *v/t* torturar; atormentar; *fig* tergiversar

toss [tɔs] *s* echada *f*; sacudida *f*; *v/t* tirar; lanzar; agitar

total ['təutl] *a* total; completo; entero; *s* total *m*; *v/t* sumar; **~itarian** [~tæli'tɛəriən] totalitario; **~ity** [~'tæliti] totalidad *f*

totter ['tɔtə] *v/i* tambalear(se)

touch [tʌtʃ] *s* tacto *m*; toque *m*; contacto *m*; rasgo *m*; ***in ~ with*** en contacto *o* comunicación con; ***out of ~*** sin noticias; *v/t* tocar; alcanzar; conmover, afectar; concernir; **~ *off*** hacer estallar; *v/i* tocar(se); **~ *down*** *aer* aterrizar; **~ *and go*** dudoso; **~ing** conmovedor; patético; **~y** susceptible; quisquilloso

tough [tʌf] fuerte, resistente; duro; rudo; vulgar; **~en** *v/t*, *v/i* endurecer(se); **~ness** tenacidad *f*; dureza *f*

tour [tuə] *s* excursión *f*; *v/t* viajar por; **~ist** turista *m*; **~ist office** oficina *f* de turismo

tournament ['tuənəmənt] torneo *m*

tousled [tauzld] despeinado

tow [təu] *s* remolque *m*; *v/t* remolcar

toward(s) [tə'wɔ:d(z)] hacia; para

towel ['tauəl] toalla *f*

tower ['tauə] *s* torre *f*; *v/i* elevarse; **~ *above*** descollar entre

town [taun] ciudad *f*; villa *f*; población *f*; **~ council** concejo *m* municipal; **~ hall** ayuntamiento *m*, *LA* municipalidad *f*

towrope ['təurəup] cable *m* de remolque

toxic ['tɔksik] tóxico

toy [tɔi] *s* juguete *m*; *v/i* jugar; juguetear

trace [treis] *s* rastro *m*; huella *f*; señal *f*; *v/t* trazar; delinear; seguir la pista de

track [træk] *s* huella *f*, camino *m*; senda *f*; vía *f* férrea; trocha *f*; ruta *f*; vereda *f*; *sp* pista *f*; ***off the beaten ~*** lugar apartado; ***on the right ~*** ir por buen camino; *v/t* rastrear; seguir la pista de

tract|ion ['trækʃən] tracción *f*; arrastre *m*; **~or** tractor *m*

trade [treid] *s* comercio *m*; negocio *m*; oficio *m*; *v/i* comerciar; traficar; *v/t* trocar; vender; **~ agreement** tratado *m* comercial; **~mark** marca *f* de fábrica; **~ union** sindicato *m*

tradition [trə'diʃən] tradición *f*; **~al** tradicional

traffic ['træfik] *s* tráfico *m*, tránsito *m*, circulación *f*; *v/i* comerciar; traficar; **~ jam** embotellamiento *m* del tráfico; **~ light** semáforo *m*

trag|edy ['trædʒidi] tragedia *f*; **~ic** ['~ʒik] trágico

trail [treil] *s* rastro *m*; pista *f*; sendero *m*; *v/t* arrastrar; *v/i* rezagarse; **~er** remolque *m*; *cine* avance *m*

train [trein] tren *m*; séquito *m*; serie *f*; cola *f*; *v/t*, *v/i* disciplinar; entrenar; formar; **~er** entrenador *m*; domador *m*; **~ing** entrenamiento *m*; formación *f*

trait [trei] rasgo *m*

traitor ['treitə] traidor *m*

tram ['træm], **~car** tranvía *m*

tramp [træmp] *s* marcha *f* pesada; caminata *f*; vagabundo *m*; *v/t*, *v/i* vagabundear; marchar; pisar con fuerza; patullar; **~le** *v/t* pisar; hollar

tranquil ['træŋkwil] tranquilo; **~lity** [~'kwiliti] tranquilidad *f*; **~lize** *v/t*, *v/i* tranquilizar(se)

transact [træn'zækt] *v/t* tramitar, despachar; **~ion** transacción *f*; negocio *m*

transatlantic ['trænzət'læntik] transatlántico

transcend [træn'send] *v/i* transcender; *v/t* exceder; **~ent** sobresaliente

transcri|be [træns'kraib] *v/t* transcribir; **~pt** ['trænskript] trasunto *m*, copia *f*; **~ption** transcripción *f*

transfer ['trænsfə:] *s* transferencia *f*; traspaso *m*; [træns'fə:] *v/t* transferir; transbordar; *v/i* trasladarse; **~able** [~'fə:rəbl] transferible

transform [træns'fɔ:m] *v/t* transformar; **~ation** transformación *f*; **~er** *tecn* transformador *m*

transfusion [træns'fju:ʒən] transfusión *f* (*de sangre*)

transgress [træns'gres] *v/t* traspasar, violar; **~ion** transgresión *f*

transient ['trænziənt] pasajero; transitorio

transistor [træn'sistə] transistor *m*

transit ['trænsit] tránsito *m*; **~ion** [~'siʒən] transición *f*; paso *m*; **~ive** *gram* transitivo; **~ory** transitorio

translat|e [træns'leit] *v/t* traducir; **~ion** traducción *f*; **~or** traductor(a) *m* (*f*)

transmi|ssion [træns'miʃən] transmisión *f*; **~t** *v/t* transmitir; **~tter** transmisor(a) *m* (*f*)

transparent [træns'pɛərənt] transparente

transpire [træns'paiə] *v/t* transpirar; *v/i* revelarse

transplant [træns'plɑ:nt] *v/t* trasplantar; **~ation** trasplante *m*

transport [træns'pɔ:t] *s* transporte *m*; *v/t* transportar

trap [træp] trampa *f*; *tecn* sifón *m*; *v/t* atrapar; aprisionar; **~door** trampa *f*; *teat* escotillón *m*

trapeze [trə'pi:z] trapecio *m*

trap|per ['træpə] cazador *m* de pieles; **~pings** arreos *m/pl*; adornos *m/pl*

trash [træʃ] *s* hojarasca *f*; cosas *f/pl* sin valor; basura *f*

travel ['trævl] *s* el viajar; *v/t*, *v/i* viajar (por); **~ agency** agencia *f* de viajes; **~(l)er** viajero(a) *m* (*f*); **~(l)er's cheque** cheque *m* para viajeros; **~(l)ing bag** maletín *m* (*de viaje*)

traverse ['trævə(:)s] *v/t* cruzar, atravesar

travesty ['trævisti] parodia *f*

trawl [trɔ:l] *v/i* pescar a la rastra; **~er** barco *m* rastreador

tray [trei] bandeja *f*

treacher|ous ['tretʃərəs] traicionero, traidor; **~y** traición *f*

treacle ['tri:kl] melaza *f*

tread [tred] *s* paso *m*; pisada *f*; *v/t*, *v/i* andar; pisar; **~le** *mec* pedal *m*

treason ['tri:zn] traición *f*

treasur|e ['treʒə] *s* tesoro *m*; *v/t* atesorar; **~er** tesorero *m*; **~y** tesoro *m*; **℃y** Ministerio *m* de Hacienda

treat [tri:t] *s* convite *m*; placer *m*; *v/t*, *v/i* tratar; convidar; **~ise** ['~iz] tratado *m*; **~ment** trato *m*; **~y** tratado *m*, pacto *m*

treble ['trebl] *a* triple; *s* tiple *m* (*voz*); *v/t*, *v/i* triplicar(se)

tree [tri:] árbol *m*

trek [trek] caminata *f*; viaje *m* largo y peligroso

tremble ['trembl] *v/i* temblar

tremendous [tri'mendəs] tremendo; formidable

trem|or ['tremə] temblor *m*; **~ulous** ['~juləs] trémulo

trench [trentʃ] trinchera *f*

trend [trend] tendencia *f*; **~y** de última moda

trespass ['trespəs] *s* intrusión *f*; transgresión *f*; *v/i* violar; infringir; **~er** transgresor(a) *m* (*f*)

tress [tres] trenza *f*

trestle ['tresl] caballete *m*

trial ['traiəl] prueba *f*; ensayo *m*; *for* proceso *m*; **on ~** *com* a prueba; *for* en juicio

triang|le ['traiæŋgl] triángulo *m*; **~ular** [~'æŋgjulə] triangular

tribe [traib] tribu *f*

tribun|al [trai'bju:nl] tribunal *m*; **~e** ['tribju:n] tribuno *m*; tribuna *f*

tribut|ary ['tribjutəri] *a*, *s* tributario *m*; *geog* afluente *m*; **~e** ['~ju:t] tributo *m*

trick [trik] *s* maña *f*; engaño *m*; truco *m*; *v/t* engañar; **~ery** trampería *f*

trickle ['trikl] *v/i*, *v/t* (hacer) gotear

tricycle ['traisikl] triciclo *m*

trident ['traidənt] tridente *m*

trifl|e ['traifl] *s* friolera *f*; bagatela *f*; postre *m* (*de bizcocho, fruta, helado y nata*); **a ~e** un poquito; *v/i* **~e *with*** jugar con; **~ing** baladí, insignificante

trigger ['trigə] gatillo *m*

trill [tril] *v/i* gorjear; trinar; *s* trino *m*

trim [trim] *a* pulcro; arreglado; *s* (buena) condición *f*; recorte *m* (*del pelo*); *v/t* arreglar; recortar; podar; afinar; **~mings** guarnición *f*; aderezos *m/pl*; accesorios *m/pl*

Trinity ['triniti] *relig* Trinidad *f*

trinket ['triŋkit] baratija *f*

trip [trip] *s* excursión *f*; viaje *m*; *v/t* echar la zancadilla a; *tecn* soltar; *v/i* tropezar; brincar

tripe [traip] *coc* callos *m/pl*

triple ['tripl] *a* triple; *v/t* triplicar; **~ts** ['~its] trillizos(as) *m* (*f*)*/pl*

tripod ['traipɔd] trípode *m*

trite [trait] trillado; vulgar

triumph ['traiəmf] *s* triunfo *m*; *v/i* triunfar; **~ant** [~'ʌmfənt] triunfante

trivial ['triviəl] trivial, común, insignificante

trolley ['trɔli] carretilla *f*

trombone [trɔm'bəun] trombón *m*

troop [tru:p] tropa *f*; banda *f*; **~er** soldado *m* de caballería

trophy ['trəufi] trofeo *m*

tropic ['trɔpik] trópico *m*; **~al** tropical; **~s** trópicos *m/pl*

trot [trɔt] *s* trote *m*; *v/i* trotar

trouble ['trʌbl] *s* molestia *f*; dificultad *f*; ***to take the ~*** tomarse la molestia; ***what's the ~?*** ¿qué pasa?; *v/t* molestar; preocupar; inquietar; **~d** inquieto; preocupado; **~some** molesto; dificultoso

trough [trɔf] abrevadero *m*

trousers ['trauzəz] pantalones *m/pl*

trousseau ['tru:səu] ajuar *m*

trout [traut] trucha *f*

truant ['tru(:)ənt] *a* holgazán; *s* tunante *m*; ***to play ~*** hacer novillos

truce [tru:s] tregua *f*

truck [trʌk] camión *m*; *f c* vagón *m*

truculent ['trʌkjulənt] agresivo; áspero

trudge [trʌdʒ] *v/i* caminar cansadamente

tru|e [tru:] *a* verdadero; legítimo; verídico; fiel; ***to come ~e*** realizarse; **~ism** tópico *m*

truly ['tru:li] verdaderamente; sinceramente; ***Yours ~*** su seguro servidor

trump [trʌmp] triunfo *m* (*en juegos de naipes*)

trumpet ['trʌmpit] trompeta *f*; **~er** trompetero *m*

truncheon ['trʌntʃən] vara *f*; porra *f*

trunk [trʌŋk] tronco *m*; baúl *m*; trompa *f* (*de elefante*); **~ call** llamada *f* interurbana

trust [trʌst] *s* confianza *f*; *com* trust *m*; *for* fideicomiso *m*; **~ee** [~'i:] fideicomisario *m*; **~ful, ~ing** confiado; **~worthy** confiable, fidedigno; **~y** leal, fidedigno

truth [tru:θ] verdad *f*; **~ful** verídico, veraz

try [trai] *s* tentativa *f*; prueba *f*; *v/t*, *v/i* probar; ensayar; tratar; **~ *on*** probarse (*ropa*); **~ *out*** someter a prueba; **~ing** difícil, penoso

T-shirt ['ti:ʃə:t] camiseta *f*

tub [tʌb] cuba *f*; tina *f*

tube [tju:b] tubo *m*; *fam* metro *m*

tuberculosis [tju(:)bə:kju'ləusis] tuberculosis *f*

tuck [tʌk] s pliegue m; v/t alforzar; recoger; ~ **up** arropar

Tuesday ['tjuːzdi] martes m

tuft [tʌft] mechón m (de pelo); manojo m

tug [tʌg] s tirón m; remolcador m; v/t remolcar; tirar de

tuition [tjuː(ː)'iʃən] cuota f de enseñanza

tulip ['tjuːlip] tulipán m

tumble ['tʌmbl] s caída f; vuelco m; v/i tumbar, caer; revolcarse; v/t tumbar; ~**r** vaso m

tummy ['tʌmi] fam barriguita f

tumo(u)r ['tjuːmə] tumor m

tumult ['tjuːmʌlt] tumulto m; ~**uous** [~'mʌltjuəs] tumultuoso

tuna ['tuːnə] atún m

tune [tjuːn] s tonada f; melodía f; in ~ mús afinado; out of ~ desafinado; v/t sintonizar; afinar; v/i armonizar; ~**up** afinamiento m (de un motor)

tunnel ['tʌnl] s túnel m

tunny ['tʌni] atún m

turbine ['təːbin] turbina f

turbulent ['təːbjulənt] turbulento

turf [təːf] s césped m

Turk [təːk] turco(a) m (f)

turkey ['təːki] pavo m; ♀ Turquía f

Turkish ['təːkiʃ] turco

turmoil ['təːmoil] desorden m, disturbio m

turn [təːn] s turno m; vuelta f; giro m; cambio m; favor m; in ~, by ~s por turnos; it is your ~ es su turno; v/t volver; dar vuelta a; girar; convertir; ~ **down** rechazar; ~ **off** apagar (luz, agua); ~ **on** poner (radio); ~ **out** echar; ~ **over** volcar; entregar; v/i dar la vuelta; girar; revolver; ponerse (agrio, triste, etc); ~ **aside** desviarse; ~ **away** volver la espalda; ~ **in** acostarse; ~ **out** resultar; ~ **up** llegar, aparecer; ~**coat** pol renegado m; ~**ing** vuelta f; ángulo m

turnip ['təːnip] nabo m

turn|off ['təːnof] salida f (del camino); ~**out** producción f (total); concurrencia f; ~**over** com volumen m de negocios; ~**stile** [~stail] torniquete m

turpentine ['təːpəntain] trementina f

turtle ['təːtl] tortuga f (de mar); ~**dove** tórtola f

tusk [tʌsk] colmillo m

tutor ['tjuːtə] preceptor m; for tutor m

TV ['tiː'viː] televisión f; **TV viewer** televidente m, f

tweed [twiːd] paño m de lana

tweet [twiːt] v/i gorjear

tweezers ['twiːzəz] pinzas f/pl

twice [twais] dos veces

twig [twig] ramita f

twilight ['twailait] crepúsculo m

twin [twin] a, s gemelo m

twine [twain] s guita f; v/t rodear; enrollar

twin-engined ['twin'endʒind] bimotor

twinkle ['twiŋkl] s centelleo m; parpadeo m; v/t, v/i (hacer) centellear; (hacer) parpadear

twirl [twəːl] s rotación f; remolino m; v/t, v/i (hacer) girar

twist [twist] torcedura f, torsión f; torcimiento m; v/t, v/i torcer(se)

twitch [twitʃ] sacudida f; tic m nervioso

twitter ['twitə] s gorjeo m; v/i gorjear (pájaros)

two [tuː] dos; to put ~ and ~ together atar cabos; ~**faced** falso; ~**fold** a doble; adv dos veces; ~**piece** de dos piezas; ~**way** aut en ambas direcciones

tycoon [tai'kuːn] magnate m industrial

typ|e [taip] s tipo m; v/t, v/i escribir a máquina; ~**ewriter** máquina f de escribir

typhoid (fever) ['taifoid] fiebre f tifoidea

typhoon [tai'fuːn] tifón m

typhus ['taifəs] tifus m

typical ['tipikəl] típico

typist ['taipist] mecanógrafo(a) m (f)

tyrann|ize ['tirənaiz] v/t tiranizar; ~**y** tiranía f

tyre ['taiə] neumático m, LA llanta f

U

udder ['ʌdə] teta f; ubre f

UFO ['juː'ef'əu] ovni m

ugly ['ʌgli] feo; repugnante

ulcer ['ʌlsə] úlcera f

ultimate ['ʌltimit] último; final; ~**ly** por último; al final

ultimatum [ʌlti'meitəm] ultimátum m

umbilical [ʌm'bilikl]: ~ **cord** cordón m umbilical

umbrella [ʌm'brelə] paraguas m

umpire ['ʌmpaiə] s árbitro m; v/t, v/i arbitrar

unabated ['ʌnə'beitid] no disminuido

unable [ʌn'eibl] incapaz

unabridged ['ʌnə'bridʒd] íntegro (libro)

unacceptable ['ʌnək'septəbl] inaceptable

unaccountable ['ʌnə'kauntəbl] inexplicable

unaccustomed ['ʌnə'kʌstəmd] insólito

unacquainted ['ʌnə'kweintid]: ~ **with** no versado en

unaffected [ʌnə'fektid] natural; sincero

unaided [ʌn'eidid] sin ayuda

unalterable [ʌn'ɔːltərəbl] inalterable

unanimous [juː(ː)'næniməs] unánime

unapproachable [ʌnə'prəutʃəbl] inabordable; inaccesible

unarmed [ʌn'ɑːmd] desarmado

unashamed ['ʌnə'ʃeimd] desvergonzado; insolente

unassuming ['ʌnə'sjuːmiŋ] modesto

unattainable ['ʌnə'teinəbl] inasequible

unauthorized [ʌn'ɔːθəraizd] desautorizado

unavoidable [ʌnə'vɔidəbl] inevitable

unaware ['ʌnə'wɛə]: be ~ of ignorar; ~**s** de improviso

unbalanced ['ʌn'bælənst] desequilibrado

unbearable [ʌn'bɛərəbl] insoportable; inaguantable

unbeatable ['ʌn'biːtəbl] imbatible

unbelievable [ʌnbi'liːvəbl] increíble

unbending ['ʌn'bendiŋ] inflexible

unbiased ['ʌn'baiəst] imparcial

unborn ['ʌn'bɔːn] nonato; no nacido aún

unbounded [ʌn'baundid] ilimitado

unbroken [ʌn'brəukən] intacto; indómito

unburden [ʌn'bəːdn] v/t descargar; aliviar

unbutton ['ʌn'bʌtn] v/t desabotonar

uncalled-for [ʌn'kɔːldfɔː] impropio; innecesario

uncanny [ʌn'kæni] misterioso; extraño

unceasing [ʌn'siːsiŋ] incesante

uncertain [ʌn'səːtn] incierto; dudoso

unchallenged ['ʌn'tʃælindʒd] incontestado

unchangeable [ʌn'tʃeindʒəbl] inmutable; invariable

unchecked ['ʌn'tʃekt] desenfrenado

uncivil ['ʌn'sivl] descortés; ~**ized** bárbaro; inculto

unclaimed ['ʌn'kleimd] no reclamado

uncle ['ʌŋkl] tío m

unclean ['ʌn'kliːn] sucio

uncomfortable [ʌn'kʌmfətəbl] incómodo; molesto

uncommon [ʌn'kɔmən] raro; extraño; poco común

uncompromising [ʌn'kɔmprəmaiziŋ] intransigente

unconcern ['ʌnkən'səːn] desinterés m; despreocupación f

unconditional ['ʌnkən'diʃənl] incondicional

unconfirmed ['ʌnkən'fəːmd] no confirmado

unconquerable [ʌn'kɔŋkərəbl] invencible

unconscious [ʌn'kɔnʃəs] inconsciente; med sin sentido; ~**ness** inconsciencia f; insensibilidad f

uncontrollable [ʌnkən'trəuləbl] ingobernable

unconventional ['ʌnkən'venʃənl] original; desenfadado

uncouth [ʌn'kuːθ] grosero; tosco

uncover [ʌn'kʌvə] v/t descubrir; destapar

uncultivated ['ʌn'kʌltiveitid] inculto; yermo

undamaged ['ʌn'dæmidʒd] indemne; ileso

undated ['ʌndeitid] sin fecha

undaunted [ʌn'dɔːntid] impávido

undecided ['ʌndi'saidid] indeciso

undeniable [ʌndi'naiəbl] innegable; incontestable

under ['ʌndə] prep debajo de; bajo; menos de; conforme a; adv debajo, bajo, abajo; ~**age** menor de edad

underclothing ['ʌndəkləuðiŋ] ropa f interior

undercurrent ['ʌndə'kʌrənt] fig tendencia f oculta

underdeveloped ['ʌndədi'veləpt] subdesarrollado

underdog ['ʌndə'dɔg] desvalido m

underdone ['ʌndə'dʌn] coc poco hecho

underestimate ['ʌndə'estimeit] v/t subestimar

undergo [ʌndə'gəu] v/t sufrir; sostener

undergraduate [ʌndə'grædjuit] estudiante m, f (universitario)

underground ['ʌndəgraund] a subterráneo; s metro m

undergrowth ['ʌndəgrəuθ] maleza f

underhanded ['ʌndə'hændid] clandestino

underline ['ʌndəlain] v/t subrayar

undermine [ʌndə'main] v/t socavar; minar

underneath [ʌndə'niːθ] adv abajo; prep bajo; debajo de

undernourished ['ʌndə'nʌriʃt] desnutrido

underpaid ['ʌndə'peid] mal pagado

underpants ['ʌndəpænts] calzoncillos m/pl

underpass ['ʌndəpɑːs] paso m inferior

underprivileged ['ʌndə'privilidʒd] desamparado

underrate [ʌndə'reit] v/t desestimar

undershirt ['ʌndəʃəːt] camiseta f

undersigned [ʌndə'saind] infrascrito m

understaffed ['ʌndə'stɑːft] corto de personal

understand [ʌndə'stænd] v/t, v/i entender; comprender; ~**able** comprensible; ~**ing** a comprensivo; s entendimiento m; inteligencia f; acuerdo m

understatement ['ʌndə'steitmənt] declaración f insuficiente

undertak|e [ʌndə'teik] v/t, v/i emprender; encargarse de; comprometerse a; ~**er** empresario m de pompas fúnebres; ~**ing** empresa f

undervalue ['ʌndə'vælju:] v/t despreciar; menospreciar

underwater ['ʌndə'wɔːtə] submarino

underway ['ʌndə'wei] en camino

underwear ['ʌndəwɛə] ropa f interior

underweight ['ʌndə'weit] de peso menor que el normal

underworld ['ʌndəwəːld] infiernos m/pl; hampa f

undesirable ['ʌndi'zaiərəbl] indeseable

undignified [ʌn'dignifaid] indecoroso

undisciplined [ʌn'disiplind] indisciplinado

undisputed ['ʌndis'pjuːtid] incontestable

undisturbed ['ʌndis'təːbd] imperturbado; inalterado

undo ['ʌn'duː] v/t deshacer; desatar; ~**ing** perdición f, ruina f

undone [ʌn'dʌn] sin hacer; desatado

undoubted [ʌn'dautid] indudable

undress ['ʌn'dres] v/t, v/i desnudarse

undue ['ʌn'djuː] indebido

undulate ['ʌndjuleit] v/t ondular; fluctuar

unearth ['ʌn'əːθ] v/t desenterrar

uneasy [ʌn'iːzi] inquieto

uneducated ['ʌn'edjukeitid] ignorante; no educado

unemploy|ed ['ʌnim'plɔid] desocupado; parado; ~**ment** desempleo m, paro m

unequal ['ʌn'iːkwəl] desigual; dispar; ~**led** incomparable; sin par

unerring ['ʌn'əːriŋ] infalible; seguro

uneven ['ʌn'iːvən] desigual

uneventful ['ʌni'ventful] sin novedad

unexpected ['ʌniks'pektid] inesperado

unfading [ʌn'feidiŋ] inmarcesible

unfailing [ʌn'feiliŋ] infalible; incansable

unfair ['ʌn'fɛə] injusto

unfaithful ['ʌn'feiθful] infiel; ~**ness** infidelidad f

unfamiliar ['ʌnfə'miljə] poco común; desconocido

unfashionable ['ʌn'fæʃnəbl] fuera de moda

unfasten ['ʌn'fɑːsn] v/t desatar

unfavo(u)rable ['ʌn'feivərəbl] desfavorable

unfeeling [ʌn'fiːliŋ] insensible, impasible

unfinished ['ʌn'finiʃt] inacabado; inconcluso; incompleto

unfit ['ʌn'fit] impropio; incapaz; inepto

unfold [ʌn'fəuld] v/t desdoblar; desplegar; desarrollar

unforeseen ['ʌnfɔː'siːn] imprevisto

unforgettable ['ʌnfə'getəbl] inolvidable

unforgiving ['ʌnfə'giviŋ] implacable

unfortunate [ʌn'fɔːtʃnit] desgraciado; desafortunado; ~**ly** desgraciadamente

unfounded ['ʌn'faundid] infundado

unfriendly ['ʌn'frendli] poco amistoso; hostil

unfurnished ['ʌn'fəːniʃt] sin amueblar

ungainly [ʌn'geinli] desgarbado

ungodly [ʌn'gɔdli] impío; fam atroz

ungovernable [ʌn'gʌvənəbl] ingobernable

ungrateful [ʌn'greitful] desagradecido; ingrato

ungrudging ['ʌn'grʌdʒiŋ] generoso; incondicional (apoyo etc)

unguarded ['ʌn'gɑːdid] desguarnecido; desprevenido

unhappy [ʌn'hæpi] infeliz, desdichado

unharmed ['ʌn'hɑːmd] ileso; sano y salvo

unhealthy [ʌn'helθi] enfermizo; insalubre

unheard-of [ʌn'həːdɔv] inaudito

unheed|ed ['ʌn'hiːdid] desatendido; ~**ing** desatento

unhesitating [ʌn'heziteitiŋ] resuelto; ~**ly** sin vacilar

unhook ['ʌn'huk] v/t desenganchar; desabrochar; descolgar

unhoped-for [ʌn'həuptfɔː] inesperado

unhurt ['ʌn'həːt] ileso; indemne

unidentified ['ʌnai'dentifaid] sin identificar

uniform ['juːnifɔːm] a uniforme; invariable; constante; s uniforme m

unify ['juːnifai] v/t unificar

unimaginable [ʌni'mædʒinəbl] inimaginable

unimportant ['ʌnim'pɔːtənt] sin importancia

uninhabit|able ['ʌnin'hæbitəbl] inhabitable; ~**ed** inhabitado; despoblado

uninjured ['ʌn'indʒəd] ileso; incólume

unintelligible ['ʌnin'telidʒəbl] ininteligible

unintentional ['ʌnin'tenʃənl] involuntario

uninteresting ['ʌn'intristiŋ] falto de interés

uninterrupted ['ʌnintə'rʌptid] ininterrumpido

uninvit|ed ['ʌnin'vaitid] no convidado; ~**ing** poco atractivo; desagradable

union ['juːnjən] unión f; sindicato m, gremio m (de obreros)

unique [juː'niːk] único

unison ['juːnizn] s unisonancia f; in ~ al unísono

unit ['juːnit] unidad f; ~**e** [~'nait] v/t unir; unificar; v/i unirse; juntarse; ♀**ed Nations** Naciones f/pl Unidas; ♀**ed States** Estados m/pl Unidos; ~**y** unidad f

univers|al [juːni'vəːsəl] universal; ~**e** [~'vəːs] universo m; ~**ity** [~'vəːsiti] universidad f

unjust ['ʌn'dʒʌst] injusto
unkempt ['ʌn'kempt] descuidado; desarreglado
unkind [ʌn'kaind] poco amable; duro
unknown ['ʌn'nəun] desconocido
unlawful ['ʌn'lɔːful] ilícito
unleash ['ʌn'liːʃ] *v/t* soltar; *fig* desencadenar
unless [ən'les] *conj* a menos que; a no ser que
unlike ['ʌn'laik] diferente; distinto; **~ly** improbable; inverosímil
unlimited [ʌn'limitid] ilimitado
unload ['ʌn'ləud] *v/t* descargar
unlock ['ʌn'lɔk] *v/t* abrir con llave
unlucky [ʌn'lʌki] desafortunado; ***to be ~*** tener mala suerte
unmanageable [ʌn'mænidʒəbl] inmanejable
unmarried ['ʌn'mærid] soltero, célibe
unmask ['ʌn'mɑːsk] *v/t* desenmascarar
unmatched ['ʌn'mætʃt] incomparable
unmerciful [ʌn'məːsiful] despiadado
unmindful [ʌn'maindful]: ***~ of*** sin pensar en
unmistakable ['ʌnmis'teikəbl] inconfundible
unmoved ['ʌn'muːvd] inalterado, impasible
unnatural [ʌn'nætʃrəl] antinatural; inhumano; desnaturalizado; perverso
unnecessary [ʌn'nesisəri] innecesario; superfluo
unnoticed ['ʌn'nəutist] inadvertido
unobserved ['ʌnəb'zəːvd] inadvertido
unobtainable ['ʌnəb'teinəbl] inasequible
unobtrusive ['ʌnəb'truːsiv] discreto, moderado
unoccupied ['ʌn'ɔkjupaid] desocupado; libre; vacante
unofficial ['ʌnə'fiʃəl] no oficial
unorganized ['ʌn'ɔːgənaizd] no organizado
unpack ['ʌn'pæk] *v/t* desempaquetar; desembalar; deshacer las maletas
unpaid ['ʌn'peid] pendiente de pago, *LA* impago
unparalleled [ʌn'pærəleld] sin par; inigualado
unpardonable [ʌn'pɑːdnəbl] imperdonable
unpaved ['ʌn'peivd] sin pavimentar
unpleasant [ʌn'pleznt] desagradable; **~ness** desavenencia *f*; disgusto *m*
unplug ['ʌn'plʌg] *v/t* desenchufar
unpopular ['ʌn'pɔpjulə] impopular
unprecedented [ʌn'presidəntid] sin precedente
unpredictable ['ʌnpri'diktəbl] imprevisible
unprejudiced [ʌn'predʒudist] imparcial
unpremeditated ['ʌnpri'mediteitid] impremeditado
unprepared ['ʌnpri'pɛəd] no preparado
unpretentious [ʌnpri'tenʃəs] sin pretensiones, sencillo
unproductive ['ʌnprə'dʌktiv] improductivo
unprofitable [ʌn'prɔfitəbl] nada lucrativo
unprovoked ['ʌnprə'vəukt] no provocado
unpublished ['ʌn'pʌbliʃt] inédito; no publicado
unqualified ['ʌn'kwɔlifaid] incapaz, incompetente; incondicional
unquestionable [ʌn'kwestʃənəbl] indiscutible
unravel [ʌn'rævl] *v/t* desenmarañar
unreal ['ʌn'riəl] irreal; ilusorio
unreasonable [ʌn'riːznəbl] irrazonable
unrelated ['ʌnri'leitid] inconexo; sin relación
unrelenting ['ʌnri'lentiŋ] inexorable, implacable
unreliable ['ʌnri'laiəbl] de poca confianza
unrepeatable ['ʌnri'piːtəbl] irrepetible
unrepentant ['ʌnri'pentənt] impenitente
unrequited ['ʌnri'kwaitid] no correspondido
unreserved [ʌnri'zəːvd] sin reservas, incondicional
unrest ['ʌn'rest] inquietud *f*; disturbio *m*
unrestrained ['ʌnri'streind] desenfrenado
unrestricted ['ʌnris'triktid] sin restricción
unripe ['ʌn'raip] verde; inmaduro
unrival(l)ed [ʌn'raivəld] sin rival; incomparable
unroll ['ʌn'rəul] *v/t* desenrollar
unruffled ['ʌn'rʌfld] tranquilo; sereno
unruly [ʌn'ruːli] revoltoso
unsafe ['ʌn'seif] inseguro; peligroso
unsaid ['ʌn'sed] sin decir
unsatisfactory ['ʌnsætis'fæktəri] insatisfactorio
unsavo(u)ry ['ʌn'seivəri] ofensivo; desagradable
unscrew ['ʌn'skruː] *v/t* desatornillar
unscrupulous [ʌn'skruːpjuləs] sin escrúpulo
unseemly [ʌn'siːmli] indecoroso
unseen ['ʌn'siːn] no visto
unselfish ['ʌn'selfiʃ] altruista; desinteresado
unsettled ['ʌn'setld] inestable; pendiente; variable; despoblado; *com* por pagar
unshaven ['ʌn'ʃeivn] sin afeitar
unshrink|able ['ʌn'ʃriŋkəbl] que no se encoge; **~ing** intrépido
unsightly [ʌn'saitli] feo
unskilled ['ʌn'skild] inexperto; **~ labo(u)r** mano *f* de obra no cualificada
unsociable [ʌn'səuʃəbl] insociable; reservado
unsold ['ʌn'səuld] sin vender
unsolved ['ʌn'sɔlvd] sin resolver
unsound ['ʌn'saund] defectuoso; erróneo
unspeakable [ʌn'spiːkəbl] indecible
unspoiled ['ʌn'spɔilt] no corrompido, intacto
unspoken ['ʌn'spəukn] tácito
unstable ['ʌn'steibl] inestable
unsteady ['ʌn'stedi] inestable; inconstante; irregular
unsuccessful ['ʌnsək'sesful] sin éxito; fracasado
unsuitable ['ʌn'sjuːtəbl] impropio
unsure ['ʌn'ʃuə] inseguro
unsuspect|ed ['ʌnsəs'pektid] insospechado; **~ing** confiado
unswerving ['ʌn'swəːviŋ] inquebrantable
untangle ['ʌn'tæŋgl] *v/t* desenmarañar
unthink|able [ʌn'θiŋkəbl] inconcebible; **~ing** irreflexivo
untidy [ʌn'taidi] desordenado; desarreglado
untie ['ʌn'tai] *v/t* desatar
until [ən'til] *prep* hasta; *conj* hasta que
untimely [ʌn'taimli] intempestivo; prematuro; ***at an ~ hour*** a deshora
untiring [ʌn'taiəriŋ] incansable
untold ['ʌn'təuld] nunca contado
untouched ['ʌn'tʌtʃt] intacto
untried ['ʌn'traid] no probado
untroubled ['ʌn'trʌbld] tranquilo
untru|e ['ʌn'truː] falso; **~th** [~'truːθ] falsedad *f*; **~thful** mentiroso; falso
unused ['ʌn'juːzd] no usado; nuevo
unusual [ʌn'juːʒuəl] insólito, extraordinario
unvarying [ʌn'vɛəriiŋ] invariable
unveil [ʌn'veil] *v/t* descubrir; quitar el velo a
unvoiced ['ʌn'vɔist] *gram* sordo
unwanted ['ʌn'wɔntid] no deseado
unwarranted [ʌn'wɔrəntid] injustificado
unwelcome [ʌn'welkəm] mal acogido; inoportuno
unwell [ʌn'wel] indispuesto, enfermizo; ***to feel ~*** sentirse mal
unwholesome ['ʌn'həulsəm] insalubre; dañino
unwieldy [ʌn'wiːldi] abultado; difícil de manejar
unwilling ['ʌn'wiliŋ] desinclinado; ***~ to*** poco dispuesto a; **~ly** de mala gana
unwind ['ʌn'waind] *v/t* desenvolver; desenredar
unwise ['ʌn'waiz] poco aconsejable, imprudente
unwittingly [ʌn'witiŋli] inconscientemente
unworthy [ʌn'wəːði] indigno
unwrap ['ʌn'ræp] *v/t* desenvolver; desempaquetar
unyielding [ʌn'jiːldiŋ] obstinado, inflexible; rígido
up [ʌp] *a* inclinado; ascendente; *adv* arriba; hacia arriba; en pie, levantado; ***~ and about*** restablecido; ***~ and down*** de arriba abajo; de un lado a otro; ***~ against*** tener que habérselas con; ***~ to now*** hasta ahora; ***what's ~?*** ¿qué pasa?; *s* ***on the ~ and ~*** cada vez mejor; ***the ~s and downs*** los altibajos *m/pl* (de la vida)
up-and-coming ['ʌpən'kʌmiŋ] *fam* joven y prometedor
upbraid [ʌp'breid] *v/t* reprochar
upbringing ['ʌpbriŋiŋ] crianza *f*; educación *f*
update [ʌp'deit] *v/t* poner al día
upgrade ['ʌpgreid] *v/t* mejorar
upheaval [ʌp'hiːvəl] trastorno *m*; *fig* cataclismo *m*
uphill ['ʌp'hil] *a* ascendente; *fig* laborioso; *adv* cuesta arriba
uphold [ʌp'həuld] *v/t* sostener
upholster [ʌp'həulstə] *v/t* tapizar; **~er** tapicero *m*; **~y** tapizado *m*
upkeep ['ʌpkiːp] mantenimiento *m*
upon [ə'pɔn] sobre; encima de
upper ['ʌpə] superior; más elevado; ***get the ~ hand*** obtener dominio sobre; **~most** más alto
upright ['ʌp'rait] vertical; derecho; recto
uprising [ʌp'raiziŋ] sublevación *f*; alzamiento *m*
uproar ['ʌprɔː] tumulto *m*
uproot [ʌp'ruːt] *v/t* desarraigar
upset [ʌp'set] *s* vuelco *m*; contratiempo *m*; *med* trastorno *m*; *v/t* volcar; desarreglar; trastornar; revolver (*el estómago*); *a* perturbado; enfadado
upshot ['ʌpʃɔt] resultado *m*
upside down ['ʌpsaid'daun] al revés
upstairs ['ʌp'stɛəz] arriba
upstart ['ʌpstɑːt] *a, s* advenedizo *m*
upstream ['ʌp'striːm] río arriba
up-to-date [ʌptə'deit] al día; moderno
upward(s) ['ʌpwəd(z)] ascendente; hacia arriba
uranium [ju'reinjəm] uranio *m*
urban ['əːbən] urbano
urbane [əː'bein] cortés; mundano
urchin ['əːtʃin] golfillo *m*
urge [əːdʒ] *s* impulso *m*; *v/t* instar; impulsar; incitar; **~nt** urgente
urine ['juərin] orina *f*
urn [əːn] urna *f*
Uruguay ['juərəgwai] el Uruguay; **~an** *a, s* uruguayo(a) *m (f)*
us [ʌs, əs] *pron* nos; (*después de preposiciones*) nosotros(as)
U.S.A. = ***United States (of America)*** EE.UU.
us|age ['juːzidʒ] uso *m*; tratamiento *m*; **~e** [juːs] *s* empleo *m*, aplicación *f*; utilidad *f*; ***it is no ~e*** es inútil; ***what is the ~e of?*** ¿para qué sirve?; [juːz] *v/t* usar; emplear; utilizar; ***~e up*** consumir; **~ed** [~sd] gastado; usado; de ocasión; [~st] acostumbrado; ***~ed to (do)*** solía (hacer); ***to get ~ed to*** acostumbrarse a; **~eful** útil; **~eless** inútil; inservible
usher ['ʌʃə], **~ette** [~'ret] acomodador(a) *m (f)*
usual ['juːʒuəl] acostumbrado; usual; ***as ~*** como de costumbre
usur|er ['juːʒərə] usurero *m*; **~y** ['~ʒuri] usura *f*
utensil [ju(ː)'tensl] utensilio *m*
uterus ['juːtərəs] útero *m*
utili|ty [ju(ː)'tiliti] utilidad *f*; ***public ~ties*** servicios *m/pl* públicos; **~ze** ['juːtilaiz] *v/t* utilizar
utmost ['ʌtməust] extremo; último; ***to the ~*** hasta más no poder
utter ['ʌtə] *a* completo, total; absoluto; *v/t* proferir; pronunciar; **~ance** pronunciación *f*; expresión *f*; **~ly** totalmente

V

vaca|ncy ['veikənsi] vacío *m*; vacante *f*; **~nt** vacante; vacío; desocupado; **~te** [və'keit] *v/t* dejar; desocupar; **~tion** vacaciones *f/pl*
vaccin|ate ['væksineit] *v/t* vacunar; **~ation** vacuna *f*
vacuum ['vækjuəm] vacío *m*; **~ cleaner** aspiradora *f*
vagabond ['vægəbɔnd] *a, s* vagabundo(a) *m (f)*
vagrant ['veigrənt] *a, s* vagabundo *m*; *fig* errante
vague [veig] vago; incierto
vain [vein] vano; vanidoso; ***in ~*** en vano
valet ['vælit] criado *m*
valiant ['væljənt] valiente
valid ['vælid] válido; **~ity** [və'liditi] validez *f*
valise [və'liːz] maleta *f*, valija *f*
valley ['væli] valle *m*
valo(u)r ['vælə] valor *m*
valu|able ['væljuəbl] valioso; **~ables** objetos *m/pl* de valor; **~ation** valuación *f*; tasa *f*; **~e** ['~juː] *s* valor *m*; ***~e added tax*** impuesto *m* sobre el valor añadido; *v/t* valorar; tasar; **~eless** sin valor
valve [vælv] válvula *f*
van [væn] camioneta *f*; furgoneta *f*
vane [vein] veleta *f*
vanilla [və'nilə] vainilla *f*
vanish ['væniʃ] *v/i* desvanecerse; desaparecer
vanity ['væniti] vanidad *f*; engreimiento *m*; **~ case** polvera *f*; neceser *m*
vapo(u)r ['veipə] vapor *m*; vaho *m*; **~ize** ['veipəraiz] *v/t* vaporizar
varia|ble ['vɛəriəbl] variable; **~nce** desacuerdo *m*; diferencia *f*; **~nt** variante *f*; **~tion** variación *f*; cambio *m*
varicose ['værikəus]: ***~ veins*** varices *f/pl*
var|iety [və'raiəti] variedad *f*; surtido *m*; **~iety show** variedades *f/pl*; **~ious** ['vɛəriəs] vario; diverso; varios
varnish ['vɑːniʃ] *s* barniz *m*; *v/t* barnizar
vary ['vɛəri] *v/t, v/i* variar
vase [vɑːz] florero *m*, vaso *m*; jarrón *m*
vaseline ['væsəliːn] vaselina *f*
vast [vɑːst] vasto; inmenso
vat [væt] tina *f*, cuba *f*
Vatican ['vætikən] Vaticano *m*
vault [vɔːlt] *s* bóveda *f*; cueva *f*; salto *m*; *v/t, v/i* saltar
veal [viːl] carne *f* de ternera
vegeta|ble ['vedʒitəbl] verdura *f*; legumbre *f*; hortaliza *f*; **~rian** [~'tɛəriən] vegetariano(a) *m (f)*; **~te** ['~eit] *v/i* vegetar; **~tion** vegetación *f*
vehemen|ce ['viːiməns] vehemencia *f*; **~t** vehemente
vehicle ['viːikl] vehículo *m*
veil [veil] *s* velo *m*; *v/t* velar
vein [vein] vena *f*
velocity [vi'lɔsiti] velocidad *f*
velvet ['velvit] terciopelo *m*
venal ['viːnl] venal
vend|er, ~or ['vendə] vendedor(a) *m (f)*; **~ing machine** distribuidor *m* automático
venera|ble ['venərəbl] venerable; **~te** ['~eit] *v/t* venerar
venereal [vi'niəriəl]: ***~ disease*** enfermedad *f* venérea
Venetian [vi'niːʃən]: ***~ blind*** persiana *f*
Venezuela [vene'zweilə] Venezuela *f*; **~n** *a, s* venezolano(a) *m (f)*
vengeance ['vendʒəns] venganza *f*; ***with a ~*** *fam* con creces
venison ['venzn] venado *m*
venom ['venəm] veneno *m* (*t fig*); **~ous** venenoso
vent [vent] *s* respiradero *m*; agujero *m*; abertura *f*; *v/t* desahogar; **~ilate** *v/t* ventilar; **~ilation** ventilación *f*
venture ['ventʃə] *s* empresa *f*; negocio *m* arriesgado; *v/i* atreverse; arriesgarse
verb [vəːb] verbo *m*; **~atim** palabra por palabra; **~ose** [~'bəus] verboso
verdict ['vəːdikt] veredicto *m*; fallo *m*; dictamen *m*
verge [vəːdʒ] *s* borde *m*; margen *m,f*; vara *f*; ***on the ~ of*** al borde de; *v/i* ***~ on*** rayar en
verify ['verifai] *v/t* verificar

vermin ['vəːmin] bichos *m/pl*; sabandijas *f/pl*
vermouth ['vəːmuːt] vermut *m*
vernacular [və'nækjulə] *s* lengua *f* vernácula; *a* vernáculo
versatile ['vəːsətail] adaptable; flexible; versátil
vers|e [vəːs] verso *m*; estrofa *f*; **~ed** versado; **~ion** ['~ʃən] versión *f*
versus ['veːsəs] contra
vertebra ['vəːtibrə] vértebra *f*
vertical ['vəːtikəl] vertical
very ['veri] *a* mismo; mero, solo; completo; *adv* mucho; muy
vessel ['vesl] vasija *f*; *mar* barco *m*
vest [vest] *s* camiseta *f*; *Am* chaleco *m*; **~ed interests** intereses *m/pl* creados
vestige ['vestidʒ] vestigio *m*
vestry ['vestri] sacristía *f*
vet [vet] *fam* veterinario *m*; veterano *m*
veteran ['vetərən] *a*, *s* veterano *m*
veterinary (surgeon) ['vetərinəri] veterinario *m*
veto ['viːtəu] *s* veto *m*; *v/t* vetar
vex [veks] *v/t* fastidiar; irritar; **~ation** irritación *f*
vibrat|e [vai'breit] *v/t*, *v/i* vibrar; **~ion** vibración *f*
vicar ['vikə] vicario *m*; párroco *m*; **~age** vicaría *f*
vice [vais] vicio *m*
vice [vais] (*prefijo*) vice; **~ president** vicepresidente *m*
vicinity [vi'siniti] vecindad *f*
vicious ['viʃəs] vicioso; depravado; cruel
victim ['viktim] víctima *f*; **~ize** *v/t* hacer víctima; tomar represalias contra
victor ['viktə] vencedor *m*; **~ious** [~'tɔːriəs] victorioso; **~y** ['~təri] victoria *f*
video ['vidiəu] vídeo *m*; **~ camera** videocámara *f*; **~ cassette** videocassette *f*; **~ disc** videodisco *m*; **~ recorder** magnetoscopio *m*
vie [vai]: **~ *with*** *v/i* competir con
view [vjuː] *s* vista *f*; perspectiva *f*; panorama *m*; opinión *f*; ***in ~*** a la vista; ***in ~ of*** en vista de; ***on ~*** expuesto; ***with a ~ to*** con miras a; *v/t* contemplar; considerar; **~er** espectador *m*; **~finder** *foto* visor *m*; **~point** punto *m* de vista
vigil ['vidʒil] vela *f*; vigilia *f*; **~ant** vigilante
vigo|rous ['vigərəs] vigoroso; **~(u)r** vigor *m*
vile [vail] vil; odioso
village ['vilidʒ] aldea *f*; pueblo *m*; **~r** aldeano(a) *m (f)*
villain ['vilən] malvado *m*; **~y** vileza *f*
vindicat|e ['vindikeit] *v/t* vindicar; justificar; **~ion** vindicación *f*; justificación *f*
vindictive [vin'diktiv] vengativo
vine [vain] parra *f*; vid *f*; **~gar** ['vinigə] vinagre *m*; **~yard** ['vinjəd] viñedo *m*
vintage ['vintidʒ] vendimia *f*; **~ wine** vino *m* añejo
viola [vi'əulə] *mús*, *bot* viola *f*
viol|ate ['vaiəleit] *v/t* violar; **~ation** violación *f*
violen|ce ['vaiələns] violencia *f*; **~t** violento
violet ['vaiəlit] *s* color *m* violado; violeta *f*; *a* violado
violin [vaiə'lin] violín *m*
VIP ['viːai'piː] = ***very important person*** persona *f* muy importante
viper ['vaipə] víbora *f*
virgin ['vəːdʒin] virgen *f*; **~ity** [~'dʒiniti] virginidad *f*
viril|e ['virail] viril; **~ity** [~'riliti] virilidad *f*
virtu|al ['vəːtʃuəl] virtual; **~e** ['~juː, '~ʃuː] virtud *f*; **~ous** ['~ʃuəs] virtuoso
virus ['vaiərəs] virus *m*
visa ['viːzə] visado *m*
vis-à-vis ['viːzə'viː] respecto a; frente a frente
visib|ility [vizi'biliti] visibilidad *f*; **~le** ['vizəbl] visible; manifiesto
vision ['viʒən] visión *f*
visit ['vizit] *s* visita *f*; *v/t* visitar; **~or** visitante *m*, *f*
visor ['vaizə] visera *f*
visual ['vizjuəl] visual; **~ize** *v/t*, *v/i* imaginar(se)
vital ['vaitl] vital; esencial; enérgico; **~ity** [~'tæliti] vitalidad *f*; **~ize** ['~laiz] *v/t* vitalizar; **~s** partes *f/pl* vitales
vitamin ['vitəmin] vitamina *f*
vivaci|ous [vi'veiʃəs] animado, vivaz; **~ty** [~'væsiti] vivacidad *f*
vivi|d ['vivid] vivo; intenso; gráfico; **~dness** claridad *f*; **~fy** ['~fai] *v/t* vivificar
voca|bulary [vəu'kæbjuləri] vocabulario *m*; **~l** ['vəukəl] vocal *f*; **~l cords** cuerdas *f/pl* vocales; **~lize** *v/t* vocalizar
vocation [vəu'keiʃən] vocación *f*
vogue [vəug] moda *f*; ***in ~*** en boga
voice [vɔis] *s* voz *f*; *v/t* expresar; hacerse eco de; **~d** [~t] *gram* sonoro
void [vɔid] *a* vacío; *for* nulo; *v/t* invalidar; desocupar
volatile ['vɔlətail] volátil
volcano [vɔl'keinəu] volcán *m*
volley ['vɔli] *s mil* descarga *f*; salva *f*; voleo *m* (*tenis*); *v/t*, *v/i sp* volear; **~ball** vóleibol *m*
volt [vəult] voltio *m*; **~age** voltaje *m*
voluble ['vɔljubl] locuaz
volum|e ['vɔljum] tomo *m*; volumen *m*; **~inous** [və'ljuːminəs] voluminoso
volunt|ary ['vɔləntəri] voluntario; **~eer** [~'tiə] *s* voluntario *m*; *v/i* ofrecerse como voluntario
voluptuous [və'lʌptʃuəs] voluptuoso
vomit ['vɔmit] *s* vómito *m*; *v/t*, *v/i* vomitar
voraci|ous [və'reiʃəs] voraz; **~ty** [~'ræsiti] voracidad *f*
vot|e [vəut] *s* voto *m*; sufragio *m*; *v/t*, *v/i* votar; **~er** votante *m*, *f*; **~ing** votación *f*
vouch [vautʃ] *v/t* atestiguar; **~ *for*** responder de; **~er** comprobante *m*; fiador *m*; **~safe** [~'seif] *v/t* conceder
vow [vau] *s* voto *m*; *v/t* hacer voto de; jurar
vowel ['vauəl] vocal *f*
voyage ['vɔiidʒ] *s* viaje *m* marítimo; travesía *f*
vulgar ['vʌlgə] vulgar; grosero; cursi; ordinario; **~ism** vulgarismo *m*; **~ity** [~'gæriti] vulgaridad *f*
vulnerable ['vʌlnərəbl] vulnerable
vulture ['vʌltʃə] buitre *m*

W

wad [wɔd] *s* fajo *m*; *mil* taco *m*; bolita *f* (*de algodón etc*)
waddle ['wɔdl] *v/t* anadear
wade [weid] *v/t*, *v/i* vadear
wafer ['weifə] barquillo *m*
waffle ['wɔfl] (*especie de*) panqueque *m*, *LA* wafle *m*
waft [wɑːft] *s* soplo *m*; *v/i* flotar
wag [wæg] *s* meneo *m*; *v/t* menear; mover (*el rabo*); *v/i* oscilar
wage [weidʒ] *s* salario *m*; sueldo *m*; *v/t* **~ *war*** hacer la guerra; **~earner** asalariado(a) *m (f)*
wager ['weidʒə] *s* apuesta *f*; *v/t*, *v/i* apostar
wag(g)on ['wægən] carro *m*; *f c* vagón *m* de carga
wail [weil] *s* lamento *m*; gemido *m*; *v/t*, *v/i* lamentarse; gemir
waist [weist] *anat* cintura *f*; **~coat** ['weiskəut] chaleco *m*; **~line** talle *m*
wait [weit] *s* espera *f*; *v/t*, *v/i* esperar; **~ *at table*** servir a la mesa; **~ *for*** esperar a; **~er** camarero *m*; **~ing** espera *f*; **~ing room** sala *f* de espera; **~ress** camarera *f*
waive [weiv] *v/t* renunciar; **~r** renuncia *f*
wake [weik] *s* estela *f* (*del barco*); velatorio *m*; *v/i* **~ *up*** despertar(se); **~ful** insomne; *fig* despierto; **~n** *v/t*, *v/i* despertar(se)
Wales [weilz] Gales *f*
walk [wɔːk] *s* paseo *m*; caminata *f*; ***to go for a ~, to take a ~*** dar un paseo; **~ *of life*** condición *f* social; profesión *f*; *v/i* andar; pasear; **~ *in*** entrar; **~ *out*** salir; *fam* declararse en huelga; *v/t* recorrer
walkie-talkie ['wɔːki'tɔːki] transmisor-receptor *m* portátil
walking| papers ['wɔːkiŋ 'peipəs] *fam* carta *f* de despido; **~ stick** nastón *m*
walkout ['wɔːkaut] *fam* huelga *f*
wall [wɔːl] pared *f*; muro *m*; muralla *f*
wallet ['wɔlit] cartera *f*
wallop ['wɔləp] *v/t fam* zurrar
wallpaper ['wɔːlpeipə] papel *m* pintado
walnut ['wɔːlnʌt] (nuez *f* de) nogal *m*
walrus ['wɔːlrəs] morsa *f*
waltz [wɔːls] *s* vals *m*; *v/i* valsar
wan [wɔn] pálido; descolorido
wand [wɔnd] vara *f*
wander ['wɔndə] *v/t* vagar, errar; **~ *about*** deambular; **~er** vagabundo *m*; **~ing** errante; nómado
wane [wein] *v/i* menguar
want [wɔnt] *s* falta *f*; necesidad *f*; ***for ~ of*** por falta de; *v/t* querer; desear; necesitar; **~ed** se busca; se necesita; *v/i* ***be ~ing*** faltar; ***be ~ing in*** estar falto (de)
war [wɔː] *s* guerra *f*; ***at ~*** en guerra
ward [wɔːd] *s* pupilo *m*; tutela *f*; sala *f*; pabellón *m* (*de hospital*); *v/t* **~ *off*** desviar; **~en** guardián *m*; **~er** carcelero *m*; **~robe** guardarropa *m*, *f*; ropero *m*; vestidos *m/pl*
ware|s [wɛəz] mercancías *f/pl*; **~house** almacén *m*; depósito *m*
warm [wɔːm] *a* caliente ; caluroso; *v/t* calentar; **~ *up*** recalentar; *v/i* **~ *up*** calentarse; **~th** [~θ] calor *m*
warn [wɔːn] *v/t* avisar; poner en guardia; amonestar; **~ing** *s* aviso *m*; advertencia *f*; *a* de aviso
warp [wɔːp] *s* urdimbre *f*; *v/t* deformar; pervertir; *v/i* torcerse; alabearse
warrant ['wɔrənt] *s* garantía *f*; *for* mandato *m* judicial; *v/t* autorizar; garantizar; **~y** garantía *f*
war|rior ['wɔriə] guerrero *m*; **~ship** buque *m* de guerra
wart [wɔːt] verruga *f*
wary ['wɛəri] cauteloso
wash [wɔʃ] *s* lavado *m*; ropa *f* para lavar; *v/t*, *v/i* lavar(se); **~ *up*** lavar los platos, *Am t* lavarse; **~able** lavable; **~ *and wear*** de lava y pon; **~er** *tecn* arandela *f*; **~ing** lavado *m*; **~ing machine** lavadora *f*
wasp [wɔsp] avispa *f*
waste [weist] *s* desperdicios *m/pl*; despilfarro *m*; basura *f*; ***a ~ of time*** una pérdida del tiempo; *a* desechado; superfluo; desolado; *v/t* malgastar; despilfarrar; *v/i* **~ *away*** consumirse; menguar; **~ful** pródigo; derrochador; **~paper basket** cesto *m* de papeles; **~ pipe** tubo *m* de desagüe
watch [wɔtʃ] *s* guardia *f*; vigilancia *f*; reloj *m*; ***to be on the ~*** estar a la mira; ***to keep ~*** estar de guardia; *v/t* mirar; observar; vigilar; *v/i* velar; **~ *for*** esperar; **~ *out*** tener cuidado; **~band** correa *f* de reloj; **~dog** perro *m* guardían; **~ful** vigilante; **~maker** relojero *m*; **~man** vigilante *m*, sereno *m*; **~word** santo *m* y seña
water ['wɔːtə] *a* acuático; *s* agua *f*; ***fresh ~*** agua *f* dulce; ***running ~*** agua *f* corriente; *v/t* regar; abrevar (*ganado*); mojar; **~ *down*** suavizar; *v/i* hacerse agua; *mar* tomar agua; ***my mouth ~s*** se me hace la boca agua; **~closet** inodoro *m*; **~colo(u)r** acuarela *f*; **~fall** salto *m* de agua; **~ing** riego *m*; **~ing can** regadera *f*; **~ing place** balneario *m*; abrevadero *m*; **~level** nivel *m* de agua; **~logged** empapado; **~mark** filigrana *f*; **~melon** sandía *f*; **~ power** fuerza *f* hidráulica; **~proof** impermeable; **~shed** *fig* momento *m* crítico; **~ skiing** esquí *m* acuático; **~spout** tromba *f* marina; **~ tank** cisterna *f*; depósito *m* de agua; **~tight** estanco; hermético; **~wheel** rueda *f* hidráulica; **~works** planta *f* de agua potable; **~y** acuoso; aguado
watt [wɔt] vatio *m*
wave [weiv] *s* ola *f*; onda *f*; ondulación *f*; *v/t*, *v/i* agitar(se); hacer señales; ondear; **~length** longitud *f* de onda
waver ['weivə] *v/i* vacilar; titubear
wax [wæks] *s* cera *f*; *v/t* encerar; (*luna*) crecer
way [wei] camino *m*; vía *f*; rumbo *m*; medio *m*; modo *m*; ***by the ~*** a propósito; ***by ~ of*** por vía de; ***go out of one's ~*** darse la molestia; ***have a ~ with people*** tener don de gentes; ***in a ~*** en cierto modo; ***lose one's ~*** extraviarse; ***on the ~*** en el camino; ***out of the ~*** lejano; aislado; ***this ~*** por acá; ***to be in the ~*** estorbar; ***to give ~*** ceder; ***to lead the ~*** enseñar el camino; ***to make one's ~*** abrirse paso; **~ *in*** entrada *f*; **~ *out*** salida *f*; ***which ~?*** ¿por dónde?; **~lay** [wei'lei] *v/t* acechar; **~ward** voluntarioso; rebelde
we [wiː, wi] *pron pers* nosotros(as)
weak [wiːk] débil; flojo; **~en** *v/t*, *v/i* debilitar(se), atenuar(se); **~ling** canijo *m*; **~ness** debilidad *f*
wealth [welθ] riqueza *f*; opulencia *f*; **~y** rico
wean [wiːn] *v/t* destetar
weapon ['wepən] arma *f*
wear [wɛə] *s* uso *m*; **~ *and tear*** desgaste *m*; *v/t* llevar puesto; calzar; vestir de; **~ *down***, **~ *out*** desgastar, cansar; *v/i* durar, resistir el uso; conservarse; **~ *away*** desgastarse
wear|iness ['wiərinis] cansancio *m*; **~isome** fastidioso; **~y** *a* cansado; fatigado; *v/t* fatigar; cansar
weasel ['wiːzl] comadreja *f*
weather ['weðə] *s* tiempo *m*; intemperie *f*; *v/t* resistir a; aguantar; **~-beaten** curtido por la intemperie; **~ chart** mapa *m* meteorológico; **~ forecast** parte *m* meteorológico; **~ vane** veleta *f*
weav|e [wiːv] *v/t* tejer; **~er** tejedor(a) *m (f)*
web [web] telaraña *f*; red *f*; alma *f* (*de riel*); *zool* membrana *f*
wed [wed] *v/t* casar; casarse con; *v/i* casarse; **~ding** boda *f*; casamiento *m*; **~ding ring** anillo *m* de boda
wedge [wedʒ] *s* cuña *f*; calce *m*; *v/t* acuñar; calzar
wedlock ['wedlɔk] matrimonio *m*
Wednesday ['wenzdi] miércoles *m*
weed [wiːd] *s* mala hierba *f*; *v/t* escardar; **~ *out*** extirpar
week [wiːk] semana *f*; **~day** día *m* laborable; *LA* día *m* de semana; **~end** fin *m* de semana; **~ly** *a* semanal; *s* semanario *m*
weep [wiːp] *v/t*, *v/i* llorar; **~ing** llanto *m*; **~ing willow** sauce *m* llorón
weigh [wei] *v/t*, *v/i* pesar; **~t** *s* peso *m*; pesa *f*; **~*ts and measures*** pesos *m/pl* y medidas; *v/t* cargar; **~tlessness** ingravidez *f*; **~t lifting** *sp* levantamiento *m* de pesas; **~ty** pesado
weir [wiə] presa *f*
weird [wiəd] extraño; misterioso; fantástico
welcome ['welkəm] *a* bienvenido; grato; *s* bienvenida *f*; *v/t* dar la bienvenida; acoger; ***you're ~!*** ¡no hay de qué!
weld [weld] *s* soldadura *f*; *v/t* soldar; **~ing** soldadura *f*
welfare ['welfɛə] bienestar *m*; prosperidad *f*; **~ state** *pol* estado *m* benefactor
well [wel] *s* pozo *m* (*agua*, *petróleo*); *arq* caja *f* de la escalera
well [wel] *a* bien; sano; ***to be o feel ~*** sentirse bien; *adv* bien; muy, mucho; ***as ~*** también, a la vez; ***as ~ as*** así como también; *interj* pues; bueno; ¡vaya!; **~-advised** bien aconsejado; **~-behaved** bien educado; **~-being** bienestar *m*; **~-bred** bien criado; **~-informed about** bien enterado de; **~-known** muy conocido; **~-meaning** bienintencionado; **~-nigh** casi; **~-off** con dinero; **~-timed** oportuno; **~-to-do** acomodado, rico
Welsh [welʃ] *a* galés; *s* idioma *m* galés; **~man** galés *m*; **~woman** galesa *f*
west [west] *a* occidental; *s* oeste *m*, occidente *m*; **~ern** occidental
wet [wet] *a* mojado; húmedo; *v/t* mojar; **~ness** humedad *f*; **~-nurse** ama *f* de cría
whack [wæk] *s* golpe *m* fuerte; *fam* tentativa *f*
whale [weil] ballena *f*
wharf [wɔːf] muelle *m*
what [wɔt] *pron* qué; cómo; el

que, la que; ~ ***about?*** ¿qué te parece?; ¿qué se sabe de?; ~ ***for?*** ¿para qué?; ***so ~?*** ¿y qué?; ***~'s new?*** ¿qué hay de nuevo?; *interj* ~ ***a!*** ¡qué!; *a interrog y rel* qué; **~ever** cualquier; todo lo que; ***or ~ever*** lo que sea

wheat [wi:t] trigo *m*

wheel [wi:l] *s* rueda *f*; volante *m (auto)*; *v/t* hacer rodar; *v/i* girar; rodar; **~barrow** carretilla *f*; **~chair** silla *f* de ruedas

whelp [welp] cachorro *m*

when [wen] *adv* ¿cuándo?; *conj* cuando; si

whenever [wen'evə] cuando quiera que; siempre que

where [wɛə] *adv* ¿dónde?; ¿adónde?; *conj* donde, adonde; **~abouts** paradero *m*

where|as ['wɛə'æz] por cuanto, visto que; mientras que; **~by** por lo cual; **~fore** por lo que; **~in** ¿en dónde?; **~on** en que

wherever [wɛə'evə] dondequiera

whet [wet] *v/t* afilar; *fig* abrir *(el apetito)*

whether ['weðə] si; sea que

which [witʃ] *pron rel e interrog* que; el, la, los, las que; lo que; el, la cual; lo cual; *a interrog y rel* ¿qué?, ¿cuál?; cuyo; el, la cual

whiff [wif] soplo *m*; vaharada *f*

while [wail] *s* rato *m*; tiempo *m*; ***for a ~*** por algún tiempo; ***in a little ~*** dentro de poco; *conj* mientras; mientras que; aun cuando; *v/t* ~ ***away*** pasar, entretener *(el tiempo)*

whim [wim] antojo *m*; capricho *m*

whimper ['wimpə] *v/i* lloriquear; gimotear

whimsical ['wimzikəl] caprichoso; extraño

whine [wain] *s* quejido *m*; gemido *m*; *v/i* quejarse; gemir

whinny ['wini] *v/i* relinchar

whip [wip] *s* fusta *f*; látigo *m*; azote *m*; *v/t* dar latigazos a; azotar; **~ped cream** crema *f*, nata *f* batida; **~ping** azotamiento *m*, paliza *f*

whirl [wə:l] *s* remolino *m*; *v/t, v/i* girar; **~pool** remolino *m*; **~wind** torbellino *m*

whisk [wisk] *s* escobilla *f*; cepillo *m*; movimiento *m* rápido; *v/t* barrer; cepillar; ~ ***away*** arrebatar; *v/i* pasar de prisa

whiskers ['wiskəz] patillas *f/pl*

whisk(e)y ['wiski] whisky *m*

whisper ['wispə] *s* susurro *m*; cuchicheo *m*; murmullo *m*; *v/t, v/i* cuchichear; susurrar

whistle ['wisl] *s* pito *m*; silbato *m*; *v/t, v/i* silbar

white [wait] *a* blanco; pálido; *s* blanco *m (del ojo)*; clara *f (del huevo)*; **~-collar worker** oficinista *m*; **~ lie** mentirilla *f*; **~n** *v/t* blanquear; **~ness** blancura *f*; **~wash** *s* blanqueo *m*; *v/t* enjalbegar; blanquear; *fig* encubrir

Whitsuntide ['witsntaid] Pentecostés *m*

whizz [wiz] *s* silbido *m*; *v/i* silbar; ~ ***by*** rehilar

who [hu:, hu] *pron interrog y rel* quien(es); el, la, lo, los, las que; el, la, los, las cual(es); ¿quién?; **~ever** quienquiera; cualquiera que

whol|e [həul] *a* todo; entero; íntegro; intacto; total; *s* todo *m*; totalidad *f*; conjunto *m*; ***on the ~e*** en general; **~ehearted** cien por cien; **~esale** *com* al por mayor; *fig* en masa; **~esaler** mayorista *m*; **~esome** salubre; **~e wheat** de trigo integral; **~ly** ['həuli] enteramente; íntegramente

whom [hu:m] *pron* a quién(es), a quien(es)

whoop [hu:p] *s* alarido *m*; *v/i* gritar; **~ing cough** tos *f* ferina

whore [hɔ:] puta *f*

whose [hu:z] *pron y a rel* cuyo, cuya; cuyos, cuyas; de quien; de quienes; *a interrog* ¿de quién?

why [wai] *adv* ¿por qué?; ¿para qué?; *conj* porque; por lo cual; *s* porqué *m*; *interj* pues; ¡toma!

wick [wik] mecha *f*

wicked ['wikid] malo; perverso; malvado

wicker ['wikə] mimbre *m*

wicket ['wikit] postigo *m*

wide [waid] ancho; extenso; vasto; **~-awake** despabilado; muy despierto; **~ly** muy, mucho; **~n** *v/t* ensanchar; extender; **~spread** difundido

widow ['widəu] viuda *f*; **~er** viudo *m*; **~hood** viudez *f*

width [widθ] anchura *f*

wife [waif] esposa *f*

wig [wig] peluca *f*

wiggle ['wigl] *v/t, v/i* menear(se) rápidamente

wild [waild] *a* salvaje; silvestre; feroz; desgobernado; descabellado; **~cat strike** huelga *f (no autorizada)*; **~erness** ['wildənis] desierto *m*; yermo *m*; **~life** fauna *f* silvestre; **~ly** desatinadamente; ferozmente

wile [wail] ardid *m*

wil(l)ful ['wilful] premeditado; testarudo; voluntarioso

will [wil] *s* voluntad *f*; intención *f*; testamento *m*; ***at ~*** a voluntad; *v/t* querer; *for* legar; **~ing** voluntario; dispuesto; **~ingness** buena voluntad *f*

willow ['wiləu] sauce *m*

wilt [wilt] *v/t, v/i* marchitar(se)

wily ['waili] astuto

win [win] *v/t, v/i* ganar; conquistar; lograr; *s sp* triunfo *m*

wince [wins] *v/i* hacer mueca de dolor; recular

winch [wintʃ] cigüeña *f*; torno *m*

wind [wind] viento *m*; aliento *m*; *med* flatulencia *f*; ***to get ~ of*** enterarse de

wind [waind] *v/t* dar cuerda a *(reloj)*; enrollar; ~ ***up*** concluir; *v/i* serpentear

wind|ed ['windid] falto de aliento; **~fall** golpe *m* de suerte; **~ing** ['waindiŋ] tortuoso; en espiral; **~ing staircase** escalera *f* de caracol

windlass ['windləs] *tecn* torno *m*

windmill ['windmil] molino *m* de viento

window ['windəu] ventana *f*; **~pane** cristal *m* de ventana; **~-shopping: *to go ~-shopping*** mirar los escaparates sin querer comprar; **~sill** alféizar *m*

wind|pipe ['windpaip] *anat* tráquea *f*; **~screen,** *Am* **~shield** parabrisas *m*; ***~screen,*** *Am* ***~shield wiper*** limpiaparabrisas *m*; **~ward** de barlovento; **~y** ventoso

wine [wain] vino *m*; **~ cellar** bodega *f*; **~grower** viticultor *m*; **~ tasting** degustación *f* de vinos

wing [wiŋ] ala *f*; *sp* extremo *m*; ***on the ~*** al vuelo; **~s** *teat* bastidores *m/pl*

wink [wiŋk] *s* guiño *m*; *v/i* guiñar; ***not sleep a ~*** no pegar ojo

winn|er ['winə] ganador(a) *m (f)*; **~ing** ganador, vencedor; *fig* cautivador; **~ing-post** poste *m* de llegada; **~ings** ganancias *f/pl*

wint|er ['wintə] *s* invierno *m*; *a* invernal; *v/i* invernar; **~ry** ['~tri] invernal; *fig* frío

wipe [waip] *v/t* limpiar; enjugar; ~ ***off*** borrar; ~ ***out*** *fig* aniquilar; borrar con

wir|e ['waiə] *s* alambre *m*; hilo *m*; telegrama *m*; *v/t* instalar alambres en; telegrafiar; **~eless** radio *f*; **~y** ['~ri] nervudo; delgado pero fuerte

wis|dom ['wizdəm] sabiduría *f*; juicio *m*; **~e** [waiz] sabio; prudente; juicioso; **~ecrack** *fam* agudeza *f*

wish [wiʃ] *s* deseo *m*; anhelo *m*; *v/t, v/i* desear; anhelar; **~ful** deseoso; **~ful thinking** espejismo *m*

wishy-washy ['wiʃiwɔʃi] flojo, débil, sin carácter

wistful ['wistful] añorante; pensativo

wit [wit] ingenio *m*; sal *f*; agudeza *f*

witch [witʃ] bruja *f*; **~craft** brujería *f*; embrujo *m*

with [wið] con; de

withdraw [wið'drɔ:] *v/t* retirar; retractar; *v/i* retirarse; **~al** retirada *f*; **~n** reservado; introvertido

wither ['wiðə] *v/t, v/i* marchitar(se)

withhold [wið'həuld] *v/t* negar; retener

with|in [wi'ðin] dentro de; al alcance de; **~out** [~'ðaut] *prep* sin; a falta de; ***to do ~out*** pasarse sin; *adv* fuera; ***from ~out*** desde fuera

withstand [wið'stænd] *v/t* resistir a

witness ['witnis] *s* testigo *m*; testimonio *m*; *v/t* atestiguar; presenciar

witty ['witi] ingenioso; gracioso

wizard ['wizəd] brujo *m*; mago *m*

wobble ['wɔbl] *v/i* tambalear(se); vacilar

woe [wəu] dolor *m*; aflicción *f*; ***~ is me!*** ¡ay de mí!

wolf [wulf] *s* lobo *m*; *v/t fam* engullir

woman ['wumən] mujer *f*; **~hood** feminidad *f*; las mujeres; **~ly** mujeril, femenino

womb [wu:m] *anat* matriz *f*; *fig* seno *m*

women's ['wiminz]: ***~ liberation*** movimiento *m* feminista; ***~ rights*** derechos *m/pl* de la mujer

wonder ['wʌndə] *s* maravilla *f*; asombro *m*; *v/i* admirarse; *v/t* preguntarse; **~ful** maravilloso

woo [wu:] *v/t, v/i* cortejar

wood [wud] madera *f*; bosque *m*; leña *f*; **~cut** grabado *m* en madera; **~cutter** leñador *m*; **~ed** arbolado; **~en** de madera; rígido; **~pecker** pájaro *m* carpintero; **~winds** *mús* maderas *f/pl*; **~work** obra *f* de carpintería

wool [wul] lana *f*; **~(l)en** de lana; **~(l)y** lanoso

word [wə:d] *s* palabra *f*; noticia *f*; ***in other ~s*** es decir; *v/t* expresar; **~ing** expresión *f*; fraseología *f*; **~ processor** procesador *m* de textos; **~y** verboso

work [wə:k] *s* trabajo *m*; obra *f*; empleo *m*; ***~ of art*** obra *f* de arte; ***at ~*** trabajando; en juego; ***out of ~*** sin trabajo; *v/t* hacer trabajar; operar; cultivar; ~ ***out*** resolver; *v/i* trabajar; funcionar; surtir efecto; **~able** practicable; **~aholic** adicto *m* al trabajo; **~day** día *m* laborable; **~er** trabajador(a) *m (f)*, obrero(a) *m (f)*; **~ing class** clase *f* obrera; **~manship** hechura *f*, confección *f*; habilidad *f*; **~s** fábrica *f*; mecanismo *m*; **~shop** taller *m*

world [wə:ld] mundo *m*; **~ly** mundano; **~ power** potencia *f* mundial; **~ war** guerra *f* mundial; **~wide** mundial

worm [wə:m] gusano *m*; lombriz *f*; **~-eaten** carcomido; apolillado

worn-out ['wɔ:n'aut] gastado; raído; agotado

worr|ied ['wʌrid] preocupado, inquieto; **~y** *s* inquietud *f*; preocupación *f*; *v/i* inquietarse; *v/t* preocupar

worse [wə:s] *a, adv* peor; ~ ***and ~*** de mal en peor; *s* algo peor; ***a turn for the ~*** empeoramiento *m*; **~n** *v/t, v/i* empeorar(se)

worship ['wə:ʃip] *s* adoración *f*; culto *m*; *v/t* adorar

worst [wə:st] *a* peor; pésimo; *adv* pésimamente; *s* lo peor, lo más malo

worth [wə:θ] *s* valor *m*; mérito *m*; precio *m*; *a* de valor; ***to be ~*** valer; ***to be ~ it*** valer la pena; **~less** sin valor; inútil; despreciable; **~while** valioso; **~y** ['~ði] digno

wound [wu:nd] *s* herida *f*; *v/t* herir

wrangle ['ræŋgl] disputa *f*; riña *f*

wrap [ræp] *v/t* envolver; cubrir; *v/i* ~ ***up*** arroparse; **~per** cubierta *f*; sobrecubierta *f (de libro)*; **~ping** envoltura *f*; **~ping paper** papel *m* de envolver

wrath [rɔθ] cólera *f*; ira *f*

wreath [ri:θ] guirnalda *f*; corona *f*

wreck [rek] *s* naufragio *m*; *fig* ruina *f*; *v/t* arruinar; **~age** restos *m/pl*; despojos *m/pl*

wrench [rentʃ] *s* arranque *m*; *med* distensión *f*; *tecn* llave *f* (inglesa); *v/t* arrancar

wrest [rest] *v/t* arrebatar (***from*** a); **~le** ['resl] *v/t* luchar con

wretch [retʃ] *s* infeliz *m*, desgraciado *m*; **~ed** ['~id] miserable; desgraciado

wriggle ['rigl] *v/i* culebrear, serpentear

wring [riŋ] *v/t* torcer; escurrir

wrinkle ['riŋkl] *s* arruga *f*; *v/t* arrugar; ***~ one's brows*** fruncir el ceño; *v/i* arrugarse

wrist [rist] *anat* muñeca *f*; **~ watch** reloj *m* de pulsera

writ [rit] escritura *f*; *for* orden *f*; mandato *m*

writ|e [rait] *v/t, v/i* escribir; ***~e down*** apuntar; ***~e off*** *com* borrar *(deudas)*; *fig* dar por perdido; ***~e out*** escribir en forma completa; extender *(cheque, etc)*; **~er** escritor(a) *m (f)*; autor(a) *m (f)*; **~e-up** crónica *f*, reportaje *m*

writhe [raið] *v/i* retorcerse

writing ['raitiŋ] letra *f*; escritura *f*; escrito *m*; ***in ~*** por escrito; **~ desk** escritorio *m*; **~ paper** papel *m* de cartas

written ['ritn] escrito

wrong [rɔŋ] *a* erróneo; equivocado; malo; injusto; inexacto; ***to be ~*** equivocarse; no tener razón; andar mal *(reloj)*; *adv* mal; al revés; ***go ~*** salir mal; *s* mal *m*; injusticia *f*; perjuicio *m*; agravio *m*; *v/t* injuriar; ofender; agraviar; **~doer** ['~du:ə] malhechor(a) *m (f)*; **~fully** injustamente

wrought [rɔ:t] forjado; labrado; **~-up** sobreexcitado

wry [rai] torcido; irónico; tergiversado; **~ face** mueca *f*

X

Xmas ['krisməs] = ***Christmas***

X-ray ['eks'rei] *v/t* hacer una radiografía; *s* rayo *m* X; radiografía *f*

xylophone ['zailəfəun] xilófono *m*

Y

yacht [jɔt] yate *m*

yam [jæm] *bot* ñame *m*, camote *m*

yap [jæp] *v/i* dar ladridos agudos

yard [ja:d] yarda *f (91,44 cm)*; patio *m*; **~stick** criterio *m*, norma *f*

yarn [ja:n] hilo *m*; *fam* cuento *m*

yawn [jɔ:n] *s* bostezo *m*; *v/i* bostezar

year [jə:] año *m*; **~ly** anual

yearn [jə:n] (**for**) *v/i* anhelar; **~ing** anhelo *m*

yeast [ji:st] levadura *f*

yell [jel] *s* grito *m*; *v/t, v/i* gritar; chillar

yellow ['jeləu] amarillo; **~ish** amarillento

yelp [jelp] *v/i* gañir; *s* gañido *m*

yes [jes] sí; ***~ indeed*** sí por cierto; ***to say ~*** asentir

yesterday ['jestədi] ayer; ***the day before ~*** anteayer

yet [jet] *conj* sin embargo; no obstante; *adv* ya *(en la pregunta)*; aún, todavía; ***as ~*** hasta ahora; ***not ~*** aún no; todavía no

yew [ju:] tejo *m*

yield [ji:ld] *s* rendimiento *m*; *com* producto *m*; cosecha *f*; *v/t* producir, rendir; admitir; ceder; *v/i* rendirse; ceder; consentir; **~ing** flexible; complaciente

yogurt ['jəugət] yogur *m*

yoke [jəuk] *s agr* yunta *f*; yugo *m*; *v/t* acoplar

yolk [jəuk] yema *f*

yonder ['jɔndə] *adv* allá

you [ju:, ju] tú; vosotros(as); usted; ustedes

young [jʌŋ] *a* joven; ***~ lady*** señorita *f*; *s* jóvenes *m/pl*; cría *f (de animales)*; **~er** más joven; menor; **~ster** ['~stə] joven *m, f*

your [jɔ:] *a pos* tu, tus, su, sus; vuestro(a, os, as); de usted(es)

yours [jɔ:z] *pron pos* tuyo(a), tuyos(as); el (la) tuyo(a), lo tuyo; los (las) tuyos(as); suyo(a), suyos(as); el (la) suyo(a), lo suyo; los (las) suyos(as); vuestro(a), vuestros(as); el (la) vuestro(a), los (las) vuestros(as); el, la, lo, los, las de usted(es)

yourself [jɔ:'self] *pron pers sing* tú mismo(a); usted mismo(a); ***by ~*** solo

yourselves [jɔ:'selvz] *pron pers pl* ustedes mismos(as); vosotros(as) mismos(as)

youth [ju:θ] juventud *f*; joven *m*; **~ful** juvenil; **~ hostel** albergue *m* juvenil

Z

zany ['zeini] alocado

zeal [ziːl] celo *m*, ardor *m*; ahínco *m*; **~ous** ['zeləs] celoso; apasionado; fervoroso

zebra ['ziːbrə] cebra *f*; **~ crossing** paso *m* de peatones

zenith ['zeniθ] cenit *m* (*t fig*)

zero ['ziərəu] cero *m*; **~ growth** crecimiento *m* cero;

below **~** bajo cero

zest [zest] deleite *m*; gusto *m*

zinc [ziŋk] cinc *m*

Zionism ['zaiənizəm] sionismo *m*

zip| fastener ['zip-], **~per** cre-

mallera *f*, *LA* cierre *m*

zippy ['zipi] brioso, vivaz

zodiac ['zəudiæk] zodíaco *m*

zone [zəun] zona *f*

zoo [zuː] parque *m* zoológico

zoolog|ical [zəuə'lɔdʒikəl]

zoológico; **~y** [~'ɔlədʒi] zoología *f*

zoom [zuːm] *v/i* volar zumbando; **~ lens** *foto* objetivo *m* zoom (*de foco variable*)

zucchini [zuˈkini] calabacín *m*

A

a to; towards (*with verbs expressing movement*); at; on, by, in (*with verbs expressing state or position*); ~ **mano** at hand; **poco ~ poco** little by little; ~ **pie** on foot; ~ **mediodía** at noon; ~ **las seis** at six o'clock; **voy ~ Londres** I am going to London; **sabe ~ limón** it tastes of lemon; ~ **la española** in the Spanish way
abad *m* abbot; **~esa** *f* abbess; **~ía** *f* abbey
abajo *adv.* down; underneath; below; *interj* down with!
abalanzar *v/t* to balance; to weigh; **~se sobre** to rush upon
abandon|ado abandoned; deserted; **~ar** *v/t* to abandon; to leave; **~o** *m* abandon; slovenliness
abani|car *v/t* to fan; **~co** *m* fan
abaratar *v/t* to cheapen
abarca *f* wooden sandal
abarcar *v/t* to include; to comprise; *LA* to monopolize
abarrotes *m/pl LA* provisions
abastar *v/t* to supply; to provide with
abastec|edor *m* supplier; **~er** *v/t* to supply; to provision; **~imiento** *m* supply; provisions; stores, stock
abasto *m* supplying
abat|ible folding; **~ido** dejected, depressed; discouraged; *com* depreciated; **~imiento** *m* depression; **~ir** *v/t* to knock down; to depress; **~irse** to loose heart; to become depressed; **~irse sobre** to swoop down on
abdica|ción *f* abdication; **~r** *v/t* to abdicate
abdomen *m* abdomen
abecedario *m* alphabet; spelling book
abedul *m* birch tree
abej|a *f* bee; **~ón** *m* drone; **~orro** *m* bumblebee
abertura *f* aperture; opening; crack
abeto *m* fir
abierto open; clear; *fig.* open, generous
abigarrado variegated; multi-colo(u)red; motley
abism|al abysmal; **~ar** *v/t* to cast down; to ruin; **~o** *m* abyss
abjurar *v/t* to abjure, to disavow
ablandar *v/t, v/i* to soften; to mollify; to mitigate; **~se** to get softer
abnega|ción *f* abnegation, self-denial; **~rse** to deny oneself
abofetear *v/t* to slap (*in the face*)
aboga|do(a) *m (f)* lawyer, barrister; **~r por** *v/i* to plead (for); to advocate
abolengo *m* ancestry; *for* inheritance
aboli|ción *f* abolition; **~r** *v/t* to abolish, to revoke
abolla|dura *f* dent; **~r** *v/t* to dent; to emboss
abomina|ble abominable; **~ción** *f* abomination; horror; **~r** *v/t* to abominate
abon|ado *m* subscriber; holder of a season ticket; **~ar** *v/t* to guarantee; to assure; *com* to pay; to credit; **~arse** to subscribe; **~aré** *m* promissory note; **~o** *m* payment; subscription; season ticket
abordar *v/t mar* to board (*a ship*); to approach, to tackle (*a person, a subject*); *v/i* to put into port
aborigen *a, m* aboriginal
aborrec|er *v/t* to hate, to abhor; **~imiento** *m* abhorrence, hatred
abort|ar *v/i* to abort; to miscarry; to fail; **~o** *m* abortion, miscarriage; monstrosity
abotonar *v/t* to button; *v/i* to bud
abovedar *v/t* to vault
abrasar *v/t* to burn (up); *agr* to parch; **~se (de, en)** *fig* to burn (with)
abraz|adera *f* bracket; clasp; **~ar** *v/t* to clasp; to embrace; to comprise; **~o** *m* embrace, hug
abrecartas *m* letter opener
abrelatas *m* can opener
abreva|dero *m* watering place; **~r** *v/t* to water (*cattle*)
abrevia|ción *f* abbreviation; shortening; **~r** *v/t* to abbreviate; to abridge; to shorten; **~tura** *f* abbreviation
abridor *m* (*tin, etc*) opener
abrig|ar *v/t* to shelter; to wrap up; to keep warm; *fig* to cherish; **~o** *m* shelter; protection; overcoat
abril *m* April
abrir *v/t* to open; to whet (*the appetite*); *v/i* to open
abrochar *v/t* to fasten; to buckle; to button; *LA* to staple
abrogar *v/t* to abrogate, to repeal
abrumar *v/t* to weigh down; to overwhelm
abrupto rugged; abrupt
absceso *m* abscess
ábside *m or f* apse
absolu|ción *f* absolution; acquittal; **~tismo** *m* absolutism; **~to** absolute; **en ~to** by no means; not at all (*in negative sentences*)
absor|ber *v/t* to absorb; **~ción** *f* absorption
abstemio(a) *m (f)* teetotaller; *a* abstemious
abstención *f* abstention
abstenerse to abstain, to refrain
abstra|cción *f* abstraction; **~cto** abstract; **~er** *v/t* to abstract; *v/i*: **~er de** to do without; **~erse** to be lost in thought
absurdo absurd
abuchear *v/t* to boo; to jeer at
abuel|a *f* grandmother; *fig* old woman; **~ita** *f fam* granny, grandma; **~ito** *m fam* grandpa; **~o** *m* grandfather; *fig* old man; **~os** *m/pl* grandparents
abulta|do bulky; **~r** *v/t* to enlarge; *v/i* to be bulky
abunda|ncia *f* abundance, plenty; **~nte** abundant, plentiful; **~r** *v/i* to abound
aburri|do boring, tiresome; **~miento** *m* boredom; tedium; **~r** *v/t* to bore; to annoy; **~rse** to be bored
abus|ar de *v/i* to abuse; to impose upon; **~ivo** improper, abusive; **~o** *m* abuse; misuse
acá here; over here; **de ~ para allá** to and fro
acaba|do *a* finished, complete; perfect; *m* finish; **~r** *v/t, v/i* to finish, to complete; to end; **~r con** to put an end to; **~r de** to have just; **él ~ de llegar** he has just arrived; **~rse** to run out of; to be all over
academia *f* academy
académico(a) *m (f)* academician; *a* academic
acaec|er *v/i* to happen; to occur; **~imiento** *m* event
acalora|miento *m* ardo(u)r; passion; anger; **~r** *v/t* to warm up; to heat; to excite; **~rse** to get overheated
acallar *v/t* to silence
acampar *v/t* to camp
acanala|do fluted; corrugated; **~r** *v/t* to groove, to flute
acantilado *m* cliff; *a* steep
acantona|miento *m* billet; **~r** *v/t mil* to quarter
acapara|dor(a) *m (f)* hoarder; monopolizer; **~miento** *m* hoarding; **~r** *v/t* to hoard; to monopolize; to corner the market in
acariciar *v/t* to caress
acarre|ar *v/t* to cart, to convey; to haul; **~o** *m* carting, cartage; transport
acaso *adv* by chance; perhaps; **por si ~** just in case; *m* chance, accident; **al ~** at random
acata|miento *m* respect; observance (*of a law*); **~r** *v/t* to respect, to treat with deference
acaudala|do wealthy; **~r** *v/t* to amass (*fortune, etc*)
acaudillar *v/t* to lead
acce|der *v/t* to accede; to agree; **~sible** accessible; **~sión** *f* accession; **~so** *m* access; entry; *med* fit, attack; **~sorio** *a, m* accessory
accident|ado troubled; rugged; **~al** accidental; **~almente** accidentally; **~e** *m* accident
acción *f* action; act; gesture; *com* share
accion|ar *v/t tecn* to set in motion; to drive; **~ista** *m, f* shareholder
acebo *m* holly
acech|ar *v/t* to spy upon; to lie in wait for; **~o** *m* spying; ambush; **cazar al ~o** to stalk
acedía *f* acidity; heartburn
aceit|e *m* oil; **~e de ricino** castor oil; **~era** *f* oil cruet; *tecn* oiler; **~oso** oily; **~una** *f* olive
acelera|ción *f* acceleration; **~dor** *m* accelerator; **~r** *v/t* to accelerate; to hasten
acelgas *f/pl* Swiss chard
acent|o *m* accent; stress; **~uar** *v/t* to stress; to emphasize
acepillar *v/t tecn* to plane; to brush
acepta|ble acceptable; **~ción** *f* acceptance; approbation; **~r** *v/t* to accept; to approve of
acequia *f* irrigation ditch
acera *f* pavement, *Am* sidewalk
acerbo harsh; sour, bitter
acerca de about; with regard to; concerning
acerca|miento *m* bringing nearer; *pol* rapprochement; **~r** *v/t* to bring near; **~rse** to approach; to come near to
acero *m* steel; **~ damasquino** damask steel; **~ inoxidable** stainless steel
acerolo *m* hawthorn
acérrimo all-out; zealous
acerta|do proper, correct; **~r** *v/t* to hit the mark; *v/i* to be right
acertijo *m* riddle; puzzle
acidez *f* acidity
ácido *m* acid; *a* acid; sour
acierto *m* good shot; success; skill
aclama|ción *f* acclamation; **~r** *v/t* to acclaim; to applaud
aclara|ción *f* explanation; **~r** *v/t* to make clear; to explain; *v/i* to clear up (*weather*)
aclimata|ción *f* acclimatization; **~r** *v/t* to acclimatize
acobardar *v/t* to intimidate; **~se** to become frightened; to flinch
acodado bent
acoge|dor welcoming, inviting; **~r** *v/t* to receive; to welcome; **~rse a** to take refuge in
acogida *f* reception
acolchar *v/t* to quilt
acomet|er *v/t* to attack; to undertake; **~ida** *f* attack; assault
acomod|ación *f* accommodation; adaptation; **~adizo** accommodating; **~ado** wealthy, well-to-do; **~ador(a)** *m (f)* usher, usherette; **~amiento** *m* agreement; **~ar** *v/t* to accommodate; to adapt; to arrange; *v/i* to suit; **~arse** to adapt oneself; **~o** *m* arrangement
acompaña|miento *m* accompaniment; escort; *teat* extra; **~r** *v/t* to accompany; to enclose (*in letter*)
acondiciona|do in (good or bad) condition; **~r** *v/t* to arrange, to prepare; *tecn* to condition
aconseja|ble advisable; **~r** *v/t* to advise; **~rse** to take advice
acontec|er *v/i* to happen; to occur; **~imiento** *m* event
acopi|ar *v/t* to gather together; **~o** *a, m* gathering; storing
acopla|dura *f*, **~miento** *m tecn* connection; coupling; **~r** *v/t* to connect; to join; to mate (*animals*); **~rse** *zool* to mate
acorazado *m* battleship
acorazonado heart-shaped
acord|ar *v/t* to decide; to agree upon; *v/i* to agree; **~arse de** to remember; **~e** *a* agreed; *m mús* chord
acordeón *m* accordion
acorralar *v/t* to round up; to pen up (*cattle*); *fig* to corner
acortar *v/t* to abridge; to shorten
acosar *v/t* to pursue; to hound; to harass
acostar *v/t* to put to bed; **~se** to go to bed; to lie down
acostumbra|do usual, customary; **~r** *v/t* to accustom; *v/i* to be in the habit of; **~rse** to become accustomed
acotar *v/t* to survey; to annotate (*a page*)
acre *a* acrid (*t fig*); sharp; sour; *m* acre
acrecentar *v/t* to promote; to increase
acrecer *v/t* to increase
acreditar *v/t* to accredit; *com* to credit; to answer for; to guarantee
acreedor *m* creditor
acribillar *v/t* to riddle (*with bullets, etc*); to pester
acróbata *m, f* acrobat
acta *f* record; minutes (*of a meeting*)
actitud *f* attitude
activ|ar *v/t* to hasten; to expedite; **~idad** *f* activity; **~o** *a* active; *m com* assets
act|o *m* act; **~or** *m* actor; **~triz** *f* actress; **~uación** *f* performance; **~ual** present; **~ualidad** *f* present time; current topic; **~ualmente** at present; presently; **~uar** *v/i* to act
acuar|ela *f* water-colo(u)r; **~io** *m* aquarium
acuartelar *v/t mil* to quarter
acuático aquatic
acuclillarse to squat
acuchillar *v/t* to knife; to stab
acudir *v/i* to come up; to present oneself; **~ a** to attend; to frequent
acuerdo *m* agreement; resolution; **de ~** in agreement; **estar de ~ con** to agree with
acumula|dor *m* storage battery; **~r** *v/t* to accumulate
acuñar *v/t* to mint; to coin
acurrucarse to huddle up, to nestle; *fig* to cower
acusa|ción *f* accusation; **~dor(a)** *m (f)* accuser; **~r** *v/t* to accuse; to acknowledge (*receipt*); *for* to indict; **~tivo** *m gram* accusative
acústica *f* acoustics
acha|car *v/t* to impute; **~que** *m* ailment
achicar *v/t* to reduce; to dwarf
achispado *fam* tipsy
adapta|ción *f* adaptation; **~dor** *m* adapter; **~r** *v/t* to adapt
adecuado adequate
adelant|ado advanced; fast (*watch*); **pagar por ~ado** to pay in advance; **~ar** *v/t, v/i* to advance; to progress; to overtake (*car*); **~arse** to take the lead; **~e** forward; ahead; **de hoy en ~e** from now on; **~o** *m* progress; advance, advance payment
adelgazar *v/t* to make slender
ademán *m* gesture; *pl* manners
además moreover; besides
adentro within; inside
adepto *m* follower; partisan
aderez|ar *v/t* to season; to adorn; **~o** *m* dressing; seasoning
adeudar *v/t* to debit; to owe; **~se** to get into debt
adhe|rencia *f* adhesion; **~rir(se)** *v/i* to adhere; **~sivo** adhesive
adición *f* addition; *LA* check (*in restaurant, etc*)
adicion|al additional; extra; **~ar** *v/t* to add
adicto *a* addicted; devoted; *m* (*drug*) addict; follower
adiestrar *v/t* to train (*horses*); to instruct
adinerado wealthy, moneyed
adiós *interj, m* good-bye
adivin|anza *f* riddle; puzzle; **~ar** *v/t* to guess; to prophesy; **~o** *m* diviner; fortune-teller
adjetivo *m* adjective
adjudicar *v/t* to adjudge; **~se** to appropriate
adjunto *a* adjoining; enclosed; *m* assistant
administra|ción *f* administration; **~dor** *m* administrator; manager; **~r** *v/t* to administer; **~tivo** administrative
admira|ble admirable; **~ción** *f* admiration; **~r** *v/t* to admire; **~rse de** to be surprised at; to wonder at
admi|sión *f* admission; acceptance; **~tir** *v/t* to admit; to accept
adob|ar *v/t* to pickle; to season; **~e** *m* adobe; **~o** *m* seasoning
adolecer *v/i* to fall ill
adolescen|cia *f* adolescence; **~te** *m, f, a* adolescent
adonde *conj* where
adónde *adv interrog* where?
adop|ción *f* adoption; **~tar** *v/t* to adopt; **~tivo** adopted
adoqu|ín *m* paving stone; **~inado** *m* paved floor
adora|ble adorable; **~ción** *f* adoration; worship; **~r** *v/t* to worship; to adore
adorm|ecer *v/t* to put to sleep; to lull; to calm; **~idera** *f* opium poppy

Spanish

adorn|ar v/t to adorn; **~o** m adornment; decoration
adqui|rir v/t to acquire; to buy; **~sición** f acquisition; purchase; **~sitivo** acquisitive; **poder** m **~sitivo** purchasing power
adrede on purpose
adscribir v/t to appoint
aduana f customs; customs duty
aducir v/t to adduce
adueñarse to take possession
adul|ación f flattery; **~ar** v/t to flatter; **~ón** a cringing; m toady
adulter|ación f adulteration; **~ar** v/t to adulterate; v/i to commit adultery
adúltero(a) m (f) adulterer(ess); a adulterous
adulto(a) a, m (f) adult
adven|edizo a newly arrived; m newcomer; **~idero** forthcoming; **~imiento** m arrival, coming
adverbio m adverb
advers|ario m adversary, opponent; **~idad** f adversity; **~o** adverse
advert|encia f advice; warning; **~ir** v/t to notice; to advise; to warn
Adviento m Advent
adyacente adjacent
aéreo aerial
aerodeslizador m hovercraft
aerodinámico aerodynamic; streamlined
aeródromo m airfield
aero|moza f LA air hostess, stewardess; **~náutica** f aeronautics; **~nave** f airship; **~puerto** m airport
afable affable; complaisant
afamado famous
afán m industry; anxiety; eagerness
afan|ar v/t to press; **~arse** to work eagerly; **~oso** arduous, difficult
afec|ción f affection; **~tación** f affectation; **~tar** v/t to affect; LA to injure; **~tivo** affective, emotional; **~to a** fond of; **~tuoso** affectionate
afeitar v/t to shave; **~se** to (have a) shave
afeminado effeminate
aferrar v/t to grasp; **~se a, en** to persist obstinately in
afianzar v/t to guarantee
afición f enthusiasm
aficion|ado a fond of; m fan; **~arse a** to take a fancy to; to become fond of
afila|dor m sharpener; **~r** v/t to sharpen, to whet; to grind
afín akin; similar; bordering
afin|ar v/t to perfect; to tune; **~idad** f affinity
afirma|ción f affirmation; **~r** v/t to affirm; **~tiva** f assent
afligir v/t to afflict, to distress; **~se** to grieve
aflojar v/t to loosen; to slacken; v/i to weaken; to diminish; **~se** to get loose
aflu|encia f inflow, influx; crowd; **~ente** m tributary; a flowing; eloquent; **~ir** v/i to flow into; to congregate
aforrar v/t to line (clothes)
afortunado fortunate
afrenta f affront; insult; **~r** v/t to insult
África f Africa; **~ del Norte** North Africa
afrontar v/t to confront; to face, to defy
afuera adv outside; outward; **~s** f/pl suburbs; outskirts
agachadiza f zool snipe
agacharse to stoop; to squat; to crouch
agalla f bot gall; **~s** pl guts, courage
agarra|dero m handle; **~r** v/t to grasp; to seize; **~rse** to grapple
agasaj|ar v/t to entertain; to regale; **~o** m lavish reception, banquet
agen|cia f agency; LA pawnshop; **~cia de viajes** travel agency; **~da** f memo book; **~te** m agent; **~te de bolsa** stockbroker; **~te de policía** policeman; **~te inmobiliario** (real) estate agent
ágil nimble; agile
agilidad f nimbleness; agility
agio m com agio, speculation
agita|ción f agitation; disturbance; **~r** v/t to agitate; to ruffle; to shake; **~rse** to flutter; to get excited
aglomerar v/t to agglomerate; to gather
agobi|ar v/t to oppress; to exhaust; to weigh down; **~o** m oppression; exhaustion
agolparse to crowd together
agonía f agony; violent pain
agonizar v/t to annoy; v/i: **estar agonizando** to be dying
agost|ar v/t to parch; **~o** m August
agota|do sold out, out of stock; out of print; **~miento** m exhaustion; **~r** v/t to exhaust; to wear out; **~rse** to give out; to be sold out
agracia|do graceful, pretty, charming; **~r** v/t to adorn; to make more attractive
agrad|able agreeable; pleasant; **~ar** v/i to please; **~ecer** v/t to thank; **muy ~ecido** much obliged; **~ecimiento** m gratitude; **~o** m affability; taste
agrandar v/t to enlarge; to increase
agrario agrarian
agravar v/t to aggravate; to make heavier
agravi|ar v/t to wrong; **~o** m offence; insult
agre|dir v/t to assault; **~sión** f aggression, assault; attack
agriarse to become sour
agrícola agricultural, agrarian
agricult|or(a) m, f farmer; **~ura** f agriculture
agridulce bittersweet
agri|etar v/t to crack, to chap; **~o** sour; acid; fig disagreeable
agrupa|ción f grouping; gathering; **~r** v/t to group; to cluster
agua f water; rain; **~ destilada** distilled water; **~ mineral** mineral water; **~ potable** drinking water; **~s abajo** downstream; **~s arriba** upstream; **~cate** m avocado; **~cero** m shower, downpour; **~nieve** f sleet
aguant|able bearable; **~ar** v/t to stand; to bear; **~arse** to contain oneself; **~e** m stamina; endurance; patience
aguar v/t to dilute
aguardar v/t to await; to wait for, to expect
aguardiente m brandy; liquor; **~ de caña** rum
aguarrás m turpentine oil
agud|eza f sharpness; **~o** sharp; acute; witty
agüero m omen
aguij|ada f spur; **~ar** v/t to spur; to goad; **~ón** m prick; sting; goad
águila f eagle
aguj|a f needle; hand (of clock); **~erear** v/t to prick; to pierce; **~ero** m hole; **~etas** f/pl muscle cramps
aguzar v/t to sharpen; **~ las orejas** to prick one's ears
ahí there; **por ~** that way, over there
ahija|da f goddaughter; **~do** m godson; **~r** v/t to adopt (children)
ahínco m eagerness; zeal
ahog|ar v/t to suffocate; to drown; **~arse** to drown; to be suffocated; **~o** m distress; med shortness of breath
ahora now; **~ bien** now then; **~ mismo** at this very moment
ahondar v/i to delve (into); v/t to deepen
ahorcar v/t to hang
ahorr|ar v/t to save; **~os** m/pl savings
ahuecar v/t to hollow (out)
ahumar v/t to smoke; to cure (meat)
ahuyentar v/t to put to flight; to frighten away
airado angry; irate
air|e m air; wind; appearance; **al ~e libre** in the open air; **con ~e acondicionado** air-conditioned; **darse ~es** to put on airs; **~oso** airy; windy; graceful; successful
aisla|miento m isolation; insulation; **~r** v/t to isolate; to insulate (heat; current)
ajar v/t to crumple; m garlic field
ajedrez m chess
ajeno belonging to another; alien; foreign; **~ de** devoid of
ajetreo m hustle and bustle
ajo m garlic
ajuar m furniture; dowry, trousseau
ajust|ado tight; right; **~ar** v/t to fit in; to arrange; **~e** m adjustment; agreement
ala f wing; brim (of hat); leaf (of table); **~ delta** hang-gliding
alabar v/t, **~se** to praise; to boast
alabearse to warp
alacrán m scorpion
alambr|ado m wire fencing; **~e** m wire
alameda f (tree-lined) avenue; poplar grove
álamo m poplar; **~ temblón** aspen
alarde m parade; show; **~ar** v/i to boast; to show off
alargar v/t to lengthen; to stretch
alarido m howl; shriek, yell
alarm|a f alarm; **~ante** alarming; **~ar** v/t to alarm
alba f dawn
albacea m executor (of will)
albahaca f basil
albañil m bricklayer; mason; **~ería** f masonry; brickwork
albaricoque m apricot
albedrío m free will; caprice
alberca f LA swimming pool
alberg|ar v/t to lodge; to put up; to shelter; **~ue** m hostel; refuge; **~ue para jóvenes** youth hostel
albóndiga f meatball
albornoz m bathrobe
alborot|adizo excitable; **~ador** agitated; riotous; **~ador** a turbulent; disorderly; m rioter; **~ar** v/t to disturb; to agitate; v/i to riot; **~o** m excitement, disturbance; uproar
alboroz|ar v/t to make merry; **~arse** to rejoice exceedingly; to exult; **~o** m merriment
álbum m album; **~ de recortes** scrapbook
albúmina f albumin
alcachofa f artichoke
alcald|e m mayor; **~ía** f mayor's office
álcali m alkali
alcan|ce m reach; pursuit; **al ~ce de** within reach or range of; **dar ~ce** to overtake; **~for** m camphor; **~tarilla** f sewer; **~zar** v/t to reach; to catch up with; LA to hand, to pass; v/i to suffice
alcaparra f caper
alcázar m fortress; citadel
alce m elk, moose
alcoba f bedroom
alcoh|ol m alcohol; **~ólico** alcoholic
Alcorán m Koran
alcornoque m cork tree
aldea f village; **~no(a)** m (f) villager
alega|ción f allegation; **~r** v/t to allege
alegoría f allegory
alegórico allegorical
alegr|ar v/t to gladden; to cheer; **~arse de** to be glad of; **~e** merry; cheerful; **~ía** f gaiety; joy
aleja|miento m removal; separation; **~r** v/t to remove; **~rse** to withdraw; to recede
alemán, alemana m, f, a German
Alemania f Germany
alenta|dor encouraging; **~r** v/t to encourage; v/i to breathe
alergia f allergy
alero m eaves; sp wing
alerta f alarm; alert; **~r** v/t to alert
aleta f small wing; zool fin, flipper
alfabeto m alphabet
alfalfa f alfalfa
alfarer|ía f pottery; **~o** m potter
alférez m second lieutenant
alfil m bishop (in chess)
alfiler m pin; **~ de seguridad** safety pin
alfombr|a f carpet; **~illa** f doormat
alforja f knapsack; saddlebag
alga f seaweed
algarabía f Arabic; fig hubbub
algazara f din, tumult
álgebra f algebra
algo pron something; adv somewhat
algodón m cotton; **~ absorbente** med cotton wool
alguacil m constable; bailiff
alguien somebody; anybody
algún some (before masculine gender nouns); **~ día** some day; **de ~ modo** somehow
algun|o(a) a some, any; **~a vez** some time; **~os días** some days; **en ~a parte** somewhere; pron somebody; pl some, some people
alhaja f jewel
alia|do(a) m (f) ally; a allied; **~nza** f alliance; **~rse** to enter into an alliance
alicates m/pl pincers; pliers
aliciente m attraction; inducement
alienar v/t to alienate
aliento m breath; **contener el ~** to hold one's breath
aligerar v/t to lighten; to shorten; to hasten
aliment|ación f food; feeding; **~ar** v/t to feed; to nourish; **~o** m food
alimenticio nourishing
alinear v/t to align
aliñar v/t to adorn; to season (food)
alisar v/t to smooth; to polish
alistar v/t to list, to enrol(l); **~se** to enlist
alivi|ar v/t to ease, to relieve; to alleviate; **~o** m relief
alma f soul; spirit
almacén m warehouse, storehouse; shop; **en ~** in store
almacen|amiento m (computer) data storage; **~ar** v/t to store; **~es** m/pl department store; **~ista** m warehouse owner
almanaque m almanac, calendar
almeja f clam
almendr|a f almond; **~o** m almond tree
alm|íbar m syrup; **~ibarado** syrupy; oversweet (t fig)
almidón m starch
almidonar v/t to starch
almirante m admiral
almizcle m musk
almohad|a f pillow; **~illa** f small cushion
almorranas f/pl hemorrhoids
alm|orzar v/i to have lunch; **~uerzo** m lunch
aloja|miento m lodging; **~r** v/t to lodge
alondra f lark
alpargata f espadrille
alp|estre Alpine; **~inista** m, f mountain climber, mountaineer; **~ino** Alpine
alpiste m bird seed
alquil|ar v/t to let, to lease; to hire out; to rent; **se ~a** to let; for rent; **~er** m rent; **de ~er** for hire
alquitrán m tar; pitch
alrededor adv around; **~ de** about; around; **~es** m/pl outskirts
alta f certificate of discharge (hospital)
altaner|ía f haughtiness; **~o** haughty; arrogant
altar m altar; **~ mayor** high altar
altavoz m loudspeaker; amplifier
altera|ción f alteration; disturbance; **~r** v/t to alter; to disturb; **~rse** to grow angry; to become upset
alterca|do m argument, altercation; **~r** v/i to dispute; to quarrel
altern|ar v/t, v/i to alternate; **~ativa** f alternative; option; **~o** alternate; elec alternating
alt|eza f height; **2eza** Highness (title); **~ibajos** m/pl ups and downs (of fortune); **~itud** f height; altitude; **~ivo** haughty; **~o** a high; tall; eminent; loud; **¡~o!** stop; **en lo ~o** at the top; **~as horas** small hours; **pasar por ~o** to overlook; to disregard; adv high; loud; loudly; **~oparlante** m LA loudspeaker; **~ura** f height; altitude; **estar a la ~ura de** to be equal to
alubia f French bean
alucina|ción f hallucination; **~r** v/t to hallucinate; to delude
alud m avalanche
aludir v/i to allude; to refer
alumbra|do m lighting; **~miento** m illumination; childbirth; **~r** v/t to light; to illuminate; to give birth to
aluminio m aluminium
alumno(a) m (f) pupil; student
aluniza|je m lunar landing; **~r** v/i to land on the moon
alusi|ón f allusion; reference; **~vo** allusive
alza f rise; **~da** f height (of horse); appeal (to a higher tribunal); **~do** raised, elevated; LA insolent; **~miento** m lifting; rising, rebellion; **~r** v/t to raise; to lift; **~rse** to go fraudulently bankrupt; to rise in rebellion; **~rse con** to steal, to make off with
allá there; over there; **más ~**

further on; **más ~ de** beyond
allana|miento m levelling; **~r** v/t to level; to flatten; to overcome; **~rse** to level out; fig to acquiesce
allegar v/t to collect; to gather together
allí there; **por ~** around there
ama f mistress (of the house); nurse; **~ de casa** housewife; **~ de cría** or **de leche** wet nurse; **~ de llaves** housekeeper
amab|ilidad f kindness; affability; **~le** nice; amiable; kind
amaestrar v/t to train; to coach; to break in (horses)
amainar v/t mar to shorten (sails); to calm; v/i to subside
amanecer m dawn; daybreak; v/i to dawn; to wake up
amansar v/t to tame
amante m, f lover
amañ|ar v/t to do cleverly; **~arse** to be expert; **~o** m cleverness; pl tools
amapola f poppy
amar v/t to love
amarar v/i aer to land on water
amarg|ar v/t to make bitter; to embitter; v/i to be bitter; **~o** bitter; harsh; **~ura** f bitterness
amarill|ento yellowish; **~o** yellow
amarra f mar cable; pl moorings; **~r** v/t to fasten; to moor
amas|ar v/t to knead; to massage; **~ijo** m kneading
amatista f amethyst
Amazonas m Amazon
ámbar m amber
ambición f ambition
ambicioso ambitious
ambiente m atmosphere; setting; **medio ~** environment
ambigüedad f ambiguity
ambiguo ambiguous
ámbito m bounds; area; ambit
ambos(as) both
ambulan|cia f ambulance; **~te** ambulant; **vendedor ~te** peddler
amenaza f threat; **~r** v/t to threaten
amenguar v/t to diminish
amen|idad f amenity; pleasantness; **~o** pleasant; light
América f America; **~ del Norte** North America; **~ Latina** Latin America
americana f jacket
americano(a) m (f), a American
amerizaje m splashdown
ametralladora f machine gun
amianto m asbestos
amiga f friend; mistress; **~bilidad** f friendliness; **~ble** friendly
amígdala f tonsil
amig|dalitis f tonsilitis; **~o** m friend, lover
aminorar v/t to reduce
amist|ad f friendship; **~arse** to become friends; **~oso** friendly
amnistía f amnesty
amnistiar v/t to grant an amnesty to
amo m master; owner; employer
amoladera f grindstone
amoldar v/t to mo(u)ld; to fashion
amonesta|ción f admonition; **~ciones** pl banns; **~r** v/t to admonish, to warn
amoníaco m ammonia
amontonar v/t to heap; to pile up
amor m love; **¡por el ~ de Dios!** for God's sake!; **~ propio** self-respect
amoral amoral
amorío m love affair
amortigua|dor m damper; **~dor de choque** shock absorber; muffler; **~r** v/t to cushion; to dampen; to muffle
amortiza|ción f amortization; **~r** v/t to pay off; to refund
ampar|ar v/t to protect; **~o** m protection; shelter
ampli|ación f amplification; extension; enlargement; **~ar** v/t to amplify; to extend; to enlarge; **~o** ample; extensive; **~tud** f amplitude; extent
ampolla f blister; bubble
amuebla|do furnished; **~r** v/t to furnish
ánade m, f duck
anadear v/i to waddle
analfabeto illiterate
análisis m or f analysis
analítico analytic
ananás m pineapple
anaquel m shelf
anarquía f anarchy
anárquico anarchistic
anatomía f anatomy
anca f rump (of horse), haunch
anciano(a) m (f) old man, old woman
ancla f anchor
anclar v/i to anchor
anch|o wide; **~oa** f anchovy; **~ura** f width; breadth
andaluz(a) m (f), a Andalusian
andamio m scaffold(ing)
anda|nte walking; errant; **~nza** f event; fortune; **~r** v/i to walk; to move; **~r a gatas** to go on all fours; **~r a tientas** to grope in the dark; **~r** m gait; **~s** f/pl stretcher; bier
andén m fc platform
andrajo m rag, tatter; pl rags, tatters
anejo m annex; a annexed
anex|ar v/t to annex; **~o** m annex, extension
anfitrión m host
ángel m angel; **~ de la guarda** guardian angel
angélico angelic
angina f angina; **~ de pecho** angina pectoris
angosto narrow
anguila f eel
ángulo m angle; **~ recto** right angle
angustia f anguish; **~r** v/t to distress
anhel|ar v/t, v/i to long for; to yearn; to breathe hard; **~o** m longing
anillo m ring; **~ de boda** wedding ring
ánima f soul
anim|ación f cheerfulness; **~ado** lively, cheerful; **~al** m animal; **~ar** v/t to animate; to encourage; **~arse** to cheer up; to revive
ánimo m spirit; courage; **¡~!** cheer up!
animos|idad f animosity; nerve; **~o** brave; spirited
aniquilar v/t to annihilate
anís m anise; aniseed
aniversario m anniversary
ano m anus
anoche last night; **~cer** v/i to grow dark; m nightfall; dusk
anomalía f anomaly
anómalo anomalous
anonimidad f anonymity
anónimo anonymous
anotar v/t to annotate; to jot down
ansi|a f anxiety; tension; yearning; **~ar** v/t to long for; **~edad** f anxiety; **~oso** anxious; eager
antagonis|mo m antagonism; **~ta** m, f antagonist
antaño last year; long ago
antártico antarctic
ante m elk; buckskin; suède leather
ante prep before; in view of; at; in the presence of; **~ todo** first of all
ante|anoche the night before last; **~ayer** the day before yesterday
antebrazo m forearm
antecede|nte a, m antecedent; **~ntes** m/pl background; **~r** v/t to precede
antecesor(a) m (f) predecessor
antedicho aforesaid
antelación f priority; precedence; **con ~** in advance
antemano: de ~ beforehand
antena f antenna; aerial
anteojos m/pl spectacles, eyeglasses
antepasados m/pl ancestors
antepecho m railing; parapet
anteponer v/t to put before
anterior former, previous; **~idad** f anteriority; priority; **con ~idad** beforehand
antes adv before; rather; sooner; **cuanto ~** as soon as possible; conj **~ bien** on the contrary; **~ de que** before
antesala f vestibule, lobby
antibiótico m antibiotic
anticipa|ción f anticipation; **con ~ción** in advance; **~r** v/t to anticipate; to advance; **~rse (a)** to take place early
anticonceptivo m contraceptive
anticua|do antiquated; obsolete; old-fashioned; **~rio** m antiquarian
antideslizante non-skid
antifaz m mask
antig|ualla f ancient relic; **~üedad** f antiquity; **~uo** ancient; antique; former; **2uo Testamento** Old Testament; **~uos** m/pl the ancients
antílope m antelope
antipático disagreeable, not nice
antirreflejo nonreflecting
antisocial antisocial
antítesis f antithesis
antoj|arse to fancy; **~o** m whim; caprice; craving
antorcha f torch
antropofagía f cannibalism
antropófago(a) m (f), a cannibal
anua|l annual; **~lidad** f annual income; annuity; **~rio** m yearbook
anublar v/t to cloud; to darken
anudar v/t to join; to knot together
anula|ción f annul(l)ment; **~r** v/t to annul(l)
anunci|ar v/t to announce; **~o** m announcement; advertisement
anzuelo m fishhook; **tragar el ~** to swallow the bait
añadi|dura f addition; **por ~** in addition; into the bargain; **~r** v/t to add
añejo old; stale; (wine) vintage
añicos m/pl small pieces
añil m indigo plant; indigo blue
año m year; **~ bisiesto** leap year; **¡Feliz 2 Nuevo!** Happy New Year!
añora|nza f longing; nostalgia; **~r** v/t to long for; to grieve for
apacentar v/t to feed (cattle); to pasture
apacib|ilidad f gentleness; **~le** gentle; placid, peaceful
apacigua|miento m appeasement; **~r** v/t to appease; to pacify
apadrinar v/t to act as godfather to; to support
apaga|do listless; dull; faded; **~r** v/t to blow out; to extinguish; to put out; to turn off; to quench (thirst); **~rse** to go out; to die down
apagón m blackout, power cut
apalear v/t to beat; to winnow
apaña|do skil(l)ful; suitable; **~dor** m sp catcher; **~r** v/t to seize; to grasp; **~rse** v/t to know the ropes; to get on
apara|dor m sideboard; **~to** m apparatus; set (radio); **~toso** ostentatious, showy
aparcamiento m parking lot
aparcar v/t, v/i to park
aparcería f sharecropping
aparear v/t to match, to level up
aparecer v/i to appear
aparej|ar v/t to prepare; to equip; **~o** m equipment; mar tackle; **~os** pl tools, gear
aparentar v/t to feign; to pretend; to seem to be
apari|ción f appearance; apparition; **~encia** f aspect; semblance
apartad|ero m fc siding; aut lay-by; road side; **~o** m post office box; a remote; distant
apartamento m flat, apartment
apart|ar v/t to separate; to remove; **~arse** to withdraw; **~e** m teat aside; paragraph; adv apart; at a distance; **~e de** except for, apart from
apasiona|do passionate; **~miento** m enthusiasm; **~r** v/t to impassion; to excite; **~rse por** to become devoted to
apatía f apathy
apea|dero m halt; stop; **~r** v/t to dismount
apeg|arse to become attached to; **~o** m affection; attachment
apela|ción f appeal; **~r** v/i to appeal; to have recourse
apellid|ar v/t to name; **~arse** to be called; **~o** m surname, last name
apenarse to grieve
apenas scarcely; hardly; barely
apéndice m appendix
apendicitis f appendicitis
apercibi|miento m preparation; provision; for summons; **~r** v/t to provide; to prepare
aperitivo m apéritif; appetizer
aperos m/pl implements, tools
apertura f opening
apestar v/t to infect with the plague; fam to annoy; to pester; v/i to stink
apet|ecer v/t to desire; to long for; **~ito** m appetite
ápice m apex, pinnacle
apicultor m beekeeper
apiñar v/t to press together
apio m celery
apisona|dora f steamroller; **~r** v/t to roll flat
aplacar v/t to placate
aplacer v/t, v/i to please
aplanar v/t to level; to flatten
aplastar v/t to crush; to squash
aplau|dir v/t to applaud; **~so** m applause
aplazar v/t to postpone; to adjourn
aplica|ción f application; **~r** v/t to apply; **~rse** to apply oneself
aplom|ar v/i to plumb; **~arse** to collapse; **~o** m aplomb; seriousness
apod|ar v/t to nickname; **~erado** m attorney, agent; representative; **~erar** v/t to empower; **~o** m nickname
apogeo m apogee
apología f defence; eulogy
apoplejía f apoplexy
aporrear v/t to beat (up); to thump (on)
aporta|ción f contribution; **~r** v/t to bring; to contribute
aposent|ar v/t to lodge; **~o** m room; lodging
apostar v/t to bet, to wager
apóstol m apostle
apóstrofo m gram apostrophe
apoy|ar v/t to support; to base; v/i to rest, to lean; **~arse** to lean; to rest; **~o** m prop; support
apreci|able appreciable; considerable; **~ación** f valuation; **~ar** v/t to estimate; to value; **~o** m esteem; estimation; valuation
aprehen|der v/t to apprehend; fig to understand; **~sión** f apprehension
apremi|ante urgent; **~ar** v/t to urge, to hurry; **~o** m urgency; pressure
aprend|er v/t to learn; **~iz** m apprentice; **~izaje** m apprenticeship
aprens|ión f fear; distrust; **~ivo** apprehensive; fearful
apresar v/t to capture; to seize
aprest|ar v/t to prepare; to make ready; **~o** m preparation
apresura|do hurried, hasty; **~r** v/t to hasten; **~rse** to make haste
apretado difficult; tightly-packed
apret|ar v/t to clasp; to press, to tighten; to harass; **~ón** m pressure; squeeze; **~ón de manos** handshake
aprieto m crush; fix; difficulty
aprisco m corral, fold
aprisionar v/t to imprison
aproba|ción f approval; **~r** v/t to approve of; to pass
apropia|ción f appropriation; **~do** appropriate; **~r** v/t to apply; to adapt; LA to appropriate; **~rse de** to take possession of
aprovecha|ble useful; **~do** economical; **~miento** m advantage; use; **~r** v/t to utilize; to take advantage of; v/i to be of use; to make progress; **~rse de** to avail oneself of
aproxima|ción f approximation; approach; **~damente** approximately; **~do** approximate; **~r** v/t, **~rse** to approach; to come near
apt|itud f aptitude; ability; **~o** apt; capable; qualified
apuesta f bet, wager
apunt|alar v/t to prop, to brace; **~ar** v/t to aim; to point at; to note down; teat to prompt; **~e** m note, notation; teat prompter; cue
apuñalar v/t to stab
apur|adamente hastily; **~ado** needy; **~ar** v/t to purify; to exhaust; LA to hurry; **~arse** to worry; to fret; **~o** m plight, need; hardship; LA haste
aquejar v/t to afflict; to ail
aquel(la), pl **aquellos(as)** a that; pl those; **aquél(la)**, pl

aquéllos(as) *pron m, f* he, she; *pl* those
aquí here; now; ~ **mismo** right here; **por** ~ (**cerca**) round here
aquiescencia *f* acquiescence; consent
aquietar *v/t* to soothe
árabe *m, a* Arab(ic)
arada *f* ploughed ground
arado *m* plough
arancel *m* tariff
arándano *m* bilberry; ~ **agrio** cranberry
araña *f* spider; ~ **de luces** chandelier
araña\|r *v/t* to scratch; **~zo** *m* scratch
arar *v/t* to plough
arbitr\|ar *v/t* to arbitrate; *sp* to referee; **~ariedad** *f* arbitrariness; **~ario** arbitrary; **~io** *m* free will
árbitro *m* umpire, referee
árbol *m* tree; *mar* mast; *tecn* arbor; shaft; ~ **de Navidad** Christmas tree
arbol\|ado *m* woodland; *a* wooded; **~eda** *f* grove
arbusto *m* shrub
arca *f* chest; ark
arcada *f* arcade
arcaico archaic
arce *m* maple tree
arcilla *f* clay
arco *m* arc; arch; bow; ~ **iris** rainbow
archiduque *m* archduke; **~sa** *f* archduchess
archipiélago *m* archipelago
archiv\|ador *m* file cabinet; **~ar** *v/t* to file; **~o** *m* register; filing department; records
arder *v/i* to burn
ardid *m* stratagem; trick
ardiente burning; ardent
ardilla *f* squirrel; ~ **listada** chipmunk; ~ **de tierra** gopher
ardor *m* ardo(u)r; heat; courage
arduo arduous; hard, tough
área *f* area; ~ **de descanso** rest area; ~ **de servicio** service area
arena *f* sand; ~ **movediza** quicksand; **~l** *m* sandy ground; pit
arenga *f* harangue; **~r** *v/i* to harangue
arenisca *f* sandstone
arenque *m* herring
arete *m* earring
argamasa *f* mortar
argénteo silver(y); silver-plated
Argentina *f* Argentina
argentino(a) *a, m (f)* Argentinian; *a* silvery
argolla *f* (large) ring; tie, bond; *sp* croquet
argüir *v/i* to discuss; to dispute
argumento *m* argument; *teat* plot
aridez *f* drought; barrenness
árido dry; barren; arid
ariete *m* (battering) ram
arisco rude; snappish; surly
aristocracia *f* aristocracy
aristócrata *m, f* aristocrat
aristocrático(a) aristocratic
aritmética *f* arithmetic
arma *f* weapon; arm; ~ **de fuego** firearm; **~da** *f* navy; **~dor** *m* shipowner; **~dura** *f* armo(u)r; framework; **~mento** *m* armament; **~r** *v/t* to arm; to assemble; to cause; to arrange
armario *m* wardrobe; cupboard
armazón *m or f* framework
armer\|ía *f* armo(u)ry; **~o** *m* gunsmith
armiño *m* ermine
armisticio *m* armistice
armonía *f* harmony
armónico harmonic
armonizar *v/t* to harmonize
aro *m* hoop; ring
aroma *m* aroma
aromático aromatic
aromatizar *v/t* to flavo(u)r
arpa *f* harp
arpía *f* harpy, shrew
arpón *m* harpoon
arque\|ar *v/t* to arch; to gauge (*ships*); **~o** *m* tonnage
arqueología *f* archeology
arqueólogo *m* archeologist
arquitect\|o *m* architect; **~ura** *f* architecture
arraig\|ar *v/i* to take root; **~arse** to settle; **~o** *m* settling; rooting in
arran\|car *v/t* to pull out; to root out; to start (*car, etc*); **~que** *m* sudden start; outburst (*of anger, etc*); *tecn* starter
arrasar *v/t* to level
arrastrar *v/t* to drag along; to carry away; **~e** *m* haulage
arrebat\|ar *v/t* to snatch away; to carry off; **~o** *m* transport of passion; rage
arrecife *m* causeway; *mar* reef
arregl\|ado orderly; moderate; **~ar** *v/t* to arrange; to adjust; **~arse** to turn out well; **~árselas** to manage; **~o** *m* arrangement; compromise; repair; **con ~o a** in accordance with
arremeter *v/t* to attack
arrenda\|dor *m* landlord; **~miento** *m* lease; rent; **~r** *v/t* to lease; to rent; **~tario** *m* lessee; tenant
arrepenti\|do repentant, sorry; **~miento** *m* repentance; **~rse** to repent; to regret
arrest\|ar *v/t* to arrest; **~arse** to dare; **~o** *m* detention; arrest; enterprise
arriate *m bot* bed
arriba above; over; up; high; upstairs; **cuesta ~** uphill; **de ~ abajo** from top to bottom; from beginning to end; **por la calle ~** up the street
arribar *v/i* to arrive
arriero *m* muleteer
arriesga\|do perilous; risky; **~r** *v/t* to risk; **~rse** to expose oneself to danger; to take a risk
arrimar *v/t* to place near; **~se** to come closer; to lean (*against*)
arrinconar *v/t* to corner
arroba *f* weight of 25 lbs.; **~miento** *m* ecstasy; **~r** *v/t* to enrapture
arrodillarse to kneel down
arrogan\|cia *f* arrogance; pride; **~te** arrogant; brave
arroj\|ar *v/t* to throw; to hurl, to fling; *com* to show; **~arse** to fling oneself; to rush; **~o** *m* daring
arrollar *v/t* to roll up; to sweep away; to run (*someone*) down
arropar *v/t* to wrap up; to tuck up
arroyo *m* stream; brook; gutter
arroz *m* rice; **~al** *m* ricefield
arruga *f* wrinkle; crease; **~r** *v/t* to wrinkle; to rumple; to crease
arruinar *v/t* to ruin; to destroy
arrull\|ar *v/t* to coo; to lull; **~o** *m* cooing; *mús* lullabye
arrumbar *v/t* to cast aside
arsénico *m* arsenic
arte *m or f* art; **bellas ~s** fine arts; **~facto** *m* appliance; contrivance
artejo *m* knuckle
arteria *f anat, fig* artery
artesan\|ía *f* handicraft; craftsmanship; **~o** *m* artisan; craftsman
artesonado *arq* coffered (*ceiling*)
ártico arctic
articul\|ación *f* articulation; *anat* joint; **~ar** *v/t* to articulate
artículo *m* article; ~ **de fondo** leading article; **~s** *pl* **de consumo** consumer goods
artifici\|al artificial; **~o** *m* art; skill; contrivance; **~oso** skil(l)ful; cunning; ingenious
artilugio *m* gadget
artiller\|ía *f* artillery; **~o** *m* gunner
artimaña *f* trick
artista *m, f* artist
arzobisp\|ado *m* archbishopric; **~o** *m* archbishop
as *m* ace
asa *f* handle; haft
asado *a* roasted; baked; **bien ~** well done; *m* roast meat
asalariado *m* employee, wage-earner
asalt\|ar *v/t* to attack; to storm; to break into; **~o** *m* assault
asamblea *f* assembly; meeting
asar *v/t* to roast
ascen\|dencia *f* ancestry; **~dente** *a* ascending; **~der** *v/i* to ascend; to climb; **~sión** *f* ascension; **~so** *m* promotion; **~sor** *m* lift, *Am* elevator
asceta *m* ascetic
ascético ascetic
asco *m* nausea; loathing; **dar ~** to sicken, to disgust
asear *v/t* to clean; to embellish
asechar *v/t* to ensnare; to trap; to ambush
asedio *m mil* siege; *com* run (*on a bank etc*)
asegura\|do *m* insured; *a* guaranteed; assured; **~r** *v/t* to secure; to insure; to fasten; to assure; **~rse** to verify
asenso *m* assent
asentar *v/t* to seat; to establish; to settle; *v/i* to be suitable; **~ al debe** to debit; **~ al haber** to credit
asentimiento *m* assent
asentir *v/i* to agree
aseo *m* cleanliness; *pl* toilet; rest rooms
asequible accessible, attainable; available
aserradero *m* sawmill
aserrar *v/t* to saw
asesin\|ar *v/t* to murder; *pol* to assassinate; **~ato** *m* murder; *pol* assassination
asesor\|(a) *m (f)* consultant; legal adviser; **~ar** *v/t* to give legal advice to, to counsel
asestar *v/t* to aim; to point; to deal (*a blow*)
aseverar *v/t* to assert
asfalto *m* asphalt
asfixiar *v/t* to asphyxiate; to suffocate
así *adv* so; thus; therefore; **~, ~** so so; **~ como** the same as; **~ como también** as well as
Asia *f* Asia; ~ **Menor** Asia Minor
asiduo assiduous
asiento *m* chair; seat; site; bottom; ~ **delantero** front seat; **tomar ~** to take a seat
asigna\|ción *f* assignment; allotment; **~r** *v/t* to assign; to ascribe; **~tura** *f* course of study; **aprobar, suspender una ~tura** to pass, to fail a school subject
asilo *m* asylum; refuge
asimilar *v/t* to assimilate
asimismo likewise
asir *v/t* to seize; to grasp
asist\|encia *f* attendance, presence; assistance; *pl* allowance; **~ente** *m* assistant; **~ir** *v/t* to help; to attend to; to serve; *v/i* to attend; to be present
asma *f* asthma
asno *m* ass
asocia\|ción *f* association; fellowship; partnership; **~do** *m* associate; partner; **~r** *v/t* to associate; **~rse** to join; to form a partnership
asolar *v/t* to destroy; to lay waste
asomar *v/t* to show; to stick out; **~se** to appear, to show (up)
asombr\|ar *v/t* to surprise; to astonish; **~arse** to be astonished; **~o** *m* astonishment; amazement
aspa *f* cross; reel; vane of windmill
aspecto *m* aspect; look; appearance
aspereza *f* acerbity; roughness
áspero rough, rugged; harsh; severe
aspiradora *f* vacuum cleaner
aspirina *f* aspirin
asque\|ar *v/t* to disgust, to revolt; **~roso** disgusting, revolting; foul
asta *f* lance; shaft; horn (*of the bull*); ~ **de bandera** flagpole
asterisco *m* asterisk
astil *m* handle
astill\|a *f* splinter; **~ar** *v/t* to splinter; to chip; **~ero** *m* shipyard
astring\|ente *m, a* astringent; **~ir** *v/t* to astringe; to compress; *fig* to bind
astro *m* star; **~logía** *f* astrology
astrólogo *m* astrologer
astro\|nauta *m* astronaut; **~nave** *f* spaceship
astronomía *f* astronomy
astrónomo *m* astronomer
astu\|cia *f* shrewdness; cleverness; **~to** astute; shrewd; cunning
asu\|mir *v/t* to assume; to take upon oneself; **~nción** *f* assumption
asunto subject; matter; business
asusta\|dizo easily frightened; **~r** *v/t* to frighten; to scare
atabal *m* kettledrum
ata\|car *v/t* to attack; **~do** *m* bundle; *a* bashful; **~dura** *f* tying; bond; **~jo** *m* shortcut; **~laya** *f* lookout, watchtower; **~que** *m* attack; **~que aéreo** air raid
atar *v/t* to bind; to fasten; to tie (up)
atareado busy; occupied
atasc\|ar *v/t* to stop up; to obstruct; **~arse** to jam; to get stuck; **~o** *m* obstruction; traffic jam
ataúd *m* coffin
ataviar *v/t* to dress up; to adorn
ateísmo *m* atheism
atemorizar *v/t* to terrify
atención *f* attention; *pl* duties, responsibilities; courtesies
atender *v/i* to attend; to pay attention to; to look after
atenerse: ~ **a** to abide by; to rely on
atenta\|do *m* criminal assault; *a* discreet; **~r** *v/t* to attempt (*a crime*)
atento thoughtful; attentive
atenua\|ción *f* attenuation; **~r** *v/t* to attenuate
ateo(a) *m (f)* atheist; *a* atheistic
aterrar *v/t* to destroy; to knock down
aterriza\|je *m* landing; **~je forzoso** *aer* emergency landing, forced landing; **~r** *v/i* to land
aterrorizar *v/t* to terrorize; to terrify
atesorar *v/t* to treasure, to hoard
atesta\|ción *f* attestation; **~dos** *m/pl for* affidavit; **~r** *v/t* to cram; to crowd; to witness; to testify
atestigua\|ción *f* testimony; **~r** *v/t* to testify, to give evidence of
ático *m* attic
atisbar *v/t* to spy on; to peep at
atizar *v/t* to poke; to trim; to rouse
atlántico Atlantic
at\|leta *m, f* athlete; **~lético** athletic; **~letismo** *m* athletics
atmósfera *f* atmosphere
atmosférico atmospheric
atolondrar *v/t* to confuse; to perplex; **~se** to become bewildered
atolla\|dero *m* obstacle; difficulty; mire; **~r** *v/i* to fall into the mire; to get stuck
atómico atomic
átomo *m* atom
atónito stupefied, dumbfounded
atonta\|do foolish; dim-witted; **~r** *v/t* to stun; to confound; **~rse** to grow stupid
atormentar *v/t* to torment
atornillar *v/t* to screw
atrac\|ador *m* gangster; hold-up man; **~ar** *v/t* to attack, to hold up
atrac\|ción *f* attraction; **~o** *m* hold-up, robbery; **~tivo** attractive
atraer *v/t* to attract; to lure
atrancar *v/t* to obstruct; to bar
atrapar *v/t* to catch; to take in
atrás backward; behind; **¡~!** get back!
atras\|ar *v/t* to slow up; to slow down; **~arse** to be late; to go slow (*watch*); **~o** *m* backwardness; delay; *pl* arrears
atravesar *v/t* to place across; to run through; to cross, to go across; **~se** to interrupt; to interfere
atreverse to dare
atrevi\|do bold; audacious; **~miento** *m* boldness, insolence
atribu\|ir *v/t* to ascribe; to attribute; **~to** *m* attribute
atril *m* music stand; lectern
atrocidad *f* atrocity; excess
atrofia *f* atrophy
atropell\|ar *v/t* to hit; to knock down; to run over; **~o** *m* accident; outrage
atroz atrocious; heinous
atuendo *m* dress, attire
atún *m* tuna
aturdi\|do giddy; distracted; **~r** *v/t* to perplex; to stun
auda\|cia *f* audacity; boldness; **~z** audacious
audición *f* hearing; audition
audi\|encia *f* audience; hearing; reception; **~tor** *m* judge; *com* auditor
auge *m* peak; apogee; popularity
augur\|ar *v/t* to augur; to predict; **~io** *m* omen
aula *f* lecture room; classroom
aull\|ar *v/i* to howl; **~ido** *m* howl

aument|ar *v/t, v/i* to raise; to increase; to augment; **~o** *m* increase
aun *adv* even; yet; although; ~ cuando even if
aún *adv* yet; still; as yet; ~ no not yet
aunque *conj* even though; although
aura *f* gentle breeze
áureo golden
aureola *f* halo
auricular *m* telephone receiver; *pl* earphones, headphones
ausen|cia *f* absence; **~te** absent
austero austere
austral southern; **2ia** *f* Australia; **~iano(a)** *m (f), a* Australian
Austria *f* Austria
austríaco(a) *m (f), a* Austrian
auténtico authentic
auto *m* sentence; edict; *pl* record of proceedings
auto *m* motorcar
auto|bús *m* bus; **~car** *m* coach; **~enfoque** *m foto* automatic focus; **~escuela** *f* driving school; **~mático** automatic; **~matización** *f* automation; **~motor** *m* Diesel train; **~móvil** *m* automobile; **~movilista** *m* motorist; **~nomía** *f* autonomy; home rule; **~pista** *f* motorway
autopsia *f* autopsy
autor *m* author
autoridad *f* authority
autoritario authoritarian
autorizar *v/t* to authorize
autorretrato *m* self-portrait
autoservicio *m* self-service
autostop *m* hitch-hiking; **~ista** *m, f* hitch-hiker
auxili|ar *a* auxiliary; *v/t* to help; **~o** *m* assistance; primeros ~os *pl* first aid
avaluar *v/t* to value; to appraise
avan|ce *m* advance; attack; **~zar** *v/t, v/i* to advance; to move forward
avar|icia *f* avarice; **~iento** avaricious; greedy; **~o** *a* miserly; mean; *m* miser
avasallar *v/t* to subdue
Avda. = avenida
ave *f* bird; ~ de paso bird of passage; ~ de rapiña bird of prey; ~s *pl* de corral poultry
avellan|a *f* hazelnut; **~arse** to shrivel; **~o** *m* hazelnut tree
avena *f* oat(s)
avenencia *f* agreement
avenida *f* avenue
avenirse a to agree to
aventajado advantageous; outstanding
aventajar *v/t* to surpass; to advance
aventur|a *f* adventure; **~ero(a)** *m (f)* adventurer, adventuress
avergonzar *v/t* to shame; **~se** to be ashamed
avería *f* damage; *tecn* breakdown
averiarse to suffer damage
averiguar *v/t* to find out, to ascertain; to inquire into
avestruz *m* ostrich
avia|ción *f* aviation; **~dor** *m* aviator; pilot; airman
aviar *v/t* to provide; to make ready; *LA* to lend
avidez *f* avidity; covetousness
ávido avid; covetous; eager
avión *m* aeroplane, *Am* airplane; ~ de reacción jet-propelled aircraft; por ~ by airmail
avíos *m/pl* tackle; kit
avis|ar *v/t* to advise; to announce; to inform; **~o** *m* notice; advice
avisp|a *f* wasp; **~ón** *m* hornet
avivar *v/t* to animate
¡ay! oh!; alas!
ayer yesterday
ayuda *f* help; **~nte** *m* assistant; **~r** *v/t* to help; to aid
ayuno *m* fast; en ~ fasting
ayuntamiento *m* town hall, city hall
azabache *m min* jet
azada *f* hoe
azafata *f* air hostess, stewardess
azafrán *m* saffron
azahar *m* orange blossom
azar *m* hazard; risk; al ~ at random; por ~ by chance
azot|ar *v/t* to whip; to thrash; to beat; **~e** *m* whip; lashing
azotea *f* flat roof
azteca *m, f, a* Aztec
azúcar *m* sugar
azucena *f* white lily
azufre *m* sulphur
azul blue; ~ celeste sky blue; ~ marino navy blue
azulejo *m* glazed tile
azuzar *v/t* to incite; to sic (*dogs*)

B

bab|a *f* spittle; saliva; **~aza** *f* slime; **~ear** *v/i* to slobber; **~ero** *m* bib
babor *m mar* port side
babosa *f zool* slug
baboso slimy; drooling
baca *f* luggage carrier (*on car roof*)
bacalao *m* cod
bacteria *f* bacterium
báculo *m* walking stick
bache *m* hole, pothole; rut
bachiller|(a) *m (f)* holder of a bachelor's degree; **~ato** *m* baccalaureate; **~ear** *v/i* to babble
bagaje *m mil* baggage
bahía *f* bay
bailar *v/i, v/t* to dance; **~ín** (**~ina**) *m (f)* dancer
baile *m* dance; ~ de sociedad ballroom dance
baja *f* fall; casualty; dar de ~ *mil* to discharge; **~da** *f* descent
baja|mar *f* low tide; **~r** *v/t* to lower; to take down; *v/i* to fall; to descend; to go down
baj|eza *f* meanness; **~ista** *m* bear (*at the stock exchange*); **~o** *a* low; short (*person*); *m mús* bass; *adv* down; below; *prep* under
bala *f* bullet; *com* bale
balada *f* ballad
baladí frivolous; trivial
balance *m* oscillation; rocking; swinging; *com* balance sheet; **~ar** *v/t* to balance; *v/i* to roll (*ship*); to sway; to waver
balancín *m* balance beam; seesaw
balanza *f* scales; balance
balar *v/i* to bleat
balazo *m* shot
balbucear *v/i* to stammer; to stutter; to babble (*baby*)
balcón *m* balcony
balde *m* bucket; de ~ gratis; free of charge; en ~ in vain; **~ar** *v/t, v/i* to wash, to flush (down)
baldío *m* waste land
baldosa *f* tile (*on floors*)
Baleares *f/pl* Balearic Isles
balística *f* ballistics
baliza *f mar* (lighted) buoy
balneario *m* spa; health resort
balón *m* ball; football
balon|cesto *m* basketball; **~mano** *m* handball
balsa *f* pool; *mar* raft; *bot* balsa wood
bálsamo *m* balsam, balm
báltico Baltic
baluarte *m* bulwark
ballena *f* whale
ballesta *f* crossbow; spring
ballet *m* ballet
bambolearse to sway
bambú *m* bamboo
banan|a *f LA* banana (tree); **~o** *m LA* banana (tree)
ban|ca *f* bench; banking; **~cario** banking; **~carrota** *f* bankruptcy; **~co** *m* bench; bank; ~co de ahorros savings bank
banda *f* sash; band; gang; **~da** *f* flock (*of birds*)
bandeja *f* tray
bandera *f* flag; banner
bandido *m* bandit
bando *m* edict; faction; party; *pl* marriage banns; **~lero** *m* bandit, brigand; **~lerismo** *m* highway robbery
banque|ro *m* banker; **~te** *m* banquet
banquillo *m* footstool; *for* dock
bañ|ador *m* bathing suit; **~arse** to take a bath; to swim (*in the sea*); **~era** *f* bathtub; **~o** *m* bath; bathroom; ~o espumoso bubble bath
baque *m* thud, thump
baqueta *f* ramrod; *pl* drumsticks
bar *m* bar; snackbar
baraja *f* pack of cards; **~r** *v/t* to shuffle (*cards*)
barandilla *f* railing
barat|ear *v/t* to sell cheap; **~ija** *f* trifle; **~o** cheap
barba *f* beard; chin
barbari|dad *f* barbarity; outrage; una ~dad an enormous amount; **~e** *f* barbarism; cruelty
bárbaro(a) *m (f)* barbarian; *a* barbarous
barbecho *m* fallow (land)
barbero *m* barber
barbilla *f* chin
barbotar *v/i* to mumble
barbudo bearded
barca *f* boat; ~ de pedales pedal boat; **~za** *f* lighter
barco *m* boat; ship; vessel; ~ de vela sailing ship
bardar *v/t* to thatch
barítono *m* baritone
barlovento: de ~ *mar* windward
barniz *m* varnish; glaze
barnizar *v/t* to varnish; to glaze
barométrico barometric
barómetro *m* barometer
barquero *m* ferryman; boatman
barquillo *m* wafer; cone (*for ice cream, etc*)
barra *f* bar (*of soap*); loaf (*of bread*)
barraca *f* hut
barranc|a *f* precipice; ravine; gully; **~o** *m* gully; *fig* difficulty
barre|dero sweeping; dragging; **~duras** *f/pl* sweepings
barrena *f* drill; auger
barrendero *m* street cleaner
barrer *v/t* to sweep
barrera *f* barrier; ~ sónica sound barrier
barriada *f* district; suburb; *LA* slum
barricada *f* barricade
barriga *f* paunch, belly
barril *m* barrel
barrio *m* district; quarter; part of a town; ~ bajo poor neighbo(u)rhood; slum
barro *m* mud; clay
barroco baroque
barroso muddy; pimply
bártulos *m/pl* belongings; implements
barullo *m* confusion; noise
bas|ar *v/t* to base; to found; **~arse en** to base one's opinion on; **~e** *f* basis; base; ~e de datos data base
básico basic
¡basta! enough!
bastante *a* enough; *LA* too much; *adv* enough; rather
bastidor *m* frame; *teat* wing
basto *a* coarse; gross; *m* packsaddle; ace of clubs; *pl* clubs (*cards*)
bastón *m* walking stick; cane
basur|a *f* rubbish; waste; **~ero** *m* dustman; garbage collector
bata *f* dressing gown; smock; housecoat
batall|a *f* battle; **~ar** *v/i* to fight; **~ón** *m* batallion
batata *f* sweet potato
bate *m* bat; **~ador** *m sp* batter
batería *f* battery; *mús* percussion instruments; ~ de cocina pots and pans
bati|do *m* **de leche** milkshake; **~dora** *f* whisk; mixer; **~r** *v/t* to beat; to strike; to whip; to whisk
batista *f* cambric
batuta *f* baton; llevar la ~ to be in command
baúl *m* trunk
bauti|smo *m* baptism; christening; **~zar** *v/t* to baptize; to christen; **~zo** *m* baptism, christening
baya *f* berry
bayeta *f* baize
bayo bay (*colour*)
bayoneta *f* bayonet
baza *f* trick (*at cards*)
bazar *m* bazaar
bazo *m anat* spleen
beat|a *f* devout woman; lay sister; **~ificar** *v/t* to beatify; **~itud** *f* blessedness; holiness; **~o** *a* happy; blessed; *m* lay brother
bebé *m* baby
bebedero *m* drinking trough; *a* drinkable
bebedizo drinkable
beb|edor *m* heavy drinker; **~er** *v/t, v/i* to drink; **~ida** *f* drink; beverage; **~ido** tipsy, half-drunk
beca *f* scholarship
becerro *m* yearling calf
bedel *m* beadle; warden
befar *v/t* to mock; to scoff
béisbol *m* baseball
beldad *f* beauty
Belén *m* Bethlehem; 2 Christmas crib; 2 *fig* bedlam
belga *m, f, a* Belgian
Bélgica *f* Belgium
bélico bellicose; warlike
beli|coso warlike; quarrelsome; **~gerancia** *f* belligerence
bell|eza *f* beauty; **~o** beautiful
bellota *f* acorn
bemol *m mús* flat
bencina *f* benzine
bend|ecir *v/t* to bless; **~ición** *f* blessing; **~ito** blessed; happy
benefic|encia *f* beneficence; **~iar** *v/t* to benefit; **~iarse** to derive benefit; to profit; **~io** *m* benefit
benemérito worthy, meritorious
benevolencia *f* benevolence; kindness
benign|idad *f* benignity; **~o** benign; mild
beodo *a, m* drunk
berberecho *m* cockle
berenjena *f* eggplant
bermejo bright red
berrear *v/i* to low; to bellow
berrinche *m fam* anger; rage
berro *m* watercress
berza *f* cabbage
bes|ar *v/t* to kiss; ~ar la mano, ~ar los pies pay one's respects to; **~o** *m* kiss
bestia *f* beast; **~l** beastly; *fam* terrific; **~lidad** *f* bestiality
besugo *m* sea bream
betún *m* bitumen; shoe polish
biberón *m* baby bottle
Biblia *f* Bible
bíblico biblical
biblioteca *f* library; **~rio** *m* librarian
bicicleta *f* bicycle
bicho *m* insect, bug; *pl* vermin; animal
bidón *m* steel drum; large can
biela *f* connecting rod
bien *adv* well; right; certainly; very; surely; más ~ rather; o ~ or else; *m* good; property; *pl* assets; ~es raíces real estate
bienaventura|do lucky; fortunate; blessed (*in Heaven*); **~nza** *f* bliss
bienestar *m* well-being; welfare
bienhechor(a) *m (f)* benefactor(-tress)
bienio *m* space of two years
bienvenida *f* welcome; dar la ~ to welcome
bifurca|ción *f* fork (*in road*); junction; **~rse** to branch off, to fork
bigamia *f* bigamy
bigote *m* moustache
bilingüe bilingual
bili|oso bilious; **~s** *f* bile
billar *m* billiards
billete *m* banknote; ticket; ~ de ida y vuelta return ticket, *Am* round trip ticket; ~ de temporada season ticket; ~ directo through ticket; ~ sencillo single ticket, *Am* one-way ticket; no hay ~s sold out; **~ro** *m* wallet; *t Am* billfold
billón *m* billion
bimotor *m* twin-engined plane
biografía *f* biography
biógrafo *m* biographer
biología *f* biology
biológico biological
biombo *m* folding screen
birrete *m* cap
bisabuel|a *f* great-grandmother; **~o** *m* great-grandfather; **~os** *m/pl* great-grandparents
bisagra *f* hinge
bisel *m* bevel
bisemanal twice-weekly
bisiesto leap (*year*)
bisniet|a *f* great-granddaughter; **~o** *m* great-grandson
bisonte *m* bison
bistec *m* (beef)steak
bisutería *f* costume jewelry
bizantino Byzantine
bizarro spirited; gallant; magnanimous
bizc|ar *v/i* to squint; to look cross-eyed; **~o** cross-eyed
bizcocho *m* biscuit; sponge-cake
blanc|o *a* white; *m* white man; target; dar en el ~o to hit the mark; en ~o blank; **~ura** *f* whiteness
blandir *v/t* to brandish
bland|o soft; mild; tender; flabby; **~ura** *f* softness; flattery
blanque|ar *v/t* to bleach; to whiten; **~o** *m* bleaching; whitewash
blasfemia *f* blasphemy
blasón *m* coat of arms; heraldry

Spanish

bledo: *no importarle a uno un ~* not to give a hoot about
blinda|je *m* armo(u)r; **~r** *v/t* to armo(u)r; *elec* to shield
bloc *m* pad (*of paper*)
bloque *m* block; **~ar** *v/t* to block up; to blockade; **~o** *m* blockade
blusa *f* blouse
bobada *f* foolishness; silly thing; foolish act
bobina *f* bobbin; spool; *elec* coil
bobo *m* simpleton; *a* stupid; foolish
boca *f* mouth; entrance; **~ *de riego*** hydrant; **~ *abajo*** face downwards; **~ *arriba*** face upwards; **~calle** *f* entrance to a street; intersection; **~dillo** *m* sandwich
bocado *m* bite; morsel; mouthful
boceto *m* sketch
bocina *f* horn; **~zo** *m* honk, hoot
bochorno *m* scorching heat; sultry weather; **~so** sultry
boda *f* wedding
bodeg|a *f* wine cellar; vault; bar; storeroom; shop; *LA* grocery; hold (*of a ship*); **~ón** *m* tavern
bofet|ada *f* slap; **~ear** *v/t* to slap in the face; to insult; **~ón** *m* blow; slap
boga *f* rowing; vogue; popularity; ***en ~*** in vogue
boicot *m* boycott; **~ear** *v/t* to boycott
boina *f* beret
bola *f* ball; marble; *pl* ballbearings; **~ *de nieve*** snowball
bole|ar *v/i* to bowl; to lie; **~ra** *f* bowling alley
bolero *m* bolero (*dance*)
bolet|a *f* admission ticket; ballot; **~ería** *f LA* ticket office; **~ín** *m* bulletin; report; **~o** *m LA* ticket
boliche *m* jack (*at bowls*); dragnet
bolígrafo *m* ball-point pen
Bolivia *f* Bolivia
boliviano(a) *m* (*f*), *a* Bolivian
bolo *m* game of ninepins
bols|a *f* bag; purse; pouch; **~a *de comercio*** stock exchange; **~a *de papel*** paper bag; **~a *de plástico*** plastic bag; **~a *del trabajo*** labo(u)r exchange; **~illo** *m* pocket; **~ista** *m* stockbroker; *LA* pickpocket; **~o** *m* purse
boll|ería *f* pastry shop; **~o** *m* small cake; bun, roll
bomb|a *f* pump; bomb; **~a *atómica*** atom bomb; **~a *de incendios*** fire engine; **~ardear** *v/t* to bomb; to bombard; **~ardero** *m* bomber plane; **~ear** *v/t mil* to shell; *LA* to fire; to dismiss; **~ero** *m* fireman
bombilla *f* light bulb
bombo *m* bass drum; *mar* lighter; ***dar ~ a*** to praise to the skies
bombón *m* sweet, *Am* candy
bonachón *m* kind person; *a* kindly; easy-going
bonaerense of *or* from Buenos Aires
bondad *f* goodness; kindness; **~oso** good; kind
bonifica|ción *f* allowance; increase; improvement; **~r** *v/t* to increase (*production*)
bonito *m* striped tunny; *a* nice; lovely; pretty
bono *m* bond; voucher
boquerón *m* large hole; opening; type of anchovy
boquete *m* gap
boquiabierto gaping; open-mouthed
boquilla *f mús* mouthpiece; cigarette holder
borbollar *v/i* to bubble
borbotar *v/i* to gush; to boil; to bubble up
borda|do *m* embroidery; **~r** *v/t* to embroider
bord|e *m* edge; border; rim; verge; ***al ~e de*** on the verge of; **~ear** *v/t* to skirt, to go round; **~illo** *m* kerb(stone), *Am* curb
bordo *m mar* shipboard; ***a ~*** on board
boreal northern
borla *f* tassel; pompon
borne *m elec* terminal
borra *f* fluff; nap, down; sediment; dregs
borrach|era *f* drunkenness; intoxication; **~o(a)** *m* (*f*) drunkard; *a* drunk
borrad|or *m* rough draft; *LA* rubber, eraser; **~ura** *f* erasure
borrar *v/t* to delete; to erase; to wipe out
borrasc|a *f* gale; storm; *fig* risk; **~oso** stormy
borrego(a) *m* (*f*) yearling lamb
borric|a *f* she-donkey; *fam* fool; **~o** *m* donkey; *fam* ass; fool
borrón *m* blot; smudge
borroso blurred; smudged
bosque *m* wood; forest
bosquej|ar *v/t* to sketch; to outline; **~o** *m* sketch
bostez|ar *v/i* to yawn; **~o** *m* yawning
bota *f* boot; wineskin; leather wine bottle; **~s *pl de goma*** rubber boots
bota|dura *f* launching; **~r** *v/t* to launch; to hurl; to fling; *LA* to throw away; to throw out; to fire; *v/i* to bounce
botánic|a *f* botany; **~o** botanic
bote *m* boat; thrust; leap; bounce; can, tin; **~ *de remos*** rowboat; **~ *plegable*** folding boat; **~ *salvavidas*** lifeboat
botella *f* bottle
botica *f* chemist's (shop), drugstore; **~rio** *m* chemist; *Am* druggist
botij|a *f*, **~o** *m* earthenware jar
botín *m* booty, loot
botiquín *m* medicine chest; first-aid kit
botón *m* button; bud
botones *m* bellboy, page
bóveda *f* vault; dome
bovino bovine
boxe|ador *m* boxer; **~ar** *v/i* to box; **~o** *m* boxing
boya *f mar* buoy; **~nte** thriving; *mar* buoyant
bozal *m* muzzle; *LA* halter
bracero *m* unskilled labo(u)rer
braga *f* diaper; hoisting rope; *pl* breeches; panties
brague|ro *m med* truss; brace; **~ta** *f* fly (*of trousers*)
bram|a *f zool* rut; **~ante** *m* twine; **~ar** *v/i* to roar; to bellow; **~ido** *m* roaring
bras|a *f* live coal; **~ero** *m* brazier
Brasil *m* Brazil
brasileño(a) *m* (*f*), *a* Brazilian
brav|o brave, courageous; fierce; rough (*sea*); **~ucón** *m* braggart; **~ura** *f* ferocity; fierceness; courage
braza *f mar* fathom; *sp* stroke; **~da** *f* armful; ***~da de espaldas*** backstroke
brazal *m* arm band
brazalete *m* bracelet
brazo *m* arm; branch
brea *f* tar; pitch
brebaje *m med* mixture; potion; draught
brécol *m* broccoli
brecha *f* breach; opening; gap
brega *f* strife; contest; **~r** *v/i* to toil, to work hard
breve *a* short; ***en ~*** soon; *m* apostolic brief; **~dad** *f* shortness; **~mente** briefly
breviario *m* breviary
brezal *m* heath; moorland
brezo *m* heather
bribón *m* loafer; knave; *a* idle; loafing
brida *f* bridle (*of a horse*); flange; clamp
brigada *f mil* brigade
brilla|nte *m* brilliant; *a* brilliant; glittering; **~ntez** *f* brilliance; **~r** *v/i* to shine; to sparkle; to glitter
brillo *m* lustre; glitter; shine; splendo(u)r
brinc|ar *v/i* to jump; to skip; to hop; **~o** *m* leap; jump
brind|ar *v/i* to drink to a person's health; *v/t* to offer; **~is** *m* toast
brío *m* strength; vigo(u)r; spirit
brioso vigorous; spirited; lively
brisa *f* breeze
británico British
broca *f* reel
brocha *f* painter's brush
broche *m* clasp; brooch
brom|a *f* joke; ***en ~a*** in fun; ***gastar una ~a*** to play a joke; **~ear** *v/i* to joke, to fool; **~ista** *m*, *f* joker; gay person
bronca *f fam* quarrel
bronce *m* bronze; **~ *amarillo*** brass; **~ *de cañón*** gun metal; **~ar** *v/t* to bronze; to tan (*skin*)
bronco rough; harsh
bronqui|al bronchial; **~tis** *f* bronchitis
brot|ar *v/i* to sprout; to spring up; *med* to break out; **~e** *m* bud; outbreak
bruj|a *f* witch; **~ería** *f* witchcraft; **~o** *m* sorcerer
brújula *f* compass; magnetic needle
brum|a *f* mist; **~oso** misty
bruñir *v/t* to polish
brus|co brusque; rough; sudden; **~quedad** *f* abruptness
brut|al brutal; brutish; *fam* fabulous; **~o** *m* brute; *a* stupid
bucea|dor *m* diver; **~r** *v/i* to dive
bucle *m* ringlet
bucólico pastoral; bucolic
buche *m* crop, maw; stomach
budín *m* pudding
buen, *apocope of* **bueno,** *used only before a masculine noun*: **~ *hombre*** good man, *or before infinitives used as nouns*: ***eso es ~ decir*** well said; **~amente** freely; easily; **~aventura** *f* good luck; **~o** good; well; all right; healthy; usable; ***¡~os días!*** good morning!; good day!; ***¡~as tardes!*** good afternoon!; ***¡~as noches!*** good night!; ***de ~as a primeras*** all of a sudden; ***por las ~as*** willingly
buey *m* ox; bullock
búfalo *m* buffalo
bufanda *f* scarf; muffler
buf|ar *v/i* to snort; to puff with rage; **~o** *m* clown; *a* clownish; comical
buhard|a *f*, **~illa** *f* attic, garret, loft
búho *m* owl
buitre *m* vulture
bujía *f* candle; spark-plug
bulbo *m bot* bulb
bulto *m* bundle; bulk; shape; swelling; bale; *LA* briefcase; ***de ~*** obvious
bulla *f* noise; chatter; uproar
bulli|cio *m* bustle; noise; din; **~cioso** noisy; lively; **~r** *v/i* to boil; to swarm, to teem
buñuelo *m* fritter; bun, doughnut
buque *m* boat; ship; **~ *de guerra*** warship; **~ *mercante*** merchantman
burbuj|a *f* bubble; **~ear** *v/i* to bubble
burdégano *m* hinny
burdel *m* brothel
burdo coarse; ordinary
burgués(esa) *m* (*f*), *a* bourgeois; middle class
burl|a *f* scoff; taunt; joke; trick; **~arse de** to scoff at; to make fun of; **~ón** *m* joker; scoffer; *a* mocking; joking
burocracia *f* bureaucracy
burócrata *m*, *f* bureaucrat
burocrático bureaucratic
burro *m* donkey; *fig* idiot; *a* stupid
bursátil of the stock exchange
busca *f* search; **~r** *v/t* to look for; to seek; to search
búsqueda *f* search
busto *m* bust
butaca *f* armchair; *teat* orchestra seat, stall
buzo *m* diver
buzón *m* letterbox, mailbox; ***echar al ~*** to post, to mail

C

cabal *a* exact; right; full; complete, thorough; *adv* perfectly; exactly
cabalgar *v/i* to ride on horseback
caballa *f* mackerel
caball|eresco chivalrous; **~ería** *f* horse; mule; cavalry; knighthood; **~eriza** *f* stable; **~ero** *m* horseman; knight; nobleman; gentleman; **~eroso** gentlemanly; **~ete** *m* easel; bridge (*of nose*); **~ito** *m* pony; ***~ito del diablo*** dragonfly; **~o** *m* horse; knight (*in chess*); *fam* heroin; ***a ~o*** on horseback; ***~o de fuerza*** horsepower; ***~o de pura sangre*** thoroughbred
cabaña *f* cabin; hut
cabece|ar *v/i* to nod; *mar* to pitch; **~o** *m* nodding; **~ra** *f* head (*of the bed, of the table*)
cabecilla *m* ringleader
cabell|era *f* wig; head of hair; **~o** *m* hair; **~udo** hairy
caber *v/i* to go in *or* into; to find room; to fit in; ***no cabe duda*** there is no doubt; ***no cabe más*** that's the limit
cabestr|illo *m med* sling; **~o** *m* halter
cabez|a *f* head; summit; lead; ***a la ~a de*** at the head of; ***~a de turco*** scapegoat; ***lavarse la ~a*** to wash one's hair; ***perder la ~a*** to lose one's head; **~ada** *f* blow on *or* with the head; nod; **~al** *m med* pad; bolster; *aut* headrest; **~ota** *m*, *f* pig-headed person; **~udo** large-headed
cabida *f* space; capacity; room
cabina *f* cabin; booth; *aer* cockpit; **~ *de teléfono*** telephone box, *Am* booth
cabizbajo downhearted, downcast; dejected
cable *m* cable; wire; **~ *de remolque*** towline
cabo *m* end; *tecn* thread; *mar* rope; handle; *geog* cape; leader; corporal; ***de ~ a rabo*** from beginning to end; ***llevar a ~*** to finish; to carry out
cabotaje *m* coastal shipping
cabra *f* goat
cabrestante *m* capstan
cabriola *f* caper; capriole
cabrito *m* kid, young goat
cacahuete *m* peanut
cacao *m* cacao
cacarear *v/i* to cackle; to brag; to boast
cacatúa *f* cockatoo
cacería *f* hunt; hunting
cacerola *f* saucepan
caciqu|e *m LA* chief; *pol* party boss; ringleader; **~ismo** *m* power of political bosses
caco *m* thief; pickpocket
cacto *m* cactus
cacharr|ería *f* crockery; **~o** *m* pot; jug; earthenware; *fam* junk; old vehicle
cachete *m* slap; blow (*in the face*)
cachiporra *f* bludgeon
cacho *m* small piece; *LA* horn (*of bull, etc*)
cachorro *m* puppy; cub; whelp
cada every; each; **~ *uno*** each one
cadáver *m* corpse
cadena *f* chain; *radio, TV* network; *fig* tie; obligation; **~ *perpetua*** life imprisonment
cadera *f* hip
cadete *m* cadet
caduc|ar *v/i* to lapse; to run out; to expire; **~idad** *f* expiry; lapse
cae|dizo falling; unsteady; **~r** *v/i* to fall; to decline; to fit; to happen; *aer* to crash; ***~r en la cuenta*** to understand; ***~rle bien*** to fit him, to suit him
café *m* coffee; café; **~ *con leche*** coffee with milk; **~ *solo*** black coffee
cafeína *f* caffeine
cafetal *m* coffee plantation
cafeter|a *f* coffee pot, percolator; **~ía** *f* café; snack-bar; **~o** *m* coffee-shop owner
caída *f* fall; downfall; slope; hang (*of clothes*); *geol* fold; *aer* crash
caimán *m* alligator
caj|a *f* box, case; safe; well (*of stairs*); ***~a de ahorros*** savings bank; ***~a de engranajes*** gearbox; **~ero(a)** *m* (*f*) bank teller; cashier; **~etilla** *f* pack (*of cigarettes*); **~ita** *f* small box; ***~ita de fósforos*** matchbox; **~ón** *m* large box; locker; drawer
cal *f* lime; **~a** *f* creek, small bay
calabacín *m bot* marrow
calabaza *f* pumpkin; gourd
calabozo *m* dungeon; prison
calada *f* soaking
calado *m* draught (*of ship*)
calamar *m* squid
calambre *m* cramp
calamidad *f* calamity
calandria *f* manglingerer; calander
calar *v/t* to soak; to drench; to perforate; *fig* to see through
calavera *f* skull; *m* madcap
calca|do *m* tracing; **~r** *v/t* to trace; to copy
calcet|a *f* (knee-length) stocking; ***hacer ~a*** to knit; **~ín** *m* sock
calcio *m* calcium
calco *m* tracing; **~manía** *f* transfer (*picture*)
calcula|dora *f* calculator; **~r** *v/t* to calculate
cálculo *m* calculation; estimate; conjecture
calder|a *f* kettle; boiler; **~illa**

f copper (*coin*); **~o** *m* small boiler
caldo *m* broth; sauce
calefacción *f* heating; ~ **central** central heating
calendario *m* calendar
calent|ador *m* heater; **~ar** *v/t* to heat; **~arse** to get hot; to warm oneself up; *LA* to get angry; **~ura** *f* fever
calibr|ar *v/t* to gauge; **~e** *m* calibre
calidad *f* quality; condition
cálido hot; warm
calidoscopio *m* kaleidoscope
caliente hot; warm
califica|ción *f* qualification; assessment; **~r** *v/t* to rate; to assess; to qualify
cáliz *m* chalice, cup
calma *f* calm; lull; **~nte** *m* sedative; **~r** *v/t* to soothe; to calm; **~rse** to abate; to quiet down
caló *m* gipsy language; slang
calor *m* heat; warmth; **hace ~** it's hot; **~ía** *f* calorie
calumnia *f* calumny, slander; **~r** *v/t*, *v/i* to slander; to libel
caluroso hot; warm; ardent
calv|icie *f* baldness; **~o** bald
calz|a *f* wedge; *pl* breeches; **~ada** *f* highway; causeway; **~ado** *m* footwear; shoes; **~ar** *v/t* to put on (*shoes*, *tires*); to wedge; **~oncillos** *m/pl* underpants
calla|do silent; quiet; secretive; **~r** *v/t* to silence; **~rse** to hold one's tongue; to be silent; **~rse la boca** to shut up
calle *f* street; **~ de dirección única** one-way street; **~ peatonal** pedestrian mall; **~ principal** main street; **~jear** *v/i* to saunter about; **~jón** *m* alley; passage; **~jón sin salida** blind alley; dead end; **~juela** *f* lane; narrow street
callo *m* corn; callus; **~so** callous, horny
cama *f* bed; **~ plegable** folding bed; **guardar ~** to be laid up; **~da** *f* litter (*of young*); *geol* layer
cámara *f* chamber; cabin; *med* stool; *aut* inner tube; **~ de comercio** Chamber of Commerce; **~ lenta** slow-motion
camarada *m* comrade
camarer|a *f* maid; waitress; **~o** *m* waiter; steward
camarilla *f* clique; faction
camar|ín *m teat* dressing room; **~ón** *m* common prawn
camarote *m* cabin; stateroom
cambalache *m fam* swap
cambi|able changeable; **~ar** *v/t* to change; to exchange; to alter; *v/i* to change; **~o** *m* change; rate of exchange; small change; **a ~o (de)** in return (for); **~o de velocidades** *aut* gearshift; **~sta** *m* moneychanger
camelo *m fam* joking; flirting
camello *m* camel
camilla *f* stretcher; litter
camin|ante *m* walker; **~ar** *v/i* to walk; to travel; **~ata** *f* long walk; **~o** *m* road; track; path; way; **en ~o** under way; **~o de** on the way to; **~o de acceso** access road; **~o troncal** main road
camión *m* lorry; *Am* truck; *LA* bus; **~ de mudanzas** removal van, *Am* moving van
camioneta *f* van
camis|a *f* shirt; **~a de noche** nightdress, nightgown; **~ería** *f* shirt shop; **~eta** *f* undershirt; **~ón** *m* nightdress
camorra *f* quarrel, brawl
campamento *m* camp
campan|a *f* bell; **~ario** *m* belfry; church tower; **~illa** *f* handbell; electric bell; tassel
campánula *f* **azul** bluebell
campaña *f* countryside; campaign
campar *v/i* to camp; to excel
campechano frank; hearty
campeón(ona) *m* (*f*) champion; **~ titular** defending champion
campeonato *m* championship
camp|ero in the open; **~esino(a)** *m* (*f*) peasant; **~estre** *a* rural; **~iña** *f* fields; countryside; **~o** *m* country; countryside; field; camp; **~o de golf** golf course *or* links; **a ~o travieso** cross-country; **~osanto** *m* cemetery
camuflar *v/t* to camouflage
can *m* dog
Canadá *m* Canada
canadiense *m*, *f*, *a* Canadian
canal *m* channel; canal; strait; **~ización** *f* canalization; **~ón** *m arq* gutter
canalla *f* mob; rabble; *m* scoundrel; rotter
canapé *m* couch, settee
Canarias *f/pl* Canary Isles
canario *m* canary
canas *f/pl* grey hair
canasta *f* basket
cancela *f* ironwork gate
cancela|ción *f* cancellation; **~r** *v/t* to cancel
cáncer *m* cancer
canciller *m* chancellor
canción *f* song; **~ de cuna** lullaby
cancionero *m* song book
cancha *f* playing field; **~ de tenis** tennis court
candado *m* padlock
candel|a *f* candle; **~ero** *m* candlestick
candente redhot
candidato *m* candidate
candidez *f* simplicity; naiveté
candil *m* oil lamp; **~ejas** *f/pl* footlights
candor *m* simplicity; candidness
canela *f* cinnamon
cangrejo *m* crab
canguro *m* kangaroo
canica *f* marble; *pl* marbles (*game*)
canícula *f* dog days
caniche *m* poodle
canijo *m* weakling
canilla *f* shinbone; tap; reel
canje *m* exchange; **~ar** *v/t* to exchange
canoa *f* canoe
canon *m mús*, *pint*, *relig* canon
canoso grey-haired
cansa|do tired, weary; **~ncio** *m* fatigue, weariness; **~r** *v/t* to tire, to weary; **~rse** to grow tired
canta|nte *m*, *f* singer; **~r** *v/t*, *v/i* to sing
cántaro *m* pitcher; jug; **llover a ~s** to rain cats and dogs
cantera *f* quarry
cantidad *f* quantity, amount
cantimplora *f* water bottle; canteen
cantina *f* canteen; wine cellar; *LA* saloon, bar
canto *m* singing; song; edge; crust (*of bread*); **~r** *m* singer
caña *f* reed; cane; stem; glass (*of beer*); **~ de azúcar** sugar cane; **~ de pescar** fishing rod; **~da** *f* gully; cattle path
cáñamo *m* hemp
cañería *f* pipeline; conduit
caño *m* pipe; tube; drain
cañón *m* gun, cannon; barrel; quill; *LA* canyon
cañon|azo *m* cannonshot; **~eo** *m* bombardment
caoba *f* mahogany
caos *m* chaos
caótico chaotic
capa *f* cloak; cape; cover; layer
capa|cidad *f* capacity; capability; **~citar** *v/t* to qualify
capataz *m* foreman, overseer
capaz capable; able; competent
capellán *m* chaplain
capilar capillary
capilla *f* chapel; choir of a church; **~ ardiente** funeral chapel
capital *a* capital; essential; important; *f* capital (*of country*); *m* capital; wealth; stock; **~ista** *m*, *f*, *a* capitalist; **~izar** *v/t* to capitalize
capitán *m* captain; **~ de puerto** harbo(u)r master
capitan|a *f* flagship; **~ía** *f* captaincy
capitulación *f* capitulation
capitular *v/i* to capitulate; to sign an agreement
capítulo *m* chapter; assembly; governing body
caporal *m* overseer; leader
capot|a *f aut* hood, bonnet; top (*of convertible*); **~e** *m* coat; overcoat; bullfighter's cape; *LA* beating; **~ear** *v/t* to get out of; to shirk
capricho *m* caprice; vagary; whim; **~so** capricious; whimsical; wayward
cápsula *f* capsule; **~ espacial** space capsule
capt|ar *v/t* to win; to attract; **~ura** *f* capture; **~urar** *v/t* to capture
capucha *f* hood
capullo *m* bud; cocoon
cara *f* face; front; surface; head (*of coin*); **~ o cruz** heads or tails; **dar ~ a** to face up to; **tener ~ de** to look like
carabina *f* carbine
caracol *m* snail; **¡~es!** good gracious!
carácter *m* character; type (*in printing*)
caracter|ístico characteristic; **~izar** *v/t* to characterize
¡caramba! heavens!; wow!; damn!
carámbano *m* icicle
caramelo *m* sweet; candy; caramel
carátula *f* mask; *LA* title page (*of book*)
carbón *m* coal; carbon; **~ de leña** charcoal
carboner|a *f* coal mine; **~ía** *f* coal yard
carbónico carbonic
carbonilla *f* cinders
carbunclo *m* carbuncle
carburador *m* carburet(t)or
carcajada *f* guffaw, burst of laughter
cárcel *f* prison, jail; *tecn* clamp
carcelero *m* jailer; warden
carcom|a *f* woodworm; **~ido** worm-eaten
cardenal *m relig*, *zool* cardinal; weal
cárdeno purplish; livid
cardíaco cardiac
cardinal cardinal
cardo *m* thistle
carear *v/t* to confront; to bring face to face
care|cer *v/i* to lack; **~ncia** *f* lack
carestía *f* scarcity; dearth; high cost
careta *f* mask; **~ antigás** gas mask
carga *f* charge; loading; load; burden; cargo; *fig* tax; **~dero** *m* loading site; **~do** loaded; laden; sultry; *elec* live; **~dor** *m* loader; stevedore; **~mento** *m* load; **~r** *v/t* to load; to burden; *elec*, *for*, *com* to charge; *v/i* to load up; to rest (*on*); **~rse a uno** to do someone in; **~rse de algo** to be full of something
cargo *m* loading; load; *com* debit; **a ~ de** in charge of; under the responsibility of
caribe Carribean
caricia *f* caress
caridad *f* charity
caries *f med* cavity, tooth decay
cariño *m* affection; kindness; **~so** affectionate; loving
caritativo charitable
cariz *m* aspect
carmesí *a*, *m* crimson
carnal carnal
carnaval *m* carnival
carne *f* flesh; meat; pulp; **~ asada** roast meat; **~ congelada** frozen meat; **~ de gallina** goose-flesh, *Am* goosebumps; **~ picada** mincemeat, *Am* ground meat
carnero *m* ram; sheep; *coc* mutton
carnet *m*: **~ de conducir** driving licence; **~ de identidad** identity card
carnicería *f* butcher's shop; butchery; bloodshed
caro dear; expensive
carpa *f* carp; *LA* tent
carpeta *f* portfolio; folder; file; *LA* desk
carpintero *m* carpenter
carrera *f* run; race; career; course; **~ de caballos** horse race; **~ de relevos** relay race
carret|a *f* cart; **~e** *m* reel; **~era** *f* (main)road; highway; **~ero** *m* cartwright; carter; **~illa** *f* wheelbarrow
carril *m* rut; furrow; lane (*of highway*); *fc* rail
carrillo *m* cheek; jowl; pulley
carro *m* cart, wagon; *LA* car; **~cería** *f* body (*of car*)
carroza *f* coach; carriage
carruaje *m* carriage
carta *f* letter; document; chart; playing card; **~ certificada** registered letter; **~ de crédito** *com* letter of credit; **~pacio** *m* satchel; briefcase
cartel *m* placard, poster; *com* cartel
cart|era *f* wallet; pocketbook; *LA* lady's handbag; briefcase; portfolio; **~ero** *m* postman
cartílago *m* cartilage
cartilla *f* booklet; certificate; primer; **leerle la ~ a** *fig* to lecture
cartografiar *v/t* to map
cartón *m* cardboard, pasteboard
cartucho *m* cartridge
casa *f* house; household; home; firm; **~ consistorial** town hall; **~ de huéspedes** boarding house; **~ pública** brothel; **en ~** at home; **~dero** marriageable; **~miento** *m* marriage
casar *v/t* to marry; to wed; *fig* to match; to join; **~se** to marry; to get married
cascabel *m* small bell
cascada *f* waterfall
casca|do worn out; cracked; **~jo** *m* gravel; grit; **~nueces** *m* nutcracker; **~r** *v/t* to break; to split
cáscara *f* shell; rind, peel; *LA* bark
casco *m* skull; helmet; hoof; fragment; hull (*of a ship*); empty bottle
caserío *m* hamlet
casero *m* landlord; proprietor; *a* domestic; homemade; home-loving
caseta *f* booth; stall
casi almost; nearly
casill|a *f* hut; lodge; pigeon-hole; *teat* box office; square
casino *m* club; casino
caso *m* case; event; occasion; matter; **en ~ de que** in case of; **en todo ~** at any rate; **hacer ~ a** to take into consideration; **hacer ~ omiso de** to ignore; **no venir al ~** to be irrelevant
caspa *f* dandruff
casquillo *m* tip; metal cap
cassette *m*, *f* cassette
casta *f* lineage; race; breed; pedigree; caste
castañ|a *f* chestnut; **~etazo** *m* snap (*of the fingers*); **~o** *m* chestnut tree; **~o de Indias** horse chestnut; **~uela** *f* castanet
castellano(a) *m* (*f*), *a* Castilian; *m* Castilian language
castidad *f* chastity
castig|ar *v/t* to punish; to correct; **~o** *m* punishment; penalty
castillo *m* castle
castizo pure; authentic
casto chaste, pure
castor *m* beaver
castrar *v/t* to prune; to geld; to castrate
castrense military
casual fortuitous; **~idad** *f* chance; accident; **por ~idad** by chance
casu|ca *f*, **~cha** *f* hovel, hut
catadura *f* sampling; taste
catalán(ana) *m* (*f*), *a* Catalan
catalejo *m* telescope, (spy)glass
catálogo *m* catalogue
Cataluña *f* Catalonia
cataplasma *m* poultice
catar *v/t* to sample; to taste; to examine; to look at
catarata *f* waterfall; *med* cataract
catarro *m* cold; catarrh
catástrofe *f* catastrophe
catecismo *m* catechism (*book*)
cátedra *f* professorship; chair (*at university*)
catedral *f* cathedral
catedrático(a) *m* (*f*) professor
categoría *f* category; group; **de ~** of importance
categórico categorical
católico(a) *m* (*f*), *a* Roman Catholic
catolicismo *m* Catholicism
catre *m* small bed; cot; **~ de tijera** camp bed
cauce *m* riverbed; channel
caución *f* caution; security
caucho *m* rubber
caudal *m* property; wealth; volume; **~oso** copious; wealthy; large (*river*)
caudill|aje *m* leadership; **~o** *m* leader
causa *f* cause; reason; *for* trial; **a ~ de** because of; **~r** *v/t* to cause; to create; to provoke
cautel|a *f* caution; prudence; **~oso** prudent; cautious, wary
cautiv|ar *v/t* to capture; **~o** *m* prisoner; captive
cauto cautious; wary
cavar *v/t* to dig
caverna *f* cavern; cave
cavidad *f* cavity; hollow
cavil|ar *v/t* to meditate upon; **~oso** distrustful
caza *f* hunt; hunting; shooting; chase; game (*animals*); **~ mayor** big game; **~dor** *m* hunter; **~dora** *f* hunting jacket

cazo *m* ladle; melting pan
cazuela *f* pan; casserole; *teat* gallery
cebada *f* barley
ceb|ar *v/t* to fatten; **~o** *m* feed; fodder
cebolla *f* onion; bulb (*of plant*)
cebra *f* zebra
cecear *v/i* to lisp
cecina *f* dried meat
ceder *v/t* to cede; to yield; to give up
cedro *m* cedar
cédula *f* document; slip (*of paper*); certificate
cegar *v/t* to blind
ceguedad *f* blindness
ceja *f* eyebrow; *fig* rim
cela|da *f* ambush; **~dor** *m* watchman; **~r** *v/t* to watch over
celda *f* cell
celebérrimo very famous
celebrar *v/t* to acclaim; to applaud; to celebrate; to say (*mass*)
célebre famous
celebridad *f* fame; celebrity
celeridad *f* speed, swiftness
celeste heavenly; celestial
celibato *m* celibacy
célibe *m, f, a* celibate; unmarried
celo *m* zeal; rut (*of animals*); sticky tape, *Am* scotch tape; *pl* jealousy; **~sía** *f* lattice; **~so** zealous; jealous
célula *f biol* cell
celulosa *f* cellulose
cementerio *m* cemetery; graveyard
cement|ar *v/t tecn* to cement; **~o** *m* cement
cena *f* supper; evening meal
cenagal *m* mire; morass
cenar *v/i* to dine; to have supper
cencerrear *v/i* to rattle; to jangle
cenicero *m* ashtray
cenit *m* zenith
ceniza *f* ashes
censo *m* census
censura *f* censorship; **~r** *v/t* to criticize; to blame; to censor
centell|a *f* spark; flash; **~ear** *v/i* to sparkle; to twinkle
centenario *m* centennial
centeno *m* rye
centígrado centigrade
centímetro *m* centimetre, *Am* centimeter
centinela *m or f* sentinel; sentry
central *f* central; head office; power station; *a* central; **~izar** *v/t* to centralize
centro *m* centre, *Am* center; **~ comercial** shopping centre, *Am* center
ceñi|do tight; **~r** *v/t* to gird; to bind; **~rse** *fig* to economize
ceñ|o *m* frown; scowl; **~udo** scowling, gruff
cepa *f* vinestock; stem; stock
cepillo *m* brush; *tecn* plane; **~ de dientes** toothbrush
cepo *m* branch; stocks, pillory; trap
cera *f* wax
cerámica *f* ceramic art; ceramics
cerca *adv* near; **~ de** *prep* near; close to
cerca|nía *f* proximity; vicinity; **~no** close; near; **~r** *v/t* to enclose; to fence; to besiege
cercenar *v/t* to cut off
cerco *m* enclosure; *mil* encirclement; siege; *LA* hedge
cerd|a *f* bristle; sow; **~o** *m* hog, pig
cereal *m, a* cereal
cerebr|al cerebral; **~o** *m* brain
ceremoni|a *f* ceremony; **~al, ~oso** ceremonious, formal
cerez|a *f* cherry; **~o** *m* cherry tree
cerilla *f* taper; match; ear wax
cero *m* zero; ***bajo ~*** below zero
cerrado closed
cerradura *f* lock
cerrajer|ía *f* locksmith's shop; **~o** *m* locksmith
cerrar *v/t* to lock; to shut; to close
cerro *m* hill
cerrojo *m* bolt (*of the door*); latch
certamen *m* competition
cert|ero sure; certain; **~eza** *f*, **~idumbre** *f* certainty
certifica|do *m* certificate; *a* registered (*letter*); **~r** *v/t* to register (*letters*); to certify
cervato *m* fawn
cerve|cería *f* brewery; bar; **~za** *f* beer; ale; ***~za de barril*** draught beer
cerviz *f* nape of the neck
cesant|e on half pay; jobless; **~ía** *f* dismissal; pension
ces|ar *v/i* to cease, to stop; **~e** *m* cease; stop; ***~e de fuego*** cease-fire
césped *m* lawn; turf
cest|a *f* basket; **~ero** *m* basketmaker; **~o** *m* basket; hamper; ***~o de papeles*** wastepaper basket
cetro *m* sceptre
ciática *f* sciatica
cicatriz *f* scar; **~ar** *v/i* to form a scar
ciclista *m, f* cyclist
ciclo *m* cycle; period
ciclón *m* cyclone
ciego blind; choked up
cielo *m* sky; atmosphere; heaven; ***¡~s!*** Good Heavens!
ciénaga *f* bog, morass
cien|cia *f* science; ***~cias*** *pl* ***naturales*** (natural) sciences; **~tífico** *a* scientific; *m* scientist; **~to** one hundred; ***por ~to*** per cent
cierre *m* fastening; closing
cierto *a* certain; true; *adv* certainly; ***por ~*** incidentally
ciervo|a *f* hind; **~o** *m* stag, hart
cifra *f* figure; number
cigarra *f* cicada
cigarr|illo *m* cigarette; **~o** *m* cigar
cigüeña *f* stork; *tecn* winch; **~l** *m* crankshaft
cilíndrico cylindrical
cilindro *m* cylinder; *impr* roller
cima *f* summit
cimentar *v/t* to lay the foundation of; to consolidate
cimiento *m* foundation
cinc *m* zinc
cincel *m* chisel; **~ar** *v/t* to engrave; to chisel
cinco five
cine(ma) *m* cinema; movies
cínico cynical
cint|a *f* ribbon; strap; ***~a adhesiva, LA ~a pegante*** adhesive tape; ***~a magnetofónica*** recording tape; ***~a métrica*** tape measure; ***~a transportadora*** conveyor belt; **~ura** *f* waist; **~urón** *m* belt; ***~urón salvavidas*** lifebelt; ***~urón de seguridad*** safety belt; *aut* seatbelt
ciprés *m* cypress
circo *m* circus
circuito *m* circuit; network; ***corto ~*** short circuit
circula|ción *f* circulation; traffic; **~r** *f* circular; *a* circular; *v/i* to circulate
círculo *m* circle; club
circundar *v/t* to (en)circle; to surround
circunstan|cia *f* circumstance; ***~cia atenuante*** extenuating circumstance; **~te** *m* bystander
ciruela *f* plum; ***~ pasa*** prune
ciru|gía *f* surgery; **~jano** *m* surgeon
cisco *m* slack; *fam* hubbub
cisma *m* schism; disagreement
cisne *m* swan
cisterna *f* cistern; watertank
cita *f* appointment; engagement; quotation; summons; **~r** *v/t* to quote; to make an appointment *or* date with
ciudad *f* city; town; **~ano(a)** *m (f)* citizen; **~anía** *f* citizenship; **~ela** *f* citadel
cívico civic; patriotic
civil civil; polite; **~ización** *f* civilization; **~izar** *v/t* to civilize
cizalla *f* shears; pliers; metal clippings
clam|ar *v/i* to cry out; **~or** *m* outcry; **~oroso** clamorous; noisy
clandestino secret; clandestine
clara *f* white of an egg; fair spell (*of weather*)
claraboya *f* skylight
clarear *v/t* to lighten; to illuminate; *v/i* to dawn; to clear up
clarete *m* claret
claridad *f* brightness; clarity; light
clarín *m* bugle
claro light; bright; clear; distinct; ***¡~!*** naturally!; of course; ***~ que sí*** of course
clase *f* class; classroom; lesson; kind; ***primera ~*** first class; ***~ media*** middle-class; ***~ obrera*** working class
clásico classic; classical
clasifica|ción *f* classification; **~r** *v/t* to classify
claudicar *v/i* to limp; to give up
claustro *m* cloister
cláusula *f* clause
clavar *v/t* to nail; to fasten; to pierce
clave *f* key; clue; *mús* clef; *arq* keystone
clavel *m* carnation
clavícula *f* collar bone
clavija *f* peg; *tecn* pin
clavo *m* nail; spike; clove; ***dar en el ~*** to hit the nail on the head
claxon *m aut* horn
clemen|cia *f* clemency; mercy; **~te** merciful
clérigo *m* priest; clergyman
clero *m* clergy; priesthood
clientela *f* clientele
clima *m* climate; **~tización** *f* air conditioning
clínica *f* clinic; hospital
clip *m* paper clip; hairpin
cloaca *f* sewer
cloquear *v/i* to cluck
cloro *m* chlorine
cloroformo *m* chloroform
club *m* club; ***~ nocturno*** night club
coagular *v/t*, **~se** to coagulate
coalición *f* coalition
coartada *f* alibi
cobalto *m* cobalt
cobard|e *m, f* coward; *a* cowardly; **~ía** *f* cowardice
cobaya *f* guinea pig
cobertizo *m* shed; shelter
cobija *f LA* blanket; **~r** *v/t* to cover; to shelter; **~se** to take shelter
cobra|dor *m* collector; **~r** *v/t* to collect (*money*); to cash; to charge (*price*); to acquire; *v/i* to get paid
cobre *m* copper
cobro *m* collection (*of money*); cashing (*of cheque*)
cocaína *f* cocaine
coc|er *v/t, v/i* to cook; **~ido** *m* stew
cocin|a *f* kitchen; stove; ***~ de gas*** gas stove; **~ar** *v/t* to cook; *v/i* to do the cooking; **~ero** *m*, **~era** *f* cook
coco *m* coconut; *fam* head; **~drilo** *m* crocodile; **~tero** *m* coconut palm
cóctel *m* cocktail
coche *m* car; *fc* coach; carriage; ***~ de alquiler*** rented car; ***~ de carreras*** racing car; ***~ fúnebre*** hearse; ***~ de turismo*** roadster
cochecito *m*: ***~ para bebé*** pram, *Am* baby carriage
cochina *f* sow; **~da** *f* dirt; filthiness; *fam* filthy thing; dirty trick
cochinillo *m* suckling pig
codazo *m* nudge
codear *v/i* to elbow; *v/t* to nudge
códice *m* codex
codici|a *f* greed; covetousness; **~ar** *v/t* to covet
código *m* code
cod|illo *m zool* knee; *tecn* elbow pipe; **~o** *m* elbow
codorniz *f* quail
coexist|encia *f* coexistence; **~ir** *v/i* to coexist
cofradía *f* guild; society
cofre *m* chest; trunk; case
coge|dor *m* dustpan; **~r** *v/t* to seize; to grasp; to catch; to collect
cogote *m* nape of the neck
cohete *m* rocket, missile; ***~ teledirigido*** guided missile; **~ría** *f* rocketry
cohibido inhibited, self-conscious
coincidencia *f* coincidence
cojear *v/i* to limp, to hobble
cojín *m* cushion
cojinete *m* **de bolas** *tecn* ball-bearing(s)
cojo lame
cok' *m* coke
col *f* cabbage; ***~ de Bruselas*** Brussels sprout
cola *f* tail; extremity; queue, *Am* line; ***hacer ~*** to queue up, *Am* to line up
colaborador *m* collaborator; co-worker
colador *m* strainer; colander
colar *v/t* to filter; to strain; **~se** to sneak in; to slip in
colch|a *f* bedspread; counterpane; **~ar** *v/t* to quilt; **~ón** *m* mattress
cole = ***colegio***
colección *f* collection
coleccionar *v/t* to collect
colect|ivo collective; **~or** *m* collector
colega *m, f* colleague
colegi|al *m* schoolboy; **~ala** *f* schoolgirl; **~o** *m* school
cólera *f* anger; wrath; *m* cholera; ***montar en ~*** to fly into a rage
coleta *f* pigtail; *fig* postscript
colga|dero *m* peg; hanger; rack; **~dura** *f* hangings; drapery; **~r** *v/t* to hang up; to hang; *v/i* to hang; to be hanging
colibrí *m* hummingbird
cólico *m* colic
coliflor *f* cauliflower
colilla *f* cigarette stub
colina *f* hill
colindante adjoining
colisión *f* collision
colmar *v/t* to heap; to fill up; to lavish
colmena *f* beehive
colmillo *m* canine tooth; fang; tusk
colmo *m* heap; height; limit; ***¡esto es el ~!*** this is the limit!
coloca|ción *f* setting; arrangement; post; job; **~r** *v/t* to put, to place; to employ; to find a job for
Colombia *f* Colombia; **2no(a)** *m (f)* Colombian
colon|ia *f* colony; **~ial** colonial; **~izar** *v/t* to colonize
color *m* colo(u)r; pigment; paint; **~ado** *m* colo(u)red; red; **~ear** *v/t* to colo(u)r; **~ete** *m* rouge
colosal colossal; gigantic
columna *f* column; pillar; ***~ vertebral*** spinal column
columpi|ar *v/t*, **~arse** to swing; **~o** *m* swing
collar *m* necklace; collar (*for animals*)
coma *f gram* comma; *m med* coma
comadre *f* godmother
comadreja *f* weasel
comadrona *f* midwife
comanda|nte *m* commander; major; **~r** *v/t* to command; to lead
comando *m mil* command
comarca *f* region; district
comba *f* curve; bend; sag; **~r** *v/t* to curve; to bend
combat|e *m* fight; battle; **~iente** *m* combatant; **~ir** *v/t, v/i* to fight; to attack
combina|ción *f* combination; woman's slip; *fc* connection; **~r** *v/t, v/i* to combine; to plan; to figure out
combustible *m* fuel; *a* combustible
comedia *f* play; drama; comedy; **~nte** *m* (comic) actor; comedian
comedido prudent; polite
comedor *m* dining room
comensal *m* dependent; table companion
comentar *v/t* to comment upon; to explain; **~io** *m* commentary; **~ista** *m* (*radio*) commentator
comenzar *v/t, v/i* to start, to commence; to begin
comer *v/t, v/i* to eat; to dine; **~se** to eat up
comercial commercial; ***centro m ~*** shopping center
comerci|ante *m, f* trader; dealer; merchant; **~ar** *v/t* to trade; to deal in; **~o** *m* business; trade; commerce; ***~o exterior*** foreign trade
comestible *a* edible; **~s** *m/pl* food
cometa *f* kite; *m* comet
comet|er *v/t* to commit; **~ido** *m* task; commitment
cómico comic; funny
comida *f* food; meal; ***~ deshidratada*** dehydrated food; ***~ liofilizada*** freeze-dried food
comienzo *m* beginning
comilón *m* glutton; big eater; *a* fond of eating
comillas *f/pl* quotation marks
comino *m* cumin; ***no me importa un ~*** I don't give a damn
comisaría *f* police station
comis|ario *m* commissary; **~ión** *f* commission
comité *m* committee
comitiva *f* suite, retinue
como *adv* how; as; like; when; in order that; because; ***¿cómo?*** *interrog* what?; how?; ***¡cómo!*** *interj* you don't say so!; ***~ no*** of course, certainly
cómoda *f* chest of drawers
comod|idad *f* comfort; convenience; **~ín** *m* joker (*card*)
cómodo comfortable; easy

compacto compact
compadecer *v/t* to pity
compadre *m* godfather
compaginar *v/t* to arrange; **~se** to agree with
compañer|ismo *m* comradeship; **~o(a)** *m (f)* comrade, companion; **~o(a) de clase** classmate; **~o de cuarto** roommate
compañía *f* company; **~ de aviación** airline; **~ naviera** shipping company
compara|ble comparable; **~ción** *f* comparison; **~r** *v/t* to compare
comparecer *v/i* to appear (*in court, etc*)
comparti|miento *m* compartment; division; **~r** *v/t* to divide; to share
compás *m* compass; *mús* measure; rhythm; **llevar el ~** to keep time
compasión *f* pity, compassion
compatib|ilidad *f* compatibility; **~le** compatible
compatriota *m, f* compatriot
compendi|ar *v/t* to summarize; to abridge; **~o** *m* summary; compendium
compensa|ción *f* compensation; **~r** *v/t* to compensate; to indemnify
compet|encia *f* competition; rivalry; competence; capacity; **~ente** competent; capable; **~idor(a)** *m (f)* rival; competitor; *a* rival; **~ir** *v/i* to compete
compilar *v/t* to compile
compinche *m* crony; chum
complac|encia *f* pleasure; satisfaction; **~er** *v/t* to please, to oblige; to comply; **~erse** to be pleased; **~iente** obliging
complejo *m, a* complex
complement|ar *v/t* to complement; to complete; **~ario** complementary; **~o** *m* complement
completar *v/t* to complete
complicar *v/t* to complicate
cómplice *m* accomplice, accessory
complicidad *f* complicity
complot *m* plot; conspiracy
compone|nda *f* compromise; **~nte** component; **~r** *v/t* to compose; to arrange; to settle; to mend
comporta|miento *m* behavio(u)r; **~rse** to behave
composi|ción *f* composition; settlement; **~tor** *m* composer
compostura *f* composure; repair
compota *f* stewed fruit; compote
compra *f* purchase; **ir de ~s** to go shopping; **~dor(a)** *m (f)* purchaser; **~r** *v/t* to purchase; to buy; *fig* to bribe
compren|der *v/t* to understand; to comprise; **~sible** comprehensible, understandable; **~sión** *f* comprehension; understanding
compres|a *f* compress; sanitary napkin; **~ión** *f* compression; **de alta ~ión** high-compression
comprimi|do *m* tablet, pill; **~r** *v/t* to compress
comproba|ción *f* proof; verification; **~nte** *m* proof; voucher; **~r** *v/t* to verify; to check; to prove
comprom|eter *v/t* to compromise; to jeopardize; to involve; **~eterse** to commit oneself; to become involved; **~iso** *m* commitment; engagement; arrangement; awkward situation
compuerta *f* hatch; flood-gate
compuesto compound
compulsión *f* compulsion
computa|dor(a) *m (f)* computer; **~dor(a) personal** personal computer; **~r** *v/t* to compute; to calculate
comulgar *v/i* to receive communion
común common; widespread; **en ~** in common; **por lo ~** usually
comunal communal
comunica|ción *f* communication; message, report; **~r** *v/t* to communicate
comuni|dad *f* community; **~ón** *f* communion
comunis|mo *m* communism; **~ta** *m, f, a* communist
con with; in spite of; **~ tal que** provided that
conato *m* endeavo(u)r; effort; *for* attempted crime
cóncavo concave
concebi|ble conceivable; **~r** *v/t* to conceive; to imagine
conceder *v/t* to concede; to grant
concej|al *m* councillor; alderman; **~o** *m* town council
concentra|ción *f* concentration; **~r** *v/t*, **~rse** to concentrate
concepción *f* idea; conception
concepto *m* notion; conception; opinion; **bajo todos los ~s** in every way
concerniente concerning
concertar *v/t* to arrange; to coordinate
concesión *f* concession, grant
concesionario *m com* licensee, concessionary; *aut* dealer
concien|cia *f* conscience; **a ~cia** conscientiously; **~zudo** conscientious
concierto *m* agreement; harmony; concert
concilia|ción *f* conciliation; affinity; **~dor** conciliatory; **~r** *v/t* to reconcile; **~r el sueño** to get to sleep
conciso concise
conclu|ir *v/t* to conclude; to infer; *v/i* to end; **~sión** *f* conclusion; **~yente** conclusive
concordar *v/t* to reconcile; to harmonize; *v/i* to agree; to tally
concordia *f* harmony; agreement
concret|ar *v/t* to sum up; to make concrete; **~arse** to limit oneself; **~o** *a* concrete; *m LA* concrete
concubina *f* concubine
concurr|encia *f* crowd; gathering; attendance; **~ido** much frequented; **~ir** *v/i* to meet; to assemble; to concur; to attend; *com* to compete
concurso *m* assembly; competition; contest
concusión *f med* concussion
concha *f* shell
cond|ado *m* earldom; county; **~e** *m* earl; count
condecora|ción *f* medal, decoration; **~r** *v/t* to decorate (*with medals, etc*)
condena *f* sentence; conviction; **cumplir ~** to serve a sentence; **~r** *v/t* to condemn; *for* to convict
condensa|ción *f* condensation; **~dor** *m* condenser; **~r** *v/t* to condense
condesa *f* countess
condescende|ncia *f* complaisance; **~r** *v/i* to comply; to yield
condición *f* condition; position; nature; **a ~ de que** on condition that
condiciona|do conditioned; **~l** conditional; **~r** *v/t* to condition; to determine
condiment|ar *v/t* to season; to spice; **~o** *m* condiment; seasoning
condiscípulo(a) *m (f)* fellow student
condole|ncia *f* condolence; **~rse** to sympathize
condominio *m* condominium
condonar *v/t* to condone
conduc|ción *f* conveyance; conduction; *aut* driving; **~ir** *v/t* to convey; to transport; to lead; to drive; **~ta** *f* conduct; behavio(u)r; **~to** *m* conduit; pipe; duct; channel; **~tor(a)** *m (f)* driver; leader; conductor (*of heat, electricity, etc*)
conectar *v/t tecn* to connect; to join
conej|era *f* rabbit warren; **~illo** *m* bunny; **~illo de Indias** guinea pig; **~o** *m* rabbit
conexión *f* connection
confección *f* concoction; preparation; ready-made article; dress-making
confeccionar *v/t* to make (ready); to prepare
confedera|ción *f* confederation; confederacy; **~r** *v/t*, **~rse** to form a confederation
conferencia *f* lecture, talk; (*long-distance*) telephone conversation; **~nte** *m, f* lecturer; **~r** *v/i* to confer together; to hold a conference
conferir *v/t* to bestow; *v/i* to discuss; to confer
confes|ar *v/t* to confess; **~ión** *f* confession; **~ionario** *m* confessional; **~or** *m* confessor
confia|do trusting, confident; unsuspecting; self confident; vain; **~nza** *f* confidence, trust; reliance; **de ~nza** reliable; **~r** *v/t* to entrust; to confide in; *v/i* to trust; to be confident
confidencia *f* confidence; **~l** confidential
configura|ción *f* shape; outline; **~r** *v/t* to shape
confinar *v/t* to confine; *v/i* **~ con** to border on
confirma|ción *f* confirmation; **~r** *v/t* to confirm
confiscar *v/t* to confiscate
confit|e *m* confectionery; sweets, *Am* candy; **~ería** *f* confectioner's shop, *Am* candy store; **~ura** *f* preserves; jam
conflicto *m* conflict; struggle
conflu|encia *f* confluence; **~ir** *v/i* (*rivers*) to meet; (*people*) to come together
conform|ar *v/t* to adjust; **~arse** to content oneself; to comply; **~e** *a* agreed; agreeing; **~e a** in accordance with; *adv* correspondingly; **~idad** *f* conformity
conforta|ble comfortable; **~nte** comforting; **~r** *v/t* to comfort
confrontar *v/t* to compare; to confront
confu|ndir *v/t* to confuse; to mix up; **~sión** *f* confusion; **~so** confused; obscure
congela|dor *m* freezer; **~r** *v/t*, *v/i* to freeze; to deep-freeze
congenia|l congenial; kindred; **~r** *v/i* to get along with
congestión *f* congestion
conglomerar *v/t*, **~se** to conglomerate
congoja *f* anguish; distress
congraciarse to ingratiate oneself
congratular *v/t* to congratulate; **~se** to be pleased
congrega|ción *f* congregation; **~r** *v/t* to gather; **~rse** to congregate; to assemble
congreso *m* congress
cónico conical
conífera *f* conifer
conjetura *f* conjecture; surmise
conjugar *v/t* to conjugate
conjun|ción *f* conjunction; **~tivo** *m* conjunctive; **~to** *a* connected; *m* whole; set; **en ~to** together; as a whole
conjura|ción *f* conspiracy; **~r** *v/i*, **~rse** to conspire
conmemorativo memorial; commemorative
conmigo with me
conmo|ción *f* commotion; unrest; **~vedor** moving; poignant; **~ver** *v/t* to move; to touch; to shake; to affect
conmuta|dor *m elec* switch; **~r** *v/t for* to commute; to change
cono *m* cone
conoc|edor(a) *a* expert; *m (f)* expert; connoisseur; **~er** *v/t* to know; to be familiar with; **~ido** well-known; **~imiento** *m* knowledge
conque so then; well then
conquista *f* conquest; **~dor** *m* conqueror; **~r** *v/t* to conquer; to win over
consabido well-known; aforesaid
consagrar *v/t* to consecrate; to devote; to sanctify
consanguíneo related by blood
consciente conscious
conscripción *f LA* conscription
consecuen|cia *f* consequence; **~te** consequent
consecutivo consecutive
conseguir *v/t* to obtain; to get; to succeed in
consej|ero *m* counsellor; adviser; **~o** *m* advice; council; advisory body; **~o de administración** board of directors; **~o de ministros** cabinet (council)
consenti|do spoilt (*child*); complaisant (*husband*); **~miento** *m* consent; **~r** *v/t* to permit; to spoil; to indulge
conserje *m* porter, janitor, doorkeeper; **~ría** *f* porter's office
conserva *f* preserved food; *pl* preserves; canned foods; **~ción** *f* conservation; maintenance; **~dor** *m pol* conservative; *a* conservative; **~r** *v/t* to preserve; to conserve; to keep up; **~torio** *m mús* conservatory
considera|ble considerable; **~ción** *f* consideration; **~do** considerate; **~r** *v/t* to consider
consigna *f* order; watchword; password; luggage-room (*at stations*); cloakroom; **~ción** *f* consignment; **~r** *v/t* to consign; to dispatch
consigo with him, with her, with you
consiguiente consequent; **por ~** consequently
consisten|cia *f* consistency; **~te** consistent
consol|ar *v/t* to console; to comfort; **~idar** *v/t*, **~se** to consolidate
consonante *f* consonant
consorte *m* partner; consort; (*law*) accomplice
conspira|ción *f* conspiracy; **~dor** *m* conspirator, plotter; **~r** *v/i* to plot; to conspire
consta|ncia *f* constancy; evidence; **dejar ~ncia de** to put on record; **~nte** constant; **~r** *v/i* to be evident; **hacer ~r** to certify
constelación *f* constellation
consternar *v/t* to dismay; to consternate
constipa|do *m* cold; **~rse** to catch cold
constitu|ción *f* constitution; **~cional** constitutional; **~ir** *v/t* to constitute; to set up
constituyente constituent
constreñir *v/t* to constrain; *med* to constipate
constru|cción *f* construction; building; **~ctor** *m* builder; **~ir** *v/t* to construct; to build
consuelo *m* consolation; solace
cónsul *m* consul
consulado *m* consulate
consulta *f* consultation; opinion; **horas** *f/pl* **de ~** doctor's consulting hours; **obra** *f* **de ~** reference book; **~r** *v/t* to consult
consumado accomplished; consummate
consum|ido lean; skinny; **~idor** *m* consumer; **~ir** *v/t* to consume; **~irse** to burn out; to waste away; **~o** *m* consumption
contab|ilidad *f* bookkeeping; accounting; **~le** *m* bookkeeper
contacto *m* contact; touch
contad|o rare; numbered; **al ~o** in cash; **~or** *m* meter (*for water, gas, etc*); accountant
contagi|ar *v/t* to contaminate; to infect; **~o** *m* contagion; corruption; **~oso** contagious
contamina|ción *f* contamination, pollution; **~ción ambiental** environmental pollution; **~r** *v/t* to contaminate; to pollute; *fig* to corrupt
contempla|ción *f* contemplation; **~r** *v/t* to contemplate; to gaze at
contemporáneo contemporary
conten|ción *f* contention; **~cioso** contentious; controversial; **~der** *v/i* to contend; to fight
conten|er *v/t* to contain; to hold; **~ido** *m* contents
content|ar *v/t* to satisfy; to please; **~arse** to be content; **~o** content; pleased
contesta|ción *f* answer; **~r** *v/t* to answer
context|o *m* context; **~ura** *f* contexture
contienda *f* dispute; struggle
contigo with you
contiguo adjacent; adjoining
continente *m* continent
contingen|cia *f* risk; contingency; **~te** *a* contingent; *m* quota; *mil* contingent
continua|ción *f* continuation; **~damente** continually; continuously; **~r** *v/t*, *v/i* to continue; **~rá** to be continued
continuidad *f* continuity
continuo constant; continuous
contorno *m* form; outline, contour; *pl* environs
contra against
contraataque *m* counterattack
contrabajo *m* contrabass
contraband|ear *v/i* to smuggle; **~ista** *m* smuggler; **~o** *m* smuggling; contraband; **pasar de ~o** to smuggle (in)
contracción *f* contraction
contrac|eptivo *m* contracep-

tive; **~orriente** *f* cross current; **~ultura** *f* counterculture
contrad|ecir *v/t* to contradict; **~icción** *f* contradiction
contraer *v/t* to contract; to enter into
contraespionaje *m* counter-espionage
contrafuerte *m arq* buttress
contraluz: a ~ against the light
contramaestre *m* boatswain
contramarcha *f tecn* reverse (gear)
contraorden *f* counterorder
contrapelo: a ~ against the grain
contraproducente self-defeating, counter-productive
contrari|ar *v/t* to go against; to annoy; **~edad** *f* setback; obstacle; vexation; **~o** contrary; ***al ~o*** on the contrary
contrarrestar *v/t* to counteract; to check
contrarrevolución *f* counter-revolution
contrasentido *m* misinterpretation; nonsense
contraseña *f* password, watchword
contrast|ar *v/t* to resist; to contrast, to be different; **~e** *m* contrast; ***en ~e con*** in contrast to
contrata *f* contract; **~r** *v/t* to engage, to hire; *sp* to sign up
contratiempo *m* mishap, setback
contrato *m* contract
contraveneno *m* antidote
contravenir *v/t* to contravene
contraventana *f* shutter (*of window*)
contribu|ción *f* contribution; tax; **~ir** *v/t* to contribute; **~yente** *m, f* contributor; taxpayer
contrincante *m* rival
control *m* control, checking; ***~ de la natalidad*** birth control; **~ador** *m* **aéreo** air traffic controller; **~ar** *v/t* to control; *com* to audit
controversia *f* controversy
contumacia *f* obstinacy; *for* contempt of court
contusión *f* bruise; contusion
convalec|encia *f* convalescence; **~er** *v/i* to convalesce
convenc|er *v/t* to convince; **~imiento** *m* conviction
conven|ción *f* convention; **~iencia** *f* conformity; convenience; **~iente** suitable; convenient; **~io** *m* agreement; convention; **~ir** *v/i* to agree; **~irse** to come to terms; to agree
convent|illo *m LA* tenement house; **~o** *m* convent
convergen|cia *f* convergence; **~te** converging
conversa|ción *f* conversation; **~r** *v/i* to converse
conver|sión *f* conversion; **~tir** *v/t* to convert
convicción *f* conviction
convidar *v/t* to invite
convincente convincing
conviv|encia *f* living together; **~ir** *v/i* to live together
convocar *v/t* to convoke
convoy *m* convoy; escort
conyugal conjugal
cónyuge *m, f* consort; husband; wife; *pl* married couple
coñac *m* brandy
coopera|ción *f* cooperation; **~r** *v/i* to cooperate; **~tiva** *f* cooperative society
coordina|ción *f* coordination; **~r** *v/t* to coordinate
copa *f* wineglass; *sp* cup; ***tomar una ~*** to have a drink
copi|a *f* copy; **~adora** *f* copying machine; **~ar** *v/t* to copy; **~oso** copious; plentiful; abundant
copla *f* couplet; song; verse
copo *m* tuft; ***~ de nieve*** snowflake; ***~s pl de avena*** oatmeal
coquet|a flirtatious; **~ear** *v/i* to flirt
coraje *m* courage; anger
corazón *m* heart; *bot* core; ***llevar el ~ en la mano*** to wear one's heart upon one's sleeve
corazonada *f* hunch; foreboding
corbata *f* necktie
corcovado hunchbacked
corchete *m* hook and eye; *impr* bracket; ***~ de presión*** snap fastener
corcho *m* cork
cordero *m* lamb
cordial friendly; **~idad** *f* cordiality; warmth; friendliness
cordillera *f* mountain range
cordón *m* cord; string; ***~ de zapato*** shoelace
cordura *f* good sense
cornada *f* goring (*by bull*)
corneja *f* crow
corneta *f* cornet; bugle; horn; *m* cornet player; bugler
cornudo *a* horned; *m fig* cuckold
coro *m* choir; chorus
corona *f* crown; **~ción** *f* coronation; **~r** *v/t* to crown
coronel *m* colonel
coronilla *f* top of the head; *fam* ***estar hasta la ~*** to be fed up
corpiño *m* bodice
corpora|ción *f* corporation; **~tivo** corporate
corpulento corpulent; stout; burly
corral *m* yard; farmyard; pen
correa *f* leather strap; leash; ***~ de ventilador*** fan belt
correc|ción *f* correction; correctness; **~to** correct; polite
corred|izo sliding; folding; **~or** *m sp* runner; *com* broker; ***~or de apuestas*** bookmaker; ***~or de bolsa*** stockbroker
corregir *v/t* to correct; to rectify; to reprimand
correo *m* mail; post office; ***a vuelta de ~*** by return mail; ***~ aéreo*** airmail; **~so** stringy, tough
correr *v/i* to run; to elapse (*time*); to flow; ***a todo ~*** at full speed; **~se** to move along; to run together
correspond|encia *f* correspondence; **~er** *v/i* to correspond; to reply; **~iente** corresponding
corresponsal *m* correspondent (*of a newspaper*)
corri|da *f* run, dash; bullfight; **~ente** *a* running; current; general; ordinary; *f* current; ***estar al ~ente*** to be informed (about); ***~ente alterna*** alternating current; ***~ente continua*** direct current; ***~ente de aire*** draught, *Am* draft
corroborar *v/t* to strengthen; to corroborate
corroer *v/t* to corrode; *geol* to erode
corromper *v/t* to corrupt; to seduce; to bribe
corrosión *f* corrosion
corrupción *f* corruption
cortabolsas *m* pickpocket
cortacésped *m* lawnmower
cortaplumas *m* penknife
cort|ar *v/t* to cut; **~e** *m* cutting; cut; style; length (*of cloth*); *f* court; entourage; yard; *LA* court of justice; ***hacer la ~e*** to court; *pl* Parliament (*in Spain*)
cortej|ar *v/t* to court, to woo; **~o** *m* courtship; wooing
cortés courteous; polite
cortesía *f* politeness; courtesy
corteza *f* bark (*of tree*); peel (*of fruit*); rind (*of cheese*)
cortijo *m* farmstead; farm
cortina *f* curtain
corto short; brief; ***a ~ plazo*** short-term
cortocircuito *m* short circuit
corvo curved, arched
corzo *m* roe-deer
cosa *f* thing; matter, business; ***otra ~*** something else; ***poca ~*** nothing much
cosech|a *f* crop; harvest; yield; **~ar** *v/t* to harvest, to reap
cos|er *v/t, v/i* to sew; **~ido** *m* sewing
cosmético *a, m* cosmetic
cósmico cosmic
cosmonauta *m* cosmonaut
cosmopolita *a, m, f* cosmopolitan
cosquill|as *f/pl* tickling; ***hacer ~as*** to tickle; ***tener ~as*** to be ticklish; **~ear** *v/t* to tickle
costa *f* coast; coastline; shore
costa *f* cost; price paid; ***a ~ de*** at the expense of
costado *m* side; flank
costar *v/i* to cost
Costa Rica *f* Costa Rica
costarriqueño(a) *a, m (f)* Costa Rican
coste *m* cost; expense; investment
costilla *f* rib
costo *m* cost; expense; **~so** high priced
costra *f* crust; *med* scab
costumbre *f* habit; practice; custom; ***de ~*** usually; ***como de ~*** as usual
costura *f* sewing; needlework; seam; ***alta ~*** haute couture
cotejar *v/t* to compare; to collate
cotidiano daily; everyday
cotiza|ción *f com* quotation; valuation; **~r** *v/t* to quote
coto *m* boundary; enclosure; landmark
coyuntura *f* joint (*of bones*); opportunity, occasion
coz *f* kick
cráneo *m* skull
cráter *m* crater
crea|ción *f* creation; **~dor** *m* maker; **~r** *v/t* to make; to create; to establish; **~tivo** creative
crec|er *v/i* to grow; to rise; **~es** *f/pl* increase; ***con ~es*** with a vengeance; **~ido** grown; **~iente** growing; crescent (*moon*); **~imiento** *m* growth; rise; ***~imiento cero*** zero growth
crédito *m* credit
credo *m* creed
crédulo credulous
cre|er *v/t* to believe; to think; **~íble** credible
crem|a *f* cream; ***~a batida*** whipped cream; **~allera** *f* zip fastener, zipper; **~oso** creamy
crepúsculo *m* twilight
cresa *f* maggot
crespo curly; displeased
cresta *f* crest; cock's comb
creyente *a* believing; *m, f* believer
cría *f* breeding
cria|dero *m* breeding place; *bot* nursery; deposit (*of minerals*); **~do(a)** *m (f)* servant; **~nza** *f* breeding; nursing; upbringing; **~r** *v/t* to raise; to nurse; to breed; to bring up; **~tura** *f* creature; infant; baby
criba *f* sieve; **~r** *v/t* to sift
crim|en *m* crime; **~inal** *a, m, f* criminal
crin *m* mane
criollo(a) creole; *LA* native, local
cripta *f* crypt
crisis *f* crisis; ***~ nerviosa*** nervous breakdown
crispar *v/t* to contract, to make twitch (*nerves, muscles*)
cristal *m* crystal; glass; windowpane; ***~ tallado*** cut glass; **~ino** clear; limpid; **~izar** *v/t* to crystallize
cristian|dad *f* Christendom; **~ismo** *m* Christianity; **~o(a)** *m (f), a* Christian
Cristo *m* Christ
criterio *m* criterion
crítica *f* criticism; critique
criticar *v/t* to criticize
crítico *m* critic; *a* critical
criticón *a* faultfinding
croar *v/i* to croak
cromo *m* chromium
crónica *f* chronicle
cronista *m* chronicler; reporter
cronología *f* chronology
cronológico chronological
croqueta *f* croquette
croquis *m* sketch; outline
cruce *m* crossing; crossroads; ***~ a nivel*** grade crossing; **~ro** *m* crossing; cruise
crucifi|car *v/t* to crucify; **~jo** *m* crucifix
crucigrama *m* crossword puzzle
crud|eza *f* crudity; rudeness; **~o** crude; raw
cruel cruel; severe; hard; **~dad** *f* cruelty; severity
cruji|do *m* creak; rustle; **~ente** crunchy; **~r** *v/i* to crackle; to creak; to rustle
cruz *f* cross; tails (*of coin*); ***~ gamada*** swastika; ***♀ Roja*** Red Cross; ***¡~ y raya!*** that's enough!; **~ada** *f* crusade; **~ado** crossed; **~ar** *v/t* to cross
cuaderno *m* notebook; copybook
cuadra *f* hall; stable; *LA* city block
cuadrado square; checkered
cuadrante *m* dial; *mat, mar* quadrant
cuadrar *v/t* to square; *v/i* to tally; to fit in; **~se** to stand at attention
cuadrilongo *a, m* oblong
cuadrilla *f* gang; band; team (*of bullfighters*)
cuadro *m* painting; picture; frame; ***~ de distribución*** switchboard
cuadrúpedo *m* quadruped
cuaja|da *f* curd; **~r** *v/i* to coagulate; to curdle; to congeal; *fig* to turn out well
cual *rel pron* (*with definite article*) who; which; *adv* as; like; such as; ***cada ~*** each one
¿cuál?, ¿cuáles? *interrog pron* which?; what?
cualidad *f* quality
cual|quier *a* (*used before nouns*) any; **~quiera** *a, sing pron* any; anyone; anybody
cuan *adv* how; **~ ... tan** as ... as
cuando when; at the time of; if; ***de ~ en ~*** from time to time; ***~ más*** at most; ***~ quiera*** whenever
¿cuándo? (*interrog*) when?
cuantía *f* quantity; importance
cuantioso large; abundant, copious
cuanto *a, pron rel* as much as; all; whatever; *adv* ***~ más barato tanto mejor*** the cheaper the better; ***en ~*** as soon as; ***en ~ a*** as to; ***~ antes*** as soon as possible
¿cuánto(a)? *interrog pron* how much; how long; how far; *pl* how many?; ***¿a ~s estamos?*** what's the date?
cuarentena *f* quarantine
cuaresma *f* Lent
cuartel *m* barracks; ***~ general*** headquarters
cuarteto *m mús* quartet
cuartilla *f* sheet (*of paper*)
cuarto *m* room; apartment; quarter; ***un ~ para*** a quarter to (*the hour*); ***(la hora) y ~*** a quarter past (*the hour*); ***~ trasero*** rump; ***sin ~*** penniless
cuarzo *m* quartz
cuatro four
cuba *f* cask; barrel; tub; drunkard; ♀ *f* Cuba
cubano(a) *a, m (f)* Cuban
cubertería *f* silverware; cutlery
cubeta *f* small vat *or* cask
cubiert|a *f* cover; lid; deck (*of a ship*); ***~a de popa*** poop deck; ***~a de proa*** foredeck; **~o** *m* cover (*at table*)
cubilete *m* dicebox; baking mold
cubito *m* **de hielo** ice cube
cubo *m* cube; pail; bucket, scuttle; ***~ de basura*** trash can
cubrecama *f* coverlet
cubrir *v/t* to cover; to cloak; **~se** to cover oneself; to put on one's hat
cucaracha *f* cockroach
cuclill|as: *sentarse en ~as* to squat; **~o** *m* cuckoo
cuchar|a *f* spoon; **~ada** *f* spoonful; **~illa** *f*, **~ita** *f* teaspoon; **~ón** *m* ladle
cuchichear *v/i* to whisper
cuchill|a *f* large kitchen knife; **~ada** *f* slash, stab; **~o** *m* knife
cuello *m* neck; collar (*of shirt, etc*)
cuenca *f* basin (*of river*); socket (*of eye*)
cuenta *f* calculation; account; bill; report; ***~ atrás*** countdown; ***~ corriente*** current account; ***a ~*** on account; ***dar ~*** to report; to account for; ***darse ~ de*** to realize; ***hacer las ~s*** to settle accounts; to sum up; ***actuar por su ~*** to act for oneself; ***tomar en ~*** to take into account
cuent|ista *m* storyteller; **~o** *m* story; tale; ***~o chino*** cock and bull story; ***~o de hadas*** fairy tale; ***~o de viejas*** old wives' tale
cuerda *f* rope; cord; chord; *mús* string; spring (*of watch or clock*); ***dar ~ a*** to wind up (*watch; clock*); ***~ floja*** tightrope; ***~ de plomada*** plumbline; ***~ de remolque*** tow line; ***~ para la ropa*** clothesline
cuerdo sane; prudent
cuerno *m* horn
cuero *m* leather; hide; skin; ***en ~s*** naked; ***~ cabelludo*** scalp
cuerpo *m* body; figure; ***~ de bomberos*** fire brigade; ***~ diplomático*** diplomatic corps
cuervo *m* raven
cuesta *f* slope; ***~ abajo*** downhill; ***~ arriba*** uphill
cuestión *f* problem; question; issue
cuestionar *v/t* to question; to discuss; to dispute; **~io** *m* questionnaire
cueva *f* cave; grotto; cellar
cuidado *m* care; worry; concern; ***tener ~*** to take care;

inter ~! careful!; take care!; **~so** careful
cuidar *v/t* to look after; to tend; *v/i* ~ **de** to take care of
culata *f* butt (*of gun*)
culebra *f* snake; ~ ***de cascabel*** rattlesnake
culmina|nte culminating; **~r** *v/i* to culminate; to peak
culo *m* bottom; buttocks; ass
culpa *f* blame; fault; **~ble** guilty; **~r** *v/t* to accuse; to blame
cultiv|ar *v/t* to cultivate; to till; **~o** *m* cultivation; *biol* culture; crop
culto *a* cultivated; cultured; elegant; learned; *m* worship; cult
cultura *f* culture
cumbre *f* top; summit
cumpleaños *m* birthday
cumpli|do *a* full; complete; polite; *m* compliment; **~miento** *m* fulfillment; completion; **~r** *v/t* to carry out; to comply (with); to reach; *v/i* to end; to expire
cúmulo *m* heap
cuna *f* cradle
cundir *v/i* to spread; to increase
cuneta *f* gutter; ditch
cuña *f* wedge
cuñad|a *f* sister-in-law; **~o** *m* brother-in-law
cuota *f* quota; share
cupón *m* coupon
cúpula *f* dome; cupola
cura *m* parish priest; *f med* cure; **~ndero** *m* quack; **~r** *v/t* to cure; **~rse** to recover
curios|ear *v/i* to snoop; **~idad** *f* curiosity; **~o** curious
cursar *v/t* to frequent a place; to take classes
cursi tasteless; showy, vulgar, cheap
cursillo *m* short course
cursiva *f* italics
curso *m* course
curtir *v/t* to tan (*hides*)
curv|a *f* curve; **~ilíneo** curvilinear
cúspide *f geol* peak
custodia *f* custody; care; safekeeping; **~r** *v/t* to guard; to watch; to look after
cutis *m* complexion; skin
cuyo(a, os, as) whose; of whom; of which

Ch

chabacan|ería *f* bad taste; shoddiness; **~o** vulgar; in bad taste
chabola *f* shack
chacal *m* jackal
chacra *f LA* small farm
cháchara *f* chatter
chacharear *v/i* to chatter
chafar *v/t* to flatten
chaflán *m* bevel
chal *m* shawl
chalado *fam* cracked (*in the head*); nutty
chalán *m* hawker; huckster
chaleco *m* waistcoat; vest; ~ ***antibalas*** bulletproof vest; ~ ***salvavidas*** life jacket
chalet *m* cottage; bungalow
chalupa *f* sloop; launch
champaña *m* champagne
champiñón *m* mushroom
champú *m* shampoo
chamuscar *v/t* to scorch; to singe
chancear *v/i* to joke; to banter
chancla *f* old shoe; slipper
chancleta *f* slipper
chanclo *m* clog; galosh
chancho *m LA* hog, pig
chanchullo *m* dirty business, swindle
chandal *m* jogging suit
changador *m LA* porter
chantaje *m* blackmail
chanza *f* joke; fun
chapa *f* sheet of metal; board; **~r** *v/t* to cover, to plate; to panel
chaparrón *m* shower; cloudburst
chapotear *v/i* to splash; to paddle
chapuce|ar *v/t* to botch; to bungle; **~ro** clumsy; shoddy (*work*)
chapurrear *v/t* to speak badly (*a language*)
chapuzar *v/i* to dive
chaqueta *f* jacket; ***cambiar*** ~ to be a turncoat
chaquete *m* backgammon
charc|a *f* pool; **~o** *m* puddle, pond
charla *f* chat; talk; **~r** *v/i* to chatter; to chat; to talk
charlatán *m* chatterbox; mountebank
charol *m* patent leather
chárter: *vuelo* *m* ~ charter flight
chas|car *v/i* to crack; to crackle; **~co** *m* trick; disappointment; **~quear** *v/t* to crack (*a whip*); to play tricks on; **~quido** *m* crack; click; snap
chato *a* snub-nosed; flattened; *m* small wineglass
chauvinista *a, m* chauvinist
chaval(a) *m (f)* boy; girl; kid
chaveta *f* cotter pin
checo(e)slova|co(a) *a, m (f)* Czechoslovak; **~quia** *f* Czechoslovakia
chelín *m* shilling
cheque *m* cheque, *Am t* check; ~ ***para viajeros*** travel(l)er's cheque, *Am t* check
chequeo *m med* check up; *aut* overhaul
chica *f* girl; maid
chicle *m* chewing gum
chico *m* boy; *a* small
chichón *m* bruise; bump
chiflado crazy
Chile *m* Chile
chileno(a) *m (f), a* Chilean
chill|ar *v/i* to yell; to scream; to shriek; **~ido** *m* scream; **~ón** shrill, noisy, loud
chimenea *f* chimney; fireplace; hearth; *mar* funnel
chimpancé *m* chimpanzee
China *f* China
chino(a) *m (f), a* Chinese
chinche *m or f* bug; bedbug
chincheta *f* drawing pin, *Am* thumb tack
chiquill|ada *f* childish speech *or* action; **~ería** *f* kids; children; **~o(a)** *m (f)* kid
chiquitín teeny
chiringuito *m* food and drink stand on the beach
chiripa *f* stroke of luck
chirriar *v/i* to chirp; to squeak; to screech (*brakes*)
chism|e *m* gossip, rumor; trifle, thing; gadget; **~ear** *v/i* to gossip; to tell tales; **~oso** gossipy
chisp|a *f* spark; **~ear** *v/i* to spark; to sparkle; **~orrotear** *v/i* to sizzle
chiste *m* joke; funny story
chivo *m* kid, goat
choca|nte shocking; startling; *LA* annoying; **~r** *v/t* to startle; to shock; to crash; *v/i* to clash; to crash
chocolate *m* chocolate
chófer *m* driver
cholo(a) *a, m (f) LA* meztizo; half-breed
chompa *f LA* pullover, sweater
chopo *m* black poplar
choque *m* shock; jolt; crash
chorizo *m* red pork sausage
chorr|ear *v/i* to gush; to spout; to drip; **~o** *m* jet; spirt; *fig* stream
choza *f* hut, shack
christmas *m* Christmas card
chubasco *m* squall; heavy shower
chul|ada *f* vulgar speech; insolence; funny thing; **~eta** *f coc* chop, cutlet; **~o** pretty, good-looking
chunga *f fam* joke; jest
chup|ar *v/t, v/i* to suck; to suck in; *LA* to drink; **~ete** *m* dummy, *Am* pacifier; **~ón** *m* sponger
churro *m* fritter; *fig* bad piece of work
chusco roguish
chusma *f* mob, rabble
chuzo *m* pike

D

daca: *toma y* ~ give-and-take
dactilografía *f* typing
dactilógrafo(a) *m (f)* typist
dádiva *f* gift
dado *m* die; *pl* dice
daga *f* dagger
daltonismo *m* colo(u)r blindness
dalle *m* scythe
dama *f* lady; gentlewoman; queen (*chess*); *pl* draughts, *Am* checkers
damasco *m* damask; *LA* apricot
damnificar *v/t* to hurt; to injure
danés(esa) *m (f)* Dane; *a* Danish
danza *f* dance; **~r** *v/i* to dance
dañ|ar *v/t* to hurt; to injure; **~ino** harmful; **~o** *m* damage; injury; **~oso** injurious
dar *v/t* to give; to grant; to yield; to strike (*the hour*); ~ ***a la calle*** to face the street; ~ ***las gracias*** to thank; ~ ***parte de*** to inform about; ~ ***un grito*** to cry out; ~ **en** *v/i* to hit upon; ***¡qué más da!*** what does it matter?
dardo *m* dart
dársena *f* quay; dock
dátil *m* date
dato *m* fact; item; *pl* particulars; data
de of; from; for; by; ***un vaso*** ~ ***agua*** a glass of water; ~ ***A a B*** from A to B; ~ ***día*** by day; ~ ***miedo*** for fear; ~ ***veras*** really; truly
deambular *v/i* to stroll
debajo *adv* underneath; below; ~ **de** *prep* under
debat|e *m* debate; **~ir** *v/t* to debate; to discuss
deb|e *m com* debit; **~er** *m* duty; obligation; debt; **~eres** *pl* homework; **~er** *v/t* to owe; *v/i* to must; to have to; **~ido** *a* fitting; due; **~ido a** owing to, due to
débil feeble; weak
debili|dad *f* feebleness; **~tar** *v/t* to weaken
década *f* decade
decadencia *f* decadence
decaimiento *m* decay; weakness; decline
decapitar *v/t* to behead
decena *f* ten
decencia *f* decency
decenio *m* decade
decente decent
decepción *f* disappointment
decepcionar *v/t* to disappoint
decible expressible
decid|ido determined; decided; **~ir** *v/t, v/i* to decide
decimal decimal
décimo *a, m* tenth
decir *v/t, v/i* to say; to tell; to speak; **es** ~ that is to say; ***¡diga!*** hello! (*on phone*); ***¡no me digas!*** you don't say!
decisi|ón *f* decision; **~vo** decisive
declamar *v/i* to hold forth; to speak out
declara|ción *f* declaration; ***~ción de renta*** tax-return; **~r** *v/t* to declare
declina|ción *f* decline; *gram* declension; **~r** *v/t gram* to decline; *v/i* to decline; to decay
declive *m* slope
decora|ción *f* decoration; **~do** *m teat* scenery; **~r** *v/t* to decorate
decoro *m* decorum; propriety
decrecer *v/i* to decrease
decrépito decrepit
decret|ar *v/t* to decree; to decide upon; **~o** *m* decree
dedal *m* thimble
dedicar *v/t* to dedicate; to devote
dedo *m* finger; ~ ***del pie*** toe; ~ ***índice*** index finger; ~ ***meñique*** little finger
deduc|ción *f* deduction; **~ir** *v/t* to deduce; to infer; to deduct
defect|o *m* defect, fault; shortcoming; **~uoso** defective
defen|der *v/t* to defend; **~sa** *f* defence, *Am* defense; safeguard; ***~sa del ambiente*** environment protection
deferencia *f* deference
deferir *v/i:* ~ **a** to defer to; to yield
deficien|cia *f* deficiency; defect; **~te** faulty
defini|ción *f* definition; **~do** definite; **~r** *v/t* to define
deform|ar *v/t* to deform; **~e** deformed; **~idad** *f* deformity
defrauda|ción *f* fraud; ***~ción fiscal*** tax evasion; **~r** *v/t* to cheat; to deceive; to defraud
defunción *f* decease, demise
degenerar *v/i* to degenerate
degollar *v/t* to decapitate
degrada|ción *f* degradation; depravity; **~r** *v/t* to degrade
degustación *f* tasting
dehesa *f* pasture, range
dei|dad *f* deity; **~ficar** *v/t* to deify
deja|do slovenly; **~r** *v/t* to leave; to abandon; to let, to allow; ***~r en paz*** to leave alone; ***~r de*** *v/i* to stop (*doing*)
dejo *m* aftertaste
del *contraction of* **de el**
delantal *m* apron
delante *adv* in front; before; ~ **de** *prep* in front of
delanter|a *f* front; front row; lead; ***llevar la ~a*** to be in the lead; **~o** *m sp* forward
delat|ar *v/t* to denounce; **~or(a)** *m (f)* informer
delega|ción *f* delegation; **~do** *m* delegate
deleit|arse *v/r:* ***~arse en*** to delight *or* revel in; **~e** *m* delight, pleasure
deletre|ar *v/t* to spell; to decipher; **~o** *m* spelling
delfín *m* dolphin
delgad|ez *f* thinness; **~o** thin; slim; slender
delibera|ción *f* deliberation; resolution; **~damente** deliberately; **~r** *v/i* to consider; to deliberate; *v/t* to decide
delicad|eza *f* delicacy; refinement; **~o** delicate; delicious; dainty; refined
delici|a *f* delight; **~oso** delicious; delightful
delimitar *v/t* to delimit
delincuen|cia *f* delinquency; **~te** *m, f* criminal
delinear *v/t* to draw; to outline
delir|ar *v/i* to rave; **~io** *m* delirium; ravings
delito *m* crime; ~ ***mayor*** felony; ~ ***menor*** misdemeano(u)r
demacrado emaciated
demagogia *f* demagogy
demanda *f* demand; petition; inquiry; lawsuit; **~nte** *m* plaintiff; **~r** *v/t* to demand; to claim; to sue
demarca|ción *f* demarcation; **~r** *v/t* to delimit; to mark out
demás *a* other; remaining; ***los, las*** ~ the others; the rest; ***por lo*** ~ as to the rest; apart from this
demasiado *a* too much; *pl* too many; *adv* too; too much
demencia *f* insanity
democracia *f* democracy
democrático democratic
demol|er *v/t* to demolish; **~ición** *f* demolition
demonio *m* demon; ***¡~s!*** hell!
demora *f* delay; **~r** *v/t* to delay; *v/i* to linger on
demostra|ción *f* demonstration; **~r** *v/t* to demonstrate; to prove
denega|ción *f* refusal; **~r** *v/t* to deny; *for* to overrule
dengue *m* affectation; ***hacer ~s*** to be finicky
denigrar *v/t* to defame; to smirch; to revile
denomina|ción *f* denomination; **~r** *v/t* to name
denotar *v/t* to denote
dens|idad *f* density; thickness; **~o** dense; thick
denta|do toothed; jagged; **~dura** *f* denture; **~r** *v/t* to indent
dentista *m* dentist
dentro inside; indoors
denudar *v/t* to denude
denuncia *f* denunciation; *for* accusation; **~ción** *f* denunciation; **~r** *v/t* to denounce; to proclaim
departamento *m* department; compartment; *LA* apartment, flat
depend|encia *f* dependence; dependency; subordination; *com* branch office; **~er** *v/i* to depend; **~iente** *m* shop assistant
deplorar *v/t* to deplore
deponer *v/t* to lay down; to depose; *for* to give evidence
deporta|ción *f* deportation; **~r** *v/t* to deport
deport|e *m* sport; **~ista** *m, f* sportsman, sportswoman; **~ivo** sporting
deposi|ción *f* removal; *for* deposition; statement; **~tar** *v/t* to deposit
depósito *m* deposit; storehouse; ~ ***de agua*** water tank; ~ ***de gasolina*** gas tank
depravado depraved
depreciar *v/t* to depreciate
depresión *f* depression
deprimi|do depressed; **~r** *v/t* to depress; to humiliate
depurar *v/t* to purify; to cleanse
derech|a *f* right; right hand; **~ista** *m, f pol* rightwinger; **~o** *m* right; law; justice; ***~o de paso*** right of way; ***~os de autor*** copyright; ***con*** ~ rightly; justly; ***de ~o*** by right; *a* right; straight
deriva *f mar* drift; **~ción** *f* derivation; origin; **~do** derivative; **~r** *v/t* to derive
derogar *v/t* to repeal; to abolish
derramar *v/t* to shed (*blood*);

derramarse to spill; to scatter; to pour out; ~se to overflow; to run over

derrame m overflow

derrapar v/i to skid

derretir v/t to melt, to dissolve; ~se to melt

derrib|ar v/t to demolish; to knock down; ~o m demolition

derrocar v/t to overthrow; to topple

derroch|ar v/t to squander; to waste; ~e m squandering

derrota f defeat; ~r v/t to defeat; to rout

derrumba|miento m collapse; cave-in; ~r v/t to tear down; ~rse to fall down; to collapse

desabotonar v/t to unbutton

desabrido tasteless; insipid

desabrigar v/t to uncover; to expose

desabrochar v/t to unclasp; to unfasten

desacat|ar v/t to be disrespectful to; ~o m disrespect; for contempt

desac|ertar v/i to err; to be wrong; ~ierto m mistake; blunder

desacomod|ado destitute; jobless; ~ar v/t to inconvenience; to dismiss (from job)

desaconsejado ill-advised

desacostumbra|do unusual; ~rse to break a habit

desacreditar v/t to discredit

desacuerdo m disagreement

desafecto m dislike; disaffection

desafia|nte defiant; ~r v/t to defy, to challenge

desafinar v/i más to be out of tune; ~se to get out of tune

desafío m challenge

desafortunado unlucky, unfortunate

desagradable disagreeable, unpleasant

desagradeci|do ungrateful; ~miento m ingratitude

desagrado m discontent, displeasure

desagraviar v/t to indemnify

desagüe m drain; outlet; draining

desahoga|do brazen; roomy; comfortable; ~r to relieve; to ease; ~rse to unburden oneself; to relax

desahogo m relief; freedom; ease

desahuci|ar v/t to evict (tenants); ~o m eviction

desaira|do unattractive; unsuccessful; ~r v/t to snub; to ignore

desal|entar v/t to discourage; ~entarse to lose heart; ~iento m discouragement; dismay

desaliñado untidy; slovenly; grubby

desalmado heartless, pitiless

desalojar v/t to dislodge, to oust

desalquilado unoccupied; not rented

desalumbrado dazzled; bewildered

desamor m coldness; indifference

desampar|ar v/t to forsake; to desert; ~o m abandonment; helplessness

desangrar v/t to bleed; ~se to lose blood; to bleed to death

desanima|do downhearted; dispirited; ~r v/t to discourage

desapacible unpleasant, disagreeable

desapar|ecer v/i to disappear; to vanish; ~ecido

missing; ~ición f disappearance

desapercibido unprepared, unprovided; unnoticed; LA inattentive

desapoderar v/t to dispossess

desaprobar v/t to disapprove of; to frown on

desaprovechado backward; unproductive

desarm|ar v/t to disarm; ~e m disarmament

desarraigar v/t to root out; to eradicate

desarregl|ado untidy; disorderly; out of order; ~ar v/t to disarrange; ~o m disorder; confusion

desarroll|ar v/t to develop; to unroll, to unwind; ~o m development; en ~o developing

desarticulado disjointed

desaseado unclean, dirty; untidy

desasos|egar v/t to disquiet; to disturb; ~iego m restlessness; anxiety

desast|re m disaster; ~roso disastrous

desatar v/t to untie; ~se to break loose; to go too far

desaten|ción f inattention; discourtesy; ~der v/t to neglect; to disregard; ~to inattentive; careless

desatinar v/t to confuse; v/i to act or speak foolishly

desaven|encia f discord; unpleasantness; ~irse to disagree

desaventajado unfavo(u)rable

desav|iar v/t to mislead; ~ío m misleading

desayun|ar v/i, ~arse to have breakfast; ~o m breakfast

desazón f insipidity; tastelessness; med discomfort

desbanda|da f disbandment; rout; ~rse to disband

desbaratar v/t to ruin; to frustrate; v/t to talk nonsense

desbocar v/i to run or flow into; ~se to run away (horse); to abuse

desborda|miento m flooding; ~r v/i, ~rse to overflow; fig to be beside oneself

descabellado dishevelled; 'rash

descabeza|do stunned; unreasonable; ~r v/t to behead

descafeinado decaffeinated (coffee)

descalabr|ar v/t to wound in the head; ~o m calamity; misfortune

descalificar v/t to disqualify

descalz|ar v/t to remove shoes; ~o barefooted

descaminado misguided

descamisado ragged

descans|ar v/i to rest; to sleep; v/t to lean; ~illo m landing; ~o m rest; relief; break; teat, sp interval

descapotable m aut convertible

descarado shameless; brazen

descarga f unloading; discharge; ~dero m wharf; ~r v/t to unload; to discharge; v/i to flow (river into sea, etc)

descargo m discharge; com credit (in accounts); for acquittal

descaro m insolence; effrontery

descarrila|miento m derailment; ~r v/i to derail

descartar v/t to discard; to reject

descen|dencia f descent;

offspring; ~der v/t to get or take down; v/i to descend; ~diente m descendant; ~so m descent; decline

descentralizar v/t to decentralize

descifrar v/t to decipher

descolgar v/t to take down (from a hook or peg); to unhook; ~se to come down

descolorar v/t to discolo(u)r

descomedido excessive; rude

descompo|ner v/t to decompose; to disarrange; to shake up; ~nerse to get out of order; to go to pieces; ~sición f decomposition; disturbance

descompuesto out of order

descon|certar v/t to disconcert, to take aback, to embarrass; to baffle; ~cierto m confusion

desconectar v/t to disconnect; to switch off

desconfia|do distrustful; suspicious; ~nza f distrust; ~r v/t to distrust

descongela|dor m defroster; ~r v/t to defrost

descono|cer v/t to fail to recognize; to ignore; to be ignorant of; ~ido a unknown; m stranger; ~imiento m ignorance; ingratitude

desconsiderado inconsiderate

desconsola|do disconsolate; ~rse to sorrow; to be grieved

descontaminación f decontamination

descontar v/t to discount; to deduct; to detract

descontenta|dizo hard to please; ~r v/t to displease

descontento dissatisfied; discontented

descontinuar v/t to discontinue

descorazonar v/t to dishearten; to discourage; ~se to lose heart

descorchar v/t to uncork

descort|és impolite; ~esía f impoliteness; discourtesy

descos|er v/t to unstitch; ~erse to blurt out; ~ido m fig babbler

descrédito m discredit

descri|bir v/t to describe; ~pción f description; ~ptivo descriptive

descuartizar v/t to carve up

descubierta: a la ~ openly; out in the open

descub|ierto a clear; open; bareheaded; poner al ~ierto to expose; ~ridor m discoverer; ~rimiento m discovery; ~rir v/t to discover; to uncover

descuento m discount

descuid|ado careless; negligent; ~arse to be neglectful; to let oneself go; not to worry; ~o m neglect; carelessness

desde prep since; from; after; ~ ahora from now on; ~ entonces since then; ~ luego at once; of course; ~ que adv since

desdecirse to retract

desdén m contempt; disdain

desdeñ|ar v/t to disdain; to scorn; ~oso disdainful, contemptuous, scornful

desdicha f misfortune; ~do unfortunate; unhappy

desdoblar v/t to unfold

desdoro m blot; stigma

dese|able desirable; ~ar v/t to desire

desech|ar v/t to reject; to discard; to throw out; ~os m/pl refuse; waste

desembalar v/t to unpack

desembaraz|ar v/t to clear; to free; ~o m freedom; naturalness

desembarc|ar v/t, v/i to put ashore; to disembark; ~o m landing

desemboca|dura f mouth (of river); ~r v/i to flow into; to lead to

desembols|ar v/t to pay out; to disburse; ~o m disbursement

desembragar v/t to disengage; to release clutch

desembrollar v/t to disentangle

desempacho m ease; confidence

desempapelar v/t to unpack; to strip (paper)

desempaquetar v/t to unpack, to unwrap

desempeñar v/t to redeem (from pawn); to extricate

desempleo m unemployment

desencadenar v/t to unchain; to liberate; ~se to break out; to break loose

desencajar v/t to dislocate; to disconnect

desencantar v/t to disenchant

desenchufar v/t to unplug

desenfad|ado free; easy; natural; ~arse to quieten down; to regain poise; ~o m ease; naturalness

desenfrena|do unbridled; unrestrained; ~rse to lose control; to give way to passion

desenganchar v/t to unhook

desengañ|ar v/t to disillusion; to undeceive; ~arse to lose illusions; to face reality; ~o m disillusion

desenla|ce m outcome; ~zar v/t to unlace; to undo

desenmascarar v/t to unmask

desenred|ar v/t to disentangle; ~o m disentanglement

desenrollar v/t to unroll

desentenderse de to pay no attention to

desenterrar v/t to unearth

desenvol|tura f naturalness; ease of manner; ~ver v/t to unfold; to unwind

desenvuelto open; free; easy; self-assured

deseo m desire; wish

desequilibr|ar v/t to unbalance; ~io m lack of balance; disorder

deser|ción f desertion; ~tar v/t, v/i to desert; ~tor m deserter

desespera|ción f despair; ~nzarse to deprive of hope; ~r v/i, ~rse to despair

desestimar v/t to belittle; to disparage

desfachatez f effrontery; cheek

desfalcar v/t to embezzle

desfallec|er v/i to faint; to weaken; ~imiento m languor; swoon

desfavorable unfavo(u)rable

desfigurar v/t to disfigure; to deface; to misrepresent

desfil|adero m narrow passage; gorge; defile; ~ar v/i to parade; to march past; ~e m parade

desflorar v/t to deflower

desgajar v/t to tear off

desgana f lack of appetite; reluctance

desgarbado ungraceful; clumsy

desgarra|do licentious; dissolute; ~dor heartbreaking; ~r v/t to tear, to rend

desgast|ado worn (out), used up; treadless (tires); ~ar v/t to wear away; to corrode; ~e m wear and tear; corrosion

desgobernar v/t to misgovern; to mismanage

desgracia f adversity; misfortune; disfavo(u)r; ~do a unlucky; wretched; unfortunate; m wretch; unfortunate person

desgreñar v/t to dishevel, to rumple, to tousle (hair)

desguarne|cer v/t to dismantle; to strip of ornaments; ~ido bare; unguarded

deshabitado uninhabited

deshacer v/t to undo; to destroy; to take apart; to unpack; ~se de to get rid of

desharrapado ragged

deshecho undone; exhausted; dissolved

deshelar v/t to thaw; to defrost

desheredar v/t to disinherit

deshielo m thaw

deshilvanado disjointed; incoherent

deshinchar v/t to reduce a swelling; to deflate; ~se to subside (swelling)

deshojar v/t to strip the leaves off

deshonesto indecent; lewd

deshonra f loss of hono(u)r, disgrace; ~r v/t to seduce; to disgrace

deshora: a ~ inopportunely, at the wrong time

deshuesar v/t to bone (meat); to stone (fruit)

desidia f laziness, indolence

desierto a deserted; uninhabited; m desert

design|ación f designation; appointment; ~ar v/t to designate; to appoint; ~io m design, plan

desigual dissimilar; unequal; uneven; ~dad f inequality; unevenness

desilusión f disappointment

desilusionar v/t to disillusion; to disappoint

desinfectar v/t to disinfect

desinflar v/t to deflate

desinter|és m lack of interest; indifference; generosity; ~esado unselfish; indifferent

desintoxicación f sobering up; detoxification

desistir de v/i to desist from; to give up

desleal disloyal, faithless; ~tad f disloyalty

desleír v/t to dissolve; to dilute

deslenguado foul-mouthed

desliz m slip, lapse; ~ar v/i to slip; to slide

deslucido unadorned; dull; inelegant

deslumbra|miento m dazzling; confusion; ~r v/t to dazzle; to puzzle; to confuse

desmán m misconduct; excess; disaster

desmandado uncontrollable

desmantelar v/t to dismantle; to abandon

desmañado clumsy

desmay|arse to faint; to lose courage; ~o m fainting fit; discouragement

desmedido excessive, disproportionate

desmejorar v/t to spoil; to impair; ~se to deteriorate; to decline; to fail (health)

desmembrar v/t to dismember; to separate

desmenti|da f denial; ~r v/t to contradict; to deny

desmenuzar *v/t* to crumble; to break into small pieces
desmesurado excessive
desmigajar *v/t* to crumble
desmilitarizado demilitarized
desmontar *v/t* to dismantle; to clear away; **~se** *v/t* to dismount
desmoralizar *v/t* to corrupt; to demoralize
desmoronar *v/t* to wear away; **~se** to decay; to crumble; to get dilapidated
desnatar *v/t* to skim (*milk*)
desnaturalizado unnatural
desnivel *m* unevenness; difference of level
desnud|ar *v/t* to strip; to denude; to undress; **~arse** to strip; **~o** *a* naked; *m* nude
desnutri|ción *f* malnutrition; **~do** undernourished
desobed|ecer *v/i* to disobey; **~iencia** *f* disobedience; **~iente** disobedient
desocupa|do idle; unemployed; unoccupied; **~r** *v/t* to vacate
desodorante *m* deodorant
desola|ción *f* desolation; affliction; **~do** distressed; **~r** *v/t* to lay waste; **~rse** to grieve
desorden *m* disorder; confusion; **~ado** untidy; **~ar** *v/t* to disorder; to disarrange
desorganiza|ción *f* disorganization; **~r** *v/t* to disorganize
desorientar *v/t* to mislead; to confuse
desovar *v/i zool* to spawn
despabila|do alert; wide-awake, smart; **~r** *v/t* to trim (*candle*); **~rse** to wake up; to grow alert
despacio slowly; gently; *LA* soft, low (*voice*)
despach|ar *v/t* to dispatch; to hasten; **~o** *m* office; dispatch
despampante *fam* stunning
desparpajo *m* ease of manner; self confidence; charm
desparramar *v/t* to scatter, to spread
despavorido terrified, panic-stricken
despectivo contemptuous; scornful; derogatory
despech|ar *v/t* to enrage; **~o** *m* spite; insolence; **a ~o de** in spite of
despedazar *v/t* to tear to pieces
despedi|da *f* farewell; dismissal; **~r** *v/t* to dismiss; to fire; **~rse** to say goodbye
despeg|ar *v/t* to unglue; to detach; **~ue** *m aer* take-off; blast-off (*of rocket*)
despeinar *v/t* to ruffle, to tousle (*hair*)
despeja|do clear; smart; cloudless (*sky*); **~r** *v/t* to clear (up); **~rse** to relax
despeluznante hair-raising
despensa *f* pantry
despeña|dero *m* precipice; crag; **~r** *v/t* to hurl down
desperdici|ar *v/t* to throw away; **~o** *m* waste; refuse
desperezarse to stretch
desperfecto *m* damage; imperfection
desperta|dor *m* alarm clock; **~r** *v/t* to wake up; **~rse** to wake up
despiadado merciless, pitiless
despierto awake; alert; smart
despilfarr|ar *v/t* to waste; to squander; **~o** *m* waste; extravagance
despist|ado absentminded; **~ar** *v/t* to mislead
desplaza|miento *m* displacement; **~r** *v/t* to displace, to move
despl|egar *v/t* to unfold; to spread; *mil* to deploy; **~iegue** *m fig* display; *mil* deployment
desplomarse to lean forward; to collapse
desplumar *v/t* to pluck (*fowl*); *fig* to fleece
despobla|do uninhabited; desert; barren; **~r** *v/t* to lay waste
despoj|ar *v/t* to despoil; to strip; **~o** *m* despoiling; plundering; *pl* leftovers
desposado newly married
desposeer *v/t* to dispossess
déspota *m* despot
despreci|able contemptible; **~ación** *f* depreciation; loss of value; **~ar** *v/t* to despise; **~o** *m* contempt
desprender *v/t* to unfasten; to separate
desprendimiento *m* detachment; **~ de piedras** rock slide
despreocupado carefree, free and easy, happy-go-lucky
desprestigiar *v/t* to disparage; **~se** to lose prestige
desprevenido unprepared
desproporcionado disproportionate
desprovisto destitute
después *adv* after; afterwards; later; **~ de** *prep* after; **poco ~** soon after
despuntado blunt
desquiciar *v/t* to unhinge; **~se** to lose one's reason
desquite *m* compensation; retaliation; *sp* return match
destaca|do prominent; outstanding; **~r** *v/t* to emphasize; *mil* to detach; **~rse** to stand out
destajo *m* piecework
destapar *v/t* to uncover
destartalado shabby
destello *m* sparkle; flash
destempla|do intemperate; dissonant; **~nza** *f* inclemency (*of weather*); intemperance; abuse; **~r** *v/t* to put out of tune; to disturb; **~rse** to get out of tune; to lose one's temper
desteñir *v/t* to remove the colo(u)r from; to fade
desterrar *v/t* to banish; to exile
destetar *v/t* to wean
destiempo: a ~ untimely; out of turn
destierro *m* exile; banishment
destilar *v/t*, *v/i* to distil(l)
destin|ar *v/t* to intend; to assign; to appoint; **~atario** *m* addressee; **~o** *m* destiny, fate; destination; employment
destitu|ción *f* dismissal; **~ir** *v/t* to dismiss
destornilla|dor *m* screwdriver; **~r** *v/t* to unscrew
destreza *f* dexterity, skill
destripar *v/t* to disembowel; *fig* to mangle
destroz|ar *v/t* to destroy; **~o** *m* destruction
destru|cción *f* destruction; ruin; **~ctivo** destructive; **~ir** *v/t* to destroy
desunir *v/t* to separate
desuso *m* disuse
desvainar *v/t* to shell; to peel
desvalido destitute, helpless
desvalijar *v/t* to rob
desval|orización *f* devaluation; **~orizar** *v/t* to devalue
desván *m* attic, garret, loft
desvanec|er *v/t* to make disappear; **~erse** to fade away; to faint; **~imiento** *m med* faintness
desvel|ar *v/t* to keep awake; **~arse** to be sleepless; **~o** *m* sleeplessness; vigilance
desventaja *f* disadvantage
desventura *f* misfortune
desvergonzado shameless, insolent
desvestirse to undress
desviar *v/t* to divert; to deflect; **~se** to deviate; to turn aside
desvío *m* by-pass; detour
desvivirse: ~ por to crave for; to give oneself up to
detall|adamente in detail, at length; **~ar** *v/t* to detail; **~e** *m* detail; **~ista** *m* retailer
detección *f* detection, monitoring
detective *m* detective
deten|ción *f* arrest; delay; **~er** *v/t* to arrest; to stop; **~erse** to stop; to delay; **~idamente** thoroughly; in detail
detergente *m* detergent
deteriorar *v/t* to spoil; **~se** to deteriorate
determina|ción *f* resolution; determination; **~r** *v/t* to determine; **~rse** to decide
detestar *v/t* to detest; to loathe
detona|ción *f* detonation; **~r** *v/i* to detonate
detrás behind; **por ~** in the back; behind one's back
detrimento *m* detriment; loss
deud|a *f* indebtedness; debt; *pl* liabilities; **~or(a)** *m* (*f*) debtor
devalua|ción *f* devaluation; **~r** *v/t* to devalue
devanar *v/t* to wind (*threads*); *v/r* **~se los sesos** to rack one's brains
devaneos *m/pl* delirium; ravings
devastar *v/t* to devastate
devoción *f* devotion; affection
devocionario *m* prayer book
devol|ución *f* return; restitution; *pl com* returns; **~ver** *v/t* to return; to give back; to restore
devorar *v/t* to devour
devoto devout, pious; devoted
día *m* day; **~ de fiesta** holiday; **~ por ~** day by day; **~ laborable** workday; **~ de semana** *LA* weekday; **al ~** up to date; **de ~** by day; **de ~ en ~** from day to day; **el ~ de mañana** *fig* in the future; **el ~ siguiente** the next day; **hoy en ~** nowadays; **buenos ~s** good morning; **todo el ~** all day; **todos los ~s** every day; **un ~ sí y otro no** every other day
diabético diabetic
diablo *m* devil
diabólico diabolical, fiendish
diafragma *m* diaphragm
diagnóstico *m* diagnosis
dialecto *m* dialect
diálogo *m* dialogue
diamante *m* diamond
diámetro *m* diameter
diapositiva *f foto* slide, transparency
diario *m* daily newspaper; diary; *a*, *adv* daily
diarrea *f* diarrhea
dibuj|ante *m* sketcher; draftsman; **~ar** *v/t* to draw; to design; **~o** *m* sketch; drawing; **~o animado** *cine* cartoon
dicción *f* diction
diccionario *m* dictionary
diciembre *m* December
dictad|o *m* dictation; **~or** *m* dictator; **~ura** *f* dictatorship
dictam|en *m* judgment; opinion; **~inar** *v/t* to judge; to express an opinion
dictar *v/t* to dictate; to pronounce
dich|a *f* happiness; **~oso** happy; fortunate
dicho *m* saying; proverb
diente *m* tooth; prong (*of fork*); tusk; fang; **~ canino** eye-tooth; **~ de león** dandelion; **~s postizos** false teeth
diestr|a *f* right hand; **~o** right; dexterous; skil(l)ful; **a ~o y siniestro** right and left, on all sides; *m* bullfighter
diet|a *f* diet; assembly; *pl* subsistence allowance; **~ético** dietary
diez ten; **~mo** *m* tithe
difama|ción *f* defamation, libel; **~r** *v/t* to defame, to libel
diferen|cia *f* difference; **~ciar** *v/t* to differentiate; *v/i* to differ; **~te** different
diferir *v/t* to defer, to delay; *v/i* to differ
difícil difficult; hard
dificult|ad *f* difficulty; **~ar** *v/t* to make difficult; **~oso** difficult
difteria *f* diphtheria
difundir *v/t* to diffuse; to spread
difunto(a) *m* (*f*), *a* deceased; dead; **día de los ♀s** All Soul's Day
difus|ión *f* diffusion; broadcasting; **~o** diffuse; widespread
dige|rir *v/t* to digest; **~stión** *f* digestion
dign|arse to deign; to condescend; **~o** deserving; dignified; **~o de** worthy of; deserving
dila|ción *f* delay; **~tación** *f* expansion; *med* dilatation; **~tar** *v/t* to dilate; to spread; to delay; **~tarse** to expand; to linger
dilema *m* dilemma
diligen|cia *f* diligence; errand; **~te** diligent
dilucidar *v/t* to elucidate
dilu|ción *f* dilution; **~ir** *v/t* to dilute
diluvio *m* deluge; flood; pouring rain
dimanar *v/i* to flow; to spring from
dimensión *f* dimension
diminu|tivo diminutive; **~to** minute; tiny
dimi|sión *f* resignation (*from a post*); **~tir** *v/t* to resign
Dinamarca *f* Denmark
dinámic|a *f* dynamics; **~o** dynamic
dinamita *f* dynamite
dínamo *f* dynamo
diner|al *m* fortune, large sum of money; **~o** *m* money; **~o en efectivo** cash
diócesis *f* diocese
Dios *m* God; **¡~ mío!** Good Heavens!; **¡por ~!** for God's sake!; **si ~ quiere** God willing
diosa *f* goddess
diploma *m* diploma
diplom|acia *f* diplomacy; **~ático(a)** *m* (*f*) diplomat; *a* diplomatic; tactful
diputa|ción *f* deputation; **~do** *m* delegate, deputy; member of parliament
dique *m* dike; dam
direc|ción *f* direction; management; board of directors; **~ción prohibida** *aut* no entry; **~tor** *a* directing; **~tor(a)** *m* (*f*) director; head; **~tor de orquesta** conductor; **~torio** *m* directory
dirigir *v/t* to direct; to address (*letter, petition*); to guide; to steer; **~se a** to speak to
discernir *v/t* to discern; to distinguish
disciplina *f* discipline; subject of study; **~r** *v/t* to discipline; to scourge
discípulo(a) *m* (*f*) disciple; pupil
disco *m* disk; phonograph record; *tel* dial; *sp* discus; **~ vertebral** spinal disk
díscolo naughty
discontinuo discontinuous
discorda|ncia *f* disagreement; **~r** *v/i* to disagree; to differ
discordia *f* discord; disagreement
discoteca *f* record store; discotheque
discreción *f* discretion; shrewdness; **a ~** at one's discretion
discrepa|ncia *f* discrepancy; **~r** *v/i* to disagree
discreto discreet; tactful; wise
disculpa *f* excuse; **~r** *v/t* to excuse; to pardon; **~rse** to apologize
discurrir *v/i* to roam; to pass, to take its course; to reflect; *v/t* to invent
discurso *m* speech; discourse
discusión *f* discussion; argument
discutir *v/t* to discuss; *v/i* to argue
diseminar *v/t* to disseminate
disentería *f* dysentery
disenti|miento *m* dissent; **~r** *v/i* to disagree
diseñ|ador *m* designer; **~ar** *v/t* to design; **~o** *m* design; model; sketch; outline
disertar *v/i* to expound; to discourse
disfraz *m* mask; disguise; fancy dress; **~ar** *v/t* to disguise
disfrutar *v/t*, *v/i* to enjoy; to have a good time
disgust|ar *v/t* to displease; **~arse** to be angry; to fall out; to be annoyed; **~o** *m* displeasure; annoyance; sorrow; unwillingness; quarrel
disidente *m*, *f* dissident
disimu|lar *v/t* to disguise; to conceal; to feign; to excuse; **~lo** *m* concealment; dissimulation
disipar *v/t* to dissipate
disminu|ción *f* diminution; decrease; **~ir** *v/t*, *v/i* to diminish
disol|ución *f* dissolution; **~uto** dissolute; **~ver** *v/t* to melt; to dissolve
disonancia *f* dissonance; discord
dispar unequal; unlike
disparar *v/t* to shoot; to discharge; to fire; **~se** to explode; to go off
disparat|ado absurd; **~e** *m* nonsense; absurdity
disparidad *f* disparity
disparo *m* shot
dispensar *v/t* to dispense; to exempt; **~io** *m* dispensary
dispers|ar *v/t* to disperse; to scatter; **~ión** *f* dispersal; dispersion
dispon|er *v/t* to dispose; to arrange; **~erse** to get ready; **~ible** available
disposición *f* disposition; arrangement; disposal
dispuesto *a* ready; arranged; disposed; **bien ~** well-disposed
disputa *f* quarrel; dispute; **~r** *v/t*, *v/i* to dispute; to debate; to quarrel
distan|cia *f* distance; **~ciar** *v/t* to place at a distance; **~te** far away, remote

Spanish

distensión f distension; med strain
distin|ción f distinction; difference; **~guido** distinguished; **~guir** v/t to distinguish; **~to** different; clear, distinct
distra|cción f distraction; diversion; entertainment; **~er** v/t to distract; **~erse** to amuse oneself; to get absentminded; **~ído** absentminded
distribu|ción f distribution; **~idor** m distributor; **~idor automático** vending machine; **~ir** v/t to distribute; to hand out
distrito m district
disturbio m disturbance
disuadir v/t to dissuade; to deter
diurno daily; bot diurnal
divagar v/i to wander; to digress, to ramble
divergencia f divergence; difference of opinion
divergir v/i to diverge; fig to disagree
divers|idad f variety; **~ión** f amusement; mil diversion; **~o** diverse; different; various
diverti|do amusing; enjoyable; **~r** v/t to amuse; **~rse** to amuse oneself; to have a good time; to make merry
divid|endo m dividend; **~ir** v/t to divide
divin|idad f divinity; **~o** divine; heavenly
divisa f badge; emblem; motto; pl foreign currency
divisar v/t to make out, to espy
divisi|ble divisible; **~ón** f division
divorci|ar v/t to divorce; to separate; **~arse** to get divorced; **~o** m divorce
divulgar v/t to divulge; to spread
dobla|dillo m hem; **~r** v/t to double; to fold; to bend; to turn (the corner); v/i to toll (bells); **~rse** to give in
doble a double; dual; **~gar** v/t to bend; to fold; to persuade; **~z** m fold; f duplicity
docena f dozen; **la ~ del fraile** the baker's dozen; **por ~** by the dozen
docente teaching; educational
dócil docile; obedient; gentle
docilidad f docility; gentleness
docto a learned; m scholar; **~r** m doctor; **~rado** m doctorate
doctrina f doctrine
document|ación f documentation; **~al** m cine documentary; **~o** m document
dogal m halter; noose
dogmático dogmatic
dogo m bulldog
dólar m dollar (U.S. money)
dole|ncia f illness; ailment; **~r** v/i to hurt; to ache; **~rse de** to pity; to be sorry for
dolor m pain; grief; ache; **~oso** painful
doloso deceitful; crafty
doma|dor m tamer (of animals); **~r** v/t to tame; to master
domesticar v/t to tame; to domesticate
doméstico domestic
domicili|ado resident; **~o** m residence
domin|ación f domination; **~ar** v/t to dominate; to subdue
domin|go m Sunday; **2go de Ramos** Palm Sunday; **~io** m dominion; control
dominó m domino, masquerade costume
don m (courtesy title used before Christian name)
don m gift; ability; **~ación** f donation; gift
donaire m grace; poise
don|ante m, f donor; **~ar** v/t to donate
doncella f virgin; maid; lady's maid
donde (interrog **dónde**) where; **~quiera** wherever
donoso witty
doña f (courtesy title used before Christian name)
dora|do golden; gilt; **~r** v/t to gild
dormidera f poppy
dormi|lón m sleepyhead; **~r** v/i to sleep; **~rse** to go to sleep, to fall asleep; **~tar** v/i to doze, to snooze; **~torio** m bedroom; dormitory
dors|al dorsal; **~o** m back
dos two; **de ~ en ~** in twos; **los ~** the two of them
dosel m canopy
dosi|ficar v/t to dose out; **~s** f dose
dot|ación f endowment; **~ado** gifted; **~ar** v/t to endow; **~e** f dowry
draga f dredger; **~minas** m minesweeper; **~r** v/t to dredge
dragón m dragon; mil dragoon
drama m play; drama
dramático dramatic
dramaturgo m playwright
drástico drastic
drenaje m drainage
drog|a f drug; **~adicto(a)** m (f) drug addict; **~uería** f drugstore
dual dual; **~idad** f duality
dúctil elastic; manageable; ductile
ducha f shower
dud|a f doubt; **sin ~a** no doubt; **~ar** v/t, v/i to doubt; **~oso** doubtful
duelo m duel; grief; mourning
duende m goblin; an unexplainable enchantment
dueñ|a f owner; mistress; **~o** m owner; master
dul|ce sweet; soft; **~zura** f sweetness; gentleness
duna f sand dune
dúo m duet
duplic|ado m duplicate; **~ar** v/t to double; to duplicate; **~idad** f duplicity
duque m duke; **~sa** f duchess
dura|ble durable; lasting; **~nte** prep during; **~nte todo el año** all year round; **~r** v/i to last; to endure
durazno m LA peach; peach tree
dureza f hardness
durmiente sleeping
duro a hard; firm; tough; m 5 peseta coin

E

ebanista m cabinetmaker; joiner
ébano m ebony
ebrio intoxicated; drunk
eclesiástico a ecclesiastical; m ecclesiastic, priest
eclipse m eclipse (t fig)
eco m echo
ecolog|ía f ecology; **~ista** m, f ecologist
economía f economy; thrift; **~ política** economics
económico economical; inexpensive
econom|ista m, f economist; **~izar** v/t to economize; to save
ecuación f equation
ecua|dor m equator; **el 2dor** Ecuador; **~torial** equatorial; **~toriano(a)** a, m (f) Ecuadorian
echa|da f cast; throw; LA boast; **~r** v/t to throw; to cast; to throw out; to pour; to spread; **~r al correo** to post; **~r abajo** to demolish; to ruin; **~r a perder** to ruin; **~r de menos** to miss; **~rse** to lie down; **~rse a perder** to go bad; to get spoiled
edad f age; epoch; **de ~ madura** middle-aged; **mayor de ~** of age; **2 Media** Middle Ages
edición f edition
edific|ar v/t to build; **~io** m building
edit|ar v/t to publish; **~or** m publisher; **~orial** m leading article; f publishing house
edredón m eiderdown; quilt
educa|ción f education; upbringing; manners; **~ción cívica** civics; **~ción física** physical education; **~r** v/t to educate; to bring up
EE.UU. = **Estados Unidos**
efect|ivamente in fact; really; **~ivo** a real; effective; m cash; **~o** m effect; purpose; pl assets; **en ~o** as a matter of fact; indeed; **~uar** v/t to carry out; **~uarse** to take place
efica|cia f efficacy; efficiency; **~z** able; efficient
efusivo effusive, affectionate
egip|cio(a) m (f), a Egyptian; **2to** m Egypt
egocéntrico egocentric
egoís|mo m egoism; **~ta** m, f egoist; a selfish
egregio eminent
egresar v/i LA to leave (school)
eje m axle; axis; fig central point; main topic; **~ tándem** dual axle
ejecu|ción f execution; **~tar** v/t to execute; to perform; **~tivo** m executive
ejempl|ar m copy; specimen; example; a exemplary; **~o** m example; **por ~o** for example
ejerc|er v/t to exercise; to practise, Am -ce; **~icio** m exercise; practice; fiscal year; **~itar** v/t to train
ejército m army
ejido m LA cooperative
ejote m LA string bean
el art m sing (pl **los**) the
él pron m sing (pl **ellos**) he
elabora|do elaborate; **~r** v/t to elaborate; to prepare
elasticidad f elasticity
elástico elastic
elec|ción f election; choice; **~cionario** LA electoral; **~tor** m elector; voter; **~torado** m electorate
electricidad f electricity
eléctrico electric; electrical
electro|domésticos m/pl household appliances; **~imán** m electromagnet; **~motor** m electromotor; **~tecnia** f electrical engineering
elefante m elephant
elegan|cia f elegance; **~te** elegant
elegi|ble eligible; **~r** v/t to choose; to elect
elemento m element; factor
elenco m catalogue; teat cast; sp team
elepé m long-playing record
eleva|ción f elevation; altitude; height; **~do** high; **~dor** m LA elevator; **~r** v/t to raise; **~rse** to rise; to be elated
eliminar v/t to eliminate
elipse f ellipse
elitista a, m, f elitist
elocuen|cia f eloquence; **~te** eloquent
elogi|ar v/t to praise; **~o** m praise; eulogy
eludir v/t to avoid; to elude
ella pron f sing (pl **ellas**) she
ello pron neuter sing it
emana|ción f emanation; **~r** v/i to emanate from
emancipar v/t to emancipate
embadurnar v/t to smear
embajad|a f embassy; **~or** m ambassador
embala|je m packing; **~r** v/t to pack
embaldosa|do m tiled floor; **~r** v/t to tile
embalse m dam; reservoir
embaraz|ada pregnant; **~ar** v/t to obstruct; to make pregnant; **~o** m pregnancy; obstacle
embarc|ación f ship; boat; embarkation; **~adero** m pier; **~ar** v/t to put on board; to embark; **~o** m embarkation
embarg|ar v/t to impede; to restrain; **~o** m embargo; seizure; **sin ~o** nevertheless; however
embarque m shipment
embaucar v/t to trick; to fool
embellecer v/t to embellish
embesti|da f assault; **~r** v/t to attack; to assail
embetunar v/t to black (shoes); to pitch
emblema m emblem; symbol
embobar v/t to fascinate; **~se** to gape; to be amazed
embocadura f mouth (of river)
émbolo m piston; plunger
embolsar v/t to pocket; to put into a purse
emborracharse to get drunk
emboscada f ambush
embotar v/t to blunt (an edge); to weaken
embotella|miento m congestion, traffic jam; **~r** v/t to bottle
embozar v/t to muffle; fig to cloak
embrag|ar v/t mar to sling; tecn to engage (a gear); **~ue** m tecn clutch
embriag|arse to get drunk; **~uez** f drunkenness; rapture
embroll|ar v/t to entangle; **~o** m tangle, muddle
embrujar v/t to bewitch
embrutecer v/t to brutalize; to coarsen
embudo m funnel
embuste m trick; fraud; **~ro** m habitual liar
embuti|do a stuffed, filled; m sausage; **~r** v/t to stuff; tecn to inlay
emerge|ncia f emergency; **~r** v/i to emerge
emigra|ción f emigration; **~do(a)** m (f) emigrant; **~r** v/i to emigrate
eminen|cia f eminence; **~te** eminent
emis|ario m emissary; **~ión** f emission; broadcast; **~ora** f broadcasting station
emitir v/t to broadcast; to emit, to give
emoción f emotion; excitement; thrill
emocion|ante exciting; **~ar** v/t to excite; to thrill
empach|ar v/t to impede; to upset; **~arse** to get embarrassed; to have indigestion; **~o** m bashfulness; indigestion; **~oso** embarrassing
empalag|ar v/t to cloy; to annoy; **~oso** oversweet; cloying; wearisome
empalm|ar v/t to couple; to join; **~e** m connection; junction
empana|da f (meat, fish, etc) pie; **~r** v/t to cover with batter or crumbs
empañar v/t to swaddle; to blur; to tarnish
empapar v/t to drench; to soak, to saturate
empapela|dor m paperhanger; **~r** v/t to wrap in paper; to paper (walls)
empaque m packing; fig air, mein; **~tar** v/t to pack; to wrap
empareda|do m sandwich; **~r** v/t to confine; to shut in
emparejar v/t, v/i to match; to pair off
emparentado related by marriage
empast|ar v/t to paste; to fill (teeth); **~e** m filling (of tooth)
empat|ar v/t to (end in a) tie; **~e** m sp draw, tie
empedernido heartless; inveterate
empedrar v/t to pave with stones
empeine m groin; instep
empeñ|ar v/t to pawn; to compel(l); **~arse** to insist; to take pains; **~o** m pledge; insistence
empeor|amiento m deterioration; **~ar** v/t to make worse; v/i to grow worse, to deteriorate
empequeñecer v/t to make smaller; to belittle
empera|dor m emperor; **~triz** f empress
emperrarse fam to get stubborn
empezar v/t, v/i to begin
empina|do steep; **~r** v/t to raise; **~r el codo** fam to drink
empírico empirical
emplasto m plaster; poultice
emplaza|miento m placement; location; **~r** v/t to place; to summon
emple|ado(a) m (f) employee; **~ar** v/t to employ; to use; **~o** m job; post; use; **modo de ~o** instructions for use
empobrecer v/t to impoverish; v/i to become poor
empolvar v/t to powder
empollar v/t to hatch; fam to study hard
emponzoñar v/t to poison
emprende|dor enterprising; bold; **~r** v/t to undertake; to take on
empresa f enterprise; company; **~rio** m contractor; manager; impresario
empréstito m (public) loan
empuj|ar v/t to push; to shove; **~e** m push; energy, drive; **~e axial** tecn thrust; **~ón** m push, shove
empuñar v/t to clutch
en in; at; into; on; upon; about; by
enaguas f/pl petticoat
enajena|ción f, **~miento** m alienation (of property); estrangement; **~ción mental** derangement; **~r** v/t to alienate
enaltecer v/t to praise; to extol
enamora|dizo quick to fall in love; **~do** a in love; **~do(a)** m (f) sweetheart; **~rse de** to fall in love with
enano(a) m (f) dwarf
enarbolar v/t to hoist
enardecer v/t to inflame; **~se** to take a passion for
encabeza|miento m heading; caption; census; **~r** v/t to head
encadenar v/t to chain

encaj|ar *v/t* to fit; to insert; **~e** *m* lace; inlaid work
encalar *v/t* to whitewash; *agr* to lime
encallar *v/i mar* to run aground; *fig* to get bogged down
encaminar *v/t* to guide; to direct; **~se** to set out for
encanecer *v/i* to grow gray
encant|ado delighted; charmed; pleased; **~ador** *a* charming; **~ar** *v/t* to enchant; to charm; to fascinate; **~o** *m* charm; spell
encañado *m* conduit (*for water*)
encapotarse to cloud over (*sky*)
encapricharse con to take a fancy to
encarar *v/i* to face; *v/t* to aim at; **~se con** to face, to stand up to
encarcelar *v/t* to imprison
encarecer *v/t* to raise the price of; to insist on, to emphasize
encarecidamente insistently
encarg|ado *m* agent; person in charge; **~ar** *v/t* to order; to charge; to entrust; **~arse de** to take charge of; **~o** *m* order; charge; commission
encarna|do red; flesh-colo(u)red; **~r** *v/t* to personify
encarnizar *v/t* to inflame; to enrage
encasar *v/t med* to set (*a bone*)
encasillar *v/t* to pigeonhole; to classify
encauzar *v/t* to channel; to lead
encend|edor *m* lighter; **~er** *v/t* to light; **~erse** to light up; to catch fire; **~ido** *m tecn* ignition; ***estar ~ido*** to be on (*light*); to be live (*wire*)
encera|do *m* oilcloth; *a* waxy; **~r** *v/t* to wax
encerrar *v/t* to shut in; to lock up
encía *f* gum (*of teeth*)
enciclopedia *f* encyclopedia
encierro *m* confinement; enclosure; prison
encima *adv* above; over; at the top; *prep* **~ de** above; on; on top of; **por ~ de todo** above all
encina *f* oak
encinta pregnant; **~do** *m* kerbstone, *Am* curb
enclavar *v/t* to nail
enclenque sickly; feeble
encoger *v/t* to contract; *v/i* to shrink; **~se** to shrink; *fig* to become discouraged; **~se de hombros** to shrug one's shoulders
encolar *v/t* to glue
encolerizar to provoke; to anger; **~se** to get angry
encom|endar *v/t* to commend; to entrust; **~endarse** to entrust oneself; **~ienda** *f* commission; charge; patronage; *LA* parcel, postal package
encono *m* ranco(u)r; ill-will
encontrar *v/t* to meet; to find; **~se** to meet; to collide; to feel; to be
encorvar *v/t* to bend; to curve; **~se** to bend down
encresparse to curl; to become agitated; to become rough (*sea*)
encrucijada *f* crossroads; ambush; *fig* quandary, dilemma
encuaderna|ción *f* binding (*of a book*); **~r** *v/t* to bind
encuadrar *v/t* to frame
encubierta *f* fraud, deceit
encub|ierto hidden; **~ridor** *m for* accessory; abettor; **~rir** *v/t* to cover up; to conceal
encuentro *m* encounter; meeting; collision
encuesta *f* inquiry; poll; **~ demoscópica** opinion poll
encumbrar *v/t* to lift; to raise; **~se** to soar
encurtidos *m/pl* mixed pickles
enchuf|ar *v/t* to connect; to plug in; **~e** *m* plug; socket; joint
ende: por ~ therefore
endeble feeble; weak
endecha *f* dirge
endémico endemic; rife
endemoniado possessed
endentecer *v/i* to teethe
enderezar *v/t* to straighten; to put right
endeudarse to run into debts
endiablado fiendish; bad-tempered; mischievous
endibia *f* endive
endiosar *v/t* to deify
endosar *v/t* to endorse
endulzar *v/t* to sweeten
endurecer *v/t*, **~se** to harden
enebro *m* juniper
eneldo *m* dill
enemi|go(a) *m* (*f*) enemy; *a* hostile; **~stad** *f* enmity
energía *f* energy; **~ nuclear** nuclear energy; **~ solar** solar energy
enérgico energetic
energúmeno *m* one possessed; wild person
enero *m* January
enervar *v/t* to enervate
enfad|arse to get angry; **~o** *m* anger; annoyance
énfasis *m* emphasis; stress
enfático emphatic
enferm|ar *v/i* to fall ill; **~edad** *f* illness; **~ería** *f* infirmary; **~ero(a)** *m* (*f*) nurse; **~izo** sickly; infirm; **~o(a)** *m* (*f*) patient; *a* ill
enfilar *v/t* to put in a row; to thread
enfo|car *v/t* to focus; **~que** *m* focusing; approach
enfrenar *v/t* to bridle (*horse*); to restrain
enfrent|amiento *m* confrontation; **~ar** *v/t* to put face to face; **~arse** to face; **~e** opposite
enfriar *v/t* to cool; **~se** to grow cold; to cool down
enfurecer *v/t* to infuriate; to enrage; **~se** to grow furious; to lose one's temper
enganch|ar *v/t* to hook; *fig* to catch; **~arse** to enlist; **~e** *m* hooking; enlisting
engañ|ar *v/t* to cheat, to deceive; **~arse** to be mistaken; **~o** *m* deceit; trick; mistake; **~oso** deceptive; misleading
engatusar *v/t* to wheedle; to coax
engendrar *v/t* to beget
englobar *v/t* to include; to comprise
engomar *v/t* to gum; to stick
engordar *v/t* to fatten; *v/i* to grow fat
engorro *m* nuisance; trouble; **~so** troublesome; awkward
engrana|je *m tecn* gear; gearing; **~r** *v/t* to gear; *v/i* to interlock
engrandec|er *v/t* to augment; to enlarge; **~imiento** *m* enlargement
engras|ar *v/t* to grease; to lubricate; **~e** *m* lubrication; lubricant
engreído conceited; stuck up
engreimiento *m* conceit
engrosar *v/t* to enlarge; to swell; *v/i* to grow fat
engrudo *m* paste
engullir *v/t* to wolf down, to gobble, to gorge
enhebrar *v/t* to thread
enhiesto (bolt) upright
enhilar *v/t* to thread; *fig* to put in order
enhorabuena *f* congratulations; ***dar la ~ a*** to congratulate
enigma *m* enigma; puzzle
enigmático enigmatic
enjabonar *v/t* to soap, to lather; *fig* to flatter
enjambre *m* swarm
enjaular *v/t* to cage
enjuagar *v/t* to rinse
enjuicia|miento *m* trial; **~r** *v/t for* to try; to judge
enla|ce *m* link; connection; liaison; **~tar** *v/t* to can; **~zar** *v/t* to join; to connect
enloquecer *v/t* to madden; *v/i* to go mad
enlosar *v/t* to pave (*with tiles or flagstones*)
enlucir *v/t* to plaster (*walls*)
enmarañar *v/t* to entangle
enmascarar *v/t* to mask
enm|endar *v/t* to correct; to reform; **~ienda** *f* emendation; amendment
enmohecerse to grow rusty *or* mo(u)ldy
enmudecer *v/t* to silence; *v/i* to be silent; to become speechless
enoj|adizo short-tempered; irritable; **~ar** *v/t* to anger; **~arse** to get angry; to get annoyed; **~o** *m* anger; annoyance
enorgullecer *v/t* to make proud; **~se** to be proud
enorm|e enormous; **~idad** *f* enormity; wickedness
enrarecerse to grow scarce
enred|adera *f bot* vine, creeper; **~ador** troublemaking; **~ar** *v/t* to entangle; to confuse; to involve; **~arse** to get entangled; **~o** *m* mess, tangle; plot
enreja|do *m* railings; trellis; **~r** *v/t* to surround with railings; to grate
enriquecer *v/t* to enrich; **~se** to grow rich
enrojecer *v/t* to make red; **~se** to blush
enrollar *v/t* to roll up
enronquecer *v/t* to make hoarse; *v/i* to grow hoarse
enroscar *v/t* to twist; to coil
ensalad|a *f* salad; **~era** *f* salad bowl; **~illa** *f* medley; patchwork
ensalzar *v/t* to praise; to exalt
ensamblar *v/t* to join; to connect; to assemble
ensanch|ar *v/t* to widen; to enlarge; **~e** *m* enlargement; widening; extension
ensangrentado blood-stained; bloodshot
ensañar *v/t* to enrage; ***~se en*** to vent one's anger on
ensay|ar *v/t* to try, to test; to rehearse; **~o** *m* test; trial; essay; *teat, mús* rehearsal
enseña|nza *f* teaching; education; schooling; tuition; **~r** *v/t* to teach; to show; **~r el camino** to lead the way
enseres *m/pl* chattels; household goods; gear
ensimismarse to fall into a reverie; *LA* to become conceited
ensordecer *v/t* to deafen; to muffle; *v/i* to go deaf
ensuciar *v/t* to soil; to foul; to pollute
ensueño *m* dream; daydream
entabl|ar *v/t* to cover with boards; *fig* to enter into; **~ar juicio** to take legal action; **~illar** *v/t med* to splint
entarimado *m* parquet flooring
ente *m* entity; being
entend|er *v/t* to understand; to think; to mean; **~ido** understood; well-informed; **~imiento** *m* understanding
entera|do knowledgeable; *LA* conceited; **~mente** entirely; **~rse** to find out
entereza *f* integrity, honesty
enternecer *v/t* to soften; to make tender
entero entire; complete
enterrar *v/t* to bury
entidad *f* entity; *pol* body
entierro *m* burial
entonar *v/t* to intone
entonces then; at that time; **¿~?** so?; **desde ~** since; then; **por ~** at that time
entorpecer *v/t* to numb; to obstruct; to make difficult
entrada *f* entry; entrance; way in; (admission) ticket; **prohibida la ~** no admittance
entrambos(as) both
entrante next; coming; **la semana ~** next week
entrañable most affectionate
entrañas *f/pl* entrails; center; nature
entrar *v/i* to enter; to go in; to begin; **~ en,** *LA* **~ a** to go into; **~ en vigencia** to come into force
entre between; among; **~acto** *m teat* interval; **~cejo** *m* space between the eyebrows; **~cortado** *m* intermittent; **~dicho** *m* prohibition
entrega *f* delivery; **~r** *v/t* to deliver; to hand over; **~rse** to surrender
entrelazar *v/t* to interlace
entremedias in between
entremeses *m/pl* hors d'oeuvres
entremeter *v/t* to place between; **~se** to interfere, to meddle
entremezclar *v/t* to intermingle
entren|ador *m sp* trainer; coach; **~ar** *v/t*, *v/i* to train
entresacar *v/t* to select; to thin out
entresuelo *m* entresol; mezzanine
entretanto meanwhile
entretejer *v/t* to interweave
entreten|er *v/t* to entertain; to keep in suspense; to hold up; **~ido** pleasant, amusing
entrever *v/t* to glimpse
entrevista *f* interview
entristecer *v/t* to sadden; **~se** to grow sad
entumecido numb; stiff
entusias|mar *v/t* to excite; to fill with enthusiasm; **~mo** *m* enthusiasm
entusiástico enthusiastic
enumerar *v/t* to enumerate
enunciar *v/t* to enunciate; to state
envainar *v/t* to sheathe
envanecer *v/t* to make vain
envas|ar *v/t* to bottle; to tin; to pack; **~e** *m* packing; container; bottle, tin
envejecerse to grow old
envenena|miento *m* poisoning; **~r** *v/t* to poison
envergadura *f* expanse; extent; scope; *aer* wingspan
envia|do *m* messenger; envoy; **~r** *v/t* to send
envidi|a *f* envy; **~ar** *v/t* to envy; **~oso** envious; jealous
envilecer *v/t* to debase
envío *m* dispatch; *com* remittance; shipment
envol|tura *f* wrapper; **~ver** *v/t* to wrap up; to envelop; *mil* to surround
enyesar *v/t* to plaster
épico epic
epidemia *f* epidemic
epidémico epidemic
epígrafe *m* title; inscription; epigraph
epiléptico epileptic
episcopado *m* bishopric
episodio *m* episode; incident
epítome *m* compendium, summary
época *f* epoch; period, time
equidad *f* equity; fairness
equilibr|ar *v/t* to balance; **~io** *m* equilibrium, balance
equinoccio *m* equinox
equip|aje *m* luggage; equipment; **~aje de mano** hand luggage; **~ar** *v/t* to fit out; to equip
equipo *m* team; kit, equipment; **~ de alta fidelidad** stereo system; hi-fi set; **~ de casa** *sp* home team
equitación *f* riding (*on horse*)
equitativo equitable; just
equivale|ncia *f* equivalence; **~nte** equivalent; **~r** *v/i* to be equivalent
equivoca|ción *f* mistake; misunderstanding; **~do** mistaken; **~rse** to be mistaken
equívoco equivocal; ambiguous
era *f* era
erección *f* establishment; erection
erguir *v/t* to raise; **~se** to straighten up
erial *m* uncultivated land
erigir *v/t* to erect; to raise; to establish
eriz|ado bristly; full; **~arse** to stand on end (*hair*); **~o** *m* hedgehog
ermita *f* hermitage; **~ño** *m* hermit
erótico erotic
erra|nte roving; **~r** *v/t* to miss; to fail; *v/i* to err; to go astray; to make a mistake; **~ta** *f impr* misprint
erróneo erroneous; wrong
error *m* mistake; error; **por ~** by mistake
eructar *v/i* to belch
erudi|ción *f* learning; **~to** learned, scholarly
erupción *f* eruption; *t med* outbreak
esbel|tez *f* slenderness; **~to** slim, slender
esboz|ar *v/t* to sketch; **~o** *m* sketch
escabech|ar *v/t* to pickle; **~e** *m* marinade
escabroso rough; craggy; harsh
escabullirse to slip away
escafandra *f* diving suit
escala *f* ladder; scale; *mar* port of call; stopover; ***hacer ~ en*** to stop at; **~fón** *m* list; register; **~r** *v/t* to scale; to climb
escaldar *v/t* to scald
escalera *f* stairs; staircase; ladder; **~ automática, ~ mecánica** escalator; **~ de incendios** fire-escape; **~ de servicio** backstairs
escalfar *v/t* to poach (*eggs*)
escalofrío *m* chill, shiver
escal|ón *m* step of a stair; rank; **~onar** *v/t* to place at regular intervals
escalpelo *m* scalpel
escam|a *f* scale (*of fish or reptile*); flake; *fig* grudge; **~oso** scaly; flaky
escamot|ar, ~ear *v/t* to make disappear; to swindle
escampar *v/i* to clear up (*sky*); *v/t* to clear out
escandalizar *v/t* to scandalize; **~se** to be shocked

escándalo *m* scandal
escandinavo *a, m* Scandinavian
escaner *m* scanner
escaño *m* bench; seat (*in Parliament*)
escapa|da *f* escape; flight; **~rate** *m* display window, shop window; **~rse** to escape; **~toria** *f* flight, escape; loophole
escape *m* escape; leak; flight; ***tubo de ~*** exhaust pipe
escarabajo *m* beetle
escarcha *f* frost; **~r** *v/t* to ice; to frost (*a cake*)
escardar *v/t* to weed
escarlat|a *f* scarlet; **~ina** *f* scarlet fever
escarm|entar *v/t* to punish severely; **~iento** *m* exemplary punishment
escarn|ecer *v/t* to ridicule; **~ecimiento** *m*, **~io** *m* derision
escarola *f* endive
escarpa *f* slope; escarpment; **~do** steep; craggy
escas|amente barely; hardly; **~ear** *v/i* to be scarce; **~ez** *f* scarcity; **~o** scarce; scanty
escayola *f med* plaster (cast)
escen|a *f* scene; **~ario** *m teat* scenery; stage
escepticismo *m* scepticism
escéptico sceptic
esclarec|er *v/t* to explain; to elucidate; to illuminate
esclav|itud *f* slavery; **~o(a)** *m* (*f*) slave
esclusa *f* lock; sluice
escob|a *f* broom; brush; **~illa** *f* whisk
escocer *v/i* to smart; to sting; **~se** to chafe
escocés(esa) *m* (*f*) Scotsman (-woman); *a* Scottish
Escocia *f* Scotland
escoger *v/t* to choose; to select; to pick out
escolar *a* scholastic; ***edad ~*** school age; *m* pupil, student
escolta *f* escort; convoy; **~r** *v/t* to escort
escollo *m* reef; pitfall; obstacle
escombr|ar *v/t* to clear of rubble; **~os** *m/pl* rubble
escond|er *v/t* to conceal; to hide; **~idas** *adv*: ***a ~idas*** secretly; **~rijo** *m* hideout; den
escopeta *f* shotgun
escoplo *m* chisel
escorbuto *m* scurvy
escoria *f* slag; dross; scum
escot|e *m* neckline; **~illa** *f mar* hatchway; **~illón** *m teat* trapdoor
escribano *m* court clerk; *LA* notary
escribi|ente *m* clerk; **~r** *v/t* to write
escrito *m* writing, document; letter; ***por ~*** in writing
escritor(a) *m* (*f*) writer
escritorio *m* desk; study, office
escritura *f* writing; *for* deed; ***la Sagrada ~*** the Holy Scripture
escrúpulo *m* scruple
escrupuloso scrupulous
escrutinio *m* scrutiny
escuadra *f mil* squad; *mar* squadron
escuálido scraggy; squalid
escuchar *v/t* to listen to
escudo *m* shield; coat of arms
escudriñar *v/t* to scrutinize; to scan; to examine
escuela *f* school; ***~ de párvulos*** kindergarten; ***~ nocturna*** night school; ***~ primaria*** elementary school
escul|pir *v/t* to sculpture; to cut; **~tor** *m* sculptor; **~tura** *f* sculpture
escupi|dera *f* spittoon; **~r** *v/t, v/i* to spit
escurri|dizo slippery; *tecn* aerodynamic; **~dor** *m* wringer; **~r** *v/t* to drain off; to wring out; **~se** to sneak off; to drip
ese, esa (*pl* **esos, esas**) *a* that; *pl* those
ése; ésa; eso (*pl* **ésos, ésas**) *pron* that one; the former; ***eso es*** that's right; ***eso sí*** yes, of course; ***por eso*** because of that
esencia *f* essence; **~l** essential
esfera *f* sphere; face (*of watch*)
esférico spherical
esfinge *f* sphinx
esforzar *v/t* to strengthen; to encourage; **~se** to make an effort; to exert oneself
esfuerzo *m* effort
esfumarse to fade away
esgrim|a *f* fencing; **~ir** *v/t* to brandish; *v/i* to fence
esguince *m* sprain (*of joint*)
eslabón *m* link
eslogan *m* slogan
esmalte *m* enamel
esmerado carefully done; painstaking
esmeralda *f* emerald
esmeril *m* emery
esmero *m* care; refinement
esmoquin *m* dinner jacket, *Am* tuxedo
espabilado bright; intelligent
espaci|ar *v/t* to space; **~o** *m* space; **~oso** spacious, roomy
espada *f* sword
espalda *f* shoulder; back
espantapájaros *m* scarecrow
espant|ar *v/t* to scare; to frighten; **~arse** to get frightened; **~o** *m* terror; shock; **~oso** frightful
Españ|a *f* Spain; **~ol(a)** *m* (*f*) Spaniard; *a* Spanish
esparadrapo adhesive tape; sticking plaster
esparci|do scattered; merry; **~r** *v/t* to scatter; to spread
espárrago *m* asparagus
espasmo *m* spasm
especia *f* spice
especial special; **~idad** *f* speciality; **~ista** *m, f* specialist; **~izar** *v/i* to specialize
especie *f* species; kind
específico specific
espect|áculo *m* show; entertainment; **~ador** *m* spectator, onlooker; viewer
especula|ción *f* speculation; **~r** *v/t* to consider; *v/i* to speculate
espej|ismo *m* mirage; illusion; **~o** *m* mirror; ***~o retrovisor*** rear view mirror
espeluznante hair-raising; lurid
espera *f* waiting; ***en ~ de*** waiting for; **~nza** *f* hope; **~r** *v/t* to hope for; to expect; to wait for; *v/i* to wait
esperma *f* sperm
espes|ar *v/t* to thicken; **~o** thick; **~or** *m* thickness
espía *m, f* spy
espiar *v/t* to spy on
espiga *f* peg; *bot* ear; *tecn* spigot
espina *f* thorn; spine; fish-bone; ***~ dorsal*** backbone, spinal column
espinacas *f/pl* spinach
espin|illa *f* shin(bone); **~oso** thorny, spiny
espionaje *m* espionage; spying
espiral *f* spiral
espíritu *m* spirit; mind; ghost; ***~ Santo*** Holy Ghost
espiritual spiritual
espléndido splendid
espliego *m* lavender
espoleta *f* wishbone; *mil* fuse
espolón *m zool, geol* spur; *arq* buttress; *mar* sea wall
esponja *f* sponge; **~rse** to glow with health
esponsales *m/pl* betrothal
espontáneo spontaneous
esporádico sporadic
espos|a *f* wife; *pl* handcuffs; **~ar** *v/t* to handcuff; **~o** *m* husband
espuela *f* spur (*t fig*)
espum|a *f* froth; foam; **~oso** frothy; foamy; sparkling (*wine*)
esputo *m* spit; spittle
esquela *f* note; ***~ de defunción*** death notice
esqueleto *m* skeleton
esquema *m* scheme; plan; chart; diagram
esquí *m* ski
esquiar *v/i* to ski
esquilar *v/t* to shear (*sheep*); to clip
esquilmar *v/t* to harvest
esquimal *a, m, f* Eskimo
esquina *f* corner (*of a street or a house*)
esquirol *m fam* strikebreaker
esquivar *v/t* to shun; to avoid
estab|ilidad *f* stability; **~ilizar** *v/t* to stabilize; **~le** stable; **~lecer** *v/t* to establish; to set up; to decree; **~lecerse** to settle down; to establish oneself; **~lecimiento** *m* establishment; institution; **~lo** *m* stable
estaca *f* stake; cudgel; **~da** *f* fencing; *mil* stockade
estación *f* season; station, stop; (*taxi*) stand; ***~ de servicio*** service station
estacion|amiento *m* parking; **~ar** *v/t, v/i* to park (*a car*); ***prohibido ~ar*** no parking
estadio *m* stadium
estad|ista *m* statesman; **~ística** *f* statistics; **~ístico** statistical; **~o** *m* state, nation; condition; rank, status; ***~o civil*** marital status; ***~o de emergencia*** state of emergency; ***~o mayor*** *mil* staff; **~os** *pl* **Unidos** United States
estadounidense *m, f* citizen of the United States
estafa *f* swindle; trick; **~dor** *m* swindler
estafeta *f* courier; district post office
estall|ar *v/i* to burst; to explode; **~ido** *m* bang; explosion; outbreak
estambre *m* worsted
estamp|a *f* print; engraving; impression; image; **~ado** *m* print (*in textiles*); **~ar** *v/t* to print; to stamp; to imprint; **~ido** *m* report (*of a gun*)
estampilla *f* rubber stamp; *LA* postage stamp
estan|car *v/t* to check; to stop; *com* to monopolize; **~carse** to stagnate; **~co** *a* watertight; *m* (state) monopoly; tobacconist; **~darte** *m* standard; banner; **~que** *m* pond; small lake
estante *m* shelf; bookcase; **~ría** *f* shelves
estaño *m* tin
estar *v/i* to be; ***~ a*** to be priced at; ***¿a cuántos estamos?*** what is today's date?; ***está bien*** all right; ***~ de viaje*** to be travelling; ***~ de más*** to be superfluous; ***~ en algo*** to understand something; ***~ enfermo*** to be ill; ***~ para*** to be in the mood for; ***está por ver*** it remains to be seen
estático static
estatua *f* statute
estatuto *m* statute; law
este *m* east
este, esta *a* (*pl* **estos, estas**) this (*pl* these)
éste, ésta *pron* (*pl* **éstos, éstas**) this one (*pl* these)
estela *f* wake (*of a ship*)
estenografía *f* stenography, shorthand
estepa *f* steppe
estera *f* mat, matting
estereo|fónico stereophonic; **~scopio** *m* stereoscope; **~tipo** *m* stereotype
estéril barren; sterile
esterili|dad *f* sterility; **~zar** *v/t* to sterilize
estétic|a *f* aesthetics; **~o** aesthetic
estevado bowlegged
estibador *m* stevedore
estiércol *m* dung; manure
estigma *m* mark; birthmark; stigma
estil|arse to be in fashion *or* use; **~o** *m* style
estilográfica: ***pluma*** *f* **~** fountain pen
estima *f* esteem; **~r** *v/t* to estimate; to esteem
estimula|nte *m* stimulant; *a* stimulating; **~r** *v/t* to stimulate; to excite
estímulo *m* stimulus; *fig* incentive
estipula|ción *f* stipulation; **~r** *v/t* to stipulate
estir|ado haughty, stiff; **~ar** *v/t* to stretch; to pull; to extend; **~ón** *m* jerk; tug; rapid growth
esto this; ***en ~*** at this moment; ***~ es*** that is to say
estocada *f* thrust (*of sword*)
estofar *v/t* to stew
estómago *m* stomach
estorb|ar *v/t* to hinder; to disturb; **~o** *m* hindrance; obstacle; nuisance
estornud|ar *v/i* to sneeze; **~o** *m* sneezing
estrado *m* dais; platform; *pl* court rooms
estrag|ar *v/t* to deprave; to pervert; **~o** *m* ruin; **~os** *pl* havoc
estrangula|ción *f* strangulation; throttling (*of an engine*); **~dor** *m tecn* choke; **~r** *v/t* to strangle; to choke; to throttle
estraperlo *m* black market
estratagema *f* stratagem; trick
estrat|egia *f* strategy; **~égico** strategic, strategical
estrech|amente tightly; closely; intimately; **~ar** *v/t* to reduce, to tighten; to take in (*clothes*); ***~ar la mano*** to shake hands; **~arse** to draw closer; to narrow; to tighten up; **~ez** *f* narrowness; tightness; poverty; **~o** *a* narrow; tight; austere; rigid; intimate; *m* strait(s), narrows
estrella *f* star; ***~ de cine*** film-star; ***~ de mar*** starfish; ***~ fugaz*** shooting star; **~do** starry; smashed; **~r** *v/t* to smash
estremec|er *v/t* to shake; **~erse** to shake; to shudder, to tremble; **~imiento** *m* shudder
estren|ar *v/t* to do *or* use for the first time; **~o** *m* first use; *teat* première
estreñi|do constipated; **~miento** *m* constipation
estrépito *m* crash; din
estrepitoso deafening
estrés *m med* stress
estribillo *m* refrain, chorus
estribo *m* stirrup
estribor *m* starboard
estricto strict; severe
estridente strident; shrill
estropajo *m* swab, mop; pan scraper; dishcloth
estropear *v/t* to hurt; to damage; to ruin; to spoil
estructura *f* structure
estruendo *m* crash, din; uproar; bustle; **~so** noisy
estrujar *v/t* to press, to squeeze out; to crush
estuche *m* case; etui; ***~ de pinturas*** paintbox
estudi|ante *m, f* student; **~ar** *v/t, v/i* to study; **~o** *m* study; studio; **~oso** studious; industrious
estufa *f* stove; heater
estupefac|ción *f* stupefaction; **~iente** *m* narcotic; drug; **~ientes** *m/pl* narcotics; **~to** stupefied
estupendo stupendous; terrific
estupidez *f* stupidity
estúpido stupid
estupro *m for* rape
etapa *f* stage; phase; period
éter *m* ether
etern|idad *f* eternity; **~o** eternal
étic|a *f* ethics; **~o** ethical
etiqueta *f* formality; etiquette; label; ***traje*** *m* ***de ~*** formal dress
Eucaristía *f* Eucharist
eufonía *f* euphony
Europa *f* Europe
europeo(a) *m* (*f*), *a* European
Euskadi Basque country
euskera *m* Basque language
evacua|ción *f* evacuation; **~r** *v/t* to evacuate
evadir *v/t* to evade, to elude
evalua|ción *f* evaluation; **~r** *v/t* to assess; to evaluate
evangelio *m* gospel
evangelizador *m* evangelist
evaporar *v/t*, **~se** to evaporate
evasi|ón *f* evasion, elusion; pretext; **~va** *f* excuse; pretext; **~vo** evasive, elusive; non-committal
evento *m* eventuality; ***a cualquier ~*** in any event
eventual accidental; possible; contingent; **~idad** *f* contingency; **~mente** possibly; by chance
eviden|cia *f* proof; **~te** evident; obvious
evitar *v/t* to avoid; to prevent
evoca|ción *f* evocation; **~r** *v/t* to evoke; to conjure up
evoluci|ón *f* evolution; development; **~onar** *v/i* to evolve; to develop
exact|itud *f* exactness; accuracy; **~o** exact; accurate; punctual
exagera|do exaggerated; overdone; excessive; **~r** *v/t* to exaggerate
exalta|do hot-headed; impetuous; **~r** *v/t* to exalt
exam|en *m* examination; inquiry; **~inar** *v/t* to examine; to investigate; to test; **~inarse** to take an examination
exangüe bloodless
exánime lifeless
exasperar *v/t* to exasperate; to irritate; **~se** to lose patience
excavar *v/t* to dig; to excavate
excede|nte *a* excessive; *m* surplus; **~r** *v/t* to exceed; to surpass
excelencia *f* excellence; excellency
excentricidad *f* eccentricity
excéntrico eccentric
excepción *f* exception

excep|cional exceptional; **~to** except; **~tuar** *v/t* to except; *for* to exempt
exces|ivo excessive; **~o** *m* excess; **~o de equipaje** excess luggage
excitar *v/t* to excite; **~se** to become excited
exclama|ción *f* exclamation; **~r** *v/i* to exclaim
exclu|ir *v/t* to exclude; **~siva** *f* exclusive interview; *com* sole right; **~sivamente** exclusively; **~sivo** exclusive
excomulgar *v/t* to excommunicate; to ban
excre|ción *f* excretion; **~mento** *m* excrement
exculpar *v/t* to exculpate; to forgive
excursión *f* excursion; outing; trip
excusa *f* excuse; apology; **~ble** excusable; **~do** *m* toilet; **~r** *v/t* to excuse; **~rse** to apologize
exen|ción *f* exemption; **~to** free from; devoid; exempt
exhalar *v/t* to exhale
exhausto exhausted
exhibi|ción *f* exhibition; **~ción-venta** sales exhibit; **~r** *v/t* to exhibit
exhortar *v/t* to exhort
exig|encia *f* demand; **~ente** demanding; exacting; **~ir** *v/t* to demand
eximir *v/t* to exempt
existen|cia *f* existence; **en ~cia** in stock; **~te** existent
existir *v/i* to exist, to be
éxito *m* success; outcome; *teat* hit; **~ de librería** best seller
éxodo *m* exodus
exonerar *v/t* to exonerate; to relieve
exorbitante exorbitant
exótico exotic
expansi|ón *f* expansion; **~vo** expansive
expatriar *v/t* to expatriate; to banish
expecta|ción *f*, **~tiva** *f* expectation; expectancy; **estar a la ~tiva** wait and see attitude
expedición *f* expedition; speed; dispatch
expedi|ente *m* resource; expedient; **~r** *v/t* to dispatch; to send; **~tar** *v/t LA* to expedite
expende|dor *m* seller; dealer; agent; **~duría** *f* shop licensed to sell tobacco and stamps
experiencia *f* experience
experiment|ar *v/t* to experience; to go through; **~o** *m* experiment
experto *m*, *a* expert
expiar *v/t* to atone for
expirar *v/i* to expire
explanar *v/t* to level
explica|ción *f* explanation; **~r** *v/t* to explain; **~tivo** explanatory
explora|dor *m* explorer; boy scout; **~dora** *f* girl scout; **~r** *v/t* to explore
explosi|ón *f* explosion; **~vo** *m*, *a* explosive
explota|ción *f* exploitation; **~r** *v/t* to exploit
expone|nte *m*, *f*, *a* exponent; **~r** *v/t* to expose; to risk; to exhibit
exportación *f* export
exporta|dor *m* exporter; **~r** *v/t* to export
exposición *f* exposition; exhibition; show
exposímetro *m foto* exposure meter
exprés *a* express; *m LA* express train
expres|ar *v/t* to express; **~ión** *f* expression; **~o** *m* express train
exprimi|dor *m* juicer; **~r** *v/t* to squeeze out; *fig* to express
expropiar *v/t* to expropriate
expuesto exposed; on display; in danger
expuls|ar *v/t* to expel, to throw out; to oust; **~ión** *f* expulsion
exquisito exquisite; excellent
éxtasis *m* ecstasy
extemporáneo untimely
exten|der *v/t* to extend; to spread; to draw up (*document*); **~derse** to extend; to reach; **~sión** *f* extension; **~so** extensive; spacious
extenua|ción *f* emaciation; **~r** *v/t* to weaken; to emaciate
exterior *a* external; exterior; *m* outside; **asuntos ~es** foreign affairs; **~izar** *v/t* to show; to make manifest
exterminar *v/t* to exterminate
externo external
extin|ción *f* extinction; **~guir** *v/t* to extinguish; **~to** extinct; **~tor** *m* fire extinguisher
extirpar *v/t* to uproot; to extirpate; to stamp out
extra|cción *f* extraction; **~er** *v/t* to extract; to mine; **~escolar** extracurricular; **~fino** superfine; **~limitarse** to go too far; **~muros** outside the city walls
extranjero(a) *m (f)* foreigner; *a* foreign; **en el ~** abroad
extrañ|ar *v/t* to surprise greatly; to find strange; *LA* to miss; **~arse de** to be greatly surprised at; **~o** odd; foreign; strange
extraordinario extraordinary; unusual; **número ~** special issue
extravagan|cia *f* oddness; folly; **~te** odd; bizarre
extraviar *v/t* to mislay; to lose; **~se** to get lost
extrema|do extreme; excessive; **~r** *v/t* to carry to the extreme
extremaunción *f* extreme unction
extremista *a*, *m*, *f* extremist
extremo *a* last; extreme; excessive; *m* extreme; end
extrovertido extroverted; outgoing
exuberancia *f* exuberante; *bot* luxuriance

F

fábrica *f* factory; plant
fabrica|ción *f* manufacture; **~nte** *m* manufacturer; **~r** *v/t* to manufacture; to make
fábula *f* fable
fabuloso fabulous
facci|ón *f* faction; **~ones** *pl* features; **~oso** factious; rebellious
faceta *f* facet
fácil easy
facili|dad *f* facility; capacity; **~tar** *v/t* to facilitate; to supply
factor *m* factor; agent; **~ía** *f* factory; agency
factura *f* invoice; **pasar la ~** to send an invoice; **~r** *v/t* to invoice; to check; **~r el equipaje** to check in luggage
faculta|d *f* faculty; permission; **~r** *v/t* to authorize; **~tivo** optional
facha *f fam* mien; aspect; appearance; **~da** *f* façade, front
faena *f* task; job; **~s** *pl* chores
faisán *m* pheasant
faj|a *f* sash; belt; corset; **~o** *m* bundle; wad, roll (*of money*)
falaz deceitful; fallacious
fald|a *f* skirt; slope (*of a mountain*); **~ero** fond of women; **~ón** *m* flap (*on clothing*)
fals|edad *f* falsehood; **~ificación** *f* forgery; **~ificado** forged; counterfeit; **~ificar** *v/t* to falsify; to forge; **~o** false; treacherous
falt|a *f* lack; deficiency; mistake; *sp* foul; **hacer ~a** to be necessary; **sin ~a** without fail; **~ar** *v/i* to be missing; to fail in; to be needed; **~o de dinero** short of money
falla *f* fault; failure; *LA* lack; **~r** *v/i* to miss; to fail; *v/t* to pronounce a sentence
fallec|er *v/i* to die; **~imiento** *m* death; decease
fallo *m* decision; sentence; **~ humano** human error
fama *f* fame; reputation; **mala ~** notoriety
famélico ravenous; starving
familia *f* family; **~r** *a* familiar; *m* relative; **~ridad** *f* familiarity; intimacy; **~rizar** *v/t* to acquaint (*with*); to accustom
famoso famous
fanático *a* fanatical; *m* fanatic; *LA* fan
fanega *f grain measure of about* 55.5 litres, *Am* liters *or* 1.59 acres
fanfarr|ón *m* boaster; braggart; **~onear** *v/i* to boast; to brag; to swagger
fango *m* mud; mire; slush
fantasía *f* imagination; fantasy; caprice; fancy
fantasma *m* phantom; ghost
fantástico fantastic
fantoche *m* puppet; marionette
farándula *f LA* show business
fardo *m* bundle; bale
farfullar *v/i* to gabble
fariseo *m* Pharisee; hypocrite
farmacéutico(a) *m (f)* pharmacist; druggist; *a* pharmaceutical
farmacia *f* pharmacy
faro *m* lighthouse; beacon; headlight (*of car*)
farol *m* lantern; street lamp
farsa *f* farce; trick; **~nte** *m* trickster; fake
fascina|ción *f* fascination; **~r** *v/t* to fascinate; to captivate
fascis|mo *m* fascism; **~ta** *m*, *f* fascist
fase *f* phase; period
fastidi|ar *v/t* to annoy; to pester; to bore; to irk; **~o** *m* annoyance; nuisance; **~oso** annoying, wearisome
fastuoso luxurious; lavish
fatal fatal; irrevocable; *fam* awful; **~idad** *f* fate; calamity; **~ismo** *m* fatalism; **~ista** *a* fatalistic; *m*, *f* fatalist
fatídico prophetic; ominous
fatig|a *f* fatigue; weariness; **~ar** *v/t* to tire; to annoy; **~oso** wearisome
fatu|idad *f* foolishness; **~o** conceited
favor *m* favo(u)r; **a ~ de** in favo(u)r of; **por ~** please; **~able** favo(u)rable; **~ecer** *v/t* to favo(u)r; to help; **~ito(a)** *m (f)*, *a* favo(u)rite
faz *f* face; *arq* front
fe *f* faith; trust; belief; **dar ~** to testify; **de buena ~** in good faith; **de mala ~** in bad faith
fealdad *f* ugliness; foulness
febrero *m* February
febril feverish; *fig* hectic
fécula *f* starch
fecund|ar *v/t* to fertilize; **~o** fertile; *fig* fruitful
fech|a *f* date; **hasta la ~a** up to now; so far; **~ar** *v/t* to date; **~oría** *f* villainy, misdeed
federa|ción *f* federation; **~l** federal
fehaciente *for* authentic
feli|cidad *f* happiness; **~cidades** *f/pl* congratulations; best wishes; **~citar** *v/t* to congratulate
feligrés *m* parishioner
feliz happy
felp|a *f* plush; **~udo** *a* plushy; *m* mat
femenino feminine
feminista *m*, *f* feminist
fenomenal *fam* great, terrific
fenómeno *m* phenomenon
feo ugly; disagreeable
féretro *m* coffin
feria *f* fair; market place
ferment|ar *v/t*, *v/i* to ferment; **~o** *m* ferment
fero|cidad *f* ferocity; **~z** fierce; savage
férreo ferrous; iron
ferretería *f* hardware store
ferro|carril *m* railway, *Am* railroad; **por ~carril** by rail; **~viario** *m* railwayman
fértil fertile; productive
ferv|iente ardent; fervent; **~or** *m* fervo(u)r; ardo(u)r
festiv|al *m* festival; **~idad** *f* festivity; **~o** festive; gay; **día ~o** holiday
fétido fetid; stinking
feto *m* f(o)etus
feudalismo *m* feudalism
fia|ble trustworthy; **~do** *adv*: **al ~do** on credit, on trust; **~dor** *m* guarantor
fiambres *m/pl* cold meats, *Am* cold cuts
fianza *f* deposit; security
fiar *v/t* to guarantee; to entrust; to sell on credit; **~se de** to trust; to rely upon
fibr|a *f* fibre, *Am* fiber; **~oso** fibrous
fic|ción *f* fiction; invention; **~ticio** ficticious
ficha *f* file; index card
fichero *m* card index; filing cabinet
fide|digno trustworthy; **~lidad** *f* faithfulness; accuracy; **alta ~lidad** high fidelity, hifi
fideos *m/pl* noodles
fiebre *f* fever; **~ del heno** hay fever
fiel faithful; loyal
fieltro *m* felt; felt hat
fiera *f* wild beast
fiesta *f* feast; festivity; party; holyday
figura *f* shape; form; **~do** figurative; **~r** *v/t* to shape; to represent; *v/i* to figure; **~rse** to imagine
fijar *v/t* to fix; to stick; to secure; **~se en** to pay attention to
fijo firm; permanent
fila *f* row, tier; line; **en ~** in a line; **~ india** single file
filete *m* fillet (*of fish or meat*); thread (*of screw*)
filia|ción *f* filiation; connection; **~l** filial
Filipinas *f/pl* Philippines
filipino(a) *a*, *m (f)* Philippine
film|ación *f cine* shooting; **~ar** *v/t* to film; **~e** *m* film
filo *m* edge; blade
filólogo *m* philologist
filón *m geol* vein; seam
filosofía *f* philosophy
filósofo *m* philosopher
filtr|ar *v/t* to filter; to strain; **~arse** to seep; **~o** *m* filter; strainer
fin *m* end, finish; aim, purpose; **a ~ de** in order to; **al ~** at last; **al ~ y al cabo** in the end; after all; **por ~** finally; **~ de semana** weekend
finado(a) *m (f)*, *a* deceased
final *m* end; *a* final; ultimate; **~idad** *f* purpose; **~izar** *v/t* to finish; *v/i* to end; **~mente** finally
finan|ciar *v/t* to finance; **~ciero** *m* financier; *a* financial; **~zas** *f/pl* finances
finca *f* landed property; *LA* farm
fineza *f* fineness; courtesy
fingir *v/t* to feign; to pretend; to fake
finiquito *m com* settlement
finlandés(esa) *a* Finnish; *m (f)* Finn
Finlandia *f* Finland
fino fine; thin; refined
firma *f* signature; *com* firm; **~r** *v/t* to sign
firme *a* firm; stable; *m* surface; **~za** *f* firmness; stability
fiscal *m* public prosecutor; *a* fiscal
fisco *m* exchequer; treasury
físic|a *f* physics; **~a nuclear** nuclear physics; **~o** *a* physical; *m* physicist
fisiología *f* physiology
fisión *f* fission; **~ nuclear** nuclear fission
fisura *f* fissure
fisonomía *f* physiognomy
fláccido flaccid, flabby
flaco thin; weak
flagelar *v/t* to flog, to lash
flagrante flagrant; **en ~** red-handed
flamante brilliant; brand-new
flamear *v/i* to blaze, to flame
flamenco *a*, *m* Flemish; Andalusian gipsy (*dance, song*); *m zool* flamingo
flanquear *v/t* to flank
flaque|ar *v/i* to weaken; **~za** *f* leanness; weakness
flash *m foto* flash
flat|o *m med* wind; **~ulencia** *f* flatulence
flauta *f* flute
fleco *m* tassel; fringe
flecha *f* arrow
flema *f* phlegm
flet|ar *v/t* to charter; *LA* to hire; **~e** *m* freight
flexib|ilidad *f* flexibility; **~le** flexible
flirtear *v/i* to flirt
floj|ear *v/i* to weaken; to slacken; **~edad** *f* weakness; idleness; **~o** weak; slack; idle; lazy
flor *f* flower; **~ecer** *v/i* to blossom; to flower; **~ero** *m* flower vase; **~ista** *m*, *f* florist
flot|a *f* fleet; **~ador** *m* float; **~ar** *v/i* to float; **~e** *m*: **a ~e** afloat
fluctua|ción *f* fluctuation; **~r** *v/i* to fluctuate
fluido *a* fluid; flowing; *m* fluid; **~ eléctrico** electric current
flu|ir *v/i* to flow; **~jo** *m* flow; flux
foca *f* seal
foco *m* focus; focal point; centre; *LA elec* bulb
fofo spongy; soft
fogata *f* bonfire
fogón *m* stove
fogon|azo *m* flash (*of gun*); **~ero** *m* stoker
fogos|idad *f* verve; vehemence; **~o** fiery; ardent
folklore *m* folklore
follaje *m* foliage
folleto *m* pamphlet, brochure
follón *a* lazy; *m* good-for-nothing; hubbub, uproar, rumpus
foment|ar *v/t* to foment; to promote; **~o** *m* encouragement; fostering
fonda *f* inn, hostelry
fondear *v/t mar* to sound; to examine; *v/i* to anchor
fondo *m* ground; bottom; depth; *pl* funds; **a ~** thoroughly
fonética *f* phonetics
fonógrafo *m LA* phonograph

Spanish

fontanero m plumber
forastero(a) m (f) stranger; visitor; outsider; a strange
forcej|ear v/i to struggle; **~eo** m struggle
forestal of the forest
forja f forge; **~do** wrought; **~r** v/t to forge; to shape
forma f form; shape; way, means; **de ~ que** so that; **de todas ~s** at any rate; **~ción** f formation; education; **~l** formal; serious; **~lidad** f formality; **~lizar** v/t to formalize; to formulate; **~r** v/t to form; to shape; **~rse** to (take) form; to develop
formidable formidable; tremendous
fórmula f formula; prescription
formulario m form, blank
foro m forum; for bar; teat upstage
forraje m forage; fodder
forr|ar v/t to line, to pad; **~o** m lining
fortalecer v/t to strengthen
fort|aleza f fortress, fort; **~ificar** v/t to fortify
fortuito fortuitous; accidental
fortuna f chance; luck; fortune, wealth; **por ~** luckily
forz|ar v/t to force; to compel; **~oso** compulsory; forcible; inevitable
fosa f grave
fósforo m phosphorus; LA match
foso m moat; ditch
foto f photo; **~copia** f photocopy; **~grafía** f photograph; **~grafiar** v/t, v/i to photograph
fotógrafo m photographer
fotómetro m photometer
fotomontaje m photomontage
fotosíntesis f photosynthesis
frac m tails; dress coat
fracas|ar v/i to fail; **~o** m failure
fracción f fraction; pol faction; splinter group
fractura f fracture
fragancia f fragrance
frágil fragile; brittle
fragment|ario fragmentary; **~o** m fragment
fragua f forge; **~r** v/t to forge (metal); to contrive
fraile m friar; monk
frambuesa f raspberry
francamente frankly
francés(esa) m (f) Frenchman (-woman); a French
Francia f France
francmasón m freemason
franco frank; com free
franela f flannel
franja f fringe
franqu|ear v/t to exempt; to free; to stamp, to frank; **~eo** m postage; **~icia** f privilege; com franchise; **~ista** pro-Franco
frasco m flask; bottle
frase f sentence; phrase
fratern|al brotherly; **~idad** f fraternity
fraud|e m fraud; **~ulento** fraudulent
fray m relig (contraction of **fraile**; before Christian names) brother
frazada f LA blanket
frecuen|cia f frequency; **~tar** v/t to frequent, to patronize; **~te** frequent
frega|dero m kitchen sink; **~r** v/t to scrub, to scour; LA to annoy, to bother
freír v/t to fry
fren|ar v/t to brake; to restrain; **~o** m brake; **~o de mano** hand brake
frente f forehead; front; **al ~** in the front; **hacer ~ a** to face (a problem); to meet (a demand)
fresa f strawberry
fres|co fresh; **~cura** f freshness; impertinence, cheek
fresno m ash tree
frialdad f coldness; indifference
fricc|ión f friction; **~ionar** v/t to rub
frigidez f coldness; frigidity
frigorífico m refrigerator
frijol m dry bean
frío cold
frioler|a f trifle; **~o** shivery, feeling the cold
frito fried
frívolo frivolous
frondoso leafy; shadowy
fronter|a f frontier; **~izo** frontier; opposite
frotar v/t to rub
fructífero productive
frugal frugal; thrifty
frunc|e m ruffle; **~ir** v/t to gather, to ruffle; to pucker; **~ir el ceño** to frown
frustrar v/t to frustrate
frut|a f fruit; **~ería** f fruit shop; **~o** m fruit, result
fuego m fire; **~s pl artificiales** fireworks
fuelle m bellows
fuente f spring; fountain
fuera outside; **por ~** on the outside; **~ de** out of; besides; **~ de juego** sp off-side; **~ de servicio** out of order; **¡~!** get out!; **~borda** outboard
fuero m jurisdiction; privilege
fuer|te a strong; vigorous; adv strongly; loudly; **~za** f strength; force; power; **a la ~za** by force; **~za mayor** act of God; **~zas pl armadas** armed forces
fug|a f flight; escape; **~arse** to flee; **~az** fugitive; passing; **~itivo(a)** m (f) fugitive
fulano so-and-so
fulgurante flashing; shining
fulminante fulminating
fullero m crook, cheat
fumar v/t, v/i to smoke; **prohibido ~** no smoking
funci|ón f function; teat performance; **~onar** v/i to function; to work; **~onario** m civil servant; official
funda f case, cover; sheath
funda|ción f foundation; **~dor** m founder; **~mento** m foundation; basis; **~r** v/t to found; to establish
fundi|ción f fusion; smelting; **~r** v/t to smelt; to fuse; **~rse** to blend, to merge
fúnebre funereal; mournful; lugubrious
funeral m funeral; **~es pl** funeral service
funesto ill-fated; dismal
funicular m funicular railway
furgón m wagon; van; f c luggage van
furgoneta f van
furi|a f fury; rage; **~oso** furious
furor m fury; rage; **hacer ~** to be all the rage
furúnculo m med boil
fuselaje m aer fuselage
fusible m elec fuse; a fusible
fusil m rifle; **~amiento** m execution by shooting
fusión f fusion; smelting; com merger
fust|a f whip; **~e** m wood; shaft; **de ~e** fig important
fútbol m football, Am soccer
futbolista m footballer, Am soccer player
fútil trivial
futuro(a) m (f) betrothed; m future; a future

G

gabán m overcoat
gabardina f gabardine; raincoat
gabinete m pol cabinet; study; small reception room
gaceta f gazette; LA newspaper
gachas f/pl porridge
gacho bent; drooping
gafas f/pl eyeglasses; **~ de buceo** diving goggles; **~ de sol** sunglasses
gait|a f bagpipe; **~ero** m bagpiper; a gaudy
gajo m branch; slice, segment (of fruit)
gala f ornament; full dress; **de ~** in full dress
galán m ladies' man; suitor; teat leading man
galano elegant; graceful
galante courteous; gallant; **~ar** v/i to flirt; **~ría** f gallantry; compliment
galápago m giant turtle
galardón m reward
galaxia f galaxy
gale|ote m galley slave; **~ra** f galley
galería f gallery; corridor
Gales m Wales
galés(esa) m (f) Welshman (-woman); a Welsh
galgo m greyhound
galimatías m gibberish
galocha f clog; galosh
galón m gallon; braid; trim; stripe (on uniform)
galop|ar v/i to gallop; **~e** m gallop
gallard|ear v/i to behave gracefully; **~ete** m pennant; **~ía** f elegance; gallantry
galleta f biscuit, cracker
gall|ina f hen; **~inero** m henhouse; bedlam; teat top gallery; **~o** m cock, rooster
gama f zool doe; mús scale; range
gamba f prawn; shrimp
gamberro m fam lout, hooligan
gamuza f chamois
gana f desire; wish; **de buena ~** willingly; **de mala ~** unwillingly, grudgingly; **tener ~s de** to feel like (doing)
ganad|ería f stock breeding; livestock; **~ero** m stockbreeder; **~o** m cattle; livestock
gana|dor m winner; gainer; **~ncia** f gain; profit; **~r** v/t to win; to earn; to gain
ganchillo m crochet (needle and work); **hacer ~** to crochet
gancho m hook; sex appeal; LA hairpin
gandul fam idle; lazy
ganga f bargain
gangrena f gangrene
gangueo m (nasal) twang
ganso m goose; gander
ganzúa f skeleton-key
gañir v/i to yelp
garabato m hook; scribble
garaje m garage
garant|ía f guarantee; security; **~izar** v/t to guarantee
garapiña|do candied; **~r** v/t to freeze; to ice, to candy
garbanzo m chick-pea; **~ negro** fig black sheep
garbo m grace; elegance; **~so** graceful; attractive
gargant|a f throat; gullet; ravine, gorge; **~ear** v/i to quaver (voice)
gárgara f gargle; **hacer ~s** to gargle
garita f sentry box; porter's lod
garra f claw, talon
garrafa f decanter; carafe
garrapata f zool tick
garrapatear v/i to scribble, to scrawl
garrocha f goad stick; sp pole
garro|tazo m blow with a cudgel; **~te** m cudgel
garúa f LA drizzle
garza f heron
gas m gas; vapo(u)r; fume; **~ lacrimógeno** tear gas; **~es pl de escape** exhaust fumes
gasa f gauze
gaseos|a f soda water; **~o** gaseous
gasfitero m LA plumber
gasolin|a f petrol, Am gas; **~era** f motorboat; petrol station, Am gas station
gasómetro m gasometer
gasta|do spent; worn out; **~dor** spendthrift; **~r** v/t to spend; to waste; to use up; to wear out
gasto m expense; **~s pl generales** com overhead
gastritis f gastritis
gastronomía f gastronomy
gat|a f she-cat; **a ~as** on all fours; **~ear** v/i to go on all fours; to climb; **~illo** m trigger; **~ito** m kitten; **~o** m cat; tecn jack; **~uno** feline
gaveta f drawer; locker
gavilla f sheaf (of corn); gang (of thieves)
gaviota f seagull
gazap|era f rabbit warren; **~o** m young rabbit; fam sly fellow; error
gazmoñero prudish; hypocritical
gaznate m gullet
gelatina f coc jelly
gemelo(a) m (f) twin; **~s** m/pl binoculars; cufflinks; **~s de campaña** field glasses; **~s de teatro** opera glasses
gemi|do m moan; groan; **~r** v/i to moan; to howl; to whine
gen m gene
genera|ción f generation; **~dor** m generator
general a general; universal; **en ~, por lo ~** in general, on the whole; m general; **~idad** f generality; majority; **~ísimo** m commander-in-chief; **~izar** v/t to generalize
generar v/t to generate
género m genus; kind, sort; cloth; material; **~s pl de punto** knitwear
generos|idad f generosity; **~o** generous; brave
geni|al gifted; talented; **~o** m temper; character; genius
genitivo m gram genitive
gente f people; folk; **~ menuda** children; small fry
gentil handsome; elegant; **~eza** f charm; courtesy; elegance
gent|ío m big crowd; **~uza** f mob
genuino genuine
geofísica f geophysics
geografía f geography
geología f geology
geólogo m geologist
geometría f geometry
geranio m geranium
geren|cia f management; **~te** m manager
geriatría f geriatrics
germ|en m germ; source; origin; **~inar** v/i to germinate
gerundio m gram gerund
gestación f gestation
gesticular v/i to gesticulate; to make faces
gest|ión f step; management (of affairs); **~ionar** v/t to negotiate; **~o** m gesture; **~or** m agent
gib|a f hunchback; hump; **~oso** humpbacked
gigante m giant; a huge; **~sco** gigantic
gilipollas m, f/pl fam idiot
gimnasi|a f gymnastics; **~o** m gymnasium
gimnástica f gymnastics
gimotear v/i to whine
ginebra f gin
ginecólogo m gyn(a)ecologist
gira f tour, excursion
giralda f weathercock
girar v/i to rotate; to turn; to spin; com to draw (check, draft); **~ en descubierto** com to overdraw
girasol m sunflower
gir|atorio revolving; **~o** m rotation; trend; com draft; **~o en descubierto** com overdraft; **~o postal** money order
gitano(a) m (f), a gipsy
glacia|l glacial; icy; fig cold, stony; **~r** m glacier
glándula f gland
glicerina f glycerine
glob|al global; **~o** m globe; **~o aerostático** balloon; **~o de ojo** eyeball; **~ular** globular; spherical
glóbulo m biol globule
glori|a f glory; heaven; bliss; **~arse** to boast; **~eta** f traffic circle; **~oso** glorious
glosa f gloss; **~r** v/t to gloss; **~rio** m glossary; comment
glotón m zool glutton; a gluttonous
glucosa f glucose
glutinoso glutinous; viscid
gnomo m gnome
goberna|dor m governor; **~nte** a governing; m, f governor; **~r** v/t to govern; to rule; to manage
gobierno m government; control
goce m enjoyment
godo(a) m (f) Goth; a Gothic
gol m goal; **~eta** f schooner
golf|illo m urchin; **~o** m geog gulf; good-for-nothing; loafer
golondrina f swallow
golos|ina f sweet; delicacy; **~o** sweet-toothed
golpe m blow; smack; clash; stroke; **de ~** all of a sudden; **~ de calor** sunstroke; **~ de estado** coup d'état; **no dar ~** not to work; **~ de fortuna** stroke of luck; **~ar** v/t to strike; to hit, to knock
gollete m neck (of bottle)
goma f gum; rubber band
góndola f gondola
gord|iflón fat; chubby; **~o** fat; stout; greasy; **~ura** f corpulence, stoutness
gorgote|ar v/i to gurgle; **~o** m gurgle
gorila m gorilla; fam thug
gorjear v/i to trill, to tweet, to warble
gorra f cap; bonnet
gorrear v/i to sponge; to freeload
gorrión m house sparrow
gorrista m sponger
gorro m cap; **~ de baño** bath cap
gorrón m cadger, leech
got|a f drop; med gout; **~ear** v/i to leak; **~eo** m dripping; leakage; **~era** f leak; gutter (of roof)
gótico Gothic
go|zar de v/i to enjoy; to

possess; **~zo** *m* joy; pleasure
graba|ción *f* recording; **~do** *m* engraving; print; **~do en madera** woodcut; **~dora** *f* (tape) recorder; **~dor-reproductor** *m* cassette player; **~r** *v/t* to engrave; to record; to tape
graci|a *f* grace; charm; witticism; **caer en ~a** to win the favo(u)r of, to please; **~as** thanks; **~as a** thanks to; **dar las ~as** to thank
grácil slender; slim
gracioso funny; charming; lively
grad|a *f* step; stair; row of seats; *agr* harrow; **~ar** *v/t* to harrow; **~erío** *m* tiers of seats; bleachers; **~o** *m* degree; step; rank; will, liking; **de buen ~o** willingly; **~uación** *f* graduation; **~ual** gradual; **~uar(se)** *v/t*, *v/i* to graduate
gráfico *m or f* graph; diagram; *a* graphic
grafito *m* graphite
gragea *f* candy sprinkles
gramátic|a *f* grammar; **~o** grammatical
gramo *m* gram(me)
gramófono *m* gramophone
grampa *f* staple; clamp
gran (*apocope of* **grande**, *used before singular m or f nouns*) large, big, great
granad|a *f* pomegranate; *mil* grenade, shell; **~o** *m* pomegranate tree
Gran Bretaña *f* Great Britain
grand|e *a* big; large; great; *m* grandee; **en ~e** in a big way; **~eza** *f* bigness; greatness; nobility; **~ioso** grandiose; grand; **~ote** huge; enormous
grane|ado granulated; **~ro** *m* granary
graniz|ada *f* hailstorm; **~ado** *m* iced fruit drink; **~ar** *v/i* to hail; **~o** *m* hail; *med* cataract
granj|a *f* farmhouse; farm; **~ear** *v/i* to gain; to win; **~ero** *m* farmer
grano *m* grain; seed; pimple
granuja *m* rogue; scoundrel
granular *v/t* to granulate; *a* granular
grapa *f* staple; **~dora** *f* stapler
gras|a *f* grease; fat; **~iento** greasy; fatty
gratifica|ción *f* gratification; bonus; **~r** *v/t* to reward; to tip; to gratify
gratis gratis; free
grat|itud *f* gratitude; **~o** pleasant; agreeable; kind; *LA* grateful
gratuito gratis; free
grava *f* gravel
grava|men *m* obligation; tax; **~r** *v/t* to burden; to impose (*tax*) upon
grave grave; serious; **~dad** *f* gravity; seriousness
gravita|ción *f* gravitation; **~r** *v/i* to gravitate
grazn|ar *v/i* to croak; to cackle; **~ido** *m* croak
Grecia *f* Greece
greda *f* clay; loam
gremio *m* guild; (trade) union
greñ|a *f* mop (of hair); **~udo** dishevel(l)ed (*hair*)
gres *m* stoneware
gresca *f* uproar; brawl
grey *f relig* congregation
griego(a) *m* (*f*), *a* Greek
grieta *f* crack; fissure; chink; *pol* rift
grifo *m* tap; faucet
grill|ete *m* shackle; fetter; **~o** *m* cricket; *pl* fetters
gringo *m* Yankee; foreigner (*in Latin America*)
gripe *f* influenza
gris grey, *Am* gray
grit|ar *v/i* to shout; **~ería** *f* shouting; **~o** *m* shout; outcry; yell
grosella *f* red currant
groser|ía *f* rudeness; coarseness; **~o** rude; discourteous; coarse
grosor *m* thickness
grotesco grotesque; ridiculous
grúa *f tecn* crane
grueso *a* bulky; thick; stout; corpulent; *m* thickness; bulk
grulla *f zool* crane
gruñi|do *m* grunt; **~r** *v/i* to grunt; to growl
gruñón *m* grumbler
grupo *m* group; **~ sanguíneo** blood group
gruta *f* cavern, grotto
guacho *m LA* orphaned
guadaña *f* scythe
gualdo *m* yellow; golden
guante *m* glove; **~s de cabritilla** kid gloves
guapo pretty; handsome; good-looking
guarda *m or f* guard; keeper; custody; **~ de playa** life-guard; **~barros** *m* mudguard; **~bosque** *m* gamekeeper; forest ranger; **~coches** *m* parking attendant; **~espaldas** *m* bodyguard; **~meta** *m sp* goalkeeper; **~polvo** *m* dust cover; **~r** *v/t* to keep; to guard; to preserve; to save; **~rropa** *m* wardrobe; *f* cloakroom
guardería *f* day care center
guardia *m* policeman; guard; *f* custody; protection; **estar de ~** to be on guard
guardián *m* keeper; custodian, warden
guardilla *f* attic, garret
guarida *f zool* lair
guarn|ecer *v/t* to garnish; to trim; to garrison; **~ición** *f* provision; garrison; *pl* harness
guarro *fam* filthy
guas|a *f* joke; irony; **~ón** joking
Guatemala *f* Guatemala
guatemalteco(a) *a*, *m* (*f*) Guatemalan
guateque *m* party; binge
guberna|mental, ~tivo governmental
guerr|a *f* war; warfare; **~a mundial** world war; **~ear** *v/i* to wage war; **~ero** *m* warrior; *a* warlike; **~illa** *f* guerrilla band; partisan; **~illero** *m* guerrilla
guía *m* guide (*person*); *f* guide; **~ telefónica** telephone directory
guiar *v/t* to guide; to steer; to drive
guij|a *f* pebble; **~arro** *m* small round pebble; **~o** *m* gravel
guillotina *f* guillotine; paper cutter
guinda *f* sour cherry
guiñ|ar *v/i* to wink; *mar* to lurch; **~o** *m* wink
guión *m gram* hyphen; script (*of film*)
guirnalda *f* garland, wreath
guisa: a ~ de in the manner of; **de tal ~** in such a way
guis|ado *m* stew; **~ante** *m* green pea; **~ar** *v/t* to cook; to stew; to prepare (*food*); **~o** *m* cooked dish
guita *f* twine, string
guitarr|a *f* guitar; **~ista** *m*, *f* guitarist
gula *f* gluttony
gusano *m* worm; grub; **~ de seda** silkworm
gust|ar *v/t* to taste; to try; *v/i* to please, to be pleasing; **~ar de** to enjoy; to relish; **~o** *m* taste; relish; **con mucho ~o** with pleasure; **~oso** *a* tasty
gutural guttural

H

haba *f* broad bean
haber *v/t* to have, to possess; *v/aux* to have; **~ escrito** to have written; **hemos leído** we have read; *v/imp* there is, there are; **debe ~ mucha gente** there must be many people; **no hay duda** there is no doubt; *v/i* **~ de** to have to; to be due to; **he de leer este libro** I've got to read this book; **~ que** it is necessary; **hay que estar puntual** it is necessary to be punctual; *m* salary; *pl com* assets
habichuela *f* kidney bean
hábil clever; able; capable
habili|dad *f* skill; ability; **~tación** *f* qualification; **~tado** *m* paymaster; **~tar** *v/t* to qualify; to equip
habita|ción *f* room; lodging; **~nte** *m, f* inhabitant; **~r** *v/t* to inhabit; to live in
hábito *m* habit; custom; *relig* vestments
habituar *v/t* to accustom; **~se** to get accustomed
habl|a *f* language; speech; **~ador** talkative; **~aduría** *f* gossip; rumor; **~ar** *v/i* to talk; to speak; to converse; **de eso ni ~ar** it's out of the question; *v/t* to speak (*a language*); **~illa** *f* gossip
hacend|ado *a* landed; *m* landowner; **~ista** *m* economist
hacer *v/t*, *v/i* to make; to create; to manufacture; to prepare; to perform; **~ caso** to consider; **~ cola** to queue, *Am* line up; **~ como si** to act as if; **~ las maletas** to pack; **~ pedazos** to break into pieces; **~ un papel** to act a part; **~ calor** to be hot (*weather*); **~ frío** to be cold (*weather*); **~se** to become; to come to be; to turn (into); **~se viejo** to grow old; **hace** since; ago; for; **hace mucho** long ago; **desde hace 3 años** for 3 years
hacia towards; **~ abajo** downwards; **~ adelante** forwards; **~ arriba** upwards; **~ atrás** backwards
hacienda *f* landed property; estate; **~ pública** federal income; **Ministerio de ♀** Ministry of Finance
hach|a *f* axe; hatchet; **~ear** *v/t* to hew
hachís *m* hashish
hada *f* fairy
hado *m* fate; destiny
halag|ar *v/t* to flatter; **~o** *m* flattery; **~üeño** flattering
halcón *m* falcon; *pol* hawk
halla|r *v/t* to find; to come across; **~rse** to find oneself (*in a place*); **~zgo** *m* find; finding; discovery
hamaca *f* hammock; deck chair
hambr|e *f* hunger; famine; starvation; **tener ~e** to be hungry; **~ear** *v/i* to starve; **~iento** hungry; starved
hamburguesa *f* hamburger
hampa *f* underworld, world of criminals
harag|án *a* idle; *m* loafer; **~anear** *v/i* to lounge around; **~anería** *f* idleness
harap|iento ragged; **~o** rag
harin|a *f* flour; meal; powder; **~a de maíz** corn meal; **~oso** mealy; floury
hart|ar *v/t* to satiate; to glut; **~o** sufficient; full; **estar ~o de** to be fed up with; to be sick of
hasta *prep* till; until; as far as; **~ luego** see you later, so long; **~ la vista** until next time; good-bye; *conj* even
hastiar *v/t* to weary; to disgust
hato *m* herd
hay there is; there are; **~ que** it is necessary; **¡no ~ de qué!** don't mention it!; you are welcome!
haya *f* beech tree
haz *f* face; surface; right side (*of cloth*); *m* sheaf; bundle
hazaña *f* exploit, feat
hebilla *f* buckle
hebra *f* thread; strand
hebroso fibrous
hectárea *f* hectare (*2.47 acres*)
hechi|cero(a) *m* (*f*) wizard; witch; *a* bewitching; **~zar** *v/t* to bewitch; to charm; **~zo** *m* spell; *a* false
hech|o made; done; complete; ready; *m* fact; **~o a mano** hand made; **~ura** *f* making; workmanship
hed|er *v/i* to stink; **~or** *m* stench
hela|da *f* frost; **~dería** *f* ice-cream shop; **~dero** *m LA* ice-cream vendor; **~do** *m* ice-cream; *a* frozen; icy; **~r** *v/t*, *v/i* to freeze, to ice; to congeal; to astonish; **~rse** to be frozen
helecho *m* fern
hélice *f* spiral; propeller
helicóptero *m* helicopter
hembra *f* female; nut (*of a screw*)
hemi|ciclo *m* semicircle; **~sferio** *m* hemisphere
hemorragia *f* h(a)emorrhage
hemorroides *f/pl* h(a)emorrhoids
henchir *v/t* to fill, to cram; **~se** to fill oneself
hend|edura *f* crack; crevice; **~er** *v/t* to cleave; to crack; to split
heno *m* hay
heráldica *f* heraldry
herb|aje *m* grass; pasture; **~icida** *m* weed-killer
hered|ad *f* estate; **~ar** *v/t* to inherit; **~era** *f* heiress; **~ero** *m* heir; **~itario** hereditary
herej|e *m, f* heretic; **~ía** *f* heresy
herencia *f* inheritance; *biol* heredity
herético heretical
heri|da *f* wound; **~do** wounded; injured; **~r** *v/t* to wound
herman|a *f* sister; **~a política** sister-in-law; **~astra** *f* stepsister; **~astro** *m* stepbrother; **~dad** *f* brotherhood; alliance; **~o** *m* brother; **~o político** brother-in-law
hermético hermetic; airtight
hermos|ear *v/t* to beautify; **~o** beautiful; **~ura** *f* beauty
héroe *m* hero
heroico heroical
heroína *f* heroine; *farm* heroin
heroinómano(a) *m* (*f*) heroin addict
herra|dura *f* horseshoe; **~je** *m* ironwork; **~mienta** *f* implement; tool; **~r** *v/t* to shoe (*horses*); to brand (*cattle*)
herrer|ía *f* smithy; blacksmith's forge; **~o** *m* smith, blacksmith
herrete *m* tag, metal tip
herrumbre *f* rust
herv|idor *m* kettle; **~ir** *v/i* to boil; to bubble; *v/t* to boil; **~or** *m* boiling; ebullition; fervo(u)r
hez *f* dregs; scum; *pl* **heces** excrements
hibernar *v/i* to hibernate
hidalgo *m* nobleman
hidráulico hydraulic
hidro|avión *m* seaplane; **~carburo** *m* hydrocarbon; **~eléctrico** hydroelectric; **~fobia** *f* rabies
hidró|filo absorbent (*cotton*); **~geno** *m* hydrogen
hiedra *f* ivy
hiel *f* gall, bile; bitterness
hielo *m* ice; **~ flotante** drift ice
hiena *f* hyena
hierba *f* grass; herb; **mala ~** weed; **~buena** *f* mint
hierro *m* iron; brand; **~ colado, ~ fundido** cast iron; **~ forjado** wrought iron
hígado *m* liver
higiénico hygienic
hig|o *m* fig; **~o chumbo** prickly pear; **~uera** *f* fig tree
hij|a *f* daughter; **~astro(a)** *m* (*f*) stepchild; **~o** *m* son; **~o político** son-in-law
hila *f* row; line; **~da** *f* row; line; **~do** *m* spinning; thread
hilera *f* row; line; rank
hilo *m* yarn, thread; wire
himno *m* hymn; **~ nacional** national anthem
hincapié: hacer ~ to take a stand; **hacer ~ en** to emphasize, to insist on
hincar *v/t* to thrust; **~se de rodillas** to kneel; to genuflect
hincha *m/f sp* fan; **~do** swollen; pompous; **~r** *v/t* to swell; to inflate; **~zón** *f* swelling
hinojo *m* fennel
hípica *f sp* equestrianism
hipnótico hypnotic
hipo *m* hiccup(s)
hipocresía *f* hypocrisy
hipócrita *m, f* hypocrite; *a* hypocritical
hipódromo *m* racecourse, hippodrome
hipopótamo *m* hippopotamus
hipoteca *f* mortgage; **~r** *v/t* to mortgage
hipótesis *f* hypothesis
hirviente boiling
hispánico Hispanic
hispanoamericano Latin American
histeria *f* hysterics
histérico hysterical
historia *f* history; story; **~dor** *m* historian
histórico historical
historieta *f* anecdote; **~s** *pl* comics
hito *m* landmark; target
hocico *m* snout, muzzle; mouth; *fam* face; **meter el ~** to meddle
hockey *m* hockey; **~ sobre hielo** ice hockey
hogar *m* hearth; home
hoguera *f* bonfire; blaze
hoja *f* leave; blade; sheet; **~ de afeitar** razor blade
hojalata *f* tin plate
hojaldre *m or f* puff pastry
hojarasca *f* dead leaves; trash
hoj|ear *v/t* to skim through a book *or* paper; **~uela** *f* small leaf; foil; pancake
¡hola! hello!
Holanda *f* Holland
holandés(esa) *m* (*f*) Dutchman (-woman); *a* Dutch

holg|ado loose; comfortable; leisurely; well-off; **~ar** *v/i* to rest; to be idle; to be unnecessary; ***huelga decir*** needless to say; **~azán** *m* idler; **~azanear** *v/i* to idle about; **~ura** *f* ampleness; enjoyment; ease; comfort
hollín *m* soot
hombr|e *m* man; **¡~e!** I say!; good gracious!; ***~e al agua*** man overboard; ***~e de estado*** statesman; **~e-rana** *m* frogman; **~ía** *f* manliness
hombro *m* shoulder
homenaje *m* homage
homicidio *m* homicide, murder
homogéneo homogeneous
homosexual *a, m, f* homosexual
hond|a *f* sling; **~o** deep; profound; **~ura** *f* depth
Honduras *f* Honduras; ***~ Británica*** British Honduras
hondureño(a) *a, m (f)* Honduran
honest|idad *f* honesty; decency; **~o** decorous; decent; chaste; honest; fair, just
hongo *m* mushroom; toadstool; fungus; bowler hat
honor *m* hono(u)r; virtue; reputation; **~able** hono(u)rable; **~ario** *a* honorary; *m* fee
honr|a *f* hono(u)r; respect; self-esteem; **~adez** *f* honesty; **~ado** honest; **~ar** *v/t* to hono(u)r; **~oso** hono(u)rable
hora *f* hour; time; ***a la ~*** on time; ***a última ~*** at the last moment; ***~ de llegada*** arrival time; ***~ de salida*** departure time; ***¿qué ~ es?*** what time is it?; ***~ punta*** rush hour; **~s** *pl* ***extraordinarias*** overtime; **~rio** *m* timetable
horca *f* gallows, gibbet; pitchfork
horcajadas: a ~ astride
horchata *f* almond milk
horda *f* horde
horizont|al horizontal; **~e** *m* horizon
hormiga *f* ant
hormigón *m* concrete
hormig|uear *v/i* to itch; to teem; **~uero** *m* anthill
hormona *f* hormone
hornillo *m* small furnace; stove; ***~ eléctrico*** hot plate
horno *m* oven; ***alto ~*** blast furnace; ***~ microondas*** microwave oven
horquilla *f* hairpin
horrendo dreadful; horrible
hórreo *m* granary
horri|ble horrible; frightful; **~pilante** horrifying, hair-raising
horror *m* horror; dread; **~izar** *v/t* to horrify; to terrify; **~oso** horrible; hideous
hort|aliza *f* vegetable; **~elano** *m* market gardener; **~icultura** *f* horticulture
hosco sullen, surly; gloomy
hospeda|je board and lodging; **~r** *v/t* to put up; to lodge; **~rse** to take lodgings
hospicio *m* hospice; poorhouse; orphanage
hospital *m* hospital; ***~ de sangre*** *mil* field hospital; **~ario** hospitable; **~idad** *f* hospitality
hostal *m* inn
hostelero(a) *m (f)* innkeeper
hostil hostile; **~idad** *f* hostility; **~izar** *v/t* to antagonize; to harass
hotel *m* hotel; villa; **~ero** *m* hotelkeeper
hoy today; ***~ en día*** nowadays; ***~ por ~*** at the present time
hoy|a *f* large hole, pit; **~o** *m* hole; cavity; pit; **~uelo** *m* dimple
hoz *f* sickle; ravine; gorge
hucha *f* large chest; piggy-bank; savings
hueco *m* hollow; *a* hollow; empty
huelg|a *f* strike; ***declararse en ~a*** to go on strike, to walk out; ***~a salvaje*** wildcat strike; **~uista** *m, f* striker
huella *f* print; mark; footprint; **~s** *pl* ***dactilares*** fingerprints
huérfano(a) *m (f)* orphan
huert|a *f* vegetable garden; irrigated land; **~o** *m* orchard; garden
hueso *m* bone; stone (*of fruit*)
huésped(a) *m (f)* guest; host, hostess
huev|era *f* egg-cup; **~o** *m* egg; ***~o duro*** hard-boiled egg; ***~o frito*** fried egg; ***~o pasado por agua*** boiled egg; **~os** *pl* ***revueltos*** scrambled eggs
hu|ida *f* flight; **~ir** *v/i* to flee; to escape
hule *m* oilcloth; *LA* rubber
hulla *f* hard coal
human|idad *f* humanity, mankind; **~idades** *pl* humanities; **~itario** humanitarian; **~o** human; humane
humear *v/i* to smoke; to emit fumes; *LA* to fumigate
humed|ad *f* moisture; dampness; **~ecer** *v/t* to moisten, to damp
húmedo moist; damp; humid
humidificador *m* air humidifier
humild|ad *f* humility; **~e** humble, meek; lowly
humillar *v/t* to humble; to humiliate; to shame
humo *m* smoke; fume
humor *m* disposition; temper; nature; mood; ***buen ~*** good mood; ***mal ~*** ill temper; bad mood; **~ada** *f* joke; **~ismo** *m* humo(u)r; **~ista** *m* humo(u)rist; **~ístico** amusing, humoro(u)s
hundi|miento *m* sinking; collapse; **~r** *v/t* to sink; to submerge; **~rse** to sink; to collapse; to vanish
húngaro(a) *m (f), a* Hungarian
Hungría *f* Hungary
huracán *m* hurricane
huraño shy; unsociable
hurón *m* ferret
hurtadillas: a ~ stealthily
hurt|ar *v/t* to steal; **~o** *m* theft; larceny
husmear *v/t* to scent, to smell out
huso *m* spindle
¡huy! *interj* ouch!

I

ibérico(a) *m (f), a* Iberian
icono *m* icon
ictericia *f* jaundice
icurriña *f* Basque national flag
ida *f* departure; trip; ***~s y venidas*** comings and goings
idea *f* idea; notion; **~l** *a, m* ideal; **~lismo** *m* idealism; **~lista** *a, m, f* idealist; **~r** *v/t* to devise; to plan
idéntico identical
identi|dad *f* identity; **~ficación** *f* identification; **~ficar** *v/t* to identify
ideología *f* ideology
idilio *m* idyll
idioma *m* language
idiomático idiomatic
idiot|a *a* stupid; *m* idiot; **~ez** *f* stupidity; idiocy
idolatría *f* idolatry
ídolo *m* idol
idóneo suitable; adequate
iglesia *f* church
iglú *m* igloo
ignomini|a *f* infamy; **~oso** ignominious; disgraceful
ignora|ncia *f* ignorance; **~nte** *m* ignorant person; *a* ignorant; **~r** *v/t* to be ignorant *or* unaware of
igual equal; same; level; ***da ~*** it makes no difference; **~ar** *v/t* to equalize; to level; **~dad** *f* equality; uniformity; evenness; **~mente** likewise
ilegal illegal
ilegible illegible
ilegítimo illegitimate
ileso unhurt
ilícito illicit; unlawful
ilimitado unlimited
ilógico illogical
ilumina|ción *f* illumination; lighting; **~r** *v/t* to light up; to illuminate; to enlighten
ilusión *f* illusion; delusion; ***¡qué ~!*** how thrilling!
ilus|ionado hopeful; excited; **~o** *m* dreamer; *a* deluded; **~orio** illusory, deceptive
ilustra|ción *f* illustration; enlightenment; **~r** *v/t* to illustrate
imag|en *f* image; likeness; **~inación** *f* imagination; fantasy; **~inar** *v/t* to imagine; **~inario** imaginary
imán *m* magnet
imbécil *a, m, f* imbecile
imitar *v/t* to imitate
impaciencia *f* impatience
impacto *m* impact; shock
impar odd (*numbers*)
imparcial impartial
impartir *v/t* to impart, to give; to convey
impasible impassive; unfeeling
impávido intrepid, undaunted
impecable impeccable, faultless
impedido invalid; crippled
impedi|mento *m* impediment; **~r** *v/t* to impede; to hinder; to prevent
impeler *v/t* to impel; to drive, to propel(l)
impenetrable impenetrable, impervious
impeniten|cia *f* impenitence; **~te** impenitent
impensado unexpected
imperativo *a, m gram* imperative
imperceptible imperceptible
imperdible *m* safety pin
imperdonable unpardonable
imperfecto imperfect
imperi|al *a* imperial; *f* top deck (*of a bus*); **~alismo** *m* imperialism; **~alista** *m* imperialist
impericia *f* inexperience; lack of skill
imperio *m* empire; **~so** imperious, imperial
impermeable *a* waterproof; *m* raincoat
impertinen|cia *f* impertinence; **~te** impertinent
imperturbado undisturbed
ímpetu *m* impetus; impetuousness; vehemence; momentum
impío godless; *fig* irreligious
implacable implacable; inexorable; unforgiving
implantar *v/t* implant; introduce
implica|ción *f* implication; **~r** *v/t* to implicate; to imply
implorar *v/t* to implore
impone|nte imposing; **~r** *v/t* to impose (*tax*); to inflict; to inspire; **~rse** to get one's way
impopular unpopular
importa|ción *f* import; **~dor** *m* importer
importa|ncia *f* importance; **~nte** important; **~r** *v/i* to be important; to matter; ***no ~*** it doesn't matter; never mind; *v/t* to import
importe *m* amount; price, value
importuno inopportune; troublesome
imposibil|idad *f* impossibility; **~itar** *v/t* to make impossible
imposible impossible
imposición *f* imposition; *com* tax; deposit
impostor(a) *m (f)* impostor
impoten|cia *f* impotence; **~te** impotent
impracticable impracticable; impassable (*of roads*)
imprecación *f* curse
impregnar *v/t* to impregnate
impremeditado unpremeditated
imprenta *f* print; printing house
imprescindible indispensable; essential
impres|ión *f* impression; print; imprint; edition; ***~ión digital*** fingerprint; **~ionante** impressive; **~ionar** *v/t* to impress; **~os** *m/pl* printed matter; **~or** *m* printer
imprevisto unforeseen
imprimar *v/t* to prime (*canvas*)
imprimir *v/t* to print; to imprint; to stamp
improbab|ilidad *f* improbability; **~le** improbable, unlikely
ímprobo dishonest; difficult
improductivo unproductive; unprofitable
impropio unsuitable; unfit; incorrect; improper
improvisar *v/t* to improvise
improvisto unexpected; unforeseen
impruden|cia *f* imprudence; **~te** imprudent; rash
impúdico immodest; shameless
impuesto *m* tax; duty; ***~ sobre la renta*** income tax; ***~ sobre el valor añadido,*** *LA* ***agregado*** value added tax
impugnar *v/t* to contradict, to oppose
impuls|ar *v/t* to propel; **~ión** *f* impulsion; propulsion; ***~ión por reacción*** jet propulsion; **~ivo** impulsive; **~o** *m* impulse
impune unpunished
impureza *f* impurity
imputa|ble imputable; **~r** *v/t* to impute; to accuse of
inacaba|ble endless; **~do** unfinished
inaccesible inaccessible
inacción *f* inaction; inertia
inaceptable unacceptable
inactiv|idad *f* inactivity; **~o** inactive
inadaptable unadaptable
inadecuado inadequate
inadmisible inadmissible
inadvert|encia *f* inadvertence; carelessness; inattention; **~ido** careless; unnoticed, unobservant
inagotable inexhaustible
inaguantable intolerable
inajenable inalienable
inaltera|ble unchangeable, unalterable; **~do** unchanged; unperturbed
inamovible unremovable
inanición *f* inanition; starvation
inanimado lifeless; inanimate
inapagable inextinguishable
inapetencia *f* lack of appetite
inaplicable inapplicable
inapreciable priceless; inestimable
inarrugable crease resistent
inarticulado inarticulate
inasequible unattainable; out of reach
inaudito unheard of
inaugura|ción *f* inauguration, opening; **~r** *v/t* to inaugurate
incandescen|cia *f* incandescence; **~te** incandescent
incansable indefatigable, untiring
incapa|cidad *f* incapacity; inability; **~citar** *v/t* to incapacitate; **~z** incapable; unable
incauto incautious; heedless
incendi|ar *v/t* to set on fire; **~ario** incendiary; **~o** *m* fire
incentivo *m* incentive
incertidumbre *f* uncertainty; insecurity
incesante unceasing; incessant
inciden|cia *f* incidence; incident; **~tal, ~te** incidental
incienso *m* incense
incierto uncertain; untrue
incinerar *v/t* to incinerate; to cremate
incipiente incipient
incisi|ón *f* incision; cut; **~vo** *a* incisive; *m* incisor (*tooth*)
incita|ción *f* incitement; provocation; **~r** *v/t* to incite
incivilizado uncivilized
inclemente inclement (*weather*); harsh; severe
inclina|ción *f* inclination; slope; bow; **~r** *v/t* to incline, to bow; to induce; **~rse** to be inclined; to lean
incluir *v/t* to include; to enclose; to comprise
inclus|ive inclusive **~ivo** inclusive; **~o** enclosed; included
incógnit|a *f* unknown quantity; mystery; **~o** *a* unknown; *m* incognito
incoheren|cia *f* incoherence; **~te** incoherent
incoloro colo(u)rless
incólume uninjured; unharmed
incomod|ar *v/t* to inconvenience; **~arse** to take the trouble; to get angry; **~idad** *f* discomfort; inconvenience; nuisance
incómodo uncomfortable; inconvenient
incompatible incompatible
incompetente incompetent; unqualified
incompleto incomplete
incomprensible incomprehensible
incomunicado isolated; in solitary confinement
inconcebible inconceivable
incondicional unconditional, unqualified
inconfundible unmistakable
incongruo incongruous
inconmovible firm; unyielding
inconquistable unconquerable
inconscien|cia *f* unconsciousness; **~te** unconscious; unaware
inconsecuente inconsequent
inconsiderado inconsiderate

inconstan|cia *f* inconstancy; **~te** unsteady; unsettled
incontable innumerable
incontesta|ble undeniable; **~do** unquestioned, unchallenged
incontinente incontinent
inconvenien|cia *f* inconvenience; indiscretion; **~te** *m* drawback, disadvantage; ***no tengo ~te (en)*** I don't mind; *a* improper; inconvenient
incorporar *v/t* to incorporate; **~se** to sit up (*in bed*); *mil* to join
incorrec|ción *f* incorrectness; discourtesy; **~to** incorrect; inappropriate
incredibilidad *f* incredibility
incredulidad *f* incredulity; scepticism
incrédulo *a* incredulous; sceptical; *m* unbeliever
increíble incredible, unbelievable
increment|ar *v/t* to augment; **~arse en valor** to appreciate; **~o** *m* increase; rise; addition
increpar *v/t* to rebuke
incriminar *v/t* to incriminate
incrustar *v/t* to incrust
incuba|dora *f* incubator; **~r** *v/t* to incubate; to hatch
inculpa|ble blameless; **~ción** *f* accusation; blame; **~r** *v/t* to accuse; to blame
incult|o uncultured; uncouth; **~ura** *f* lack of culture
incumb|encia *f* duty; **~ir** *v/i* to be incumbent on
incurable incurable
incurrir *v/i* to incur
incursión *f mil* raid; incursion
indaga|ción *f* investigation; **~r** *v/t* to investigate
indebido undue; illegal
indecen|cia *f* immodesty; indecency; **~te** immodest; indecent
indecible unspeakable
indecis|ión *f* indecision; **~o** irresolute; undecided
indecoroso unseemly
indefectible unfailing
indefenso defenceless, *Am* defenseless
indefini|ble indefinable; **~do** indefinite; undefined
indeleble indelible
indemn|e unhurt; undamaged; **~izar** *v/t* to indemnify; to compensate
independiente independent
indescriptible indescribable
indeseable undesirable
indeterminado irresolute; indeterminate
India: ***la ~*** India
indica|ción *f* sign; indication; hint; **~dor** *m* indicator, pointer; ***~dor de camino*** roadsign; **~r** *v/t* to indicate; **~tivo** *a, m gram* indicative
índice *m* index; pointer; forefinger
indicio *m* indication; sign
indiferen|cia *f* indifference; apathy; **~te** indifferent; apathetic
indígena *a, m, f* native
indigente destitute
indigest|ión *f* indigestion; **~o** indigestible
indign|ación *f* indignation; **~ar** *v/t* to irritate; **~arse** to become indignant; **~o** unworthy; ignoble
indio(a) *m (f), a* Indian
indirect|a *f* insinuation; **~o** indirect; roundabout
indisciplinado undisciplined
indiscre|ción *f* indiscretion; **~to** indiscreet
indisculpable inexcusable
indiscutible unquestionable, indisputable
indispensable indispensable
indis|poner *v/t* to indispose; to upset; ***~poner con*** to set against; **~ponerse** to fall ill; **~posición** *f* indisposition; **~puesto** indisposed; unwell
indisputable indisputable; evident
indistinto indistinct; vague; dim
individu|al individual; **~alidad** *f* individuality; **~o(a)** *m (f), a* individual
indiviso undivided
indócil unruly; intractable
indocumentado without identification
índole *f* character; nature; kind
indolente indolent
indomable indomitable; untam(e)able
inducción *f (elec)* induction
inducir *v/t* to induce
indudable doubtless
indulgen|cia *f* indulgence; **~te** indulgent; lenient
indult|ar *v/t* to pardon; to exempt; **~o** *m* pardon
indumentaria *f* clothing; apparel
industria *f* industry; manufacturing; trade; skill; **~l** *m* industrialist; *a* industrial; **~lizar** *v/t* to industrialize
inefica|cia *f* inefficiency; **~z** inefficient; ineffectual
ineludible unavoidable
inencogible unshrinkable
inep|cia *f* stupidity; ineptitude; **~to** inept, unfit
inequívoco unequivocal
inercia *f* inactivity
inesperado unexpected
inestab|ilidad *f* instability; **~le** unstable; unsettled
inevitable unavoidable, inevitable
inexacto inaccurate
inexhausto unused; inexhaustible
inexistencia *f* non-existence
inexperto inexperienced; unskilled
inexplicable unexplainable, inexplicable
inexpresable inexpressible
inexplorado unexplored
infalib|ilidad *f* infallibility; **~le** infallible
infama|r *v/t* to defame; to slander; **~torio** slanderous
infam|e infamous, vile; **~ia** *f* baseness; infamy
infan|cia *f* infancy; childhood; **~te** *m* infant; prince; **~til** infantile; childish; **~tería** *f* infantry
infarto *m med* infarct; ***~ del miocardio*** heart attack
infatigable tireless
infecci|ón *f* infection; **~oso** infectious
infectar *v/t* to infect
infecundo sterile; infertile
infeliz unhappy
inferencia *f* inference
inferior inferior; lower; subordinate; **~idad** *f* inferiority
inferir *v/t* to infer; to lead to
infernal infernal; hellish
infiel unfaithful
infiern|illo *m* chafing dish; **~o** *m* hell, inferno
infiltrar *v/t* to infiltrate
ínfimo lowest
infini|dad *f* infinity; **~to** infinite; endless
inflación *f* inflation; swelling
inflacionista inflationary
inflama|ble inflammable; **~ción** *f* combustion; inflammation; **~r** *v/t* to ignite; to inflame; **~rse** to catch fire
inflar *v/t* to inflate; **~se** to swell; to become inflated
inflexi|ble inflexible; unbending, rigid; **~ón** *f* inflection
infligir *v/t* to inflict
influen|cia *f* influence; **~te** influential
influ|ir *v/t* to influence; **~jo** *m* influx; influence; **~yente** influential
información *f* information
informal unreliable; unconventional; **~idad** *f* irregularity; unreliability
inform|ar *v/t* to inform; **~ática** *f* data processing; computer science; **~ativo** informative; **~e** *m* report; *a* shapeless
infortunio *m* bad luck; misfortune
infracción *f* infringement; violation (*of laws etc*)
infrarrojo infrared
infrascrito undersigned
infrecuente infrequent
infringir *v/t* to infringe; to violate
infructuoso fruitless
infundado unfounded
infundir *v/t* to inspire with; to infuse
ingeni|ar *v/t* to think up; **~árselas** to shift, to manage
ingeni|ería *f* engineering; **~ero** *m* engineer; **~o** *m* inventiveness; talent; wit; **~osidad** *f* ingenuity; **~oso** ingenious
ingenuo ingenuous, naive
ingerir *v/t* to swallow; to ingest
Inglaterra *f* England
ingle *f* groin
inglés(esa) *m (f)* Englishman (-woman); *a* English
ingrat|itud *f* ingratitude; **~o** ungrateful, unthankful; thankless
ingravidez *f* weightlessness
ingrediente *m* ingredient
ingres|ar *v/i* to enter; to be admitted; *v/t* to deposit (*money*); **~o** *m* entrance; *pl* earnings; receipts
inhábil unskil(l)ful; clumsy
inhabilitar *v/t* to disable, to disqualify
inhabita|ble uninhabitable; **~do** uninhabited
inherente inherent
inhibir *v/t* to inhibit
inhospitalario inhospitable
inhumano inhuman
inhumar *v/t* to bury (*a body*)
inicia|l initial; **~r** *v/t* to initiate; **~tiva** *f* initiative; ***~tiva privada*** private enterprise
inicuo iniquitous; wicked
inigualado unparalleled
inimaginable unimaginable
ininteligible unintelligible
ininterrumpido uninterrupted, continuous
iniquidad *f* iniquity
injerir *v/t* to insert; **~se** to interfere, to meddle
injert|ar *v/t* to graft; **~o** *m* graft
injuri|a *f* outrage; affront; **~ar** *v/t* to insult; **~oso** insulting; offensive
injust|icia *f* injustice; **~o** unjust; unfair
inmaculado immaculate
inmaduro unripe; *fig* immature
inmanejable unmanageable
inmediat|amente immediately; **~o** immediate
inmejorable excellent; unsurpassable
inmen|so immense; **~surable** immeasurable
inmerecido undeserved
inmigra|ción *f* immigration; **~r** *v/i* to immigrate
inminente imminent
inmobiliario pertaining to real estate
inmoderado immoderate
inmodesto immodest
inmoral immoral; **~idad** *f* immorality
inmortal immortal; **~idad** *f* immortality
inmóvil immobile, motionless
inmovilizar *v/t* to immobilize
inmuebles *m/pl* real estate
inmundo filthy; *fig* impure
inmunidad *f* immunity
inmutable changeless; immutable
innato innate, inborn
innecesario unnecessary
innegable undeniable
innoble ignoble, base
innocuo innocuous, harmless
innovar *v/t* to innovate
innumerable innumerable; countless
inobediente disobedient
inocen|cia *f* innocence; **~te** innocent; naïve
inocular *v/t* to inoculate
inodoro *a* odo(u)rless; *m* lavatory
inofensivo harmless
inoficial unofficial
inolvidable unforgettable
inopinado unexpected
inoportuno inconvenient; ill-timed; unwelcome
inoxidable stainless, unrustable
inquebrantable firm, inalterable
inquiet|ante disquieting; **~ar** *v/t* to trouble; **~arse** to worry; **~o** worried; uneasy; **~ud** *f* uneasiness; restlessness
inquilino(a) *m (f)* tenant
inquina *f* dislike; grudge
inqui|rir *v/t* to investigate; to enquire into; **~sición** *f* inquisition; **~sitivo** inquisitive
insaciable insatiable
insalubre unhealthy
insano unhealthy; insane
insatisfactorio unsatisfactory
inscri|bir *v/t* to inscribe; **~pción** *f* inscription
insect|icida *m* insecticide; **~o** *m* insect
insegur|idad *f* insecurity; **~o** insecure
insensat|ez *f* folly; **~o** stupid; foolish
insensible insensible; insensitive, unfeeling
insertar *v/t* to insert
inservible useless
insidioso insidious
insign|e distinguished; **~ia** *f* badge; *pl* insignia
insignifican|cia *f* insignificance; **~te** insignificant
insincero insincere
insinuar *v/t* to insinuate; **~se** to ingratiate oneself
insipidez *f* insipidity
insípido insipid; tasteless
insist|encia *f* insistence; **~ente** insistent; **~ir** *v/i* to insist
insociable unsociable
insolación *f* sunstroke
insolen|cia *f* insolence; **~te** impudent; insolent
insólito unusual
insolven|cia *f* insolvency; **~te** insolvent; bankrupt
insomn|e sleepless, wakeful; **~io** *m* insomnia
insondable unfathomable
insonor|izado soundproof; **~o** soundless; soundproof
insoportable intolerable, unsufferable, unbearable
insospechado unsuspected
insostenible indefensible
inspec|ción *f* inspection; **~cionar** *v/t* to inspect; **~tor** *m* inspector; superintendent; supervisor
inspira|ción *f* inspiration; **~r** *v/t* to inspire
instala|ción *f* installation; **~r** *v/t* to set up; to install; **~rse** to establish oneself
instan|cia *f* petition; rebuttal; *for* instance; plea; **~te** *m* instant; ***al ~te*** instantly, immediately
instantáne|a *f* snapshot; **~o** instantaneous; ***café ~o*** instant coffee
instar *v/t* to urge; to press
instigar *v/t* to instigate; to urge
instint|ivo instinctive; **~o** *m* instinct
institu|ción *f* institution; establishment; **~ir** *v/t* to institute; to establish; **~to** *m* institute; school; **~triz** *f* schoolmistress; governess
instru|cción *f* education; instruction; teaching; training; **~ctivo** instructive; **~ido** educated; learned; **~ir** *v/t* to instruct, to teach; to train
instrumento *m* instrument; ***~ de cuerda*** stringed instrument; ***~ de viento*** wind instrument
insubordina|do insubordinate; rebellious; **~rse** to rebel
insuficiente insufficient; inadequate
insufrible insufferable
insulina *f* insulin
insult|ar *v/t* to insult; to affront; **~o** *m* insult
insumergible unsinkable
insuperable insuperable
insur|gente insurgent; rebel; **~rección** *f* insurrection
intacto intact; untouched
intachable blameless; irreproachable
integr|al *a* integral; *f mat* integral; **~ar** *v/t* to integrate; **~idad** *f* integrity; honesty
íntegro entire; complete
intel|ecto *m* intellect; **~ectual** intellectual; **~igencia** *f* intelligence; **~igente** intelligent
intemperie *f* harsh weather; ***a la ~*** out in the open
intempestivo untimely; ill-timed
intención *f* intention; ***con ~*** deliberately
intencionado deliberate; ***bien ~*** well-meaning
intens|idad *f* intensity; strength; **~ivo** intensive; **~o** intense
intento *m* intent; attempt; aim, intention
intercalar *v/t* to interpolate
intercambio *m* interchange; exchange
interceder *v/i* to intercede
interceptar *v/t* to intercept
interdicción *f* prohibition
interés *m* interest; ***intereses*** *pl* ***creados*** vested interests
interes|ado(a) *m (f)* interested party; *a* interested; mercenary; **~ante** interesting; **~ar** *v/t* to interest; **~arse por** to take an interest in
interestatal interstate
interferencia *f* interference; *pl* atmospherics (*radio*)
interino temporary; provisional; interim
interior *m* inside; interior; *a* internal; inner; **~idades** *f/pl* personal affairs
interjección *f gram* interjection

interlocutor(a) *m (f)* speaker
intermedi|ario intermediary; **~o** *m* interval; *sp* half-time
interminable endless
intermitente *a* intermittent; *m aut* blinker
internacional international
intern|ado *m* boarding school; **~ar** *v/t* to intern; **~arse en** to go deeply into; **~o(a)** *m (f)* boarding pupil; *a* internal
interpelar *v/t* to appeal to; to address
interponer *v/t* to interpose
interpreta|ción *f* interpretation; explanation; **~r** *v/t* to interpret
intérprete *m, f* interpreter
interrogar *v/t* to interrogate; to question; *for* to examine
interru|mpir *v/t* to interrupt; **~pción** *f* interruption; **~ptor** *m elec* switch
intervalo *m* interval; gap
interven|ción *f* intervention; *med* operation; **~ir** *v/i* to intervene; *v/t* to audit; **~tor** *m* auditor; inspector
interviú *f* interview
intestin|al intestinal; **~o** *m* intestine
intim|ar *v/t* to hint; **~arse** to become intimate; **~idad** *f* intimacy; privacy
intimidar *v/t* to intimidate; to frighten
íntimo innermost; intimate
intoleran|cia *f* intolerance; **~te** intolerant
intoxica|ción *f* poisoning; **~r** *v/t* to poison
intraducible untranslatable
intranquil|izar *v/t*, **~izarse** to worry; **~o** restless; uneasy; worried
intransigente uncompromising; *t pol* die-hard
intransitable impassable
intransitivo intransitive
intratable unsociable
intrépido intrepid; daring
intriga *f* intrigue; **~r** *v/t* to intrigue; to fascinate; *v/i* to intrigue, to scheme
intrincado intricate; entangled
introduc|ción *f* introduction; **~ir** *v/t* to introduce
intromisión *f* interference
intrus|ión *f* intrusion; **~o** *m* intruder; *a* intrusive
intui|ción *f* intuition; **~r** *v/t* to intuit; **~tivo** intuitive
inunda|ción *f* flood; deluge; **~r** *v/t* to flood; to inundate
inusitado unusual; uncommon
inútil useless
invadir *v/t* to invade
inválido *m* invalid
invariable invariable; unchanging, unvarying
invasión *f* invasion
invencible invincible
inven|ción *f* invention; discovery; **~tar** *v/t* to invent; **~tariar** *v/t* to inventory; **~to** *m* invention; **~tor** *m* inventor
invern|áculo *m* greenhouse; **~adero** *m* winter quarters; hothouse; **~al** *a*: **estación** *f* **~al** winter resort; **~ar** *v/i* to spend the winter; **~izo** wintry
inverosímil improbable
inver|sión *f* inversion; investment; **~so** inverse; inverted; opposite; **~tido** *a, m* homosexual; **~tir** *v/t* to invert; to reverse; to turn upside down; *com* to invest
investiga|ción *f* research; investigation; **~r** *v/t* to investigate
investir *v/t* to invest; to confer upon
inveterado inveterate
invicto unconquered
invierno *m* winter
inviola|ble inviolable; sacred; **~do** inviolate
invita|ción *f* invitation; **~do(a)** *m (f)* guest; **~r** *v/t* to invite
invocar *v/t* to invoke
involuntario involuntary, unintentional
inyec|ción *f* injection; **~tar** *v/t* to inject
ir *v/i* to go; to move; to travel; to suit; **~ haciendo algo** to begin doing something; **va anocheciendo** it is beginning to grow dark; **~ a** to go to; to intend to; **voy a hacer unas compras** I am going to do some shopping; **~ a buscar** to fetch; **~ a pie** to walk; **~ en tren** to go by train; **¡qué va!** nonsense!; **¡vaya!** is that so?, really!; **~se** to go away
ira *f* anger; **~cundo** angry; irascible
iris *m* iris; rainbow
Irlanda *f* Ireland
irlandés(esa) *m (f)* Irishman (-woman); *a* Irish
ironía *f* irony
irónico ironical
irracional irrational
irradia|ción *f* radiation; **~r** *v/t* to radiate
irrazonable unreasonable
irreal unreal; **~idad** *f* unreality; **~izable** unattainable; unrealizable
irreconciliable irreconcilable
irreemplazable irreplaceable
irreflexivo unthinking
irregular irregular; abnormal; uneven; **~idad** *f* irregularity; unevenness
irreparable irreparable; beyond repair
irrespetuoso disrespectful
irresuelto irresolute; wavering
irrevocable irrevocable
irrigación *f t med* irrigation
irris|ión *f* derision; **~orio** derisory
irrita|ble irritable; short-tempered; **~r** *v/t* to irritate; to anger
irrompible unbreakable
isla *f* island; **~s** *pl* **Baleares** Balearic Islands; **~s Canarias** Canary Islands; **~s Malvinas** Falkland Islands
Islam *m* Islam
islámico Islamic
islandés(esa) *m (f)* Icelander
Islandia *f* Iceland
isl|eño(a) *m (f)* islander; **~ote** *m* small barren island
israelí *a, m, f* Israeli
istmo *m* isthmus
Italia *f* Italy
italiano(a) *m (f)*, *a* Italian
itinerario *m* itinerary
I.T.V. = **inspección técnica de vehículos** vehicle inspection
I.V.A. = **impuesto sobre el valor añadido** value-added tax
izar *v/t* to hoist
izquierda *f* left side; left hand
izquierdista *m, f* leftist

J

jabalí *m* wild boar
jabalina *f* wild sow; javelin
jabón *m* soap
jabon|aduras *f/pl* soapsuds; **~ar** *v/t* to soap; *fam* to reprimand; **~era** *f* soap dish; **~ero** *m* soap maker
jaca *f* pony
jacinto *m* hyacinth
jacta|ncia *f* boasting; **~rse** to boast; to brag
jadear *v/i* to pant; to gasp
jaez *m* harness; **jaeces** *pl* trappings
jaguar *m* jaguar
jalar *v/t, v/i LA* to pull
jale|a *f* jelly; **~o** *m* hullabaloo; racket
jamás never; **nunca ~** never
jamón *m* ham
Japón *m* Japan
japonés(esa) *a, m (f)* Japanese
jaque *m* check (*in chess*); **~ mate** checkmate
jaqueca *f* headache, migraine
jarabe *m* syrup; sweet drink; **~ contra la tos** cough syrup
jarcias *f/pl mar* rigging
jardín *m* garden; **~ botánico** botanical garden; **~ de infancia** nursery school; **~ zoológico** zoo
jardinero(a) *m (f)* gardener
jarr|a *f* jar; pitcher; **~o** *m* jug; pitcher; **~ón** *m* urn; flower vase
jaspeado speckled
jaula *f* cage; cell
jauría *f* pack of hounds
jazmín *m* jasmine
jef|atura *f* leadership; headquarters; **~e** *m* chief; leader; employer; boss; **~e de estación** stationmaster; **~e del estado** chief of state; **~e de tren** conductor
jengibre *m* ginger
jeque *m* sheik
jerarquía *f* hierarchy
jerez *m* sherry
jerga *f* jargon
jeringa *f* syringe
jersey *m* jersey; jumper, *Am* sweater
jesuita *m* Jesuit
jinete *m* horseman
jira *f* strip (*of cloth*); picnic; tour; **~fa** *f* giraffe
jocoso jocose; merry
jorna|da *f* working day; day's journey; **de ~da completa** full-time; **~l** *m* wage; day's pay; **~lero** *m* day labo(u)rer; worker
joroba *f* hump; **~do** *m* hunchbacked
jota *f* jot, bit; **no entender ni ~** not to understand a bit
joven *m, f* young man; young girl; young (*of animals*); *a* young; **~cito(a)** *m, f* youngster
joy|a *f* jewel; gem; **~ería** *f* jewelry shop; **~ero** *m* jewel(l)er; jewelcase
jubila|ción *f* retirement; pension; **~r** *v/t* to pension off; **~rse** to retire (*from job*)
jubileo *m* jubilee
júbilo *m* joy; rejoicing
judaico Judaic; Jewish
judía *f* bean; **~ verde** green bean
judicial legal; judicial
judío(a) *m (f)* Jew; Jewess; *a* Jewish
juego *m* game; sport; play; set (*of dishes, etc*); **en ~** at stake; **~ de prendas** forfeits; **fuera de ~** offside; **hacer ~** to match; **~ limpio** fair play; **~ sucio** foul play
juerga *f* spree; binge; **ir de ~** to go out and live it up
jueves *m* Thursday
juez *m* judge
juga|da *f* play; move; stroke; throw; **~dor(a)** *m (f)* player; gambler; **~r** *v/t, v/i* to play; to gamble
jugo *m* juice; sap; substance; **~so** juicy
juguet|e *m* toy; plaything; **~ear** *v/i* to joy; to gambol; **~ón** playful; frisky
juicio *m* judg(e)ment; sense; opinion; **fuera de ~** out of one's mind; **~so** sensible; prudent
julio *m* July
jumento *m* donkey
junco *m bot* rush; junk (*boat*)
jungla *f* jungle
junio *m* June
junt|a *f* board; council; meeting; **~a directiva** board (*of directors*); **~a de accionistas** stockholders' meeting; **~ar** *v/t* to join; to connect; **~arse** to meet; to assemble; **~o** *a* joined; together; close; *adv* near; close; at the same time; **~o a** next to; **~ura** *f* joint; juncture; *tecn* seam
jura|do *m* jury; juror; **~mentar** *v/t* to swear in; **~mento** *m* oath; **~mento falso** perjury; **prestar ~mento** to take an oath; **~r** *v/t, v/i* to swear; to curse
jurídico juridical; legal
juris|dicción *f* jurisdiction; **~ta** *m, f* jurist; lawyer
just|amente *adv* justly; exactly; just, precisely; **~icia** *f* justice; **~iciero** just; severe; **~ificar** *v/t* to justify; **~ipreciar** *v/t* to appraise; **~o** *a* just; exact; tight-fitting; *adv* tightly
juven|il juvenile; youthful; **~tud** *f* youth
juzga|do *m* court of justice; tribunal; **~r** *v/t, v/i* to judge; to pass judg(e)ment

K

karate *m* karate
kero|seno, ~sén *m* kerosene
kilo|gramo *m* kilogram; **~metraje** *m* distance in kilometres
kilómetro *m* kilometre, *Am* kilometer
kilovatio *m* kilowatt
kiosco *m* kiosk; stand; newsstand

L

la *art f* the; *pron pers f* her; it
laberinto *m* labyrinth, maze
labia *f* glibness, fluency; **tener mucha ~** to have the gift of gab
labio *m* lip; brim (*of a cup*); edge
labor *f* work, labo(u)r; farming; needlework; **~ de equipo** teamwork; **~able** workable; **~ar** *v/t* to work; to till (*soil*); **~atorio** *m* laboratory; **~ioso** laborious; (*person*) hardworking
labr|ado *m* wrought; hewn; **~ador** *m* ploughman; farm labo(u)rer; **~antío** arable; **~anza** *f* cultivation (*of land*); **~ar** *v/t* to farm, to till; to work; **~iego** *m* farm hand; peasant
laca *f* shellac, lacquer; hair spray; **~ para uñas** nail polish
lacayo *m* footman
lacio limp; straight (*hair*)
lacr|ar *v/t* to seal with sealing wax; to injure (*health*); **~e** *m LA* sealing wax
lacri|mógeno tear-producing; **gas** *m* **~mógeno** tear gas; **~moso** tearful; lachrymose
lacta|ncia *f* lactation; **~r** *v/t* to nurse; *v/i* to suckle
lácteo milky
ladear *v/t* to tilt; *v/i* to deviate; **~se** to lean; to incline
lad|era *f* slope; **~o** *m* side; **al ~o** near, at hand; **al ~o de** beside; **~o a ~o** side by side; **de ~o** sideways
ladr|ar *v/i* to bark; **~ido** *m* barking
ladrillo *m* brick
ladrón(ona) *m (f)* thief
lagart|ija *f* small lizard; **~o** *m* lizard
lago *m* lake
lágrima *f* tear
laguna *f* lagoon; gap
laico lay; secular
lamenta|ble regrettable, deplorable; **~r** *v/t* to lament; to regret; **~rse** to wail
lamento *m* lament; wail
lamer *v/t* to lick
lámina *f* lamina; sheet (*of metal*); engraving plate
lamina|do laminated; rolled; **~r** *v/t* to laminate; to roll (*metal*)
lámpara *f* lamp; light; tube (*radio*); **~ de destello** *foto* flash bulb; **~ de soldar** blowtorch
lamparilla *f* small lamp; nightlight
lana *f* wool
lance *m* throw; cast; event; move; **~ro** *m* lancer
lancha *f* launch; small boat; lighter; **~ automóvil** motor launch; **~ neumática** rubber dinghy; **~ salvavidas** lifeboat
langost|a *f* locust; lobster; **~ino** *m* crawfish; prawn
languide|cer *v/i* to languish; to pine; **~z** *f* languor
lánguido languid
lanza *f* spear; lance; **~dera** *f* shuttle; **~dor** *m sp* pitcher; **~r** *v/t* to launch; to throw, to cast; **~rse** to rush; **~rse de morro** *aer* to nose-dive
lapicero *m* pencil case
lápida *f* tablet; memorial stone; **~ sepulcral** tombstone
lápiz *m* pencil; **~ de labios** lipstick
lapso *m* lapse; fall
larga: a la ~ in the long run; **~rse** to leave; to make off
largo long; free; liberal; **a ~ plazo** *com* long-term; **a lo ~ de** alongside; along; **¡~ de aquí!** get out!; **~metraje** *m* feature film
larguero *m* door jamb; *sp* crossbar
largueza *f* liberality; length
laring|e *f* larynx; **~itis** *f* laryngitis
lascivo lascivious; sensual, lewd
lástima *f* pity; **dar ~** to inspire compassion; **¡qué ~!** what a pity!
lastim|ar *v/t* to wound; to hurt; to offend; to pity; **~oso** pitiful; pitiable
lastre *m* ballast
lata *f* can; tin; *fam* nuisance; **dar la ~** to be a nuisance
lateral lateral; side
latido *m* throb; beat; throbbing
latifundio *m* large estate
latigazo *m* lash *or* crack of a whip
látigo *m* whip
latín *m* Latın
latinoamericano(a) *m (f)* Latin American
latir *v/i* to beat; to throb
latitud *f* latitude
lat|ón *m* brass; **~oso** *fam a* annoying, boring
latrocinio *m* theft; robbery
laudable laudable
lava|bo *m* washbasin, *Am* sink; lavatory; **~dero** *m* washing place; **~do** *m* washing; **~do del cerebro** brainwashing; **~dora** *f* washing machine
lavanda *f* lavender

lavandería *f* laundry
lavaparabrisas *m* windshield washer
lavar *v/t* to wash; **~ en seco** to dry clean; **~ y marcar** shampoo and set; **~se las manos** to wash one's hands
lavavajillas *m* dishwasher (*machine*)
laxante *m* laxative
laya *f* spade
laz|ada *f* bow, knot; **~o** *m* slip-knot; tie; bow (*of ribbons*); *fig* link; bond
le *pron pers* him; you; to him; to her; to it; to you
leal loyal; **~tad** *f* loyalty
lec|ción *f* lesson; **~tor(a)** *m* (*f*) reader; **~tura** *f* reading
leche *f* milk; **~ de manteca** buttermilk; **~ desnatada** skimmed milk; **~ en polvo** powdered milk; **~ra** *f* dairymaid; milk can; **~ría** *f* dairy; **~ro** *m* milkman
lecho *m* bed; river-bed
lechón *m* suckling pig
lechuga *f* lettuce
lechuza *f* barn-owl
leer *v/t*, *v/i* to read
lega|ción *f* legation; **~do** *m* legacy; legate
legal legal; lawful; **~izar** *v/t* to legalize
lega|r *v/t* to bequeath; **~tario** *m* legatee
legendario *a* legendary
legible legible, readable
legión *f* legion
legisla|ción *f* legislation; **~dor** *m* legislator; *a* legislative; **~tivo** legislative; **~tura** *f* term of a legislature
legitim|ar *v/t* legitimize; legalize; **~idad** *f* legitimacy; lawfulness
legítimo legitimate; lawful
lego *m* lay brother; layman; *a* lay, secular
legua *f* league (*5.5 km*); **~ marítima** sea-mile
legum|bre *f* vegetable; **~inoso** leguminous
lejan|ía *f* distance; **~o** distant; remote
lejía *f* lye; *fam* reprimand
lejos *adv* far away; far off; **a lo ~** in the distance; **desde ~** from a distance; **~ de** far from
lema *m* motto; catchword; slogan; theme
lencería *f* linen (goods); linen shop; lingerie
lengua *f* tongue; language; **~ materna** mother tongue; **tirar de la ~** to make talk
lenguado *m* sole
lenguaje *m* language; idiom; diction
lengüeta *f* tongue (*of shoe, etc*); flap; barb (*of dart*)
lente *m or f* lens; **~s** *pl* spectacles, glasses; **~s de contacto** contact lenses
lentej|a *f* lentil; **~uela** *f* spangle
lentillas *f/pl* contact lenses
lent|itud *f* slowness; **~o** slow
leña *f* firewood; **~dor** *m* woodcutter, lumberjack
león *m* lion; **~ marino** sea lion
leopardo *m* leopard
lepra *f* leprosy
lerdo dull, slow; clumsy
lesión *f* injury; lesion
lesionar *v/t* to injure
letal lethal
letanía *f* litany
letárgico lethargic
letr|a *f* letter; handwriting; words, lyrics (*of a song*); **~a de cambio** bill of exchange; draft; **~ negrilla** *impr* bold face; **~ado** *m* lawyer; *a* learned; **~ero** *m* sign; notice; placard
leva *f* press; *mil* levy; *tecn* cam
levadura *f* yeast, leaven; **~ de cerveza** brewer's yeast
levanta|miento *m* lifting; raising; rising, rebellion; **~miento de pesos** *sp* weight lifting; **~r** *v/t* to raise; to lift; **~rse** to rise; to get up; to stand up
levante *m* east; east wind
leve light; slight
léxico *m* lexicon
ley *f* law; standard; fineness (*of gold etc*); **~ marcial** martial law
leyenda *f* legend; caption
liar *v/t* to tie; **~se** to get involved
liber|ación *f* liberation; **~al** liberal; **~ar** *v/t* to liberate; to free; **~tad** *f* liberty; freedom; **~tador** *m* liberator; **~tar** *v/t* to liberate, to release; to set free
libertin|aje *m* licentiousness; **~o** *m* libertine
libra *f* pound; **~ esterlina** pound sterling
libra|dor *m* *com* drawer; **~r** *v/t* to free; to exempt; *com* to draw; **~rse de** to get rid of
libre free
librer|ía *f* bookshop; **~o** *m* bookseller
libro *m* book; **~ de bolsillo** paperback; **~ de consulta** reference book; **~ mayor** ledger
licencia *f* permit; **~ de manejar** *LA* driving licence, *Am* driver's license; **~ por enfermedad** sick leave; **~do** *m* licentiate; *LA* lawyer; **~r** *v/t* to permit; to license; *mil* to discharge; **~rse** to take a degree
lícito legal; lawful
licor *m* liquor; liqueur
lid *f* contest; dispute; **~iar** *v/i* to fight; *v/t* to fight (*bulls*)
líder *m* leader
liebre *f* hare
lienzo *m* linen cloth; canvas
liga *f* garter; league; **~dura** *f* ligature; **~mento** *m* ligament; **~r** *v/t* to bind; **~rse** to join together; to combine; **~s** *f/pl* suspenders; **~zón** *f* linking; union
liger|eza *f* lightness; levity; **~o** light; fast; flighty
lignito *m* lignite
lija *f* dogfish; **papel de ~** sandpaper
lila *f* lilac (*flower and colo[u]r*)
lima *f* lime; file; **~ para las uñas** nail file; **~dura** *f* filing; **~r** *v/t* to file, to polish
limero *m* lime tree
limitar *v/t* to limit
límite *m* limit; **~ de velocidad** speed limit
limítrofe bordering
limo *m* slime
limón *m* lemon
limonero *m* lemon tree
limosna *f* alms
limpia|botas *m* bootblack; **~dientes** *m* toothpick; **~parabrisas** *m* windscreen (*Am* windshield) wiper; **~r** *v/t* to clean; to cleanse; **~r en seco** to dry clean
limpi|eza *f* cleanliness; cleaning; **hacer la ~eza** to clean; **~o** clean; tidy
limusina *f* limousine
linaje *m* lineage; class
linaza *f* linseed
lince *m* lynx
linchar *v/t* to lynch
lind|ante adjoining; **~ar** *v/i* to border; **~e** *m* boundary
lind|eza *f* prettiness; **~o** pretty; beautiful; **de lo ~o** a lot; wonderfully
línea *f* line; **~ aérea** airline; **~ de montaje** *tecn* assembly line
linea|l lineal; **~r** *v/t* to draw lines on
linfa *f* lymph
lingote *m* ingot
lingüista *m* linguist
lingüístic|a *f* linguistics; **~o** linguistic
lino *m* flax; linen
linóleo *m* linoleum
linterna *f* lantern; **~ eléctrica** flashlight
lío *m* bundle; intrigue; *fam* mess, jam
liofilización *f* freeze drying
liquida|ción *f* *com* liquidation; **~r** *v/t* to liquefy; *com* to liquidate
líquido *m*, *a* liquid
lira *f* *mús* lyre
lírico lyrical
lirio *m* lily
lirón *m* *zool* dormouse
lisiado disabled, crippled
liso smooth; even; **~ y llano** plain, simple
lisonj|a *f* flattery; **~ero** flattering
lista *f* list; strip; slip (*of paper*); **~ de correos** general delivery; **~ de precios** price list
listo clever; quick; ready
litera *f* litter; berth; *f c* couchette
litera|rio literary; **~tura** *f* literature
litig|ar *v/i* to dispute; **~io** *m* dispute; lawsuit
litografía *f* lithography
litoral *m* littoral; seashore; coast
litro *m* litre, *Am* liter
liturgia *f* liturgy
liviano fickle; *LA* light (*clothing, food*)
lívido livid
lo *art* the; *pers pron of* **él** him, it; **~ bueno** the good; **no ~ hay** there isn't any; **~ mío** what is mine; **~ que** how
lobo *m* wolf; **~ de mar** sea dog; **~ marino** seal
lóbulo *m* lobe
local *m* premises; site; *a* local; **~idad** *f* place; seat (*in the theatre*); locality; **~izar** *v/t* to localize
loción *f* wash; lotion
loco *a* mad; *m* madman; **volverse ~** to go mad
locomo|ción *f* locomotion; **~tora** *f* locomotive, engine
locuaz talkative; garrulous
locura *f* madness
locutor *m* radio announcer; commentator
lodo *m* mud; **~so** muddy
lógic|a *f* logic; **~o** logical
logr|ar *v/t* to achieve; to succeed in; **~o** *m* achievement; gain; success
lombarda *f* red cabbage
lombriz *f* earthworm
lomo *m* loin; back; ridge (*of a mountain*)
lona *f* canvas
lonche *m* *LA* lunch; **~ría** *f* *LA* snack bar
Londres *m* London
longaniza *f* pork sausage
longitud *f* length; **~ de onda** wave length
lonja *f* exchange; market; slice
loro *m* parrot
los (las) the (*pl*); *pron pers* them
losa *f* flagstone; slab
lote *m* share; lot; **~ría** *f* lottery
loza *f* crockery
lubrica|nte *m* lubricant; **~r** *v/t* to lubricate, to oil
lucera *f* skylight
lucerna *f* chandelier
lucero *m* bright star
lucidez *f* lucidity; brightness; brilliancy
lúcido lucid, clear
luci|do brilliant; splendid; successful; **~érnaga** *f* glow-worm; **~rse** to dress up; to shine
lucio *m* *zool* pike
lucro *m* gain, profit
lucha *f* fight; struggle; **~ libre** wrestling; **~r** *v/i* to fight; to struggle; to wrestle
luego *adv* immediately; then; later; **¡hasta ~!** so long!; **~ que** after; **desde ~** of course
lugar *m* place; spot; position; *fig* reason; **en primer ~** in the first place; **dar ~ a** give rise to; **en ~ de** instead of
lúgubre dismal, gloomy
lujo *m* luxury; **~so** luxurious
lumbre *f* fire; brightness
luminoso luminous
luna *f* moon; mirror; plate glass; **~ de miel** honeymoon
lunar *a* lunar; *m* mole; beauty spot
lunático *a* lunatic; *m* lunatic, madman
lunes *m* Monday
luneta *f* lens; **~ trasera** *aut* rear window
lupa *f* magnifying glass
lúpulo *m* *bot* hop; hops
lustrabotas *m* *LA* bootblack
lustr|e *m* gloss; polish; **~oso** shining
luto *m* mourning; **estar de ~** to be in mourning
luz *f* light; daylight; **dar a ~** to give birth to; **salir a ~** to come to light; (*book*) to be published; **~ de carretera** bright lights; **~ de cruce** dimmers; **~ de población** parking lights; **a todas luces** anyway

Ll

llaga *f* wound; sore; ulcer; **~r** *v/t* to wound
llama *f* flame; sudden blaze; *zool* lama
llama|da *f* call; knock; signal; *impr* reference (mark); **~da de larga distancia** trunk call, *Am* long distance call; **~miento** *m* call; **~r** *v/t* to call; to summon; to invoke; *v/i* to knock *or* ring at the door; **~rse** to be named; **¿cómo se ~ Ud.?** what's your name?; **~tivo** gaudy; showy
llamear *v/i* to blaze
llan|a *f* trowel; flat land; **~amente** clearly; plainly; simply; **~o** flat, even; level; plain, simple
llanta *f* rim (of wheel); *LA* tyre, *Am* tire
llanto *m* weeping; flood of tears
llanura *f* evenness; flatness; plain
llave *f* key; *tecn* wrench; faucet; tap; bolt; *elec* switch; *mús* key; **~ inglesa** monkey wrench; **~ maestra** pass-key; **~ de tuercas** spanner; **~ro** *m* key ring
llavín *m* latch key
llega|da *f* arrival; **~r** *v/i* to arrive; to come; to reach; **~r a ser** to become; **~r a las manos** to come to blows
llenar *v/t* to fill; to stuff; to occupy; to satisfy
lleno *a* full; complete; **de ~** fully; *m* fill, plenty; *teat* full house
lleva|dero tolerable; **~r** *v/t* to carry; to take; to bring; to lead (*a life*); to wear (*clothes*); to spend (*time*); to keep (*books*); to bear; to endure; **~r a cabo** to complete; to carry out; **~r adelante** to push ahead with; **~r puesto** to wear; **~rse** to take away; to carry off; **~rse bien con** to get on well with
llor|ar *v/i* to cry; to weep;to bewail, to mourn; **~iquear** *v/i* to snivel, to whimper; **~ón(ona)** *m* (*f*) weeper; *a* always weeping; **~oso** tearful
llovediz|o leaky; **agua ~a** rain water
llov|er *v/i* to rain; **~er a cántaros** to rain cats and dogs; **~iznar** *v/i* to drizzle
lluvi|a *f* rain; **~oso** rainy

M

maca *f* bruise (*on fruit*); spot; flaw
macabro macabre
macarrones *m/pl* macaroni
macarse to rot (*fruit*)
macedonia *f* **(de frutas)** fruit salad
maceta *f* flowerpot
macis *f* *coc* mace
macizo *a* solid, massive; *m* mass, bulk; flowerbed
macha|car *v/t* to pound; to crush; *v/i* to harp (*on*); **~do** *m* hatchet
machete *m* machete
machina *f* crane, derrick
macho *m* male; man; hook (*for an eye*); *a* male; manly; virile
machucar *v/t* to pound; to bruise
machucho elderly; judicious
madeja *f* skein
mader|a *f* wood; timber; *m* Madeira wine; **~a laminada** plywood; **~ero** *m* timber merchant; **~o** *m* beam (*of timber*); *fam* blockhead
madr|astra *f* stepmother; **~e** *f* mother; *fig* origin; **~e patria** mother country; **~e política** mother-in-law; **~eperla** *f* mother-of-pearl; **~eselva** *f* honeysuckle
madriguera *f* burrow; den
madrileño(a) *m* (*f*) inhabitant of Madrid
madrina *f* godmother; **~ de boda** bridesmaid
madruga|da *f* dawn; early morning; **de ~da** very early; **~dor(a)** *m* (*f*) early riser; **~r** *v/i* to rise very early
madur|ar *v/t* to ripen; to think out; *v/i* to ripen; *fig* to mature; **~ez** *f* maturity; ripeness; **~o** mature; ripe; **de edad ya ~a** middle-aged
maestr|a *f* schoolmistress; teacher; **~ía** *f* mastery; title of a master; **~o** *a* masterly; *m* schoolmaster; master; **~o de ceremonias** master of ceremonies; **~o de obras** builder; foreman
mafia *f* Mafia
magia *f* magic
mágico magic; magical
magisterio *m* teaching profession
magistra|do *m* magistrate; **~l** magisterial; masterly; **~tura** *f* judicature
magnánimo magnanimous
magnético magnetic
magneti|smo *m* magnetism; **~zar** *v/t* to magnetize
magnetofón *m* tape recorder
magnetoscopio *m* video recorder
magnífico magnificent; excellent
magnitud *f* magnitude
mago *m* magician; wizard;

los Reyes ~s the Three Wise Men
magro lean
magulladura *f* bruise
mahometano *a, m* Mohammedan
maíz *m* maize; Indian corn
maizal *m* maize field, *Am* corn field
majader|ía *f* silliness; annoyance; **~o** annoying, tiresome
majest|ad *f* majesty; **~uoso** majestic
majo(a) *m* (*f*) attractive man *or* woman; *a* good looking; pretty
mal *a apocope of* **malo**, *used before masculine nouns*; **un ~ consejo** a bad advice; *m* evil; harm; illness, disease; damage; **parar en ~** to come to a bad end; **~ de mar** seasickness; **~ de vuelo** airsickness; *adv* badly; hardly; **de ~ en peor** from bad to worse; **¡menos ~!** just as well!
malabarista *m, f* juggler
malaconsejado ill-advised
malacostumbrado having bad habits; spoiled
malagradecido unthankful, ungrateful
malandante unfortunate
malaventura *f* misfortune
malbaratar *v/t* to squander
malcasado unhappily married; unfaithful (*in marriage*)
malcontento discontented
malcriado ill-bred
maldad *f* wickedness
maldecir *v/t* to curse
maldición *f* curse
maldito wicked; bad; accursed; **¡~ sea!** confound it!, damn!
malecón *m* pier, jetty
maléfico harmful
malentendido *m* misunderstanding
malestar *m* malaise; uneasiness; *med* discomfort; *pol* unrest
malet|a *f* suitcase; bag; **hacer la(s) ~a(s)** to pack; **~ero** *m aut* boot, *Am* trunk; **~ín** *m* small case, travel(l)ing bag
malevolencia *f* ill will
malévolo malevolent
maleza *f* undergrowth, scrub, shrubbery
malgastar *v/t* to waste, to squander
malhablado foulmouthed
malhecho *a* ill made; *m* misdeed; **~r** *m* malefactor
malhumorado bad-tempered; cross; peevish
malici|a *f* malice; cunning; **~oso** malicious; suspicious
maligno malignant
malintencionado ill-disposed
mal|o bad; evil; ill; unpleasant, naughty; **a las ~as** *LA* by force; **estar de ~as** to be in a bad mood; **ponerse ~o** to fall ill
malogra|do abortive; frustrated; **~r** *v/t* to waste; to lose; to upset; to ruin; **~rse** to fail; to come to an untimely end; *LA* to break down (*machine*)
malogro *m* failure; waste
malparir *v/i* to miscarry
malquerer *v/t* to dislike
malsano unhealthy
malta *f* malt
maltratar *v/t* to ill-treat
malva *f bot* mallow
malvado wicked
malvavisco *m* marshmallow
malversación *f* embezzlement
malla *f* mesh; network
Mallorca *f* Majorca
mamá *f* mamma; mummy
mama *f* breast; **~r** *v/t, v/i* to suck
mameluco *m fam* simpleton; rompers
mamífero *m* mammal
mampostería *f* masonry
manada *f* flock; herd
mana|ntial *m* spring; fountain; well; source; **~r** *v/i* to flow; to spring from
manc|ar *v/t* to cripple; **~o** one-armed; one-handed
mancomunidad *f* association; community; union
man|cornas, ~cuernas *f/pl LA* cufflinks
mancha *f* stain; spot; **~r** *v/t* to stain
mand|ado *m* order; mandate; errand; **~amiento** *m relig* commandment; order; **~ar** *v/t, v/i* to order; to command; to bequeath; to send; to rule
mandarina *f* tangerine; mandarin orange
mandat|ario *m* agent; **~o** *m* order; command; *pol* mandate; rule
mandíbula *f* jaw
mand|o *m* command; **~o a distancia** remote control; *pl* controls; **~ón** imperious; domineering
manecilla *f* hand (*of watch*)
manej|ar *v/t* to handle; to wield; to manage; *LA* to drive; **~o** *m* handling; management
manera *f* manner; way; *pl* manners; **de ~ que** so that; **de ninguna ~** by no means
manga *f* sleeve; hose; *mar* beam; **tener ~ ancha** to be broadminded
mango *m* handle; **~near** *v/i* to meddle
manguera *f* water hose
manguito *m* muff; *tecn* sleeve
manía *f* mania; craze; **~co** *m* maniac; *a* mad
maniatar *v/t* to handcuff
manicomio *m* lunatic asylum, mental hospital
manicura *f* manicure
manifesta|ción *f* manifestation; declaration; *pol* demonstration; **~nte** *m* public demonstrator; **~r** *v/t* to show; to declare
manifiesto *m* manifest; *a* evident; obvious
manilla *f* bracelet; handcuff; hand (*of clock*); **~r** *m* handlebar
maniobra *f* handiwork; man(o)euvre; operation; trick; **~r** *v/t, v/i* to handle; to man(o)euvre
manipula|ción *f* manipulation; **~r** *v/t, v/i* to handle; to manipulate
maniquí *m* mannequin
manivela *f* crank
mano *f* hand; forefoot; coat (*of paint*); hand (*at cards*); **~ de obra** labo(u)r, manpower; **a ~** at hand; **a una ~** of one accord; **de segunda ~** second hand; **echar una ~ a** to lend a hand to; **estrechar la ~** to shake hands; **mudar de ~s** to change hands; **~jo** *m* bunch; **~pla** *f* mitten; **~sear** *v/t* to handle, to finger; to paw; **~tazo** *m* slap
mansión *f* mansion; abode
manso meek; gentle; tame
mant|a *f* blanket; plaid; **~ear** *v/t* to toss up in a blanket
mantec|a *f* fat; *LA* butter; **~a de cerdo** lard; **~oso** buttery; fat
mantel *m* tablecloth; **~ería** *f* table linen
manten|er *v/t* to maintain; to keep; to support; **~erse** to sustain oneself; **~imiento** *m* maintenance; support
mantequ|era *f* churn; butter dish; **~ero** *m* dairyman; **~illa** *f* butter
mant|illa *f* mantilla; *pl* baby clothes; **~o** *m* cloak; **~ón** *m* shawl
manual *a* manual; handy; **trabajo** *m* **~** manual labo(u)r; *m* handbook, manual
manu|brio *m* crank; handle; **~factura** *f* manufacture; **~scrito** *m* manuscript; *a* handwritten; **~tención** *f* maintenance; maintaining; support
manzan|a *f* apple; block of houses; **~illa** *f* camomile; manzanilla wine; **~o** *m* apple tree
maña *f* skill; cleverness
mañana *f* morning; tomorrow; **por la ~** in the morning; **pasado ~** the day after tomorrow; **~ por la ~** tomorrow morning
mañoso skil(l)ful; clever
mapa *m* map; **~ de carreteras** road map; **~ meteorológico** weather chart
mapache *m* racoon
maquilla|je *m* make-up; **~rse** to make up (*face*)
máquina *f* machine; engine; apparatus; locomotive; **~ de afeitar** safety razor; **~ de coser** sewing machine; **~ de escribir** typewriter; **~ de venta automática** vending machine; **~ fotográfica** camera; **~ tragaperras** slot machine
maquin|ación *f* machination; **~aria** *f* machinery; **~ista** *m f c* engine driver; operator, machinist
mar *m or f* sea; **~ de fondo** ground swell; **en alta ~** on the high seas; **en el ~** at sea; **hacerse a la ~** to put out to sea; **la ~ de** a lot of; **por ~** by sea
maraña *f* thicket; tangle
maravill|a *f* marvel; **~arse** to wonder; to marvel; **~oso** marvel(l)ous
marca *f* mark; trademark; brand; standard; **de ~** excellent; **~ de fábrica** trade mark; **~dor** *m* scoreboard; **~pasos** *m med* pacemaker; **~r** *v/t* to mark; to score (*a hit, a goal*); to dial (*telephone*); to designate; to stamp
marco *m* frame; standard
marcha *f* march; progress; departure; *tecn* motion, working; **~ atrás** reverse gear; **poner en ~** to put into gear; **~r** *v/i* to go; *tecn* to run; to work; **~r en vacío** *tecn* to idle; **~rse** to leave, to clear out
marchitarse to wither, to wilt
mare|a *f* tide; **~a baja** low-tide; **~ado** seasick; dizzy; giddy; **~ar** *v/t fig* to annoy; **~arse** to get seasick; **~jada** *f* swell (*of the sea*); *fig* commotion; **~o** *m* seasickness; *fam* vexation
marfil *m* ivory
margarina *f* margarine
margarita *f* daisy
margen *m* margin; border; *f* bank (*of river*)
marginados *m/pl*: **los ~** the disenfranchised
marica *f* magpie; *m fam* milksop, effeminate man
marido *m* husband
marimacho *m* tomboy; mannish woman
marin|a *f* navy; seamanship; **~ero** *a* seaworthy; *m* sailor; **~o** marine
marioneta *f* puppet, marionette
maripos|a *f* butterfly; **~ear** *v/i* to flit about
mariquita *f* ladybird
mariscal *m* marshall; **~ de campo** field marshall
marisco *m* shellfish; *pl* sea food
marisma *f* salt marsh (*on the sea*)
marítimo maritime
marmita *f* cooking pot
mármol *m* marble
marmota *f* marmot; **~ de Alemania** hamster; **~ de América** ground hog
maroma *f* thick rope
marqués *m* marquis
marquesa *f* marchioness
marquesina *f* marquee; canopy
marran|a *f* sow; *fig* slut; **~o** *m* hog; *fam* dirty person
marrón brown
marroquí *a, m, f* Moroccan; *m* morocco (*leather*)
Marruecos *m* Morocco
marsopa *f* porpoise
martes *m* Tuesday; **~ de carnaval** Shrove Tuesday, Mardi Gras
martill|ar *v/t* to hammer; **~o** *m* hammer
martinete *m* drop hammer; pile driver
mártir *m* martyr
martiri|o *m* martyrdom; **~zar** *v/t* to torment
marzo *m* March
mas *conj* but; however; although
más more; most; besides; plus; **nada ~** nothing else; **~ bien** rather; **~ o menos** more or less; **a lo ~** at most; **a ~ tardar** at the latest; **por ~ que** however much; **no ~ que** only; **los ~** the majority
masa *f* mass; bulk; dough
masaj|e *m* massage; **~ista** *m, f* masseur, masseuse
mascar *v/t* to chew; *fam* to mumble
máscara *f* mask; disguise; face mask
masculino masculine; male
masón *m* freemason
masticar *v/t* to masticate, to chew
mástil *m* mast; post; pole
mastín *m* mastiff
mata *f* bush; scrub
mata|dero *m* slaughterhouse; **~dor** *m* killer; **~nza** *f* slaughter; **~r** *v/t* to kill; **~sanos** *m fam* quack doctor
mate *a* dull; matte; *m* checkmate; maté tea
matemátic|as *f/pl* mathematics; **~o** *m* mathematician; *a* mathematical
materia *f* matter; material; subject; **~ prima** raw material; **~l** *a* material; *m* material; ingredient; **~lista** *m, f* materialist; *a* materialistic
matern|idad *f* maternity; motherhood; maternity hospital; **~o** motherly; maternal
matinal morning; matutinal
matiz *m* tint; shade; **~ar** *v/t* to colo(u)r; to shade; to tint; to match
matón *m* bully
matorral *m* thicket
matrícula *f* list; register; *aut* licence, *Am* license; plate number
matricularse *v/t* to matriculate; to enrol(l)
matrimonio *m* matrimony, marriage; couple
matriz *f* matrix; womb; *tecn* mould
matrona *f* matron
maullar *v/i* to mew, to meow
máxima *f* maxim
máxim|e especially; **~o** *a* highest; greatest; *m* maximum
maya *a* Mayan; *m, f* Maya; *f bot* daisy
mayo *m* May
mayonesa *f* mayonnaise
mayor *a* greater; bigger; older; major; **~ de edad** of age; **al por ~** wholesale; *m* chief; *mil* major; **~es** *m/pl* ancestors; elders
mayordomo *m* steward; butler
mayoría *f* majority
mayorista *m* wholesaler
mayúscula *f* capital letter
maza *f* mace
mazapán *m* marzipan
mazmorra *f* dungeon; jail
mazorca *f* **de maíz** corncob
me *pron pers* me; to me; myself
mear *v/i* to piss
mecáni|ca *f* mechanics; **~co** *m* mechanic; engineer; *a* mechanical
mecanismo *m* mechanism
mecanografía *f* typewriting
mecanógrafo(a) *m* (*f*) typist
mece|dora *f* rocking chair; **~r** *v/t* to rock; to swing
mech|a *f* wick; fuse; lock (*of hair*); **~ero** *m* burner (*of lamp*); cigarette lighter; shoplifter; **~ón** *m* lock (*of hair*); bundle (*of threads*)
medalla *f* medal
médano *m* sand dune
media *f* stocking; *LA* man's sock; *mat* mean; **hacer ~** to knit; **los ~** *m/pl* (the) media
media|ción *f* mediation; **~do** half-full; **a ~dos de enero** in the middle of January; **~dor** *a* mediating; *m* mediator; **~no** middle; medium; average; mediocre
medianoche *f* midnight
media|nte *a* intervening; *prep* by means of; **~r** *v/i* to be in the middle; to mediate
medic|amento *m* medicine; drug; **~ina** *f* medicine
medición *f* measurement
médico *a* medical; *m* physician, doctor; **~ de urgencia** emergency doctor
medid|a *f* measure(ment); **a ~a que** at the same time as; **hecho a la ~a** made to measure; **~or** *m LA* meter
medio *a, adv* half; middle; **a ~ camino** halfway; **en ~ de** in the middle of; **de por ~** half; between; **por ~ de** by means of; *m* middle; half; means, way; **~s** *pl* means; resources; **~s de comunicación** mass media
mediocre mediocre
mediodía *m* midday; south
medir *v/t* to measure
meditar *v/t, v/i* to meditate; to ponder
mediterráneo *m* Mediterranean Sea; ~ *a* Mediterranean
medrar *v/i* to grow; to flourish
medroso timorous
médula *f anat* marrow; **~ espinal** spinal cord
medusa *f* jellyfish
megafonía *f* P.A. system
mejill|a *f* cheek; **~ón** *m* mussel
mejor better; finer; superior; (*with definite article*) best; **lo ~** the best thing; **a lo ~** maybe, as like as not; **tanto ~** so much the better; **~a** *f* improvement; **~ar** *v/t, v/i* to improve; **~ía** *f* improvement

melancolía f melancholy
melaza f molasses
melena f long hair; mane
melocotón m peach
melodía f melody
melón m melon
meloso sweet; syrupy
mella f notch; gap; ~r v/t to nick, to notch
mellizo(a) m (f), a twin
membrana f membrane; zool web
membrete m note; letterhead
membrillo m quince
memor|ándum m memorandum; notebook; ~ia f memory; petition; report; pl memoirs; ~izar v/t to memorize
mención f reference, mention
mencionar v/t to mention; sin ~ to say nothing of, not to mention
mendi|gar v/t to beg; ~go m beggar
mene|ar v/t to shake; to wag, to move; ~arse to move; to be active; ~o m shaking; wagging
menester m job; errand; ~es pl duties; business; ser ~ to be necessary; ~oso needy, destitute
menestra f vegetable stew
mengua f decline; decrease; ~nte a decreasing; f ebb tide; waning (of moon); ~r v/i to diminish; to decrease, to dwindle; to wane
menor smaller; less; minor; younger; ~ de edad under age; al por ~ retail
menos adv less; least; fewer; fewest; a ~ que unless; ~ de less than; m mat minus (sign); prep except
menos|cabo m detriment; damage; ~preciar v/t to despise; to belittle; to undervalue; ~precio m scorn; contempt
mensaje m message; ~ro(a) m (f) messenger
mensual monthly; ~idad f monthly salary or allowance
mensurable measurable
menta f mint; peppermint
mental mental; ~idad f mentality
mente f mind; intellect; cambiar de ~ to change one's mind
mentecato m fool
mentir v/i to lie; ~a f lie, falsehood; ~illa f white lie, fib; ~oso(a) m (f) liar; a untruthful, lying
mentís m denial; dar un ~ a to deny; to give the lie to
mentón m chin
menú m menu
menud|ear v/t to repeat; v/i to happen frequently; ~illos m/pl giblets (of fowls); ~o small; a ~o often
meñique m little finger
meollo m marrow; fig core
merca|dear v/i to trade; ~dería f LA merchandise; ~do m market; market place; ~do común common market; ~do negro black market; ~ncía f merchandise, goods; commodity; ~ntil mercantile, commercial
merced f mercy; favo(u)r; grace; vuestra ~ your hono(u)r, your worship; a la ~ de at the mercy of
mercenario m mercenary soldier; a mercenary
mercería f dry goods store
mercurio m mercury
merece|dor deserving, worthy; ~r v/t to deserve; to merit; ~ido deserved
merendar v/i to take a snack;

to lunch
merengue m meringue
meridiano m meridian
meridional southern
merienda f snack; light meal; lunch
mérito m merit; worth
meritorio meritorious
merluza f hake
merma f shrinkage; loss; waste; ~r v/i to decrease, to become less
mermelada f jam, marmalade
mero a mere, pure, simple; m zool grouper
mes m month
mes|a f table; desk; poner la ~a to set the table; ~eta f tableland; plateau; ~illa f side table
mesón m inn
mestizo(a) m (f), a halfbreed
mesura f moderation; restraint; ~do moderate; restrained
meta f goal; objective; aim; m goalkeeper
metal m metal; mús brass
metálico a metallic; m specie, coin; en ~ in cash
meteoro m meteor; ~logía f meteorology
meter v/t to put in; to insert; to stake; to invest; ~se to interfere; to intrude; ~se con to pick a quarrel with; ~se en to get into
meticuloso meticulous
metódico methodical
método m method
metrall|a f shrapnel; ~eta f submachine gun
métrico metric, metrical
metro m verse (poetry); metre, Am meter; underground, subway
metrópoli f metropolis
metropolitano m metropolitan
mexicano(a) a, m (f) Mexican
México m Mexico
mezcla f mixture; blend; ~r v/t to mix; to mingle
mezcolanza f fam hotchpotch; jumble
mezquin|dad f niggardliness; meanness; ~o wretched; mean; miserable, petty; puny
mezquita f mosque
mí pron pers me
mi pron pos (pl mis) my
miaja f crumb
mico m long-tailed monkey
microbio m microbe
micrófono m microphone
microprocesador m microprocessor
microscopio m microscope
miedo m fear, dread; de ~ wonderful; awful; tener ~ to be afraid; ~so timorous; afraid
miel f honey
miembro m member; limb
mientras while; ~ que so long as; ~ tanto meanwhile, in the meantime
miércoles m Wednesday
miga f crumb; ~ja f small crumb
migración f migration
migraña f migraine
mijo m millet
mil a thousand
milagro m miracle; ~so miraculous
mili|cia f militia; ~ciano m militiaman; ~tante militant; ~tar m soldier; a military; v/i pol to be a party member; mil to serve
milla f mile; ~ náutica nautical mile
millón m million

millonario m millionaire
mimar v/t to pet, to fondle; to spoil, to pamper
mimbre m wicker
mimeógrafo m mimeograph
mímico mimic
mina f mine; fig storehouse; ~r v/t to mine; to excavate
miner|al m, a mineral; ore; ~ía f mining; ~o m miner
miniatura f miniature
minifalda f miniskirt
mínim|o minimum; smallest; ~um m minimum
minino m pussy(-cat)
minist|erial ministerial; ~erio m ministry; ♀erio de Comercio Board of Trade; ♀erio de Hacienda Treasury; ♀erio de Relaciones Exteriores Foreign Office; ~ro m minister; primer ~ prime minister
minoría f minority
minucios|idad f thoroughness; ~o minutely; precise
minúscula f small letter
minusválidos m/pl the handicapped
minuta f rough copy; list; memo; menu; pl minutes
minutero m minute hand
minuto m minute
mío, mía, míos, mías mine
miope short-sighted, near-sighted
mira f sight; aim; con ~s a with an eye to; ~da f look; echar una ~da a to take a look at; ~do considerate; ~dor m lookout point; ~r v/t to look; to watch; to consider; ~r por to look after
mirasol m sunflower
mirlo m blackbird
mirón m onlooker; busybody
mirto m myrtle
misa f mass; ~ del gallo midnight mass
misceláneo miscellaneous
miser|able miserable, wretched; mean; niggardly; ~ia f misery; poverty; ~icordia f mercy
mísero wretched
misi|ón f mission; ~onero m missionary
mismo same, similar; -self; very; aquí ~ right here; yo ~ I myself; el ~ rey the same king; el rey ~ the king himself; lo ~ the same thing; lo ~ da it is all the same; lo ~ que just like
misterio m mystery; ~so mysterious
místico mystic
mitad f half; middle; a ~ del camino midway; a ~ del precio at half price; cortar por la ~ to cut down the middle
mitigar v/t to mitigate
mitin m meeting
mito m myth
mitra f mitre
mixto mixed
mobiliario m furniture
mocedad f youth; correr sus ~es to sow one's wild oats
moción f motion; movement
moco m mucus; ~so a snotty-nosed; m impudent youngster
mochila f knapsack
moda f fashion; de ~ fashionable
modales m/pl manners
model|ar v/t to model; ~o m model; pattern; f model, mannequin
modera|ción f moderation; ~r v/t to moderate; ~rse to control oneself
modern|izar v/t to modernize; ~o modern
modest|ia f modesty; ~o modest

módico moderate; reasonable (prices)
modifica|ción f modification; ~r v/t to modify
modismo m idiom; idiomatic expression
modista f dressmaker; milliner
modo m way; mode, method; manner; de ~ que so that; de otro ~ otherwise, or else; de ningún ~ by no means; de todos ~s at any rate, by all means
modula|ción f modulation; ~ción de frecuencia frequency modulation; ~r v/i to modulate
módulo elec, aer module
mofa f mockery; ridicule; derision; ~rse de to mock at
mofeta f skunk
mohín m grimace
moho m mo(u)ld, mildew; rust; ~so musty; rusty
moja|do wet; soaked; damp; ~r v/t to wet; to soak; ~rse to get soaked
mojigato(a) m (f) hypocrite; a hypocritical; prudish
mojón m landmark
molde m mo(u)ld; form; cast; ~ar v/t to mo(u)ld; to shape
molécula f molecule
moler v/t to grind; to mill; to annoy; ~ a palos to beat up
molest|ar v/t to annoy; to upset; to trouble; ~arse to take the trouble; ~ia f trouble; annoyance; ~o troublesome; annoying
molin|ero m miller; ~illo m hand mill; coffee grinder; ~o m mill; ~o de viento windmill
molleja f gizzard
mollera f crown of the head
moment|áneo momentary; ~o m moment; a cada ~ at every moment; al ~o immediately; de ~ at the moment
momia f mummy
mona f female monkey; fam hangover; ~cal monastic; ~cillo m acolyte; ~da f silly thing; silliness; lovely thing; pretty child
monar|ca m monarch; sovereign; ~quía f monarchy
monasterio m monastery
monda f pruning; paring; ~dientes m toothpick; ~duras f/pl peelings, parings; ~r v/t to peel; to cleanse; to prune
moned|a f coin; money; currency; ~ero m wallet; coin purse
monetario monetary
monigote m grotesque figure
monitor m monitor
monj|a f nun; ~e m monk
mono m monkey; a pretty; cute
monóculo m monocle
monólogo m monologue
monopatín m skateboard
monopoli|o m monopoly; ~sta m monopolist; ~zar v/t to monopolize (t fig)
monotonía f monotony
monstruo m monster; ~sidad f monstrosity; ~so monstrous; freakish
monta f mounting; significance; mat total; ~cargas m hoist; lift (for baggage); ~discos m disc jockey; ~do mounted; ~dor m fitter; ~je m assembly; installing
montañ|a f mountain; ♀as f/pl Rocosas Rocky Mountains; ~és(esa) m (f) highlander; ~oso mountainous
montar v/i to mount; to ride;

~ a caballo to ride a horse; ~ en bicicleta to ride a bicycle; ~ en cólera to fly into a rage; v/t to mount; to ride; to assemble
monte m mountain; hill; woodland; wilds; ~ alto forest; ~ bajo scrub; ~ de piedad pawnshop
montería f hunting, chase
montículo m mound
montón m heap, pile
montura f mount; saddle
monumento m monument; memorial
monzón m, f monsoon
moño m knot; bun; tuft
moqueta f moquette; carpet
mora f mulberry; blackberry
morada f dwelling
morado purple
moral f morale; ethics; m black mulberry tree; a moral; ~eja f moral; maxim; lesson
mórbido soft; morbid; diseased
morboso morbid
morcilla f black sausage; teat gag
mord|az pungent; biting; ~aza f gag; tecn clamp; ~edura f bite; ~er v/t to bite; ~iscar v/t to nibble
moren|a f zool moray; ~o brown-skinned; dark
morera f white mulberry tree
morfina f morphine
morir v/i to die
morisco Moorish
moro(a) m (f) Moor; a Moorish
morosidad f slowness; com delinquency
morral m nosebag (horse); knapsack
morriña f sadness; blues; homesickness
morro m snout; headland
morsa f walrus
mortaja f shroud
mortal mortal; fatal; ~idad f mortality; death rate
mortero m mortar
mortífero deadly
mortificar v/t to mortify
mosaico m mosaic; relig Mosaic
mosca f fly; soltar la ~ to give money
moscardón m hornet
moscatel muscatel (grape or wine)
mosquea|do spotted; ~rse to take offense
mosquit|ero m mosquito net; ~o m mosquito; gnat
mostaza f mustard
mosto m must, new wine
mostra|dor m counter; (hotel) desk; ~r v/t to show; to display
mote m catchword; nickname
motín m riot; mutiny
motiv|ar v/t to cause; to motivate; ~o m motive; motif; con ~o de on the occasion of
moto|cicleta f motorcycle; ~nave f motor ship; ~r a tecn motive; anat motor; m motor; engine; ~r de fuera de borda outboard motor; ~r de reacción jet engine; ~rista m motorist
motriz motive; moving
move|dizo shifting; unsettled; loose; ~r v/t, ~rse to move
movible movable
movi|lidad f mobility; ~lización f mobilization; ~lizar v/t to mobilize; ~miento m movement; motion; mús movement
moz|a f girl, lass; ~albete m lad; ~o m young man; serv-

mucama 74

Spanish

ant; waiter; **~o de hotel** porter
mucama *f LA* maid
mucos|a *f* mucous membrane; **~o** mucous
muchach|a *f* girl; **~o** *m* boy
muchedumbre *f* crowd
mucho *a* a lot; much; *pl* many; **con ~** by far; *adv* a lot; a great deal, considerably; **~ más** much more; **~ mejor** far better; **~ menos** let alone
muda *f* change of clothing; *zool* mo(u)lt; **~nza** *f* move, removal; **~r** *v/t, v/i* to change; **~rse** to change; to move
mud|ez *f* dumbness; **~o** dumb; mute
mueble *m* piece of furniture; *pl* furniture
mueca *f* face; grimace; **hacer ~s** to pull (*Am* make) faces
muela *f* millstone; molar tooth
muelle *m* spring (*of watch, etc*); quay; wharf; dock
muérdago *m* mistletoe
muert|e *f* death; **de mala ~e** awful; **~o(a)** *a* dead; *m (f)* dead person
muestra *f* pattern; sample
muestrario *m* collection of samples
mugi|do *m* lowing (*of cattle*); **~r** *v/i* to low; to moo; to bellow
mugr|e *f* grime, dirt; **~iento** grimy, filthy
mujer *f* woman; wife; **~iego** womanizer
mul|a *f* mule; **~adar** *m* rubbish heap; **~o** *m* mule
mulato(a) *m (f), a* mulatto
muleta *f* crutch; red cloth used by bullfighters
multa *f* fine; **~r** *v/t* to fine
multicopista *f* duplicator
multinacionales *f/pl* multinational corporations
múltiple manifold, multifarious
multiplicar *v/t* to multiply
multitud *f* crowd, multitude
mund|ano worldly; **~ial** world-wide; **~o** *m* world; **todo el ~o** everybody
munición *f* ammunition
municip|al municipal; **~alidad** *f* municipality; **~io** *m* town
muñeca *f* wrist; doll; dressmaker's model
muñón *m* stump (*of an amputated limb*); pivot
mural *a, m* mural
muralla *f* wall; rampart
murciélago *m* bat
murmullo *m* rustle; murmur
murmurar *v/i* to murmur; to criticize; to ripple (*of water*)
muro *m* wall
muscul|ar, ~oso muscular
músculo *m* muscle
muselina *f* muslin
museo *m* museum
musgo *m* moss
música *f* music
musical musical
músico *m* musician
musitar *v/i* to mumble
muslo *m* thigh
mustio sad; withered
musulmán(ana) *m (f), a* Moslem
muta|bilidad *f* mutability; **~ción** *f* mutation; change
mutila|do(a) *m (f)* cripple; disabled person; **~r** *v/t* to mutilate; to mangle
mutismo *m* muteness
mutualidad *f* mutuality; mutual benefit society
mutuo mutual
muy very; **~ señores nuestros** Dear Sirs (*in letters*)

N

nabo *m* turnip; *arq* newel
nácar *m* mother-of-pearl
nac|er *v/i* to be born; to sprout; to spring, to start; **~iente** nascent; growing; rising (*sun*); **~imiento** *m* birth; origin, beginning
naci|ón *f* nation; **2ones Unidas** United Nations
nacional national; **~idad** *f* nationality; **~izar** *v/t* to nationalize; to naturalize
nada *f* nothingness, nothing; *pron* nothing; **de ~** you are welcome; not at all; **~ de eso** none of that; **~ más** nothing else
nada|dor(a) *m (f)* swimmer; **~r** *v/i* to swim; to float
nadie nobody; no one; **~ más** nobody else
nafta *f* naphtha
nailon *m* nylon
naipe *m* playing card
nalgas *f/pl* buttocks
nana *f* lullaby; *fam* granny
naranj|a *f* orange; **~ada** *f* orangeade; **~al** *m* orange grove; **~o** *m* orange tree
narciso *m* daffodil
narcótico *m* narcotic; drug; *a* narcotic
narcotizar *v/t* to drug; to dope
nari|gudo big-nosed; **~z** *f* nose; nostril; bouquet (*of wine*); **sonarse las ~ces** to blow one's nose; **tabicarse las ~ces** to hold one's nose
narra|ción *f* narration, story; tale; **~r** *v/t* to narrate, to recite; **~tiva** *f* narrative
nata *f* cream; **~ batida** whipped cream
natación *f* swimming
natal native, natal; **~icio** *m* birthday; **~idad** *f* birthrate
nat|ividad *f* nativity; **~ivo(a)** *m (f)* native; indigenous; *a* natural; **~o** native
natural *a* natural; fresh, raw; *m, f* native; *m* nature, temperament; **al ~** without additives; as it is; **~eza** *f* nature; **~eza muerta** still life; **~idad** *f* naturalness; **~ismo** *m* naturalism; **~izar** *v/t* to naturalize
naturismo *m* nudism
naufrag|ar *v/i* to be shipwrecked; **~io** *m* shipwreck
náufrago(a) *m (f)* shipwrecked person; *a* shipwrecked
náusea *f* nausea; disgust
náutic|a *f* navigation, seamanship; **~o** nautical
navaja *f* jackknife; penknife; razor
nav|al naval; **~e** *f* ship; nave (*of church*); **~e espacial** space ship; **~egador** *m* navigator; **~egante** *a* navigating; *m aer* navigator; **~egar** *v/i* to navigate; to sail; **~egar en tabla** to surf
Navidad *f* Christmas Day
naviero *m* shipowner
navío *m* ship; **~ de guerra** warship
neblina *f* mist
nebuloso cloudy; misty
neces|ario necessary; **~er** *m* vanity case; **~idad** *f* necessity; **~itado** poor; needy; **~itar** *v/t* to want; to need
necio foolish, silly
necrología *f* obituary
nefasto ominous; unlucky
nega|ción *f* negation; denial; **~r** *v/t* to deny; to refuse; to prohibit; **~tiva** *f* denial; refusal; **~tivo** *a* negative; *m foto* negative
negligen|cia *f* negligence; neglect; carelessness; **~te** careless; negligent
negoci|ación *f* negotiation; business transaction; **~ante** *m* businessman; dealer; **~ar** *v/i* to trade; to negotiate; **~o** *m* occupation; business
negr|o *m* negro; *a* black; **ponerse ~o** to get angry; **~ura** *f* blackness
nene(a) *m (f)* baby, child
neón *m* neon
nervio *m anat* nerve; sinew; energy; *arq, bot* rib; **~so** nervous
neto neat; pure; *com* net
neumático *m* tyre, *Am* tire; *a* pneumatic
neurótico neurotic
neutral neutral; **~idad** *f* neutrality
neutro neutral; *gram* neuter
neutrón *m quim* neutron
nev|ada *f* snowfall; **~ar** *v/i* to snow; **~era** *f* ice box; **~oso** snowy
ni *conj* neither, nor; **~ esto ~ aquello** neither this nor that; **~ siquiera** not even
Nicaragua *f* Nicaragua
nicaragüense *a, m, f* Nicaraguan
nicho *m* niche, recess
nido *m* nest
niebla *f* fog; mist; haze
niet|a *f* granddaughter; **~o** *m* grandson
nieve *f* snow
nilón *m* nylon
ningún *a* (*apocope of* **ninguno** *used before masculine nouns*) no, not one; **de ~ modo** by no means
ningun|o(a) *a* no, not one, not any; **~a cosa** nothing; **de ~a manera** in no way; *pron* none, no one, nobody; **~o de ellos** none of them
niñ|a *f* girl; **~era** *f* nanny; **~ez** *f* childhood; **~o** *m* boy; **desde ~o** from childhood; **~o prodigio** infant prodigy
níquel *m* nickel
níspero *m* medlar (*tree and fruit*)
nítido bright, spotless; *foto* sharp
nitrógeno *m* nitrogen
nivel *m* level; **~ de agua** water level; **~ sonoro** noise level; **~ar** *v/t* to level; to grade
no no, not; **~ más** no more; **~ sea que** lest
noble noble; highborn; **~za** *f* nobility; aristocracy
noción *f* idea; notion
nocivo harmful; noxious
nocturno nocturnal
noche *f* night; evening; **buenas ~s** good evening; good night; **por la ~** at night; **de la ~ a la mañana** overnight; **2buena** *f* Christmas Eve; **~ vieja** New Year's Eve
nodriza *f* wet nurse
nog|al *m*, **~uera** *f* walnut (*tree or wood*)
nombr|amiento *m* appointment; **~ar** *v/t* to name; to appoint; **~e** *m* name; title; **~e de pila** Christian name, first name; **~e de soltera** maiden name
nomeolvides *f* forget-me-not
nómina *f* payroll
nomina|l nominal; **~tivo** *m* nominative
non odd, uneven (*number*)
nopal *m* prickly pear
nordeste *m* northeast
noria *f* chain pump; ferris wheel (*at fairs*)
norma *f* norm; standard; rule; **~l** normal
noroeste *m* northwest
norte *m* north; **~americano(a)** *m, f* North American (*U.S.A.*); **~ño** northern
norueg|o(a) *m (f), a* Norwegian; **2a** *f* Norway
nos *pron pers* us; each other
nosotros(as) *pron pers pl* we, ourselves; us
nostalgia *f* nostalgia; homesickness
nota *f* note; annotation; mark (*in school*); *com* account; bill; **tomar ~** to take note
nota|ble noteworthy, notable; **~r** *v/t* to note, to notice; to observe; to take down; **~rio** *m* notary
notici|a *f* piece of news; notice; information; *pl* news; **~ar** *v/t* to notify; to inform; **~ario** *m* newsreel; *radio, TV* newscast
notificar *v/t* to notify
notorio well-known
novato(a) *m (f)* beginner
novedad *f* novelty; latest news *or* fashion; **sin ~** as usual
novel|a *f* novel; story; fiction; **~a policíaca** detective story; **~ista** *m, f* novelist
novia *f* bride; fiancée; **~zgo** *m* engagement
novicio(a) *a* inexperienced; *m (f)* novice
noviembre *m* November
novill|a *f* heifer; **~ada** *f* fight with young bulls; **~o** *m* young bull; steer; **hacer ~os** to play truant
novio *m* bridegroom; fiancé; **los ~s** *pl* the bride and groom
nub|e *f* cloud; film (*on the eye*); **~ecita** *f* small cloud; **~lado** cloudy
nuca *f* nape of the neck
nuclear nuclear
núcleo *m* nucleus
nud|illo knuckle; **~o** *m* knot; **~oso** gnarled
nuera *f* daughter-in-law
nuestro(a, os, as) *pron pos* our, ours
nueva *f* piece of news; **~mente** again; recently
nueve nine
nuevo new; novel; further; **de ~** all over again
nuez *f* walnut; nut; **~ de Adán** Adam's apple; **~ moscada** nutmeg
nul|idad *f* nullity; incompetence; annul(l)ment (*of marriage*); **~o** null, void
numera|ción *f* numeration; **~ción romana** Roman numerals; **~dor** *m mat* numerator; **~r** *v/t* to number; to count
numérico numerical
número *m* number; figure; **sin ~** countless
numeroso numerous
nunca never; **~ jamás** never again; **casi ~** hardly ever
nuncio *m relig* nuncio; messenger
nupcia|l nuptial, bridal; **~s** *f/pl* wedding, nuptials
nutria *f* otter
nutri|ción *f* nutrition; **~do** abundant; copious; **~r** *v/t* to nourish; to feed; **~tivo** nutritious

Ñ

ñandú *m* American ostrich
ñaño *LA* intimate; spoiled
ñapa *f LA* bonus; tip
ñaque *m* odds and ends; junk
ñoñ|ería *f* spinelessness; bashfulness; **~o** insipid; spineless; shy; fussy

O

o or; either
oasis *m* oasis
obed|ecer *v/t* to obey; **~iencia** *f* obedience; **~iente** obedient
obertura *f mús* overture
obes|idad *f* fatness; **~o** fat
obisp|ado *m* episcopate; **~o** *m* bishop
obje|ción *f* objection; **~tar** *v/t* to object; to oppose; **~tivo** *m* objective; **~tivo zoom** *foto* zoom lens; *a* objective; **~to** *m* object; thing; purpose
oblicuo oblique; slanting
obliga|ción *f* obligation; duty; *pl com* bonds, securities; **~r** *v/t* to oblige, to bind; **~rse** to commit oneself; **~torio** compulsory
oblongo oblong
obr|a *f* work; creation; structure; building site; **~a de arte** work of art; **~a de consulta** reference work; **~a maestra** masterpiece; **~as** *pl* **públicas** public works; **~ar** *v/t* to work; to manufacture; *v/i* to act; to behave; **~ero(a)** *m (f)* worker; **~ero calificado** skilled worker
obsceno obscene, indecent
obscur|ecer *v/t* to darken; to obscure; *v/i* to get dark; **~o** dark; obscure
obsequi|ar *v/t* to entertain, to present with; **~o** *m* courtesy; gift; attention; **~oso** attentive, obliging
observa|ción *f* observation; remark; **~dor(a)** *m (f)* observer; *a* observant; **~r** *v/t* to observe, to remark; to watch; to regard; **~torio** *m* observatory
obsesión *f* obsession
obstáculo *m* obstacle
obsta|nte: no ~nte nevertheless; however; **~r** *v/i* to obstruct, to hinder
obstina|ción *f* obstinacy, stubbornness; **~do** obstinate, stubborn; **~rse (en)** to persist (in)
obstruir *v/t* to obstruct; **~se** to be blocked
obten|ción *f* attainment; **~er** *v/t* to obtain; to attain
obtura|dor *m aut* throttle; *foto* shutter; **~r** *v/t* to stop up; to plug
obús *m* shell; howitzer
obvio obvious, evident
oca *f* goose
ocasión *f* occasion; **de ~** second-hand
ocasiona|l accidental; **~r** *v/t* to cause
ocaso *m* sunset; decline; west
occident|al western; occidental; **~e** *m* west
oceánico oceanic
océano *m* ocean; **2 Atlántico** Atlantic Ocean; **2 glacial Ártico** Arctic Ocean; **2 Pacífico** Pacific Ocean
ocio *m* leisure; idleness; **~so** idle; inactive; useless
octubre *m* October
ocul|ar *a* ocular; *m* eyepiece; **~ista** *m* oculist
ocult|ar *v/t* to conceal; to hide; **~o** hidden; occult
ocupa|ción *f* occupation; **~nte** *m, f* occupant; **~r** *v/t* to occupy; **~rse en** to look after; to be engaged in
ocurr|encia *f* occurrence; incident; witticism; **~ir** *v/i* to occur; to happen
ocho eight
odi|ar *v/t* to hate; **~o** *m* hatred; **~o de sangre** feud; **~oso** hateful, odious
odontólogo(a) *m (f)* odontologist
odorífero aromatic, fragrant
oeste *m* west

ofen|der *v/t* to offend; to insult; **~derse** to take offence, *Am* offense; **~sa** *f* offence, *Am* offense; **~siva** *f* offensive; **~sivo** offensive; **~sor(a)** *m (f)* offender; *a* offending
oferta *f* offer; proposal; *com* **~ y demanda** supply and demand
ofici|al *a* official; *m* officer; official; clerk; **~ar** *v/i* to officiate; **~na** *f* office; **~na de turismo** tourist office; **~na principal** head office; **~nista** *m, f* clerk; white-collar worker; **~o** *m* trade; profession; work; **~oso** officious
ofre|cer *v/t* to offer; to present; **~cerse** to volunteer; to offer oneself; **~cimiento** *m* offer; **~nda** *f* offering
oftalmólogo *m* oculist
ofuscar *v/t* to mystify; to confuse
oí|ble audible; **~da** *f* hearing; **de ~das** by hearsay; **~do** *m* ear; sense of hearing; **de ~do** by ear
¡oiga! *tel* hello!
oír *v/t* to hear; to listen
ojal *m* buttonhole
¡ojalá! *interj* if only it would; *conj* **~ que** I wish; if only
ojea|da *f* glance, glimpse; **~r** *v/t* to eye, to have a look at
ojera *f* dark ring under the eye
ojete *m (sewing)* eyelet
ojo *m* eye; eye of the needle; **¡~!** look out!; **~ amoratado** black eye; **a ~s cerrados** blindly
ola *f* wave; **~ de marejada** tidal wave; **la nueva ~** the new wave
oleada *f* big wave; surge, swell; *fig* wave
óleo *m* oil; oil painting
oleoducto *m* oil pipeline
oler *v/t* to smell; to scent; *v/i* to smell; **~ a** to smell of
olfat|ear *v/t, v/i* to smell; **~o** *m* sense of smell
oliv|a *f* olive; olive tree; **~ar** *m* olive grove; **~o** *m* olive tree
olmo *m* elm tree
olor *m* smell, odo(u)r
olvid|adizo forgetful; **~ar** *v/t* to forget; **~o** *m* forgetfulness; oblivion
olla *f* stew pot; saucepan; **~ de presión** pressure cooker
ombligo *m anat* navel
omi|sión *f* omission; carelessness; **~tir** *v/t* to omit
omnipotente omnipotent
omnisciente omniscient
omóplato *m* shoulder blade
ond|a *f* wave *(sea, hair, radio)*; **~a acústica** sound wave; **~ear** *v/i* to wave; to ripple; to undulate; **~ulado** wavy; waved; undulated
onza *f* ounce
opaco opaque
opción *f* option; choice; **en ~** as an option
ópera *f* opera
opera|ción *f* operation; *com* transaction; **~dor** *m* operator; *cine* camera-man; **~r** *v/t* to operate; **~rio** *m* operative; worker
opereta *f* operetta
opin|ar *v/t* to be of the opinion; **~ión** *f* opinion; **cambiar de ~ión** to change one's mind; **en mi ~ión** in my opinion; **~ión pública** public opinion
opio *m* opium
opo|ner *v/t* to oppose; **~nerse** to object; to be opposed; **~sición** *f* opposition; **~sitor(a)** *m (f)* opponent; competitor
oportun|idad *f* opportunity; **~ista** *m, f* opportunist; **~o** opportune; convenient
oposición *f* resistance; contrast; competitive exam *(for a job)*
opr|esión *f* oppression; **~esivo** oppressive; **~imir** *v/t* to oppress; to press
optar *v/t* to opt; to choose
óptic|a *f* optics; **~o** *a* optical; *m* optician
optimis|mo *m* optimism; **~ta** *m, f* optimist; *a* optimistic
óptimo best; very good
opuesto opposite; contrary
opulen|cia *f* opulence; **~to** opulent; rich
oración *f* speech; prayer; sentence
oráculo *m* oracle
ora|dor(a) *m (f)* orator; speaker; **~l** oral; **~r** *v/i* to make a speech; to pray
oratorio *m relig* oratory; chapel; *mús* oratorio
orbe *m* world; globe
órbita *f* orbit; **estar en ~** to be in orbit
orden *m* order; **~ del día** agenda; **en ~** in order; **llamar al ~** to call to order; *f* order, command; **~ de pago** money order; **por ~ de** on the orders of; **~ación** *f* arrangement; disposition; **~ador** *m* computer; **~ador de viaje** on-board computer; **~anza** *f* statute; ordinance; *m mil* orderly; **~ar** *v/t* to put in order; to order, to arrange; to command; to ordain; **~arse** to be ordained
ordeñar *v/t* to milk
ordinal ordinal
ordinario ordinary, vulgar; coarse; common
oreja *f* ear; tab *(of shoe)*
orfanato *m* orphanage
orfebre *m* goldsmith; silversmith; **~ría** *f* gold *or* silver work
organillo *m* barrel organ
organi|smo *m* organism; **~sta** *m, f* organist; **~zación** *f* organization; **~zar** *v/t* to organize
orgánico organic
órgano *m* organ
orgullo *m* pride; **~so** proud
orient|ación *f* orientation; **~al** oriental; **~ar** *v/t* to position; to guide someone; **~e** *m* orient; **el ≈e** the East, the Orient; **≈e Medio** Middle East; **≈e Próximo** Near East
orificio *m* orifice; hole
origen *m* origin; source
origina|l original; odd; **~r** *v/t* to originate; **~rse** to spring from
orilla *f* edge; bank, shore, riverside; **a ~s de** on the banks of
orina *f* urine; **~r** *v/t, v/i* to urinate
oriundo native (of)
orla *f* border, edging; **~r** *v/t* to border, to edge
orna|mento *m* ornament; **~r** *v/t* to adorn
oro *m* gold; **~ batido** gold leaf
oropel *m* tinsel
orquesta *f* orchestra
orquídea *f* orchid
ortiga *f* nettle
orto|doncia *f* orthodontics; **~doxo** orthodox; **~grafía** *f* spelling; **~pedista** *m, f* orthop(a)edist
oruga *f* caterpillar
orzuelo *m med* sty
os *pron pers* you; to you
osad|ía *f* boldness; daring; **~o** bold
oscila|ción *f* oscillation; **~r** *v/i* to swing; to oscillate
oscur|ecer *v/t* to darken; *fig* to confuse; *v/i* to grow dark; **~o** dark
oso *m* bear; **~ blanco** polar bear
ostenta|r *v/t* to show off; to flaunt; **~tivo** ostentatious
ostra *f* oyster
otoño *m* autumn, fall
otorga|miento *m* granting, conferring; *for* deed; **~r** *v/t* to grant, to confer
otorrinolaringólogo(a) *m (f)* ear, nose and throat doctor
otr|o(a, os, as) other; another; **¡~a!** *teat* encore!; **~o día** another time; **~a cosa** something else; **~a vez** again; **~os tantos** as many
ovación *f* ovation
oval, ~ado oval
ovario *m anat* ovary
oveja *f* sheep; ewe
ovillo *m* ball *(of wool)*
ovni = **objeto volante no identificado** UFO (unidentified flying object)
oxidar *v/t*, **~se** to oxidize; to rust
oxígeno *m* oxygen
oyente *m, f* listener; hearer
ozono *m* ozone

P

pabellón *m* pavilion; ward *(in hospital)*; *mil* bell tent; **~ de música** bandstand
pacer *v/i* to graze
pacien|cia *f* patience; **~te** *m, f, a* patient
pacifi|cación *f* peace, pacification; **~cador(a)** *m (f)* peacemaker; **~car** *v/t* to pacify; to appease; **~carse** to calm down
pacífico peaceful, pacific
pacifista *m, f* pacifist
pacotilla *f* trash, rubbish; **de ~** of poor quality
pact|ar *v/t* to contract; to agree to; **~o** *m* pact
padec|er *v/t* to suffer from; to tolerate; **~imiento** *m* suffering
padr|astro *m* stepfather; *fig* obstacle; **~e** *m* father; priest; *pl* parents; ancestors; **≈e Santo** Holy Father *(the Pope)*; **≈e Nuestro** Lord's Prayer, Our Father; **~ino** *m* godfather; best man
padrón *m* census; register; *tecn* pattern; *fig* stain, blot
pag|a *f* salary, pay; **~adero** payable; **~ador(a)** *m (f)* payer
pagano(a) *m (f), a* pagan, heathen
pagar *v/t* to pay; to repay; **por ~** *com* unpaid; **~é** *m* promissory note; IOU
página *f* page *(of a book)*
pago *m* payment; **~ al contado** cash payment; **~ a cuenta** payment on account; **~ a plazos** instal(l)ment plan
país *m* country; land; region; **≈ Vasco** Basque country; **los ~es subdesarrollados** underdeveloped countries
paisa|je *m* landscape; **~no(a)** *m (f)* fellow countryman (-woman); civilian; **vestido de ~no** in civilian clothes
Países *m/pl* **Bajos** Netherlands
paja *f* straw
pájaro *m* bird; sly fellow; **~ cantor** song bird; **~ carpintero** woodpecker
paje *m* page; cabin boy
pala *f* shovel; spade; blade *(of oar)*
palabr|a *f* word; **~a por ~a** word for word; verbatim; **~ota** *f* swearword
palacio *m* palace
palad|ar *m* palate; taste; relish; **~ear** *v/t* to taste
palanca *f tecn* lever; bar; **~ de cambio** gearshift
palangana *f* washbasin
palco *m teat* box
palenque *m* palisade
palet|a *f* small shovel; **~o** *m* rustic
palia|r *v/t* to palliate; to lessen; **~tivo** palliative
palide|cer *v/i* to pale, to turn pale; **~z** *f* pallor
pálido pale
palillo *m* toothpick; *pl* chopsticks; castanets
palique *m* small talk
paliza *f* beating; thrashing
palm|a *f bot* palm tree; palm leaf; palm of the hand; **dar ~as** to clap hands; **~ada** *f* pat, slap; **~adas** *f/pl* applause; **~ar** *m* palm grove; **~atoria** *f* small candlestick; **~era** *f* palm tree; **~o** *m* span *(measure of length, 8 inches)*; **~o a ~o** inch by inch
palo *m* stick; pole; cudgel; *(card)* suit; **~ de golf** golf club
palom|a *f* pigeon; dove; **~ar** *m* pigeon house; dovecot; **~itas** *f/pl* **(de) (maíz)** popcorn
palpa|ble evident, palpable; **~r** *v/t* to touch, to feel; to grope along
palpitación *f* palpitation
paludismo *m* malaria
pampa *f* pampa, prairie
pan *m* bread; loaf; **~ de jengibre** gingerbread; **~ de oro** *tecn* gold leaf; **~ integral** whole wheat bread
pana *f* corduroy; **~dería** *f* bakery; **~dero** *m* baker
panal *m* honeycomb
Panamá *m* Panama
panameño(a) *a, m (f)* Panamanian
pancarta *f* placard
pandereta *f* tambourine
pandill|a *f* gang, pack *(of thieves)*; clique; **~ero** *m LA* gangster
panecillo *m* roll *(bread)*
panfleto *m* pamphlet
pánico *m* panic
panqueque *m LA* pancake
panta|leta *f LA* panties; ladies' underpants; **~lón** *m* trousers
pantalla *f* screen; lampshade
pantan|o *m* marsh; swamp; reservoir; **~oso** marshy
pantera *f* panther
pantorrilla *f* calf *(of the leg)*
panty *m* tights, *Am* panty hose
panz|a *f* paunch, belly; **~udo** pot-bellied
pañal *m* (baby's) nappy, *Am* diaper; **~es** *pl* swaddling clothes
pañ|ería *f* draper's shop, *Am* dry goods store; **~o** *m* cloth; duster; **~o de cocina** dishcloth; **~o higiénico** sanitary napkin; **~os** *pl* **menores** underclothes, underwear; **~uelo** *m* handkerchief; kerchief
papá *m* father; daddy
papa *m* pope; *f LA* potato; **~do** *m* papacy
papagayo *m* parrot
papamoscas *m* flycatcher
papel *m* paper; *teat* part, role; *pl* (identification) papers; documents; **~ carbón** carbon paper; **~ de cocina** paper towels; **~ de envolver** brown paper; **~ de estaño** tinfoil; **~ de fumar** cigarette paper; **~ higiénico** toilet paper; **~ de lija** sandpaper; **~ de seda** tissue paper; **~ moneda** paper money; **~ pintado** wallpaper; **~ secante** blotting paper; **~era** *f* wastepaper basket; **~ería** *f* stationer's; **~ero** *m* stationer; **~eta** *f* card; check; slip of paper; **~ucho** *m* scurrilous article; worthless paper
paperas *f/pl* mumps
papilla *f* pap
paquete *m* packet; parcel; **~s** *pl* **postales** parcel post
par *m* pair; couple; peer; **sin ~** matchless; *a* even *(of numbers)*; equal; *f* par; **a la ~** equally
para for; intended for; to; **~ que** in order that; **estar ~** to be about to; **¿~ qué?** what for?; **~ que** in order that, so that
parabrisas *m* windscreen, *Am* windshield
paracaídas *m* parachute
paracaidista *m* parachutist
parachoques *m* bumper
para|da *f* stop; stopping place; **~da discrecional** request stop; **~da de taxis** taxi stand; **~dero** *m* whereabouts; *LA* busstop, railway stop; **~do** *a* motionless; *LA* standing up; unemployed; *m* unemployed worker
paradoja *f* paradox
paradójico paradoxial
parador *m* inn; tourist hotel
parafina *f* paraffin
paraguas *m* umbrella
Paraguay: el ~ Paraguay
paraíso *m* paradise; heaven
paraje *m* place, spot; situation
paralel|a *f* parallel; **~o** parallel
parálisis *f* paralysis
paralítico paralytic
páramo *m* moor; bleak plateau
parapeto *m* breastwork, parapet
parar *v/t* to stop; to check *(progress)*; *v/i* to stop; to stay; to end up; **~ en** to result in; **~se** to stop; *LA* to stand
pararrayos *m* lightning conductor
parásito(a) *m (f)* parasite
parasol *m* sunshade
parcela *f* parcel, plot (of ground); **~r** *v/t* to allot; to parcel out
parcial partial, one-sided; **~idad** *f* partiality; bias
parco sparing; frugal
parche *m* sticking plaster; patch
pard|o dark; brown; **~usco** greyish; drab
parec|er *m* opinion; appearance; looks; **a mi ~er** in my opinion; **al ~er** apparently; *v/i* to appear; to seem; **~erse** to resemble; **~ido** *a* like, similar; **bien ~ido** good-looking; *m* resemblance, likeness
pared *f* wall
pareja *f* couple; pair; partner
parente|la *f* relations, parentage; **~sco** *m* kinship
paréntesis *f* parenthesis; brackets
paria *m, f* outcast, pariah
paridad *f* parity, equality
pariente *m, f* relative
parir *v/t, v/i* to give birth
paritorio *m* delivery room
parl|amentar *v/i* to converse; **~amento** *m* parliament; **~anchín** *m, f* chatterbox; **~otear** *v/i* to prattle, to chatter
paro *m* lock-out; unemployment; *zool* titmouse
parodia *f* parody, travesty

parón *m* stop, delay
parpadear *v/i* to blink, to twinkle
párpado *m* eyelid
parque *m* park; **~ de atracciones,** *LA* **de diversiones** amusement park; **~ infantil** playground; **~ nacional** national park; **~ zoológico** zoo
parquímetro *m* parking meter
parra *f* climbing vine
párrafo *m* paragraph
parrilla *f* grill; grate
párroco *m* parish priest
parroquia *f* parish; parish church; **~no(a)** *m* (*f*) parishioner
parsimonia *f* frugality
parte *f* part; share; *for* party; side; **de ~ de** from; on behalf of; **de ~ a ~** through and through; **en ~** partly; **en todas ~s** everywhere; **por otra ~** on the other hand; **la mayor ~** most of; **~s** *pl anat* parts; *m* report; message; **~ meteorológico** weather forecast
participa|ción *f* share; participation; announcement; **~r** *v/t* to inform, to notify; *v/i* to participate; to share
participante *m, f* participant
participio *m gram* participle
partícula *f* particle
particular particular; special; private; **~idad** *f* particularity, peculiarity; **~izar** *v/t* to specify
partida *f* departure; certificate; *com* item; shipment; game (*of cards*); entry (*in a register*); **~ de matrimonio** marriage certificate; **~rio(a)** *m* (*f*) partisan, follower
parti|do *m pol* party; match, game (*in sport*); profit; **sacar ~do de** to take advantage of; **tomar ~do** to make a decision; to take sides; **~r** *v/t* to part, to divide, to split; to break; to cut (*cards*); *v/i* to depart; **a ~r de hoy** from now on
partitura *f mús* score
parto *m* childbirth; **estar de ~** to be in labo(u)r
párvul|ario *m* nursery school; **~o** *a* small; tiny; *m* small child
pasa *f* raisin; **~ de Corinto** currant
pasado *a* past; **~ de moda** old-fashioned, out of fashion; **~ mañana** the day after tomorrow; *m* past
pasador *m* bolt; pin; smuggler
pasaje *m* passage; voyage; fare; **~ro(a)** *m* (*f*) passenger
pasamano *m* banister, handrail
pasaporte *m* passport
pasar *v/t* to pass; to cross; to surpass; to hand; to transfer; to smuggle; to undergo; to endure; to overlook; **~lo bien** to have a good time; **~ por alto** to ignore; to overlook; *v/i* to pass; to manage; to go past; to end; **~ de** to exceed; **~ a** to proceed; **~ por** to be reputed; **¿qué pasa?** what's the matter?; what's the trouble?; **~se** to go over; **~se sin** to do without, to dispense with
pasatiempo *m* pastime
pascua *f* Passover; **♀ del Espíritu Santo** Pentecost; **♀ de la Navidad** Christmas; **♀ de Resurrección** Easter
pase *m* permit; pass
pase|arse to go for a walk; **~o** *m* walk; stroll; **dar un ~o** to take a walk
pasillo *m* corridor
pasión *f* passion
pasiv|idad *f* passivity; **~o** *m com* liabilities; debit; *a* passive
pasm|ar *v/t* to stun; to amaze, to astonish; **~o** *m* amazement; **~oso** amazing
paso *m* pace; step; passing; gait; walk; **~ a nivel** grade crossing; **~ de peatones** pedestrian crossing; **~ superior** *f c* overpass; **a pocos ~s** at a short distance; **de ~** in passing; **abrirse ~** to make one's way; **ceder el ~** to make way; **marcar el ~** to mark time; **salir del ~** to get out of a difficulty
pasota *m, f fam* unconcerned, indifferent person; dropout
pasta *f* paste; dough; *pl* pastry; cookies; **~ de dientes** toothpaste
pastel *m* cake; pie; **~ería** *f* pastry shop; pastry; **~ero** *m* pastry cook
pastilla *f* tablet; cake (*of soap*); cough drop, lozenge
pasto *m* grazing; pasture; food; **~r(a)** *m* (*f*) shepherd(ess); **~ral** pastoral
pastoso pasty, doughy
pata *f* foot; leg; paw; **~s de gallo** crow's feet; **a cuatro ~s** on all fours; **~s arriba** upside down; **meter la ~** *fig* to put one's foot in it; **~da** *f* stamp (*with the foot*); kick
patán *m* rustic; lout
patata *f* potato
patear *v/t, v/i* to kick; to stamp
patent|e *f* patent; warrant; *a* patent, evident; **~izar** *v/t* to make evident
patern|al fatherly; paternal; **~idad** *f* paternity; **~o** paternal
patético moving, pathetic
patíbulo *m* gallows
patillas *f/pl* side whiskers; sideburns
patín *m* skate; **~ de ruedas** roller skate
patin|adero *m* skating rink; **~ador(a)** *m* (*f*) skater; **~aje** *m* skating; **~aje artístico** figure skating; **~ar** *v/i* to skate; to skid; **~eta** *f* scooter
patio *m* courtyard; *teat* pit
pato *m* duck; **pagar el ~** to be the scapegoat
patológico pathological
patraña *f* fake, swindle
patria *f* fatherland; native country
patrimonio *m* patrimony
patrio native; **~ta** *m, f* patriot; **~tero** *m* jingoist
patriótico patriotic
patriotismo *m* patriotism
patrocin|ador *m* patron, sponsor; **~ar** *v/t* to sponsor; **~io** *m* patronage; protection
patrón *m* patron; protector; landlord; boss; standard; (*sewing*) pattern
patron|a *f* patroness; landlady; **~ato** *m* trust; trusteeship; foundation
patrulla *f* patrol; squad; **~r** *v/t, v/i* to patrol
paulatinamente gradually
pausa *f* pause; rest; **~damente** leisurely, slowly; **~do** calm; slow; **~r** *v/i* to pause
pauta *f* rule; pattern; model
pava *f* turkey hen; **pelar la ~** to carry on a flirtation
paviment|ar *v/t* to pave; **~o** *m* pavement; paving
pavo *m* turkey; **~ real** peacock; **~nearse** to swagger, to show off
pavor *m* terror; dread
payas|ada *f* clowning; **~o** *m* clown
paz *f* peace, tranquillity
peaje *m* toll
peatón *m* pedestrian
peca *f* freckle
peca|do *m* sin; **~dor(a)** *m* (*f*) sinner; **~minoso** sinful
pecera *f* fish bowl
peculiar peculiar; **~idad** *f* peculiarity
pechera *f* shirt front
pecho *m* chest; breast; bosom; slope; *fig* courage; **dar el ~** to breast feed; **tomar a ~** to take to heart
pechuga *f* breast (*of fowls*)
pedag|ogía *f* pedagogy; **~ogo** *m* teacher
pedal *m* pedal; **~ear** *v/i* to pedal
pedante pedantic; **~ría** *f* pedantry
pedazo *m* piece, fragment
pedernal *m* flint
pedestal *m* pedestal
pedestre pedestrian
pediatra *m* pediatrician
pedicuro(a) *m* (*f*) chiropodist
pedi|do *m* demand; request; *com* order; **~r** *v/t* to ask for; to request; to demand; to sue for; *com* to order
pedo *m fam* fart; **soltar ~s** to fart
pedr|ada *f* hit with a stone; **~egoso** stony; **~ejón** *m* boulder; **~isco** *m* hailstorm
peg|a *f* gluing; sticking; *fig* difficulty; **~adizo** sticky; **~ado a** attached to; **~ajoso** sticky; **~ar** *v/t* to stick; to glue; to beat; **~ar fuego a** to set on fire; **no ~ar los ojos** not to sleep a wink; **~ar un tiro a** to shoot; **~arse** to adhere; to stick to; **~atina** *f* sticker; **~ote** *m* sticking plaster; *fam* sponger; **~otear** *v/i fam* to sponge
pein|ado *m* hairdo; **~ador** *m* dressing gown; **~adura** *f* combing; **~ar** *v/t* to comb; to search; **~e** *m* comb
pelad|o shorn; peeled; **~uras** *f/pl* parings
pelar *v/t* to peel; to cut the hair off; to shear; to pluck (*fowls*); *fig* to fleece
peldaño *m* step (*of staircase*); rung (*of ladder*)
pelea *f* fight; quarrel; **~r** *v/i* to fight; to quarrel
pelele *m* dummy; simpleton
peleter|ía *f* furrier's shop; **~o** *m* furrier
pelícano *m* pelican
película *f* film; movie; **~ muda** silent film
peligr|ar *v/i* to be in danger; **~o** *m* risk; peril; **correr ~o** to run a risk; **~oso** dangerous
pelillo *m* annoying trifle; **echar ~s al mar** to bury the hatchet; **pararse en ~s** to stick at trifles
peli|negro black-haired; **~rrojo** redheaded
pel|o *m* hair; *tecn* fibre, *Am* fiber, filament; down (*of birds, fruit*); nap (*of cloth*); coat (*of animals*); **no tener ~os en la lengua** to be very outspoken; **por los ~os** by the skin of one's teeth; **tomar el ~o** to pull one's leg, to tease; **~ón** hairless; penniless
pelot|a *f* ball; **~a vasca** pelota (*ballgame*); **~ear** *v/t* to audit (*accounts*); *v/i* to knock a ball about; to argue
pelotón *m* tuft of hair; *mil* squad; **~ de ejecución** firing squad
pelu|ca *f* wig; **~do** hairy, shaggy; **~quería** *f* hairdresser's shop; **~quero(a)** *m* (*f*) hairdresser; barber
pelusa *f* fluff; down (*on fruit*)
pellej|a *f*, **~o** *m* skin; hide; **salvar el ~o** to save one's skin
pellizc|ar *v/t* to pinch; to nip; **~o** *m* pinch, nip
pen|a *f* grief, sorrow; punishment, penalty; **~a capital** capital punishment; **a duras ~as** with great trouble; **valer la ~a** to be worthwhile; **~ado** *m* convict; *a* grieved; laborious; **~al** penal; **~ar** *v/t* to punish; **~arse** to grieve
pencazo *m* whiplash
pendenciero quarrelsome
pend|er *v/i* to hang; to dangle; **~iente** *a* pending; **~iente de pago** unpaid; *f* slope, hill; *m* earring
péndulo *m* pendulum
pene *m* penis
penetra|ción *f* penetration; insight; **~nte** penetrating; piercing; **~r** *v/t* to understand; to penetrate
penicilina *f* penicillin
península *f* peninsula
penique *m* penny
peniten|cia *f* penitence; penance; **~ciaría** *f* penitentiary; **~te** penitent
penoso distressing; arduous; unpleasant
pensa|do deliberate, premeditated; **bien ~do** well-intentioned; **poco ~do** ill considered; **~dor(a)** *m* (*f*) thinker; **~miento** *m* thought; thinking; *bot* pansy; **~r** *v/t* to think; to intend; **~r en** to think of; **~tivo** thoughtful, pensive
pensi|ón *f* pension; rent; boarding house; **~onar** *v/t* to pension; **~onista** *m, f* pensioner; boarder
pentecostés *m* Whitsuntide, Pentecost
penúltimo penultimate, next to last
penumbra *f* semi-darkness
penuria *f* poverty, need
peñ|a *f* rock; crag; group of friends; **~asco** *m* crag, cliff; **~ón** *m* large rock
peón *m* foot-soldier; *LA* farmhand, peon; pawn (*chess*)
peonza *f* spinning top
peor *a, adv* worse; worst; **de mal en ~** from bad to worse
pepin|illos *m/pl* gherkins; **~o** *m* cucumber; **no me importa un ~o** I couldn't care less
pepita *f* pip; seed (*of fruit*); nugget
pequeñ|ez *f* smallness; trifle; pettiness; **~o** little; small
pera *f* pear; goatee; **~l** *m* pear tree
perca *f* perch (*fish*)
percance *m* misfortune, accident, mishap
percatarse de to realize, to notice
percep|ción *f* perception; **~tible** perceptible; **~tivo** perceptive
percibir *v/t* to collect (*taxes*); to receive; to perceive, to notice
percusión *f* percussion
percha *f* rack; coat stand
perd|er *v/t* to lose; to waste; to miss; **echarse a ~er** to be ruined; **~erse** to get lost; to pass out of sight *or* hearing; **~ición** *f* perdition; ruin
pérdida *f* loss; **~s y ganancias** *f/pl* profit and loss
perdido lost; wasted; stray; incorrigible
perdiz *f* partridge
perdón *m* pardon; mercy; **¡~!** sorry!
perdonar *v/t* to forgive; **¡perdóneme!** excuse me!
perdurar *v/i* to endure; to last
perece|dero perishable; **~r** *v/i* to come to an end; to perish; to die
peregrin|ación *f* pilgrimage; **~ar** *v/i* to go on a pilgrimage; **~o(a)** *m* (*f*) pilgrim; *a* migratory
perejil *m* parsley
perenne perennial; **de hoja ~** evergreen
perentorio peremptory, decisive
perez|a *f* laziness, idleness, sloth; **~oso** *a* lazy, idle; *m zool* sloth
perfección *f* perfection
perfeccionar *v/t* to perfect; to improve
perfecto perfect, complete
perfidia *f* perfidy, treachery
pérfido perfidious, disloyal
perfil *m* profile, outline; **~ar** *v/t* to profile; to outline; **~arse** to take shape; to show one's profile
perfora|dora *f* hole puncher; **~dora neumática** pneumatic drill; **~r** *v/t* to punch; to perforate; to drill
perfum|ar *v/t* to scent; **~e** *m* perfume; **~ería** *f* perfume shop
pergamino *m* parchment
pericia *f* skill; expertness, know-how; **~l** expert
perico *m* parakeet
periferia *f* periphery
perilla *f* doorknob; goatee; **~ de la oreja** earlobe
periódico *m* newspaper; *a* periodical
periodi|smo *m* journalism; **~sta** *m* journalist
período *m* period
peripecia *f* vicissitude
perito *m* expert
perjudic|ar *v/t* to harm; to damage; **~ial** harmful
perjuicio *m* damage; hurt
perjur|ar *v/i* to commit perjury; **~io** *m* perjury; **~o** *m* perjurer
perla *f* pearl
permane|cer *v/i* to remain; to stay; **~ncia** *f* permanency; stay; sojourn; **~nte** *f fam* perm; *a* permanent
permi|sible permissible; **~sivo** permissive, tolerant; **~so** *m* permission; leave; **con ~so** if I may; excuse me; **~tir** *v/t* to permit; to allow
permuta *f* exchange; barter; **~ción** *f* exchange, interchange; **~r** *v/t* to exchange
pernicioso harmful; pernicious
perno *m* bolt
pernoctar *v/i* to spend the night
pero but, yet
perogrullada *f fam* truism, platitude
perpendicular perpendicular
perpetrar *v/t* to perpetrate
perpetuo perpetual
perplej|idad *f* perplexity; **~o** perplexed
perr|a *f* bitch; *pl fam* small change; **~era** *f* kennel; drudgery; **~illo** *m* small dog; *mil* trigger; **~illo de falda** lap dog; **~ito caliente** *m* hot dog; **~o** *m* dog; **~o de aguas** spaniel; **~o de lanas** poodle; **~o de presa** bulldog; **~o guardián** watchdog; **~o pastor** sheepdog
persa *m, f, a* Persian
persecución *f* persecution; pursuit; harassment
perseguir *v/t* to pursue; to harass, to persecute
perseverar *v/i* to persevere, to persist

persiana *f* Venetian blind
persignarse to cross oneself
persisten|cia *f* persistency; **~te** persistent
persona *f* person; individual; *teat* character; **en ~** in person; **~je** *m* personage; **~l** *a* personal, private; *m* personnel; **~lidad** *f* personality; **~rse** to appear personally
personifica|ción *f* personification; **~r** *v/t* to personify
perspectiva *f* perspective, outlook, prospect
perspica|cia *f* perspicacity; sagacity; **~z** perspicacious, shrewd
persua|dir *v/t* to persuade; **~sivo** persuasive; inducing
pertene|cer *v/i* to belong; to appertain; to concern; **~ncia** *f* ownership; property
pértiga *f* pole
pertina|cia *f* stubbornness; **~z** stubborn, obstinate
pertinente pertinent; *for* concerning
pertrechar *v/t*, **~se** *mil* to equip; to supply; to store
perturba|ción *f* disturbance; **~r** *v/t* to confuse, to agitate, to perturb
Perú: el ~ Peru
peruano(a) *m (f)*, *a* Peruvian
perver|sión *f* perversion; **~so** perverse; **~tido** *m* pervert; **~tir** *v/t* to pervert, to corrupt
pesa *f* weight; *sp* shot; dumbbell; **~dez** *f* heaviness; sluggishness; **~dilla** *f* nightmare; **~do** heavy; massive; tedious; fat; **~dumbre** *f* sorrow; grief
pésame *m* condolences; **dar el ~** to express one's condolences
pesar *v/t* to weigh; to afflict; *v/i* to weigh; to be heavy; to be important; *m* sorrow, grief; **a ~ de** in spite of; **a ~ de todo** all the same, nevertheless; **~oso** sorry, regretful
pesca *f* fishing; **~dería** *f* fish shop; **~dero** *m* fishmonger; **~do** *m coc* fish; **~dor** *m* fisherman; **~r** *v/t*, *v/i* to fish; to catch, to angle
pescuezo *m* neck
pesebre *m* manger; stall
peseta *f* peseta (*Spanish currency unit*)
pesimista *m*, *f* pessimist
pésimo worst; vile, abominable
peso *m* weight; burden; heaviness; balance, scales; *LA* peso (*currency unit*)
pesquisa *f* inquiry; investigation
pestañ|a *f* eyelash; **~ear** *v/t* to wink; to blink
pest|e *f* pest; plague; stench; **~ífero** foul; **~ilencia** *f* pestilence
pestillo *m* door latch; bolt
petaca *f* cigar(ette) case
pétalo *m* petal
petard|ear *v/t* to swindle; *v/i aut* to backfire; **~o** *m* firecracker; *mil* petard; *fam* swindle
petición *f* petition; demand
petirrojo *m* robin
petrificar *v/t* to petrify
petróleo *m* petroleum, (mineral) oil
petulan|cia *f* arrogance; **~te** haughty, arrogant
pez *m* fish (*living*); *f* pitch, tar; **~ gordo** *fam* bigwig
pezón *m* stalk; nipple
pezuña *f* hoof
piadoso pious; devout
piano *m* piano; **~ de cola** grand piano
piar *v/i* to chirp, to peep
pica *f* pike; **~da** *f* sting; bite
picadero *m* riding school
picadillo *m* minced meat
picado *a* pricked; *m aer* dive
picadura *f* prick; sting; bite
picante hot, strongly spiced; biting
picaporte *m* door knocker; latch; door-handle
picar *v/t* to prick; to sting; to bite; to chop, to mince; **~ en** to verge on; **~se** to be moth-eaten; to turn sour; to become choppy (*sea*); *fam* (*drugs*) to get a fix, to shoot up
pícaro *a* sly, crafty; base; roguish; *m* rogue; rascal
picazón *f* itch, itching
pico *m* beak, bill (*of a bird*); peak, summit; pick; spout (*of teapot*); woodpecker; **a las tres y ~** a little after three
picotazo *m* peck of a bird
pictórico pictorial
pichón *m* young pigeon
pie *m* foot; trunk (*of tree*); stem (*of plant*); support; **a ~** on foot; **al ~ de la letra** literally; **buscar tres ~s al gato** to split hairs; **en ~** standing; upright; **dar ~** to give cause; **de ~s a cabeza** from head to foot; **estar de ~** to be standing; **ponerse en ~** to stand up
piedad *f* piety; devoutness; mercy; pity
piedra *f* stone; hail; **~ arenisca** sandstone; **~ caliza** limestone; **~ imán** lodestone
piel *f* skin; hide; leather
pienso *m* fodder; feed; thought; **ni por ~** by no means
pierna *f* leg; **dormir a ~ suelta** to sleep soundly
pieza *f* piece; *tecn* part; room; **de una ~** in one piece; **~ de repuesto** spare part
pigmento *m* pigment
pijama *m* pyjamas, *Am* pajamas
pila *f* heap, stack; basin; water trough; *relig* font; *elec* battery; pile
pilar *m* pillar; trough
píldora *f* pill; **~ anticonceptiva** birth control pill
pilón *m* trough; basin; loaf (*sugar*); mortar
pilot|ar *v/t* to pilot; to drive; to steer; **~o** *m* pilot; driver
pilla|je *m* plunder; **~r** *v/t* to pillage, to plunder; *fam* to catch
pillo *m* rascal; knave
piment|ero *m* pepper plant; pepper pot; **~ón** *m* red pepper
pimient|a *f* black pepper; **~o** *m* green pepper; chili pepper
pimpollo *m* shoot; bud
pinar *m* pine grove
pincel *m* paint brush
pinch|ar *v/t* to prick, to puncture; **~azo** *m* prick; puncture (*t aut*)
pingüe greasy; *fig* fat (*profits, etc*)
pin|güino *m* penguin; **~ito** *m* first step; **hacer ~itos** to toddle
pino *m* pine tree; **~cha** *f* pine needle
pinta *f* spot, mark; appearance; **tener buena ~** to look good; **~do** spotted; speckled; **~r** *v/t* to paint; to depict; **~rse** to make up one's face
pintor|(a) *m (f)* painter; **~esco** picturesque
pintura *f* painting; paint
pinzas *f/pl* tweezers; forceps; tongs; claws (*of crabs, etc*)
pinzón *m* finch
piña *f* pineapple; pine cone
piñón *m* pine kernel; *tecn* pinion
pío *a* pious, devout; *m zool* cheeping
piojo *m* louse; **~so** lousy, mean
pionero *m* pioneer
pipa *f* pipe; cask; *pl* sunflower seeds
pique *m* pique, resentment; **echar a ~** *v/t* to sink; **irse a ~** to sink; to be ruined
piquete *m* prick; *mil* picket
piragua *f* canoe
pirámide *f* pyramid
pirat|a *m* pirate; **~ear** *v/i* to pirate; **~ería** *f* piracy
Pirineos *m/pl* Pyrenees
pirop|ear *v/t*, *v/i* to compliment (*a woman*); **~o** *m* compliment
pis *m fam* piss; **hacer ~** to piss, to pee
pisa *f* treading; **~da** *f* footstep; footprint; **~papeles** *m* paperweight; **~r** *v/t* to step on; to tread on; to trample
piscina *f* swimming pool
piscolabis *m* snack
piso *m* floor; flooring; pavement; stor(e)y; flat, apartment; **~ bajo** ground floor
pisón *m* rammer
pisotear *v/t* to trample on
pista *f* track; trail; scent; ring (*of the circus*); **~ de aterrizaje** runway; **~ de baile** dance floor; **~ de esquiar** ski run; **~ de patinaje** skating rink; **~ de tenis** tennis court
pistol|a *f* pistol; **~ero** *m* gangster, gunman
pistón *m* piston
pit|ar *v/t* to blow (*whistle*); *LA* to smoke; *v/i* to whistle; to boo; to honk horn; **~illera** *f* cigarette case; **~illo** *m* cigarette; **~o** *m* whistle; *aut* horn
pitón *m* protuberance, lump; spout (*of jar*); *LA* nozzle; *bot* young shoot
pizarra *f* slate; blackboard
pizca *f* bit; crumb; dash; pinch (*of salt, etc*)
placa *f* plate; plaque; **~ de matrícula** *aut* number *or* license plate; **~ giratoria** turntable
place|ntero pleasant; **~r** *m* pleasure; *v/t* to please
plácido placid
plaga *f* scourge; calamity; plague; **~r** *v/t* to infest
plagio *m* plagiarism
plan *m* plan; project; attitude; **~ de estudios** curriculum; **en ese ~** in that way
plana *f impr* page; **primera ~** front page; **a ~ y renglón** line for line
plancha *f* iron; **~do** ironed; **~r** *v/t* to iron
planea|dor *m aer* glider; **~r** *v/i* to glide; *v/t* to plan, to design
planeta *m* planet
planicie *f* plain
planificar *v/t* to plan
plano *m* plan; plane; map; **primer ~** foreground; *a* level, flat; smooth
plant|a *f* plant; sole (*of the foot*); stor(e)y; **~ar** *v/t* to plant; **~arse** to stop (*animal*); to stand firm
plantear *v/t* to outline, to state; to propose, to present
plantel *m* nursery garden
plantilla *f* staff, personnel; inner sole (*of a shoe*)
plantío *m* planting; *bot* bed
plañi|dera *f* mourner; **~r** *v/i* to weep, to lament
plasma *m* plasma
plástico *a*, *m* plastic
plata *f* silver; *LA* money
plataforma *f* platform; **~ de lanzamiento** launching pad (*for rockets*)
plátano *m* banana; plane tree
platea *f teat* stalls, *Am* orchestra floor
plate|ado silverplated; silvery; **~ro** *m* silversmith
plática *f* conversation; sermon
platicar *v/i* to talk, to chat
platija *f* plaice
platillo *m* saucer; small dish; *pl* cymbals; **~ volante** flying saucer
platino *m* platinum
plato *m* dish; plate; course
playa *f* shore; beach
plaza *f* (public) square; market place; post; **~ de armas** parade ground; **~ de toros** bullring; **~ mayor** main square; **sentar ~** *mil* to enlist
plazo *m* term; due date; instal(l)ment; period; **a ~s** on credit, by instal(l)ments; **corto ~** short notice
pleamar *f* high tide
pleb|e *f* common people, the masses; **~eyo** *a*, *m* plebeian; commoner; **~iscito** *m* referendum
plega|ble, ~dizo folding; collapsible; **~r** *v/t* to fold; to pleat
plegaria *f* prayer
pleito *m* lawsuit; *fig* dispute, controversy
plen|amente fully; **~ario** plenary; **~ipotencia** *f* full powers; **~itud** *f* plenitude; fullness; **~o** full; complete; **en ~o día** in broad daylight; **en ~o invierno** in the middle of winter
pleuresía *f* pleurisy
pliego *m* sheet (*of paper*); sealed letter *or* document
pliegue *m* fold, crease
plisar *v/t* to pleat
plomo *m* lead; lead weight
plum|a *f* feather; quill; pen; nib; **~a estilográfica** fountain-pen; **~aje** *m* plumage; **~azo** *m* feather pillow; **~ero** *m* feather duster; **~ón** *m* down; feather bed
plural *m* plural
pluralidad *f* majority
pluriempleo *m* holding various jobs; moonlighting
plusvalía *f com* appreciation; surplus value
pobla|ción *f* population; town; **~do** *m* town; village; inhabited place; **~r** *v/t* to populate, to people; to settle; to stock; **~rse** to fill with
pobre *a* poor; *m*, *f* poor person; beggar; **~za** *f* poverty
pocilga *f* pigsty
poción *f* potion; dose (*of medicine*)
poco *a* little; scanty; *adv* little, not much; **dentro de ~** shortly; presently; **~ más o menos** more or less; **~ a ~** little by little; **por ~** nearly; **tener en ~** to think little of
pocho discolo(u)red; pale
poda *f* pruning; **~r** *v/t* to prune
poder *m* power; authority; strength; might; **~ notarial** power of attorney; **en ~ de** *com* in possession of; **plenos ~es** full authority; *v/t*, *v/i* to be able; **a más no ~** to the utmost; **no ~ con** to be unable to bear
poder|ío *m* power; authority, dominion; wealth; **~oso** powerful
podri|do rotten; corrupt; **~rse** to rot, to putrefy
poe|ma *m* poem; **~sía** *f* poetry; poem; **~ta** *m* poet
poético poetic
polaco(a) *a* Polish; *m (f)* Pole
polarizar *v/t* to polarize
polea *f* pulley
polémica *f* polemics
policía *f* police; *m* policeman; **~co** of the police
polígamo *m* polygamist
polilla *f* moth
politécnico polytechnic
polític|a *f* politics; policy; **~a exterior** foreign policy; **familia ~a** in-laws; **~o** political; polite
póliza *f* certificate; draft; *com* policy; **~ de seguro** insurance policy
polizón *m* stowaway; tramp
polizonte *m fam* copper, policeman
polo *m* pole; *sp* polo
polonés(esa) *m (f)*, *a* Polish
Polonia *f* Poland
poltrón idle, lazy
polución *f* pollution
polv|areda *f* dust cloud; **~era** *f* vanity case; **~o** *m* dust; powder; *pl* toilet powder; **estar hecho ~** to be worn out; **~o(s) de levadura** baking powder; **~o(s) de talco** talcum powder
pólvora *f* gunpowder
polvoriento dusty
poll|a *f* pullet; *fam* chick, young girl; **~ada** *f* hatch of chickens; **~ería** *f* poultry shop; **~o** *m* chicken; *fam* youngster; **~uelo** *m* chick
pomelo *m* grapefruit
pómez: piedra *f* **~** pumice stone
pomp|a *f* pomp; show; **~a de jabón** soap bubble; **~oso** magnificent; grandiose; pompous
pómulo *m* cheekbone
ponche *m* punch (*drink*)
poncho *m LA* poncho, cloak, blanket
pondera|ción *f* deliberation; consideration; **~r** *v/t* to weigh; to ponder
poner *v/t* to put; to place; to set (*a table*); to lay (*eggs*); to give (*name*); to turn on; to put on; to cause; to set to; **~ en claro** to make clear; **~ en duda** to doubt; **~ en marcha** to start (*an engine*); **~se** to become, to get; to set (*the sun*)
poniente *m* west; west wind
pontifica|do *m* pontificate; **~l** pontifical
ponzoñ|a *f* poison; **~oso** poisonous
popa *f mar* stern; **de ~ a proa** fore and aft; totally
populacho *m* populace, mob
popular popular; **~idad** *f* popularity; **~izarse** to become popular
poqu|edad *f* paucity; timidity; **~ito** very little
por by; for; through; as; across; for the sake of; on behalf of; *mat* times; **escrito ~** written by; **pasamos ~ París** we travel via Paris; **~ la mañana** in the morning; **se vende al ~ mayor** it is sold wholesale; **~ ciento** percent; **~ docena** by the dozen; **~ adelantado** in advance; **~ escrito** in writing; **~ ahora** for now; **¡~ cierto!** sure!; **~ si acaso** just in case
porcelana *f* porcelain; china
porcentaje *m* percentage
porción *f* portion; part
porche *m* porch, portico
pordiosero *m* beggar
porfía *f* persistence; competition
porfiado obstinate
pormenor *m* detail; **~izar** *v/t* to detail

pornografía *f* pornography
poro *m* pore; **~so** porous
porque because; in order that
porqué *m* cause, reason; **¿por qué?** *interrog* why?; what for?
porquer|ía *f* dirt; rubbish; dirty business; **~o** *m* swineherd
porra *f* cudgel; truncheon; club; **mandar a la ~** to kick out; **~zo** *m* blow, thump; bump
porro dull, stupid; *fam joint (drugs)*
portaaviones *m* aircraft carrier
portada *f* doorway; porch; front; title page
portador(a) *m (f)* bearer
portaequipajes *m* boot, *Am* trunk; luggage rack
portal *m* porch; vestibule; door of house; gate; **~ón** *m mar* gangway
portamonedas *m* purse
portarse to behave
portátil portable
portavoz *m* spokesman
portazgo *m* toll
portazo *m* slam of a door
porte *m* carriage; postage; behavio(u)r; **~ franco** postage prepaid
porter|ía *f* porter's lodge; *sp* goal; **~o(a)** *m (f)* porter, janitor, concierge; superintendent; *sp* goalkeeper
pórtico *m* porch; arcade
portilla *f* porthole
Portugal *m* Portugal
portugués(esa) *m (f)*, *a* Portuguese
porvenir *m* future
posad|a *f* inn, hostel; **~ero** *m* innkeeper
posar *v/i* to pose; to perch *(birds)*
pose|edor(a) *m (f)* possessor; owner; **~er** *v/t* to possess; to own; **~ído** possessed; **~sión** *f* possession; ownership; **~sivo** possessive
posib|ilidad *f* possibility; **~ilitar** *v/t* to make possible; **~le** possible
posición *f* position; rank
positivo positive
posponer *v/t* to place behind; to postpone; to subordinate
postal postal; **(tarjeta)** *f* **~** postcard
pos(t)data *f* postscript
poste *m* post; pillar; pole; **~ de llegada** *sp* winning post; **~ indicador** signpost
postergar *v/t* to postpone; to pass over
posteri|dad *f* posterity; **~or** subsequent; rear; back
pos(t)guerra: de ~ postwar
postigo *m* wicket; shutter
postizo *a* false; artificial; *m* false hair
postra|do prone; prostrate; **~r** *v/t* to overthrow; to prostrate
postre *m* dessert; **~mo, ~ro** last; rear
postular *v/t* to claim; to postulate
póstumo posthumous
postura *f* posture, pose, position; *com* bid; stake
potable drinkable
potaje *m* vegetable stew
pote *m* pot; jar
poten|cia *f* power; potency; horsepower; **~cia mundial** world power; **~cial** *m* potential; capacity; *a* potential; **~te** powerful; potent
potesta|d *f* power; jurisdiction; **~tivo** facultative
potr|a *f* filly; **~ero** *m* pasture; paddock; *LA* cattle ranch; **~o** *m* foal, colt
poza *f* puddle; pool
pozo *m* well; **~ de mina** pit; shaft
práctica *f* practice, custom
practica|ble feasible; **~nte** *m* apprentice; **~r** *v/t* to practice; to perform
práctico *m mar* pilot; *a* practical; workable
prad|era *f* meadowland; **~o** *m* field, meadow
pragmático pragmatic
preámbulo *m* preamble
precario precarious
precaución *f* precaution
precavido cautious, wary
precede|ncia *f* precedence; priority; preference; **~nte** *m* precedent; **sin ~nte** unprecedented; *a* preceding; prior; **~r** *v/t* to precede; to have priority over
precepto *m* precept; order; rule; **~r** *m* tutor
preciar *v/t* to value; to appraise
precint|ado presealed; prepackaged; **~o** *m* sealed strap
precio *m* price; cost; worth; value; esteem; **~ fijo** fixed price; **~so** precious; valuable; *fig* lovely
precipi|cio *m* precipice; **~tación** *f* **radiactiva** fallout; **~tar** *v/t* to precipitate; to hasten; **~tarse** to rush; to dash
precis|amente precisely; **~ar** *v/t* to define exactly, to specify; to need; **~ión** *f* precision; accuracy; need; **~o** precise; necessary
preconizar *v/t* to recommend; to favo(u)r; to foresee
precoz precocious
precursor(a) *m (f)* forerunner; precursor
predecesor *m* predecessor
predecir *v/t* to predict
predestinar *v/t* to predestine
prédica *f* sermon
predica|dor(a) *m (f)* preacher; **~mento** *m* category; *LA* predicament; **~r** *v/t*, *v/i* to preach
predicción *f* prediction
predilec|ción *f* predilection; **~to** favo(u)rite
predio *m* landed property; estate
predisposición *f* predisposition
predomin|ar *v/t* to predominate; **~io** *m* predominance; superiority
prefabricado prefabricated
prefacio *m* preface, prologue
prefecto *m* prefect
preferen|cia *f* preference; **localidad de ~cia** *teat* reserved seat; **~cia de paso** *aut* right of way; **~te** preferential
preferi|ble preferable; **~r** *v/t* to prefer
prefijo *m* prefix
pregón *m* announcement; cry *(of traders)*
preguerra *f* prewar period
pregunta *f* question; **hacer una ~** to ask a question; **~r (por)** *v/t*, *v/i* to ask (for); **~rse** to wonder
prehistórico prehistoric
preju|icio *m* prejudice; **~zgar** *v/t* to prejudge
prelado *m* prelate
preliminar *a* preliminary; *m* preliminary
preludio *m* prelude
prematuro premature; untimely
premedita|ción *f* premeditation; **~do** premeditated; deliberate; **~r** *v/t* to premeditate
premi|ar *v/t* to reward; to award a prize to; **~o** *m* prize; *com* premium; **~o gordo** first prize
premisa *f* premise; assumption
premura *f* pressure, urgency
prenda *f* pledge; token; forfeit; **en ~** in pawn; **~ perdida** forfeit; *pl* talents; **~r** *v/t* to pawn; to please
prende|dor *m* clasp; brooch; **~r** *v/t* to seize; to catch; *LA* to switch on; **~r fuego** to catch fire; **~ría** *f* pawnshop
prensa *f* press; **~do** *m* sheen *(on material)*; **~r** *v/t* to press
preñado *a* pregnant with; full of; *m* pregnancy
preocupa|ción *f* worry; **~do** preoccupied, worried; concerned; **~r** *v/t* to worry; to preoccupy; **~rse** to worry; to concern oneself; to take an interest in
prepara|ción *f* preparation; **~r** *v/t* to prepare; **~rse** to get *or* make ready; **~tivo** *a* preparatory; **~tivos** *m/pl* preparations
prepondera|ncia *f* preponderance; **~r** *v/i* to prevail
preposición *f gram* preposition
prerrogativa *f* prerogative; privilege
presa *f* capture; prey, quarry; dam, weir
presagi|ar *v/t* to presage; **~o** *m* presage, omen
présbita far-sighted
presbítero *m* priest
prescindir de *v/i* to do without, to dispense with
prescri|bir *v/t* to prescribe; **~pción** *f* prescription; **~to** prescribed
presencia *f* presence; bearing; appearance; **~ de ánimo** presence of mind; **~r** *v/t* to attend; to be present at, to witness
presenta|ción *f* introduction; presentation; **~dor(a)** *m (f)* *TV* moderator; **~r** *v/t* to introduce; to present; to display; **~rse** to present oneself; to turn up
presente *a* present; **al ~** at present; **tener ~** to bear in mind, to keep in view; *m* present *(t gram)*
presenti|miento *m* premonition; presentiment; **~r** *v/t* to have a presentiment of
preserva|ción *f* preservation; conservation; **~r** *v/t* to preserve; **~tivo** *a*, *m* preservative; *m* condom
presiden|cia *f* presidency; chairmanship; **~te** *m* president; chairman
presidi|ario *m* convict; **~o** *m* prison; *mil* garrison
presidir *v/t* to preside over
presilla *f* fastener; clip
presión *f* pressure; **a ~** *tecn* under pressure; **~ atmosférica** air pressure; **~ sanguínea** blood pressure
preso *m* prisoner; *a* captured
presta|ción *f* lending; loan; **~do** loaned; **pedir ~do** to borrow; **~dor(a)** *m (f)* lender; **~mista** *m* moneylender, pawnbroker
préstamo *m* loan
presta|r *v/t* to lend; **~tario** *m* borrower
prestidigitador *m* conjurer, magician
prestigio *m* prestige; **~so** famous, renowned
presto quick; ready
presu|mido conceited; presumptuous; **~mir** *v/t* to presume; to surmise; *v/i* to show off; to be conceited; **~nción** *f* presumption; **~nto** presumed, supposed; **~ntuoso** conceited; presumptuous; pretentious
presupuesto *m* budget
presuroso hasty; prompt
preten|der *v/t* to seek; to claim; to attempt; to pretend; to pay court to; **~dido** alleged; **~diente** *m* claimant; suitor; **~sión** *f* claim; pretension
pretérito *m*, *a* preterit(e); past
pretexto *m* pretext
prevalecer *v/i* to prevail; to take root
prevaricar *v/i* to act dishonestly; to fail in one's duty
preven|ción *f* prevention; warning; foresight; **~ir** *v/t* to prepare; to warn; to foresee; to prevent; **~irse** to get ready; to be prepared; **~tivo** preventive
prever *v/t* to foresee; to forecast
previo *a* previous, prior; *prep* after, following
previs|ión *f* foresight; forecast; **~or** farsighted; thoughtful
prieto blackish, dark; *LA* brunette
prima *f* female cousin; *com* premium; bounty
primacía *f* primacy
primado *m* primate
primario primary
primavera *f* spring; *bot* primrose
primer|amente in the first place; **~izo** *m* beginner; **~o(a)** *a* first; primary; foremost; **~ ministro** prime minister; **de ~a** first rate; first class; **de ~a mano** first hand; **en ~ lugar** firstly; **~os auxilios** first aid; *adv* first; rather
primitivo primitive
primo *m* cousin; **~ hermano, ~ carnal** first cousin; *a mat* prime; **~génito** first-born
primor *m* excellence; beauty; ability; **~oso** excellent; exquisite; skil(l)ful
princ|esa *f* princess; **~ipado** *m* principality; **~ipal** *a* principal; main; *m* chief
príncipe *m* prince; **~ heredero** crown prince
principi|ante *m*, *f* beginner; **~ar** *v/t* to begin; **~o** *m* beginning; principle; **al ~o** at first; **a ~os del mes** at the beginning of the month
pring|ar *v/t* to dip in fat; to baste; **~oso** greasy; sticky
prioridad *f* priority
prisa *f* haste, hurry, speed; **a toda ~** as quickly as possible; **darse ~** to hurry, to make haste, to be quick; **tener ~** to be in a hurry
prisión *f* prison, jail; imprisonment
prisionero(a) *m (f)* prisoner; captive
prism|a *m* prism; **~ático** prismatic; **~áticos** *m/pl* binoculars
priva|ción *f* privation; loss; want; **~do** private; personal; **~r** *v/t* to deprive; to prohibit; **~tivo** privative; special, exclusive
privilegi|ar *v/t* to privilege; **~o** *m* privilege; sole right
pro *m or f* profit; benefit; **en ~ de** for, on behalf of
proa *f mar* bow; prow; **de ~ a popa** from stem to stern
probab|ilidad *f* probability; likelihood; **~le** probable; likely
proba|r *v/t* to test; to try; to prove; to taste, to sample; **~torio** probative
probeta *f* test tube; **niño-~** *m* test tube baby
probidad *f* integrity; probity
problem|a *m* problem; **~ático** problematic
proced|encia *f* origin; **~ente** fitting; lawful; **~ente de** coming from; **~er** *v/i* to proceed; to be right; to behave; **~er a** to proceed to; to start; **~er contra** to proceed against; **~er de** to proceed from; to originate in; *m* behavio(u)r; **~imiento** *m* process; procedure; *for* proceedings
proces|ador *m* **de textos** word processor; **~ar** *v/t* to prosecute; to put on trial; **~ar datos** to process data; **~o** *m* process; prosecution; *for* trial, lawsuit
proclama|ción *f* proclamation; **~r** *v/t* to proclaim
procura|dor *m* attorney; solicitor; **~r** *v/t* to try; to seek; to cause
prodigar *v/t* to squander; to lavish
prodigio *m* prodigy; wonder; miracle; **~so** prodigious; wonderful
pródigo prodigal; lavish; **~(a)** *m (f)* spendthrift
produc|ción *f* production; output; **~ción en serie** mass production; **~ente** *a* producing; *m* producer; **~ir** *v/t* to produce; to yield; to cause; to generate; **~tivo** productive; **~to** *m* product; produce; proceeds; yield; **~tor(a)** *m (f)* producer
proeza *f* exploit, heroic deed
profano *a* profane; **~(a)** *m (f)* layman (laywoman)
profecía *f* prophecy
proferir *v/t* to utter
profes|ar *v/t* to profess; to feel; to practise, *Am* practice *(a profession)*; **~ión** *f* profession; **~ional** professional; **~or(a)** *m (f)* teacher; professor; **~orado** *m* teaching staff; teaching profession; **~oral** professorial
profet|a *m* prophet; **~izar** *v/t* to predict, to prophesy
profund|idad *f* depth; **~izar** *v/t* to deepen; to study thoroughly; **~o** profound; deep
profus|ión *f* profusion; abundance; **~o** profuse, abundant
programa *m* program(me); **~ción** *f* programming
progres|ar *v/i* to progress; **~ivo** progressive; **~o** *m* progress
prohibi|ción *f* prohibition; **~r** *v/t* to prohibit; **~tivo** prohibitive
prohijar *v/t* to adopt
prójimo *m* neighbo(u)r; fellow being
proletari|ado *m* proletariat; **~o** *m*, *a* proletarian
prolijo prolix; long-winded
prólogo *m* prologue
prolongar *v/t* to prolong; to extend
promedio *m* average
prome|sa *f* promise; **~tedor** promising; **~ter** *v/t* to promise; **~tido(a)** *m (f)* fiancé(e), betrothed
prominente prominent
promiscuo promiscuous; in disorder
promoción *f* promotion; advancement; **la ~ de** the class of
promontorio *m* cape; headland
promo|tor *m* promoter; **~ver** *v/t* to promote; to foster; to provoke

promulgar *v/t* to promulgate; to publish officially
pronombre *m* pronoun
pronosticar *v/t* to foretell
pronóstico *m* forecast; prediction; *med* prognosis; **~ del tiempo** weather forecast
prontlitud *f* promptness, dispatch; **~o** *a* prompt; fast; ready; *adv* quickly; soon; early; **por lo ~o** for the time being; **tan ~o como** as soon as
pronuncia|ción *f* pronunciation; **~miento** *m* military revolt; **~r** *v/t* to pronounce; to utter
propaga|ción *f* propagation; spreading; **~nda** *f* propaganda; **~ndista** *m, f* propagandist; **~r** *v/t* to spread; to propagate
propens|ión *f* propensity, leaning, inclination; **~o** inclined, prone
propiamente properly
propicio favo(u)rable; propitious
propie|dad *f* ownership; property; special quality; **es ~dad** copyright; **~tario(a)** *m (f)* proprietor (-tress); landowner
propina *f* tip; gratuity
propio own; proper; suitable; typical; selfsame; **el ~ rey** the king himself
proponer *v/t* to propose
proporción *f* proportion; symmetry
proporciona|do proportionate; proportioned; **~r** *v/t* to provide; to adjust
proposición *f* proposition; proposal
propósito *m* purpose; object; **a ~** by the way; on purpose; **¿a qué ~?** to what end?; **de ~** on purpose; **fuera de ~** beside the point
propuesta *f* offer; proposal
propuls|ar *v/t* to propel; **~ión** *f* propulsion; propelling; **~or** *m* propellent
prorrat|a *f* quota, share; **~ear** *v/t* to apportion; **~eo** *m* allotment
prórroga *f* prolongation; extension (*of time*)
prorrogar *v/t* to prorogue; to extend (*in time*)
prosa *f* prose
prosáico prosaic; matter-of-fact
proscri|bir *v/t* to prohibit; to proscribe; to banish; **~to** *m* outlaw; *a* banned; outlawed
prose|cución *f* prosecution; pursuit; **~guir** *v/t* to go on with, to continue; *v/i* to continue; to resume
prospecto *m* prospectus
prosper|ar *v/i* to prosper, to thrive; **~idad** *f* prosperity
próspero prosperous
prostitu|ir *v/t* to prostitute; to debase; **~ta** *f* prostitute
protagonista *m, f* protagonist; main character
protección *f* protection
prote|ctor *a* protecting; protective; *m* protector; **~ger** *v/t* to protect; **~gido(a)** *m (f)* protégé(e)
protesta *f* protest; **~ción** *f* protestation; **~nte** *m, f* Protestant; *a* protesting; **~r** *v/t, v/i* to protest
protesto *m com* protest (*of a bill*)
protocolo *m* protocol; etiquette
prototipo *m* prototype, model
protuberancia *f* protuberance
provecho *m* profit; **¡buen ~!** bon appétit!; **~so** profitable
provee|dor(a) *m (f)* purveyor; supplier; **~r** *v/t* to supply; to provide
provenir de *v/i* to arise from; to originate in
proverbio *m* proverb
providencia *f* providence; forethought; foresight
provincia *f* province; **~l** provincial; **~no(a)** *m (f)*, *a* provincial
provisión *f* supply; provision; store; *pl* provisions
provisional temporary, provisional
provoca|ción *f* provocation; **~r** *v/t* to provoke; to annoy; to tempt; to cause
próxim|amente shortly; **~o** near; close; next; **el mes ~o** next month
proyec|ción *f* projection; **~tar** *v/t* to plan; to project; **~til** *m* projectile; missile; **~to** *m* plan; project; **~tor** *m cine* projector; searchlight
pruden|cia *f* prudence; **~te** prudent; cautious
prueba *f* proof; evidence; test; trial; *foto* proof; **~ de alcohol** alcohol level test; **~ de fuego** *fig* acid test; **a ~ de agua** waterproof; **a ~ de bala** bulletproof; **~ eliminatoria** *sp* heat; **poner a ~** to test
prurito *m* itch
psicología *f* psychology
psicológico psychological
psicoterapia *f* psychotherapy
psiquíatra *m* psychiatrist
psiquiatría *f* psychiatry
púa *f* barb; tooth (*of a comb*); sharp point; **alambre m de ~s** barbed wire
pubertad *f* puberty
publica|ción *f* publication; **~r** *v/t* to publish
públicamente in public
publicidad *f* publicity; *com* advertising
público *m* public; audience; *a* public; common
puchero *m* cooking pot; stew; **hacer ~s** to pout
púdico chaste
pudor *m* modesty; decency; shame; **~oso** modest; bashful
pudrir *v/t* to rot; to vex; **~se** to rot; to decay
pueblo *m* nation; people; (country) town; village
puente *m* bridge; **~ colgante** suspension bridge; **~ levadizo** drawbridge
puerc|a *f* sow; **~o** *m* hog; wild boar; **~o espín** porcupine; *a* filthy
pueril puerile, childish
puerro *m* leek
puerta *f* door; entrance; **~ giratoria** swing(ing) door
puerto *m* port; mountain pass; **~ franco, ~ libre** free port
Puerto *m* **Rico** Puerto Rico
puertorriqueño(a) *a, m (f)* Puerto Rican
pues since; because; then; well; **ahora ~** now then; **~ bien** well then, very well; **~ sí** well, yes
puesta *f* setting (*of the sun*); stake (*at cards*); **~ a punto** *aut* tune-up
puesto *m* place; stand (*on the market*); post; job; **~ de periódicos** news stand; **~ de socorro** first aid station; *a* dressed; arranged; **~ que** *conj* since; inasmuch as
pugilato *m* boxing; fight
pugna *f* battle; struggle; **~r** *v/i* to fight, to strive
puja|nte strong; vigorous; **~nza** *f* strength; vigo(u)r; **~r** *v/i* to struggle; to bid
pulcr|itud *f* neatness; **~o** neat; tidy; exquisite
pulga *f* flea; **tener malas ~s** to be bad tempered
pulga|da *f* inch; **~r** *m* thumb
puli|do neat; polished; **~mentar** *v/t* to polish; **~mento** *m* gloss; **~r** *v/t* to polish
pulm|ón *m* lung; **~ón de acero** iron lung; **~onía** *f* pneumonia
pulóver *m LA* pullover
pulpa *f* pulp
pulpo *m* octopus
pulsa|ción *f* pulsation; throb; *mús* touch; **~dor** *m* pushbutton; **~r** *v/t* to play (*stringed instrument*); *v/i* to throb
puls|era *f* bracelet; **~o** *m* pulse; **tomar el ~o** to feel the pulse
pulular *v/i* to abound; to swarm
pulverizar *v/t* to pulverize
pulla *f* cutting remark, taunt
punción *f med* puncture
pundonor *m* point of hono(u)r
puni|ble punishable; **~ción** *f* punishment
punt|a *f* point; tip; nib; end; promontory; **en la ~a de la lengua** on the tip of the tongue; **sacar ~a a** to sharpen; **~ada** *f* stitch; **~apié** *m* kick; **~ear** *v/t* to dot; *mús* to plunk; **~ería** *f* aim; marksmanship; **~iagudo** sharp; **~illa** *f* lace edging; tack; **de ~illas** on tiptoe; **~o** *m* point; dot; full stop; nib (*of pen*); sight (*in firearms*); stitch (*in sewing*); **hacer ~o** *v/t, v/i* to knit; **a ~o de** about to (*do*), on the point of (*doing*); **~o de partida** starting point; **~o de vista** viewpoint; **~o y coma** semicolon; **en ~o** sharp; exactly
puntuación *f* punctuation
puntual punctual; **~idad** *f* punctuality; **~izar** *v/t* to fix; to describe in detail; **~mente** punctually
puntuar *v/t* to punctuate
punz|ada *f* prick; puncture; stab (*of pain*); **~ar** *v/t* to prick; to pierce
puñad|a *f* blow with the fist; **~o** *m* handful; bunch
puñal *m* dagger; **~ada** *f* stab (*with a dagger*; *of pain*)
puñetazo *m* punch
puño *m* fist; cuff; hilt; handle
pupa *f* pimple; blister
pupil|a *f* pupil (*of the eye*); **~o** *m* ward
pupitre *m* school desk
puramente purely
puré *m* purée; **~ de patatas** mashed potatoes
pureza *f* purity
purga *f* purge; purgative; **~nte** *m* purgative; laxative; **~r** *v/t* to purge; **~rse** to take a purgative; **~torio** *m* purgatory
purificar *v/t* to purify; to cleanse
puro *a* pure, unmixed; *m* cigar
púrpura *f* purple
pus *m* pus
pusilánime pusillanimous; cowardly
pústula *f* pustule; pimple
puta *f* whore
putrefacto putrid; rotten
pútrido putrid; rotten
puya *f* goad
P.V.P. = **precio de venta al público** retail price

Q

que *rel pron* who; whom; which; that; what; *conj* as; that; than; **¡~ venga!** let him come!; **~ yo sepa** as far as I know; **más ~** more than; **dice ~ sí** he says yes
qué *interrog pron* what?; which?; **¿por ~?** why?; **¿para ~?** what for?; **¿y ~?** so what?; what then?; **¿~ hora es?** what's the time?; *interj* what a!; how!; **¡~ niño!** what a child!; **¡~ difícil!** how difficult!
quebra|da *f* ravine; **~dero** *m* **de cabeza** headache; worry; **~dizo** brittle; fragile; **~do** *a* broken; *com* bankrupt; *m mat* fraction; **~ntamiento** *m* fracture, break; **~ntar** *v/t* to break; to crack; to shatter; **~nto** *m* weakness; grief; exhaustion; **~r** *v/t* to break; to bend; *v/i* to go bankrupt; **~rse** to get broken; *med* to be ruptured
queda *f* curfew; **~r** *v/i* to remain; to stay; to be left; **~r bien** to come out well; **~r en hacer algo** to agree to do something; **~rse** to remain; to stay; **~rse con** to keep
quehaceres *m/pl* jobs; duties; **~ de casa** household chores
quej|a *f* complaint; moan; grudge; **~arse** to moan; to whine, to complain; **~ido** *m* moan, whine
quema *f* burning; fire; **~dura** *f* scald; burn; **~dura del sol** sunburn; **~r** *v/t* to burn; to scorch; to scald; to blow (*fuse*); **~rse** to burn; to be very hot; to feel very hot
quemarropa: a ~ pointblank
querella *f* quarrel; dispute; **~rse** *for* to lodge a complaint
querer *v/t* to want, to wish; to love; to like; to need; **~ decir** to mean; **sin ~** unintentionally
querido dear; beloved
queso *m* cheese; **~ crema** cream cheese; **~ de bola** Edam cheese
quicio *m* pivot hole; frame jamb; **sacar de ~** to exasperate (*person*); to exaggerate the importance of (*thing*)
quiebra *f* crack; fissure; *com* bankruptcy, failure
quien *rel pron* (*pl* **quienes**) who; whom; **hay ~ dice** there are those who say; **~quiera** (*pl* **quienesquiera**) whoever; whosoever
quién *interrog pron* (*pl* **quiénes**) who?
quiet|o quiet; calm; **~ud** *f* stillness; repose
quijada *f* jawbone
quijot|esco quixotic; bizarre; **~ismo** *m* quixotism
quilate *m* carat
quilla *f* keel
quimera *f* chimera; dispute, quarrel
químic|a *f* chemistry; **~o** *m* chemist; *a* chemical
quincalla *f* hardware
quincena *f* fortnight; **~l** fortnightly
quinielas *f/pl* (*football*) pool
quinina *f* quinine
quinta *f* country house; *mil* conscription
quintillizos *m/pl* quintuplets
quiosco *m* kiosk; booth; street stand
quiquiriquí *m* cock-a-doodle-doo
quirófano *m med* operating room
quirúrgico surgical
quisquill|a *f* trifling dispute; **~oso** touchy; fastidious; hair-splitting
quiste *m* cyst
quita|esmalte *m* nail polish remover; **~manchas** *m* stain remover; **~nieves** *m* snow-plough, *t Am* -plow; **~sol** *m* sunshade
quita|r *v/t* to take away; to take off; to deprive of; to avert; to remove; *mat* to subtract; **~rse** to take off (*hat, clothes*); **~rse de en medio** to get out of the way
quite *m* parry; dodge
quizá, quizás perhaps, maybe

R

rábano *m* radish; **~ picante** horseradish
rabi|a *f* rage; *med* rabies; **~ar** *v/i* to rage; **~ar por** to long eagerly for; **~eta** *f* fit of temper
rabino *m* rabbi
rabioso rabid; furious
rab|o *m* tail; tail end; **con el ~o entre las piernas** *fam* ashamed; crestfallen; **~udo** long-tailed
racial racial
racimo *m* bunch; cluster
raciocinio *m* reasoning
ración *f* ration; portion
racional rational; **~ista** *m, f, a* rationalist
raciona|miento *m* rationing; **~r** *v/t* to ration
racha *f* gust (*of wind*); run (*of luck*); **~ de victorias** winning streak
radar *m* radar
radia|ción *f* radiation; **~ctivo** radioactive; **~dor** *m* radiator; **~r** *v/i* to radiate; *v/t* to broadcast
radica|l *a* radical; *m gram, mat* radical; **~r** *v/i* to take root; to be located
radio *m* radius; radium; *f or m* broadcasting, radio; **~difusión** *f* broadcasting; **~grafía** *f* X-ray; **~grama** *m* radiotelegram; **~logía** *f* radiology; **~rreceptor** *m* radio receiver; **~terapia** *f* radiotherapy; **~yente** *m, f* listener
raer *v/t* to scrape; to grate
ráfaga *f* gust, flurry, squall (*of wind*); flash (*of light*)
raído scraped; threadbare, worn-out; barefaced
raí|z *f* root; origin; **~z cuadrada** square root; **a ~z de** as a result of; **de ~z** by the root; **echar ~ces** to take root
raja *f* crack; splinter; slice (*of fruit*); **~r** *v/t* to split; to chop; to slice
ralo thin (*liquid*); sparse
rall|ar *v/t* to grate; **~o** *m tecn* rasp
rama *f* branch; **en ~** raw (*cotton, etc*); **andarse por las ~s** to beat about the bush; **~l** *m* strand (*of a rope*); branch line (*of a railway*)
ramera *f* whore, prostitute
ramificarse to branch off
ramillete *m* bouquet; centerpiece; collection
ramo *m* small branch; bunch (*of flowers*); field of art *or* science; line of business
rampa *f* ramp
ramplón vulgar
rana *f* frog
rancio rancid; rank, stale
ranch|ero *LA* rancher; **~o** *m mil, mar* mess; settlement; *LA* ranch
rango *m* rank; class
ranura *f* groove
rapaz *a* greedy; rapacious; *m* youngster; brat
rapé *m* snuff (*tobacco*)
rapidez *f* rapidity; speed
rápido *m* express train; *a* speedy; rapid

rapiña *f* robbery with violence; **de ~** of prey (*birds*)
rapos|a *f* vixen; fox; *fam* cunning person; **~o** *m* fox
rapt|ar *v/t* to kidnap; **~o** *m* kidnapping; abduction
raqueta *f* racket; **~ de nieve** snowshoe
raquítico *med* rachitic; rickety; feeble; stunted
rar|eza *f* rarity; oddity; peculiarity; **~ificar** *v/t* to rarefy; **~o** rare; uncommon; *fig* strange; notable; **~a vez** seldom
ras *m* levelness; **~ con ~** level; **a ~ de** on a level with
rasar *v/t* to graze; to skim; to level
rasca|cielo *m* skyscraper; **~dor** *m* rasp, scraper; hairpin; **~r** *v/t* to scratch; to scrape
rasgar *v/t* to tear; to rip
rasgo *m* feature; trait, characteristic; **a grandes ~s** in outline
rasg|ón *m* tear; rip; **~uear** *v/t, v/i* to strum (*guitar, etc*); **~uño** *m* scratch
raso *m* satin; *a* flat; plain; cloudless (*sky*)
raspa|dura *f* rasping; *pl* scrapings; **~r** *v/t* to rasp; to scrape
rastra *f* trail; track; rake
rastr|ear *v/t* to trail; to track; **~eo** *m* dredging; tracking; **~ero** creeping; **~illo** *m* rake; **~o** *m* scent; track; trace; rake; **~ojo** *m* stubble
rata *f* rat
rate|ar *v/t* to apportion; to pilfer; *v/i* to creep; **~ría** *f* pilfering; **~ro** *m* thief; pickpocket
ratifica|ción *f* ratification; **~r** *v/t* to ratify; to confirm
rato *m* while; (short) time; **un ~** awhile; **largo ~** a long time; **a ~s** from time to time; **~s libres** spare time; **pasar un mal ~** to have a bad time
ratón *m* mouse
ratonera *f* mousetrap
raya *f* line; stripe; streak; dash; parting (*of hair*); ray (*fish*); **~do** striped; **~r** *v/t* to line; *v/i* to border
rayo *m* ray; beam; spoke; thunderbolt; **~ láser** laser beam; **~ del sol** sunbeam
rayón *m* rayon
raza *f* race; breed; **~ humana** human race, mankind
razón *f* reason; cause; information; message; rate; **a ~ de** at the rate of; **con ~** rightly, with good reason; **dar ~ de** to inform about; **tener ~** to be right; **~ social** trade name
razona|ble reasonable; **~r** *v/i* to reason
reacción *f* reaction; **~ en cadena** chain reaction
reaccionar *v/i* to react; **~io(a)** *m (f)*, *a* reactionary
real real; genuine; royal
reali|dad *f* reality; truth; **en ~dad** in fact; as a matter of fact; **~zar** *v/t* to carry out, to accomplish; to put into practice
realmente really; actually
realzar *v/t* to heighten, to enhance; *tecn* to emboss
reanimar *v/t* to revive; to encourage
reanud|ación *f* resumption; **~ar** *v/t* to resume
reapar|ecer *v/i* to reappear; **~ición** *f* reappearance
rearm|ar *v/t, v/i* to rearm; **~e** *m* rearmament
reasumir *v/t* to resume; to take up again
rebaja *f* diminution; *com* rebate, reduction; **~r** *v/t* to lower; to reduce; to diminish; to discount
rebanada *f* slice (*of bread*)
rebaño *m* flock; herd
rebasar *v/t* to exceed; to overflow; to better (*a record*)
rebatir *v/t* to repel; to refute
rebel|arse to rebel; to revolt; **~de** *m* rebel; *a* rebellious; **~día** *f* rebelliousness; *for* default; contempt of court; **~ión** *f* rebellion
reblandecer *v/t* to soften
rebobinar *v/t* to rewind (*tape etc*)
reborde *m* flange; border
rebosar *v/i* to run over; **~ de** to overflow with
rebot|ar *v/i* to bounce; to rebound; *fam* to annoy; **~e** *m* rebound; **de ~e** on the rebound
rebozar *v/t* to muffle up; to dip *or* coat (*meat or fish*) in flour (*before frying*)
rebusca *f* careful search; **~do** affected; recherché; elaborate
rebuznar *v/i* to bray
recabar *v/t* to claim (*responsibility, etc*); to obtain by entreaty
recado *m* message
reca|er *v/i* to relapse; **~ída** *f* relapse
recalentar *v/t* to warm up; to overheat
recámara *f LA* bedroom
recambio *m* spare part; refill
recargar *v/t* to reload; to recharge; to overcharge
recata|do cautious; shy; **~r** *v/t* to conceal
recauda|ción *f* collection (*of funds, taxes*); **~dor** *m* collector; **~r** *v/t* to collect (*taxes, etc*); to gather
recel|ar *v/t* to fear; to suspect; **~o** *m* fear; suspicion; misgiving; **~oso** suspicious
recep|ción *f* reception; admission; receipt; **~cionista** *m, f LA* receptionist; **~tivo** receptive
recesión *f* (*economic*) recession
receta *f med* prescription; recipe (*cooking, etc*); **~r** *v/t* to prescribe
recib|idor(a) *m (f)* receiver; recipient; **~imiento** *m* reception; **~ir** *v/t* to receive; to accept; **~o** *m com* receipt; **acusar ~o** to acknowledge receipt
recicla|ble recyclable; **~je** *m* recycling
recién *adv* (*apocope of* **reciente**) recently; newly; **~ casado** newlywed; **~ nacido** newborn
reciente recent; new; modern; **~mente** recently; just
recinto *m* precinct; enclosure
recio strong, robust; harsh; bulky
recipiente *m* receptacle; recipient
reciprocar *v/t* to reciprocate
recíproco reciprocal
recita|l *m* recital; reading; **~r** *v/t* to recite
reclama|ción *f* claim; demand; complaint; **~r** *v/t* to claim, to demand
reclinar *v/t*, **~se** to recline, to lean back
reclu|ir *v/t* to shut in; **~sión** *f* seclusion; imprisonment; **~so(a)** *m (f)* prisoner
recluta *m* recruit; **~r** *v/t* to recruit; to levy
recobrar *v/t*, **~se** to recover; to regain
recodo *m* bend; curve
recog|er *v/t* to pick up; to collect; to gather; to harvest; **~ida** *f* retirement; withdrawal; harvesting; **~ida de basuras** garbage collection
recolec|ción *f* collection (*money*); gathering; harvesting; compilation
recomenda|ble recommendable; **~ción** *f* recommendation; advice; **~r** *v/t* to recommend; to request
recompensa *f* reward; **~r** *v/t* to recompense; to compensate
reconcentrar *v/t* to concentrate
reconcilia|ción *f* reconciliation; **~r** *v/t* to reconcile; **~rse** to become reconciled
reconoc|er *v/t* to recognize; to admit; to inspect, to examine; **~ido** recognized; accepted; **estar ~ido** to be grateful; **~imiento** *m* recognition; inspection; *med* examination
reconquista *f* reconquest
reconstitu|ir *v/t*, **~irse** to reconstitute; to reconstruct; **~yente** *m* restorative, tonic
reconstruir *v/t* to reconstruct; to rebuild
reconvención *f* reprimand; reproach
récord *m sp* record
recorda|r *v/t* to remind; to remember; **~torio** *m* reminder
recorr|er *v/t* to travel; to run over, to cover (*a distance*); **~ido** *m* journey; distance covered; run
recor|tar *v/t* to cut away; to cut out; to reduce; to clip; **~tes** *m/pl* clippings
recosta|do reclining; lying down; **~rse** to lie down; to rest
recrea|ción *f* recreation; break, recess (*at school*); **~rse** to amuse oneself
recreo *m* amusement; recreation, pastime; break, recess (*at school*)
recrudecer *v/i* to break out again
recta *f* straight line
rectángulo *m* rectangle
rectificar *v/t* to correct; to rectify
rect|itud *f* rectitude; **~o** straight; honest
rector *m* head; principal; rector; *a* ruling; governing; **~ía** *f* parsonage, rectory
recuento *m* count, tally; recount; *com* inventory
recuerdo *m* memory; remembrance; souvenir; *pl* regards
recular *v/i* to recoil
recupera|ble recoverable; **~r** *v/t*, **~rse** to recover; to retrieve; to recuperate
recur|rir *v/i* to resort (to); to revert; **~so** *m* recourse; *for* appeal; *pl* resources, means
recusar *v/t for* to reject
rechaz|ar *v/t* to reject; to repel; to refuse; **~o** *m* rebound; *fig* repulse
rechifla *f* catcall; hooting
rechinar *v/i* to grate; to creak; to gnash (*teeth*)
rechoncho *fam* chubby
red *f* net; netting; network, web; **~ ferroviaria** the railway system
redac|ción *f* editing; wording; editorial staff; **~tar** *v/t* to compose; to edit; to write; **~tor(a)** *m (f)* editor
redecilla *f* hair net
reden|ción *f* redemption; **~tor** *m* redeemer
redimir *v/t* to redeem
rédito *m* interest; return; proceeds
redoblar *v/t* to double; to bend back
redond|ear *v/t* to round; to make round; **~earse** to become affluent; **~el** *m* arena; **~o** round; circular; *fig* clear, categorical
reduc|ción *f* reduction; **~ido** reduced; small; limited; **~ir** *v/t* to diminish; to reduce; **~irse** to boil down; to have to economize
reducto *m* redoubt
reelección *f* reelection
reelegir *v/t* to reelect
reembols|ar *v/t* to reimburse, to pay back; **~o** *m* reimbursement; refund
reemplaz|ar *v/t* to replace; **~o** *m* replacement
reexpedir *v/t* to forward (*mail*)
refer|encia *f* reference; **~ir** *v/t* to report; **~irse (a)** to refer (to)
refin|amiento *m* refinement; **~ar** *v/t* to refine; to purify; **~ería** *f* refinery
refle|ctor *m* reflector; *a* reflecting; **~jar** *v/t* to reflect; *v/i* to reflect, to think; **~jo** *m* reflex; reflection; **~xión** *f* reflection; meditation; **~xionar** *v/i* to meditate, to reflect; **~xivo** reflective; thoughtful; *gram* reflexive
reflu|ir *v/i* to flow back; **~jo** *m* ebb (*tide*); *fig* retreat
reforma *f* reform; **♀ Reformation**; **~ agraria** land reform; **~r** *v/t* to reform; to improve
reforzar *v/t* to strengthen, to reinforce
refract|ar *v/t opt* to refract; **~ario** refractory; obstinate; rebellious
refrán *m* proverb; slogan
refregar *v/t* to rub; *fam* to harp on; to rub in
refrenar *v/t* to rein in; to restrain; to curb
refrendar *v/t* to legalize; to countersign
refresc|ar *v/t* to refresh; to renew; **~o** *m* refreshment; cool drink
refriega *f* fray, scuffle
refrigera|dor(a) *m (f)* refrigerator; **~r** *v/t* to cool
refrigerio *m* snack; refreshment
refuerzo *m* strengthening
refugi|arse to take refuge; **~o** *m* refuge, shelter
refundir *v/t* to recast; to contain; to rearrange
refunfuñ|ar *v/i* to snarl; to growl; **~o** *m* grumble, growl
refutar *v/t* to refute
rega|dera *f* watering can; sprinkler; **~dío** *m* irrigated land
regal|ado dirt cheap; **~ar** *v/t* to give (away); **~ía** *f* prerequisite; privilege; **~o** *m* present
regaliz *m* liquorice, *Am* licorice
regaña|dientes: a ~dientes reluctantly; **~r** *v/t* to reprimand; to scold; to nag (at); *v/i* to protest; to growl
regar *v/t* to water; to irrigate
regate|ar *v/t, v/i* to haggle; **~o** *m* haggling; bargaining
regazo *m* lap
regenerar *v/t* to regenerate
regen|tar *v/t* to govern; to manage; **~te** *m, f* regent
régimen *m* régime; government; *med* diet
regio royal, regal
región *f* region; part, area
regir *v/t* to govern; to manage; *v/i* to prevail; to be in force (*law*)
registr|ar *v/t* to record; to register; to examine; to search; **~o** *m* register; registration; recording; search; list
regla *f* ruler (*for drawing lines*); rule; regulation; *med* menstruation; **en ~** in order; **~ de cálculo** slide rule; **~mentar** *v/t* to regulate; **~mento** *m* rules and regulations; by-laws
regocij|arse to be merry; to rejoice; **~o** *m* rejoicing; merriment, mirth
regoldar *v/i* to belch
regordete *fam* plump; chubby
regres|ar *v/i* to return; **~o** *m* return
reguero *m* irrigation ditch
regula|ción *f* regulation; control; **~dor** *m* regulator; throttle, control knob; **~r** *v/t* to regulate; to control; *a* regular; medium; so-so; **~ridad** *f* regularity; **~rizar** *v/t* to regularize
rehabilitar *v/t* to rehabilitate; to restore
rehacer *v/t* to do again; to remake
rehén *m* hostage
rehusar *v/t* to refuse; to decline
reimpresión *f* reprint
rein|a *f* queen; **~ado** *m* reign; **~ar** *v/i* to reign; to prevail
reincidencia *f* relapse
reino *m* kingdom, realm; reign; **♀ Unido** United Kingdom
reír *v/i* to laugh; **~se de** to laugh at
reiterar *v/t* to repeat
reivindicación *f* claim; *for* recovery
rej|a *f* window grating; grille; railing; **~a de arado** plough share; **~as** *pl* bars; **entre ~as** behind bars; **~illa** *f* small grating; wickerwork; lattice; *elec* grid
rej|ón *m* lance (*of bullfighter*); **~oneador** *m* mounted bullfighter who uses the *rejón*
rejuvenecer *v/t* to rejuvenate
relaci|ón *f* relation; relationship; narration; account; *pl* relations; connections; courtship; **~onar** *v/t* to relate; to connect
relajarse to relax
relámpago *m* flash; lightning
relampaguear *v/i* to lighten; to flash
relatar *v/t* to relate, to report
relativ|idad *f* relativity; **~o** relative
relato *m* report; narrative
relegar *v/t* to banish; to relegate
relev|ante outstanding; **~ar** *v/t* to relieve; to replace; to emboss; to exonerate; **~o** *m mil* relief; *sp* relay
relieve *m* (*art*) relief; **poner de ~** to set off; to emphasize
religión *f* religion
religios|a *f* nun; **~o** *a* pious; religious; *m* monk
relinch|ar *v/i* to neigh; to whinny; **~o** *m* neighing
reliquia *f* relic
reloj *m* clock; watch; **~ de arena** hourglass; **~ de caja** grandfather's clock; **~ de cuarzo** quartz watch; **~ de cuclillo** cuckoo clock; **~ de pulsera** wrist watch; **~ de sol** sundial; **~ería** *f* watchmaker's (shop); clockmaking; **~ero** *m* watchmaker
reluci|ente brilliant; glossy;

~r *v/i* to shine; to glitter
relumbrón *m* glare
rellen|ar *v/t* to refill; to stuff; to pad; **~o** *m* stuffing; filling; padding
remach|ar *v/t* to rivet; **~e** *m* rivet
remada *f* stroke (*in rowing*)
remanente *m* remainder; residue
remanso *m* backwater
remar *v/i* to row
rematar *v/t* to finish; to knock down (*auction*); to conclude; *v/i* to end; to terminate; **~e** *m* end; conclusion; highest bid; sale (*at auction*); *LA* auction; **de ~e** to top it off
remedar *v/t* to imitate, to copy
remedi|ar *v/t* to remedy; to repair; **~o** *m* remedy; **no hay ~o** it can't be helped
remend|ar *v/t* to patch; to darn; to mend; **~ón** *m* cobbler
remero *m* oarsman
remesa *f com* remittance; consignment; **~r** *v/t com* to remit; to send
remiendo *m* patch; darning; mending
remilgarse to be affected
remilgo *m* affectedness; finickiness
remira|do cautious, prudent; **~r** *v/t* to review; to inspect
remisión *f* remission; remittance
remiso remiss; slack; indolent
remit|ente *m, f* sender; **~ir** *v/t* to send, to remit
remo *m* oar
remoj|ar *v/t* to soak; **~o** *m* steeping, soaking
remolacha *f* beet; beet root; **~ azucarera** sugar beet
remol|cador *m* tugboat; **~car** *v/t* to tug; to draw
remolino *m* whirlpool; eddy; flurry, whirl
remolque *m* towline; towrope; *aut* trailer; **a ~** in tow
remontar *v/t* to surmount (*obstacle, etc*); to frighten away (*game*); **~se** to rise; to amount (*to*); to go back (*to*)
remordimiento *m* remorse, compunction
remoto remote, outlying; ***control*** *m* **~** remote control
remover *v/t* to remove; to stir
remunera|ción *f* remuneration; **~dor** remunerative; **~r** *v/t* to remunerate; to reward
renac|er *v/i* to be reborn; **~imiento** *m* rebirth; revival; **♀** Renaissance
renacuajo *m* tadpole
rencor *m* ranco(u)r; spite; **~oso** rancorous; spiteful
rendi|ción *f* surrender; profit; **~do** submissive; humble; ***estar* ~do** to be worn out
rendija *f* crack; chink; crevice
rendi|miento *m* return; yield; weariness; submission; **~r** *v/t* to render; to return; to yield; to surrender; **~r *el alma*** to give up the ghost; **~rse** to surrender; to give up
renega|do *m* renegade, turncoat; *a* wicked; **~r** *v/t* to deny; to disown; *v/i* to turn renegade
renglón *m* line (*of letters, of merchandise, etc*); **a ~ *seguido*** right after
reno *m* reindeer
renombr|ado famous; **~e** *m* fame, renown
renova|ción *f* renewal; **~r** *v/t* to renew
rent|a *f* income, revenue; interest; annuity; **~a *vitalicia*** life annuity; **~as *pl públicas*** revenue; **~ar** *v/t* to yield; **~ista** *m, f* stockholder
renuncia *f* renunciation; **~r** *v/t* to renounce
reñir *v/i* to quarrel
reo *m* offender; criminal; *for* defendant; *a* guilty
reojo: *mirar de* ~ to look askance (at)
reorganizar *v/t* to reorganize
repara|ción *f* repair; reparation; **~r** *v/t* to repair; to make good; to restore; to remedy; *v/i* **~r (en)** to stop (at); to notice, to pay attention to
reparo *m* remark; criticism; ***poner* ~s** to make objections
repart|ición *f* division; distribution; **~ir** *v/t* to distribute; **~o** *m* delivery (*mail*); *teat* cast
repas|ar *v/t* to pass again; to revise; to go over; to check; **~o** *m* revision, review; *tecn* overhaul
repatriar *v/t* to repatriate
repel|ente repulsive; **~er** *v/t* to repel; to refute
repent|e *m* start; sudden movement; **de ~e** suddenly, all at once; **~ino** sudden; swift
repercu|sión *f* repercussion; **~tir** *v/i* to rebound
repertorio *m* repertory; repertoire
repeti|ción *f* repetition; **~r** *v/t* to repeat
repi|car *v/t* to ring (*bells*); to peal; **~que** *m* ringing; chime, peal
repisa *f* shelf; mantelpiece; **~ *de ventana*** windowsill
replantar *v/t* to replant
replantear *v/t* to restate (*a problem*)
replegar *v/t* to refold; **~se** *mil* to fall back
repleto replete; full to the brim; crowded
réplica *f* answer; retort
replicar *v/i* to reply; to retort
repliegue *m* fold; *mil* falling back
repoblación *f* repopulation
repollo *m* cabbage
reponer *v/t* to replace; **~se** to recover
reporta|je *m* report, article; **~r** *v/t* to restrain; to carry
reportero *m* reporter
reposacabezas *m* head rest
reposado poised; restful; calm
reposición *f* replacement; recovery (*health*); *for* restoration; *teat* revival
reposo *m* rest
repostería *f* confectionery; confectioner's shop
repren|der *v/t* to reprimand; **~sible** reprehensible, objectionable; **~sión** *f* censure; reprimand
represalia *f* retaliation; reprisal
represar *v/t* to dam (up)
representa|ción *f* representation; *teat* performance; **~nte** *m, f* agent; representative; **~r** *v/t* to represent; to perform (*plays*); to play (*a role*); to declare; to express; **~rse** to imagine; **~tivo** representative
represión *f* repression; suppression
reprim|enda *f* reprimand; **~ir** *v/t* to repress; to restrain
reprobar *v/t* to censure; to reprove
réprobo(a) *m (f)* reprobate
reproch|ar *v/t* to reproach; to censure; **~e** *m* reproach
reproduc|ción *f* reproduction; **~ir** *v/t* to reproduce
reptil *m* reptile
república *f* republic; **♀ *Dominicana*** Dominican Republic
republicano(a) *m (f), a* republican
repudia|ción *f* rejection; **~r** *v/t* to repudiate
repuesto *m* spare part; store, stock; *a* recovered
repugna|ncia *f* repugnance; aversion; **~nte** repugnant; loathsome; **~r** *v/t* to oppose; to conflict with
repulsa *f* refusal; rebuke; **~r** *v/t* to reject; to refuse
repulsi|ón *f* repulsion; **~vo** repulsive
reputa|ción *f* reputation; **~r** *v/t* to repute; to estimate
requebrar *v/t* to court; to flirt with
requemar *v/t* to burn; to scorch; *fig* to inflame (*blood*)
requeri|miento *m* notification; requirement; *for* summons; **~r** *v/t* to require, to necessitate; to notify; to investigate
requesón *m* cottage cheese; curd
requiebro *m* flirtatious remark
requis|ar *v/t mil* to requisition; **~ición** *f mil* requisition
res *f* head of cattle; beast
resaber *v/t* to know thoroughly
resabi|arse to acquire bad habits; **~do** very well known; *fam* pretentious; **~o** *m* nasty taste; ***tener* ~os *de*** to smack of
resaca *f mar* undertow; *fam* hangover; *fig* backlash
resaltar *v/i* to jut out; to stand out
resarcir *v/t* to indemnify
resbal|adizo slippery; **~ar** *v/i* to slip, to slide; to skid; **~ón** *m* slip; error
rescatar *v/t* to release; to ransom; to rescue; **~e** *m* ransom; ransom money
rescindir *v/t* to annul; to rescind
rescoldo *m* embers
resecar *v/t* to dry thoroughly; to parch
reseco parched
resenti|do bitter; resentful; **~miento** *m* resentment; grudge; **~rse** to resent; to be affected (*by*)
reseña *f* summary; short survey; **~r** *v/t* to review
reserva *f* reserve; reticence; *for* reservation; *mil* reserve; **con ~** in confidence; **sin ~** freely; frankly; **~do** cautious; reserved; **~r** *v/t* to reserve
resfria|do *m* cold (*illness*); **~rse** to catch cold
resfrío *m* cold (*in the head*)
resguard|ar *v/t* to shelter; to defend; to protect; **~o** *m* protection; shelter; voucher
resid|encia *f* residence; **~encial** residential; **~ente** *m, f* resident; **~ir** *v/i* to reside; to dwell
residuo *m* residue; remainder
resigna|ción *f* resignation; acquiescence; **~r** *v/t* to give up; **~rse** to resign oneself
resina *f* resin
resisten|cia *f* resistance; endurance; strength; **~te** strong; resistant; tough
resistir *v/i*, **~se** to resist; to offer resistance; *v/t* to endure; to withstand
resolución *f* resolution; determination; resoluteness; courage; solving; **en ~** in short, to sum up
resolver *v/t* to resolve; to decide; to solve; **~se** to resolve itself; to work out
resona|ncia *f* resonance; **~r** *v/i* to resound; to ring; to echo
resoplar *v/i* to snort, to puff
resorber *v/t* to reabsorb
resorte *m tecn* spring; *fig* resource
respald|ar *v/t* to back, to endorse; **~o** *m* back (*of a chair, etc*); backing; support
respect|ivo respective; **~o** *m* relation; **~o a** *or* **de** with regard *or* respect to
respet|able respectable; **~ar** *v/t* to respect; **~o** *m* respect; **~uoso** respectful
respir|ación *f* respiration; breathing; **~adero** *m* vent; air valve; **~ar** *v/i* to breathe; **~atorio** respiratory; **~o** *m* breathing; reprieve, rest, respite
respland|ecer *v/i* to shine; to glitter; **~eciente** resplendent; gleaming; shining; **~or** *m* splendo(u)r
respond|er *v/t, v/i* to answer, to reply; to respond; to be responsible; **~er a** to answer, to obey; *med etc* to respond to; **~er de** to answer for; **~ón** pert, impudent
responsab|ilidad *f* responsibility; **~le** responsible
respuesta *f* answer, reply
restablec|er *v/t* to reestablish; to restore; **~imiento** *m* restoration; recovery (*from illness*)
restante remaining; **los ~s** the rest
restañar *v/t* to stanch (*flow of blood*)
restar *v/t* to subtract; to deduct
restaura|nte *m* restaurant; **~r** *v/t* to restore; to repair
restitu|ción *f* restitution; **~ir** *v/t* to restore; to return
resto *m* rest; remainder; *pl* remains; *coc* leftovers; **~s *mortales*** mortal remains
restregar *v/t* to rub; to scrub
restri|cción *f* restriction; limitation; **~ctivo** restrictive; **~ngir** *v/t* to restrict
resucitar *v/t* to resuscitate; *v/i* to return to life
resuelto resolute; bold
resulta|do *m* result; outcome; ***dar* ~do** to produce results; **~r** *v/i* to result; to turn out
resum|en *m* summary; **en ~en** in brief; in short; **~ir** *v/t* to summarize, to sum up
resurgi|miento *m* resurgence; revival; **~r** *v/i* to revive; to reappear
retablo *m* altarpiece; retable
retaguardia *f* rearguard
retal *m* remnant; clipping
retama *f bot* genista; broom
retard|ar *v/t* to retard; to delay; to slow up; **~o** *m* delay
retazo *m* remnant; *pl* odds and ends
retén *m* reserve; store; *tecn* catch, stop
reten|ción *f* retention; **~er** *v/t* to retain; to keep back
reticente reticent
retina *f anat* retina
retintín *m* tinkling; jingle
retir|ada *f* withdrawal; retreat; **~ar** *v/t* to withdraw; to retire; **~o** *m* retirement; retreat; seclusion
reto *m* challenge; threat; *LA* insult
retocar *v/t* to retouch; to touch up (*photographs*)
retoño *m bot* shoot, sprout
retoque *m* retouching; finishing touch
retorcer *v/t* to twist; **~se** to writhe
retórica *f* rhetoric
retorsión *f* twisting
retractar *v/t*, **~se** to retract; to recant
retráctil retractable
retra|er *v/t* to bring back; *fig* to dissuade; **~ído** retiring; unsociable; **~imiento** *m* withdrawal, retreat
retrasar *v/t* to delay; to defer; to put off; *v/i* to be slow (*watch*); **~se** to be delayed; to be late; to be slow (*watch*)
retraso *m* delay; timelag; lateness; **con ~** late
retrat|ar *v/t* to portray; to describe; **~arse** to be photographed *or* portrayed; **~o** *m* picture; portrait
retreta *f mil* retreat; tattoo
retrete *m* lavatory; toilet
retroactivo retroactive
retroce|der *v/i* to go back; to recede; **~so** *m* backward motion
retrospectivo retrospective
retruécano *m* pun
retumbar *v/i* to resound; to rumble
reuma *m*, **~tismo** *m* rheumatism
reuni|ón *f* gathering; meeting; **~ón *en la cumbre*** summit meeting; **~r** *v/t* to join; to unite; **~rse** to meet; to get together
reválida *f* final examination
revalidar *v/t* to confirm; to ratify
revancha *f* revenge
revelar *v/t* to reveal; to develop (*photographs*)
revender *v/t* to retail; to resell
revent|ar *v/i* to burst; to break; to explode; **~ón** *m* bursting; explosion; *aut* blowout; great effort
reverberar *v/i* to reverberate; (*light*) to play, to be reflected
reveren|cia *f* reverence; respect; **~ciar** *v/t* to venerate; to revere; **♀do** *relig* Reverend
revers|ible *med* reversible; **~o** *m* reverse; back, other side
revertir *v/i for* to revert
revés *m* reverse; back; wrong side; misfortune; *sp* backhand (*stroke*); **al ~** upside down; inside out; backwards
revestir *v/t* to put on; to wear; *tecn* to cover, to coat, to line; **~se de** to assume, to muster up
revis|ar *v/t* to revise; *tecn* to overhaul; **~ión** *f* revision; **~or** *m* censor; **~or *de cuentas*** auditor; *a* revising
revista *f* review; periodical; magazine; *teat* revue; ***pasar* ~** to review
revoca|ción *f* revocation; abrogation; **~r** *v/t* to revoke; to repeal
revolcar *v/t* to knock down; to tread upon; **~se** to wallow
revolotear *v/i* to flit, to flutter around
revoltoso unruly; rebellious; naughty
revoluci|ón *f* revolution; revolt; **~onario(a)** *a, m (f)* revolutionary
revólver *m* revolver
revolver *v/t* to turn over; to stir up; to disturb; to upset; *v/i* to revolve; **~se** to turn round; to turn over; to change
revoque *m* whitewashing
revuelo *m* commotion, disturbance

revuelt|a *f* revolt; turn; bend (*in road*); **~o** disturbed; upset
rey *m* king; **los ~es Magos** the Three Wise Men; **~erta** *f* quarrel, row
rezaga|do *m* latecomer; *mil* straggler; **~r** *v/t* to leave behind; **~rse** to fall behind, to straggle
rez|ar *v/i* to pray; to say prayers; to read (*paragraphs, etc*); **~o** *m* prayer
rezumar *v/i* to leak out
ría *f* estuary
riachuelo *m* brook, stream
riber|a *f* beach, shore; **~eño** riverside
ribete *m* edging (*sewing*); *fig* trimmings; *pl* streak, touch
ricino *m* castor-oil plant
rico rich; plentiful; delicious
ridiculizar *v/t* to ridicule; to make fun of
ridículo ridiculous, ludicrous
riego *m* irrigation, watering
riel *m f c* rail
rienda *f* rein; **a ~ suelta** at full speed; freely; **dar ~ suelta a** to give free rein to
riesgo *m* risk; danger
rifa *f* raffle; lottery; **~r** *v/t* to raffle; *v/i* to quarrel, to fight
rigidez *f* rigidity
rígido rigid
rigor *m* rigo(u)r; sternness; stiffness; hardness; **de ~** prescribed by the rules; obligatory; **~oso** rigorous
riguros|idad *f* severity; **~o** rigorous; strict
rima *f* rhyme; **~r** *v/i* to rhyme
rímel *m* mascara
rincón *m* corner; angle; remote place
rinoceronte *m* rhinoceros
riña *f* quarrel
riñón *m* kidney
río *m* river; stream; **~ abajo** downstream; **~ arriba** upstream
ripio *m* debris; rubbish; rubble; padding (*in speech or writing*)
riqueza *f* wealth; riches
risa *f* laugh; laughter; **morirse de ~** to laugh one's head off
risco *m* cliff, bluff
risueño pleasant; smiling
rítmico rhythmical
ritmo *m* rhythm
rito *m* rite
rival *m, f* rival; competitor; **~izar** *v/i* to compete; **~izar con** to rival
rivera *f* brook; creek
riz|ador *m* curling iron; **~ar** *v/t* to curl; to ripple; **~o** *m* curl; ripple; *aer* loop
robar *v/t* to rob; to plunder; to steal
roble *m* oak; **~do** *m* oak grove
robo *m* theft; robbery
robust|ecer *v/t* to strengthen; **~o** robust, strong; hardy
roca *f* rock
roce *m* friction; rubbing
rocia|da *f* sprinkling; spray; **~r** *v/t* to sprinkle; to spray
rocín *m* work horse, hack
rocío *m* dew
rockero *m fam* rocker; rock singer
rocoso rocky
roda *f mar* stem
rodaballo *m* turbot
roda|da *f* rut, wheel track; **~ja** *m* small wheel; disk; **~je** *m* set of wheels; *cine* shooting, filming; **~r** *v/i* to roll; to revolve; to run on wheels; **~r una película** to shoot a film
rode|ar *v/i* to make a detour; *v/t* to encompass; to surround; **~o** *m* roundabout way; detour; **ir por ~os** to beat around the bush
rodilla *f* knee; **de ~s** kneeling
rodillo *m* roller; rolling pin
roe|dor *a* gnawing; *m* rodent; **~r** *v/t* to gnaw; to nibble
roga|ción *f* request; **~r** *v/t* to beg; to ask, to request
rojizo reddish, ruddy
rol *m* roll, list; *teat* role, part
rojo red
rollizo plump; buxom
rollo *m* roll; cylinder; long, boring talk; **en ~** rolled (up)
roman|a *f* steelyard; **~o** *a, m* Roman
romance *m* Romance (*language*); ballad; **~ro** *m* ballad collection
romanticismo *m* romanticism
romántico romantic
romer|ía *f* pilgrimage; *fig* excursion; **~o** *m* pilgrim; *bot* rosemary
rompe|cabezas *m* puzzle; riddle; **~huelgas** *m* strike breaker; *fam* scab; **~olas** *m* breakwater; **~r** *v/t* to break; to break up; to break through; to tear; *v/i bot* to burst (open); **~r a** to begin to
ron *m* rum
roncar *v/i* to snore; to roar
ronco hoarse
ronda *f* round (*of cards, drinks etc*); beat (*of policeman*); **~r** *v/t, v/i* to patrol; to prowl
ron|quedad *f* hoarseness; **~quido** *m* snore
ronrone|ar *v/i* to purr; **~o** *m* purring
roñ|a *f* rust (*in metals*); scab (*in sheep*); crust (*of filth*); **~oso** scabby; filthy; *fam* mean, stingy
ropa *f* clothes; clothing; **~ blanca** linen; **~ de cama** bedclothes; **~ interior** underclothes; underwear; **a quema ~** point blank
ropero *m* wardrobe
rosa *f* rose; rose colo(u)r; **~do** pink; rose-colo(u)red; **~l** *m* rosebush; **~rio** *m* rosary
rosbif *m* roast beef
rosca *f* screw thread; (*turn of a*) spiral; ring, circle
roseta *f* nozzle (*of watering can*); rosette
rosquilla *f* ring-shaped pastry
rostro *m* face; aspect; countenance; *mar* beak; *zool* rostrum
rota|ción *f* rotation; **~tivo** rotary; revolving
roto broken; shattered; chipped; torn; **~r** *m* rotor
rótula *f* kneecap
rotulador *m* felt pen
rotular *v/t* to label; to mark
rótulo *m* sign; mark; label
rotundo round; forthright; categorical
rotura *f* fracture; break; **~r** *v/t* to break up (*new ground*)
roza|dura *f*, **~miento** *m* chafing; friction; **~r** *v/t* to scrape, to rub; to grub up; to graze; **~rse** to rub shoulders (*with*)
roznar *v/i* to bray
rubéola *f* German measles
rubí *m* ruby
rubi|a *f* blonde (*woman*); station wagon; **~o** blond; golden
ruborizarse to blush; to flush
rúbrica *f* red mark; flourish (*of signature*)
rubricar *v/t* to sign with flourish *or* initials
rud|eza *f* rudeness; **~o** rude
rueda *f* wheel; circle; **en ~** in a ring; **~ de prensa** press conference
ruego *m* request
rufián *m* ruffian, lout; pimp
rugi|do *m* bellow; roar; **~r** *v/i* to roar; to howl
ruibarbo *m* rhubarb
ruido *m* noise; din; **mucho ~ y pocas nueces** much ado about nothing; **~so** noisy
ruin mean; base; vile; **~a** *f* ruin; collapse; *pl* ruins; wreck; **~oso** ruinous, dilapidated; worthless
ruiseñor *m* nightingale
rul|eta *f* roulette; **~os** *m/pl* hair curlers; **~ota** *f* caravan, trailer
Rumania *f* Rumania
rumano(a) *a, m* (*f*) Rumanian
rumbo *m* direction; *mar* course; **ir con ~ a** to go in the direction of
rumiar *v/t* to ruminate
rumor *m* murmur, mutter; rumo(u)r
ruptura *f* break; rupture
rural rural; rustic
Rusia *f* Russia
ruso(a) *m* (*f*), *a* Russian
rústic|o rustic; rural; simple; **en ~a** paperback (*books*)
ruta *f* route
rutina *f* routine; **~rio** routine, everyday

S

S.A. = **Sociedad Anónima** Ltd., *Am* Inc.
sábado *m* Saturday; Sabbath
sabana *f LA* prairie, savannah
sábana *f* sheet (*for the bed*)
sabandija *f* bug; *pl* vermin
sabañón *m* chilblain
saber *v/t* to know; to know how to; to be able; **hacer ~** to inform; **~ de** to know about; **que yo sepa** to my knowledge; **~ a** *v/i* to taste of; to smack of; **a ~** namely; *m* knowledge; learning
sabi|duría *f* wisdom; **~o** wise; learned
sablazo *m* slash with a sword; *fam* sponging
sabor *m* taste; flavo(u)r; **~ear** *v/t* to savo(u)r; to taste
sabot|aje *m* sabotage; **~ear** *v/t* to sabotage
sabroso tasty; juicy; delicious
saca *f* taking out; extraction; exportation; **~corchos** *m* corkscrew; **~grapas** *m* staple puller; **~puntas** *m* pencil sharpener; **~r** *v/t* to take out; to draw out; to bring out; to extract; to get; to obtain; to turn out; to produce; **~r adelante** to bring up (*child*); to carry on
sacarina *f* saccharin
sacerdo|cio *m* priesthood, ministry; **~te** *m* priest
saciar *v/t* to satiate
saco *m* sack; bag; *LA* jacket; **~ de dormir** sleeping bag
sacramento *m* sacrament
sacrific|ar *v/t* to sacrifice; **~io** *m* sacrifice
sacrilegio *m* sacrilege
sacrist|án *m* sexton; **~ía** *f* vestry, sacristy
sacro holy; sacred; **~santo** sacrosanct
sacudi|da *f* shake; jerk; shock; blast; **~r** *v/t* to shake; to jerk; to rock; **~rse** to shake off; to get rid of
saeta *f* arrow; dart; hand of a clock; religious flamenco chant
sagaz astute; sagacious; shrewd
sagrado holy, sacred
sainete *m teat* short farce; one-act play
sajón(ona) *m* (*f*), *a* Saxon
sal *f* salt; wit; **~es** *pl* **aromáticas** smelling salts
sala *f* hall; large room; drawing room; **~ de espera** waiting room; **~ de estar** living room, sitting room; **~ de operaciones** operating room
sal|ado salted; salty; charming; *LA* unlucky; **~ar** *v/t* to salt; **~ario** *m* salary; wage
salaz salacious, prurient
salchich|a *f* pork sausage; **~ón** *m* salami
sald|ar *v/t com* to settle; to liquidate; **~o** *m com* balance; settlement; clearance; sale; **~o deudor** debit balance
salero *m* salt-cellar, salt shaker; *fam* wit; charm
salida *f* departure, start; exit, way out; rising (*of the sun*); *com* sales potential; outlet; **dar ~ a** to vent (*anger etc*); *com* to put on the market, to sell; **~ de emergencia** emergency exit
saliente protruding
salina *f* salt mine
salir *v/i* to go out; to leave; to depart; to appear; to rise (*sun*); to prove; to come out; **~ bien** to succeed; **~ para** to leave for; **~se** to overflow; to leak; **~se con la suya** to get one's own way
salitre *m* saltpetre, *Am* saltpeter
saliva *f* saliva, spittle
salmo *m* psalm
salmón *m* salmon
salmuera *f* brine
salón *m* salon, parlo(u)r; lounge; **~ de baile** ballroom; **~ de belleza** beauty parlo(u)r; **~ de té** tearoom
salpicadero *m aut* dashboard
salpicar *v/t* to splash; to spatter
salpullido *m med* rash
salsa *f* sauce; gravy
salta|montes *m* grasshopper; **~r** *v/i* to jump; to spring; to leap; to burst; *v/t* to skip; to jump over
saltea|dor *m* highwayman; robber; **~r** *v/t* to hold up
salto *m* leap; jump; hop; dive; **~ de agua** waterfall; **~ mortal** somersault
salu|bre healthy, salubrious; **~d** *f* health; well-being; *relig* salvation; **~dable** salutary; **~dar** *v/t* to greet; to salute; **~do** *m* greeting; **~dos** *m/pl* best wishes
salva *f mil* salvo
salva|ción *f* salvation; **~dor** *m* savio(u)r; rescuer; **~dor** *relig* Savio(u)r; **~guardia** *f* safe conduct; **~je** wild; savage; **~r** *v/t* to save; to rescue; **~rse** to escape; **~vidas** *m* life-belt
salvedad *f* reservation; proviso
salvia *f bot* sage
salvo *a* safe; *adv* save; except; **a ~** in safety; **~ que** unless; except that
salvoconducto *m* safe conduct
san (*apocope of* **santo,** *used before masculine names*) Saint; **~ Nicolás** Santa Claus
sanar *v/t* to cure, to heal
sanatorio *m* nursing home; sanatorium
sanc|ión *f* sanction; *sp* penalty; **~ionar** *v/t* to sanction
sandalia *f* sandal
sandía *f* watermelon
sanea|miento *m* drainage; sanitation; *for* guarantee; **~r** *v/t* to put in sewers; to repair; to drain (*land*); *for* to indemnify
sangr|ante bleeding; **~ar** *v/t, v/i* to bleed; **~e** *f* blood; **a ~e fría** in cold blood; **~ía** *f* bleeding; wine punch; **~iento** bloody; bloodstained
sanguijuela *f* leech
sanguíneo sanguinary
san|idad *f* health; public health; **~idad pública** public health; **~itario** sanitary; **~o** healthy; **~o y salvo** safe and sound
santa *f* female saint
santiamén: en un ~ in a jiffy
sant|idad *f* sanctity; holiness; **~ificar** *v/t* to sanctify; to consecrate; **~iguarse** to cross oneself; **~o** *a* holy, saintly; *m* saint; name's day, saint's day; **~o y seña** password; **~uario** *m* sanctuary
saña *f* fury
sapo *m* toad
saque *m* service (*tennis, etc*); **~ de meta** goal kick (*soccer*)
saque|ar *v/t* to plunder; **~o** *m* pillage; looting
sarampión *m* measles
sarcasmo *m* sarcasm
sarcófago *m* sarcophagus
sardina *f* sardine
sargento *m* sergeant
sarn|a *f* itch; *zool* mange; **~oso** mangy
sartén *f* frying pan
sastre *m* tailor
Satanás *m* Satan
satánico satanic
satélite *m* satellite
satén *m* satin
satinado glossy
sátira *f* satire
satírico satirical
satisfac|ción *f* satisfaction; **~er** *v/t* to satisfy; to gratify; to pay (*debts*); **~torio** satisfactory
saturar *v/t* to saturate
sauce *m* willow; **~ llorón** weeping willow
saúco *m* elder tree
savia *f* sap
sazón *f* ripeness; seasoning; opportunity; **a la ~** at that time; **en ~** ripe
sazonado seasoned; ripe; witty
se *pron 3rd person, m or f, sing or pl used as:* **1.** *reflexive pronoun* himself, herself, itself, themselves; **él ~ cortó** he cut himself; **ella ~ dijo** she said to herself; **2.** *reflexive verb:* **afeitarse** to shave oneself; **morirse** to die (*slowly*); **~ rompió la pierna** he broke his leg; **3.** *replacing the dative* le, les *of the pers pron when immediately followed by the accusative cases* lo, la, los, las: **~ las dí** I gave them to him (her, them); **4.** *the impersonal form* one; some; people; **~ dice** it is said; **~ sabe** it is known; **~ habla español** Spanish spoken; **~ perdió el dinero** the money was lost; **5.** each other, one another; **ellos ~ aman** they love each other
sebo *m* tallow, suet; grease
sec|a *f* drought; dry season; **~ador** *m* dryer; **~ano** *m* dry land; **~ante** *m* blotting paper; **~ar** *v/t* to dry (up)
secci|ón *f* section; **~ón transversal** cross-section; **~onar** *v/t* to divide up
secesión *f* secession
seco dry; curt; dull; bare; **a secas** plainly, simply, just
secre|ción *f* secretion; **~tar** *v/t* to secrete; **~tario(a)** *m* (*f*)

secretary; **~to** *m* secret; *a* secret; confidential
secta *f* sect; **~rio(a)** *m (f), a* sectarian
sector *m* sector; ~ ***privado*** *com* private sector
secuaz *m* follower; partisan
secuela sequel; aftermath
secuencia *f* sequence
secuestr|ar *v/t* to seize; to kidnap; **~o** *m* kidnapping
secular secular; age-old; **~izar** *v/t* to secularize
secundar *v/t* to second; to help; **~io** secondary
sed *f* thirst; ***tener*** ~ to be thirsty
seda *f* silk
seda|nte *m* sedative; *a* soothing; **~tivo** *m* sedative
sede *f* seat (*of government, etc*); *relig* see; ***la Santa*** ♀ the Holy See
sedería *f* silk shop; silks
sedici|ón *f* sedition; **~oso** seditious; mutinous
sediento thirsty
sedimento *m* sediment
sedoso silken, silky
seduc|ción *f* seduction; enticement; **~ir** *v/t* to seduce; to entice; **~tor** *m* seducer
sega|dora *f* reaper; mower; ***~dora trilladora*** *f agr* combine; **~r** *v/t* to mow; to reap
seglar *m* layman; *a* secular
segmento *m* segment
seguida: *en* ~ at once, immediately; **~mente** consecutively, successively
seguido *a* continued; successive; straight; ***3 días ~s*** 3 days in a row; *adv* ***todo*** ~ straight ahead
segui|dor *m* follower; **~r** *v/t* to follow; to chase; *v/i* to go on (*doing something*)
según *prep* according to; ~ ***lo que dice*** from what he says; *adv* depending on; ~ ***y como***, ~ ***y conforme*** depending on how; it depends
segund|ero *m* second hand (*of a watch or clock*); **~o** *a, m* second; ***de ~a clase*** second class; ***de ~a mano*** second-hand; ***en ~o lugar*** secondly
segur|amente surely; **~idad** *f* safety; security; **~o** *m com* insurance; ***~o de incendios*** fire insurance; ***~o de responsabilidad civil*** third-party insurance; *a* safe, secure; ***estar ~o de que*** to be sure that
seis six
selec|ción *f* selection; choice; **~cionar** *v/t* to select; **~tivo** selective; **~to** select; choice
selv|a *f* forest; jungle; **~ático** wild
sell|ar *v/t* to stamp; to seal; to conclude (*a treaty, etc*); **~o** *m* stamp; seal; ***~o de caucho*** *or* ***de goma*** rubber stamp; ***~o de correo*** postage stamp
semáforo *m* traffic light
semana *f* week; **~l** weekly; **~rio** *m* weekly paper
semblante *m* appearance; aspect; countenance, face
sembrar *v/t* to sow; to spread (*news*)
semeja|nte similar; like; **~nza** *f* resemblance, similarity; **~r** *v/i* to resemble
semen *m* semen; **~tal** *m* stud animal
semestr|al half-yearly; **~e** *m* semester; half-yearly pay
semi *prefix* half; semi; **~círculo** *m* semicircle; **~dormido** half asleep; **~esfera** *f* hemisphere
semilla *f* seed
seminario *m* seminary
semita *m* Semite
sémola *f* semolina
senado *m* senate; **~r** *m* senator
sencill|ez *f* simplicity; **~o** *a* simple; plain; frank; *m LA* small change
send|a *f*, **~ero** *m* footpath
sendos(as) one for each
senectud *f* old age
seno *m* bosom; breast; womb; *fig* bosom
sensaci|ón *f* sensation; feeling; emotion; **~onal** sensational
sensat|ez *f* good sense; **~o** sensible, wise
sensib|ilidad *f* sensibility; sensitivity; **~le** sensitive; emotional; susceptible; perceptible; *med* tender, sore
sensorio sensory
sensual sensual
sentado seated; settled; ***dar por*** ~ to take for granted
sentar *v/t* to seat; to set, to establish; *v/i* to fit; to suit; ~ ***bien*** to fit; to agree with (*food*); **~se** to sit down; ***¡siéntese!*** be seated!
sentencia *f for* sentence; dictum, saying; **~r** *v/t for* to sentence
sentido *m* sense; interpretation; direction; ***en cierto*** ~ in a sense; ***de doble*** ~ two-way (*traffic*); ~ ***común*** common sense; ***perder el*** ~ to lose consciousness
sentimental sentimental; emotional
sentimiento *m* sentiment; feeling; grief; regret
sentir *v/t* to feel; to experience; to perceive; to regret, to be sorry about; *m* feeling; **~se** to feel; to resent; *LA* to get angry
seña *f* sign; token; *pl* address; ***~s personales*** personal description; **~l** *f* sign; signal; mark; *com* deposit; ***~l de carretera*** road sign; ***~l digital*** fingerprint; **~lar** *v/t* to point out; to indicate; to mark
señor *m* gentleman; master; owner; lord; mister; sir; *pl* gentlemen; ***muy ~es nuestros*** dear sirs; **~a** *f* lady; mistress; madam; **~ear** *v/t* to dominate; **~ía** *f* lordship; **~il** lordly; noble; **~ío** *m* dominion; mastery; **~ita** *f* young lady; miss
señuelo *m* lure
separación *f* separation
separa|do separate; ***por ~do*** separately; **~r** *v/t* to separate; to sort; to remove
septentrional northern
septiembre, setiembre *m* September
sepulcro *m* tomb; sepulchre, *Am* sepulcher
sepult|ar *v/t* to bury; **~ura** *f* burial; tomb; grave
sequ|edad *f* dryness; barrenness; curtness; **~ía** *f* drought
séquito *m* retinue, entourage
ser *v/i* to be; to exist; ***de ~ así*** if so; ***a no ~ por*** were it not for; ***es que*** the fact is that; ***sea lo que sea*** be that as it may; *m* essence; being; ~ ***humano*** human being
seren|ar *v/t* to calm; **~arse** to calm down; **~ata** *f* serenade; **~idad** *f* serenity; composure; **~o** *a* calm; composed, serene; *m* night watchman
seri|al *m radio, TV* serial; **~e** *f* series; ***en ~e*** mass (*production*)
serio serious; sober; grave; ***en*** ~ in earnest; seriously
sermón *m* sermon
serp|entear *v/i* to wind; to meander; **~iente** *f* serpent, snake; ***~iente de cascabel*** rattlesnake
serranía *f* mountainous region
serr|ar *v/t* to saw; **~ín** *m* sawdust
servi|ble useful; **~cial** obliging; **~cio** *m* service; good turn; ***de ~cio*** *mil* on duty; **~cios** *pl* restrooms, lavatories; ***~cios públicos*** public utilities; **~dor** *m* servant; ***su seguro ~dor*** yours truly; **~dumbre** *f* (staff of) servants; servitude; **~l** slavish; menial
servilleta *f* table napkin
servir *v/t* to serve; to oblige; *v/i* to be in service; **~se** to help oneself
sesg|ar *v/t* to cut obliquely; **~o** *m* slant; (*sewing*) bias; ***al ~o*** obliquely; on the bias
sesión *f* session; sitting; ***levantar la*** ~ to adjourn
seso *m* brain; sense; judgment; ***devanarse los ~s*** to rack one's brains
seta *f* mushroom
seto *m* hedge; ~ ***vivo*** quickset hedge
seud|o pseudo; **~ónimo** *m* pseudonym
sever|idad *f* severity; **~o** severe
sex|o *m* sex; **~ual** sexual; **~ualidad** *f* sexuality
si *m mús* si, ti, B note; *conj* if; when; whether; ***como*** ~ as if; ~ ***bien*** although; ~ ***no*** if not; otherwise
sí *pron, reflexive form of the third person*: himself, herself, itself, oneself, themselves; ***de por*** ~ on its own account; by itself; ***fuera de*** ~ beside oneself; ***volver en*** ~ to regain consciousness
sí *adv* yes; indeed; ***por ~ o por no*** in any case; ***¡eso ~ que no!*** absolutely not
siderurgia *f* siderurgy, iron and steel industry
sidra *f* cider
siega *f* harvesting
siembra *f* sowing
siempre always; ever; ~ ***que*** whenever; provided that; ***como*** ~ as usual; ***lo de*** ~ the usual; ***para*** ~ for ever, for good
sien *f anat* temple
sierpe *f* serpent
sierra *f* saw; mountain range
siesta *f* hottest time of the day; afternoon nap; siesta
siete seven
sífilis *f* syphilis
sifón *m* siphon
sigilo *m* secrecy
sigla *f* symbol, abbreviation
siglo *m* century
signa|rse to cross oneself; **~tura** *f* library number; *impr* signature
significa|ción *f*, **~do** *m* significance; meaning, sense; **~r** *v/t* to mean; to indicate; **~tivo** significant
signo *m* sign; symbol; ~ ***de admiración*** exclamation point; ~ ***de interrogación*** question mark; ~ ***de puntuación*** punctuation mark
siguiente following; next
sílaba *f* syllable
silba|r *v/t* to hiss at; *v/i* to whistle; **~tina** *f LA* catcall; **~to** *m* whistle
silenci|ador *m* silencer; *tecn* muffler; **~o** *m* silence; **~oso** silent; soundless
silueta *f* outline; silhouette
silv|estre wild; rustic; **~icultura** *f* forestry
sill|a *f* chair; saddle; ***~a plegadiza*** camp stool; ***~a de ruedas*** wheelchair; **~ón** *m* easy chair, armchair
sima *f* abyss
símbolo *m* symbol
simetría *f* symmetry
simiente *f* seed
símil like, similar
simil|ar similar; **~itud** *f* similarity, resemblance
simpatía *f* liking
simpático attractive; nice
simpatizar *v/i* to have a liking for; to sympathize
simpl|e simple; mere; ordinary; **~eza** *f* simplicity; stupidity; **~icidad** *f* simplicity; **~ificar** *v/t* to simplify
simular *v/t* to simulate, to pretend
simultáneo simultaneous
sin without; ~ ***embargo*** nevertheless, however
sinagoga *f* synagogue
sincero sincere
sincronizar *v/t* to synchronize
sindica|lismo *m* syndicalism; **~to** *m* syndicate; trade union
sinfín *m* endless amount, great number
sinfonía *f* symphony
singular *a* unique; singular; extraordinary; *m gram* singular
siniestr|ado damaged; hurt in an accident; ***zona ~ada*** disaster area; **~o** *a* sinister; *m* disaster; catastrophe, accident
sinnúmero *m* great number *or* amount
sino *m* fate; *conj* but; except; only; ***no sólo ...*** ~ not only ... but
sinónimo *m* synonym
sinrazón *f* wrong; injustice
sinsabor *m* trouble; insipidness
sintaxis *f* syntax
sintético synthetic
síntoma *m* symptom
sintonizar (con) *v/t* to tune in
sinvergüenza *m, f* scoundrel, brazen person
sionismo *m* Zionism
siquiera *adv, conj* at least; even; although, even though; ***ni*** ~ not even
sirena *f* siren; mermaid
sirvient|a *f* maid servant, housemaid; **~e** *m* servant
sisa *f* pilfering; **~r** *v/t* to pilfer; to take in (*dresses*)
sistem|a *m* system; **~ático** systematic
siti|ar *v/t* to lay siege to, to besiege; **~o** *m* siege; place, spot; site
situa|ción *f* situation; **~r** *v/t* to situate; to place; to locate
so under; below; ~ ***pena de*** under penalty of
sobaco *m* armpit
sobar *v/t* to knead; to handle; to fondle; *LA* to flatter
soberan|ía *f* sovereignty; **~o(a)** *m (f), a* sovereign
soberbi|a *f* pride; haughtiness; **~o** haughty; arrogant
soborn|ar *v/t* to bribe; to corrupt; **~o** *m* bribery
sobra *f* surplus; **~dillo** *m arq* penthouse, sloping roof; **~r** *v/t* to exceed; *v/i* to be left over; to be more than enough
sobre *m* envelope; *prep* on; upon; on top of; over; above; about; ~ ***las tres*** about three o'clock; ~ ***todo*** above all
sobrecama *m* bedspread
sobrecarg|ar *v/t* to overload; to overcharge; **~o** *m mar* supercargo
sobrecejo *m* frown
sobrecoger *v/t* to startle
sobrecubierta *f* jacket (*of book*)
sobredicho above mentioned
sobredosis *f* overdose
sobre(e)ntender *v/t* to understand; to infer
sobrehumano superhuman
sobremanera exceedingly
sobremesa *f* tablecloth; after the meal
sobrenatural supernatural
sobreocupación *f* overbooking
sobrepasar *v/t* to surpass
sobrepeso *m* overweight
sobreponer *v/t* to superimpose
sobreprecio *m* surcharge
sobrepujar *v/t* to surpass; to outdo
sobresali|ente outstanding; **~r** *v/i* to excel(l); to protude
sobresalt|ar *v/t* to startle; to frighten; **~o** *m* sudden fright; shock
sobrestante *m* overseer, supervisor; foreman
sobrestimar *v/t* to overrate
sobretiempo *m* overtime
sobretodo *m* overcoat
sobrevenir *v/i* to happen unexpectedly
sobrevivi|ente *a* surviving; *m* survivor; **~r** *v/t, v/i* to survive; to outlive
sobriedad *f* sobriety, temperance
sobrin|a *f* niece; **~o** *m* nephew
sobrio sober; temperate
socarrón cunning; sly; mocking
socav|ar *v/t* to undermine; **~ón** *m arq* sudden collapse; *min* tunnel
soci|able sociable; friendly; **~al** social; **~alismo** *m* socialism; **~alista** *m, f, a* socialist; **~alizar** *v/t* to socialize; **~edad** *f* society; company; ***alta ~edad*** high society; ***~edad anónima*** *com* joint stock company; ***~edad de control*** holding company; **~o** *m* partner; member; ***~o comanditario*** *com* silent partner; ***~o de honor*** honorary member; ***~o de número*** full member; **~ología** *f* sociology
socorr|er *v/t* to help; **~o** *m* help
soez vulgar, coarse, base
sofá *m* sofa
sofisticado sophisticated
sofoc|ar *v/t* to choke, to smother; to stifle; to suffocate; to extinguish; **~o** *m* suffocation; *fig* embarrassment
soga *f* rope
soja *f* soya
sojuzgar *v/t* to subdue
sol *m* sun; sunlight; ***tomar el*** ~ to sunbathe
solamente only
solapa *f* lapel; **~do** deceitful, sly
solar *m* plot, building site; manor house; **~iego** ancestral (*of house*)
solaz *m* solace; relaxation
soldado *m* soldier; ~ ***raso*** buck private
solda|dura *f* soldering, welding; **~r** *v/t* to solder, to weld
soleado sunny
soledad *f* solitude, loneliness; lonely place
solemne solemn
solemnizar *v/t* to solemnize; to celebrate
soler *v/i* to be accustomed to; ***suele venir temprano*** he usually comes early

Spanish

Spanish

solera *f* prop, support; ***vino de ~*** vintage wine
solicitar *v/t* to petition; to apply for
solícito solicitous
solicitud *f* application (*for a job, post*); **a ~** on request, on demand
solid|aridad *f* solidarity; **~ez** *f* solidity
sólido solid; stable; hard
soliloquio *m* soliloquy
solista *m, f mús* soloist
solitari|a *f* tapeworm; **~o** solitary
solo *a* alone; *m mús* solo
sólo only
solomillo *m* sirloin
soltar *v/t* to unfasten; to release; **~se** to get loose; **~se a** to begin to
solter|o(a) *a* unmarried; *m* (*f*) bachelor; spinster; **~ón** *m* old bachelor; **~ona** *f* old maid, spinster
soltura *f* ease; agility
solu|ble soluble; **~ción** *f* solution; **~cionar** *v/t* to solve
solven|cia *f* solvency; **~te** solvent
solloz|ar *v/i* to sob; **~o** *m* sob, sobbing
sombr|a *f* shadow; shade; darkness; **~ear** *v/t* to shade, to overshadow; **~erera** *f* hatbox; **~erería** *f* hat shop; millinery; **~ero** *m* hat; ***~ero de copa*** top hat, silk hat; **~ía** *f* shady spot; **~illa** *f* parasol; sunshade; **~ío** gloomy; shady
somero superficial; brief
someter *v/t* to submit
somnámbulo *m* sleepwalker
somnífero *m* sleeping pill
son *m* sound; tune; **a ~ de** to the sound of
sond|a *f mar* lead, sounding line; *med* probe; **~ear** *v/t* to sound; to explore; to probe; **~eo** *m* sounding; poll, survey
soneto *m* sonnet
sónico sonic
sonido *m* sound
sonor|o sonorous, resonant; clear; *gram* voiced; ***banda ~a*** sound track
sonr|eír *v/i*, **~eírse** to smile; **~isa** *f* smile
sonrojar *v/t* to make blush; **~se** to blush
sonsonete *m* singsong voice; rhythmical raps *or* taps
soñ|ar *v/t, v/i* to dream; **~oliento** sleepy, drowsy
sop|a *f* soup; **~era** *f* soup tureen
sopl|ar *v/i* to blow; *fam* to squeal; **~ete** *m* blowtorch; **~o** *m* puff; gust; blow; **~ón** *m* informer
soport|ar *v/t* to support; to hold up; to endure; to bear; **~e** *m* support
sorb|er *v/t* to suck; to absorb; **~o** *m* sip
sordera *f* deafness
sórdido sordid; nasty, dirty
sordo deaf; *gram* unvoiced; **~mudo(a)** *m* (*f*) deaf-mute
soroche *m LA* altitude sickness
sorprende|nte surprising; **~r** *v/t* to surprise
sorpresa *f* surprise
sorteo *m* raffle; drawing (*of lottery, tickets*)
sortija *f* finger ring
sosa *f quím* soda
sosegar *v/t* to calm
sosiego *m* tranquil(l)ity; quiet
soslayo: al ~ sideways; obliquely; sidelong (*glance*)
soso insipid; dull
sospech|a *f* suspicion; **~ar** *v/t, v/i* to suspect; **~oso** suspicious
sostén *m* support; upkeep; brassière
sosten|er *v/t* to support; to hold (*opinion, conversation, etc*); **~erse** to support oneself; **~imiento** *m* support; maintenance
sota *f* jack; knave (*in cards*)
sotana *f* cassock
sótano *m* cellar; basement
soto *m* grove, thicket
soviético Soviet
su *pron poss 3rd pers m, f sing* (*pl* **sus**) his, her, its, your, their; one's
suav|e smooth; soft; **~idad** *f* smoothness; softness; **~izar** *v/t* to soften
subalterno *a, m* subordinate; auxiliary
subarr|endar *v/t* to sublet; **~iendo** *m for* sublease
subasta *f* auction
subconsciencia *f* subconscious
subdesarrollado underdeveloped
súbdito(a) *m* (*f*) subject
subibaja *f* seesaw
subi|da *f* climb; rise; increase; **~do** deep, bright (*colo[u]r*); **~r** *v/i* to go up; to rise; to move up; *v/t* to raise; to lift up; to go up; **~rse a, en** to get on, into
súbit|amente, ~o all of a sudden
subjuntivo *m* subjunctive
subleva|ción *f* insurrection, uprising; **~rse** to rebel
sublime sublime
submarin|ismo *m* scuba diving; **~o** *m* submarine; *a* underwater
subordinar *v/t* to subordinate; to subject
subproducto *m* by-product
subrayar *v/t* to underline; to emphasize
subsanar *v/t* to correct; to compensate for; to excuse
subscribir *v/t* to subscribe to; to endorse; *com* to underwrite
subsidi|arias *f/pl* feeder industries; **~ario** subsidiary; **~o** *m* subsidy; ***~o de paro*** unemployment insurance
subsiguiente subsequent
subsist|encia *f* subsistence; **~ir** *v/i* to live, to subsist; to endure
substancia *f* substance; essence; **~l** substantial; considerable
substitu|ir *v/t* to substitute; **~to(a)** *m* (*f*), *a* substitute
subterfugio *m* subterfuge
subterráneo subterranean
subtítulo *m* subtitle; caption
suburb|ano suburban; **~io** *m* suburb
subvención *f* subsidy; grant
subversivo subversive
succión *f* suction
suce|der *v/i* to succeed; to follow; to occur; **~sión** *f* succession; issue; **~sivo** successive; **~so** *m* event; incident; outcome; **~sor** *m* successor
suci|edad *f* dirtiness; dirt; **~o** dirty
suculento succulent; luscious
sucumbir *v/i* to succumb; to yield
sucursal *f* branch office; subsidiary
sud *m* south; **~americano** South American
sudadera *f LA* jogging suit
sudar *v/i* to perspire; to sweat
sud|este *m* southeast; **~oeste** *m* southwest
sudor *m* sweat
Suecia *f* Sweden
sueco(a) *m* (*f*) Swede; *a* Swedish
suegr|a *f* mother-in-law; **~o** *m* father-in-law
sueldo *m* salary; wage
suelo *m* soil, earth; ground; floor; land; bottom
suelto *a* loose; free; detached; *m* loose change
sueño *m* sleep; dream; ***conciliar el ~*** to get to sleep; ***tener ~*** to be sleepy
suero *m* serum; whey
suerte *f* fate, destiny; luck; ***echar ~s*** to draw lots; ***mala ~*** hard luck
suéter *m* sweater
sufijo *m* suffix
sufrag|ar *v/t* to defray; to assist; **~io** *m* franchise; suffrage
sufri|do long-suffering; patient; **~miento** *m* suffering; tolerance, patience; **~r** *v/t* to suffer; to put up with
sugerir *v/t* to suggest
sugestivo suggestive
suicid|a *m, f* suicide; **~arse** to commit suicide; **~io** *m* suicide
Suiza *f* Switzerland
suizo(a) *m* (*f*), *a* Swiss
sujetador *m* fastener; clip; brassière
sujetapapeles *m* (paper) clip
sujet|ar *v/t* to secure, to hold; to subject; **~o** *m* subject; topic
sulfúrico sulfuric
suma *f* sum; **en ~** in short; **~mente** extremely, highly; **~r** *v/t* to summarize; to amount to; to add up to; **~rio** summary
sumergi|ble submergible; **~r** *v/t*, **~rse** to submerge; to sink
suministr|ar *v/t* to supply; **~o** *m* supply
sumi|sión *f* submission; **~so** submissive; obedient
sumo supreme; extreme; ***a lo ~*** at the most
suntu|ario luxury; **~oso** sumptuous, luxurious
supera|ble surmountable; **~r** *v/t* to exceed; to surmount; to surpass
superávit *m com* surplus
superfici|al superficial; **~e** *f* surface
superfluo superfluous
superhombre *m* superman
superintendente *m* superintendent; overseer
superior *m* superior; *a* better; finer; superior; **~idad** *f* superiority
superlativo *a, m* superlative
supermercado *m* supermarket
supersónico supersonic
supersticioso superstitious
supervivencia *f* survival
suplantar *v/t* to supplant
suplement|ario supplementary; **~o** *m* supplement; ***~o dominical*** Sunday newspaper supplement
súplica *f* entreaty; petition
suplicar *v/t* to implore
suplicio *m* torture; torment
suplir *v/t* to supplement; to replace
suponer *v/t* to suppose; to assume
suprem|acía *f* supremacy; **~o** supreme
supr|esión *f* suppression; **~imir** *v/t* to suppress; to abolish; to eliminate
supuesto supposed; assumed; ***por ~*** of course
supurar *v/i* to suppurate, to fester
sur *m* south
surc|ar *v/t* to furrow; **~o** *m* furrow; groove
surgir *v/i* to spout; to issue forth; to arise
surti|do *m* assortment; *a* assorted; **~dor** *m* fountain; jet; ***~dor de gasolina*** gas pump; **~r** *v/t* to supply; to stock; ***~r efecto*** to produce the desired effect; *v/i* to spout
susceptib|ilidad *f* susceptibility; **~le** susceptible; touchy; sensitive
suscitar *v/t* to stir up
suscribir *v/t* to subscribe
susodicho aforesaid
suspen|der *v/t* to suspend; to hang up; to fail; **~sión** *f* suspension; **~so** suspended; amazed
suspicacia *f* distrust; suspicion
suspir|ar *v/i* to sigh; **~o** *m* sigh
sustan|cia *f* substance; **~tivo** *m* substantive
sustent|ar *v/t* to support; to maintain; **~o** *m* maintenance; sustenance
sustitu|ir *v/t* to substitute; to replace; **~to(a)** *m* (*f*), *a* substitute
susto *m* fright; shock
sustra|cción *f* subtraction; **~er** *v/t* to subtract; to deduct
susurr|ar *v/i* to whisper; to murmur; to rustle; **~o** *m* whisper
sutil subtle; fine, thin; **~eza** *f* subtlety; artifice
sutura *f med* suture
suyo(a) (*pl* **suyos, as**) *pron pos 3rd person, m and f*, his, hers, theirs, one's; his own, her own, their own; **de ~** in itself; ***salirse con la suya*** to get one's way

T

tabaco *m* tobacco
tábano *m* horsefly, gadfly
tabern|a *f* tavern; inn; **~ero** *m* innkeeper
tabique *m* partition wall
tabl|a *f* board; plank; slab; list; *mat* table; ***a raja ~a*** at any price; ruthlessly; ***~a a vela*** surfboard; ***~a de materias*** contents (*of book, etc*); ***~a de multiplicar*** multiplication table; ***~a de planchar*** ironing board; **~ado** *m* wooden platform; stage; **~ero** *m* planking; board; counter; drawing board; ***~ero de instrumentos*** dashboard; **~eta** *f* tablet; lozenge; **~illa** *f* small board; *med* splint; **~ón** *m* thick plank; beam; ***~ón de anuncios*** notice board, *Am* bulletin board
tabú *m* taboo
taburete *m* stool
tacaño stingy, niggardly
tacita *f* small cup
tácito tacit
taciturno taciturn; silent; melancholy
taco *m* stopper; plug; wad (*in cannon*); billiard cue; calendar pad; pad (*of paper or tickets*); *fam* curse word; ***echar ~s*** *fam* to swear heavily
tacón *m* heel
tacon|azo *m* clicking of the heels; **~ear** *v/i fam* to walk with a tapping of the heels
táctica *f* tactics; gambit
tacto *m* tact; sense of touch; feel
tach|a *f* defect; fault; stain; flaw; ***sin ~a*** flawless; **~ar** *v/t* to find fault with; to cross out (*writing*); **~ón** *m* deleting mark (*in writing*); **~uela** *f* tack
tafetán *m* taffeta
tahur *m* gambler
taimado crafty, shifty
taj|a *f* cut; **~da** *f* slice; *fam* hoarseness; **~r** *v/t* to cut; to chop
tajo *m* cut; gash; cleft, ravine
tal (*pl* **tales**) such, so as; certain; so; thus; ***~ cual*** such as; ***~ vez*** maybe, perhaps; ***con ~ que*** provided that; ***¿ qué ~?*** how are you?; ***un ~ González*** a certain Gonzalez
tala *f* felling of trees; *fig* destruction
taladr|ar *v/t* to bore; to drill; **~o** *m* borer; gimlet, drill
talar *v/t* to fell (*trees*); *fig* to devastate
talco *m* talc; talcum powder
taleg|a *f* bag; sack; *pl* fortune; **~o** *m* bag, sack
talento *m* talent; **~so** gifted
talón *m* heel (*of foot*); *com* coupon; voucher; stub
talonario *m* stub book
talla *f* carving; sculpture; height; cut (*of diamond*); **~do** carved; **~r** *v/t* to carve; to cut (*precious stones*); to value; to appraise; **~rín** *m* noodle
talle *m* figure; waist; **~r** *m* workshop; ***~r de reparaciones*** repair shop
tallo *m* stalk; stem
tamaño *m* size
tambalear *v/i* to stagger, to totter; to sway, to lurch
también also; too; as well
tambor *m* drum; *anat* eardrum; drummer; **~ilear** *v/i* to drum (*with the fingers*); (*rain*) to patter
Támesis *m* Thames
tamiz *m* fine sieve; **~ar** *v/t* to sift
tampoco neither; not either
tan (*apocope of* **tanto**) so; such; as; ***~ grande como*** as big as; ***~ sólo*** only; ***¡qué cosa ~ bonita!*** what a beautiful thing!
tanda *f* turn; shift; relay
tang|ente *f* tangent; **~ible** tangible
tanque *m* tank; reservoir
tante|ar *v/t* to test; to measure; to examine; *v/i* to keep the score; **~o** *m* calculation; score (*in games*); **al ~o** by guesswork
tanto *a* so much; as much; *pl* so many; as many; ***~ como*** as much as; *adv* so much; so long; so far; so often; ***no es para ~*** it's not that bad; ***por lo ~*** therefore; ***~ más*** all the more; ***~ mejor*** all the better; *m* certain quantity *or* sum; so much; point *or* score (*in games*); *com* rate; ***~ por ciento*** percentage; ***otro ~*** as much more; ***estar al ~*** to be informed; *conj* ***con ~ que*** provided that; ***en ~ que*** while
tapa *f* lid; cover; cap; flap (*of envelope*); cover (*of book*); **~cubos** *m* hubcap; **~dera** *f* lid; cover; **~r** *v/t* to cover; to cover up; to put a lid on; to stop up (*hole*)
tapete *m* rug
tapia *f* mud wall
tapicería *f* tapestry
tapiz *m* tapestry; **~ado** *m* upholstery; **~ar** *v/t* to hang with tapestry; to upholster; to carpet
tapón *m* plug; stopper
taquigrafía *f* shorthand
taquígrafo(a) *m* (*f*) stenographer
taquil|la *f* booking office; box office; **~lero** *m* booking clerk
taquimecanógrafa *f* shorthand typist

taquímetro *m* speedometer
tara *f com* tare
tara|cear *v/t* to inlay; **~rear** *v/t* to hum (*a tune*)
tarda|nza *f* delay; **~r** *v/i* to be late; to take a long time; **a más ~r** at the latest
tarde *f* afternoon; **¡buenas ~s!** good afternoon!, good evening!; *adv* late; too late; **de ~ en ~** from time to time; **~ o temprano** sooner or later
tardío late; slow
tarea *f* task; job; duty
tarifa *f* tariff
tarima *f* platform; dais
tarjeta *f* card; **~ de crédito** credit card; **~ de embarque** boarding card; **~ de identidad** identity card; **~ de visita** visiting card; **~ postal** postcard
tarro *m* jar; *LA* top hat
tarta *f* tart; cake; **~ nupcial** wedding cake
tartamudear *v/i* to stammer
tasa *f* rate; assessment; measure; **a ~ de** at the rate of; **~ción** *f* valuation; **~r** *v/t* to rate, to tax; to fix a price for
tatas: andar a ~ to go on all fours
tatuaje *m* tattoo(ing)
taurino bullfighting
taxi *m* taxi cab; **~sta** *m* taxi driver
taz|a *f* cup; cupful; **~ón** *m* large cup; bowl; basin
té *m* tea
te *pron pers and refl* you; to you; yourself (*familiar*) *form*)
tea *f* torch
teatro *m* theatre, *Am* theater; **~ de títeres** Punch and Judy show
tebeos *m/pl* comics
tecl|a *f* key (*of the piano, typewriter, etc*); **~ado** *m* keyboard
técnic|a *f* technique; **~o** *m* technician; *a* technical
tecnología *f* technology
tecnólogo *m* technologist
tech|ado *m* roof; **~ar** *v/t* to roof; **~o** *m*, **~umbre** *f* ceiling; roof
tej|a *f* tile; **~ado** *m* (*tiled*) roof; **~ar** *v/t* to tile
tej|edor *m* weaver; **~er** *v/t* to weave; *LA* to knit; **~ido** *m* texture; fabric, cloth
tejo *m* yew tree
tejón *m* badger
tela *f* cloth, fabric; film; **~s** *pl* **del corazón** heartstrings; **~r** *m* loom; **~raña** *f* spider's web, cobweb
tele = **televisión**
telediario *m TV* daytime news program
teledirigido remote controlled
teleférico *m* cable railway
telefonazo *m* ring, telephone call
telefonear *v/t*, *v/i* to telephone
telefonema *m* telephone message
telefónico telephonic
teléfono *m* telephone; **llamar por ~** to telephone
telegrafiar *v/t* to wire; to cable
telegráfico telegraphic
telégrafo *m* telegraph
telegrama *m* telegram, cable
teleimpresor *m* teleprinter
telenovela *f* soap opera
telepático telepathic
telesc|ópico telescopic; **~opio** *m* telescope
telesilla *f* chair lift
telesquí *m* ski lift
televi|dente *m* TV viewer; **~sar** *v/t* to televise; **~sión** *f* television; **ver (por) ~sión** to watch television; **~sión por cable** cable TV; **~sor** *m* television set
telón *m teat* curtain
tema *m* subject; theme; topic
tembl|ar *v/i* to tremble; **~or** *m* tremor; trembling; **~or de tierra** earthquake; **~oroso** trembling; shaky
tem|er *v/t*, *v/i* to fear; **~erario** reckless; rash; **~eridad** *f* rashness; **~eroso** timorous; **~ible** dreadful; **~or** *m* fear
tempera|mento *m* temperament; **~ncia** *f* temperance; **~r** *v/t* to temper; to moderate; **~tura** *f* temperature
tempes|tad *f* storm; tempest; **~tuoso** stormy
templa|do temperate; moderate; lukewarm, tepid; mild; *mús* in tune; **~nza** *f* temperance; mildness; **~r** *v/t* to temper; to moderate; *mús* to tune
temple *m* state of weather; mood; temper (*of metals*)
templo *m* temple; church
temporada *f* season; **~ alta** high season
temporal *m* stormy weather; *a* temporary
temprano early
tena|cidad *f* tenacity; **~cillas** *f/pl* curling tongs; **~z** tenacious; tough; resistant; **~zas** *f/pl* forceps; pincers
tendedero *m* clothesline
tende|ncia *f* tendency; **~r** *v/i* to tend; to incline; *v/t* to stretch; to spread; to hang out (*washing*); **~r la mano** to reach out one's hand; **~rse** to stretch oneself out; to lie down
ténder *m fc* tender
tender|ete *m* booth; (market) stand; **~o** *m* shopkeeper
tendón *m* sinew; tendon
tenebros|idad *f* gloom; darkness; **~o** dismal; dark; gloomy
tenedor *m* fork; holder, bearer; **~ de libros** bookkeeper
tener *v/t* to have; to possess; to own; **~ dos años** to be two years old; **~ en mucho** to esteem; **~ entendido** to understand; **~ presente** to bear in mind; **~ por** to take for; **~ que** to have to
tenia *f* tapeworm
teniente *m* lieutenant
tenis *m* tennis
tenor *m* tenor, tone; *mús* tenor
tensión *f* tension; stress; rigidity; **~ sanguínea** blood pressure
tentación *f* temptation
tentáculo *m* tentacle; feeler
tenta|dor tempting; **~r** *v/t* to touch, to feel; to grope for; to tempt; **~tiva** *f* try, attempt; **~tivo** tentative
tenue thin; tenuous
teñir *v/t* to dye; to tinge
teología *f* theology
teor|ético theoretical; **~ía** *f* theory
tepe *m* sod
terapéutico therapeutic
tercer|mundista (of the) Third World; **~ mundo** *m* Third World
terciopelo *m* velvet
terco obstinate
tergiversar *v/t* to misrepresent; to twist (*words*)
termal thermal
termina|ción *f* termination; **~nte** final; categorical, definite; **~r** *v/t*, *v/i* to finish; **~rse** to end
término *m* end; ending; conclusion; term; expression; landmark; **~ medio** average; middle way; **~ técnico** technical term; **en primer ~** in the first place; **en último ~** finally
termo *m* thermos (*flask*)
termómetro *m* thermometer
terner|a *f* heifer calf; veal; **~o** *m* bull calf
terno *m* suit (*of clothes*); set of three
ternura *f* tenderness
terraplén *m* embankment
terrateniente *m* land owner
terraza *f* terrace
terremoto *m* earthquake
terreno *m* ground; soil; terrain
terrestre earthly; terrestrial
terrible frightful; terrible
terrífico terrifying
territori|al territorial; **~o** *m* territory
terrón *m* clod; patch of ground; lump
terror *m* terror; dread; **película de ~** horror film; **~ífico** terrifying; **~ismo** *m* terrorism; **~ista** *m* terrorist
terso smooth
tertulia *f* small party, gathering
tesis *f* thesis; **~ doctoral** doctoral dissertation
tesón *m* insistence; tenacity
tesor|ería *f* treasury; exchequer; **~ero** *m* treasurer; **~o** *m* treasure
testa|mento *m* will; **~r** *v/i* to make a will
testarudo obstinate; stubborn
testículo *m* testicle
testi|ficar *v/t* to testify; to depose; **~go** *m* witness; **~go ocular** eyewitness; **~monio** *m* testimony
teta *f* breast; teat; nipple
tetera *f* teapot, teakettle
tétrico gloomy; sullen
textil textile
texto *m* text
textura *f* texture
tez *f* complexion; skin
ti *pron 2nd pers sing* you
tía *f* aunt
tibia *f* tibia
tibio lukewarm
tiburón *m* shark
tiempo *m* time; period; epoch; weather; *gram* tense; *mús* time, tempo; **a ~** in time; **a su ~** in due course; **hace buen ~** it is fine (weather); **hace ~** some time ago; **~ libre** free time
tienda *f* shop; tent; **~ de campaña** army tent
tienta *f med* probe; cleverness; sagacity; **andar a ~s** to grope
tiento *m* feel; touch; tact; wariness
tierno tender; affectionate
tierra *f* earth; world; land; country; **tomar ~** *aer* to land; **~ adentro** inland; **~ firme** mainland; **♀ Santa** Holy Land
tieso stiff, rigid; taut
tiesto *m* flower pot
tifo *m* typhus
tifoidea *f* typhoid fever
tifón *m* typhoon
tifus *m* typhus
tigre *m* tiger; **~sa** *f* tigress
tijeras *f/pl* scissors
tijeretear *v/t* to snip, to cut
tild|ar *v/t* to cross out; *fig* to brand as; **~e** *f* tilde (*as in ñ*)
tilo *m* linden
tim|ador *m* swindler; **~ar** *v/t* to cheat; to swindle
timbal *m* kettledrum
timbr|ar *v/t* to stamp; **~e** *m* stamp; bell; timbre (*of voice*); **~e de alarma** alarm bell
timidez *f* timidity
tímido timid, shy
timo *m* swindle
timón *m mar, aer* helm; rudder
timonel *m* steersman, coxswain
tímpano *m* kettledrum; eardrum
tina *f* large jar; vat; tub
tinglado *m* shed; *fam* scheme
tinieblas *f/pl* darkness
tino *m* skill, knack; **a buen ~** by guesswork; **sin ~** immoderately; foolishly
tint|a *f* ink; dye; tint; shade; **saber de buena ~a** *fam* to have on good authority; **~e** *m* dyeing; tint; **~ero** *m* inkwell
tintín *m* tinkle; jingle
tintinear *v/t* to tinkle; to jingle; to clink
tinto *a* dyed; stained; *m* red wine; **~rería** *f* dyer's shop; dry cleaner's; **~rero** *m* dyer
tintura *f* dye; stain; tincture; smattering; **~ de yodo** iodine
tío *m* uncle; fellow
tiovivo *m* merry-go-round
típico typical
tiple *m* soprano, treble
tipo *m* type; model; *com* rate (*of interest, exchange, etc*); *fam* fellow; **~grafía** *f* printing; typography
tira *f* long strip; strap; **~ y afloja** tug-of-war
tira|da *f* throw; cast; distance; printing, edition; **~do** dirt cheap; **~dor** *m* shooter; marksman
tiran|ía *f* tyranny; **~o** *m* tyrant
tirante *m* strap; brace; *a* tense; *pl* braces, *Am* suspenders; **~z** *f* tautness; tension
tirar *v/t* to throw, to fling; to throw away; to fire (*a shot*); *v/i* to pull; to attract; **~ de** to pull
tiritar *v/i* to shiver
tiro *m* throw; shot; length; range; **errar el ~** to miss one's aim; **~ al blanco** target practice; **~ con arco** archery
tiroides *m anat* thyroid
tirón *m* pull; tug; **de un ~** at a stretch
tiroteo *m* firing; skirmish
tísico consumptive
tisis *f med* consumption
títere *m* puppet; marionette
titubear *v/i* to stagger; to hesitate, to waver; to stammer
titula|do entitled; titled; qualified; **~r** *v/t* to entitle; to name; *m* headline
título *m* title; diploma; right; **a ~ de** by way of
tiza *f* chalk
tiznar *v/t* to stain; to smudge
toalla *f* towel
tobera *f* nozzle
tobillo *m* ankle
tobogán *m* toboggan; slide
tocadiscos *m* record player; **~ automático** jukebox
tocado *m* head-dress; hairstyle; *a fam* crazy; touched; **~r** *m* dressing table; ladies' room
toca|nte touching; **~nte a** with regard to, concerning; **~r** *v/t* to touch; to feel; to play (*an instrument*); to ring (*a bell*); to touch upon; to move; *v/i* to touch; to be up (*to*); to border; **~r a su fin** to be at an end
tocayo *m* namesake
tocino *m* bacon
tocón *m* stub, stump
todavía still, yet; **~ no** not yet
todo *a* all; entire; whole; complete; every; **~ aquel que** whoever; **~s los días** every day; *adv* totally; entirely; **ante ~** first of all; **con ~** notwithstanding; **del ~** entirely; absolutely; **sobre ~** above all; *m* all; whole; *pl* everybody
todopoderoso almighty
toldo *m* awning; *LA* Indian hut
tolera|ble tolerable; passable; **~ncia** *f* tolerance; **~r** *v/t* to tolerate
toma *f* taking; *mil* capture; *tecn* inlet; outlet; *foto, cine* shot, take; **~corriente** *m tecn* plug; **~dura** *f* **de pelo** *fam* practical joke; **~r** *v/t* to take; to seize; to grasp; to have (*food, drink*); **~r cariño a** to grow fond of; **~r a mal** to take (*something*) the wrong way; *v/i LA fam* to drink; **toma y daca** give and take
tomate *m* tomato
tomavistas *m* motion picture camera
tomillo *m* thyme
tomo *m* volume
ton *m*: **sin ~ ni son** without rhyme or reason; **~alidad** *f mús* tonality; key; **~alidad mayor, menor** major, minor key
tonel *m* barrel; cask
tonela|da *f* ton; **~je** *m* tonnage
tónic|a *f mús* tonic; keynote; **~o** *a, m* tonic
tono *m* tone; pitch; **de buen ~** elegant
tont|ería *f* silliness; foolishness; **~o** silly; stupid
top|ar *v/t* to bump against; **~arse con** to meet, to run into; **~e** *m* butt, end; buffer; **hasta el ~e** up to the brim
tópico *m* commonplace; cliché; *LA* topic
topo *m* mole; *fam* awkward person
topógrafo *m* topographer
toque *m* touch; chime; blast; *mil* bugle call; **los últimos ~s** the finishing touches
torbellino *m* whirlwind; *fam* lively person
torc|er *v/t* to twist; to bend; to sprain; to distort; *v/i* to turn; **~erse** to become twisted; to sprain; **~ido** twisted, bent
tordo *m* thrush
tore|ar *v/i* to fight bulls; *v/t* to fight (*the bull*); to tease; to elude; **~o** *m* bullfighting; **~ro** *m* bullfighter
toril *m* bull pen
torment|a *f* storm; thunderstorm; **~o** *m* torment; torture; **~oso** stormy
torna|r *v/t* to give back; to transform; *v/i* to go back; to return; **~rse** to become; to change into
tornasol *m* sunflower
torneo *m* tournament
torn|illo *m* screw; **~iquete** *m* turnstile; **~o** *m* lathe; winch, windlass; revolution, turn; **en ~o a** about, around
toro *m* bull
toronja *f* grapefruit
torpe slow; heavy; dull; **~za** *f* heaviness; dullness
torre *f* tower; steeple; turret; (*chess*) rook; high-rise building; **~ de control** *aer* control tower
torrente *m* torrent
tórrido torrid
torta *f* cake; pie; *fam* slap
tortazo *m fam* sock, punch, clout
tortilla *f* omelette
tórtol|a *f* turtledove; **~o** *m fig* sweetheart
tortuga *f* tortoise; turtle
tortuoso winding

Spanish

tortura *f* torture, anguish; **~r** *v/t* to torture
tos *f* cough; **~ *ferina*** whooping cough
tosco crude, rude
toser *v/i* to cough
tosta|da *f* toast; **~do** sunburnt, tanned; **~dor** *m* toaster; **~r** *v/t* to toast; to roast (*coffee*); to tan (*in the sun*)
tostón *m* toasted bread cube; *fig* bore
total total, complete; **~idad** *f* totality; **~itario** totalitarian; **~mente** totally
tóxico toxic
toxicómano(a) *m* (*f*) drug addict
traba *f* bond; lock; obstacle; fetter
trabaj|ador(a) *m* (*f*) worker; *a* industrious, hardworking; **~ar** *v/t*, *v/i* to work; to till (*soil*); **~ar con** *fig* (get to) work on; **~ar por** to strive to; **~o** *m* work; employment; **~os** *pl* ***forzados*** hard labo(u)r
traba|lenguas *m* tongue twister; **~r** *v/t* to link; to tie up; **~r *amistades*** to make friends
trac|ción *f* traction; **~tor** *m* tractor
tradici|ón *f* tradition; **~onal** traditional
traduc|ción *f* translation; **~ir** *v/t* to translate; **~tor(a)** *m* (*f*) translator
traer *v/t* to bring; to cause
trafica|nte *m* dealer; trader; **~r** *v/i* to trade; to deal
tráfico *m* traffic; *com* trade
traga|dor(a) *m* (*f*) glutton; **~luz** *m* skylight; **~monedas** *m*, **~perras** *m* slot machine; **~r** *v/t* to swallow; to gulp down; ***no poder* ~r** not to be able to stand (*someone*)
tragedia *f* tragedy
trago *m* drink; swallow; ***echarse un* ~** to have a drink; ***mal* ~** misfortune; hard time
trai|ción *f* treason; **~cionar** *v/t* to betray; **~dor(a)** *m* (*f*) traitor; betrayer; *a* treacherous
traído worn, threadbare
traje *m* dress; suit; **~ *de baño*** swimsuit; bathing suit; **~ *de etiqueta*** full dress, evening dress; **~ *sastre*** women's suit
trajín *m* bustle, hustle
trajinar *v/t* to carry from place to place; *v/i* to bustle about
trama *f* weft; *fig* plot; intrigue; **~r** *v/t* to weave; *fig* to plot
tramitar *v/t* to negotiate
trámite *m* step, move; *pl* legal formalities
tramo *m* section (*of road*); flight (*of stairs*)
tramp|a *f* trap, snare, pitfall; **~ear** *v/i* to cheat
trampolín *m* springboard
tramposo *a* deceitful; *m* crook; swindler
trancar *v/t* to bar (*a door*)
trance *m* critical situation; ***a todo* ~** at all cost; ***en* ~ *de*** in the act of
tranquil|idad *f* tranquillity; stillness; **~izar** *v/t* to calm; **~o** calm; quiet
transacción *f* agreement, compromise; *com* transaction
transatlántico *a* transatlantic; *m* liner
transbord|ador *m* ferry (boat); **~ar** *v/t* to transship; to transfer; **~o** *m* transfer
transcribir *v/t* to transcribe; to copy
transcur|rir *v/i* to elapse; **~so** *m* course (*of time*)
transeúnte *m* passer-by
transfer|encia *f* transfer; **~ir** *v/t* to transfer
transforma|ción *f* transformation; **~dor** *m elec* transformer; **~r** *v/t* to transform
tránsfuga *m mil* deserter
transfu|ndir *v/t* to transfuse; **~sión** *f* transfusion; **~*sión de sangre*** blood transfusion
transgredir *v/t* to transgress
transición *f* transition
transig|ente accommodating; **~ir** *v/i* to give in; to compromise
transistor *m* transistor
transita|ble passable; **~r** *v/i* to travel
tránsito *m* passage; transit; ***en* ~** en route
transitorio transitory
translúcido translucent
transmi|sión *f* transmission; **~sor** *m* transmitter, sender; **~tir** *v/t* to transmit; to broadcast
transparen|cia *f* transparency; **~te** transparent
transpirar *v/i* to transpire; to perspire
transport|ar *v/t* to transport; **~e** *m* transport; *fig* rapture; **~e *colectivo*** public transportation
transvers|al transversal; **~o** transverse
tranvía *m* tramway; streetcar
trapear *v/t LA* to mop (*the floor*)
trapecio *m* trapeze; *mat* trapezoid
trapero *m* rag dealer
trapisonda *f* deception; brawl
trap|ito *m* small rag; **~o** *m* rag; cloth; ***soltar el* ~o** *fam* to burst out laughing *or* crying
tráquea *f anat* windpipe
traque|tear *v/i* to clatter; *v/t* to handle roughly; to rattle; **~teo** *m* rattle, clatter
tras after; behind; besides; **~ *de*** in addition to; ***uno* ~ *otro*** one after the other
trascenden|cia *f* transcendence; consequence; **~tal** of highest importance; momentous
trasegar *v/t* to decant; to turn upside down
traser|a *f* back; rear; **~o** *m* buttock; rump; *a* hind; rear
trasfondo *m* background
trashumar *v/i* to migrate from one pasture to another
trasiego *m* decanting; disarrangement
trasla|dar *v/t* to move; to remove; **~do** *m* move; transfer; **~parse** *v/r* to overlap
traslu|cirse *v/r* to shine through; **~z** *m*:**al ~z** against the light
trasnochar *v/i* to spend the night; to keep late hours
traspapelar *v/t* to mislay
traspas|ar *v/t* to move; to pass over; to cross over; to transfer (*business*); **~o** *m* move; transfer, conveyance; violation (*of law*)
trasplant|ar *v/t* to transplant; **~arse** to emigrate; **~e** *m med* transplant
trasquilar *v/t* to shear; to crop (*hair*) badly
trast|ada *f* dirty trick; mischief; **~azo** *m* whack, thump; **~e** *m* fret (*of a guitar*); ***dar al* ~e *con*** *fam* to finish with; **~ear** *v/t* to play (*a guitar, etc*); *v/i* to move things; **~o** *m* old piece of furniture; trash; junk; *fam* worthless person; *pl* tools; implements
trastorn|ar *v/t* to confuse; to upset; to overturn; **~o** *m* confusion; upheaval; disorder; derangement
trasunto *m* transcript, copy
trata *f* slave trade; **~do** *m* treatise; agreement; *pol* treaty; **~miento** *m* treatment (*t med*); form of address; **~r** *v/t* to treat; to address (*someone*); *v/i* **~r *de*** to try; to deal with; **~*rse con uno*** to have to do with someone; **~*rse de*** to be a question of; ***¿ de qué se* ~?** what is it about?
trato *m* treatment; manner; behavio(u)r; dealings; form of address; ***de fácil* ~** easy to get on with; ***cerrar un* ~** to strike a bargain
través *m* bias; traverse; ***a(l)* ~ *de*** across; through
traves|ero *a* crosswise; *m* bolster; **~ía** *f* crossing; passage; voyage
travesura *f* mischief, lark, prank
travieso mischievous; naughty
trayecto *m* road, route; distance; stretch; journey; trajectory
traz|a *f* sketch; plan; **~ar** *v/t* to trace; to sketch; to devise; **~o** *m* outline
trébol *m* clover; **~es** *m/pl* (*cards*) clubs
trecho *m* distance; stretch; *fam* bit, piece; ***de* ~ *en* ~** at intervals
tregua *f* truce; respite
tremendo dreadful
trementina *f* turpentine
trémulo tremulous
tren *m* train; outfit; show; **~ *directo*** through train; **~ *de aterrizaje*** landing gear; **~ *de enlace*** connecting train; **~ *de mercancías*** goods train
trenza *f* plait, tress; braid; pigtail; pony tail; **~r** *v/t* to plait; to braid
trepar *v/i* to climb
trepida|ción *f* vibration; **~r** *v/i* to vibrate; to shake
tres three
triángulo *m* triangle
tribu *f* tribe
tribuna *f* platform; **~l** *m* tribunal; court of justice
tribut|ar *v/t* to pay (taxes); **~ario** *m* taxpayer; *a* tributary; **~o** *m* tribute
triciclo *m* tricycle
tricornio *m* three-cornered hat
trienio *m* period of three years
trig|al *m* wheat field; **~o** *m* wheat
trilla|do *agr* threshed; *fig* hackneyed, stale; **~r** *v/t* to thresh
trillizos *m/pl* triplets
trimestral quarterly
trinar *v/i* to trill; to warble
trincar *v/t* to break up; *mar* to lash; *v/i fam* to drink
trinch|ar *v/t* to carve; to slice; **~era** *f mil* trench; trench coat
trineo *m* sleigh; sled(ge)
Trinidad *f relig* Trinity
trinitaria *f bot* pansy
tripa *f* gut; intestine; *coc* tripe
triple triple
trípode *m* tripod
tríptico *m* triptych
tripulación *f* crew
trisca *f* crunch; racket; **~r** *v/i* to stamp; to romp about
trismo *m* lockjaw
triste sad; **~za** *f* sadness
triturar *v/t* to grind
triunf|ar *v/i* to triumph; **~o** *m* triumph; win, victory; (*cards*) trump
trivial trivial, commonplace; **~idad** *f* triviality
trocar *v/t* to exchange; to turn into
trocha *f* by-path; *LA f c* gauge
trofeo *m* trophy
trole *m* trolley
tromba *f* whirlwind; **~ *marina*** waterspout
trombón *m mús* trombone
tromp|a *f mús* horn; trunk of an elephant; **~azo** *m* bump; severe blow; **~eta** *f* trumpet
trona|da *f* thunderstorm; **~r** *v/i* to thunder
tronco *m* trunk
trono *m* throne
tropa *f* troop; *mil* rank and file; *pl* troops
tropel *m* crowd; confusion; ***de* ~, *en* ~** in a mad rush
trop|ezar *v/i* to stumble; **~*ezar con*** to run into; **~ezón** *m* slip, mistake; blunder; **~iezo** *m* stumbling; trip
tropical tropical
trópico *geog* tropic
tropiezo *m* stumble; *fig* obstacle
trot|amundos *m* globe trotter; **~ar** *v/t*, *v/i* to trot; **~e** *m* trot
trozo *m* piece; bit
truco *m* trick
trucha *f* trout
trueno *m* thunder
trufa *f* truffle
truhán *m* swindler, cheat, crook
tú *pers pron 2nd pers sing* you
tu (*pl* **tus**) *poss pron m*, *f* your
tuberculosis *f* tuberculosis
tub|ería *f* tubing; piping; **~o** *m* tube; pipe; **~*o de desagüe*** overflow pipe; **~*o de ensayo*** test tube
tuerca *f tecn* nut
tuert|o crooked; one-eyed; ***a* ~*as o a derechas*** by hook or by crook
tuétano *m anat* marrow
tufo *m* vapo(u)r; stench
tul *m* tulle; **~ipán** *m* tulip
tullido disabled, crippled
tumba *m* tomb; shake, jolt; somersault
tumbar *v/t* to knock down; **~se** to lie down
tumbo *m* violent fall; ***dar* ~s** to stagger
tumor *m* tumo(u)r
tumultuoso tumultuous
tuna *f bot* prickly pear; *mús* student music group
tunante *m* rogue, rascal
túnel *m* tunnel; **~ *de lavado*** car wash
túnica *f* tunic; robe
tupé *m* toupee; *fam* cheek
turba *f* crowd; peat
turbante *a* perturbing; *m* turban
turbar *v/t* to disturb; to upset; **~se** to be disturbed; to get confused
turbina *f* turbine
turbulento turbulent
turco(a) *m* (*f*), *a* Turk
turis|mo *m* tourism; roadster; **~ta** *m*, *f* tourist
turn|ar *v/i* to alternate, to take turns; **~o** *m* turn; ***por* ~*os*** by turns
turquesa *f* turquoise
Turquía *f* Turkey
turrón *m* nougat
tutear *v/t* to address familiarly as "tú"
tutor *m* guardian; tutor
tuyo(a) *poss pron; 2nd pers m*, *f* yours; *relig* thine

U

u (*before words beginning with* o *or* ho) or
ubicación *f* location; situation
ubre *f* udder
Ud. = ***usted***
ufanarse to boast
ujier *m* usher
úlcera *f* ulcer
ulcer|arse to fester; **~oso** ulcerous
ulterior farther; further; later; subsequent
ultimar *v/t* to conclude; to finish; *LA* to finish off
último last; final; latest; utmost
ultraj|ante outraging; **~ar** *v/t* to outrage; to insult; **~e** *m* outrage
ultramar: *de* ~ overseas; **~inos** *m/pl* groceries
ultranza: *a* ~ at all costs
ulular *v/i* to howl; to hoot
umbral *m* threshold
umbr|ío, ~oso shady; shadowy
un (*apocope of* **uno**) *m*, **una** *f indef art* a, an
unánime unanimous
unanimidad *f* unanimity
unción *f* anointment
undular *v/i* to undulate
ungüento *m* ointment; salve
único only; sole, unique; ***hijo* ~** only child
uni|dad *f* unity; *tecn* unit; **~do** united; joined; **~ficar** *v/t* to unify, to unite
uniform|ar *v/t* to make uniform; **~e** *a* uniform; unvarying; *m* uniform; **~idad** *f* uniformity
uni|ón *f* union; unity; **~r** *v/t* unite; **~rse** to join together
unísono unisonous; ***al* ~** in unison
univers|al universal; **~alidad** *f* universality; **~idad** *f* university; **~itario** *a* university; *m* university student; **~o** *m* universe
uno(a) *a* one; *pl* some; a few; *pron m*, *f* one, someone; **~ *y otro*** both; ***cada* ~** each one; **~ *a* ~** one by one
unt|ar *v/t* to rub; to spread (*butter on bread*); to smear (*with grease*); **~o** *m med* ointment, unguent; **~uoso** greasy
uña *f* nail; talon; claw; hoof; ***comerse las* ~s** to bite one's nails; ***ser* ~ *y carne*** to be inseparable
uranio *m* uranium
urban|idad *f* politeness; manners; **~ización** *f* housing estate, planned community; **~o** urbane; urban
urbe *f* large city, metropolis
urdimbre *f* warp
urdir *v/t* to warp (*yarn*); *fig* to plot; to scheme
urgen|cia *f* urgency: ***salida* *f* *de* ~*cia*** emergency exit; **~te** urgent
urinario *a* urinary; *m* urinal
urna *f* urn; ballot box
urraca *f* magpie
urticaria *f* nettle rash
Uruguay *m* Uruguay; **2o(a)** *m* (*f*) Uruguayan
usa|do used; worn; accustomed; **~nza** *f* usage; custom; **~r** *v/t* to use; to make use of; **~rse** to be in fashion; to be in use
uso *m* use; employment; ***al* ~** in keeping with custom
usted you
usua|l customary; **~rio** *m* user
usufructo *m for* usufruct; use
usur|a *f* usury; **~ero** *m* usurer; profiteer

utensilio *m* implement; tool; utensil
útero *m med* uterus
útil *a* useful; **~es** *m/pl* tools, implements; **~es de escritorio** stationery
util|idad *f* usefulness, utility; **~itario** utilitarian; **~izable** utilizable; **~izar** *v/t* to utilize; to use
utopía *f* Utopia
uva *f* grape; **~ de Corinto** currant; **~ espina** gooseberry; **~ pasa** raisin

V

vaca *f* cow; *coc* beef
vacaciones *f/pl* vacation; holiday
vacan|cia *f* vacancy; **~te** vacant
vaciar *v/t* to empty
vacila|ción *f* hesitation; **~nte** vacillating; hesitant
vacío *a* empty; vacant; *m* vacuum
vacuna *f* vaccine; **~ción** *f* vaccination; **~r** *v/t* to vaccinate
vad|ear *v/t* to ford; **~o** *m* ford
vagabund|ear *v/i* to rove; to loiter; **~o** *m* tramp; vagrant; *a* idle; roving
vagar *v/i* to rove; to wander
vago *adj* vague; indefinite; *m* vagabond; tramp
vagón *m* carriage; railroad car; **~-cama** sleeping car; **~ de cola** caboose; **~ restaurante** dining car
vagoneta *f* van; open truck
vahído *m* dizziness
vaho *m* vapo(u)r
vaina *f* sheath; husk, pod; *LA fam* nuisance
vainilla *f* vanilla
vaivén *m* swinging; rocking; ups and downs (*of fortune*); *tecn* shuttle movement
vajilla *f* crockery; table service
vale *m com* voucher; promissory note; **~ de correo, ~ postal** money order; **~dero** valid
valentía *f* courage, valo(u)r
valer *v/t* to be worth; to cost; **~ la pena** to be worth while; **¡no vale!** it is no good!; **¿cuánto vale?** how much is it?; **~se de** to avail oneself of; **¡válgame Dios!** bless my soul!
valeroso brave; strong
valía *f* worth; value
validez *f* validity
válido valid
valiente brave; valiant; strong; excellent
valija *f* case; mail bag
val|ioso valuable; wealthy; **~or** *m* value; price; courage, valo(u)r; *pl com* securities; bonds; **~or nominal** face value; **~oración** *f* valuation; **~orar, ~orizar** *v/t* to value; to appraise
vals *m* waltz
válvula *f* valve; **~ de seguridad** safety valve
valla *f* fence; barrier; *sp* hurdle
valle *m* valley
vanagloriarse to boast
vanguardia *f mil* vanguard, van
van|idad *f* vanity; uselessness; **~idoso** vain; **~o** useless; pointless; **en ~o** in vain
vapor *m* steam; vapo(u)r; steamer; **~izar** *v/t* to vaporize
vaquero *m* cowhand
vara *f* stick; rod; pole; Spanish measure; **~r** *v/t* to beach; **~rse** *mar LA* to be stranded
varia|ble variable; changeable; **~ción** *f* variation; change; **~do** varied; **~r** *v/t* to vary; to change; to modify; *v/i* to vary; to differ
varicela *f* chicken pox
varicoso varicose
variedad *f* variety; **función *f* de ~es** variety show
varilla *f* thin stick, wand; rib; rod; **~je** *m* ribbing
varios various; several
varón *m* male; man
varonil manly
vasc|o(a) *m (f)*, *a* Basque; **~uence** *m* Basque language
vas|ija *f* vessel; **~o** *m* glass
vástago *m bot* shoot; sprout; *fig* offspring
vasto vast, immense
vaticinio *m* prophecy
vatio *m* watt
vecin|al neighbo(u)ring; **~dad** *f*, **~dario** *m* vicinity; neighbo(u)rhood; **~o(a)** *m (f)* neighbo(u)r; citizen; resident
veda *f* prohibition; closed season; **~r** *v/t* to prohibit
vega *f* fertile plain
vegeta|ción *f* vegetation; **~l** *m* vegetable; plant; *a* vegetable; **~r** *v/i fig* to vegetate; **~riano(a)** *m (f)*, *a* vegetarian
vehemen|cia *f* vehemence; **~te** vehement; passionate
vehículo *m* vehicle
veintena *f* score, about twenty
vejez *f* old age
vejiga *f* bladder; **~ de la bilis** gall bladder
vela *f* candle; watch, vigil; *mar* sail; **barco *m* de ~** sailing ship; **~ mayor** mainsail; **en ~** awake; **~da** *f* vigil; soirée; **~do** veiled; **~r** *v/t* to watch; *v/i* to stay awake; **~torio** *m* wake
velero *m* sailing boat
veleta *f* weather vane; *fig* fickle person
velo *m* veil
velocidad *f* speed; velocity; *aut* gear; **a toda ~** at full speed; **~ de crucero** cruising speed
veloz speedy, fast
vell|o *m anat* down; **~ón** *m* fleece; sheepskin; **~oso, ~udo** hairy
vena *f* vein
venado *m* stag; deer; venison
venal mercenary, venal
vencedor(a) *m (f)* conqueror; winner; *a* winning
venc|er *v/t* to overcome; to conquer; *v/i* to win; *com* to fall due, to expire; **~ido** defeated; *com* due, payable; **darse por ~ido** to acknowledge defeat; **~imiento** *m com* maturity
venda *f* bandage; **~r** *v/t* to bandage; to swathe
vendaval *m* strong wind; gale
vende|dor(a) *m (f)* seller; salesman; retailer; **~r** *v/t* to sell; to market
vendible marketable
vendimia *f* vintage; grape harvest
veneno *m* poison; venom; **~so** poisonous; venomous
venerar *v/t* to venerate; to worship
venéreo venereal
Venez|uela *f* Venezuela; **2olano(a)** *m (f)* Venezuelan
venga|nza *f* vengeance, revenge; **~r** *v/t* to avenge; **~rse de** to take revenge on; **~tivo** revengeful; vindictive
venia *f* permission, leave; pardon; *LA* salute
venida *f* coming; arrival
venir *v/i* to come; to arrive; **~ a menos** to come down in the world; **~ a ser** to turn out to be; **~ bien** to suit; **~ de** to come from; **~se abajo** to collapse; to fall down
venta *f* sale; selling; **de ~** for sale; **precio *m* de ~** selling price
ventaj|a *f* advantage; **~oso** advantageous
ventan|a *f* window; **~a de la nariz** nostril; **~al** *m* large window; **~illa** *f*, **~illo** *m* small window
ventarrón *m* gale
ventila|ción *f* ventilation; **~dor** *m* ventilator; fan; **~r** *v/t* to ventilate; *fig* to discuss
ventis|ca *f* snowstorm; blizzard; **~quero** *m* snowstorm; glacier
ventoso windy
ventrílocuo *m* ventriloquist
ventrudo potbellied
ventur|a *f* luck; happiness; **a la ~a** at random; **por ~a** by chance; **~oso** fortunate
ver *v/t* to see; to look at; to notice; to understand; **¡a ~!** let's see!; **hacer ~** to show; **tener que ~ con** to have to do with
veranea|nte *m, f* summer vacationist; **~r** *v/i* to spend the summer holidays
veraneo *m* summer vacation
verano *m* summer
veras *f/pl*: **de ~** truly; really
veraz truthful
verbena *f* traditional fair on the eve of a saint's day
verbo *m* verb; **~so** verbose, long-winded
verdad *f* truth; **~ero** real, authentic
verd|e green; unripe; **¡están ~es!** sour grapes!; **~or** *m* greenness, verdure; **~oso** greenish
verdugo *m* hangman
verdu|lero(a) *m (f)* greengrocer; **~ra** *f* greens; fresh vegetables
vereda *f* lane; path; *LA* pavement
veredicto *m* verdict; finding
vergonzoso shameful; bashful
vergüenza *f* shame; bashfulness; disgrace; **¡qué ~!** what a disgrace!, shame!
verídico truthful
verificar *v/t* to verify; to confirm; **~se** to prove true; to take place
verja *f* iron railing; grille, grating
vermut *m* vermouth; *LA teat, cine* afternoon performance
verosímil likely, plausible
verosimilitud *f* probability
verraco *m* boar
verruga *f* wart
versa|do versed; proficient; **~r** *v/i* to go around; **~r sobre** to treat of
versátil versatile
versión *f* version; translation; interpretation
verso *m* verse
vértebra *f* vertebra
verte|dero *m* dumping place, rubbish heap; **~r** *v/t* to pour (out); to spill; to shed; *v/i* to flow; to run
vértice *m* vertex
vertiente *f* slope
vertiginoso dizzy; giddy
vesícula *f* vesicle; blister
vestíbulo *m* vestibule; lobby
vestido *m* dress; clothing
vestigio *m* trace; vestige
vestir *v/t* to clothe; to dress; *v/i* to look elegant; to dress; **~ de** to wear; **~se** to dress; to get dressed
vestuario *m* wardrobe; changing room; cloakroom
veterano *m* veteran; *a* experienced
veterinario *m* veterinary surgeon, *Am* veterinarian
veto *m* veto
vez *f* time; occasion; turn; **a la ~** at the same time; **a su ~** in his turn; **alguna ~** sometimes; **cada ~** every time; **de ~ en cuando** from time to time; **en ~ de** instead of; **rara ~** seldom; **tal ~** perhaps; **una ~** once; **una ~ que** since; **a veces** sometimes; **muchas veces** often; **pocas veces** rarely, seldom; **repetidas veces** time and again
vía *f* road; track, route; *fig* manner; **~ férrea** railway; **por ~ aérea** by airmail; **por ~ marítima** by sea; **por ~ de** by way of; **2 Láctea** Milky Way
viable practicable
viaj|ante *m, f* travel(l)er; **~ar** *v/i* to travel; **~e** *m* journey; *mar* voyage; **~e de ida y vuelta** round trip; **~e de novios** honeymoon; **~e de negocios** business trip; **¡buen ~e!** have a good trip!; bon voyage!; **~ero** *m* travel(l)er
víbora *f* viper
vibra|ción *f* vibration; **~dor** *m* vibrator; **~r** *v/i* to vibrate
vicario *m* vicar; curate
vicepresidente *m* vice-president
vici|ar *v/t* to spoil; to corrupt; **~o** *m* vice; bad habit; **~oso** vicious; depraved
vicisitud *f* vicissitude
víctima *f* victim
victimar *v/t LA* to kill
victori|a *f* victory; **~oso** victorious
vid *f* grapevine
vida *f* life; **en la ~** never in my life; **¡por ~ mía!** upon my soul!
vidente *m, f* seer
vídeo *m* video
video|cámara *f* video camera; **~cassette** *m* video cassette; **~disco** *m* video disk
vidrier|a *f* stained glass window; **~o** *m* glazier
vidrio *m* glass; **~ tallado** cut glass; **~so** glassy (*eyes, etc*)
viejo(a) *a* old; ancient; *m (f)* old man (woman)
viento *m* wind; **hace ~** it is windy; **~s *pl* alisios** trade winds
vientre *m* abdomen; belly
viernes *m* Friday; **2 Santo** Good Friday
viga *f* beam; girder
vigen|cia *f* validity; operation; **estar en ~cia** to be in force; **~te** in force; valid
vigía *f* lookout (post), watchtower
vigilan|cia *f* vigilance; **~te** *a* vigilant; *m* watchman; shopwalker
vigilar *v/t* to watch over; to look after
vigilia *f* vigil, watch
vigor *m* vigo(u)r; strength; force, effect; **en ~** valid; in force; **~oso** vigorous
vil vile; base; **~eza** *f* vileness; villainy
vilo: en ~ suspended; uncertain
villa *f* town; municipality
villancico *m* Christmas carol
villorrio *m* hamlet; little village
vinagre *m* vinegar; **~ra** *f* vinegar cruet, castor; *LA* heartburn
vincular *v/t* to connect; to link; *for* to entail
vínculo *m* bond; tie
vino *m* wine; **~ de Jerez** sherry; **~ de la casa** house wine; **~ generoso** full-bodied wine; **~ de solera** vintage wine; **~ tinto** red wine
viñ|a *f*, **~edo** *m* vineyard
viola *f mús* viola; *bot* viola
viol|ar *v/t* to violate; to rape; **~encia** *f* violence; **~entar** *v/t* to force; **~entarse** to force oneself; **~ento** violent
violeta *f* violet
viol|ín *m* violin; **~ón** *m* double bass; **~oncelo** *m* cello
virar *v/i mar* to tack; to veer
virg|en *f* virgin; **~inidad** *f* virginity
viril virile, manly; **~idad** *f* virility; manhood
virtu|al virtual; **~d** *f* virtue; **~oso** virtuous
viruela *f* smallpox
virulen|cia *f* virulence; **~te** virulent
virus *m* virus
visa *f LA*, **visado** *m* visa
visaje *m* grimace
visar *v/t* to visa (*passport*); to endorse
vísceras *f/pl* viscera; guts
viscos|idad *f* viscosity; **~o** sticky; viscous
visib|ilidad *f* visibility; **~le** visible; evident
visión *f* vision, sight
visit|a *f* visit; **~ar** *v/t* to visit; to call on; **~eo** *m* frequent visiting
vislumbr|ar *v/t* to glimpse; **~e** *f* glimpse, glimmer
viso *m* sheen (*of cloth*)
visón *m* mink
visor *m foto* viewfinder
víspera *f* eve; **~s** *f/pl* evensong; **en ~s de** on the eve of
vista *f* sight; vision; eyesight; aspect; **a la ~** in sight; **de ~** by sight; **en ~ de** in view of; **está a la ~** it is obvious; **hasta la ~** so long; **hacer la ~ gorda** to pretend not to see; **perder de ~** to lose sight of; *m* customs officer; **~zo** *m* glance; **echar un ~zo** to glance at
visto: ~ bueno approved; O.K.; **está ~** it is clear; **por lo ~** apparently
vistoso showy; attractive
visual visual
vital vital; **~icio** lifelong; for life; **~idad** *f* vitality
vitamina *f* vitamin
viticultura *f* grape growing
vitorear *v/t* to acclaim
vítreo glassy; vitreous
vitrina *f* showcase
vituper|ar *v/t* to vituperate; **~io** *m* vituperation; censure
viud|a *f* widow; **~edad** *f* widow's pension; **~ez** *f* widowhood; **~o** *m* widower
viva *f* cheer; **¡~!** hurrah!; long live!
viva|cidad *f* vivacity; brilliance; **~racho** vivacious, gay; **~z** witty; lively
víveres *m/pl* provisions
vivero *m* hatchery; *bot* nursery
viveza *f* liveliness
vivien|da *f* dwelling; housing; **~te** living
viv|ificar *v/t* to vivify; to revitalize; **~ir** *v/t, v/i* to live; to live through; **¿quién vive?** *mil* who goes there?; **~o** alive, living; lively; vivid, bright
Vizcaya *f* Biscay
vizconde *m* viscount; **~sa** *f* viscountess
vocab|lo *m* word; **~ulario** *m* vocabulary
vocación *f* vocation; calling
vocal *f* vowel; *m* voting member; *a* vocal; **~izar** *v/i* to vocalize; to articulate

voce|ar *v/i* to shout; to announce; **~río** *m* shouting
vociferar *v/i* to shout; to vociferate
vola|dizo *arq* projecting; **~or** flying; **~ura** *f* explosion; blast
vola|nte *m* steering wheel; flywheel; balance (*of watch*); handbill; badminton; flounce; **~r** *v/i* to fly; to run fast; to pass quickly; *v/t* to blow up; to blast
volátil volatile; changeable
volcán *m* volcano
volcánico volcanic
volcar *v/t* to overturn; to upset; to empty out
voleibol *m* volleyball
voleo *m sp* volley
voltaje *m* voltage
volte|ar *v/t* to turn; to revolve; to turn upside down; *LA* to turn over; *v/i* to roll over; **~reta** *f* somersault
voltio *m* volt
volum|en *m* volumen; **~inoso** voluminous
volunta|d *f* will; intention; desire; **a ~d** at will; **de buena ~d** with pleasure; **~rio** *a* voluntary; *m* volunteer
voluptuos|idad *f* voluptuousness; **~o** voluptuous
volver *v/t* to turn; to replace; to return; *v/i* to return; **~ loco** to drive mad; **~ atrás** to turn back; **~ a hacer algo** to do something again; **~ en sí** to regain consciousness; **~se** to turn, to become
vomitar *v/t* to vomit, to

throw up
vómito *m* vomiting
voraz voracious
vos *pron pers LA regional* you
vot|ación *f* voting; (*total*) vote; **~ar** *v/t* to vote for; *relig* to vow; **~o** *m* vote, ballot; *relig* vow; *pl* wishes
voz *f* voice; noise; word; **a una ~** unanimously; **dar voces** to shout; **en alta ~** aloud
vuelco *m* overturning; spill
vuelo *m* flight; flare (*of a dress*); *arq* projecting part; **al ~** on the wing; **~ de enlace** connecting flight
vuelta *f* turn; walk; bend, curve; reversal; *sp* lap; **a ~ de correo** by return mail; **a la ~** around the corner; overleaf; **dar una ~** to take a stroll; **dar ~s** to go round, to revolve; **estar de ~** to be back; **poner de ~ y media** to insult; to call names
vuestro(a, os, as) *pron pos* your, yours
vulgar common; ordinary, vulgar; **~idad** *f* vulgarity
vulnera|ble vulnerable; **~r** *v/t* to damage, to harm

W

wáter *m* lavatory, toilet
whisk(e)y *m* whisk(e)y

X

xenófobo(a) *m (f)*, *a* hater of foreigners, xenophobe
xilófono *m* xylophone

Y

y and
ya already; now; at once; soon, presently; **~ no** no longer; **~ que** since; as; **¡~!** oh, I see!; **~ ... ~** now ... now; **¡~ lo creo!** indeed!; of course!
yace|nte lying; **~r** *v/i* to lie; to lie in the grave
yacimiento *m* deposit; bed (*of minerals*); **~ petrolífero** oil field
yapa *f LA* bonus, extra
yarda *f* yard (*measure*)
yate *m* yacht
yedra *f* ivy
yegua *f* mare
yelmo *m* helmet
yema *f* yolk (*of egg*); *bot* bud; **~ del dedo** tip of the finger
yermo uncultivated, desert, waste
yerno *m* son-in-law
yerro *m* error, mistake
yes|ería *f* plaster work; **~o** *m geol* gypsum; plaster; plaster cast; **~o mate** plaster of Paris
yo *pron pers* I
yodo *m* iodine
yogur *m* yogurt
yola *f* yawl
yugo *m* yoke *t fig*
Yugo(e)slavia *f* Yugoslavia
yugo(e)slavo(a) *m (f)* Yugoslav; *a* Yugoslavian
yunque *m* anvil
yunta *f* yoke (*of oxen*)
yute *m* jute

Z

zafar *v/t mar* to untie, to loosen, to clear; **~se** to run away
zafir(o) *m* sapphire
zagal *m* lad, youth; shepherd
zagual *m* paddle
zaguán *m* hallway, entrance
zaguero rear; lagging behind
zahurda *f* pigsty
zaino *fig* false; treacherous
zalamería *f* flattery
zalema *f* salaam; bow
zamarro *m* sheepskin jacket
zambo(a) *m (f) LA* half Indian – half black
zambullirse to dive, to plunge
zampar *v/t* to hurl; to gobble; to put away hurriedly
zanahoria *f* carrot
zan|ca *f* long leg, shank; **~cada** *f* stride; **~cadilla** *f* tripping; trick; trap; **~co** *m* stilt; **~cudo** *a* long-legged
zangamanga *f fam* trick
zángano *m zool* drone; *fig* sponger
zanja *f* ditch; trench; *LA* gully
zanquear *v/i* to waddle; to stride along
zapa *f mil* spade; **~dor** *m mil* sapper; **~r** *v/t* to sap
zapat|ería *f* shoeshop; **~ero** *m* shoemaker; **~illa** *f* slipper; **~o** *m* shoe
zar *m* czar
zaragata *f fam* quarrel; brawl
Zaragoza Saragossa
zarandear *v/t* to sift; to sieve
zarcillo *m* tendril

zarpa *f* paw; **~r** *v/i* to weigh anchor, to set sail
zarrapastroso ragged
zarza *f* bramble; **~mora** *f* blackberry
zarzuela *f* operetta, light opera
zigzaguear *v/i* to zigzag
zócalo *m arq* socle
zoco *m* public square; clog
zodíaco *m* zodiac
zona *f* zone; district; **~ de pruebas** testing ground; **~ tórrida** torrid zone
zonzo *LA* silly, foolish
zoología *f* zoology
zoológico zoological
zopenco dull, stupid
zopilote *m LA* buzzard
zopo crooked, malformed (*foot, hand*)
zoquete *m* block of wood; *fam* blockhead
zorr|a *f* vixen; *fig* cunning person; *fam* slut; tart; **~o** *m* fox
zozobra *f mar* capsizing; *fig* worry; **~r** *v/i* to founder; to be in danger
zueco *m* wooden shoe, clog
zumb|ar *v/i* to buzz, to hum; to drone; *v/t* to joke with; **~arse de** to make fun of; **~ido** *m* buzzing; **~ido de oídos** buzzing in the ears
zumo *m* juice
zurcir *v/t* to darn; to mend
zurdo left-handed
zurrar *v/t* to spank, to thrash; *tecn, fam* to tan
zurrir *v/i* to hum; to rattle; to grate
zutano *m* so-and-so

Numerals
Numerales
Cardinal Numbers — *Cardinales*

0 cero, *nought, zero*
1 uno(a) *one*
2 dos *two*
3 tres *three*
4 cuatro *four*
5 cinco *five*
6 seis *six*
7 siete *seven*
8 ocho *eight*
9 nueve *nine*
10 diez *ten*
11 once *eleven*
12 doce *twelve*
13 trece *thirteen*
14 catorce *fourteen*
15 quince *fifteen*
16 dieciséis *síeteen*
17 diecisiete *seventeen*
18 dieciocho *eighteen*
19 diecinueve *nineteen*
20 veinte *twenty*
21 veintiuno *twenty-one*
22 veintidós *twenty-two*
30 treinta *thirty*

31 treinta y uno *thirty-one*
40 cuarenta *forty*
50 cincuenta *fifty*
60 sesenta *sixty*
70 setenta *seventy*
80 ochenta *eighty*
90 noventa *ninety*
100 ciento, cien *a (or one) hundred*
101 ciento uno *hundred and one*
200 doscientos *two hundred*
300 trescientos *three hundred*
400 cuatrocientos *four hundred*
500 quinientos *five hundred*
600 seiscientos *six hundred*
700 setecientos *seven hundred*
800 ochocientos *eight hundred*
900 novecientos *nine hundred*
1000 mil *a (or one) thousand*
1976 mil novecientos setenta y seis *nineteen hundred and seventy-six*
2000 dos mil *two thousand*
100 000 cien mil *a (or one) hundred thousand*
500 000 quinientos mil *five hundred thousand*
1 000 000 un millón *a (or one) million*
2 000 000 dos millones *two millions*